Taxation
and self-assessment

Incorporating the Finance Act 1997

16th Edition 1997

Peter Rowes
BSc. (Econ), FCA, ATII

Letts Educational
Aldine Place
London W12 8AW
Tel: 0181-740 2266
Fax: 0181-743 8451
e-mail: mail@lettsed.co.uk

Acknowledgements

The author would like to express thanks to the following for giving permission to reproduce past examination questions and forms.

Institute of Chartered Accountants in England and Wales (ICAEW)

Chartered Association of Certified Accountants (ACCA)

Chartered Institute of Management Accountants (CIMA)

Institute of Taxation (INST T)

Controller of Her Majesty's Stationery Office

Note

The provisions of the Finance Act 1997 have been incorporated in this edition.

A CIP catalogue record for this book is available from the British Library

ISBN 1 85805 311 0
Copyright Peter Rowes © 1997
Formerly published by D P Publications

Typeset by Kai, Nottingham

Printed by WM Print,
Walsall, W Midlands, WS2 9NE

Contents

Preface   v

Abbreviations and Statutes   vii

Summary of main changes 1997/98   viii

Part I: Income tax

1	General principles	3
2	Administration	8
3	Personal allowances and reliefs I	25
4	Personal allowances and reliefs II	33
5	Charges on income and interest paid	40
6	Income from savings I – taxed income	47
7	Income from savings II – gross income	52
8	Income from employment I – Schedule E	59
9	Income from employment II – international aspects	78
10	Income from employment III – PAYE	85
11	Income from UK land and property – Schedule A	93
12	Income from foreign investments – Schedule D Case IV and V	99
13	Income from other sources – Schedule D Case VI	103
14	Income from self-employment – Schedule D Case I and II	104
15	Income from self-employment – basis of assessment	117
16	Income from self-employment – change of accounting date	128
17	Capital allowances	135
18	Relief for trading and capital losses	161
19	Partnership taxation	172
20	Personal investment I – pensions and retirement annuities	181
21	Personal investment II – miscellaneous	186
22	Estate and trust income	191
23	National Insurance contributions and Social Security	197
	Income tax: end of section questions and answers	204

Part II: Corporation tax

24	General principles	219
25	The charge to corporation tax	226
26	Capital allowances	236
27	Charges on income – Quarterly returns	238
28	Qualifying distributions ACT and FII	245
29	Relief for losses	254
30	Close companies	263
31	Corporation tax rates and the small company	271
32	Groups and consortia	276
33	International aspects	291
34	Miscellaneous	300
	Corporation tax: end of section questions and answers	306

Part III: Taxation of chargeable gains

35	General principles	325
36	The basic rules of computation	329
37	Land and chattels	339
38	Stocks and securities	349
39	Taxable persons	362
40	Chargeable occasions	368
41	Gifts – holdover relief	373
42	Business assets and businesses	378
	Taxation of chargeable gains: end of section questions and answers	388

Part IV: Inheritance tax

43	General principles	397
44	Basic rules of computation	404
45	General exemptions and reliefs	410
46	Principles of valuation	417
47	Business property relief	424
48	Agricultural property and woodlands relief	427
49	Settlements	430
	Inheritance tax: end of section questions and answers	436

Part V: Value Added Tax

50	General principles	445
51	The VAT system	453
52	Special schemes for retailers	463
53	VAT worked examples	467

Part VI: Elements of tax planning

| 54 | Elements of tax planning | 475 |

Part VII: Case law

| 55 | Case law | 483 |

| **Index** | | 495 |

Preface

Aims of the manual

1. The main aim of this book is to provide a thorough basic knowledge of taxation covering Income Tax, Corporation tax, Taxation of Chargeable Gains, Inheritance Tax, and Value Added Tax.

    It has been written for students of the following:

    Chartered Association of Certified Accountants

    Level 2: Paper 7 The Tax Framework
    Level 3: Paper 11 Tax Planning

    Chartered Institute of Management Accountants

    Stage 3: Business Taxation

    Institute of Chartered Accountants in England and Wales

    PE 1   Elements of Taxation
    PE 2   Advanced Taxation

    Institute of Chartered Secretaries and Administrators

    Part IV

    Institute of Taxation

    Association of Taxation Technicians – all papers

    Associateship examination – all papers (introductory text)

    Association of Accounting Technicians

    Level 3: Taxation options

    Institute of Company Accountants

    Level 2: Paper 8
    Level 4: Paper 16

    Association of International Accountants

    Module F: Paper 16 Taxation and Tax Planning

    Universities and Colleges

    Foundation courses in Accounting – Taxation papers

    Accounting and Business Studies Degrees – Taxation papers

Need

2. a) This is a comprehensive text which covers the principles of the five taxes in some depth, within a single volume.

    b) The legal framework of each branch of taxation is important and this is provided with numerous illustrative examples of the practical operation of statute and case law.

    c) At the tax planning level taxation is an integrated discipline as decision making frequently requires a consideration of several aspects of taxation. This manual provides a foundation on which that integrated approach can be developed, as covered by Part VI of the book.

Approach

3. a) For each of the five branches of taxation studies this book should provide the student with:

    i) A knowledge of relevant statutory law

    ii) A knowledge of the case law developed to interpret statutory law.

    It should enable him to apply these legal principles to practical problems and prepare the necessary computations, and to understand the importance of the planning.

    b) Each of the branches of taxation is introduced by a general principles chapter which outlines the main features of each tax. Subsequent chapters develop the principles in detail with examples.

    c) Illustrative examples form an important feature of this text. At the end of each chapter and each section (except the introductory text) there are questions with answers for student self-testing. Also provided are further questions, the answers to which are contained in a separate supplement which can be obtained direct from the publishers by lecturers recommending the manual as a course text.

    This edition incorporates the provisions of the Finance Act 1997.

    Peter Rowes
    May 1997

Abbreviations and statutes

Abbreviations

ACT	Advance corporation tax	PAYE	Pay as you earn
All.ER	All England Reports	PRT	Petroleum revenue tax
BSI	Building society interest	RPI	Retail prices index
CAA	Capital Allowances Act 1990	Sch.	Schedule
CFC	Controlled foreign company	STC	Simons tax cases
CGT	Capital gains tax	STI	Simons tax intelligence
CIHC	Close Investment Holding company		
CIR	Commissioners of Inland Revenue	TA 1988	Income and corporation taxes Act 1988
CT	Corporation tax		
CTAP	Corporation tax accounting period	TC	Tax cases
		TCGA 1992	Taxation of chargeable gains Act 1992
DTR	Double taxation relief		
		TMA 1970	Taxes Management Act 1970
FA 1997	Finance Act 1997		
FII	Franked investment income	VAT	Value added tax
FP	Franked payment		
IBA	Industrial building allowance		
IHT	Inheritance tax		

Statutes

Part I	Income tax	Income and Corporation Taxes Act 1988 and Finance Act 1997
Part II	Corporation tax	do.
Part II	Capital Gains Tax	Taxation of Chargeable Gains Act 1992.
Part IV	Inheritance Tax	Inheritance Tax Act 1984
Part V	Value Added Tax	Value Added Tax Act 1994
—	Capital Allowances	Capital Allowances Act 1990

Summary of main changes 1997/98

Part I. Income tax

1. Personal reliefs

	1997/98 £	1996/97 £
a) Personal allowance	4,045	3,765
Married couple's allowance	* 1,830	* 1,790
Allowances: Aged 65–74		
Personal allowance	5,220	4,910
Married couple's allowance	* 3,185	* 3,115
Abatement of relief where income exceeds	15,600	15,200
Allowances: aged 75+		
Personal allowance	5,400	5,090
Married couple's allowance	* 3,225	* 3,115
Abatement of relief where income exceeds	15,600	15,200
Additional personal allowance for children	* 1,830	* 1,790
Wife's bereavement allowance	* 1,830	* 1,790
Blind person's allowance	1,280	1,250

b) The allowances marked with an asterisk (*) allowed at the 15% rate are given as a deduction in computing the tax liability.

2. Income tax rates

	1997/98	1996/97
Lower rate	20%	20%
Basic rate	23%	24%
Higher rate	40%	40%
Single rate trusts	34%	34%

3. Taxable bands

For 1997/98 the lower rate band has been extended by £200 to £4,100 and the basic 23% rate band £400 to 22,000.

Taxable income £	Band £	1997/98 Rate %	Tax payable on band £	Cumulative Tax £
0 – 4,100	4,100	20	820	820
4,100 – 26,100	22,000	23	5,060	5,880
26,101 – –		40	–	–

4. Class IV National Insurance

	1997/98	1996/97
Taxable band	7,010–24,180	6,860–23,660
Rate of tax	6%	6%
Maximum payable	£1,030.20	£1,008.00
Maximum deduction	–	–

From 1996/97 the 50% deduction is abolished.

5. Mortgage interest relief

The maximum loan for home purchase qualifying for tax relief remains at £30,000. From 6th April 1995 this relief is restricted to 15%.

6. Fuel scale rates

	1997/98 £	1996/97 £
Car fuel (petrol) scale		
1,400cc	800	710
1,401cc–2,000cc	1,010	890
2,001cc+	1,490	1,320
Car fuel (diesel) scale		
1,400cc	740	640
1,401cc–2,000cc	740	640
2,001cc+	940	820

7. **Fixed profit car scheme**

   With effect from 5th April 1997 the following rates apply:

	Pence per business mile	
Engine capacity	**up to 4,000 miles**	**over 4,000 miles**
0 – 1,000	28.0	17.0
1,001 – 1,500	35.0	20.0
1,501 – 2,000	45.0	25.0
2,001 –	63.0	36.0

8. **Company Vans Scale benefit**

   For 1997/98 the scale charges for private use of a company van are as follows:

	Age of Van	
	< 4 years old £	> 4 years old £
Scale charge	500	350

9. **PAYE and National Insurance Thresholds**

	1997/98		1996/97	
	PAYE £	**NI £**	**PAYE £**	**NI £**
Weekly pay	78.00	62.00	72.40	61.00
Monthly pay	338.00	269.00	313.75	264.00

10. **Official rates of interest**

    These rates apply from the dates shown:

Applicable from	Official Beneficial Loan Rate		
6 Jan 94	7.50%	6 Jun 96	7.00%
6 Nov 94	8.0%	6 Nov 96	6.75%
6 Oct 95	7.75%		
6 Feb 96	7.25%		

11. **Self-assessment**

    1996/97 is the first year to which self-assessment applies. This is also a transitional year for income assessed on a P.Y. basis. In general the transitional year will be assessed on 50% of the income of the two years ending in 1996/97.

12. **Savings income**

    Savings income such as bank interest, building society interest and NSB interest will be taxed at either 20% or 40% with effect from 6 April 1996. This procedure is the same as that which already applies to dividends.

Part II. Corporation tax

1. **Rates**

   The rates for the financial year 1997 are as follows:

	FY 1997 – 31.3.98	FY 1996 – 31.3.97
Full rate	33%	33%
Small company rate	23%	24%
Marginal bands	(£300,000 – £1,500,000)	(£300,000 – £1,500,000)
Marginal fraction	$1/40$	$9/400$

   The small company rate has been reduced from 24% to 23% for the 1997 FY.

2. **ACT**

   The rate of ACT for 97/98 is fixed at 20% of the distribution which gives a fraction of $\frac{20}{80}$ ie $\frac{1}{4}$

Part III. Capital gains tax

1. **Exemption**

   The annual exemption for individuals for 1997/98 is £6,500 per person (1996/97 £6,300).

   The lower rate of income tax applies to chargeable gains in appropriate circumstances.

Part IV. Inheritance tax

1. Rates

For chargeable transfers made on or after 6th April 1996 the IHT death rates are as follows:

On or after 6th April 1997		On or after 6th April 1996	
£	%	£	%
0 – 215,000	–	0 – 200,000	–
215,001 –	40	200,000 –	40

Part V. Value added tax

1. Registration

Registration levels applicable from 27.11.1996.

	£
Taxable turnover in previous 12 months	48,000
Taxable turnover in next 30 days	48,000

2. Deregistration

The annual limit for deregistration £46,000. From 27.11.1996.

3. VAT Fuel rates 1997/98

The following rates apply to VAT accounting periods beginning on or after the 6th April 1995, ie the first Return Period after that date.

Engine size (cc)	3 Month period				1 Month period			
	Scale charge diesel	VAT due per car	Scale charge petrol	VAT due per car	Scale charge diesel	VAT due per car	Scale charge petrol	VAT due per car
	£	£	£	£	£	£	£	£
1400 or less	185	27.55	200	29.78	61	9.08	66	9.82
More than 1400 but not more than 2000	185	27.55	252	37.53	61	9.08	84	12.51
More than 2000	235	35.0	372	55.40	78	11.61	124	18.46

The above rates are the same as those for income tax purposes and benefits in kind.

Part I

Income Tax

1   General principles

Introduction

1. In this chapter the main features of the income tax system are outlined, all of which are developed in detail in later chapters. It begins with some basic expressions. A summary of taxable income, its classification and basis of assessment is then provided. The remainder of the chapter deals with the principle tax deduction at source, and non taxable income. A summary of tax rates, personal allowances and reliefs relating to 1997/98 is given at the end.

Basic expressions

2. **The Income Tax Year 1997/98**

   This runs from the 6th April 1997, to the 5th April 1998, and is also known as the fiscal year. Assessments to income tax are made by reference to income tax years and are known as years of assessment.

   Tax Rates

   Rates of income tax for an income tax year are determined annually in the Finance Act. A summary of the rates from the FA 1997 are shown at the end of this chapter.

   Taxable Persons

   Income tax is charged on the income of individuals, partners and trusts resident in the UK. Non residents deriving any income from a UK source are also chargeable to income tax.

   Taxable Income

   Income on which income tax is payable is known as taxable income and this consists of the sum of income from all taxable sources, less deductions for charges on income paid, and personal allowances and reliefs other than those given in terms of tax as a deduction.

   Schedular System

   The system of taxation of income by reference to the classification of income under different groups or 'Schedules'.

Summary of taxable income 1997/98

		£	£
Income			
Income from employment	– salaries, wages, pensions etc	–	
	– benefits in kind	–	
Income from self-employment	– business income less capital allowances	–	
Income from savings	– dividends	–	
	– bank/building society interest	–	
Income from UK land and property		–	
Income from foreign investments		–	
			–
Deductions			
Personal allowance		–	
Covenants to charities		–	
Pension contributions – self employed			–
Gift aid		–	–
Total net taxable income			–
Tax payable	Lower rate – 20%	–	
	Basic rate – 23%	–	
	Higher rate – 40%	–	–
Allowances and reliefs given in terms of tax			
Personal allowances – MCA, APA, WBA		–	
Enterprise Investment Scheme		–	
Venture capital trusts		–	
Notional tax on investment income		–	–
Income tax due			–

The following points should be noted at this stage:

a) The undermentioned items are given relief at restricted rates:

		1997/98	1996/97
i)	Married couple allowance	15%	15%
ii)	Additional personal allowance	15%	15%
iii)	Widows bereavement allowance	15%	15%
iv)	Maintenance deduction	15%	15%
v)	Mortgage interest relief (MIRAS)	15%	15%
vi)	Medical insurance payments	23%	24%

Items i) to iv) are given relief by way of a deduction from the total tax liability for the year and not as a deduction in computing Net taxable income.

Mortgage interest relief at the 15% rate is given by deduction at source. Medical insurance payment relief is given at 23% by deduction at source.

b) Income from employment and self employment is after the deduction of any 'allowable expenses'.

c) With effect from 6th April 1996 savings income in general is subject to income tax at either the 20% or 40% rate. Where the income is received after deduction of income tax, such as bank and building society interest, the rate of 20% is applied at source.

3. The classification of income into earned and unearned income is only necessary in respect of the computation of relevant earnings for Personal Pension Plans and existing retirement annuity relief (see Chapter 20).

The nature of income

4. For income tax purposes, most income has been classified into what are known as Schedules, the rules applicable to which are contained in the Taxes Act 1988. A summary of the Schedules is given below with a brief description of the type of income designated within each Schedule. A more detailed analysis of each Schedule is contained in later chapters.

Classification of income by income tax schedule

Schedule A	Profits of a business letting property in the UK
Schedule D	
Case I	Profits of a trade carried on in the UK
Case II	Profits of a profession or vocation carried on in the UK
Case III	Bank interest, annuities
Case IV	Income from overseas securities
Case V	Income from overseas possessions
Case VI	Other annual profits
Schedule E	
Case I to III	Income received from employment and offices of profit
Schedule F	Dividends received from UK companies.

Income from savings

5. The following is a summary of the tax on income from savings in respect of the year 1997/98.

	Tax at source %	Tax on income %
Building society interest*	20	20–40
Bank interest*	20	20–40
Loan/debenture interest*	20	20–40
Interest on government securities*	20	20–40
National Savings Bank interest*	–	20–40
Dividends*	20	20–40
Covenant income	23	20–23–40
Trust income	23–34	20–23–40

Notes

i) For items marked with an asterisk there is no liability at the 23% rate.

ii) The income taxed at source is grossed up for income tax purposes and any higher rate is assessed on the gross income.

iii) Dividend income has been subject to the 20%/40% rate since 1993/94.

iv) In the case of bank and building society interest an individual can register to receive the interest gross in appropriate circumstances.

Basis of assessment

6. In order to ascertain an individual's taxable income for any given year of assessment, it is necessary to first identify his income with a particular income tax schedule and then apply the appropriate rules.

   With effect from 1997/98 all sources of income are assessed on a current years basis. 1996/97 is a transitional year towards self assessment in which all sources of income are taxed on either a current year basis or by reference to transitional provisions. For 1995/96 and earlier years a taxpayer could have taxable income arising on previous years basis and also on a current years basis as illustrated in the summary below.

Basis of assessment

		1997/98 et seq	1996/97	1995/96
Schedule A		CY	CY	CY
Schedule D	Case I and II	CY	TY	PY
	Case III	CY	TY	PY
	Case IV	CY	TY	PY
	Case V	CY	TY	PY
	Case VI	CY	CY	CY
Schedule E	Case I to III	CY	CY	CY
Schedule F		CY	CY	CY
Building society interest (unless Case III)		CY	CY	CY
Bank deposit interest (unless Case III)		CY	CY	CY

Notes

i) CY = Current year. TY = Transitional year. PY = Preceding year

ii) All new sources of income arising under Schedule D Case I or II, III, IV and V on or after 6th April 1994 are assessed on a current year basis from the beginning.

PAYE system

7. It should also be noted that a substantial proportion of all Schedule E income tax is in fact collected under what is known as the Pay As You Earn system. The main features of this system are covered in Chapter 10.

Due dates for payment – 1997/98

8. Under the new system for self assessment the taxpayer will automatically be required to make two payments on account and a third balancing payment to meet any outstanding tax. In respect of 1997/98 the position is as follows:

31st January 1998	First payment on account based on tax assessed for 1996/97. This will include the first instalment of Schedule D Case I and II, Cases III and IV and Schedule A.
31st July 1998	Second payment on account based on tax assessed for 1996/1997. This will include the second instalment of Schedule D Case I and II.
31st January 1999	Final balancing payment including tax at higher rates on taxed income and capital gains tax.

   For details see Chapter 2.

Due dates for payment – to 1995/96

9.

Source	Normal due dates
Schedule A	1st January in the year of assessment
Schedule C	By deduction at source
Schedule D	
Case I and II	1st January in year of assessment, and 1st July in the following year of assessment in two equal instalments
Case III	1st January in year of assessment
Taxed investment income including building society interest Schedule D	Higher rate 1st December in the following year of assessment
Case IV and V	1st January in year of assessment. But income from a foreign trade, profession or vocation, and foreign pensions, in two instalments as for Schedule D case I or II.
Case VI	1st January in the year of assessment
Schedule E	Normally collected under PAYE, and due when deducted

Flat rate

10. The Flat rate applies to the income of discretionary trusts and is 34% for 1997/98.

Non-taxable income

11. The following types of income are exempt from taxation:

a) The first £70 of interest on deposits with the National Savings Bank held in the Ordinary Accounts. Husband and wife may each claim £70 on separate accounts. Interest on investment accounts of the NSB, and on accounts with Trustee Savings Banks are fully taxable.

b) Interest on all National Savings Certificates.

c) Interest and bonuses on Save As You Earn (SAYE) certified contractual savings schemes.

d) Premium bond prizes.

e) Interest on certain government securities held by non residents.

f) Job release allowances if paid within one year of normal retirement age.

g) Compensation for loss of employment up to £30,000.

h) Redundancy payments.

i) War widows' pensions.

j) Interest payable on damages for personal injury or death.

k) Gambling winnings and competition prizes.

l) Scholarship awards and other educational grants.

m) Payments for services in the armed forces relating to:
    i) Wound and disability pensions
    ii) Service grants, bounties and gratuities
    iii) Annuities and additional pensions paid to holders of the Victoria Cross, George Cross and other gallantry awards.

n) Long service awards to employees, subject to certain limitations. (See Chapter 7).

o) Certain social security benefits such as: child benefit, family income supplement, maternity benefit and grant, attendance allowance, mobility allowance. Unemployment benefit and statutory sickness benefit are taxable.

p) Widow's payment of £1,000.

q) Up to £81.73 (£4,250 p.a.) per week of gross rent paid on furnished lettings on the taxpayers only or main residence.

r) Outplacement counselling.

Tax rates 1997/98

First £4,100 of Taxable Income   20%
Basic rate   23%
Higher rate   40%

Taxable Income £	Band £	Rate %	Tax Payable on Band £	Cumulative Tax £
0 – 4,100	4,100	20	820	820
4,101 – 26,100	22,000	23	5,060	5,880
26,100 –		40		

Flat rate 1997/98

Discretionary trust income   34%

Personal allowances 1997/98

	£	Relief at 15% rate
Personal allowance	4,045	
Married couples allowance	1,830	✓
Allowances aged 65–74:		
Personal age allowance	5,220	
Married couples age allowance	3,185	✓
No age allowance if income over – single		
– married		
Abatement income level	15,600	
Allowance aged 75–:		
Personal age allowance	5,400	
Married couples age allowance	3,225	✓
No age allowance if income over – single		
– married		
Abatement income level	15,600	
Additional personal allowance for children	1,830	✓
Wife's bereavement allowance	1,830	✓
Blind persons allowance	1,280	

National insurance 1997/98

Retirement pension – single person   3,247
Class 4 contributions – self-employed
6.0% of profits between 7,010–24,180
Maximum liability   1,030.20

2   Administration

1. This chapter provides an outline of the administrative features of the income tax system.

    The first part of the chapter deals with the general organisational background followed by sections concerned with the new self-assessment arrangements which apply for the first time into 1996/97.

    The second part of the chapter deals with the appeals procedures, and the assessment and payment rules applicable to 1995/96. A specimen Tax Return for 1997 is included as an appendix.

Inland revenue

2. Income tax is administered by the Commissioners of Inland Revenue or as they are normally called the Board of Inland Revenue who are responsible to the Treasury. The Board operates in regional and district offices through Inspector of Taxes and Collectors of Taxes. The former are primarily responsible for the issue of Tax Returns and the assessment of income tax, while the latter are concerned with the collection of assessed amounts. A continuous reorganisation of the organisation is taking place which envisages the following changes:

    a) Local tax and collection offices will be restructured into Taxpayer Service Offices and Taxpayer District Offices.

    b) Taxpayer Service Offices will deal with changes to PAYE code numbers and personal reliefs, issue of assessments and preliminary collection services. It is anticipated that most taxpayers will only have to deal with this office.

    c) Taxpayer District Offices will carry out compliance work such as the examination of some business accounts, corporation tax, PAYE, Audit and local collection work.

Tax returns

3. The first self assessment Tax Return issued in April 1997 consists of the following:

    1) The tax return headed – Tax Return for the year ended 5th April 1997

    2) The opportunity to request supplementary pages where appropriate

    - Employment
    - Share schemes
    - Self employment
    - Partnership
    - Land and property
    - Foreign
    - Trusts etc
    - Capital gains
    - Non residence etc

    Income from all sorces and capital gains for the year ended 5th April 1997 are required together with a claim for allowances.

Self assessment 1996/97 et seq

4. The following is a summary of the main administrative features of the section of self assessment.

    a) For individuals and partnerships the first year to which self assessment applies is 1996/97.

    b) In April 1997 the revised self assessment tax return issued consists of one main return and 9 supplementary pages

    c) The tax return contains a section for the self-calculation of the tax due or repayable.

    d) There are two key dates for the filing of tax returns.

    i)   By the 30th September following the end of the tax year for those taxpayers who require the Inland Revenue to compute the tax payable.

    ii) By the 31st January following the end of the tax year for taxpayers who wish to make their own calculation of tax due.

    e) Thus for 1996/97 the two filing dates are 30th September 1997 for I.R. calculation and 31st January 1998 for taxpayer calculation.

f) Failure to file a tax return on or before 31st January 1998, in respect of 1996/97 will incur an automatic fixed penalty of £100. If the return is still outstanding 6 months after the filing date a further £100 penalty will be incurred unless a daily penalty has been approved by the Commissioners.

g) Under the new system the obligation to pay tax is not linked to the issue of assessments as at present. Instead the taxpayer will be automatically required to make two payments on account and a third balancing payment to meet any tax outstanding.

h) The first payment on account is due on the 31st January of the income tax year in question. The second payment on account is due on the 31st July following the end of the income tax year. The balancing payment is due on the 31st January following the end of the income tax year.

i) The payments on account are contained in a Self Assessment – Statement of Account which shows the due dates for payment and contains a payslip.

j) Where the tax payable is expected to be lower in the year of assessmwnt than in the previous year the taxpayer can make a claim to reduce the payments on account.

Year of assessment 1996/97 – Summary of Events

5. I   31. 1. 1997   1st Payment on account   –   Computed by reference to 1995/96 relevant amount

II   31. 7. 1997   2nd Payment on account   –   Computed by reference to 1995/96 relevant amount

III 30. 9. 1997   File 1997 Tax return   –   I.R. to compute tax payable for 1996/97

IV   31. 1. 1998   File 1997 Tax return   –   Taxpayer to compute tax payable for 1996/97

V   31. 1. 1998   Balance payment due   –   Balance of any tax due for 1996/97

Due dates for payment – 1996/97

6. 31st January 1997   First payment on account – in general 50% of the relevant amount for the preceding income tax year i.e. 1995/96.

31st July 1997   Second payment on account – in general 50% of the relevant amount for the preceding income tax year i.e. 1995/96.

31st January 1998   Balancing payment/repayment including any capital gains tax due for 1996/97.

Payments on Account

7. The following general points should be noted:

i) Under the Regulations taxpayers will not need to make POAs if

a) their income tax (and NIC) liability for the preceding year – net of tax deducted at source or tax credits on dividends – is less than £500 in total or

b) more than 80% of their income tax (NIC) liability for the preceding year was met by deduction of tax at source or from tax credits on dividends.

ii) The most common ways of paying tax by deduction are through Pay As You Earn (PAYE), the sub-contractors' deduction scheme, and tax paid on interest received.

iii) The first tax year to which POAs apply in 1996/97. This is a transitional year for which there are special rules. POAs for the year 1996/97 are worked out by reference to only certain types of income assessed for 1995/96. For this reason the second limit – the percentage test – does not apply to 1996/97. Both limits will operate for 1997/98 onwards.
POAs are due by 31st January in the tax year and by 31st July after its end.

iv) Payments on account apply for the first time in 1996/97. The 1996/97 POAs are based on certain income tax (and Class 4 NIC) liabilities for 1995/96. (The liabilities which are ignored are most employment and pension income, and investment income from shares or which is paid after deduction of tax at source.) The 1996/97 POAs will be due for payment on 31st January 1997 and 31st July 1997. In December 1996 the Inland Revenue notified relevant taxpayers of the amounts they should pay by those dates.

v) For 1997/98 onwards income tax and NIC liability (net of tax deducted at source and tax credits) for the preceding year will determine whether or not payments on account are needed. If they are due, they will normally be half the tax (NIC) liability for the preceding year, net of tax deducted at source and tax credits. The first payment on account is due on 31st January in the tax year and the second on 31st July after its end. Where taxpayers consider their tax (NIC) bill (net of tax deducted at source and tax credits) for the current year will be lower than that for the previous year, they may claim to reduce their POAs accordingly.

vi) Where payments on account do not meet the entire tax (NIC) liability – net of tax deducted at source and tax credits – for a tax year, a final payment will be due by 31st January after the end of the tax year. Where they exceed the final tax liability, a repayment will arise.

Example

Mr. X's self assessment for 1997/98 shows:

profits	£50,000	tax deducted	nil
interest (gross)	3,000	tax deducted	£600
Total	53,000		600

His total tax and NIC bill turns out to be

tax	£15,000	
NIC	500	15,500

So his payment due for 1997/98 is   14,900

The £500 test does not relieve Mr. X of the need to make POAs so he has to consider the percentage test.

Mr. X has to make POAs for 1998/99 because his tax deducted at source (£600) is not more than 80% of his total liability (£15,500).

Each payment on account for 1998/99 will be half his payment due for 1997/98 i.e. £7,450.

Relevant Amount – 1996/97

8. The relevant amount for 1995/96 comprises:

Total 1995/96 tax and NIC on   – Schedule D cases I to VI

– Schedule A

– Schedule E Direct Collection Assessments

Excluded from the above is higher rate tax on taxed income, capital gains tax, and on any other type of Schedule E income.

Where total relevant amount is less than £500.00 no payment on account is required. For general rules see below.

Payments on account in respect of 1996/97

31st January 1997	–	50% × 1995/96 Schedule D case I & II + NIC class IV
	+	100% Schedule A; Schedule D cases III – VI
31st July 1997	–	50% × 1995/96 Schedule D cases I & II + NIC class IV.

Balancing Payment

31st January 1998   –   Balance of any tax due for 1996/97 including capital gains tax.

Example

P has the following income tax and capital gain tax liabilities agreed for 1996/97 based on his 1997 Tax Return.

	£
Schedule D case I & NIC	25,000
Capital Gains Tax	1,000

The relevant amount for 1995/96 has been agreed in the sum of £18,000 all attributable to Schedule D case I income.

Show the payments of the tax to be made in respect of the year 1996/97.

Solution

P. Tax liability for 1996/97

		£
31st January 1997	50% × Relevant amount 1995/96	
	= 50% × 18,000	9,000
31st July 1997	50% × Relevant amount 1995/96	
	= 50% × 18,000	9,000
31st January 1998	Balance of tax due	8,000
		26,000

Note:

The total tax due for 1996/97 is

		£
	Income tax	25,000
	Capital gain tax	1,000
		26,000
Less Payment on account (1995/96 relevant amount)		18,000
	Balance due	8,000

Surcharges on income tax – 1996/97

9. In addition to any interest that may arise on any tax paid late there will also be a scheme of surcharges to encourage prompt payments: the initial surcharge will be 5% of any tax unpaid after 28 days from the due date for payment. The surcharge will be 5% of any tax unpaid at that date.

   Where any tax remains unpaid more than 6 months after the due date for payment then a further surcharge of 5% of the tax due will be charged.

   The surcharge will be payable in respect of any tax which is shown due in any self assessment (whether calculated by the taxpayer or the Inland Revenue) but which is not covered by any P.O.A. or balancing payment.

Interest on under and overpayments

10. A charge to interest will automatically arise on any tax paid late whether in respect of income tax, NIC or capital gains tax in respect of:

    i) any payment on account

    ii) any balancing item

    iii) any tax payable following an amendment to self assessment whether made by the taxpayer or the Inland Revenue

    iv) any tax payable in a discovery assessment by the I.R.

    Interest will arise from the due dates for payment to the date on which payment is finally made for payments on account and balancing payments.

    For amendments to self assessments the interest charge will run from the annual filing date for the income tax year i.e. the 31st January following the end of the income tax year. Interest on any overpayments of tax will be paid automatically.

Example

    M has the following data relating to 1995/96 and 1996/97.

		1995/96 £	1996/97 £
Schedule D Case I tax due		5,000	6,000
Payments made	1 April 1997		2,500
	31 July 1997		1,500
	2 March 1998		2,000

    Calculate the amounts on which interest will be charged and show the interest period.

Solution

Amount Payable £	Amount Paid £	Due date	Actual date	Interest Period £	Interest amount
2,500	2,500	31.1. 97	1. 4. 97	1. 2. 97 – 31. 3. 97	2,500
2,500	1,500	31.7. 97	31. 7. 97	1. 8. 97 – 1. 3. 98	1,000
2,000	2,000	31.1. 98	2. 3. 98	1. 2. 98 – 1. 3. 98	2,000

Notes:

i) As the first POA was late interest will automatically be charged for the interest period shown.

ii) As the second POA was not fully met interest will be charged from the 1st August 1997 to the settlement date of 1st March 1998.

iii) As the final balancing amount was not paid on the due date there will be an automatic surcharge of 5% on the balance due i.e £1,000 × 5% = £50.

NB w.e.f 31st January 1997 the following interest rates apply:

Interest on tax due (income tax and capital gains tax)	8.5%
Repayment supplement	4.0%

Appeals – organisational structure

11. The main structure of the appeal system in England and Wales may be illustrated as follows:

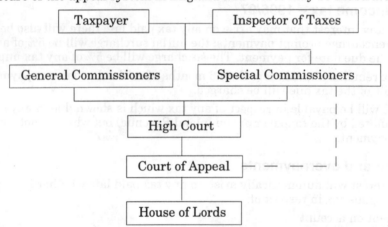

a) General Commissioners for the purposes of income tax are usually appointed from local business or professional people. They are unpaid, but can obtain repayment of normal expenses. A Clerk to the General Commissioners, who is legally qualified, is also appointed to give advice and assistance.

b) Special Commissioners are officials appointed by the Lord Chancellor who must be Barristers, Advocates or Solicitors of not less than 10 years standing. They hear appeals singly except where the Presiding Special Commissioner (one of the Special Commissioners so designated by the Lord Chancellor) decides that more than one is required.

c) In general an appeal may be made to either the General or Special Commissioners. However, an election to appeal to the Special Commissioners can be disregarded by the General Commissioners. This may arise, for example, where the Inspector of Taxes refers the taxpayer's election to appeal to the Special Commissioners, to the General Commissioners for their consideration and they direct accordingly.

d) There are specific circumstances where an appeal is only dealt with by the Special Commissioners eg

    i)   Sec 47 TMA 1970 – Value of unquoted shares

    ii)   Sec 739 TA 1988 – Transfer of assets abroad

e) The General Commissioners may arrange to transfer an appeal to the Special Commissioners if the latter agree. This may occur where an appeal before the General Commissioners is of a complex nature or, could necessitate a lengthy period of time for consideration.

f) Either the taxpayer or the Inspector of Taxes may appeal from the Commissioners to the High Courts. There is a further right of appeal to the Court of Appeal, and where leave is granted to the House of Lords. On an order made by the Lord Chancellor, certain classes of appeal from the decisions of the Special Commissioners may be referred directly to the Court of Appeal.

g) Changes are planned with respect to appeals, costs and reporting of the Special Commissioners in due course.

h) The FA (No2) 1992 contains provisions which enable changes to the names and structure of the appeal system to be made by statutory instrument.

i) Hearings of the Special Commissions are now published.

Appeals – system

12. The following points arise under this heading:

a) Where an assessment is issued the taxpayer is given 30 days within which to appeal against the assessment where he is not in agreement with its contents.

b) A late appeal may be accepted by the Inspector of Taxes where there is reasonable excuse for delay, but if he does not accept the late appeal it must be referred by him to the Commissioners for their decision. TMA Sec 49. If they do not accept the late appeal there is no further appeal to the High Court.

c) Where an appeal is made the grounds of the appeal must be stated in writing to the Inspector of Taxes whose address is on the Notice of Assessment.

d) If an appeal is made any tax due is respect of the assessment remains payable unless an application to postpone payment is also made. See below.

e) Appeals may be settled by mutual agreement between the taxpayer (or his Agent) and the Inspector of Taxes under Sec 54 TMA 1970 and in practice this is the most common method adopted. In these circumstances the assessment becomes 'final and conclusive' as if the Commissioners had themselves determined the appeal. However the appellant can repudiate this agreement within 30 days if he notifies the Inspector accordingly.

f) Where agreement cannot be reached with the Inspector of Taxes the case may be taken before the Commissioners for their deliberation.

g) An appeal against an assessment is to be determined by a hearing before the Commissioners. Upon determination of the appeal, the Commissioners may confirm, reduce or increase the assessment as appropriate subject to an appeal by either party to the High Courts Sec 50 (6)&(7) TMA 1970.

Due dates for payment – to 1995/96

13.

Source		Normal due dates
Schedule A		1st January in the year of assessment
Schedule C		By deduction at source
Schedule D	Case I & II	1st January in year of assessment, and 1st July in the following year of assessment in two equal instalments.
	Case III	1st January in year of assessment Higher rate 1st December in the following year of assessment.
Taxed investment income including Building Society interest		
	Case IV & V	1st January in year of assessment. But income from a foreign trade, profession or vocation, and foreign pensions, in two instalments as for Schedule D case I or II
	Case VI	1st January in the year of assessment
Schedule E		Normally collected under PAYE and due when deducted.

Note: From 1996/97 new dates for payment will apply.

Penalties – from 1996/97

14.

a) Failure to give notice of chargeability to income or capital gains tax within 6 months after end of year of assessment (TMA 1970 s 7).

Amount not exceeding tax assessed for that year and not paid before 1 February following that year.

b) Failure to comply with notice requiring return for income tax or capital gains tax (TMA 1970 s 93).

Initial penalty of £100; and, upon direction of Commissioners, further penalty not exceeding £60 for each day on which failure continues after notification of direction; if failure continues after six months following filing date, and no application for a direction has been made, a further penalty of £100.

In addition, if failure continues after first anniversary of filing date, and there would have been a liability to tax shown in the return, a penalty not exceeding the liability that would have been shown in the return.

If the taxpayer can prove that the liability to tax shown in the return would not have exceeded the sum of penalties above, those penalties taken together are not to exceed that amount.

c) Failure to retain records as required by TMA 1970 s 12B (1) (TMA 1970 s 12B (5)).

Penalty not exceeding £3,000.

d) Falsification of documents (TMA 1970 s 20BB).

On summary conviction, a fine not exceeding the statutory maximum (£5,000); on conviction on indictment, imprisonment for a term not exceeding 2 years or a fine or both.

Mitigation of penalties

15. The penalty figure will usually be a percentage of the tax underpaid or paid late and in practice the Inspector never seeks a penalty of more than 100% of the tax. That figure is reduced, by negotiation with reductions based on the following criteria:

Disclosure   –   a reduction of up to 20% or up to 30% for voluntary disclosure

Cooperation   –   a reduction of up to 40%

Gravity   –   a reduction of up to 40%

The penalty together with the amount of tax underpaid plus interest is incorporated in a formal letter to the taxpayer which also encloses details of the procedures for payment.

Where the terms of the settlement contract are agreed to by the taxpayer formal proceedings cannot be undertaken by the Revenue. If the taxpayer does not make an 'offer to settle' then assessments to cover the tax interest and penalties will be raised subject to the normal appeals procedures.

Error or mistake relief TMA Section 33

16. Relief can be claimed in writing against any over-assessment due to an error or mistake (including an omission) in any return on statement. The relief must be claimed within 6 years of the end of the year of assessment which the assessment in which the assessment was made and is given where the return or statement was incorrect.

The payment is determined by the Board with appeal to the Special Commissions, and on a point of law to the High Court.

• Student self-testing question

A has the following data relating to 1995/96 & 1996/97.

	1995/96	1996/97
Schedule D Case I	16,000	18,000
Capital gains tax	1,500	2,000
Schedule A	2,500	4,000
Higher rate on investment income	1,000	1,500
Total tax due	21,000	25,500

Calculate the tax payments for 1996/97 and the due dates for payments.

Solution

1996/97 payments and due dates

	31. 1. 97	31. 7. 97	31. 1. 98	Total
Schedule D Case I	8,000	8,000		16,000
Schedule A	2,500			2,500
Balance 25,500 – 18,500	–	–	7,000	7,000
	10,500	8,000	7,000	25,500

Notes:

i) *Schedule A for 1995/96 is payable wholly on the 31st January 1997 and not apportioned.*

ii) *Capital gain tax and higher rate tax on investment income for 1996/97 is included in the balance payment of £7,000.*

• Questions without answers

1. From the following information relating to 1995/96 & 1996/97 complete the payments to be made in respect of 1996/97.

	1995/96	1996/97
Schedule D Case I tax paid	15,000	18,000
Schedule A paid	1,000	2,000
Capital gain tax paid	1,200	3,000
Higher rate on investment income paid	3,000	1,000

2. The statement of Account for J received on December 18th 1996 showed total Payment on account for 1996/1997 due of £5,500.

J paid the sum of £2,000 on the 31st March 1997 and £3,500 on the 31st August 1997. Assuming a rate of interest of 10% compute the amount of interest which will be automatically assessed on J.

Appendix to chapter 2

Tax Return
for the year ended 5 April 1997

FINAL DRAFT

Please read this page first

The green arrows and instructions will guide you through your Tax Return

This Notice requires you by law to send me a Tax Return for the year from 6 April 1996 to 5 April 1997. Give details of all the income and capital gains on which you may be charged to tax using:

- this form and any supplementary pages you need; **OR**
- other Inland Revenue-approved forms; **OR**
- the Electronic Lodgement Service (ELS).

Make sure your Tax Return reaches me by:

- **30 September 1997**
  - if you want me to calculate your tax, **OR**
  - include any tax you owe (up to £1,000) in next year's tax code, **OR**
- **31 January 1998** if you want to calculate your tax and do not want any tax you owe included in next year's tax code.

You are liable to automatic penalties if your Tax Return does not reach me by 31 January 1998. You face interest and surcharge on any tax you pay late.

All Tax Returns will be checked. Please remember that there are penalties for supplying false information.

Your new Tax Return

I have sent you pages 1 to 8 of your Tax Return.

- Page 2 tells you about supplementary pages for some types of income and gains. For example; there are pages for employment, and for self-employment income.
- Pages 3 and 4 are for details of other income, for example pensions and savings.
- Page 5 is for claiming reliefs .
- Page 6 is for claiming allowances.
- Pages 7 and 8 are for other information.

I have included any supplementary pages I think you need after page 8. You are responsible for making sure you have the right ones. Use page 2 to check.

I have also sent you:

- a Tax Return Guide to help you fill in your Tax Return - read pages 2 and 3 of the guide before you start, and
- a Tax Calculation Guide to help you calculate your tax if you want to.

If you need help:

- refer to your Tax Return Guide, **OR**
- ring the number above - most queries can be answered by telephone, **OR**
- when the office is closed, phone our Helpline on 0000 000000 (open 7 days a week until 10pm), **OR**
- if you do not want to explain your query on the phone, call in at a Tax Enquiry Centre - look under 'Inland Revenue' in the phone book.

SA100

Please turn over

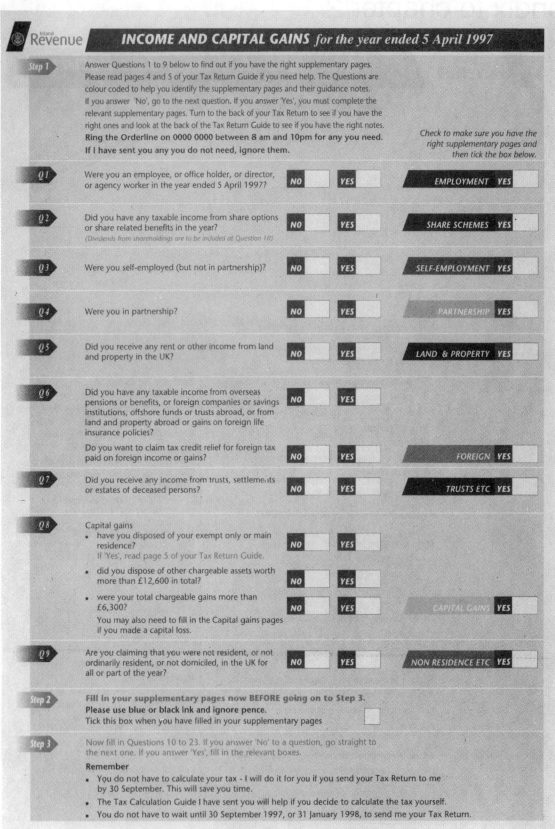

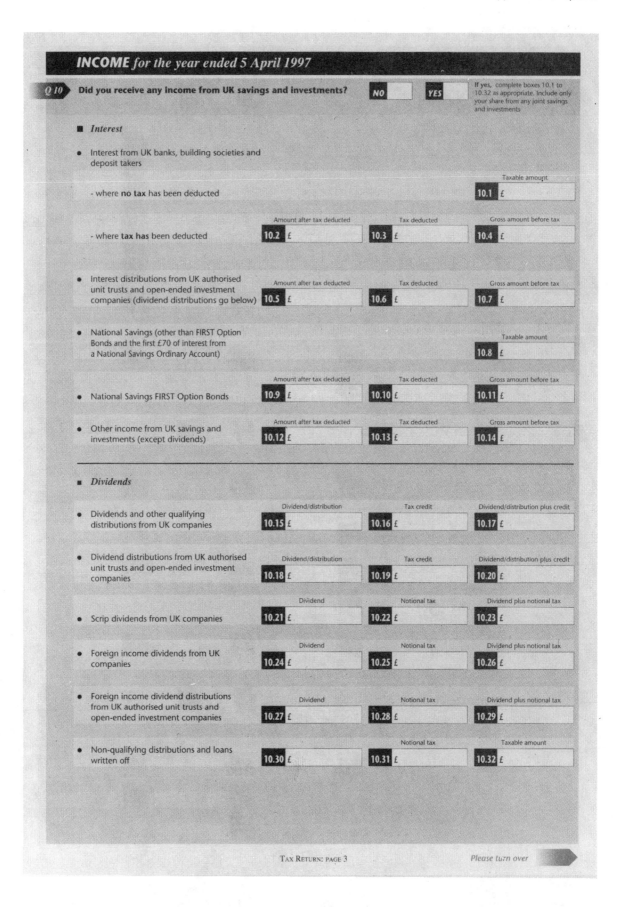

INCOME *for the year ended 5 April 1997, continued*

Q11 Did you receive a UK pension, retirement annuity or Social Security benefit?   NO [ ]   YES [ ]   If yes, complete boxes 11.1 to 11.13 as appropriate

■ *State pensions and benefits*

	Taxable amount for 1996-97
● State Retirement Pension	**11.1** £
● Widow's Pension	**11.2** £
● Widowed Mother's Allowance	**11.3** £
● Industrial Death Benefit pension	**11.4** £
● Unemployment Benefit, Income Support and Jobseeker's Allowance	**11.5** £
● Invalid Care Allowance	**11.6** £
● Statutory Sick Pay and Statutory Maternity Pay paid by the Department of Social Security	**11.7** £

	Tax deducted	Gross amount before tax
● Taxable Incapacity Benefit	**11.8** £	**11.9** £

■ *Other pensions and retirement annuities*

	Amount after tax deducted	Tax deducted	Gross amount before tax
● Pensions (other than State pensions) and retirement annuities	**11.10** £	**11.11** £	**11.12** £

	Amount after tax deducted
● Exemption/deduction - see notes in your Tax Return Guide	**11.13** £

Q12 Did you receive any of the following kinds of income?   NO [ ]   YES [ ]   If yes, complete boxes 12.1 to 12.12 as appropriate

	Income receivable	Exempt amount	Income less exempt amount
● Taxable maintenance or alimony	**12.1** £	**12.2** £	**12.3** £

	Number of years		Amount of gain
● Gains on UK life insurance policies (without notional tax)	**12.4**		**12.5** £

	Number of years	Notional tax	Amount of gain
● Gains on UK life insurance policies (with notional tax)	**12.6**	**12.7** £	**12.8** £

	Amount
Corresponding deficiency relief	**12.9** £

	Amount received	Notional tax	Amount plus notional tax
● Refunds of surplus additional voluntary contributions	**12.10** £	**12.11** £	**12.12** £

Q13 Did you receive any other income which you have not already entered elsewhere on your Tax Return?   NO [ ]   YES [ ]   If yes, complete boxes 13.1 to 13.6 as appropriate
Make sure you fill in any supplementary pages before answering Question 13.

	Amount after tax deducted	Tax deducted	Amount before tax
● Other income	**13.1** £	**13.2** £	**13.3** £

	Losses brought forward	Loss used in 1996-97
	13.4 £	**13.5** £

	Losses sustained in 1996-97
	13.6 £

TAX RETURN: PAGE 4

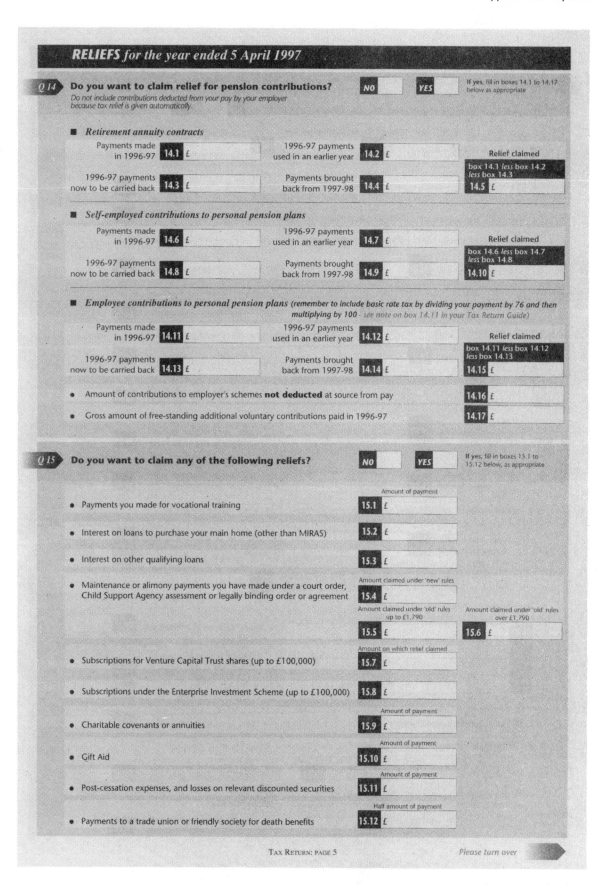

RELIEFS *for the year ended 5 April 1997*

Q14 Do you want to claim relief for pension contributions? NO YES If yes, fill in boxes 14.1 to 14.17 below as appropriate

Do not include contributions deducted from your pay by your employer because tax relief is given automatically.

■ *Retirement annuity contracts*

| Payments made in 1996-97 | 14.1 £ | 1996-97 payments used in an earlier year | 14.2 £ | Relief claimed |
| 1996-97 payments now to be carried back | 14.3 £ | Payments brought back from 1997-98 | 14.4 £ | box 14.1 less box 14.2 less box 14.3 14.5 £ |

■ *Self-employed contributions to personal pension plans*

| Payments made in 1996-97 | 14.6 £ | 1996-97 payments used in an earlier year | 14.7 £ | Relief claimed |
| 1996-97 payments now to be carried back | 14.8 £ | Payments brought back from 1997-98 | 14.9 £ | box 14.6 less box 14.7 less box 14.8 14.10 £ |

■ *Employee contributions to personal pension plans* (remember to include basic rate tax by dividing your payment by 76 and then multiplying by 100 - see note on box 14.11 in your Tax Return Guide)

| Payments made in 1996-97 | 14.11 £ | 1996-97 payments used in an earlier year | 14.12 £ | Relief claimed |
| 1996-97 payments now to be carried back | 14.13 £ | Payments brought back from 1997-98 | 14.14 £ | box 14.11 less box 14.12 less box 14.13 14.15 £ |

● Amount of contributions to employer's schemes **not deducted** at source from pay 14.16 £

● Gross amount of free-standing additional voluntary contributions paid in 1996-97 14.17 £

Q15 Do you want to claim any of the following reliefs? NO YES If yes, fill in boxes 15.1 to 15.12 below, as appropriate

Amount of payment
● Payments you made for vocational training 15.1 £

● Interest on loans to purchase your main home (other than MIRAS) 15.2 £

● Interest on other qualifying loans 15.3 £

● Maintenance or alimony payments you have made under a court order, Child Support Agency assessment or legally binding order or agreement Amount claimed under 'new' rules 15.4 £

Amount claimed under 'old' rules up to £1,790 15.5 £ Amount claimed under 'old' rules over £1,790 15.6 £

Amount on which relief claimed
● Subscriptions for Venture Capital Trust shares (up to £100,000) 15.7 £

● Subscriptions under the Enterprise Investment Scheme (up to £100,000) 15.8 £

Amount of payment
● Charitable covenants or annuities 15.9 £

Amount of payment
● Gift Aid 15.10 £

Amount of payment
● Post-cessation expenses, and losses on relevant discounted securities 15.11 £

Half amount of payment
● Payments to a trade union or friendly society for death benefits 15.12 £

ALLOWANCES *for the year ended 5 April 1997*

Q 16 *You get your personal allowance of £3,765 automatically. If you were born before 6 April 1932, enter your date of birth in box 21.4 to get age-related allowances. Fill in other boxes as appropriate.*

Do you want to claim any of the following allowances? NO YES If yes, fill in boxes 16.1 to 16.28 as appropriate

Date of registration (if first year of claim)	Local authority (or other register)

■ *Blind person's allowance* 16.1 / / 16.2

■ *Transitional allowance* (for some wives with husbands on low income if claimed in earlier years)

● Tick to claim and give details in the 'Additional information' box on page 8 please 16.3
(see page 23 of your Tax Return Guide for what is needed)

● If you want to calculate your tax enter amount of transitional allowance you can have in box 16.4 16.4 £

■ *Married couple's allowance - if you are a married man* - *see page 24 of your Tax Return Guide*

● Wife's full name 16.5

● Date of marriage (if after 5 April 1996) 16.6 / /

● Wife's date of birth (if before 6 April 1932) 16.7 / /

● Tick box 16.8 if you and your wife have allocated half the allowance to her 16.8

● Wife's tax reference (if known, please) 16.9

● Tick box 16.10 if you and your wife have allocated all the allowance to her 16.10

■ *Married couple's allowance - if you are a married woman* - *see page 23 of your Tax Return Guide*

● Date of marriage (if after 5 April 1996) 16.11 / /

● Husband's full name 16.12

● Tick box 16.13 if you and your husband have allocated half the allowance to you 16.13

● Husband's tax reference (if known, please) 16.14

● Tick box 16.15 if you and your husband have allocated all the allowance to you 16.15

■ *Additional personal allowance* (available in some circumstances if you have a child living with you - *see page 24 of your Tax Return Guide*)

● Name of the child claimed for 16.16

● Child's date of birth 16.17 / /

● Tick if child lives with you 16.18

● Name of university etc/type of training if child 16 or over on 6 April 1996 and in full time education or training 16.19

Shared claims
Name and address of other person claiming

16.20

Postcode

● Enter your share as a percentage 16.21 %

● If share not agreed, enter number of days in year ended 5 April 1997 child lived with

- you 16.22 days

- other person 16.23 days

■ *Widow's bereavement allowance*

● Date of your husband's death 16.24 / /

■ *Transfer of surplus allowances* - *see page 25 of your Tax Return Guide before you fill in boxes 16.25 to 16.28*,

● Tick if you want your spouse to have your unused allowances 16.25

● Tick if you want to have your spouse's unused allowances 16.26

Please give details in the 'Additional information' box on page 8 (*see page 25 of your Tax Return Guide to see what is needed*)
If you want to calculate your tax enter the amount of the surplus allowance you can have.

● Blind person's surplus allowance 16.27 £

● Married couple's surplus allowance 16.28 £

TAX RETURN: PAGE 6

OTHER INFORMATION *for the year ended 5 April 1997*

Q17 Have you had any 1996-97 tax refunded directly by your Tax Office or Unemployment Benefit Office? `NO` `YES` If yes, enter the amount of the refund here

17.1 £

Q18 Do you want to calculate your tax? `NO` `YES` If yes do it now and then fill in boxes 18.1 to 18.9 below. Your Tax Calculation Guide will help

- Unpaid tax for earlier years included in your tax code for 1996-97   **18.1** £
- Tax due for 1996-97 included in your tax code for a later year   **18.2** £
- Total tax due for 1996-97 *(put the amount in brackets if an overpayment)*   **18.3** £
- Unpaid tax for earlier years   **18.4** £
- Overpaid tax for earlier years   **18.5** £
- Your first payment on account for 1997-98   **18.6** £

Tick box 18.7 if you are making a claim to reduce your payments on account and say why in the 'Additional information' box **18.7**   Tick box 18.8 if you do **not** need to make payments on account **18.8**

- 1997-98 tax you are reclaiming now   **18.9** £

Q19 Do you want to claim a repayment if you have paid too much tax? `NO` `YES` If yes, fill in boxes 19.1 to 19.12 as appropriate

(If you tick 'No', I will set any amount you are owed against your next tax bill.)

Should the repayment/payment be sent

- to you? *(tick box and go to Question 20)* **19.1**

or

- your bank or building society account or other nominee *(tick box and fill in boxes 19.3 to 19.7 or boxes 19.3 to 19.12 as appropriate)?* **19.2**

Please give details of your (or your nominee's) bank or building society account for repayment

Name of bank or building society **19.3**	
Branch sort code **19.4**	— —
Account number **19.5**	
Name of account **19.6**	
Building society ref. **19.7**	

Fill in boxes 19.8 to 19.12 if you want the repayment to be made to someone other than yourself (a nominee).

Name

I authorise **19.8**

If you want your repayment to be made to your agent tick box 19.9 **19.9**

Agent's ref. for you **19.10**

Nominee's address **19.11**

Postcode

to receive on my behalf the amount due

This authority must be signed by you. A photocopy of your signature will not do. **19.12**

Signature

Q20 Are your details on the front of the form wrong? `NO` `YES` If yes, please make any corrections on the front of the form

Q21 Please give other personal details in boxes 21.1 to 21.4

Please give a daytime telephone number if convenient. It is often quicker to phone if we need to ask you about your Tax Return.

Your telephone number **21.1**

Say if you are single, married, widowed, divorced or separated **21.3**

or, if you prefer, your agent's telephone number **21.2**

Date of birth **21.4** / /

(also give your agent's name and reference in the 'Additional information' box on page 8)

If you were born before 6 April 1932, or you have ticked the 'Yes' box in Question 14, or you are claiming relief for Venture Capital Trust subscriptions

Please turn over

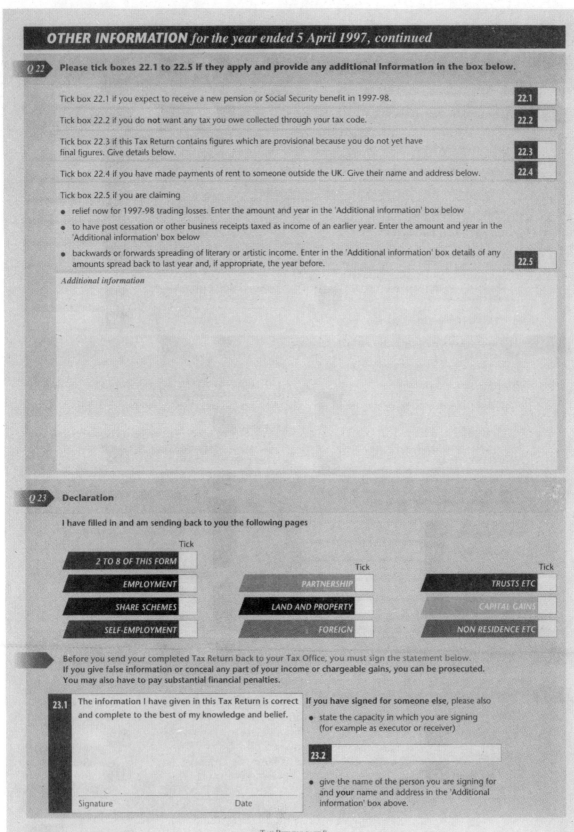

OTHER INFORMATION *for the year ended 5 April 1997, continued*

Q 22 Please tick boxes 22.1 to 22.5 if they apply and provide any additional information in the box below.

Tick box 22.1 if you expect to receive a new pension or Social Security benefit in 1997-98. **22.1**

Tick box 22.2 if you do **not** want any tax you owe collected through your tax code. **22.2**

Tick box 22.3 if this Tax Return contains figures which are provisional because you do not yet have final figures. Give details below. **22.3**

Tick box 22.4 if you have made payments of rent to someone outside the UK. Give their name and address below. **22.4**

Tick box 22.5 if you are claiming

- relief now for 1997-98 trading losses. Enter the amount and year in the 'Additional information' box below
- to have post cessation or other business receipts taxed as income of an earlier year. Enter the amount and year in the 'Additional information' box below
- backwards or forwards spreading of literary or artistic income. Enter in the 'Additional information' box details of any amounts spread back to last year and, if appropriate, the year before. **22.5**

Additional information

Q 23 Declaration

I have filled in and am sending back to you the following pages

Tick

2 TO 8 OF THIS FORM

EMPLOYMENT

SHARE SCHEMES

SELF-EMPLOYMENT

Tick

PARTNERSHIP

LAND AND PROPERTY

FOREIGN

Tick

TRUSTS ETC

CAPITAL GAINS

NON RESIDENCE ETC

Before you send your completed Tax Return back to your Tax Office, you must sign the statement below. If you give false information or conceal any part of your income or chargeable gains, you can be prosecuted. You may also have to pay substantial financial penalties.

23.1 The information I have given in this Tax Return is correct and complete to the best of my knowledge and belief.

Signature   Date

If you have signed for someone else, please also

- state the capacity in which you are signing (for example as executor or receiver)

23.2

- give the name of the person you are signing for and **your** name and address in the 'Additional information' box above.

3 Personal allowances and reliefs I

Introduction

1. This chapter is concerned with the main features of the system of independent taxation in relation to the personal allowances for individuals and the married couple's allowance. Other aspects are covered in the next chapter.

List of topic headings

2. Computational Rules - allowances and reliefs at the 15% rate

   Husbands and wives
   Personal allowance (PA)
   Married couple's allowance (MCA)
   Transfer and allocation of the married couple's allowance
   Personal age allowance (PAA)
   Married couple's age allowance (MCAA)
   Married couple's allowance – year of marriage
   Wives with excess allowances.

Computational Rules - Allowances and reliefs at the 15% rate

3. The following allowances are only eligible for income tax relief at the rate of 15% for 1997/98.

MCA	Married couple's allowance
MCAA	Married couple's age allowance
APA	Additional personal allowance
WBA	Wife's bereavement allowance

   Relief for these allowances is given by way of a tax deduction in computing the final income tax liability. These deductions cannot reduce the liability to less than nil so that a repayment attributable to these allowances is not possible.

   The above are not deducted from Statutory Total Income to arrive at taxable income as are:

PA	Personal allowance
BPA	Blind person's allowance

Husbands and wives

4. The main features of the system of independent taxation for husbands and wives are as follows.
   a) Husband and wife are treated as separate taxpayers each completing their own tax returns and responsible for their own tax liabilities.
   b) The income of the wife is not aggregated with that of the husband for income tax purposes.
   c) Each spouse is entitled to the full basic rate band of income tax and the lower rate band.
   d) Both spouses receive a personal allowance which is available for set-off against earned and unearned income. The amount of the allowance is increased for persons over 65, and again for those over 75. As a general rule the personal allowance is not transferable but there are some transitional provisions where this can take place.
   e) The married couple's allowance is claimed by the husband the amount being increased where one of the spouses is over 65, and again where the spouses age is over 75. The married couple's allowance is transferable to the wife, and can be allocated between spouses.
   f) Each person entitled to the personal age allowance will also be entitled to the annual income limit of £15,600 for 1997/98. Married couples both eligible for the personal age allowance will therefore each be entitled to an income limit of £31,200.
   g) The personal allowance available to an elderly wife can be used against a pension obtained as a result of her husband's contributions for national insurance.
   h) Under Sec 835 TA 1988 reliefs may be deducted from any income, to the taxpayers best advantage, but in most cases there is no obvious benefit in utilising one source in preference to another.
   i) The main legislation concerned with personal reliefs is contained in Section 256 to 275 of the TA 1988. Changes in the rates of personal reliefs are contained in the annual Finance Acts.

Personal allowance (PA) 1997/98 £4,045 (1996/97 £3,765)

5. This allowance is given automatically to all individuals male or female, single or married. There are higher rates of personal allowance for people over the age of 65 and these are discussed below under Section 7. The personal allowance is deducted from statutory total income in arriving at the taxable income of each individual, and is thus given relief at the taxpayers marginal rate of tax.

    In general the personal allowance is not transferable.

> **Example**

A who is single has a salary income from employment for 1997/98 of £29,045.
Compute his income tax liability for 1997/98.

Solution	**Income tax computation 1997/98**	
Earned income		**£**
Schedule E		29,045
Personal allowance		4,045
Taxable income		25,000
Tax liability	4,100 @ 20%	820
	20,900 @ 23%	4,807
	25,000	5,627

Note

With income from employment there would normally be some taxation already collected by way of the PAYE system which reduces the balance due accordingly.

Married couple's allowance (MCA) 1997/98 £1,830 – 15% (1996/97 – £1,790)

6. A married man can claim the married couple's allowance provided that his wife is actually living with him in the year of assessment. Husband and wife are treated for tax purposes as living together unless:

    a) They are separated under an Order of the Court or by a deed of separation or

    b) They are in fact separated in such circumstances that the separation is likely to be permanent.

    Married couples are be able to choose how to allocate the MCA between them, subject to the right of the wife to claim 50% of the allowance if she so wishes. See 7 below.

    Relief for the MCA is restricted to tax at the rate of 15% wef 6th April 1995, and is given as a deduction in computing the total tax liability.

    In the year of marriage the married couple's allowance is claimable by the husband on a pro rata basis, see section 11 below.

> **Example**

Mr & Mrs X both aged under 65 have been married for a number of years and their incomes for 1997/98 are as follows:

	£
Mr X Schedule E	24,045
Mrs X Schedule E	5,045

Compute the tax liabilities for 1997/98.

Solution	**Income tax computation 1997/98**		**Mr X**	**Mrs X**
			£	**£**
Schedule E			24,045	5,045
Personal allowance			4,045	4,045
Taxable income			20,000	1,000
Tax payable:				
4,100	1,000	@ 20%	820	200
15,900	–	@ 23%	3,657	–
20,000	1,000		4,477	200
Deduct MCA relief 1,830 @ 15%			274	–
Tax due			4,203	200

Notes

i) The tax is calculated separately for husband and wife and there is no aggregation.

ii) The PA for the wife is available for set-off against her own total income.

iii) The MCA is a separate allowance claimed by the husband, but see note 7 below.

iv) The MCA is limited to relief at the lower rate of 15% and given as a deduction in computing the total tax liability.

v) Each spouse is responsible for the payment of his / her own respective tax liability.

Transfer and allocation of the married couple's allowance

7. With effect from 6th April 1993 the following rules apply:

a) A wife can elect, without reference to her husband, to receive 50% of the *basic* married couple's allowance, (MCA).

b) A husband and wife can jointly elect that the whole of the MCA is deducted from the wife's income instead of the husband's.

c) The election must be made in writing *before* the beginning of the year of assessment to which it is to apply.

d) In the absence of any of the elections mentioned in (a) and (b) above, the husband will be entitled to full allowance and be able to give notice of a transfer of any excess of the allowance over his total income as before. Total income for this purpose is determined ignoring the following reliefs.

i) Loan interest payable under MIRAS

ii) Personal pension scheme contributions paid by the husband as an employee and on which basic rate income tax relief has been given at source

iii) Private medical insurance contract premiums from which basic rate income tax has been deducted at source. FA 1989 Sec 54(5).

An application to transfer unused MCA must be made in writing by the husband to the Inland Revenue within six years after the end of the year of assessment concerned. Once accepted the transfer is irrevocable for that year.

It should be noted that the amount which may be transferred in this way is not restricted to the MCA (as it is in (a) and (b) above) but includes any additional allowance given where either spouses over the age of 65 in the year of assessment ie the MCAA.

Example

Mr & Mrs T both under 65 years of age have the following data relating to 1997/98:

	Mr T (£)	Mrs T (£)
Schedule E	4,045	34,045

An election has been made to transfer the whole of the MCA to Mrs T for 1997/1998.
Compute the tax payable for 1997/98.

Solution

Income tax computation 1997/98

	Mr T £		Mrs T £
Schedule E	4,045		34,045
Personal allowance	4,045		4,045
Taxable income	NIL		30,000
Tax payable:			
	–	4,100 @ 20%	820
		22,000 @ 23%	5,060
		3,900 @ 40%	1,560
	–	30,000	7,440
Less MCA relief at 15%	–	1,830 @ 15%	274
Tax payable	NIL		7,166

The personal age allowance (PAA)

8.

	1997/98	**1996/97**
Age 65–74	£5,220	£4,910
Age 75–	£5,400	£5,090

For taxpayers over the age of 65 at any time during the year of assessment a higher personal allowance is available, and there is a further additional amount for those aged 75 and over. The increased level of allowances is available even if the taxpayer dies before the specified age if he would have attained that age in the year of assessment.

The full amount of the PAA may be claimed where the total income after charges (ie statutory total income) is not greater than £15,600.

Total income includes any encashment of a single premium bond (see Chapter 21).

Charges include covenants to charities and pension payments made by self-employed individuals.

Where the income after the charges is greater than £15,600 then the PAA is reduced by half the excess until the basic personal allowance becomes more beneficial.

Income limits (single person or married woman)

		Minimum	**Maximum**
		£	**£**
Age 65–74		15,600	17,950
Age 75–		15,600	18,310
Age 65–74	5,220 – 1/2 (17,950 – 15,600) = £4,045		
Age 75	5,400 – 1/2 (18,310 – 15,600) = £4,045		

Whatever the level of income of the taxpayer, the personal allowance can never be reduced below the basic personal allowance for a person under 65, ie £4,045 for 1997/98.

> **Example**

K who is 66 and single has income from employment in 1997/98 of £13,000 and a state retirement pension of £4,000.

Compute K's income tax liability for 1997/98.

Solution   **K's income tax computation 1997/98**

		£	£
Schedule E	Salary		13,000
	Pension		4,000
Statutory total income			17,000
PAA		5,220	
Less 1/2 (17,000–15,600)		700	4,520
Taxable income			12,480
Tax payable:			
	4,100 @ 20%		820
	8,380 @ 23%		1,927
	12,480		
Tax payable			2,747

The married couple's age allowance (MCAA) – 15% rate relief

9.

	1997/98	**1996/97**
Age 65–74	£3,185	£3,115
Age 75–	£3,225	£3,155

a) A married man can claim the higher level of married couple's allowance where:

  i) *Either* the husband or the wife are over the age of 65, *or*

  ii) Both husband and wife are over the age of 65. The amount of the allowance then depends on the age of the older of the husband or wife in the year of assessment eg

	Husband	Wife	MCAA	
			£	
Age	55	65	3,185	(wife aged 65)
	65	80	3,225	(wife aged 75+)
	80	55	3,225	(husband aged 75+)

b) The full amount of the allowances (ie PAA and MCAA) is reduced by 1/2 of the excess where the husband's income exceeds £15,600. Note that the wife's income never affects the level of the MCAA. Where the husband's MCAA is reduced by reason of his total income it can never be reduced below the basic married couple's allowance for couples under the age of 65, which is £1,830 for 1997/98, except in the year of marriage.

In applying the reduction in the MCAA the following rules should be used:

i) First – reduce the PAA until it reaches the level of the PA for people under the age of 65.

ii) Second – reduce the MCAA until it reaches the level of the MCA for people under the age of 65.

The above has the effect of preserving as late as possible any MCAA which can be transferred to the spouse.

If the husband cannot use all the MCAA the unused amount can be transferred to his wife.

c) An election by both husband and wife to transfer the basic MCA can be made in accordance with the rules noted in 6 above.

d) For 1997/98 the MCAA is given relief at 15% as a deduction in computing the tax liability.

10. | **Example**

Mr Z is aged 66 and his wife aged 77. In the year 1997/98 Mr Z has Schedule E income of £18,400 and Mrs Z has Schedule E income of £24,045.

Compute the tax payable by Mr and Mrs Z for 1997/98.

Solution   **Mr Z income tax computation 1997/98**

	£	£
Schedule E		18,400
Reduction in total allowances 1/2 (18,400 − 15,600) =	1,400	
PAA	5,220	
Less reduction	1,400	
PA (Basic PA)	3,800	4,045
Taxable income		14,355
Tax payable:		
4,100 @ 20%		820.00
10,255 @ 23%		2,358.65
14,355		3,178.65
Less deduction for MCAA 3,000 @ 15%		450.00
		2,728.65

Mrs Z income tax computation 1997/98

	£	£
Schedule E		24,045
PAA	5,400	
Less 1/2 (24,045 − 15,600)	4,222	
∴ Basic PA claimed	1,178	4,045
Taxable income		20,000
Tax payable:		
4,100 @ 20%		820
15,900 @ 23%		3,657
20,000		
Tax due		4,477

Notes

i) The PAA of £5,400 for Mrs Z is reduced, but as this is less than the basic PA for 1997/98 of £4,045 the latter becomes the amount of the allowance.

ii) The PA (or PAA) is available for set-off against both earned and unearned income.

iii) The level of Mrs Z's income has no effect on the MCAA claimed by her husband.

iv)

MCAA for 74+ is		3,225
Less reduction for excess	1,400	
Less reduction in PA (5,220 – 4,045)	1,175	225
		3,000

Married Couple's Allowance – Year of marriage

11.

		1997/98	1996/97
MCA		1,830	1,790
MCAA	65-74	3,185	3,115
MCAA	75+	3,225	3,115

A married couple's allowance is claimed by the husband providing that for the year of assessment his wife is living with him. In the year of marriage the appropriate married couple's allowance is reduced by one twelfth for every completed tax month from 6th April to the date of the marriage. A tax month goes from 6th of the month to the 5th of the next month, so there is a monthly deduction as follows:

				Monthly deduction
MCA		$\dfrac{1,830}{12}$	=	£152.50
MCAA	65 – 74	$\dfrac{3,185}{12}$	=	£265.42
MCAA	75 –	$\dfrac{3,225}{12}$	=	£268.75

An election can be made to transfer the MCA to the spouse in accordance with the rules noted in section 7. above.

Example

A aged 23 marries Miss T aged 23 on 21st October 1997.

	£
Married couple's allowance	1,830
Less $\frac{6}{12}$ths (six complete months) ie 6 × 152.5	915
Net allowance	915

Example

B aged 58 marries Mrs T aged 66 on 6th June 1997.

	£
Married couple's age allowance	3,185
Less $\frac{2}{12}$ths (two complete months) ie 2 × 265.42	531
Net allowance	2,654

Note

B is entitled to the MCAA for a wife aged 65, even though he is less than 65 years of age. The married couple's allowance is determined by reference to the age of the oldest spouse.

D aged 68 marries Miss T aged 76 on 4th April 1998.

	£
Married couple's age allowance	3,225
Less $\frac{11}{12}$ths (eleven complete months) ie 11×268.75	2,956
Net allowance	269

Note
In this case the maximum MCAA is allowed by reference to Miss T's age, ie 75+
The following additional points should be noted:
i)   For the year of marriage, separate tax returns are required.
ii)   In the year of marriage, a man can disclaim the married couple's allowance, which would normally be beneficial where he is otherwise entitled to the additional personal allowance for children. Both allowances are only available for relief at 15% rate for 1997/98.

Wife with excess allowances

12.   The wife's personal allowance is not transferable to her husband under the system of independent taxation and this in fact maintains the rules applicable to the pre-1990/91 regime.

• Student self-testing question

A and Mrs A have been married for a number of years. A is aged 59 and Mrs A becomes 65 on 1st July 1997.

The following data relates to 1997/98.

	Mr A £	Mrs A £
Schedule E salary	24,045	
Schedule E state pension (own entitlement)		2,500
Schedule E (pension former employer)		14,500

Compute the tax payable for 1997/98 for Mr and Mrs A.

Solution

Mr A Income tax computation 1997/98

	£
Schedule E	24,045
Less PA	4,045
Taxable income	20,000
Tax payable:	
4,100 @ 20%	820
15,900 @ 23%	3,657
20,000	4,477
Less deduction for MCA 1,830 @ 15%	274
Balance payable	4,203

Mrs A Income tax computation 1997/98

	£	£
Schedule E state pension		2,500
Schedule E (pension former employer)		14,500
		17,000
PAA	5,220	
Less 1/2 (17,000 − 15,600) ie 1/2 × 1,400	700	4,520
Taxable income		12,480
Tax payable:		
4,100 @ 20%		820.00
8,380 @ 23%		1,927.40
12,480		
Balance payable		2,747.40

Notes

i) *Mr A is entitled to the married couple's allowance of £3,185 as his wife is 65 during the year of assessment, but this is restricted to the basic £1,830, as his income is greater than £15,600 and the marginal relief.*

ii) *Mr A is not entitled to the PAA as he is not 65 during the year of assessment.*

iii) *Mrs A is entitled to the personal age allowance for persons aged 65 as she attained that age during the year of assessment 1997/98*

• Questions without answers

1. Mr and Mrs A, both aged 50, have the following data for the year 1997/98:

	Mr A £	Mrs A £
Schedule E income	32,045	6,045

Compute the tax liabilities for 1997/98.

2. Z aged 60 is married to Mrs Z aged 73. In respect of the year ended 5th April 1998 they have the following data:

	Z £	Mrs Z £
Schedule E income	29,545	–
State pension		2,700
Company pension		10,345

Compute the tax liabilities for 1997/98.

3. Mr and Mrs Q are both under the age of 65. During 1997/98 they have the following income:

	Q £	Mrs Q £
Schedule E	1,500	18,545

Compute the tax liability for 1997/98.

4   Personal allowances and reliefs II

Introduction

1.   This chapter deals with further aspects of the personal allowances and reliefs available to individuals under the system of independent taxation. A list of topic headings is given below.

List of topic headings

2.   Additional personal allowance for children. (APA)
Blind person's allowance
Widow's bereavement allowance
Medical insurance payments
Year of death of husband
Year of death of wife
Year of permanent separation or divorce
After year of permanent separation or divorce
Non-residents
Charitable gifts and donations.

Additional personal allowance for children 1997/98 £1,830 – 15% (1996/97 - £1,790)

3.   This allowance is available to widows, widowers, and other individuals not entitled to the married couple's allowance, eg a single parent. The relief is available providing the claimant has living with him either his own child, (including an adopted child), or any other child, eg a brother or sister, under sixteen on the 6th April 1997 who is maintained by him. If the child is over the age of sixteen on 6th April 1997 the relief is only available if the child is in full time education.

A child who enrols on a two year YTS training programme will normally qualify.

The relief is also available to a married man if his wife is unable to look after herself throughout the year because of permanent illness or disablement.

When two or more people can claim for the same child, eg where the parents are separated or divorced, then the allowance is divided between them. The allowance is one amount however many children are maintained.

If a person is entitled to any part of the MCA in the same year of assessment as he claims APA then the latter is reduced accordingly. Relief for APA is restricted to tax at the rate of 15% for all tax payers and is deducted from the total liability.

Example

A, a single person aged 35, looks after his brother George who is aged 11. A has a salary for 1997/98 of £16,045. On 7th October 1997 A marries Miss J aged 32. Miss J has employment income of £10,045.

Compute the tax payable by Mr A and Miss J for 1997/98.

Solution   **Mr A Income Tax computation 1997/98**

	£	£
Schedule E salary		16,045
Less PA		4,045
Taxable income		12,000
Tax payable		
4,100 @ 20%		820
7,900 @ 23%		1,817
12,000		2,637
Less deduction for APA 1,830 @ 15%		274
		2,363

Note:

If A claims the MCA this will be 1,830 – (6/12ths × 1,830) = £915. It will clearly be more advantageous to claim the full additional personal allowance of £1,830 rather than the reduced MCA, as both are only allowed at the rate of 15%.

Miss J Income Tax computation 1997/98

	£
Schedule E	10,045
Less PA	4,045
Taxable income	6,000
Tax payable	
4,100 @ 20%	820
1,900 @ 23%	437
6,000	
Balance payable	1,257

Blind person's allowance 1997/98 £1,280 (1996/97 £1,250)

4. This allowance is available to any person who is on the local authority blind person's register. Where both husband and wife are blind then each can claim the allowance. If either the husband or the wife cannot fully use the amount of their blind allowance then the balance can be transferred to the other spouse. This rule applies whether or not the spouse receiving the transferred allowance is a registered blind person. A notice to transfer any unused allowance must be made in writing to the Inspector of Taxes within six years of the end of the year of assessment. This allowance is deducted from total income to arrive at taxable income, and is thus given relief at the taxpayers marginal rate of tax.

> **Example**

K who is widow, aged 55 is a registered blind person. She has two sons under the age of 16 at school, and a daughter aged 21 who lives with her mother in order to help maintain the home. K's income for the year 1997/98 consists of the following.

	£
Widow's pension	3,300
Wages for part-time employment (gross)	10,025 (PAYE deducted £1,310)

Compute K's income tax liability for 1997/98.

Solution   **K Income Tax computation 1997/98**

		£
Schedule E wages		10,025
Widow's pension		3,300
		13,325
Personal allowance	4,045	
Blind person's allowance	1,280	5,325
Taxable income		8,000
Tax payable		
4,100 @ 20%		820
3,900 @ 23%		897
8,000		1,717
Less PAYE	1,310	
APA 1,830 @ 15%	274	1,584
Balance due		133

Note

Only one additional personal allowance is available, whatever the number of dependents, with relief for 1997/98 @ the rate of 15%.

Widow's bereavement allowance 1997/98 £1,830 – 15%. (1996/97 - £1,790)

5. In the year of the death of her husband a widow is entitled to this allowance providing that she has lived with her husband at sometime during the year. This allowance is also available for the next income tax year providing that she has not remarried before the commencement of that tax year. The allowance is in addition to any other allowances available to the widow. See 7 below.

From the 6th April 1995 relief for this allowance is restricted to the rate of 15% for all taxpayers, and is deducted from the total tax liability.

Medical insurance – basic rate relief for 1997/98

6. In accordance with Sec 54–57 FA 1989, tax relief is available in respect of medical insurance payments the main features of which are as follows:

    a) Relief is available for payments made under a private medical insurance contract. The contract must be approved by the Inland Revenue.

    b) The person insured must:
        i)   Be aged over 60. For married couples only one of the spouses need be over 60.
        ii) Resident in the UK at the time of payment.

    c) Relief is not available if the person making the payment does so out of funds provided by someone else, or where he is already entitled to relief eg under a company contract for employees.

    d) Tax relief is given to the person actually making the payments so that a relative could make the payments on behalf of his elderly parents, and claim the tax relief.

    e) Basic rate income tax is deducted at source by the payer.

    f) Husband and wife are each entitled to the relief which must be set against their own income.

    g) From 5th April 1994 payments are excluded from all income tax computation.

Year of death of husband

7. The following points should be noted under this heading:

    Husband

    a) A full married couple's allowance is available.

    b) A full personal allowance is available.

    c) Total income up to the date of death less allowances and reliefs for the whole year are ascertained and any tax due is payable from the husband's estate.

    Wife

    a) A full personal allowance is available.

    b) Widow's bereavement allowance is available.

    c) Where an election has not been made to transfer all or part of the MCA to the wife, then in the year of her husband's death the whole of the MCA must first be set against the husband's income. The balance of any MCA not used against the husband's income up to the date of his death is available for set off against widow's income.

    d) An additional personal allowance is available where there is a child living with the widow.

Example

T aged 55 died on 5th October 1997 and his salary to the date of death was £4,200. Mrs T aged 56 is employed and for the income tax year 1997/98 has the following data:

	£
Schedule E salary	13,045
Widow's pension	1,800
Widow's payment	1,000

Compute the income tax liabilities of T and Mrs T for 1997/98.

Solution

T deceased Income tax computation 1997/98
(6.4.97 to 5.10.97)

	£
Schedule E salary	4,200
PA	4,045
Taxable income	155
Tax payable 155 @ 20%	31.00
MCA 207 @ 15%	31.00
Tax due	–

Mrs T Income tax computation 1997/98

	£	£
Schedule E Salary		13,045
Widow's pension		1,800
		14,845
PA		4,045
Taxable income		10,800
Tax payable		
4,100 @ 20%		820
6,700 @ 23%		1,541
10,800		2,361
Less deduction bereavement allowance 1,830 @ 15%	274	
Less deduction MCA (1,830 – 207) @ 15%	243	517
Balance due		1,844

Notes

i)   The widow is entitled to the bereavement allowance and a personal allowance and the balance of the MCA not used by her husband. (1,830 – 207 = 1,623).

ii) The widow's payment of £1,000 is not taxable, whereas the widow's pension is taxed as Schedule E income.

Year of death of wife

8.   In the year of the death of a wife the husband is entitled to the full amount of the married couple's allowance at the rate appropriate. The additional personal allowance may be claimed in the tax year following the death of a wife if the husband is maintaining an 'eligible child'.

Year of permanent separation or divorce

9.   The following points should be noted:

a)   A married woman is treated for tax purposes as living with her husband unless either they are separated under a Court Order, or deed of separation, or they are in fact permanently separated. The Inland Revenue treat the separation as likely to be permanent if the parties have been living apart for one year.

b)   In the year of permanent separation or divorce, the husband can claim the full married couple's allowance.

c)   The wife can claim the additional personal allowance for the year of separation if she has a child maintained by her after she separates from her husband. She would also be entitled to the normal personal allowance.

> **Example**

P and his wife Q both under age 65 decide to separate permanently with effect from the 6th August 1997 and notify the Inland Revenue of their decision. Q will not be maintained by her husband after the separation. In respect of the year 1997/98 the tax returns of P and Q showed the following:

	P £	Q £
Schedule E Earnings	14,045	8,045

Compute the income tax liabilities of P and Q for 1997/98.

Solution

P income tax computation 1997/98

		£
Schedule E		14,045
Personal allowance		4,045
Taxable income		10,000
Tax payable		
4,100 @ 20%		820
5,900 @ 23%		1,357
10,000		2,177
Deduction for MCA 1,830 @ 15%		274
Tax payable		1,903

Q income tax computation 1997/98

		£
Schedule E		8,045
Less PA		4,045
Taxable income		4,000
Tax payable		
4,000 @ 20%		800

After year of permanent separation or divorce

10. If a husband and wife separate permanently before 6th April 1990 and the husband made voluntary payments to maintain his wife in 1989/90 then if he continues to do so he can claim a married couple's allowance. The MCA will continue until either:

   a) i) The husband stops making the voluntary payments or

   ii) The marriage is officially terminated.

   b) Where relief is given for the voluntary maintenance payments in the circumstances described above no part of the MCA can be transferred to the separated wife.

   For maintenance payments see Chapter 5.

Non-resident's personal reliefs

11. With effect from 6th April 1990 a 'qualifying non-resident' can claim full personal allowances against his UK income. Under the pre 1990/91 system a proportion of allowances could be claimed by reference to the ratio of the UK source income to the total world income. See Chapter 9.

Charitable gifts and donations

12. a) **Gift aid**

   Gifts of money made to charities are eligible for income tax relief at both the basic and higher rate. The main features of the scheme are as follows:

   i) The donor making the payment to a charity must provide the recipient with a tax deduction certificate (Form R185). This is the authority required by the Inland Revenue to repay to the charity tax deducted at source.

   ii) If the donor makes a payment of say £1,155 (net) to a charity then effects of this are:

   1) The donor is deemed to have made a gross payment of £1,500 from which basic rate income tax of 23% (not 20% rate) has been deducted at source ie £1,500 @ 23% = £345.

   2) The charity can claim back the £345 deducted at source.

   3) The donor is eligible for relief at the higher rate (where relevant) on the full £1,500 ie $17\% \times £1,500 = £255$. Total relief £345 (deducted at source) + £255 = £600.00.

   iii) Gifts already qualifying for relief under the payroll deduction scheme or by way of covenant cannot also qualify for relief.

   iv) The minimum limit for gifts made is £250.00. There is no maximum limit.

   b) **Payroll deduction scheme for charities**

   An employee can obtain income tax relief on donations to a charity up to £1,200 for 1997/98. The employer is responsible for making payments to the charity, and uses the 'net pay arrangements' in computing the employees PAYE liability. See Chapter 10.

c) **Covenanted gifts to charities**

Covenants entered into for a recognised charity are allowed as a deduction against the higher rates of taxation and the charity can normally obtain a repayment of the basic rate of income tax deducted at source. See Chapter 5.

• Student self-testing question

A who is aged 45 and a widower maintains his 3 children all under the age of 16 at home. On 12th October 1997 A marries Miss J aged 42. For the year to 5th April 1998 the following data applies:

	A £	Miss J £
Salary	36,045	9,045

A pays medical insurance of £300 (net) in respect of an approved medical insurance contract taken out by his father aged 67. Miss J looks after her elderly mother aged 75, and makes a voluntary payment to her of £100 per month.

Calculate the tax payable by A and Miss J for 1997/98.

Solution   **A Income tax computation 1997/98**

		£
Schedule E salary		36,045
Less PA		4,045
Taxable income		32,000
Tax payable	4,100 @ 20%	820
	22,000 @ 23%	5,060
	5,900 @ 40%	2,360
	32,000	8,240
Less deduction for APA 1,830 @ 15%		276
Balance payable		7,964

Miss J Income tax computation 1997/98

		£
Schedule E salary		9,045
Less PA		4,045
Taxable income		5,000
Tax payable		
	4,100 @ 20%	820
	900 @ 23%	207
	5,000	
Balance payable		1,027

Notes

i)   *A would claim the additional personal allowance of £1,830 rather than the proportionate amount of the married couple's allowance which would be $\frac{1,830}{2}$ = £915. Both are restricted to relief at the rate of 15%.*

ii) *A is entitled to relief in respect of the medical insurance premium paid on behalf of his father. As income tax is deducted at source at the BR and relief is limited to that rate, the gross amount is ignored in computing the taxable income.*

iii) *There is no dependent relative allowance available for Miss J's contribution to her mother's maintenance.*

• Questions without answers

1. Q died on 5th October 1997 at the age of 67. Mrs Q is aged 55. In respect of the year to 5th April 1998 the following data applies:

	Q £	Mrs Q £
Schedule E salary (to 5.10.97)	3,000	–
Widow's payment		1,000
Widow's pension		3,045
Mrs Q's salary		9,000

   Compute the income tax liabilities for 1997/98.

2. F who is single is a registered blind person, aged 50, who has living with her an adopted child aged 12. F's income for 1997/98 consists of the following:

	£
Wages from employment	9,200
Social security mobility allowance	1,500

   Compute F's income tax liability for 1997/98.

5   Charges on income and interest paid

Introduction

1. Charges on income is the term used to describe what are known as 'annual payments' which together with the special provisions relating to interest payments, form the basis of this chapter. The first part of the chapter deals with the computational aspects of annual payments, and the second half with payments of interest.

Annual payments

2. Under Sec 348–350 TA 1988, these are payments which possess the quality of annual recurrence, are not voluntary transactions, and are usually supported by a legal obligation such as a Court order, or deed of covenant.

    Annual payments are not charges on income unless they fall within the following categories:

    a) Made in pursuance of existing obligations;

    b) Payments of interest;

    c) Covenanted payments to a charity;

    d) Payments made for bone fide commercial reasons in connection with the payer's trade, profession or vocation.

Maintenance payments made after 14th March 1988 – Relief at 15%

3. The main features are noted below.

    a) Payments are made gross without deduction of income tax. They are not a charge on income.

    b) The recipient is not chargeable to income tax in respect of maintenance payments.

    c) The payer obtains income tax relief on payments to a divorced or separated spouse but not payments made to children. Relief is available until the recipient remarries. For 1997/98 this is limited to £1,830.

    d) Payments of a voluntary nature will not normally be available for tax relief.

    e) From 6th April 1994 the relief for qualifying maintenance payments is given by way of a deduction in computing the tax liability, known as the 'maintenance deduction'.

    f) For 1997/98 relief is given at the 15% rate.

Example

P is required under a court Order dated 28th March 1997 to pay his former wife, Q, the sum of £2,000 by way of maintenance for 1997/98 and subsequent income tax years. P's other income consists of Schedule E salary of £22,045. P and Q are both aged 45.

Compute P's income tax for 1997/98.

Solution   **P's Income Tax computation 1997/98**

		£	£
Schedule E			22,045
Personal allowance			4,045
Taxable income			18,000
Tax payable			
	4,100 @ 20%		820
	13,900 @ 23%		3,197
	18,000		4,017
Less Maintenance deduction. 1,830 @ 15%			274
			3,743

Notes

i) *P pays maintenance to his wife of £2,000 for 1997/98 and obtains tax relief on £1,830 @ the 15% rate ie £274.00.*

ii) *P's former wife will not be charged to income tax in respect of the £2,000, which she receives gross.*

Covenants

4. A covenant is a legally binding agreement whereby the covenantor agrees to transfer a part of his income to another person. In order to be deductible at all as an annual payment the following conditions must apply:

   a) The deed must be irrevocable

   b) It must be capable to exceeding 6 years: 3 years for covenants to a charity.

   Income tax at the basic rate is deducted at source by the payer.

   The recipient is in receipt of net income which has already suffered income tax at source and may therefore obtain a repayment in appropriate circumstances.

5. **Charitable covenants**

   Covenants entered into for a recognised charity are allowed as a deduction against the higher rates of taxation and the charity can normally obtain a repayment of the basic rate income tax deducted at source.

6. **Non charitable covenants – made on or after the 15th March 1988**

   For new covenants made by an individual on or after the 15th March 1988 the position is as follows:

Payer	–	No tax relief
Recipient	–	Not liable to taxation.

Computational rules for annual payments and interest

7. a) If made after deduction of basic rate income tax, and allowed as a charge on income against the higher rates deduct the gross amount as a charge on income and add on basic rate tax to the total liability (eg covenants to charities). This is sometimes called 'extended basic rate'.

   b) If made after deduction of 15% income tax rate and excluded from all income tax computations, ignore completely. This rule applies to Mortgage Interest payments under MIRAS.

   c) Where mortgage interest is paid gross the following rules should be followed:

      i) Do not deduct as a charge on income.

      ii) Deduct tax at the 15% rate from the total tax payable for the year.

   d) If made after deduction of basic rate income tax and excluded from all income tax computations, ignore completely. This applies to medical insurance payments.

> **Example**

T who is married has Schedule E income of £17,045 for 1997/98. His wife has salary income of £11,045. T makes covenanted payments of £1,000 (gross amount) to a registered charity and £500 (gross amount) to his mother, both were entered into in May 1992.

Compute the income tax liability for 1997/98 for T and Mrs T who are both aged less than 65.

Solution **Income Tax computation 1997/98**

	T £	Mrs T £
Earned Income		
Salaries	17,045	11,045
Less covenant to charity	1,000	–
Statutory Total Income	16,045	11,045
Personal allowance	4,045	4,045
Taxable income	12,000	7,000

	T £	Mrs T £
Tax payable 4,100 / 4,100 @ 20%	820	820
7,900 / 2,900 @ 23%	1,817	667
12,000 7,000	2,637	1,487
Add income tax on covenant to charity	230	–
	2,867	1,487
Less deduction of MCA (1,830 @ 15%)	274	–
Total tax payable	2,593	1,487

Notes

i)   *The covenant to T's mother is not allowed as a deduction.*

ii) *The covenant to the charity is allowed at all rates and the basic rate deducted at source is therefore added back to arrive at the total tax payable by T, ie 1,000 @ 23% = £230.*

Annual payments for business purposes

8.   Payments made by an individual for bona fide commercial reasons in connection with his trade profession or vocation are charges on income paid.

Royalty payments made in connection with a patent used in an individual's trade are paid after deduction of basic rate income tax at source. The gross amount is allowed against the basic and higher rates of the payer.

Interest payments (MIRAS) – 15% relief 1997/98

9.   **Relevant loan interest**

Where relevant loan interest is paid in the UK by a 'qualifying lender' to a 'qualifying borrower' then the borrower:

a)   Deducts and retains income tax from the payments, even if not liable to income tax.

b)   Relief for the interest *at the higher rates* is not allowed from 1991/92.

c)   With effect from 6th April 1995 relief by way of deduction is restricted to the rate of 15%.

d)   Mortgage interest is not to be deducted in computing total income for income tax purposes.

This is the essence of what is known as the 'MIRAS' scheme or mortgage interest relief at source.

Relevant loan interest includes interest on a loan for the purchase of land, which includes buildings, a caravan or house boat.

At the time the interest is paid the property must be the only or main residence of the borrower.

Relief for interest on loans in respect of a residence for a dependent relative made before 5th April 1988 is also available.

Relief for interest on loans for improvements, made before the 5th April 1988 is also still available.

Interest on a loan by a person in job related accommodation, to purchase a house which he intends to live in as a main residence, is also relevant loan interest, this includes a self employed person.

A qualifying lender is a person included in the list in **Sec 376 TA 1988**, or incorporated in subsequent statutory instruments and includes: building societies, local authorities, banks, the Post Office, and insurance companies.

A qualifying borrower is generally any individual who pays relevant loan interest, except employees of foreign governments.

Total loans eligible for relief cannot exceed £30,000 and for loans made after the 31st July 1988, the limit applies to a residence, rather than a borrower.

Interest on a bridging loan up to £30,000 for a 12-month period can normally be obtained, additionally, when an individual moves from one house to another.

Mixed loans, involving both the purchase of a house and say a business, are not within the MIRAS system.

Example

10. Z has Schedule E income of £27,045 for the year 1997/98. He pays mortgage interest of £1,600 (net under the MIRAS) on a loan used to buy his home. Z is single.

Compute Z's income tax liability for 1997/98.

Solution   **Income Tax computation 1997/98**

		£
Earned income		
Schedule E		27,045
Personal allowance		4,045
		23,000
		£
Taxation liability	4,100 @ 20%	820
	18,900 @ 23%	4,347
	23,000	
Tax payable		5,167

Note

Mortgage interest relief has been ignored in the computation. It is only allowed at the rate of 15% which is given by way of deduction at source.

Extended basic rate

11. a) The additional tax payable at basic rate in respect of charges is known as 'extended basic rate'. This practice is usually followed in Inland Revenue Schedule E Assessments.

Example

V has Schedule E income of £31,045 for 1997/98. He pays £1,540 net by way of covenant to a registered charity.

Compute V's income tax liability for 1997/98.

Solution   **V Income tax computation 1997/98**

		£
Earned income		
Schedule E		31,045
Less covenant 1,540 ÷ 0.77		2,000
		29,045
Less PA		4,045
		25,000
Taxation liability	4,100 @ 20%	820
	20,900 @ 23%	4,807
	25,000	5,627
Add income tax on covenant		460
Tax payable		6,087

Using the extended basic rate method the position would be:

		£
Earned income		31,045
Less personal allowance		4,045
Taxable income		27,000
Taxation liability:	4,100 @ 20%	820
20,900 + 2,000 =	22,900 @ 23%	5,267
	27,000	
Tax payable		6,087

Note: The covenant does not appear as a deduction in the computation but the basic rate band is extended (by £2,000 in this case) to give the same effect.

b) The 'extended basic rate' method is used in Schedule E assessments for the following transactions:
    Covenants to charities
    Gift aid payments
    Personal pension payments where tax is deducted at source, ie employee Personal pension plans.

Mortgage interest paid 'gross'

12. Where mortgage interest is paid outside the MIRAS scheme the position is as follows:

i) Relief at the 15% rate on the gross interest (subject to the £30,000 maximum) is given as a deduction in computing the total income tax payable.

ii) The gross interest is ignored in the income tax computation other than as (i) noted above.

Limited loans

13. Where the total amount of the loans used for a qualifying purpose exceeds £30,000, then the interest allowed is limited accordingly.

> **Example**

K paid interest during 1997/98 in respect of £60,000, taken out in 1992 to purchase his own residence. Interest £5,600 gross.

Calculate the interest allowed for tax purposes and the total interest paid to the lender.

Solution   **Income Tax computation 1997/98**

Loan interest paid £5,600.

Proportion attributable to maximum loan of £30,000 $= \dfrac{30,000}{60,000} \times 5,600 = £2,800$

Income tax deducted at source of 15% = 15% × £2,800 = £420

Net payment of mortgage interest by K:

		£
Miras	2,800 – 420	2,380
Excess		2,800
Total interest paid		5,180

Joint borrowers

14. Where the joint borrowers are husband and wife living together a single limit of £30,000 applies. If they are not husband and wife living together a single level of £30,000 still applies on the loan, and applies to the residence, rather than the borrower.

Mortgage interest relief for husband and wife – allocation of interest

15. The following points should be noted under this heading:

a) A husband and wife are entitled to claim income tax relief on the amount of interest they each pay on a qualifying loan, within the joint total ceiling of £30,000. For 1997/98 this would be at the rate of 15%.

b) If the loan is in joint names then within the limit, the amount of interest will normally be shared equally. Where the loan is in one person's name then the allowable interest will normally be given to that person.

c) In order to vary the above general arrangements, the couple can jointly elect for an 'allocation of interest'. The effect of the election is that the allowable interest can be allocated between them in any way they choose. Thus a wife could be allocated the whole of the interest relief even though the loan is in the sole name of the husband.

d) The allocation of interest election (Form 15 1990) is subject to the following rules:

    i) It must be signed by both husband and wife.

    ii) The election must be made within 12 months of the end of the income tax year to which it relates.

    iii) Once made the election will remain until changed or withdrawn.

    iv) Either partner can withdraw the election, but both partners must jointly elect for any change.

Other qualifying interest payments

16. Interest due in the UK on a loan used for any of the under-mentioned purposes is payable without deduction of income tax, and allowed as a gross charge against total income, and the higher rate of income tax. The £30,000 limit does not apply to loans under this heading.

    a) To purchase plant or machinery for use in a partnership or employment.

    b) To purchase an interest in or make a loan to a partnership, where the taxpayer would not be a limited partner.

    c) Loans made in acquiring an interest in a co-operative enterprise as defined in section 2 of the Industrial Common Ownership Act 1976.

    d) To pay inheritance tax. Relief is available for one year only.

    e) To acquire ordinary shares or make loans to a close company, but not a close investment company. The borrower must with his associates:

        i) Have a material interest in the company, ie more than 5% of the ordinary share capital or be entitled to more than 5% of the assets on a notional rounding up, or

        ii) If having less than a 5% interest, have worked for the greater part of his time in the management of the company.

Note

Interest in respect of the profits from the lettings of property in the UK is deductible as an expense in computing taxable income with effect from 5th April 1995 for income tax purposes.

Class IV national insurance contributions – to 1995/96

17. An individual can deduct 50% of his class IV national insurance contributions from total income which for 1995/96 is based on the following:

7.3% × profits in between £6,640 and £22,880. Maximum relief is $\dfrac{1,185.52}{2}$ = £592.76.

With effect from 6th April 1996 the rate is reduced to 6.0% but there is no 50% deduction from total income. See Chapter 23 for details.

Business loan interest

18. Interest paid on loans for business purposes is charged as an expense of trading, and not as a charge on income. This applies to bank loan or overdraft interest, providing the loan is used wholly and exclusively for the purposes of trade.

The special rules concerning relevant interest do not apply to companies. Annual interest not paid to a bank, such as debenture interest, is paid after deduction of basic rate income tax by a company. See Chapter 27.

• Student self-testing question

1. T who is married has the following data relating to 1997/98.

	£
Schedule E earnings T	30,245
Mrs T Schedule E	7,045
T pays mortgage interest after deduction of income tax under MIRAS of	1,600

On 6th April 1997 T paid £924 (Net) under a deed of covenant to a recognised charity.

Compute the income tax liability for 1997/98 of T and Mrs T, both aged 55.

Solution

Income Tax computation 1997/98

	T £	Mrs T £
Earned income		
Schedule E. T	30,245	–
Schedule E. Mrs T	–	7,045
	30,245	7,045
Less Charitable covenant (gross) 924 ÷ 0.77	1,200	– –
	29,045	7,045
Personal allowance	4,045	4,045
Taxable income	25,000	3,000
Taxation liability:		
4,100 / 3,000 @ 20%	820	600
20,900 / @ 23%	4,807	–
25,000 / 3,000	5,627	600
Add BR tax on covenant (1,200 @ 23%)	276	–
	5,903	600
Less deduction for MCA 1,830 @ 15%	274	–
Tax payable	5,629	600

Notes

i) The MIRAS interest is ignored as the rate of 15% is deducted at source.

ii) As the covenant is allowed at the higher rate, basic rate income tax deducted at source is added back in the computation.

• Question without answer

A who is a widower has the following data relating to 1997/98.

	£
Schedule E earnings	42,045
Mortgage interest paid under MIRAS (gross)	2,900

A has two children, one aged 20 who is attending full-time education, and the other aged 13 is at school.

The eldest is in receipt of covenanted income entered into in 1997/98 from his father of £770 net. A also has a covenant with Oxfam which he entered into in 1990 for an amount of £2,000 (gross).

Compute A's income tax liability for 1997/98.

6 Income from savings I – taxed income

Introduction

1. This chapter is concerned with the taxation of savings income which is normally received after deduction of tax at source.

   The treatment of other savings income received gross and taxed under Schedule D case III is dealt with in the next chapter.

Bank/building society interest etc – 20% rate

2. a) With effect from 6th April 1996 the lower rate of 20% applies to the following savings income:

   > interest on National Savings products
   > interest from banks and building societies
   > interest from government securities
   > interest on corporate loan stocks and other securities
   > purchased life annuities
   > interest distributions from authorised unit trusts.

   b) Where the taxpayer is only taxable at the lower rate of 20% or basic rate of 23%, then there will be no further liability. The 20% deduction at source is deemed to have satisfied the full charge.

   c) For higher rate taxpayers the 40% rate applies to the gross income with due allowance for the lower rate deduction at source.

   d) Those taxpayers who receive taxed interest will be able to claim the 20% deduction by way of repayment.

   e) Savings income (including dividends – see below) are to be treated as the top slice of an individual's taxable income, leaving out of account:

   i)   any termination payment relating to an office or employment

   ii) any chargeable events arising from non qualifying life policies.

   f) The tax treatment of interest received is now the same as that for dividends which has been in operation since 1993/94.

   g) Provided application is made on Form R85 (1990) then an individual resident in the UK can register with the bank or building society to receive the interest gross if he or she is not liable to income tax.

   h) A separate application to register must be made for each building society or bank account or share of joint account.

   i) If an account is for a child under 16 a parent of guardian will need to sign the registration form.

   j) The basis of assessment is the actual year and not the preceding year for all interest received (Net).

Interest paid gross

3. The following forms of investment still pay interest gross:

   a) certificates of deposit and sterling or foreign currency time deposits, provided that the loan is not less than £50,000 and is repayable within five years;

   b) taxable National Savings investments (other than first option bonds);

   c) general client accounts with banks and building societies operated by solicitors or estate agents;

   d) accounts held at overseas branches of United Kingdom banks and building societies;

   e) bank and building society accounts where the owner is not ordinarily resident in the United Kingdom and has made a declaration to that effect;

   f) bank and building society accounts in the names of companies, clubs, societies and charities;

   g) loans from unincorporated borrowers; and

   h) $3\frac{1}{2}$ per cent War loan.

Dividends received from UK companies – 1993/94 et seq

4.
i) Dividends received from UK companies are net amounts to which is attached a tax credit of 20% of the dividends.

ii) The net dividend received plus the tax credit of 20% is the gross dividend payment.

iii) For the taxpayer with taxable income in the 20% or 23% band there is no further liability to income tax.

iv) For higher rate taxpayers the gross amount of the dividend is liable to income tax at the 40% rate, 20% of which has been deducted at source.

v) The tax credit of 20% can be reclaimed by any taxpayer in appropriate circumstances.

vi) Dividend income is taxed on an 'actual basis' under Schedule F.

vii) All dividend income is treated as the top slice of income in all cases, but see (iii) above.

viii) In effect there is a new income tax relief of 20% on dividend income, but the higher rate of 40% still applies in appropriate circumstances.

ix) For details of 'scrip dividends' see Chapter 21.

Example

Z Who is single has Schedule E income of £16,045 for 1997/98, and UK Dividend income net of £4,000 compute Z's income tax liability for 1997/98.

Solution   **Z income tax computation 1997/98**

Schedule E	16,045
Dividends (gross) $\frac{4000}{0.8}$	5,000
	21,045
PA	4,045
Taxable Income	17,000
4,100 @ 20%	820
7,900 @ 23%	1,817
12,000	2,637
5,000 @ 20% (dividends)	1,000
17,000	3,637
Less Income tax on dividends	
5,000 @ 20%	1,000
Tax due	2,637

Notes

i) *Check:*

Taxable income excluding dividends		12,000	
Tax on 4,100 @ 20%	820		
Tax on 7,900 @ 23%	1,817	2,637	
Tax on dividends of 20% paid at source		1,000	3,637

ii) *As basic rate taxpayers the dividend is only taxable at the 20% rate and there is no further income tax to pay on this source of income.*

Example

P who is married has the following income for 1997/98:

Schedule E	19,045
Building society interest (net)	4,000
UK dividends (net)	8,000

Compute P's income tax liability for 1997/98.

Solution **P income tax computation 1997/98**

Schedule E			19,045
BSI (gross) $\dfrac{4,000}{0.8}$			5,000
Dividends (gross) $\dfrac{8,000}{0.8}$			10,000
			34,045
PA			4,045
Taxable Income			30,000
4,100 @ 20%			820
10,900 @ 23%			2,507
11,100 @ 20%			2,220
26,100			
3,900 @ 40%			1,560
30,000			7,107
Less Income tax on BSI	1,000		
Less Income tax on dividends	2,000		
Less deduction MCA @ 15%	274		3,274
			3,833

Notes:

i) *Check:*

Taxable income excluding lower rate income		15,000
Income tax @ 20% × 4,100	820	
Income tax @ 23% × 10,900	2,507	3,327
Less Income tax on MCA		274
		3,053

Income tax at higher rate on dividends:	
3,900 @ (40% − 20%) =	780
	3,833

ii) *That part of the savings income attributable to the basic rate band is only taxed at the 20% rate. The part attributable to the higher rate band is taxed at the 40% rate which in this case is £15,000 – £11,100= £3,900.*

Example

J who is single aged 49 has the following income for the year ended 5th April 1998.

Schedule E salary	£3,200
Bank interest (net)	£2,000

Compute J's income tax for 1997/98.

Solution **J's Income Tax liability 1997/98**

	£
Schedule E	3,200
Bank interest (gross) $\dfrac{2,000}{0.8}$	2,500
	5,700
P Allowance	4,045
Taxable income	1,655
Tax payable	
1,655 @ 20%	331
Less income tax on bank interest	500
Repayable	(169)

Notes:
i)   *The tax credit attached to the bank interest is 20% of the payment.*
ii) *Repayment of income tax is also at the 20% rate*

Personal equity plans

4. Under the provisions of Sec 333, and Schedule 29 TA 1988, UK resident individuals aged 18+ may invest up to £6,000 in a general PEP approved fund and £3,000 in a single corporate PEP.

The main features of the scheme are as follows:

a) Up to £6,000 can be invested p.a. in approved general PEP funds and £3,000 in a single 'company PEP'.

b) Dividends and interest accruing, which are not decreed to be part of the £9,000 annual limit are reinvested in the PEP fund and tax reclaimed by the fund managers on behalf of investor.

c) If the plans are kept then on a subsequent disposal the dividend/interest received is exempt from income tax, and the disposal does not give rise to a charge to capital gains tax.

d) Husband and wife can each invest up to £9,000.

e) With effect from 6th April 1993 the tax credit on dividends is 20% of the payment and from 6th April 1996 the 20% interest rate applies to interest received.

See Chapter 21 for further details.

• Student self-testing question

The following information relates to the Tax Returns of A and Mrs A.

Year ended 5th April

	1997 £	1998 £
A salary	12,700	19,945
Mrs A salary	13,676	14,045
Taxed dividends (net) A	350	480
Bank interest (net) A	300	400
Mortgage interest paid (net) A (MIRAS)	852	750
Covenant to Oxfam (gross) A	1,800	2,000

Calculate the income tax liability of A and Mrs A for 1997/98.

Solution — Income tax computation 1997/98

	£	A £	Mrs A £
Earned income			
A salary		19,945	–
Mrs A salary		–	14,045
Unearned income			
Dividends (gross) 480/.80	600		
Bank interest 400/.80	500	1,100	–
		21,045	14,045
Charges on income			
Covenant to Oxfam		2,000	–
		19,045	14,045
Personal allowance		4,045	4,045
Taxable income		15,000	10,000
Taxation charged			
4,100 / 4,100 @20%		820	820
9,800 / 5,900 @ 23%		2,254	1,357
13,900 / 10,000		3,074	2,177
1,100 — Tax on dividends and bank interest @ 20%		220	
15,000 10,000			
		3,294	2,177
Less Income tax on savings income at source	220		
MCA @ 15%	274	494	
		2,800	2,177
			–
Add income tax on covenant 2,000 @ 23%		460	
Tax payable		3,260	2,177

• Questions without answers

1. X has the following income for 1997/98.

	£
Schedule E salary	28,045
Dividends (net)	3,600
Building society interest (net)	1,200

    X is married and pays £2,000 (gross) to a registered charity.

    Compute X's income tax liability for 1997/98: X is aged 65 on 5th April 1998 and his wife is aged 55.

2. Miss J received the following income during the year ended 5th April 1998.

	£
UK dividends	800
Building society interest	600
Interest on 8% Treasury Stock	1,200

    All income is shown net of any tax deducted.

    Calculate the net tax chargeable and the repayment due to Miss J for 1997/98.

3. Mr B received £800 from a building society account during 1997/98. He had no other income during the year. On 1st January 1998 he paid £924 (net) under a Deed of Covenant to a registered charity.

    Calculate the tax payable by Mr. B for the year ended 5th April 1998.

7 Income from savings II – gross income

Introduction

1. This chapter is concerned with the taxation of savings income received gross and taxable as case III income. For new sources arising on or after 6th April 1994 and existing sources from 6th April 1997 the current year basis of assessment applies. Although mainly case IV income, the accrued income scheme is dealt with in this chapter.

Taxable income – case III

2. In accordance with Sec 18(3) TA 1988, income tax is chargeable under this schedule on any interest annuity or other annual payment received by the taxpayer. The following income received gross is assessed under this schedule.

   a) Interest on certain government securities such as 3½% War Loan, 9½% British Savings Bonds, and all securities held on the National Savings Stock Register, and purchased through a Crown Post Office, interest on Capital Bonds.

   b) Interest on accounts with the National Savings Bank. Interest on an Ordinary account is exempt up to £70 p.a. for husband and wife, ie £140 in total. However, the full amount of any interest on an investment account is taxable.

   c) Interest paid gross by a building society or bank on a qualifying term deposit of more than £50,000.

   d) Interest paid to non residents.

   Income is taxed on an arising basis which means when it is either received or enures for the benefit of the taxpayer. Where payment is made by cheque then the income arises when the sum is credited to the account of the drawee, see *Parkside Leasing Ltd v Smith* 1984 STI 740. There are no permitted deductions for expenses from case III income; see *Shaw v Tonkin* 1987. However charges on income can be deducted from this source, in the same way as they can be deducted from other income.

Savings income – lower rate 20%

3. With effect from 6th April 1996 savings income arising under Schedule D Case III is taxed at the 20% rate in the same way as other taxed savings income discussed in the previous chapter. Where the taxpayer is not taxable at the higher rate, the 20% liability is the only rate charged.

Basis of assessment – sources after 5th April 1994 – existing 1997/98

4. **Current year basis** – Income arising in the year of assessment.

   Thus for the year 1997/98 the taxable income is the income arising between the 6th April 1997 and 5th April 1998.

   All new sources of income which pay interest gross arising on or after the 6th April 1994 are taxed on a current year basis.

   Existing sources will move on to a current year basis in 1997/98.

   > **Example**

   T opens a NSB Investment account on the 1st May 1994 with interest credited as follows:

	1994	1995	1996	1997
June	150	220	325	375
December	200	300	405	425

   Compute the assessments for 1994/95, to 1997/98.

Solution

		£
1994/95	current year basis	350
1995/96	current year basis	520
1996/97	current year basis	730
1997/98	current year basis	800

Note

If the account had been opened prior to 6th April 1994 as a new source, with the first interest arising after that date, the current year basis would still apply.

Transitional year 1996/97

5. For any income source arising before 6th April 1994 the profits assessed in 1996/97 will be 50% of the profits arising in the 24 month period 6th April 1995 to 5th April 1997.

   Where 1995/96 has been taxed on an actual basis by reason of an election under Section 66 TA 1988, then 1996/97 will be assessed on the profits of the 12 month period to 5th April 1997.

   Where a source ceases in 1996/97 or 1997/98 then the old rules apply throughout including any revisions of 1995/96 and 1996/97.

Example

P opens an NSB investment account on the 27th February 1992 and interest credited to the account was:

	1992	1993	1994	1995	1996	1997
	£	£	£	£	£	£
June	70	98	82	90	110	100
December	100	96	88	94	80	95

Compute the assessments for all available years.

Solution

			£	
Assessments	1992/93	actual	170	
	1993/94	actual	194	
	1994/95	PY	194	Revised to actual 170
	1995/96	PY	170	
	1996/97	½(184 + 190)TY	187	
	1997/98	CY	195	

Notes

i) *The first year of assessment was 1992/93 and not 1991/92 when the account was opened.*

ii) *The taxpayer option applies to 1994/95. See 6 below.*

iii) *1996/97 is the transitional year and the assessment is on 50% of the 2 years ended 5th April 1997.*

Example

T has the following income for the last two income tax years:

	1995/96	1996/97
	£	£
Salary	9,750	10,750
National savings bank interest:		
Ordinary account	120	130
Investment account	200	350

T is married and pays mortgage interest of £2,250. T's wife receives bank interest of £4,000 (net) in 1996/97, and £1,000 in 1995/96, net of income tax. The National Savings Bank Ordinary Account was opened in 1990. The Investment Account was opened on 1st May 1994.

Compute the income tax liability for 1996/97 of Mr and Mrs T.

Solution

Income Tax computation 1996/97

	Mr T	Mr T	Mrs T
	£	£	£
Schedule E. T		10,750	–
Schedule D case III:			
NSB Ordinary a/c (250 ÷ 2) − 70 TY	55		
NSB Investment a/c CY	350	405	–
Bank interest $4,000 \times \dfrac{100}{80}$		_____	5,000
		11,155	5,000
Personal allowance		3,765	3,765
Taxable income		7,390	1,235

Taxation charged $\quad 3,900 + 405 =$

		Mr T	Mrs T
4,305 /1,235 @ 20%		861.00	247.00
3,085 / – @ 24%		740.40	–
7,390 1,235		1,601.40	247.00
Less Income tax deducted from bank interest		–	1,000.00
Less MCA @ 15% × 1,790		268.00	–
Tax payable / (Repayable)		1,333.40	(753.00)

Notes

i)   As there is no relief except at source, the mortgage interest has been ignored here.
ii) Income tax deducted from the bank interest is at the 20% rate.
iii) The NSB Investment Account is taxed on a current year basis from 1994/95 onwards.
iv) The case III income for 1996/97 is taxed on a transitional basis.

Basis of assessment – existing sources to 1995/96

6. **Normal basis** – Income of the preceding income tax year.

Thus for the year 1995/96 the taxable income is that arising between the 6th April 1994 and the 5th April 1995.

There are special rules for the years when a source of income first arises and when it ceases. As regards the former the first year of assessment is determined by the date the income first arises and not the date of the acquisition of the source. The final year of assessment is determined by the date the source is disposed of, and not the date of the final receipt of income, where these differ.

Opening years	1st year	Income arising in the first year.
	2nd year	Income arising in the second year. If the income first arose on the 6th April in the first year, then the second year will be on a preceding year basis.
	3rd year	Income of the preceding year.
	4th year	Income of the preceding year.

The taxpayer has the right to elect for an actual basis of assessment for the first year in which the preceding year is used, and this will normally arise in respect of the third year.

Closing years	Final year	Actual income arising in the final year.
	Penultimate year	Preceding year basis unless the Inland Revenue adjust this year to an actual basis.

When additions or disposals are made to an existing source of income, the opening and closing rules should be applied as if they are distinct sources. If a source ceases to yield any income for 6 consecutive years, a claim can be made to apply the cessation basis as if the source had closed, when the income last arose. Should the income arise again then it will be treated as a new source.

> **Example**

P opens an NSB investment account on the 27th February 1991 and interest credited to the account until it was closed on 30.12.1995 was:

	1991	1992	1993	1994	1995
	£	£	£	£	£
June	70	98	82	90	110
December	100	96	88	94	80

Compute the assessments for all available years.

Solution			£	
Assessments	1991/92	actual	170	
	1992/93	actual	194	
	1993/94	preceding year	194	
	1994/95	do.	170	
	1995/96	actual final year	190	
	1993/94	revised	170	Taxpayers option
	1994/95	do.	184	Inland revenue decision.

Note

The first year of assessment was 1991/92 and not 1990/91 when the account was opened.

Securities – the accrued income scheme (TA 1988 Sec 713–715)

7. The main features of the taxation of accrued income, which applies to the 'transfer' of 'securities' are noted below. In essence interest is apportioned between the old and the new owners so that the former is charged to tax on interest up to the date of the settlement, and the latter on interest accruing from that date.

   a) **Securities** This includes any loan stock or securities, whether issued by a UK body or not, such as:

      Company debentures and loan stock, secured or not
      Government securities
      Local authority or other public authority stocks.

      The following are not securities for this purpose:

      Shares in a company
      National savings certificates
      Certificates of deposit.

   b) **Transfer** This means transfer by way of sale, exchange, gift or otherwise. A deemed transfer occurs on death of an individual and where an appropriation to/from trading stock takes place.

   c) **Sale with accrued interest (cum dividend)** (ie with the right to receive the next interest payment). If securities are transferred cum div the transferor is deemed to have received as accrued income an amount equal to the accrued proportion, ie

      $$\text{Accrued proportion} = \frac{A}{B} \times \text{interest payable on the securities on the interest date next following the settlement day}$$

      A = number of days in the 'interest period' (normally a 6 or 12 month period) up to and including the settlement day of the transfer.

      B = total number of days in the interest period. The transferee is entitled to relief of the same amount which would be deducted from the interest payment when received.

   d) **Sale without accrued interest (ex dividend)** Where securities are transferred without the interest accruing, the transferor is entitled to a credit known as the rebate proportion, ie

      $$\text{Rebate proportion} = \frac{A}{B} \times \text{interest payable on the securities on the interest date next following B the settlement day}$$

      A and B are as defined above in (c).

      The transferee is treated as receiving an income equal to the rebate proportion.

   e) **Income tax treatment** The main points here are:

      i) If the net effect of the adjustments to be made in an interest period is an increase in taxable income, then this is taxed as case VI income receivable on the last day of the interest period.

      ii) If the net effect of the adjustments in an interest period is to decrease the taxable income, then this is taken as reducing the next income receipt taxable as case III income.

      iii) The accrued interest is treated as arising at the end of the interest period in which the transaction takes place, and not the date of the disposal.

   f) **Exemptions** The following transfers are excluded from the scheme:

      i) Transfers by individuals (husband and wife are treated separately), personal representatives and trustees of mentally disabled persons, or persons in receipt of an attendance allowance, where the holding is 'small'.

Small means having a nominal value not exceeding £5,000 per spouse on any day in the year of assessment in which the interest period ends, or the previous year of assessment.

ii) Transfers by persons neither resident or ordinarily resident in the UK in the chargeable period in which the transfer is made. Chargeable period means year of assessment or accounting period for companies.

iii) Transfers of government securities which are exempt from UK income tax if paid to a non resident under Sec 47 TA 1988, such as $3\frac{1}{2}$% War Loan.

8. | **Example**

J purchased £2,000 $9\frac{3}{4}$% Treasury Stock on 1st April 1997 cum dividend. Show the income tax computation if the stock is sold to Q.

i) Ex dividend on 22nd July 1997: settlement date 28th July 1997

ii) Cum dividend on 30th June 1997: settlement date 7th July 1997

iii) Ex dividend on 22nd January 1998: settlement date 4th February 1998

Interest is payable on 10th February and 10th August

Assume that both J and Q owned chargeable securities with a nominal value in excess of £5,000 throughout the relevant years.

Solution   **Income Tax Computations 1997/98**

i) Number of days in interest period   181
    do.   from 10.2.97–1.4.97   50
    do.   10.2.97–28.7.97   168
    Interest payable 10th April 1997 – £97.50
    Purchased 1st April 1997

    Accrued proportion $= \dfrac{50}{181} \times £98.00$ $= £27$

    Sold ex div 22nd July 1997

    Rebate proportion $= \dfrac{181-168}{181} \times £98.00 = £7$

    Interest received 10th August 1997   £98
    Less Accrued proportion   £27
            Rebate proportion   £7   £34
    Schedule D case III   £64

Note

The case III income is equal to the actual interest accrued over the time the investment is held viz:

$$\frac{168-50}{181} \times 98 = £64$$

ii) Number of days from 10th February 1997
    to 7th July 1997   147
    Sale cum div 30th June 1997   £
    Accrued proportion on sale
    $\dfrac{147}{181} \times 98$ 80
    Less accrued proportion on acquisition
           on 1st April 1997 as in (i) above   27
    Schedule D case VI   53

Note

The case VI income is equal to Actual interest accrued over the time the investment is held although J does not actually receive an interest payment viz:

$$\frac{147-50}{181} \times 98 = 53$$

iii) Sale 22nd January 1998 ex div

		£	£
Interest period to 10th August 1997			
As per (i) above:			
Interest received		98	
Less Accrued proportion	27		
Rebate proportion	7	34	64
Interest period to 10th February 1998			
Interest received 10th February 1998		98	
Rebate interest on disposal			
Number of days in interest period	184		
do. from 10.8.97 to 4.2.98 = 178			

$$\frac{184 - 178}{184} \times 98 = \frac{6}{184} \times 98$$

		£	£
		3	95
Schedule D case III			159

Deep discount securities

9. A deep discount security is a redeemable security (not a share) issued by a company where the difference between the issue price and the redemption price (the discount) is:

a) > 15% of the amount payable on redemption, or

b) > 1/2% for each complete year between the date of issue and date of redemption.

Where a person disposes of a deep discount security then he is treated as deriving an income element chargeable as Schedule D case III income (or where appropriate case IV). The income is deemed to arise in the year of assessment in which the disposal takes place and it is not taxed therefore on the preceding year basis which is the normal basis for case III.

The income element is calculated by reference to the formula:

$$\left(\frac{(A \times B)}{100}\right) - C$$

A = the issue price (adjusted for any previous income elements)
B = % yield to maturity date
C = the amount of annual interest if any payable on the security.

Where the deep discount security falls within the 'Chargeable Provisions' of the Sch. 4 TA 1988, (coupon stripping and deep discounts) then the holder may be subject to income tax on the income annually.

• Student self-testing question

A, who is married, has earned income for the year 1997/98 of £28,295. He has bank interest Net of £3,000, and his wife receives building society interest of £5,224. A pays mortgage interest of £750 after deduction of income tax, in respect of a loan to buy his house under MIRAS.

Compute the income tax liability for 1997/98 of A and his wife.

Solution

Income tax computation 1997/98

		A £	Mrs A £
Earned income			
Schedule E. A		28,295	–
Bank interest (gross) $\frac{3,000}{.80}$		3,750	–
Building society interest (gross) $\frac{5,224}{.80}$		–	6,530
		32,045	6,530
Less Personal allowance		4,045	4,045
Taxable income		28,000	2,485
Taxation charged	5,950 / 2,485 @ 20%	1,190	497
	20,150 @ 23%	4,635	–
	1,900 @ 40%	760	–
	28,000	6,585	497
Less tax credits:	bank interest	750	–
	building society interest	–	1,306
Tax payable		5,835	(809)
Less MCA @ 15%		274	–
Tax Payable (repayable)		5,561	(809)

Note

A's 20% band is equal to 4,100 + (3,750 – 1,900) = 5,950.

• Questions without answers

1. R has the following investments:

   a) Deposit account with Bank first opened in January 1993. Interest credited to the account as follows:

	1993 £	1994 £	1995 £	1996 £	1997 £
June	225	200	120	210	300
December	210	300	180	220	320

   b) Deposit with National Savings Bank (investment account) first made in April 1994.

	1994 £	1995 £	1996 £	1997 £
Interest – December	300	350	420	500

   c) Deposit with building society made in January 1994.

	1994 £	1995 £	1996 £	1997 £	1998 £
Interest – March	70	180	200	305	410

   Calculate the income tax assessments for all years up to 1997/98.

2. Miss K received the following income during the year ended 5th April 1998.

	£
UK dividends	8,000
Building society interest	720
Interest on 8% Treasury Stock	600
NSB interest investment account opened 1995	700

   All income is shown net of any tax deducted.

   You are required to calculate the net tax chargeable for 1997/98.

3. Mr W is 81 and married. During 1997/98 he received the following income :

	£
State and works pensions	7,800
Dividends (net)	1,200
Building society interest (net)	3,000

   Calculate the income tax payable by/repayable to Mr W for 1997/98.

8   Income from employment I – Schedule E

Introduction

1. This chapter is concerned with the taxation of income from employment.

    The major part deals with the meaning of taxable emoluments and benefits in kind. A summary of benefits is provided showing in broad terms the taxable effects on higher – and lower-paid employees.

    The remainder of the chapter deals with other income taxable under Schedule E. Some overseas aspects of Schedule E are considered in the next chapter.

Summary of taxable income

2. Tax under this schedule is charged in respect of the following income.

    Emoluments from an office or employment including benefits in kind, less expenses.
    Pensions paid by the state or from private superannuation funds.
    Payments on retirement or removal from office.
    Benefits from profit sharing schemes.
    Certain social security payments.

Basis of assessment

3. The assessment is based on the emoluments received in the year of assessment, whenever earned.

Case	Year of assessment
I and II	Full amount of emoluments received in respect of an office or employment.
III	Full amount of emoluments received in the UK in respect of an office or employment.

    ### Meaning of receipt

    Emoluments are treated as being received at the time of the earliest of the following events.

    a) When payment is made of, or on account of, the emoluments.

    b) When a person becomes entitled to payment of, or on account of, the emoluments.

    c) Where a person is a director of a company:
        i)   When sums on account of the emoluments are credited in the company's accounts and records.
        ii) When the amount of the emoluments for a period is determined before the end of a period.
        iii) When the amount of the emoluments is not known and determined until after the end of the period, when it is so determined.

    ### Director

    A director is defined for Schedule E purposes as follows.

    a) A member of the board of directors of a company.

    b) A single director or similar person who manages the affairs of a company.

    c) Each member, where the company's affairs are managed by the members themselves.

    d) Any person in accordance with whose directions or instructions the company's directors are accustomed to act except where that person is acting in a professional capacity.

Emoluments

4. Under Sec 19 TA 1988 tax is charged in respect of any office or employment on emoluments therefrom, under one of three cases. The classification into cases is determined mainly by the domicile and residence of the taxpayer, and the location of his employment.

    ### Office

    This can be defined as a position with duties attached to it which do not change with the holder. It is the emoluments which go with the office that are taxable. Examples of office holders are: a judge; a trustee or executor; a town clerk; a company director or secretary. An inspector of public meetings was held not to hold an office, see *Edwards* v *Clinch* HL 1981 STI.

Employment

This is usually taken to be evidenced by a contract of employment or service, as required for example under the Employment Protection (Consolidated) Act 1978. On the other hand a contract for services rendered is normally associated with self employment, the rewards of which are assessable under Schedule D case I or II. See *Fall v Hitchen* 1972 49 TC 433. *Hall v Lorimer* 1992 CA STC 23.

Emolument

This is defined in section 131 to include all salaries, fees, wages, perquisites and profits whatsoever. 'Perks' or benefits in kind are defined below.

The following are typical taxable emoluments:

wages or salaries; overtime pay; bonus payments; holiday pay; commissions; fees; honoraria; tips; cost of living allowances; meal vouchers in excess of 15p per day; incentive prizes awarded to employees for reaching sales or performance targets.

Gifts and voluntary payments

5. In general gifts and voluntary payments unconnected with an employment are not taxable, but see the examples noted below.

   a) Reasonable gifts made by an employer in connection with marriage or retirement are not taxable.

   b) Long service awards are not taxed providing that they are not cash; the award is in respect of not less than 20 years service; no similar payment has been made during the previous 10 years; and the cost to the employer does not exceed £20 for each year of service. A cash award would be taxable.

   c) Benefit matches for sports personnel are not taxed providing that they are not a condition of their employment contract. See *Reed v Seymour* 1927 HL 11 TC 625 and *Moorhouse v Doorland* 1954 CA 36 TCI. However transfer signing on fees are taxable emoluments.

   d) An award of £130 to a bank clerk for passing his professional examinations was held to be a non taxable gift. See *Ball v Johnson* 1971 47 TC 155.

   e) £1,000 paid by the Football Association to each of the members of the 1966 England world cup team was held to be a gift and not remuneration. *Moore v Griffiths* 1972 48 TC 338.

   f) Tips of a taxi driver were held to be taxable in *Calvert v Wainwright* 1947 27 TC 475.

   g) The Easter offerings given to a vicar in response to an appeal made by his Bishop were held to be taxable. See *Cooper v Blakiston HL* 1908 5 TC 347.

   h) Gifts from third parties costing not more than £100 in any tax year are not taxable, by concession.

   i) Payments to a footballer to join his new club were held to be taxable as emoluments under Sec 14 TA 1988 ie as a payment on retirement or removal from office. The inducement fee was also held to be taxable as emoluments from an employment. *Shilton v Wilmhurst* 1990 HL STC.

The taxation of benefits as emoluments

6. The taxation of benefits in kind as emoluments depends upon placing a value on the goods and services that are provided at less than full cost, for an employee. This is achieved as follows.

   a) In respect of employees earning less than £8,500 p.a., unless provided otherwise by statute, benefits are taxable if they can be converted into moneysworth, at their secondhand value. See *Tenant v Smith* 1892 HL 3 TC 158. and *Wilkins v Rogerson* 1961 39 TC 344.

   Benefits which cannot be converted into moneysworth are therefore in principle not taxable, eg interest free loans, or the private use of a company car.

   b) For directors and employees earning £8,500 or more, benefits are taxable whether or not they can be converted into moneysworth. The general charging provisions are contained in Sec 154 TA 1988, and these state that benefits are to be valued at the cost to the employer, or in accordance with a prescribed rate or scale eg private cars.

   c) For directors and all employees there are prescribed scales of benefit values, or the cost to the employer is used eg accommodation, season tickets and transport vouchers.

   d) Following the decision in *Pepper v Hart* HL 1992 STC 898 it appears that benefit in hand may be valued on the marginal cost principle, and not on an average cost basis.

Directors and employees earning £8,500 or more

7. Some of the rules under this topic only apply to what are described as 'directors and employees earning £8,500 or more' or simply P11D employees. These include the following.

   a) Any employee whose total remuneration, plus expenses and benefits paid or provided, is greater than £8,500 p.a.

   b) Any director holding more than 5% of the company's ordinary shares.

   c) A full time working director owning 5% or less of the ordinary share capital, if his total remuneration is greater than £8,500.

   Employers must complete a return (form P11D) of payments, benefits, etc each year in respect of all directors and employees earning £8,500 or more, unless a dispensation is obtained.

   In general any benefit provided for the members of the family or household of an employee are treated as if they were provided for the employee personally. The term family or household covers the employee's spouse, children and their spouses, his parents, servants, dependants and guests.

Dispensations

8. Where the company is able to explain to the inspector of taxes its arrangements for paying expenses and providing benefits, and satisfy them that they would all be fully covered by the expenses claim under Section 198 TA 1988, then it is possible to obtain a 'dispensation'. The practical effect of this is that details of the expenses covered need not be entered on the form P11D or on the employer's annual return or on the employees tax return.

   The nature of the expenses covered by the dispensation depends to some extent on the particular circumstances, but they can cover:

   travelling and subsistence
   cost of entertaining incurred wholly and exclusively for business
   mileage allowances (provided they are less than the FPCS rates)
   subscriptions to professional bodies related to employment
   telephone rentals to employees on call outside normal hours.

   In general dispensations are more difficult to obtain for director/family controlled companies.

Determination of £8,500 level

9. The determination of the £8,500 level may be illustrated as follows:

	£
Salary less pension contributions	–
Commission	–
Reimbursed expenses	–
Benefits in kind	–
	– Higher paid level > £8,500
Less allowable expense deduction	–
Schedule E assessment	–

   Note that the determination of the level of earning for a director and employee earning £8,500 or more includes the value of benefits in kind as if he were a higher paid employee and before any expense deductions permitted under Sec 198 TA 1988.

   Example

   K has the following data relating to 1997/98.

	£
Salary	5,200
Commission	1,500
Travelling expenses reimbursed to K	1,050
Car benefit (based on value of car)	1,580
Car fuel benefit (all private petrol paid for by K)	–
	9,330

As the total remuneration plus expenses and benefits is greater than £8,500, K is taxable as a person earning more than £8,500.

If the travelling expenses were paid direct by K's employers and not reimbursed to him, then they would not be included in determining the £8,500 level and therefore K would not be taxed in that capacity.

Summary of benefits 1997/98

10.

Class of Benefit	Directors and employees earning more than £8,500	Employees earning less than £8,500
Private use of employer's car (see below).	Cash equivalent	Not taxable providing some business use
Mobile telephones	£200 p.a.	ditto
Accommodation (see below).	Can be wholly or partly exempt, otherwise taxed on annual value plus expenses paid	Can be wholly or partly exempt: otherwise taxed on annual value plus expenses paid
Board and lodging	Taxed on cost to the employer	Tax free unless received in cash
Industrial clothing	Tax free	Tax free
Suits and clothing	Taxed on cost to employer	Taxed on secondhand value
Medical insurance	Premiums paid by employer taxable	Exempt
Beneficial loans (see below)	Generally taxable with some exceptions	No taxable benefit
Cash vouchers, saving certs.	Full value taxable	Full value taxable
New share option schemes	Not subject to income tax, CGT on final disposal	Not subject to income tax CGT on final disposal
Savings related share options	Not subject to income tax, CGT on final gain	Not subject to income tax CGT on final gain
Profit sharing schemes	Limited tax free benefit	Limited tax free benefit
Luncheon vouchers	Tax free up to 15p per day	Tax free up to 15p per day
Subsidised meals	Tax free if generally available	Tax free if generally available
Other assets loaned	20% of market value when first provided	Not taxable
Other assets transferred	Taxed on net increase in value	Taxed on second hand value
Season tickets and transport vouchers.	Taxed on cost to the employer	Taxed on cost to the employer
Private sick pay	Taxed on amount received	Taxed on amount received
Scholarships provided by reason of employment	Taxed on cost to employer	Not taxable
Employer-subsidised nursery facilities	Taxed on cost to employer	Not taxable
Loan written off	Taxed on full value	Taxed on full value
Workplace nurseries	Not taxable	Not taxable
In-house sports facilities	Not taxable	Not taxable

Private motor cars 1997/98 – car benefit

11. With effect on and from 6th April 1994 a new system of calculating the benefit in kind attributable to private motor cars was introduced.

The main features are as follows.

1. The benefit is calculated as follows.

	£
35% × List price of car	X
Less discount:	
$\frac{1}{3}$ for business miles 2,500 – 18,000	X
$\frac{2}{3}$ for business miles > 18,000	
	X
Less $\frac{1}{3}$ for cars > 4 years old	X
Cash equivalent	X
Less payment for private use	X
Assessable benefit	X

2. List price is the published price when first registered plus the list price of any 'extras' provided with the car. If the car has no published price a 'notional value' will be used.

3. Where the car is more than 15 years old at the end of the income tax year of assessment then its value if more than £15,000 is taken to be £15,000.

4. The maximum value of any car is limited to £80,000.

5. The mileage figures are reduced proportionally if the car is not available for any part of the year.

6. Where the employee makes a capital contribution to the cost of the car, then, subject to a maximum of £5,000, the amount is deducted from the list price.

7. Where an employee is required to make a capital contribution to the employer for private use of the car then this is deducted from the cash equivalent subject to a lower limit of zero.

Car scale benefit 1997/98

Age of car on 5th April	Under 4 years	Over 4 years
	% of List price	
Business mileage		
0 – 2,500	35.00	23.33
2,501 – 17,999	23.33	15.55
18,000 –	11.67	7.78

Example

A has a Vauxhall company car for 1997/98 first registered in April 1996 with a list price of £12,000. Business mileage is 10,000 p a.

Compute the cash equivalent for 1997/98.

Solution

Cash equivalent 1997/98

List price × 35% = 12,000 × 35%	4,200
Less discount $\frac{1}{3}$ (mileage 2,500 – 18,000)	1,400
Cash equivalent	2,800
Per table £12,000 × 23.33%	2,800

Example

K has a Rolls Royce company car made available for 1997/98. The car when first registered in June 1995 had a list price of £130,000. Business mileage is 20,000 miles p.a. K pays £4,000 p.a. to the company for his private use.

Compute the cash equivalent for 1997/98.

Solution   Cash equivalent 1997/98

List price (restricted) £80,000 × 35%	28,000	
Less Discount $\frac{2}{3}$ (Business mileage > 18,000)	18,666	
Cash equivalent	9,334	(= 80,000 × 11.67% per table)
Less contribution by K	4,000	
Assessable benefit	5,334	

Private motor cars 1997/98 – fuel benefit

12.

Engine size cc	Scale charge	
	Petrol	*Diesel*
	£	£
0 – 1400	800	740
1401 – 2000	1,010	740
2001 –	1,490	940

Notes:

i)   The petrol benefit is reduced to nil where *all* private petrol is paid for by the employee/director.

ii)   Age is determined by reference to the age at the end of the relevant year of assessment ie 5th April 1998 for 1997/98.

iii)   Employers (not employees) are required to pay NIC at the main rate of 10.0% (1997/98) on cars provided for private use of employees earning more than £8,500 p.a. This liability is assessed on an annual basis using the car scale and fuel rates quoted above, and collected in June following the previous tax year.

iv)   Where one car is used jointly by two or more employees a separate liability can arise in respect of each user.

Example

A is employed by Beta Ltd and is provided with a 2500 cc Rover car which cost £15,000 on 1st January 1995. A used the car during 1997/98 covering 20,000 miles of which 15,000 were business miles. Beta Ltd paid for all fuel, business and private. A pays £300 to the company each year for the use of the car.

Calculate the value of any car benefit for 1997/98.

Solution   A – Value of motor car benefits 1997/98

	£
Motor car benefit 35% × £15,000	5,250
Less discount $\frac{1}{3}$	1,750
Cash equivalent	3,500
Less contribution	300
	3,200
Motor fuel benefit	1,490
Total	4,690

Note

If the contribution by A of £300 had been made towards the private fuel cost but did not cover all the charge the total value of the benefits would have been £3,500+ £1,490 = £4,990

Fixed profit car scheme

13. With effect from 6th April 1990 FPCS rates were introduced where an employer pays an employee a mileage allowance for business use of the employee's own car.

Pence per business mile 1997/98

Engine capacity	up to 4,000 miles	over 4,000 miles
up to 1000	28.0	17.0
1,001 –1,500	35.0	20.0
1,501 – 2,000	45.0	25.0
2,001 –	63.0	36.0

Any payment received in excess of the ceiling is taxable.

The scheme is optional and employers/employees do not have to use the FPCS system. Instead a normal claim for expenses under Schedule E can be made by the employee.

Relief for interest on a loan for the purchase of a car is not included in the FPCS rates.

Company vans

14. With effect from the 6th April 1993 any employee benefiting from the private use of an employer-provided van pays income tax on the following standard amounts:

Age of van 1997/98

	under 4 years old	over 4 years old
	£	£
Scale charge	500	350

These charges apply to vans of less than 3,5 tonnes in weight (gross). Heavier vehicles will not be taxed unless they are used wholly or mainly for the employees' benefit.

There is no separate charge for fuel provided for private use.

Accommodation

15. Value of benefit (directors and all employees)

Where any individual (ie with earnings above and below the £8,500 threshold) is provided with living accommodation then subject to certain exemptions noted below, he is liable to tax on the value of the benefit which is equal to:

Gross value + Cost of ancillary services – Employee's contribution – business use.

Gross value is the gross rating value of the property occupied, or the rent, if any, paid by the person providing the accommodation.

Cost of ancillary services is the total of any expenses incurred in providing services such as heating, lighting, rates, domestic services or gardening, and the provision of furniture.

Employee's contribution means any rent paid by an employee.

Business use means the proportion of any benefit attributable to business use.

Total exemption from gross value

An individual is not taxed on the gross value of the accommodation providing it is:

a) necessary for the proper performance of his duties, or
b) for the better performance of his duties, and in general provided for others, or
c) required for security reasons.

A full time working director with less than 5% interest in a company is eligible for the exemption under (a) and (b) but not under (c). All other directors are ineligible for any exemption.

Partial exemption from ancillary costs benefit

If an individual is exempted under any of the categories noted above, then the taxable value of all ancillary services is limited to a maximum of 10% of net assessable emoluments for the year, ie remuneration benefits etc (excluding ancillary benefits) less any amount paid by the employee for use of the services.

Net emoluments (ignoring the benefit in question) are after deducting allowable expenses, superannuation and approved pension scheme payments and capital allowances.

> **Example**

Q is an employee of T plc occupying a house with a gross value of £1,000, which is exempt accommodation.

The employer pays the following expenses:

	£
Heating and lighting	1,200
Gardening	800
Domestic servant's wages	500
Furniture costing	10,000

Q's salary for the year 1997/98 is £42,000 and he pays the company £3,000 for the use of the house.

Calculate the value of the benefit for 1997/98.

Solution   **Value of accommodation benefit 1997/98**

i) Gross value of property exempted   –
    Ancillary services:

Heating and lighting	1,200	
Domestic service	500	
Gardening	800	2,500
Use of furniture 20% × 10,000		2,000
		4,500

ii) Q – Emoluments £42,000 × 10%   4,200
    Benefit restricted to the lower ie   4,200
    Less contribution paid by Q   3,000
    Schedule E benefit   1,200

Notes

i)   *The furniture is valued as an asset loaned to an employee, at 20% of its market value when first provided, ie £10,000.*

ii) *If Q's occupation was non exempted the value of his benefit would be the gross value plus expenses ie £1,000 plus £4,500 less contribution of £3,000 ie £2,500. The emolument restriction does not apply in this case.*

Accommodation costing more than £75,000

16. An extra taxable emolument arises where the following occurs.

   a) The cost of providing accommodation is greater than £75,000, and

   b) The living accommodation is provided for a person by reason of his office or employment, and

   c) The occupier is liable to a taxable benefit in respect of accommodation, as outlined in the previous section. If the employee is exempt from the 'gross value' charge noted above he is also exempted under this heading.

   d) The additional value is determined from:

   Appropriate % × [cost or deemed cost – £75,000] – contribution by taxpayer

   Appropriate % = the official rate of Interest in force on the 6th April of the year of assessment. For 1997/98 it is 6.75% (1996/97 7.25%)

   Cost   = cost of acquisition + cost of improvements carried out before year of assessment.

   Contribution   = the amount by which any rent paid by tenant is greater than the gross value of the accommodation.

> **Example**

J plc acquired a property in October 1996 for £260,000 which had a gross rateable value of £10,000. In May 1997 improvements costing £25,000 were incurred. On 7th April 1997, Z the marketing director, occupied the property paying a rent of £5,000 p.a. He paid £10,000 towards the original cost.

Calculate the value of the taxable benefits in kind for 1997/98.

Solution

	£	£
1997/98. Value of accommodation benefit:		
Gross value of property	10,000	
Less rent paid	5,000	5,000
Additional value of accommodation:		
Cost of accommodation	250,000	
Less exempt amount	75,000	
	175,000	
6.75% × 175,000 =		11,812
		16,812

Notes

i)   The £16,812 would be emoluments of Z for 1997/98 chargeable to income tax.

ii)   The improvement expenditure of £25,000 will fall into the computation of the additional value for 1998/99.

iii) As the rent paid by Z is less than the gross value there is no deduction in the computation of the additional value.

iv)   The official rate of interest at the 6th April 1997 was 6.75%.

v)   Where the property is not occupied throughout the year the change is pro-rated.

vi)   Additional value is [(260,000 - 10,000) – 75,000] × 6.75% = £11,812.

Assets other than cars – private use

17. Where assets are made available for use by directors and employees earning £8,500 or more then the annual benefit is calculated as follows.

  a) Land and property (other than accommodation) is valued at a market rent.

  b) Other assets eg a company van, are valued at 20% of the original market value or if higher, the rental paid by the employer.

Assets transferred to an employee

18. If an asset made available to a director or employee earning £8,500 or more is subsequently acquired by that person then the assessable benefit on the acquision is the greater of:

  a) the excess of the current market price over the price paid by the employee and,

  b) the excess of the market value when first provided for use by the employee, less any amounts assessed as annual benefits (at 20%) over the price paid by the employee.

Beneficial loans (Sec. 160 TA 1988)

19. Where an individual is provided with an interest free or cheap loan then in general the benefit derived from such an arrangement is taxable. Employees earning less than £8,500 p.a. are not assessable since the benefit is not convertible into cash.

The following are the main features:

  a) The loan giving rise to the benefit to an employee or his relative must be obtained by reason of an employment.

  b) The assessable amount is calculated by two methods, (see below) using the **official rate of interest** less any interest actually paid by the employee.

  c) Official rates of interest in the last two years have been:

6th January 1994	–	5th November 1994	7.50%
6th November 1994	–	5th October 1995	8.00%
6th October 1995	–	5th February 1996	7.75%
6th February 1996	–	5th June 1996	7.25%
6th June 1996	–	5th November 1996	7.00%
6th November 1996	–		6.75%

d) No benefit will arise where the interest on such a loan would normally qualify for tax relief such as:

    i) a loan for the purchase of the taxpayers main residence not exceeding £30,000

    ii) a loan for the purchase of plant or machinery for use in employment.

e) If the value of the loan outstanding during the year does not exceed £5000, there will be no charge from 1994/95.

Methods of calculation

20. I. Average method

    a) This method averages the loan over the tax year by reference to the opening and closing balances at the beginning and end of the year (or date of creation and discharge) and applies the official rate to this amount.

    b) Interest paid if any on the loan is deducted from the amount computed in (a) above to determine the amount chargeable to tax.

    c) This method is applied automatically unless an election is made, either by the taxpayer or the inspector of taxes, to apply the second method.

    d) Where the company's accounts year does not coincide with the tax year then it will usually be necessary to make the calculations by reference to two accounting periods.

Example

Z Ltd makes an interest free loan to R, one of its higher paid employees on the 1st October 1997 of £24,000, repayable by 8 quarterly instalments of £3,000, payable on the 1st January, April, July and October. The first payment is made on the 1st January 1998. Calculate the assessable benefit for 1997/98. Assume an average official rate of interest of 8.0% throughout the year.

Solution	**Computation of interest benefit**	
		£
1.10.1997	Loan granted	24,000
5.4.1998	Balance of loan outstanding	
	24,000 – 6,000	18,000
		42,000

Average loan outstanding

$$\frac{42,000}{2} \qquad 21,000$$

Period of loan

1.10.1997–5.4.1998 = 6 months. (ie completed tax months)

Interest $8\% \times \dfrac{6}{12} \times 21,000 =$ 840

Assessable benefit 1997/98   840

21. II. Alternative method

    a) Under this method the interest is calculated on the balance outstanding on a day to day basis, using the official rate of interest.

    b) Any interest paid is deducted from the amount calculated in (a) above.

Example

Using the data relating to Z Ltd in the previous example, calculate the assessable benefit under the alternative method.

Solution   **Computation of interest benefit**

		£	£
1.10.1997	Loan granted	24,000	
1.1.1998	Loan repayment	3,000	
		21,000	

Number of days from 1.10.1997 to 1.1.1998 = 92

Interest 92/365 × 8.0% × 24,000   484

1.1.1998	Balance outstanding	21,000	
1.4.1998	Loan repayment	3,000	
5.4.1998	Balance outstanding	18,000	

		£	
Number of days from	1.1.1998 to 1.4.1998 =	90	
do.	1.4.1998 to 5.4.1998 =	5	
Interest	90/365 × 8.0% × 21,000		414
	5/365 × 8.0% × 18,000		20
Assessable benefit 1997/98			918

Relief for expenses

22. The following may be deducted from emoluments in arriving at an assessable income under Schedule E.

a) Expenses permitted under Sec 198 TA 1988, being incurred wholly and exclusively and necessary for the performance of the duties of the office or employment; for example, industrial clothing; tools of trade. Travelling expenses from home to place of business are not permitted deductions, see *Ricketts* v *Colquhoun* 1926 10 TC 118. *Parikh* v *Sleeman* 1988 STC 580; see also *Elderkin* v *Hindmarsh* 1988 STC 267. *Fitzpatrick* v *IRC* 1992 STI 456.

b) With effect from 6th April 1998 the position regarding employees' travel and subsistence is to be redefined. The main features of the proposals are:

   i) to give site-based employees relief for travel and subsistence expenses incurred as a result of their employment

   ii) to give relief for the *additional* cost of the business journey in triangular travel. A deduction will be available for the net additional cost an employee incurs as a result of travelling between home and a temporary place of work. Any saving realised by an employee through not undertaking normal commuting will be offset against the cost of travel between home and the temporary workplace.

   iii) to extend the present time limit for a posting to qualify as a temporary place of work from 12 months to 24 months.

c) Those permitted specifically by statute eg fees and subscriptions to professional bodies, section 201; contributions to exempt approved pension schemes, Section 592.

d) Capital allowances on plant or machinery provided by the employee in order to perform his duties may be deducted, eg a private car, or office equipment, or car used under the FPCS scheme.

None of the above are charges on income which can be deducted from total income, and not just employment income.

Liability insurance relief

23. With effect from 1995/96 income tax relief is available to employees and directors for payments they make to secure indemnity insurance against liability claims arising from their job or to meet uninsured work-related liabilities. Relief is also extended to situations where the employer or a third party pays the insurance which would otherwise give rise to a benefit in kind. The cost of the insurance is deducted as an expense from the Schedule E income tax in the year in which the payment is made.

Relief is extended to payments made by ex-employees for periods of up to six years after the year in which employment ceases.

Employees' incidental expenses paid by employer

24. Payments by employers of certain miscellaneous personal expenses incurred by employees are exempt from income tax and N.I.C. from 6th April 1995.

The exemption covers incidental expenses such as newspapers, telephone calls, home and laundry bills incurred by employees when they stay away from home overnight on business.

Payments of up to £5.00 a night in the UK (£10.00 outside UK) are tax free. However, if the employer pays sums greater than these limits then the whole amount becomes taxable.

Removal expenses and benefits

25. With effect from the 5th April 1993 certain payments and benefits received by reason of an employment are not to be treated as an emolument for Schedule E purposes.

This applies to:

i) sums paid to an employee, or to a third party on behalf of an employee in respect of quantifying removal expenses, and

ii) any qualifying removal benefit provided for the employee or to members of his or her family or household (including sons and daughters in law, servants, dependants and guests).

Qualifying removal expenses comprise the following.

1) Expenses disposal, ie legal expenses, loan redemption penalties, estate agents' or auctioneers' fees, advertising costs, disconnection charges, and rent and maintenance etc. costs during an unoccupied period, relating to the disposal of his or her interest (or of the interest of a member of his or her family or household) in the employee's former residence.

2) Expenses of acquisition, ie legal expenses, procurement fees, survey fees, Registry fees, stamp duty and connection charges, relating to the acquisition by the employee (or by a member of his or her family or household) of an interest in his or her new residence.

3) Expenses of abortive acquisition, ie expenses which would have been within category 2 above but for the interest not being acquired, for reasons beyond the control of the person seeking to acquire it or because that person reasonably declined to proceed with it.

4) Expenses of transporting belongings, ie expenses, including insurance, temporary storage and disconnection and reconnection of appliances, connected with transporting domestic belongings of the employee and of members of his or her family or household from the former to the new residence.

5) Travelling and subsistence expenses (subsistence meaning food, drink and temporary accommodation). These are restricted to:

   a) such costs of the employee and members of his or her family or household on temporary visits to the new area in connection with the change;

   b) the employee's travel costs between his or her former residence and new place of work;

   c) costs of temporary living accommodation for the employee;

   d) the employee's travel costs between his or her former residence and such temporary accommodation;

   e) the travel costs of the employee and members of his or her family or household between the former and new residences;

   f) certain costs incurred to secure continuity of education for a member of the employee's family or household who is under 19 at the beginning of the year of assessment in which the commencement of change of duties etc. take place.

6) Bridging loan expenses, ie interest payable by the employee (or by a member of his or her family or household) on loan raised at least partly because there is a gap between the incurring of expenditure in acquiring the new residence and the receipt of the proceeds of the disposal of the former residence. Interest on so much of the loan as either

   a) exceeds the market value of his or her interest (or the interest of a member of his or her family or household) in the former residence (at the time the new residence is acquired), or

   b) is not used for the purpose of either redeeming a loan raised by the employee on his or her former residence or acquiring his or her interest) or the interest of a member of his or her family or household) in the new residence is excluded.

7) Duplicate expenses, ie net expenses incurred as a result of the change in the replacement of domestic goods used at the former residence but unsuitable for use at the new residence.

Qualifying removal benefits consist of benefits or services corresponding to the seven headings noted above, with the restriction that the provision of a car or van for general private use is excluded from category 5 above.

The amount of the qualifying removal expenses is limited to a maximum of £8,000.

Payroll deductions for charities

26. An employee can obtain income tax relief on donations to a charity, and for 1997/98 the maximum is £1,200 for payments after 6th April 1997. The main features of the scheme, contained in Sec 202 TA 1988, are as follows:

a) Schemes are operated through charity agencies which must be approved by the Inland Revenue.

b) Employers are legally bound to pay the donation over to the agency charity and they may not be refunded to the employee.

c) Payments made by deed of covenant are not included in the scheme. However, an employee can still make a covenanted donation, subject to the normal requirements, in addition to any made under the payroll scheme.

d) The employer will make the deduction of the donation before PAYE is applied, in the same way that pension contributions are dealt with under the 'net pay' arrangements. The amount of the contributions made each year will not appear on the employee's P.60.

e) National Insurance contributions at the appropriate rate are payable on the gross pay before deduction of any charitable donations.

f) Pensioners can be incorporated into the scheme provided that they are subject to PAYE.

The following are some of the agencies approved by the Inland Revenue:

Dr Barnardo's
United Way Payroll Giving Service
Charities Aid Foundation
Wales Council for Voluntary Action
Scottish Council for Voluntary Organisation
Northern Ireland Council for Voluntary Action
Federation of Master Builders (South West Region).

Emoluments and overseas employment

27. This aspect of the subject is dealt with in the next chapter.

Payments on retirement or removal from office

28. The main provisions concerned with the taxation of payments for loss of employment are contained in Sec 148 and 188 TA 1988, and these include the following:

a) First   £30,000   exempt
   Excess over   £30,000   taxed in full

b) Complete or partial exemption is available for terminal payments which relate to any foreign service.

c) General exemption applies to payments made:
   i)   on the death or permanent disability of an employee
   ii)   to benefits provided under a pension scheme
   iii) to terminal payments made to members of the armed forces.

> **Example**

N, a single man, retires as a director of T plc on the 1st October 1997 and receives the sum of £35,000 by way of ex gratia payment.

N's other income for 1997/98 is a salary of £7,045, and bank interest of £3,200 (net).

Calculate the tax payable on the terminal payment.

Solution

N's Income Tax computation 1997/98

	£	£
Schedule E salary		7,045
Bank interest gross 3,200 ÷ 0.8		4,000
Terminal payment	35,000	
Less exempt amount	30,000	5,000
		16,045
Personal allowance		4,045
Taxable income		12,000
Tax Payable 4,100 @ 20%		820
4,000 @ 20%		800
3,900 @ 23%		897
12,000		2,517
Less deducted at source on bank interest		800
Tax payable		1,717

Note Tax payable on the terminal payment is £5,000 @ 23% i.e. £1,150. The 23% rate is the marginal rate in this case.

Outplacement counselling

29. This involves the provision of services normally paid for by the employer, for employees who are or become redundant, to help them find new work.

For expenditure incurred after the 16th March 1993 the expenditure will be exempt from tax whether or not it exceeds the £30,000 limit for redundancy payments.

Pensions

30. Any pension paid to a former employee is taxable as earned income on the recipient. This includes payments from company operated schemes, from schemes operated by assurance companies, and voluntary payments where there is no formal pension scheme.

If the scheme is approved by the Inland Revenue then any contributions made by the employee are deductible from taxable earnings. The company's contributions are also allowed as an expense in computing taxable profits.

Pensions paid by the state are taxable as earned income of the recipient and these include: retirement pensions, widows' pensions and service pensions.

Benefits from approved profit-sharing schemes

31. A company can establish an approved profit-sharing scheme whereby money is allocated to trustees to purchase shares in the company, on behalf of its employees. After a minimum period of two years the shares can be appropriated to the employee. Income tax is payable depending upon how long the shares are retained by the employee.

Period	% original value liable to income tax
Disposal before 3rd anniversary	100%
on or after 3rd anniversary	75%

Note: The above rules apply after the royal assent to the Finance Bill 1996. Prior thereto the nil rate applied after five years.

If the shares are disposed of at a price greater than their original value then a capital gains tax liability will arise on the employee. The maximum value of shares which can be allocated per person in any one year of assessment is the greater of £3,000, or 10% of salary, subject to an overall maximum of £8,000 a year.

Social security benefits

32. The following benefits are taxable under this heading:

Unemployment benefit (Job seeker's allowance)

Invalidity care allowance

Supplementary benefit when paid to unemployed persons or strikers

Statutory maternity pay

Widow's pension, but not the widow's payment of £1,000

Old person's pension

Retirement pension

Statutory sick pay.

Executive share options schemes (Section 185–187 sch. 9 TA 1988)

33. Under these schemes, if approved, an employee is given the right to buy shares at a fixed price which will not be subject to income tax if retained for a requisite period. The main features of these schemes are as follows.

a) The price of the shares is fixed at not less than the market value, at the time the employee gets his or her option.

b) The shares must form part of the ordinary share capital of the company.

c) Employee participants in the scheme must work at least 20 hours a week for the company, and full time working directors must work at least 25 hours a week.

d) Options are limited in value to £30,000 on the value of the shares under option.

e) There is no income tax liability on the grant of the option or on any increase in the value of the shares providing that the option is used at least three years and no more than ten years after the employee obtained it.

f) On the eventual disposal of the shares then the normal rules of capital gains tax apply.

g) A savings-related share option scheme is also available with similar rules to those noted above.

h) Approved schemes are not limited to quoted shares but include shares in a company which is not controlled by other companies.

Profit-related pay 169–184 TA 1988 – (to 31.12.1999)

34. Income tax relief is to be available for private sector employees who are members of approved registered schemes where there is a clear relationship between the PRP and the profits of the business in general. The main features are as follows.

a) At least 80% of employees must be covered by the scheme.

b) Profits are to be calculated by reference to profits after taxation as defined in the Companies Act 1985, subject to limited adjustments.

c) Tax relief is limited to the lower of the following:

    i) 20% × employee's pay for the profit period

       less pension contributions and payroll giving to charities

       plus PRP for the profit period.

    ii) £4,000: 1998 – £2,000: 1999 – £1,000: 2,000 – nil

    iii) the actual payment of PRP for the profit period regardless of when paid.

Total pay is after deduction of superannuation and payroll deductions, and has the same meaning as for PAYE purposes, plus PRP payments.

Note P.R.P. is to be phased out gradually by 1st January 2000.

> **Example**

A receives the following from his employer Q Ltd in respect of the year ended 5th April 1998:

	£
Salary	25,000
PRP for the profit period	5,000

A is married and pays pension contributions of £1,200 and £800 under the charitable payroll deduction scheme.

Compute the tax payable for 1997/98.

Solution   **A's Income tax computation 1997/98**

	£	£
Schedule E salary		25,000
		5,000
		30,000
Less Pension contribution	1,200	
Charitable donations	800	2,000
		28,000
Less PRP exemption (see Note)		4,000
		24,000
Personal allowance		4,045
Taxable income		19,955
Tax payable 4,100 @ 20%		820
15,855 @ 23%		3,647
19,955		4,467
Less deduction for MCA @ 15% = 1,830 @ 15%		274
		4,193

Notes

i)   *PRP exemption is the lower of:*

   a)   *20% [(25,000 – 2,000) + PRP]*
   = 20% × (23,000 + 5,000)
   = £5,600

   b)   *£4,000 for APs commencing in calendar year 1997.*

   Exemption is ∴ 100% × £4,000 = £4,000.

ii)   *£1,000 of the PRP payment of £5,000 is taxable.*

• Student self-testing question

N, who is single, is the marketing director for Z plc and for 1997/98 he had the following data:

	£
Schedule E earnings	91,805
Building society interest (received)	4,000

N has a 1995 2000cc diesel company car which had a list price of £15,000 when first registered in May 1995. His average mileage on business is 12,000 miles a year. He regularly travels overseas for the company and during 1997/98 spent a total of 136 days abroad. All motor expenses are borne by the company.

N occupies a company house which cost £223,148 in October 1994. The gross value of the property less rent paid by N amounted to £5,000 for 1997/98.

Calculate the taxable income of N for 1997/98 and the tax payable. Official rate 6.75%.

Solution   **Computation of benefits in kind 1997/98**

	£	£
Accommodation		
Gross value less contribution by N		5,000
Additional value:		
Original cost	223,148	
Less exempt amount	75,000	
	148,148	
6.75% × £148,148 =		10,000
		15,000
Car benefit: List price × 35% = 15,000 × 35%	5,250	
Less discount $\frac{1}{3}$	1,750	
	3,500	
Fuel benefit – diesel	740	4,240

Income tax computation 1997/98		£
Schedule E		91,805
Benefits in kind – accommodation	15,000	
– motor car	4,240	19,240
		111,045
Building society interest (gross)		5,000
		116,045
Personal allowance		4,045
Taxable income		112,000
Tax payable: 4,100 @ 20%		820
22,000 @ 23%		5,060
85,900 @ 40%		34,360
112,000		40,240
Less income tax on building society interest		1,000
Tax borne		39,240

Note

There is no special deduction from earnings for limited overseas visits.

• Questions without answers

1. S is employed as a salesman by Q Ltd whose accounts for the last three years to 31st March show, the following payments to S:

	Salary £	Bonus £	Total £
Year to 31.3.1998	7,500	5,200	12,700
Year to 31.3.1997	6,950	4,212	11,162
Year to 31.3.1996	5,875	4,275	10,150

The bonus is paid in the August following the year end.

In addition to his salary and bonus, the Form P11D completed in respect of the year 1997/98 showed the following:

	£
Travelling expenses	3,500
Medical insurance	600
Beneficial loan free of interest	
Loan made 5.11.1997	10,000
Balance outstanding 5.4.1998	10,000
Car list price when new	18,000
First registered 1. 3.1995	
Make 2000cc Ford Sierra	
Business mileage 15000	
All fuel ie business and private paid for by company	

S is married with two children who attend private school, fees amounting to £5,500 p.a. being paid for by S's mother.

The following additional information is contained in S's income tax returns:

		Year to 5.4.1997 £	Year to 5.4.1998 £
Building society interest (net)	S.	491	400
Bank interest (net)	S.	700	480
Mortgage interest (MIRAS net)	S.	875	3,000

You are required to compute S's income tax liability for 1997/98. Assume an average official rate of interest of 8%.

2. A who is single retires from T Ltd on the 1st September 1997 and receives by way of ex gratia payment the sum of £100,000. In respect of 1997/98 A's other income was a salary of £10,000 and Schedule A income of £14,045.

Compute the amount of tax attributable to the terminal payment of £100,000.

Inland Revenue

P11D *Return of expenses payments and benefits* 1996-97

Note for employer
Complete this form for a director, or an employee who earned at a rate of £8,500 a year or more during the year 6 April 1996 to 5 April 1997.
Do not include expenses and benefits covered by a dispensation or PAYE settlement agreement. Read the P11D (Guide) and booklet 480,
[Chapter 24] before you complete the form. Send the completed P11D and form P11D(b) to the Tax Office. The forms must reach the Tax
Office by 6 July 1997. You must give a copy of this information to the employee/director by the same date.
The term employee is used to cover both directors and employees throughout the rest of this form.

Employer's details

Employer's name

PAYE tax reference

Employee's details

Employee's name	Works number or Department	Tick here if a director	National Insurance number

Note for employee
Please keep this form in a safe place as you may not be able to get a duplicate. You will need it for your personal records and to complete your 1996-97 Tax
Return if you get one. The box numbers on the form correspond to those on the employment pages of the Return. On this form P11D some boxes have the same
numbering, for example 1.12. If there are entries in these boxes, you should add them all together and then include the total figure in the appropriate box on the Return,
unless you think some other figure is appropriate. Your 1997-98 tax code may need to be adjusted to take account of the information given on this form.

A Assets transferred (cars, property, goods or other assets)

	Cost / Market value	Amount made good or from which tax deducted	Cash equivalent
Description of asset _____	£	– £	= **1.12** £

B Payments made on behalf of the employee

	Amount paid
Description of payment _____	**1.12** £
Tax on notional payments not borne by the employee within 30 days of receipt of each notional payment	**1.12** £

C Vouchers and credit cards

	Gross amount	Amount made good or from which tax deducted	Taxable payment
Value of vouchers and payments made using credit cards or tokens	£	– £	= **1.13** £

D Living accommodation

Cash equivalent of accommodation provided for the employee or his/her family/household.	**1.14** £

E Mileage allowance

	Gross amount	Amount made good or from which tax deducted	Taxable payment
Car and mileage allowances paid for employee's car	£	– £	= **1.15** £

F Cars and car fuel

If more than one car was made available to the employee, give details for each car and enter the total cash equivalent for all cars in box 1.16. If more
than two cars were made available, either at the same time or in succession, please give details on a separate sheet.

	Car 1			Car 2		
Make and model						
Date first registered						
	From		To	From		To
Dates the car was available						

Business mileage used in calculation for this car
If the car was unavailable for part of the year
the business mileage limits are reduced proportionately
Tick one box only for each car

Car 1			Car 2		
2,499 or less	2,500 to 17,999	18,000 or more	2,499 or less	2,500 to 17,999	18,000 or more
☐	☐	☐	☐	☐	☐

	Car 1	Car 2
List price of the car (If there is no list price or it is a classic car, employers see booklet 480; employees see leaflet IR 133)	£	£
Price of optional accessories fitted when the car was first made available to the employee	£	£
Price of accessories added after the car was first made available to the employee	£	£
Capital contributions (maximum of £5,000) the employee made towards the cost of the car or accessories	£	£
Amount paid in the year by the employee for private use of the car	£	£
Total car benefit charge for all cars available in 1996-97.	**1.16** £	
Total car fuel benefit charge for all cars available in 1996-97.	**1.17** £	

P11D(1997) BMSD 11/96

23386 12.96 Niceday Stationery & Print Limited   BMSD11/96   W0P0044

Please turn over

G Vans

Cash equivalent of all vans made available for private use. **1.18** £

H Interest free and low interest loans

If the total amount outstanding on all loans does not exceed £5,000 at any time in the year there is no need to complete this section.

	Loan 1	Loan 2
Purpose of the loan(s) using code shown in P11D Guide		
Number of joint borrowers (if applicable)		
Tick the box if the loan is within MIRAS	☐	☐
Amount outstanding at 5 April 1996 or at date when loan was made if later	£	£
Amount outstanding at 5 April 1997 or at date when loan was discharged if earlier	£	£
Maximum amount outstanding at any time in the year	£	£
Total amount of interest paid by the borrower in the year to 5 April 1997 – enter "NIL" if none was paid	£	£
Date loan was made or discharged in the year to 5 April 1997 where applicable		
Cash equivalent of loan(s) - *after deducting interest paid*	**1.19** £	**1.19** £

I Mobile telephones

Cash equivalent of all mobile telephones provided. **1.20** £

J Private medical treatment or insurance

	Cost to you	Amount made good or from which tax deducted	Cash equivalent
Private medical or dental treatment or insurance	£	– £	= **1.21** £

K Qualifying relocation expenses payments and benefits (Non qualifying expenses should be entered at P below)

Excess over £8,000 of all qualifying relocation expenses payments and benefits for each move. When calculating the excess you should take into account any qualifying items from last year. **1.22** £

L Services supplied

	Cost to you	Amount made good or from which tax deducted	Cash equivalent
Services supplied to the employee	£	– £	= **1.22** £

M Assets placed at the employee's disposal

	Annual value plus expenses incurred	Amount made good or from which tax deducted	Cash equivalent
Description of asset _____	£	- £	= **1.22** £

N Shares

Tick the box if during the year there have been share-related benefits for the employee ☐

O Other items

	Cost to you	Amount made good or from which tax deducted	Cash equivalent
Subscriptions and professional fees	£	- £	= **1.22** £
Other items - please describe _____	£	- £	= **1.22** £

	Tax paid
Income tax paid but not deducted from the director's remuneration	**1.22** £

P Expenses payments made to, or on behalf of, the employee

	Gross amount	Amount made good or from which tax deductd	Taxable payment
Travelling and subsistence payments	£	- £	= **1.23** £
Entertainment – *if you are a trading organisation, read P11D Guide and enter either "√" or "x" as appropriate here* ☐	£	- £	= **1.23** £
General expenses allowance for business travel	£	- £	= **1.23** £
Payments for use of home telephone	£	- £	= **1.23** £
Non-qualifying relocation expenses (those not in section K)	£	- £	= **1.23** £
Other expenses - please describe_____	£	- £	= **1.23** £

9 Income from employment II – international aspects

Introduction

1. This chapter is concerned with some of the more common features of income tax arising from overseas situations. It begins with an outline of the concepts of residence and domicile which are fundamental in determining liability to income tax. The meaning of these concepts is then considered with examples. The main headings of this chapter are:

Residence
Ordinary residence
Domicile
Emoluments and overseas employment
British subjects and others resident abroad
UK residents working overseas – 100% deduction.

Residence

2. Residence of a taxpayer is not defined in the UK tax statutes so that the meaning is largely determined by case law and the practical rules which have been developed by the Inland Revenue. The main factors to be taken into consideration in determining whether or not an individual is resident in the UK are as follows:

a) **Physical presence in the UK during the tax year**

This is usually a prerequisite so that if a person does not actually set foot in the UK during a tax year then he or she is not likely to be considered resident. See *Reed v Clark* 1985 STC 323. Temporary absence abroad does not affect a UK citizen's residence. Sec 334 TA 1988.

b) **Six months stay in the UK**

If a person is present in the UK for at least six months (ie 183 days) then he or she is deemed to be resident. The count is made of the total number of days whether or not there are successive visits, with the days of arrival and departure usually being ignored. Sec 336 TA 1988.

c) **Accommodation in the UK**

The rules whereby if a person has accommodation available for his or her use in the UK then he or she is deemed to be resident in any year in which he or she sets foot inside the UK whether he or she owns the accommodation or not, are abolished with effect from the 6th April 1993.

d) **UK director working abroad**

A person who works mainly abroad and also carries out the functions of a director in the UK could be deemed resident unless the duties were regarded as incidental to the overseas employment.

The Inland Revenue will not regard attendance at board meetings in the UK as incidental where the directorship is with the company employing him or her abroad and that office carries with it executive responsibilities requiring him or her to be overseas.

However, where the directorship is non-executive in the UK with a separate subsidiary and unconnected, or only tenuously connected, then attendance at that company's board meetings will not be regarded as incidental.

Where accommodation is available in the UK the location of that property relative to the place where the duties are to be performed could be important where loss of non-resident status might otherwise be at risk.

Ordinary residence

3. Ordinary residence is generally equivalent to being habitually resident in a particular country. The main determinants are as follows.

a) Habitual or customary residence as opposed to occasional residence taking one tax year with another. *IRC v Lysaght* 1928 13 TC 511.

b) A visitor will be regarded as ordinarily resident (and resident) if his or her visits for four consecutive tax years have averaged three months or more per tax year.

c) Visitors to the UK for study or educational purposes are treated as resident and ordinarily resident from the date of arrival if the stay is expected to last four years. If not, the individual is treated as being ordinarily resident at the beginning of the fifth year.

Domicile

4. This is a concept of general law quite distinct from nationality and implies that a person has a permanent place of residence often connected with his or her place of birth. There are three kinds of domicile: domicile of origin, domicile of choice and domicile of dependence.

    a) **Domicile of origin**

    A person automatically acquires a domicile at birth and this is normally the domicile of his or her father and not necessarily the country where he or she is born. It follows that a person may be a domicile of a country which in fact he or she never visits. The domicile of origin is retained until it is superseded by either a domicile of choice or of dependence.

    b) **Domicile of choice**

    This is voluntary choice of domicile which can be made by any individual in the UK on attaining the age of 16 or marries under that age. To be effective
    i) the individual must take up residence in the country concerned, and
    ii) there must be an intention to remain indefinitely in the country concerned.

    Extended residence in a country without intention is not sufficient to change a domicile.

    Where a domicile of choice is lost, for example, where the person ceases to be permanently resident in a country, then his or her domicile of origin is revived.

    c) **Domicile of dependence**

    This concept used to apply to married women who, on marriage, acquired the domicile of their husband and were unable to acquire a domicile of choice. Under the provision of the Domicile and Matrimonial Proceedings Act 1973, this dependence was abolished and married women have a place of domicile determined in the same way as men.

    Infants under age (i.e. under 16 or age of marriage if earlier) have a domicile of dependence, normally their father's domicile.

Emoluments and overseas employment

5. Tax under Schedule E is charged under three cases depending in the main on the residence status of the employee and the place where the duties are performed.

    Case I

    This applies to persons resident and ordinarily resident in the UK. The charge is in respect of emoluments received from employments wherever the duties are performed. There is a deduction permitted of 100% for duties performed wholly or partially overseas.

    Case II

    This applies to persons not resident in the UK, or if resident, not ordinarily resident in the UK. The charge is in respect of duties performed in the UK only. Emoluments in respect of duties performed abroad are taxable on the remittance basis of Case III.

    Case III

    This applies to persons resident, whether ordinarily resident or not, so far as the emoluments do not fall within Case I or Case II. The charge is on the emoluments received in the UK (the remittance basis) in respect of overseas duties.

    A person resident but not ordinarily resident performing duties in the UK is taxed under Case II. A person resident and ordinarily resident performing duties in the UK is taxed under Case I.

    The following charts illustrate the position more fully.

6.

Non-foreign emoluments

UK residence Status of employee in year of assessment	Duties of employment performed wholly or partly in UK		Duties of employment performed wholly outside UK
	Duties in UK	Duties outside UK	
Resident and ordinarily resident	Case I All emoluments	Case I Less 100% deduction for 365 days in qualifying period	Case I Less 100% deduction for 365 days in qualifying period
Resident but not ordinarily resident	Case II	Case III Remittance basis	Case III Remittance basis
Not resident	Case II	No UK tax liability	No UK tax liability

Foreign emoluments

UK residence Status of employee in year of assessment	Duties of employment performed wholly or partly in UK		Duties of employment performed wholly outside UK
	Duties in UK	Duties outside UK	
Resident and ordinarily resident	Case I	Case I	Case III Remittance basis
Resident but not ordinarily resident	Case II	Case III Remittance basis	Case III Remittance basis
Not resident	Case II	No UK tax liability	No UK tax liability

Note

Foreign emoluments are those of a person not domiciled in the UK from an employer not resident in the UK.

British subjects and others resident abroad

7. A non-UK resident is subject to income tax on UK sources of income, which may be mitigated to some extent by double taxation agreements. In principle the position ignoring any double taxation relief is as follows:

UK pensions. Pensions payable as retirement pensions are taxed at source.

Gilt-edged securities. Income from certain British Government securities is exempt from UK tax. The list contained in Sec 47 TA 1988 includes 3 1/2% War Loan which together with securities held or on the NSB Register have the interest paid gross. Interest on securities outside the list are not exempt from UK tax.

UK rental income. Rent on UK property payable to a non-resident is subject to deduction of income tax at source by the payer. Tax is deducted from the business profits from lettings in the UK.

Bank and building society interest. Bank and Building society interest may be paid gross to non-residents who have filed a declaration to that effect with the Inland Revenue.

By way of concession no action is usually taken to pursue this liability to income tax except in so far as it can be recovered by set off in a claim to relief in respect of taxed income in the UK.

UK Dividends. The payment of UK company dividends to non-residents is invariably covered by a double taxation agreement which can provide for the whole or a part of the tax credit to be paid. For dividends paid after 5th April 1993 the maximum tax credit is 20% of the dividend payment.

Personal allowances

8. a) Non-UK residents are not normally entitled to claim allowances but certain classes of non-residents can claim, and these are listed below:

        Commonwealth citizens (including a British citizens) or citizens of the Republic of Ireland

        Missionaries of any UK missionary society

        People employed in the services of the Crown or Crown Protectorate

        Residents of the Channel Islands or Isle of Man

Former UK residents who are abroad for reasons of health

Foreign residents entitled under a double taxation agreement – in general these only apply where the income is *not* derived from interest, dividends or royalties

All nationals of states within the European Economic Area.

b) The following points should be noted.
i) Non-residents claiming allowances can set them against any income chargeable to UK tax.
ii) The blind person's allowance will not normally be claimable.
iii) Where a husband is not resident in the UK but qualifies for the married couple's allowance then any unused surplus can be transferred to the wife.

In calculating the surplus which can be transferred, only the UK taxable income is taken into consideration.

Limit on income chargeable on non-residents

9. From 1996/96 income tax chargeable on the total income of a non-UK resident (apart from income from a trade or profession carried on through a branch or agent, or under Schedule A) is not to exceed the aggregate of the following:

i) the tax which would otherwise be chargeable if excluded income and any personal allowances due were both disregarded.

ii) the tax deducted from so much of the 'excluded income' as is subject to deduction at source, including tax credits.

Excluded income is income chargeable under Schedule D Case III and Schedule F, Case IV and certain Social Security benefits (including state pensions).

Example

A, who is single, is a UK non-resident British subject working in France with the following data relating to 1997/98:

Salary from French company	1,500,000 F. francs
Building society interest (net)	£20,000

Compute A's UK income tax liability for 1997/98.

Solution   **A's UK income tax liability 1997/98**

		£
BSI (gross)		25,000
Personal allowance		4,045
Taxable income		20,955
Tax payable	4,100 @ 20%	820
	16,855 @ 20%	3,371
	20,955	4,191
Less income tax deducted at source		5,000
Repayable		(809)

Notes
i) *The BSI can be paid gross to non-residents.*
ii) *A's foreign emolument income is totally ignored in computing his UK tax liability.*
iii) *The maximum tax chargeable would be £5,000.00 in this case.*

UK residents working overseas – 100% deduction

10. Individuals who are resident and ordinarily resident in the UK may qualify from Schedule E emoluments related to an overseas employment in accordance with Sec 192 TA 1988. The following are the main points to be noted.

a) The duties performed wholly or partly outside the UK must consist of at least 364 days during a qualifying period.

b) A qualifying period may consist wholly of days absent from the UK or days absent plus days spent in the UK

c) No single period spent in the UK may exceed 62 days continuously.

d) At the date of arrival in the UK during the qualifying period, the total number of days spent in the UK since the qualifying period began must not exceed one sixth of the total period. The one sixth test is applied on the day immediately prior to the return to the UK.

e) The day of departure is a day of absence but the day of arrival is not.

f) A day of absence from the UK must involve absence at midnight on that day.

g) The 100% deduction only applies to emoluments for duties performed outside the UK so that any remuneration for UK duties remains liable to UK tax without the deduction unless such duties can be regarded as 'incidental to the overseas employment'. In general it appears that 'reporting to or receiving instructions from Head Office' can be regarded as incidental duties.

The following additional points should be noted.

a) Where a person goes abroad to work and the time abroad spans a complete income tax year then non-residence exemption can be claimed for the whole period of absence providing any return visits do not exceed the 91 days annual average.

b) Self-employment abroad does not give rise to a claim under the 100% deduction rules noted above.

c) Other income arising in the UK will remain accessible to the UK income tax whatever the residence of the person.

Example

T is the Marketing Director for ADKAY LTD, a UK resident company. He makes frequent long trips abroad and during the 18 months to 31st January 1997 his record is as follows:

Leaves UK	21.8.95	Returns UK	17.12.95
Leaves UK	17.1.96	Returns UK	2.2.96
Leaves UK	9.2.96	Returns UK	31.1.97

Calculate the qualifying periods.

Solution   **Qualifying period for overseas visits**

Date of departure	Date of return	Days out	Days in	Cumulative total	1/6th	Total days in
21.8.95	17.12.95	118	–	118	–	–
17.1.96	2.2.96	16	31	165	28	31

(17.12.95–16.1.96)

Since the cumulative total of time spent in the UK is greater than one sixth then the period is broken and a new qualifying period starts on 17th January 1996.

17.1.96	2.2.96	16	–	16	–	–
9.2.96	31.1.97	356	7	379	63	7

Since the total period of absence exceeds 364 days T has established a qualifying period of absence entitling him to the 100% deduction from his emoluments earned for the period.

Non-resident entertainers and sportspeople

11. Legislation contained in Sec 555 TA 1988 ensures that basic rate income tax is to be deducted from payments made to non-resident entertainers or sportspeople in respect of UK appearances.

a) The rules apply to tennis players, golfers, motor racing drivers, pop and film stars, actors, musicians and similar persons.

b) Payments from which income tax must be deducted include fees and prizes and other payments made for promotional activities associated with the non-resident's appearance in the UK.

c) Payments made to third parties on behalf of the entertainer or sportsperson are within the scope of the rules.

• Student self-testing question

P, who is the European Sales Manager of TO plc, a UK resident company, was sent to work in Belgium on 1st November 1996 in order to establish a Sales Office to promote the company's products throughout Europe. P returned to the UK from time to time to report on developments and his dates of departure and arrival were as follows:

Dates of departure	**Dates of Return**
1st November 1996	20th December 1996
2nd January 1997	4th April 1997
1st May 1997	16th July 1997
1st August 1997	10th November 1997

P is married and pays mortgage interest of £1,500 (net) in the year to 5th April 1998 on a mortgage of £26,000 on his private residence. P's salary for the year ended 5th April 1998 amounted to £35,000. P has a company car first registered in May 1995 which cost £15,000 and has a cylinder capacity of 2249cc. During the year ended 5th April 1998 business mileage amounted to 9,800 miles. All petrol for business and private use is paid for by the company.

Compute P's income tax liability for 1997/98.

Solution   **P's income tax computation 1997/98**

		£	£
Schedule E			
			35,000
Car scale $35\% \times 15,000 = 5,250 - \frac{1}{3}$		3,500	
Car fuel		1,490	4,990
			39,990
Less relief for overseas earnings			
Period from 6.4.97–9.11.97			
$\frac{218}{365} \times 39,990$			23,884
			16,106
Less personal allowance			4,045
Taxable income			12,061
Tax payable	4,100 @ 20%		820.00
	7,961 @ 23%		1,831.03
	12,061		2,651.03
less deduction for MCA 1,830 @ 15%			274.00
			2,377.03

Notes

i) *Qualifying periods for overseas earnings*

Date of departure	Date of return	Days out	Days in	Cumulative total	1/6th	Total days in
1.11.96	20.12.96	49	–	49	–	–
2.1.97	4.4.97	93	13	155	26	13
1.5.97	16.7.97	76	27	258	43	40
1.8.97	10.11.97	101	16	375	63	56

The following conditions are met:

a) *Periods in the UK do not amount to more than one sixth of the total period nor more than 62 consecutive days.*

b) *There is a continuous qualifying period of more than 364 days.*

ii) *The 100% deduction is applied to the emoluments as apportioned on a time basis so that the amount eligible for the deduction for 1997/98:*

$$\frac{218}{365} \times 39,990 = £23,884$$

iii) *The whole of the earnings for a qualifying period attracts the 100% deduction even though part may relate to UK duties.*

• Questions without answers

1. Q, who is resident, ordinarily resident and domiciled in the UK, provides the following information in respect of his journeys abroad as Sales Manager of a UK company.

Left UK 12 April 1996	Returned	15 May 1996
Left UK 9 June 1996	Returned	29 September 1996
Left UK 29 October 1996	Returned	5 May 1997
Left UK 9 June 1996	Returned	7 September 1997

   Determine whether or not Q qualifies for the 100% deduction from overseas earnings and if so, the date of commencement and cessation of the qualifying period.

2. Norman Hibbert and his wife are both British subjects resident in Spain. Mr Hibbert works for a firm of Spanish estate agents selling holiday homes to British holidaymakers. His wife Sally works as a part-time courier for a travel company. Their annual salaries are £25,000 and £13,500 respectively.

   For 1997/98 their UK sources of income are:

   a) Building society interest (Net) £4,000 (Mr Hibbert).

   b) Income from £20,000 $12\frac{1}{2}$% debentures in Thornton & Co. Ltd, a UK company, Mr Hibbert.

   c) Income from £5,000 $3\frac{1}{2}$% War Loan left to Mrs Hibbert by her mother in 1983.

   You are required to calculate the income tax repayable to Mr and Mrs Hibbert by the UK Inland Revenue for 1997/98.

   (ACCA)

3. Walter Smith, aged 59, is employed by Global Products plc as a sales manager. Walter is resident, ordinarily resident and domiciled in the UK. During the period from 1 October 1995 to 31 January 1997, Global Products plc sent Walter to three different overseas countries in order to set up new sales offices. His itinerary was as follows:

1 October 1995 to 30 April 1996	Working in the country of Arcadia.
1 May 1996 to 30 June 1996	On holiday in the UK.
1 July 1996 to 31 October 1996	Working in the county of Bellum.
1 November 1996 to 15 December 1996	On holiday in the UK.
16 December 1996 to 31 January 1997	Working in the county of Cadang.

   From 1 February 1997 onwards, Walter worked in the UK. Global Products plc paid for all of Walter's travel and subsistence expenses whilst he was abroad. These amounted to £8,800, £4,100 and £2,500 for the trips to Arcadia, Bellum and Cadang respectively. The company also paid the travel expenses of £2,600 when Walter's wife visited him in Cadang during January 1997.

   Walter is paid a salary of £36,500 p.a. by Global Products plc. His only other income is building society interest of £7,200 (net) p.a.

   You are required to calculate Walter's taxable income for 1996/97 before personal allowances.

   (ACCA)

10 Income from employment III – PAYE

Introduction

1. The Pay As You Earn system of deducting income tax at source applies to Schedule E income *(see Chapter 7)* from offices or employments such as wages, salaries, bonuses, benefits in kind and pensions. The system is operated by employers who collect the income tax on behalf of the Inland Revenue.

    National Insurance contributions which are related to employees' earnings *(see Chapter 23)* are also collected under the PAYE system.

    The system does not apply to self-employed individuals.

Taxable pay

2. For the purposes of tax deduction pay includes the following:

    a) salaries, wages, fees, bonuses, overtime, commissions, pensions, honoraria etc whether paid weekly or monthly

    b) holiday pay

    c) christmas boxes in cash

    d) terminal payments *(see Chapter 8)*

    e) statutory sick pay *(see Chapter 23)*.

    In general, benefits in kind, other than cash benefits are taken into account by adjustment of the employees' coding notice (see below) rather than by being treated as pay, see 7 below.

Net pay arrangements

3. In calculating taxable pay, the employer must deduct any contribution to a pension scheme on which the employee is entitled to relief from tax as an expense. This includes company AVCs, *see Chapter 19*. The agreement applies only to schemes which have been approved by the Pensions Scheme Office of the Inland Revenue. The net pay scheme also applies to the payroll deduction scheme for gifts to charities.

Outline of the PAYE system

4. In order to operate the PAYE system every employer requires the following:

    a) code numbers for employees

    b) tax tables

    c) tax deduction working Sheet P11 (1993)

    d) forms for operation of the system.

Code numbers

5. a) All employees, including Directors and some pensioners, are allocated a code number which is based on the personal allowances, reliefs and charges on income available to individuals, as evidenced by the information contained in their Tax Return. In appropriate cases the code number also takes into consideration other factors such as untaxed interest and tax underpaid or overpaid in previous years.

    The actual code number is equal to the sum of all allowances and reliefs, less the last digit, rounded down. Thus a married man with no other allowances or charges is entitled to a personal allowance of £4,045 plus a married couple's allowance of £1,830 ie £5,875, less an allowance restriction of £639 in respect of the MCA. (see 6 below)

    ie 5,875 – 639 = 5,236 = 523 H.

Deductions Working Sheet P11	Year to 5 April 19**96**

Employer's name P. G. R. LTD.

Tax Office and reference

BIRMINGHAM 193 1200/007

National Insurance contributions

Earnings recorded in column 1a should not exceed the Upper Earnings Limit

For employer's use	Earnings on which employee's contributions payable **Whole pounds only** 1a	Total of employee's and employer's contributions payable 1b	Employee's contributions payable 1c	Earnings on which employee's contributions at contracted-out rate payable included in col. 1a **Whole pounds only** 1d	Employee's contributions at contracted-out rate included in column 1c 1e	Statutory Sick Pay in the week or month included in column 2 1f	Statutory Maternity Pay in the week or month included in column 2 1g	Statutory Maternity Pay recovered 1h	Month no
	Bt £ fwd	Bt £ fwd	Bt £ fwd	Bt £ fwd	Bt £ fwd	Bt £ fwd	Bt £ fwd	Bt £ fwd	Bt fwd Mth 7
	1000	182 24	80 04						8
									9
									10
									11
									12

▲ SSP total   ▲ SMP total

Enter the NI Contribution Table Letter here ▼

End of Year Summary

	1a	1b	1c	1d	1e
A					

Complete only for occupational pension schemes newly contracted-out since 1 January 1986.
Scheme contracted-out number

S	4					

Employee's surname *in CAPITALS* SPENDTHRIFT		First two forenames JOHN RICHARD	

National Insurance no. TZ 14 79 03	Date of birth *in figures* Day 02 Month 12 Year 64	Works no. etc. 48	Date of starting *in figures* Day Month Year
Tax code † 352L	Amended code †		Date of leaving *in figures* Day Month Year
	Wk/Mth in which applied		

PAYE Income Tax

Week no	Pay in the week or month including Statutory Sick Pay/Statutory Maternity Pay 2	Total pay to date 3	Total free pay to date (Table A) 4a	*K codes only* Total additional pay 4b	Total taxable pay to date i.e. column 3 *minus* column 4a or column 3 *plus* column 4b 5	Total tax due to date as shown by Taxable Pay Tables 6	*K codes only* Tax due at end of current period Mark refunds 'R' 6a	*K codes only* Regulatory limit i.e. 50% of column 2 entry 6b	Tax deducted or refunded in the week or month. Mark refunds 'R' 7	*K codes only* Tax not deducted owing to the Regulatory limit 8	For employer's use
Bt fwd wk 30		7000				1141 91					
31											
32											
33											
34											
35	1000 00	8000 00	2352 72		5647 28	1305 08			163 17		
36											
37											
38											
39											
40											
41											
42											
43											
44											
45											
46											
47											
48											
49											
50											
51											
52											
§											

Pay and Tax totals
Previous employments ◄
This employment ◄
Mark net refund 'R' ►

Where you are using a K code enter the total of the amounts in column 7 for this employment.

Employee's Widow's & Orphans/Life insurance contribution in this employment

† If amended cross out previous code.
§ Complete this line if pay day falls on 5 April (in leap years 4 & 5 April).

Please keep this form for at least 3 years after the end of the year to which it relates, or longer if you are asked to do so.

Printed by St Ives Direct, St Ives plc, WOB 0065, 12/95

87

b) Some of the letters used at present after a code number are as follows:

H   Basic personal allowance plus married couple's allowance or additional personal allowance

L   Basic personal allowance

P   Personal allowance for those aged 65 – 74

V   Personal allowance for those aged 65 – 74 plus the MCAA

K   An amount to be added to pay

T   This is for all other cases in which the number V would follow the number but the taxpayer notifies the tax office that he or she does not wish to use one of the letters.

c) The following special codes are also used:

BR   This means that tax is to be deducted at the basic rate.

F   This code, followed by a number means that the tax due on a social security benefit, eg retirement pension, or widow's pension or allowance, is to be collected from the taxpayers earnings from employment.

NT   This means that no tax is to be deducted.

D   This code followed by a number means that the pension/benefit is more than the allowances.

OT   This code means that no allowances have been given.

Deductions from allowances in code numbers

6. The following items may be deducted in arriving at the code number:

a) State benefits or pension

b) Income from property

c) Unemployment benefit

d) Untaxed interest

e) Taxable expense allowances and benefits in kind

f) Excessive basic rate adjustment where too much tax is paid at the basic rate and not enough at the higher rate

g) Tax underpaid in earlier years

h) Taxed investment income at the higher rate

i) Allowance restriction. This is for allowances and reliefs at a lower rate eg MCA, MCAA, APA and maintenance payments. For 1997/98 the MCA restriction is £639.

     i.e. $(1,830 - 639) \times 23\% = £274; \ 1,830 \times 15\% = £274$

K Codes

7. With effect from 6th April 1993 a system of 'K' codes has been introduced where there is a negative coding allowance, which usually arises where the non-PAYE income, eg benefits in kind, are greater than the allowances due.

The excess is added to the taxable pay on the tax deduction sheet (P11) and taxed accordingly.

Tax tables (on following page)

8. The following tables are in general use:

Pay adjustment tables.

These show the proportion of the employee's allowances, as determined by his or her code number, for each week cumulatively from 6th April to the pay date.

Taxable pay tables B, C, D – .

Tax is deducted weekly (monthly for monthly paid persons) by reference to tables which show the tax due to date when a particular code number is used. Table B shows the tax due at the basic rate and the deduction for the lower rate and Tables C and D at the higher rate of 40%.

To give the benefit of tax at the 20% rate subtraction tables are provided.

Tax deduction working sheet

9. The deductions working sheet (P11) 1995 contains particulars relating to income tax payable, National Insurance contributions and statutory sick pay, and columns for the K codes.

A specimen deduction working sheet is reproduced (on the previous pages) and completed for period 8 in respect of JR Spendthrift who has a code number of 352L. Extracts of the Tables A and B, and National Insurance tables are also reproduced.

Pay

a) Pay due for the month of December 1995 is determined at £1,000 and entered in Column 2 and added to the total pay to date (Column 3) from the previous 6th April 1995.

b) With a code number of 352L, the Pay adjustment table for period 8 shows an amount of £2,352.72 due to date which is entered in Column 4(a).

c) Total free pay is deducted from the total pay to date to obtain the total taxable pay to date Column 5.

d) Total tax due to date on the total taxable pay to date is obtained from Table B £1,411.75 less relief at the lower rate to date of £106.67.

e) Tax deducted or refunded in the month (Column 7) is the difference between the total tax due brought forward from period 7 (£1,141.91) and the amount computed to period 8 (£1,305.08), ie £163.17.

PAYE tax tables 1995/96

Free pay to date table A

Pay adjustment table

Code	Month 8 Nov 6–Dec 5 £	Month 9 Dec 6–Jan 5 £	Month 10 Jan 6–Feb 5 £
352	2,352.72	2,646.81	2,940.90

Taxable pay tables

Table B

	Total taxable pay to date £	Total tax due to date(BR) £	Deduction lower rate £
Month 8	5,647	1,411.75	106.67
9	6,353	1,588.25	120.00
10	7,059	1,764.75	133.34

National Insurance contribution tables 1995/96
(Not contracted out contributions)

Table A

Gross pay (month) and employer's contributions payable £	Total of employee's contributions payable £	Employee's contributions payable £	Employer's contributions payable £
1,000	182.24	80.04	102.20
1,100	202.44	90.04	112.40

National Insurance contributions

10. These are determined by reference to the scale rates as indicated in Chapter 21 and for a non-contracted out employee (Class 1) the amounts as per the NI contribution and SSP rate tables are

Monthly pay £1,000	Table A	Employee	80.04
		Employer	102.20
		Total	182.24

Where the exact gross pay is not included in the tables the next lowest figure is taken.

Statutory sick pay

11. Where any amount of sick pay is paid to an employee then this is entered in Column 1d and accumulated. SSP is included in gross pay for the purposes of both deduction of income tax and National Insurance contributions. 100% of the gross amount of any SSP entered on the deduction working sheet, together with an extra amount to compensate for the employer's NIC paid in the SSP called 'NIC compensation on SSP' is deductible from the total NIC due for the period if their SSP payments for an income tax month exceed 13% of their Class I contributions for that month. *See Chapter 22.*

Forms for use with PAYE

12.	P6	Notice to employer of code or amended code.
	P9	Notice to employers of changed code for the coming year.
	P9D	Return of expenses payments, fees, bonuses etc for an employee to whom form P11D is not applicable.
	P11D	Return of expenses payments, benefits etc to or for directors and higher paid employees.
	P14	End of year return of pay, tax and National Insurance contributions for each employee.
	P45	Part 1. Particulars of employee leaving
		Part 2. Employee leaving – copy of employer's certificate.
		Part 3. New employee – particulars of old employment.
		Part 4. Retained by employee.
	P11 1993	Deduction Working Sheet.
	P46	Notice to Inland Revenue of employees without a P45.
	P46 (CARS)	Details of change of cars available for private use.
	P35	Employer's annual statement, declaration and certificate.
	P60	Employer's certificate of pay and tax deductions to be given to employee at the end of the year.

Payment of tax

13. Income tax and National Insurance contributions (employer's and employee's) are due for payment to the Collector of Taxes not later than the 19th day of each month. Thus the tax and NIC due for period 8, 1997, which covers the period from 6th November to 5th December, is payable on or before the 19th December 1997.

The National Insurance payable is reduced by any statutory sick pay payments paid during the month.

Specially printed Payslip Booklets are issued to all employers for the purposes of recording payments and rendering payments to the Collector of Taxes.

Where an employer falls in arrears with his or her monthly payments of tax and National Insurance contributions deducted from employees then the Collector of Taxes can issue a notice to an employer estimating the amount unpaid. This becomes enforceable unless the estimated amount or the actual liability is paid within 7 days.

For periods beginning after 5th April 1995 employers whose average monthly payments to the Collector of Taxes of PAYE and NIC are less than £600.00 (1994/95 £450.00) in total are allowed to pay quarterly. Payments will be due on the following dates: 19th July, 19th October, 19th January and 19th April. Similar arrangements apply to contractors in the construction industry.

Interest on late payment of tax

14. From the 19th April 1993 late payments of PAYE (income tax, Class 1 and 1A NIC contributions) for the year 1992/1993 onwards are charged interest at the prescribed rate.

Interest is also charged on late payments of Class IV NICs.

Late payments of monthly or quarterly PAYE within the year are not subject to an interest charge for the time being.

Bonus and commission payments

15. As a general principle taxable pay is assessed in the year in which it is paid under the rules of Schedule E introduced by the FA 1989 as outlined in Chapter 8.

Thus, for example, where J has a salary of £10,000 for 1996/97 and earns a commission of an additional £5,000 for that year which is only ascertained and paid in July 1997, then the commission is assessable in the tax year 1997/98.

Directors' remuneration

16. The rules of taxation under Schedule E by reference to the emoluments received apply to directors and all other employees. *See Chapter 8.*

PAYE regulations

17. Detailed regulations for the operation of PAYE are provided under Sec 204 TA 1970 by means of Statutory Instruments, the most important being SI 1993 No. 744. Where failure to operate PAYE takes place it is the employer who is primarily responsible for making good any deficit and an assessment under Regulation 29 (1) subject to appeal may be issued for recovery. If the determined amount is not paid within 90 days then the CIR may direct under Regulation 26 that the tax should be recovered from an employee/director. This can arise where the Commissioners of Inland Revenue are of the opinion that the employee/director received his or her emoluments knowing that the employer has wilfully failed to deduct tax. In general wilful means 'with intention or deliberate' – see *R v IRC Chisholm* 1981 STC 253.

In *R v CIR ex parte Keys and Cook* 1987 QB. DT. 25.5.87 the controlling directors of a company which failed to deduct income tax under the PAYE system from their remuneration were held to be liable for that tax under Regulation 26(4) Income Tax (Employments) Regulations 1973 (now consolidated into the 1993 Regulations).

PAYE audits

18. The main regulations enabling the Inland Revenue to undertake an audit are as follows:

a)   Income Tax (Employments) Regulations 1993 (ST 1993/744)
b)   Social Security (Contributions) Regulations 1979 (SI 1979/591).

These provide that wherever called upon to do so by any authorised officer of the Inland Revenue, the employer must produce at his or her premises to that officer for inspection of the following.

All wages sheets, deduction working sheets and other documents and records whatsoever relating to the calculation or payment of emoluments of his employees, or to the deduction of tax from such emoluments or to the amount of earnings related contributions payable in respect of their emoluments. Since the regulations clearly refer to emoluments, which as defined by Sec 131 TA 1988 includes 'perquisites and profits whatsoever' then the audit can easily be extended to embrace compliance with all aspects of benefits in kind, P11 Ds and related matters.

End of year returns

19. At the end of the income tax year the employer must complete and return to the tax office the following forms:

> Form P35: P35SC (sub-contractors)
> Form P14.

The P35 is the employer's Annual Statement, Declaration and Certificate, which is signed by the employer and returned to the tax office by 19th May following the end of the income tax year.

The back of Form P35 contains a summary of the deduction card totals for the year, while the front contains a list of questions concerning payments for casual employment, expenses and Forms P11D etc. Form P14 is an end of year summary made out in respect of each employee for whom a tax deduction card has been used. This form is in triplicate and the two top copies, one marked DSS copy, must be sent to the tax office by 19th May following the end of the tax year. The third copy is the employee's P60 certificate, and shows his or her total pay and deductions for the income tax year.

From 6th April 1995 an automatic penalty will arise if end of year returns (P14, P35, P38/38A) are late. The statutory deadline is the 19th May but for this year only there is a concessionary extension of 14 days to the 2nd June 1995. The penalty is £100 per month (or part) per unit of 50 employees. Where forms P11D are required then these must be returned to the tax office before 6th June following the end of the tax year.

Employers and self-assessment

20. For 1996/97 the following is a summary of the effects of self-assessment on employers.

a)   Employee forms P60 detailing pay and tax to be issued by 31st May 1997.
b)   New four-part P45 to be issued. Employee to retain Part 4.
c)   Copies of form P11D and P9D to be issued to employees by 6th July 1997.
d)   Forms P14 and P35 to be sent to the Inland Revenue by 6th July 1997.
e)   Forms P11D and P9D to be sent to the Inland Revenue by 6th July 1997.
f)   Penalties for filing an incorrect or incomplete form P11D can amount to £300 per return.
g)   Additional penalties can be imposed for failure to comply with the new regulations.

Thresholds for PAYE and National Insurance

21.		1997/98 £	1996/97 £
PAYE	Weekly	78.00	72.40
	Monthly	338.00	313.75
National Insurance	Weekly	62.00	61.00
	Monthly	269.00	264.00

• Student self-testing question

T's P60 for the year 1997/98 shows total gross pay of £30,500. He is employed as a sales manager with a salary of £12,000 p.a. for 1997/98. In addition he receives commission paid by reference to the profits shown by the company's accounts amounting to:

		£	
Year ended 31st December 1996		18,500	– paid June 1997
do. 31st December 1997		23,000	– paid June 1998

Tax deducted under PAYE for the year 1997/98 amounted to £6,100. Code 404L was finally operated.

T has no other income but paid mortgage interest under MIRAS of £2,250 on the mortgage of his private residence for 1997/98

Compute the Schedule E liability for 1997/98.

Solution   **Income tax computation 1997/98**

			£
Schedule E salary			12,000
Commission paid June 1997			18,500
			30,500
Personal allowance			4,045
			26,455
	4,100 @ 20%		820
	22,000 @ 25%		5,060
	355 @ 40%		142
Tax payable	26,455		6,022
Less deducted by PAYE			6,100
Amount overpaid			78

Note The code number 404L is the basic single person's code for 1997/98.

• Questions without answers

1. Using the deduction working sheet for JR Spendthrift shown in the earlier part of this chapter work out the income tax payable and National Insurance contributions due if he earns a gross salary for the next two months as follows:

	£
1996 Period 9 December	1,000
1997 Period 10 January	1,000

2. Mrs P has the following data relating to 1996/97.

	£
Salary	15,000
BSI (net)	75

Her husband receives an invalidity pension of £1,500, and a works pension of £2,250.
An election for the MCA to be transferred to Mrs P has been made for 1996/97.
Compute the coding notice for Mrs P for 1996/97. Assume that the works pension has not been coded out.

11 Income from UK land and property – Schedule A

Introduction

1. The rules applicable to Schedule A are radically changed under the FA 1995 with effect on and from the 6th April 1995 for income tax purposes. However, for corporation tax purposes the existing provisions apply as noted in Chapter 25.

   This chapter deals with the new provisions including computational examples.

Basis of charge

2. a) Tax is charged on the annual profits or gains arising from any business carried on for the exploitations, as a source of rents or other receipts, of any estate interest, or rights in or over land in the UK.

   Receipts in relation to land includes:
   i) any payment in respect of any licence to occupy or otherwise use any land, or in respect of the exercise of any further right over land.
   ii) rent charges, ground annuals and feu duties and any other annual payments derived from land.

   b) The following are not taxed under Schedule A, but Schedule D, Case I.
   i) Profits or gains from the occupation of any woodlands managed on a commercial basis.
   ii) Farming and agriculture.
   iii) Mines, quarries and similar concerns.

   c) Furnished accommodation previously taxed as case VI income is now taxed as Schedule A business profits, and this includes furnished holiday lettings.

   d) The letting of caravans on fixed sites and house boats on fixed moorings is chargeable under Schedule A.

Basis of assessment

3. The basis of assessment under Schedule A is the annual profits or gains arising in the income tax year. It will not be possible to use an 'accounts basis' of assessment from 1995/96.

Computation of taxable profits

4. a) All profits or gains of a Schedule A business are to be computed in accordance with the rules applicable to a trading business under Schedule D, Case I.

   b) Property situated in the UK is to be pooled regardless of the type of lease or whether or not it is furnished accommodation.

   c) Any business expenditure incurred in earning the profits from letting is to be deducted from the total pooled income, and is subject to the same rules for allowable expenditure as apply to Case I trading income.

   d) Capital allowances available are given as an expense chargeable against property income so that the adjusted taxable profits are after capital allowances.

   e) As capital allowances are not available for plant and machinery let in a dwelling house the renewals basis or the wear and tear allowance for furnished lettings (currently 10% of annual rents less rates), other capital allowances are available for plant and machinery e.g. as part of the office equipment used for estate management.

   f) Interest payable in respect of a Schedule A business is allowed as a deduction in calculating the profits of the business under the same rules as apply to other expenses incurred for the purposes of the business.

   g) Rental business losses must be carried forward and set against future profits from the same rental business.

> **Example**

Z purchased a freehold factory site on the 6th April 1996 which he lets for an annual rental of £15,000 payable in advance on the usual quarter days. First payment due 6th April 1996 covered the period to 24th June 1996. Property expenses paid by Z for the year to 5th April 1997 amounted to £2,500 and interest paid on a loan to purchase the factory was £3,500.

Capital allowances for the 12 months to 5th April 1997 have been agreed at £2,000.

Compute Z's Schedule A business income for 1996/97.

Solution

Z's Schedule A business income 1996/97

	£	£
Rents receivable		15,000
Less expenses:-		
Property expenses	2,500	
Loan interest	3,500	6,000
Adjusted Profit		9,000
Less capital allowances		2,000
Taxable profits		7,000

Notes

i) The rents received are computed on an accruals basis.

ii) Schedule A business income is investment income and not 'earned income'.

Transitional provisions

5. As part of the move to the new Schedule A rules there are a number of transitional adjustments which may need to be made to compensate for double-counting of receipts and expenses and gaps in basis periods.

   The receipts or expenses may be double-counted as the accruals system is introduced in 1995/96 and any necessary adjustment can be made in the 1995/96 assessment by agreement with the Inland Revenue.

   Gaps in the basis period will normally arise where the assessments have not been based on a fiscal year basis.

Lease premiums

6. One way of looking at lease premiums is to regard them as a capitalised part of future rental income which would otherwise have been received by way of annual rent. They include any sum whether payable to the immediate or a superior landlord, arising in connection with the granting of a lease, but not arising from an assignment, of an existing lease.

   Under an assignment the lessee takes the position of the original lessee, with the same terms and conditions.

   Where a lease is granted (but not assigned) at a premium, for a period not exceeding 50 years, then the landlord is deemed to be in receipt of a rental income equal to the premium, less an allowance of 2% of the premium for each complete year of the lease remaining, excluding the first 12 month period.

> **Example**

B granted a lease for 24 years of its warehouse to a trader on the following terms:

A lease premium of £12,000 to be paid on 1.5.1996 and an annual rent of £1,000.

Allowable expenditure for the year 1996/97 was £5,800.

Schedule A business income 1996/97

	£	£
Lease premium	12,000	
Less $2\% \times 12{,}000 \times (24 - 1)$		
ie $1/50 \times 12{,}000 \times 23$	5,520	6,480
Annual rent		1,000
		7,480
Less allowable expenses		5,800
Taxable profits		1,680

In effect the lease premium is discounted by reference to its duration, and the longer the unexpired portion, the greater the discount. Thus if a lease had 49 years to run the discount would be:

$$(49 - 1) \times 2\% \text{ ie } 96\%.$$

The amount of the taxable premium may also be determined by use of the formula where:

$$P - \frac{P \times Y}{50}$$

P = amount of premium paid; Y = number of completed 12 months other than the first.

A premium on a lease for a period greater than 50 years would not be taxed as Schedule A income. If the lease premium is paid by instalments the full amount, less the discount, is taxable in the usual way. However, if hardship can be proved the tax may be paid over a period not exceeding 8 years, by Sec 34 TA 1988.

Sub-leases and assignments

7. The creation of a sub-lease out of the main or head lease for a premium would give rise to a liability, but not an assignment of that lease. Where a charge to taxation arises from the granting of a lease at a premium, and this is followed by the lessee granting a sub-lease at a premium, then any liability arising on the second occasion is reduced, as shown in the example below.

Example

J grants a lease for 20 years to M for a premium of £10,000. After occupying the premises for five years, M grants a sub-lease to another person for a period of 10 years at a premium of £6,000.

Show the computation of J's and M's liability under Schedule A.

Solution **Computation of J's liability under Schedule A**

	£
Lease premium	10,000
Less 2% × 10,000 × (20 − 1) ie 38% × 10,000	3,800
	6,200

Computation of M's liability

	£
Lease premium	6,000
Less 2% × 6,000 × (10 − 1) ie 18% × 6,000	1,080
	4,920

$$4,920 - \left(\frac{\text{Duration of sub lease}}{\text{Duration of head lease}} \times \text{Schedule A income on main lease premium of J, ie 6,200} \right)$$

4,920 − [10/20 × 6,200] ie 1,820

The amount of the lease premium assessed on M is therefore £1,820.

Lease premiums and the lessee

8. Where the lessee makes a payment of a lease premium on the granting of a lease, then a proportion of that premium may be set against the following:

   a) any trading income, providing the premises are used for business purposes, Sec 87 TA 1988

   b) any rental income or lease premium received from any sub lease granted by the lessee.

In effect the amount of the premium assessed as income of the lessor can be charged as an expense of trading, the taxable portion being spread over the remaining life of the lease.

Example

S is granted a lease of premises to be used for trading purposes, for a period of 20 years at an annual rent of £600 p.a. and an initial lease premium of £32,000.

	£
Lease premium	32,000
Less 2% × 32,000 × (20 − 1) ie 38% × 32,000	12,160
Lease premium charged on lessor	19,840

Relief available to S is $\dfrac{19840}{20}$ ie £992 p.a.

Furnished holiday lettings. Sec 503–504 TA 1988

9. a) The commercial letting of furnished holiday accommodation chargeable under Schedule A is treated as carrying on a trade.

  b) To be eligible as 'qualifying accommodation' the following requirements must be met.

   i) The accommodation must be let by the owner to a tenant who has use of the furniture.

   ii) There must be a commercial letting carried on with a view to the realisation of profit.

   iii) The accommodation must be available for commercial letting to the public generally as holiday accommodation for periods which amount in total to not less than 140 days p.a.

   iv) The periods for which the holiday accommodation is so let amount to at least 70 days.

   v) For a period comprising at least 7 months (which need not be continuous, but includes the period of 70 days mentioned in (iv) above) it is not normally in the same occupation for a continuous period exceeding 31 days.

   vi) Averaging may be used in determining the 70 day test in respect of all or any of the properties let by the same person. A claim to this effect must be made within two years of the end of the year of assessment or accounting period to which this is to apply.

  c) Allowable expenditure deductible in computing trading income from the commercial letting of furnished holiday accommodation is the same as that for Schedule D case I and accordingly the same rules of computation apply.

10. The following provisions apply to trading income from the commercial letting of holiday accommodation, as they do to Schedule D Case I or II trading income.

  a) Income is earned income therefore eligible for personal pension plans. *(See Chapter 20.)*

  b) Capital allowances are available on eligible expenditure. *(See Chapter 17.)*

  c) Loss reliefs are available. *(See Chapter 18.)*

  d) Relief for pre-trading expenditure is available. *(See Chapter 14.)*

  e) CGT relief for replacement of business assets *(see Chapter 42),* transfer of business on retirement *(see Chapter 42)* and relief for gifts of business assets *(see Chapter 41).*

Where a person has qualifying holiday accommodation in a year of assessment and other holiday accommodation which does not fulfil the 70 day letting test then an averaging of the whole accommodation can be made if an election is made within two years of the year of assessment.

Example

Z owns and lets holiday bungalows none of which are let to the same person form more than thirty days. In respect of 1997/98 the following information is provided about the lettings:

	Days available	Days let
Bungalow A	190	82
Bungalow B	150	48
Bungalow C	150	95
Bungalow D	135	85

Determine which of the bungalow lettings are 'qualifying accommodation'.

Solution

Bungalow D   This does not qualify as it does not satisfy the 140 day test even though its lettings are more than 70 days. It cannot be used in any averaging.

Bungalow A   This satisfies both tests.

Bungalow C   This satisfies both tests.

Bungalow B   This fails the 70 day letting test. However it can be averaged with bungalow C to qualify:

$$\frac{95 + 48}{2} = \frac{143}{2} \quad = 71 \text{ days}$$

The income from bungalows A, B and C will therefore be treated as trading income for 1997/98.

Furnished accommodation

11. Rents from furnished accommodation are assessed under Schedule A.

Relief for depreciation of furniture and fittings, (ie plant and machinery for capital allowances purposes) may be given in respect of each asset on the 'renewals method', or as an agreed 10% deduction from net rent.

Net rent is gross rent receivable less charges and services normally borne by the tenant, but in fact borne by the landlord, such as council tax, water and sewerage rates.

Capital allowances as such cannot be claimed in respect of house property.

Rent a room

12. With effect from 1997/98 householders can let rooms in their own house for £4,250.00 (previously £3,350) pa tax free provided it is furnished accommodation with the following effects.
   a) Gross rents up to £4,250 p.a. are exempt.
   b) Gross rents greater than £4,250 are taxable as follows:
      i) pay tax on excess rent ie (rent – £4,250)
      ii) pay tax on gross rents less expenses including capital allowances.

A claim must be made for the exemption not to be applied in writing within one year of the tax year to which it is to apply.

It is possible for the income to be taxed under Case I where the taxpayer is deemed to be carrying on a trade, and provides substantial services in connection with the letting eg. meals, cleaning, laundry, and goods and services of a similar nature.

Non-resident landlords

13. The following is a summary of the rules which apply from 6th April 1996 in respect of rents paid to non-resident landlords.
   a) When rent is paid to a non-resident landlord then the letting agent, or if there is no agent the tenant, must deduct income tax from the rent at the basic rate.
   b) The tax deducted is based on the net rent remitted to the landlord, ie after expenses.
   c) Returns on a quarterly basis must be sent to the IR Accounts office together with the necessary tax due within 30 days of the end of the quarter (31st March, 31st June, 31st September and 31st December).
   d) A tenant is obliged to deduct tax unless:
      i) the rent does not exceed £5,200 p.a.
      ii) he or she has received a notice from FICO telling him or her not to deduct tax
      iii) he or she pays rent to an agent.
   e) FICO (Inland Revenue's Financial Intermediaries and Claims Office) may grant an application to receive rents gross from the non-resident landlord subject to certain conditions concerning past and future compliance with tax rules and regulations.

Schedule A to 5th April 1995

13. The system of taxing Schedule A income from property prior to 6th April 1995 is substantially retained for corporation purposes and is included in Chapter 25.

• Student self-testing question

Mrs T has a bungalow which was used for commercial letting as furnished holiday accommodation during 1997/98. The Schedule A trading profits amounted to £6,045.

She is responsible for all the organisation and management of the lettings.

Mr T has Schedule E income of £23,045 and taxed bank interest of £2,400 (net). Mrs T has Schedule E income of £10,000.

Compute T's income tax liability for 1997/98 and that of Mrs T.

Solution

Income Tax computation 1997/98

	T	Mrs T
	£	£	£
Earned income			
Schedule E T		23,045	10,000
Schedule A Mrs T		–	6,045
Unearned income			
Interest (gross) 2,400 ÷ 0.8		3,000	–
		26,045	16,045
Personal allowance		4,045	4,045
Taxable income		22,000	12,000
Income tax charged		£	£
4,100 + 3,000 = 7,100 / 4,100 @ 20%		1,420	820
14,900 / 7,900 @ 23%		3,427	1,817
22,000 12,000		4,847	2,637
Less income tax deducted from bank interest	600.00		
Deduct MCA @ 15%	274.00	874	–
Tax payable		3,973	2,637

• Question without answer

V is a technical representative for K plc. In respect of the year to 5th April 1998 he had Schedule E earnings of £15,000 and the use of a company car. V's form P11D for 1997/98 showed the following information.

	£
Travelling and subsistence	5,170
Car list price when new	13,000

Car details:

First registered 1.4.1995;	1600cc Cavalier
Business mileage 20,000 miles;	All private petrol mileage paid for by V

V's wife had bank interest (net) of £400 in respect of 1997/98 and income from the letting of furnished holiday accommodation of £2,750. The furnished holiday accommodation consists of two furnished caravans, both of which were available for lettings from the 12th April 1997 to the 31st October 1997. During that period actual lettings, none of which were to the same person for more than 30 days, consisted of the following:

CARAVAN A	CARAVAN B
21.4.97 – 30.4.97	21.4.97 – 28.4.97
7.7.97 – 20.8.97	14.7.97 – 7.8.97
27.8.97 – 12.9.97	14.8.97 – 31.8.97

All dates of letting are inclusive.

Compute the income tax liability in respect of 1997/98 for Mr and Mrs V.

12 Income from foreign investment – Schedule D Cases IV and V

Introduction

1. This chapter is concerned with the taxation of income arising outside the UK from securities and possessions. These terms are first defined under the heading of general principles and then follows the basis of assessment for new and existing sources of income. The nature of double taxation relief is illustrated with a computational example.

General principles

2. In accordance with Sec 18 TA 1988, income arising from securities outside the UK is taxed under Case IV. Income from a security means income from a mortgage or debenture, but not from stocks or shares.

    Income arising from possessions is taxed under Case V by the same section, and this includes income from trades, professions or vocations, income from stocks and shares, and bank interest, and property. Emoluments from any form of overseas employment, as noted in Chapter 8, are taxable as Schedule E income, but overseas pensions are Case V income.

Basis of assessment – sources arising after 5th April 1994 existing 1997/98

3. Current year basis – Income arising in the year of assessment.

    For new sources of income arising on or after the 6th April 1994 the general rule for the current year basis applies and Case IV and V income is taxed on the income of the year of assessment.

    Where the remittance basis applies then tax is charged on the amount of profit received in the UK in the tax year of assessment.

    Foreign trades which would have been taxed as Case I/II income if carried on in the UK are subject to the same basis rules as apply for Case I/II. The accounting period rules, treatment of capital allowances and loss reliefs applicable to Case I/II income also apply in these circumstances.

    Case V profits or losses from properties outside the UK are not combined with the Schedule A rental business profits or losses. They are taxed separately and losses on one cannot be set against profits of the other.

Transitional year 1996/97

4. For any income source arising before 6th April 1994, the profits assessed in 1996/97 will be 50% gross of the profits arising, or received, in the 24 month period to 5th April 1997.

    Where 1995/96 has been assessed on an actual basis then the profits assessed in 1996/97 will be profits of the12 month period to 5th April 1997.

    Where a source ceases in 1996/97 or 1997/98, the existing rates will apply throughout including any revision of 1995/96 and 1996/97.

Basis of assessment – existing sources to 1995/96

5. a) The normal basis of assessment for both Cases IV and V is the income of the preceding year, with special rules for the opening and closing periods, as for Case III income.

    b) The income assessable is the income arising in the previous year. However, where the recipient is not domiciled or resident in the UK, then the remittances of the previous year form the basis of the assessment.

    c) Foreign pensions or annuities are subject to 10% reduction unless the remittance basis is used.

    d) Income from foreign trades, professions or vocations is computed in the same way as income arising under Schedule D Case I or II.

    e) From 6th April 1995 interest paid on a loan to buy property is deductible in computing net rents.

Summary of assessment 1995/96

Income	Arising basis	Remittance basis
Investment income		
Resident but not domiciled in UK	–	Amount remitted
Other cases	Full amount arising	–
Foreign pensions		
Resident but not domiciled in UK	–	Amount remitted
Other cases	Full amount arising	–
less 10%		
Foreign trades etc		
Resident but not domiciled in UK	–	Amount remitted
Other cases	Full amount arising	–

For guidance on the meaning of domicile or residence *see Chapter 9*.

An individual must be resident in the UK to be taxable under Case IV or V, as non-residents are only taxable in respect of their UK source income.

Double taxation relief

6. If a UK resident has income taxable under Case IV or V which has suffered foreign taxation, then as the same income will also be chargeable to UK income tax, there is normally some measure of relief available to prevent charging the same income twice.

   In the first instance, relief may be available under what are known as double taxation treaties or conventions. These are agreements made between the UK and foreign countries which specify the manner in which various classes of income received by, say, a UK resident from another country are taxable, and the extent to which credit is allowed for any foreign tax suffered. The latter is referred to as double taxation relief. Where this relief is not available under any treaty or there is no treaty then in accordance with Sec 790 TA 1988, an equivalent amount of 'unilateral relief' is normally available.

7. Double taxation relief can be obtained by a UK resident in respect of his or her foreign income in the following ways:

   a) By being exempted from any foreign taxation on the income, under the double tax convention.

   b) By deducting any foreign tax suffered from the gross amount of the foreign income, leaving the 'net amount' to be assessed to UK tax.

   c) By charging the gross amount of the overseas income to UK taxation, and claiming as a credit the amount of any foreign tax suffered. This is the most common method used.

   Double tax relief is limited to the lower of the foreign tax suffered and the UK tax at the taxpayer's marginal rate of taxation, on that income.

Example

T, who is single, is resident and domiciled in the UK, has the following income:

	Year to 5.4.97	Year to 5.4.98
Schedule E	8,500	11,245
Building society interest (net)	1,491	1,600
Schedule D Case V:		
Net securities interest – investment made 1995	850	1,000
Foreign tax on securities	150	200
Rents (net) investment made May 1995	550	900
Foreign tax on rents	400	700

Compute T's income tax liability for 1997/98.

Solution

Income Tax computation 1997/98

	£	£
Earned income		
Schedule E		11,245
Unearned income		
B.S.I. 1,600/.80	2,000	
Schedule D :		
Case IV Interest (gross) CY	1,200	
Case V Rents (gross) CY	1,600	4,800
		16,045
Personal allowance		4,045
Taxable income		12,000

Taxation charged:	4,100 + 2,000 = 6,100 @ 20%	1,220
	5,900 @ 23%	1,357
	12,000	2,577
Less double tax relief		568
		2,009
Less income tax on B.S.I.		400
Tax payable		1,609

Notes

	£	£
i) *Double tax relief.*		
Rent, foreign tax suffered	*700*	
UK tax at the marginal rate 1,600 = 23%	*368*	
The lower amount of UK tax		*368*
Dividends, foreign tax suffered	*200*	
UK tax at the marginal rate 1,200 = 23%	*276*	
The lower amount of foreign tax		*200*
Total		*568*

ii)   *In this example, although the highest rate of UK taxation is taken against the highest foreign taxed income, the rents, there remains unrelieved foreign taxation of:*

$$£700 - £368 \text{ ie } £332$$

iii)   *Foreign income arising after 6th April 1994 is taxed on a current year basis.*

• Student self-testing question

Z, who is married, has the following data relating to the year 1997/98.

	£
Schedule E salary	20,045
Rent from letting apartment in Spain acquired 1995	
(after foreign taxes of £1,300)	1,700
B.S.I. (net)	800
Mortgage interest paid by A under MIRAS	850

Mrs Z's only income is a foreign pension received of £9,000

Compute the income tax liability of Z and Mrs Z for 1997/98.

Solution

Income tax computation 1997/98

		Z	Mrs Z
	£	£	£
Earned income			
Z Schedule E		20,045	–
Mrs Z foreign pension	10,000		
Less 10% deduction	1,000	–	9,000
Z Schedule D Case V rent CY	3,000		
BSI 800 ÷ 0.8	1,000	4,000	–
			9,000
		24,045	9,000
Personal allowance		4,045	4,045
Taxable income		20,000	4,955

Taxation charged:

4,100 + 1,000 =	5,100 / 4,100 @ 20%	1,020.00	820.00
	14,900 / 855 @ 23%	3,427.00	196.65
	20,000 / 4,955	4,447.00	1,016.65
Less double tax relief		690.00	–
		3,757.00	1,016.65
Less : Income tax on BSI	200.00		
Deduct MCA @ 15% × 1,830	274.00	474.00	
Tax payable		3,283.00	1,016.65

Notes

i) *The double tax relief on £3,000 is the lower of:*

Foreign tax suffered	1,300	
UK tax at marginal rate: 3,000 @ 23%	690	ie 690

ii) *The foreign pension paid to Mrs Z is subject to the 10% deduction for 1997/98.*

13 Income from other sources – Schedule D Case VI

Introduction

1. This chapter deals with the taxation of 'miscellaneous profits' under Case VI of Schedule D. Prior to 1995/96 furnished accommodation and the Rent a Room scheme were taxed under the rules of Schedule D Case VI. As these have now been transferred to Schedule A, the Case VI taxable income scope is reduced considerably.

General principles

2. Tax under this schedule is charged in respect of any annual profits or gains not falling under any other case of Schedule D, and not charged by virtue of any other schedule. This does not mean that all profits not otherwise charged are taxable under this case, and the following points should be noted.

   a) Profits arising from capital transactions are not annual profits taxable under this case.

   b) Where isolated transactions take place, then if they are not construed as being 'an adventure in the nature of trade', and thus taxable as Case I trading income, they may escape liability from Case VI. See *Leeming* v *Jones* 1930 15 TC 333 and *Hobbs* v *Hussey* 1942 24 TC 152.

   c) Only profits or gains identified with those specified in the previous five cases are taxable under Case VI. For this reason voluntary gifts are not taxable as Case VI income.

3. Tax is also chargeable on income specifically mentioned in the Taxes Acts as Case VI income such as:

   a) income from furnished lettings to 1994/95. *See Chapter 11.*

   b) capital profits arising on the sale of patents rights, Sec 524 TA 1988.

   c) certain transactions in land or an artificial nature, Sec 776 TA 1988.

Basis of assessment

4. The basis of assessment is the actual income arising in the income tax year, less any expenses incurred in earning that income. Capital allowances cannot be claimed in respect of 'plant and machinery', but the renewals basis may be available.

   Losses under Case VI can be set against other Case VI profits, but not against any other class of income. They may be carried forward to subsequent years and used against Case VI income.

Accrued income scheme

5. For details of the provisions concerning accrued income taxable under Schedule D Case VI *see Chapter 7 Income from savings*.

14 Income from self-employment I – Schedule D Cases I and II

Introduction

1. In this chapter the determination of business income for taxation purposes is examined. A summary of the order in which the topic is considered is given first. This is followed by an analysis of the main principles within each topic heading. A comprehensive illustration of the adjustment of profits for tax purposes appears at the end of the chapter. The basis of assessment is dealt with in the next chapter.

List of topic headings

2. Schedule D Case I and II income
   The concept of trading
   Taxable receipts
   General principles for deduction of expenditure
   Allowable expenditure
   Non-allowable expenditure
   Asset values for tax purposes
   Adjustment of profits
   Schedule D Case I and II income

3. Income derived from a business in the form of profits is chargeable to income tax where the business is conducted by an individual, either as a sole trader or in partnership with someone else. Where the business is undertaken by an incorporated person, such as a company, then corporation tax is chargeable on the profits, and not income tax.

   In accordance with Sec 18 TA 1988, tax under this schedule is charged on the annual profits or gains arising or accruing to any person residing in the UK from any trade, profession or vocation, whether carried on in the UK or elsewhere.

   Case I deals with any trade, and Case II with any profession or vocation. Trade is defined to include any 'manufacture, adventure, or concern in the nature of trade'. By Sec 53 TA 1988 all farming and market gardening in the UK are treated as carrying on a trade.

The concept of trading

4. As Lord Wilberforce pointed out in the case of *Ransome* v *Higgs* 1974 STC 539 'everyone is supposed to know what trade means so Parliament, which wrote this into the law in 1799, has wisely abstained from defining it'.

   The Royal Commission on the taxation of profits and income in 1955 listed 'six badges of trade' which are generally used in determining what is an adventure in the nature of trade. These are:
   a) the subject matter of the realisation
   b) the length of the period of ownership
   c) the frequency or number of similar transactions by the same person
   d) supplementary work on or in connection with the property realised
   e) the circumstances that were responsible for the realisation
   f) motive.

5. The present day meaning must therefore be deduced from a mixture of previous legal decisions, accepted practice and the 'badges of trade'. The following is a summary of some general points.
   a) Betting and gambling are not generally regarded as trading unless carried on by an authorised bookmaker.
   b) The fact that a trade is illegal does not mean that it is therefore not taxable.
   c) Where transactions are concluded within a year they may nevertheless be regarded as 'annual profits or gains'. See *Martin* v *Lowry* 1926 11 TC 297.
   d) Isolated transactions can amount to trading if they are of a commercial nature. See *Salt* v *Chamberlain* 1979 STC 750, *Wisdom* v *Chamberlain* 1968 45 TC 92. *Rutledge* v *CIR* 1929 14 TC 490. *Marson* v *Morton*. The Times 7.8.1986. *Kirkham* v *Williams* STC 1989.

e) All farming and market gardening carried on in the UK are treated as carrying on a trade.

f) Changes in the activities of a trade may amount to the establishment of a separate trade for tax purposes. See *Gordon Blair* v *CIR* 1962 40 TC 358, *DIK Transmissions (Dundee) Ltd* v *CIR* 1980 STI 784, *Cannon Industries Ltd* v *Edwards* 1965 42 TC 625.

g) The commercial letting of holiday accommodation which complies with the provisions of Sec 503–504 TA 1988 is taxable under Schedule D Case VI but treated in all other respects as Case I trading income. *See Chapter 12.*

Taxable receipts

6. In general profits arising from 'capital transactions' are not treated as income for the purposes of Schedule D Case I, although they may be taxable under some other tax, such as capital gains tax. Any profit on the disposal of a fixed asset would not therefore be subject to income tax, and conversely, any loss arising would not be allowed as a business expense.

   Where a person receives a sum of money which is paid under a legal obligation in return for goods or services provided in the normal course of trade, then this is clearly a trading transaction, chargeable to taxation. However, where the receipt does not arise from any contractual obligation, and the person has given nothing in return, then this may be regarded as a non-taxable receipt. Some general types of transaction are considered below.

Exchange profit and loss

In general exchange profits and losses arising from trading transactions will be chargeable to taxation whereas those relating to capital or non-trading transactions will not be chargeable.

See *Imperial Tobacco of Gt. Britain & Ireland Ltd* v *Kelly* 1943 25 TC 292; *Davies* v *The Shell Co of China Ltd* 1951 32 TC 133; *Pattison* v *Marine Midland Bank Ltd* 1983 CA STC 269. *Beauchamp* v *FW Woolworth plc* 1989 HL STC. New provisions affecting companies in effect treat all exchange gains and losses as taxable or allowable as a trading expense.

Insurance claims

On the whole, insurance compensation received in connection with damage or loss to a fixed asset is not taxable as a trading receipt. Claims under personal accident insurance, and claims relating to any loss on a current asset are generally taxable.

See *Green* v *Gliksten J & Son Ltd* 1929 14 TC 394; *Gray & Co Ltd* v *Murphy* 1940 23 TC 225; *Keir & Cawden Ltd* v *CIR* 1958 38 TC 23.

Compensation and voluntary payments

If these transactions arise in the ordinary course of trade then they are taxable on the recipient. If they are voluntary ex gratia payments, arising outside the domain of trading, then they are generally not taxable.

See *Murray* v *Goodhews* 1978 STC 191, *CIR* v *Falkirk Ice Rink Ltd* 1975 STC 434; *Simpson* v *John Reynolds & Co (Insurance) Ltd* 1975 ALL.E.R 245, *Poulter* v *Gayjon Processes Ltd* 1985 STI 30.

Regional development grants

Where a regional development grant is made to a person carrying on a trade profession or vocation which would otherwise be taxable as a trading receipt then under Sec 92 TA 1988 it is not a taxable receipt. Regional development grants are those made under the provisions of Part II of the Development Act 1982.

General principles for deduction of expenditure

7. In arriving at the taxable trading income of a business, a deduction is allowed for expenditure which satisfies the following criteria:

   a) it is not precluded under Sec 74 TA 1988, or

   b) it is expressly allowed such as redundancy payments, under Sec 579 TA 1988.

   Section 74 is entitled 'General rules as to deductions not allowable' and this provides a framework for what is and what is not allowable, since by implication, items not included in the section are presumed to be allowable. There are 15 parts to this section, and the most important are 74(a) and 74(f). In effect these provide that any business expenditure must satisfy two tests to be allowable:

   a) it must be revenue and not capital expenditure, and

   b) it must be incurred wholly and exclusively for the purposes of trade.

While an acceptable division between capital and revenue can normally be determined on sound accounting principles, it does not follow that such a treatment by itself will suffice to pass the interpretation meant by the section. Case law has supplied most of the guidance on this matter, and the words of Viscount Cave in *Atherton* v *British Insulated and Helsby Cables Ltd* 1925 10 TC 155, are the most frequently quoted:

> 'when an expenditure is made not only once and for all but with a view to bringing into existence an asset, or an advantage for the enduring benefit of a trade, I think that there is a very good reason for treating such expenditure as properly attributable not to revenue, but to capital'.

The following Court decisions provide some idea of the importance and range of these two sections.

1. *Regent Oil Co Ltd* v *Strick* 1966 43 TC 1. Payments made to acquire leases were held to be capital payments.

2. *IRC* v *Carron Co* 1968 45 TC 65. Expenditure incurred in modifying the company's charter was held to be revenue expenditure.

3. *Mitchell* v *Noble (BW) Ltd* 1927 11 TC 373. Compensation paid to a permanent director in consideration for his retirement was held to be revenue expenditure.

4. *Associated Portland Cement Mfs Ltd* v *Kerr* 1946 27 TC 103. Payments to retiring directors in consideration of covenants not to carry on similar business were held to be capital.

5. *The Law Shipping Co Ltd* v *IRC* 1924 12 TC 103. Repair expenditure at the time of purchase of a ship, necessary to enable it to remain as a profit earning asset, was held to be capital.

6. *Odeon Associated Theatres Ltd* v *Jones* 1972 48 TC 257. Repair expenditure incurred at the time of the purchase of the cinema, not necessary to make the asset commercially viable, was held to be revenue.

7. *Strong & Romsey Ltd* v *Woodfield* 1906 5 TC 215. Damages and costs of injuries to a guest, caused by a falling chimney were held to be non revenue expenditure.

8. *Smiths Potato Estates Ltd* v *Bolland* 1948 30 TC 267. Legal and accountancy expenses of an income tax appeal were held to be non revenue expenses.

9. *Morgan* v *Tate & Lyle Ltd* 1954 35 TC 367. Expenses incurred to prevent the nationalisation of their industry were held to be allowable deductions.

10. *Copeman* v *Flood (William) & Sons Ltd* 1941 24 TC 53. Sums paid as director's remuneration are not necessarily expended wholly and exclusively for the purposes of trade.

11. *ECC Quarries Ltd* v *Watkins* 1975 STC 578. Abortive expenditure on planning permission was held to be capital expenditure.

12. *Tucker* v *Granada Motorway Services Ltd* 1979 STC 393. A sum paid to secure a change in the lease of a service station was held to be capital.

13. *Garforth* v *Tankard Carpets Ltd* 1980 STC 251. When a mortgage made to secure loans to a connected company was foreclosed, the sum paid over was held to be not allowable.

14. *CS Robinson* v *Scott Bader Co Ltd* 1980 STC 241. The salary, expenses and social costs of an employee, seconded to a foreign subsidiary, were held to be allowable expenses of the parent company.

15. *Dollar* v *Lyons* 1981 STC 333. Payments made to children for work on a farm were held to be pocket money and not a trading expense.

16. *Walker* v *Joint Credit Card Co Ltd* 1982 STI 76. Payments to a competitor to cease carrying on business were held not to be expenses of trading.

17. *Whitehead* v *Tubbs (Elastic) Ltd* 1983 STI 496. A sum of £20,000 paid to ICFC to obtain release from the terms of a loan agreement was held to be capital expenditure.

18. *Watkiss* v *Ashford, Sparkes and Harward* 1985 STC. Expenditure on partnership lunches was held to be not deductible. Annual conference costs were, however, deductible.

19. *Jeffs* v *Ringtons Ltd* 1985 STC 809. Company payments to set up a trust fund to acquire shares for the benefit of employees were held to be revenue expenditure and not capital.

20. *Mackinlay* v *Arthur Young McClelland Moore & Co* 1988. Removal expenses of £8,658 paid to two partners were held not to be allowable in determining the firm's Case II profits.

21. *Rolfe* v *Wimpey Waste Management* 1988 STC The company acquired land sites to be used for its waste disposal business. The annual charge to profit and loss account in respect of the amount filled was held to be capital expenditure. Decision upheld CA 1989.

22. *Donald Fisher (Ealing) Ltd* v *Spencer* ST1 Feb 1989. A sum received by way of compensation in connection with a rent review was held to be taxable as a trading receipt.

Allowable expenditure – a summary

8. Subject to the general principles noted above, the following is a list of the most common items of expenditure which are allowed as an expense in computing taxable trading income.
   1. Cost of materials, components and goods purchased for resale.
   2. Gross wages and salaries, and employer's NIC.
   3. Redundancy payments.
   4. Ex gratia payments and compensation for loss of office.
   5. Pension scheme contributions to approved schemes – actually paid in year.
   6. Rent business rates and telephone.
   7. Fuel and power.
   8. Printing and stationery.
   9. Vehicle and aircraft running and maintenance expenses.
   10. Repairs and renewals, see below.
   11. Bad and doubtful debts, see below.
   12. Travelling and accommodation expenses for business purposes, eg sales representatives, trade fairs and conferences.
   13. Advertising and promotional expenditure.
   14. Bank interest.
   15. Leasing payments.
   16. Hire purchase interest.
   17. Patent renewal fees and expenses, see below.
   18. Insurance of assets, employees, goods etc.
   19. Legal expenses arising from trading, such as debt collection, see below.
   20. Professional charges such as audit fees and consultancy charges, but not those concerned with the acquisition of an asset.
   21. Training expenditure.
   22. Welfare expenditure for employees.
   23. Subscriptions and donations, see below.
   24. Losses and defalcations of employees, see below.
   25. Penalty payments for late delivery of goods.
   26. Pre-trading expenditure of a revenue nature, incurred up to seven years before trading.
   27. Incidental costs of obtaining loan finance, see below.
   28. Expenditure on waste disposal.
   29. Gifts to educational establishments.
   30. Loan relationship losses – companies only.

Non-allowable expenditure – a summary

9. The following is a list of the most common items of expenditure which are not generally allowed as an expense in computing trading income.
   1. Depreciation of fixed assets and losses on disposals.
   2. Professional charges concerned with a taxation appeal.
   3. General provisions against future expenditure such as those for doubtful debts, pension schemes, furnace relinement, or for preventive maintenance.
   4. Legal expenses on the acquisition of an asset.
   5. Entertainment except staff functions.
   6. Losses and defalcations by directors.
   7. Repairs which involve any improvement or amount to a renewal.
   8. Fines for illegal acts.
   9. Political donations.
   10. Non-trading losses.
   11. Penalties, interest or surcharge arising from VAT.

12. Unpaid emoluments *(see Chapter 25)*.

13. Council tax.

14. Payments induced by blackmail or extortion after 30th November 1993.

Rent paid to non-resident

10. Where net rental profits are paid to a non-resident landlord then basic rate income tax must be deducted at source from these payments and accounted for to the Inland Revenue (under Section 43 TA 1988). *See Chapter 11 section 13.*

    Failure to so deduct does not mean that the income tax can be recouped from the future rental payments. *Tenbry Investments L v Peugeot Talbot Co Ltd* 1992 STC 791.

Entertainment expenses and gifts

11. Under Sec 577 TA 1988, expenses of this nature are not allowed unless they are incurred for the entertainment or of one's own staff, and in the latter case, this must not be incidental to the approval of any kind of hospitality to others. Where an employer bears the cost of an annual Christmas party, or similar function such as a staff dinner and dance, which is open to the staff generally, then the Revenue will not in practice seek to tax any relevant benefit in kind, where the expenditure is modest. In this context expenditure of the order of £75.00 per annum for each employee or guest will generally be regarded as modest. If the total expenditure is at the lower end of the range indicated, it need not be included on the form P11D. This limit does not apply to the amount allowed as a business expense.

    Gifts of any kind given by way of entertainment are also disallowed except small gifts which

    a) carry a prominent advertisement

    b) are not food drink or tobacco

    c) do not amount in value to more than £10.00 per person p.a.

    In accordance with Sec 577 TA 1988, gifts made to a body of persons or trust established for charitable purposes only are allowed provided that they are incurred 'wholly and exclusively' for the purposes of trade.

Repairs and renewals

12. Improvements to premises are not allowed under Sec 74(g) TA 1988, but repairs occasioned by normal wear and tear would be deductible. Repair is not defined but has been held to amount to 'restoration or replacement of subsidiary parts', whereas a renewal is the reconstruction of the entirety, meaning not the whole but substantially the whole. A renewal would therefore be regarded as capital expenditure and not allowed as a trading expense. As noted in the *Odeon Theatre* case above, repairs to newly acquired premises, necessary to make them usable, would also be disallowed.

Patent fees and expenses

13. In accordance with Sec 83 TA 1988, deduction as an expense is allowed for any fees paid or expense incurred in obtaining for the purposes of a trade:

    a) the grant of a patent or extension of a patent period

    b) the registration of a design or trade mark.

    Expenditure on any abandoned or rejected application for a patent is also allowable.

Bad and doubtful debts

14. Sec 74(i) TA 1988 provides that bad debts proved to be such are allowed as a deduction, and doubtful debts are also allowed in so far as they are respectively estimated to be bad. Thus a provision for specific bad debts is allowable, but not a general provision based on some overall percentage of outstanding debtors.

    Where a debt is incurred outside the trading activities of the business, eg loans to employees written off, then any loss arising will not be allowable. This would also apply to any bad debts arising from the sale of any fixed assets.

    Under Sec 94 TA 1988, any bad debts recovered are treated as trading receipts in the period when received.

Pension scheme contributions

15. Sums paid to an approved exempt pension scheme are allowed as a deduction. Approved in this sense means by the Inland Revenue, who have created a separate department known as the Pension Schemes Office which deals with the approval of all schemes. The sums must be actually paid and not just provided for, to make good any deficit in the pension scheme.

Redundancy payments/outplacement counselling

16. Payments made to employees under the Employment Protection (Consolidated) Act 1978 are permitted deductions, and any rebates received are taxable as trading income. Payments made outside the provisions of the Act are also in general, allowed. See *O'Keeffe* v *Southport Printers Ltd* 1984 STI 381, where payments made to employees on the cessation of trade were held to be allowable.

Training costs

17. From the 6th April 1987 expenditure by employers on training for new work or skills undertaken by employees about to leave or those who have already left is allowed as a trading expense if not already so treated.

Employees must undertake a qualifying course of training which must have a duration of at least one year. Sec 588 TA 1988.

Legal expenses

18. In general legal charges incurred in maintaining existing trading rights are allowable, and this would include costs of debt recovery, settling disputes, preparation of service agreements, defence of title to business property, and damages and costs arising from the normal course of trade.

As already noted, legal costs incurred in contesting an income tax appeal were held to be not allowable. However, accounting and legal expenses incurred in seeking taxation advice would normally be allowed.

Expenses concerned with the acquisition of an asset would not be allowed, but those arising in connection with the renewal of a short lease (ie having a life less than 50 years) are in practice permitted.

The legal costs of raising or altering any share capital of a company are disallowed, but not those relating to loan capital.

Losses and defalcations

19. Any loss not arising from the trade, or not incurred wholly and exclusively for the purposes of trade, will not be allowable as a deduction in computing taxable profits. Two sub-sections to Sec 74 give substance to this principle and indicate types of loss which are not deductible:

a) Any loss not connected with or arising out of the trade, profession or vocation, (74(e)).

b) Any sum recoverable under an insurance or contract of indemnity, (74(1)).

With regard to losses arising from the sorts of risks that are usually insured against such as fire, burglary, accident or loss of profits, then the loss sustained is allowable if arising from the trade, eg loss of stocks, and any compensation received must be treated as a trading receipt.

Where assets are involved then any loss arising would be of a capital nature and not allowable as a deductible expense.

Losses arising from defalcations or embezzlement by an employee would normally be allowable.

See *English Crown Spelter Co Ltd* v *Baker* 1908 5 TC 327; *Milnes* v *J Beam Group Ltd* 1975 STC 487; *Roebank Printing Co Ltd* v *CIR* 1928 13 TC 864; *Curtis* v *Oldfield J & G* Ltd 1925 9 TC 319.

Waste disposal expenditure

20. The FA 1990 has introduced new provisions relating to expenditure on the disposal of waste materials and site restoration.

a) **Preparation expenditure**

Expenditure incurred in the preparation of a waste disposal site for the deposit of waste materials (including expenditure on earth works) is allowed as an expense in computing trading profits, in accordance with the following formula:

$$(A - B) \times \left(\frac{C}{C + D} \right)$$

A = Site preparation expenditure at any time not previously allowed as an expense of trading or being eligible for capital allowances.

B = Amount of expenditure allowed under this heading in previous period of account.

C = Volume of waste deposited during the period of account.

D = Unused capacity of the site at the end of the period of account.

Where any of the expenditure in A was incurred before the 6th April there is a reduction as follows:

$$A \text{ is reduced by } E \times \left(\frac{F}{F + G} \right)$$

E = Site expenditure incurred before 6th April 1989.

F = Volume of waste materials deposited before 6th April 1989.

G = Unused capacity of the site at the 6th April 1989.

b) **Restoration payments**

Where a person makes a restoration payment on or after 6th April 1989 then it is allowed as an expense in computing trading profits provided that:

i) it has not been allowed as a trading expense in any previous period of account, and

ii) it does not represent capital expenditure eligible for capital allowances.

A site restoration payment is one made in connection with a site which ceased to be used for waste disposal before the payment was made.

Post-cessation expenditure

21. For payments made after 28th November 1994 in connection with a trade that has been permanently discontinued, relief is available for payments made wholly and exclusively

   a) in remedying defective work done, goods supplied or services rendered

   b) in meeting legal and professional charges.

   The relief is available within seven years of the discontinuance for self-employed individuals.

   Relief is given primarily against an individual's total income for the year but where this is insufficient it may be set against any chargeable gains for that year.

Miscellaneous items

22. **Remuneration**

   Bona fide salaries to employees and directors, including commissions and bonuses, are allowable if they are incurred for the purposes of trade. See *Copeman* v *Flood* 1941 24 TC 53.

   Subscriptions and donations

   Subscriptions to trade associations or other bodies for the purposes of trade would be allowable, but not those unconnected with trade, or involving entertainment of a non-deductible nature. Where the payment is for the benefit or welfare of employees it will usually be allowed, eg a donation to a hospital or convalescent home which is used by employees of the firm. Gifts to registered charities are allowed if made for the purposes of trade.

   Where a donation is the subject of a legal contract such as a covenant then it is not a business expense but a charge on the taxpayer's total income.

   Employees seconded to charities

   When an employer seconds an employee temporarily to a charity, then any expenditure attributable to that employment by the employer is deductible as a business expense.

   This provision is extended to persons seconded to educational bodies where the expenditure is incurred between 26.11.1986 and 14.4.1997. Sec 86 TA 1988.

Costs of loan finance

Incidental costs of obtaining loan finance (including convertible loan stock) are allowed as a deduction in computing trading income, and this includes: fees, commissions, advertising, printing and stationery, but not stamp duty.

Pre-trading expenditure

Expenditure incurred within seven years (five years prior to 1st April 1993) prior to the actual commencement of trading is allowed if the expenditure would have been allowed as a trading expense had trading taken place during that period. *See Chapter 18.*

Gifts to educational establishments

Where a person carrying on a trade, profession or vocation makes a gift of plant and machinery to an educational establishment on or after 19th March 1991, then the proceeds of sale can be treated as zero.

Post-cessation receipts

Where an individual ceases to trade and in the following seven years incurs post-cessation expenditure then this can be set against the individuals income or capital gains in the year of the payment.

Capital allowances

For businesses commencing on or after 6th April 1994 and all businesses w.e.f 1997/98 capital allowances are deducted in arriving at the adjusted profits for the purposes of Schedule D Case I or II.

Asset values for tax purposes

23. Fixed assets

Fixed assets such as land and buildings or plant and machinery, fixtures and fittings etc, do not usually affect the determination of taxable trading income, except where the cost of an asset is charged against income, or in so far as there is a charge for depreciation. In the former case, the cost would be disallowed as capital, whether or not capital allowances are available. With regard to the charge for depreciation, then this is not allowed as a business expense, however computed. Where leasehold property is acquired then an allowance determined by reference to any premium paid is generally available, *see Chapter 11.*

Long-term investments

Long-term investments held as a fixed asset do not give rise to any particular problems as they are normally non-trading assets, and any surpluses or deficits arising from annual revaluations are not brought into the computation of taxable income. Realisations would require capital gains tax consideration, however.

Where the investments are trading assets then they will be valued on the same basis as other current assets.

Current assets

Current assets held by a business for the purposes of its trade would normally be valued for accounts purposes at the lower of cost or net realisable value. The same principles are applied for taxation purposes, but there are some special factors relating to stock and work in progress.

Stock and work in progress

The following is a summary of the position with regard to the valuation of stock and WIP.

1. In the absence of statutory authority stocks should be valued at the lower of cost or market value. Market value means selling price less selling expenses, and not replacement value. See *CIR* v *Cock Russell & Co Ltd* 1949 29 TC 287: *BSC Footwear Ltd* v *Ridgway* 1971 47 TC 495.

2. Consistency of method of valuation does not of itself guarantee that a correct method of valuation has been used. See *BSC Footwear* v *Ridgway* case noted above.

3. Overhead expenditure does not have to be included in the valuation of work in progress or finished stocks, however desirable this may be for accounting purposes. See *Duple Motor Bodies* v *Ostime* 1961 39 TC 537.

4. Standard cost values may be used but due allowance for variances from standard must be made where they are material.

5. In general neither the base stock method nor the LIFO method of stock valuation is an acceptable method of valuation for taxation purposes. See *Partrick* v *Broadstone Mills Ltd* 1953 35 TC 44; *Minister of National Revenue* v *Anaconda American Brass Ltd* 1956 AC

6. Where there is a change in the method of valuation from one valid basis to another, then the opening and closing stocks in the current period must be valued on the same basis. A valid basis of valuation is one which does not violate the tax statutes as interpreted by the Courts, and which is recognised by the accounting profession.

   If the charge is from one valid basis to another then the opening stock of the current period must be equal to the closing stock of the previous period. Thus if the new valuation gives rise to a surplus in that previous period it will be taxable, and if a deficit, a repayment can be claimed.

7. Where a trade is discontinued, then in accordance with Sec 100 TA 1988, stock must be valued at an open market price, or if sold to another trader, at realised selling price.

   Where the trade is discontinued on or after the 29th November 1994 the stock must be valued on an 'arms length basis' if the purchaser and the vendor are connected persons.

Intangible assets

Under this heading are included goodwill, patents and trade marks, copyrights and know how. There are no special problems of valuation, and most of them give rise to a claim for capital allowances, *see Chapter 17.*

Trading stock consumed

Where a trader takes goods from the trading stock for personal consumption or consumption by his or her household, then it must be valued at the retail selling price, see *Sharkey* v *Wernher* 1955 36 TC 275.

Adjustment of profits

24. The following is a comprehensive example of the adjustment of profits for the purposes of Schedule D Case I.

   > **Example**

   F has been in business for a number of years as a retailer, and his trading and profit and loss account for the year ended 31st October 1997 is:

	£	£
Sales		175,827
Cost of sales		145,319
Gross profit		30,508
Wages and salaries	5,829	
Light and heat	2,751	
Rent	1,980	
Motor expenses	2,588	
Repairs and renewals	3,500	
General expenses	1,082	
Bad debts	130	
Printing, telephone, stationery	1,150	
Depreciation	900	
Salary for F	5,000	24,910
		5,598
Profit on sale of car	110	
Bank interest received	528	638
Trading profit		6,236

   Notes

   1. *The top floor of the premises is occupied by F and his family as living accommodation and a disallowance of 1/3 of relevant expenditure has been agreed.*

   2. *Repairs and renewals comprise:*

External painting of whole building	*1,500*	
Internal decorating of shop	*750*	
New deep freeze	*1,250*	*3,500*

3. General expenses comprise:

Staff Christmas party	325	
Entertaining	287	
Trade journals	125	
Daily newspapers	84	
Subscription to trade association	52	
Subscription to golf club	175	
Other allowable expenditure	34	1,082

4. Bad debts account:

	£		£
Trade debts w/off	73	Provisions b/f: general	250
Provisions c/f:		specific	100
general	300	Bad debt recovered	18
specific	125	Profit and loss a/c	130
	498		498

5. 25% of the telephone calls of £132 has been agreed as private use.

6. Total motor mileage for the year amounted to 16,000 miles, of which 4,000 was attributed to private use.

Compute the Schedule D Case I adjusted profits assessable in the year 1997/98, ie the profits to 31st October 1997.

Solution
Income tax computation 1997/98

	£	£
Schedule D Case I adjustment of profits		
Trading profit per accounts		6,236
Add back non-allowable expenditure:		
Light and heat 1/3 private use	917	
Rent 1/3 private use	660	
Motor expenses 1/4 private use	647	
Repairs and renewals: 1/3 external painting	500	
deep freeze	1,250	
General expenses: entertaining	287	
daily newspapers	84	
subscription to golf club	175	
Bad debt, increase in general provision	50	
Telephone 1/4 × 132	33	
Depreciation	900	
Salary for F	5,000	10,503
		16,739
Less non-trading income:		
Profit on sale of car	110	
Bank interest (net)	528	638
Adjusted profit		16,101

Notes

i)   1/3 of all the expenses relating to the private accommodation have been added back.

ii)   The deep freeze is an asset and not revenue expenditure.

iii)   Entertainment is not allowed as a business expense.

iv)   Daily newspapers and the subscription to the golf club are not allowable business expenditure.

v)   The increase in the general provision for bad debts is not allowed.

vi)   Depreciation is not allowed as an expense of trading.

vii)   F's salary on account of profits is not an expense of trading as he is the proprietor.

viii)   The bank interest received would be taxable as investment income.

ix)   The profit on the sale of the car is not a taxable trading receipt.

x)   The profits for this year to 31st October 1997 will be taxed on a current year basis in 1997/98.

• Student self-testing question

J and his wife are partners in a grocery business whose results for the year to 31st March 1998 are as follows.

	£	£
Sales		250,000
Less cost of goods consumed		204,822
Gross profit		45,178
Expenses:		
Wages to employees	14,250	
Wages to Mrs J	3,500	
Heating and lighting	1,109	
Rates and insurance	2,130	
Printing and stationery	157	
Bad debts	1,259	
Motor expenses	1,710	
Depreciation	391	
Repairs and renewals	2,800	
Legal expenses	1,200	
Accountancy fees	575	
General expenses	3,900	
Mortgage interest	1,100	34,081
		11,097
Other income:		
Profit on sale of refrigerator	386	
Garage rents	1,200	
Bank deposit interest	187	
Discounts received	591	
VAT refund	426	
PAYE refund	91	2,881
Net profit		13,978

Notes

i) *Bad debts account*

	£		£
General provision c/f	500	General provision b/f	400
Specific provision c/f	226	Specific provision b/f	250
Cash takings stolen by		Trade debt recovered	31
former employee	1,075	Profit and Loss Account	1,259
Trade debt written off	139		
	1,940		1,940

ii) Business mileage is estimated at 7,500 miles out of a total of 10,000 miles for the year.

iii) Repairs and renewals include:

	£
New cash register	550
Repointing exterior wall	395
Installation of burglar alarm system	1,200

iv) Legal expenses comprise:

	£
Renewal of lease	575
Preparation of will for J	75
Obtaining probate for J's mother	550

v) Mortgage interest is paid in connection with the purchase of J's house.

vi) J and his wife have consumed goods at a cost of £1,000 which has not been adjusted for in the accounts. Assume a gross profit percentage of 20%.

vii) *General expenses comprise:*

	£
Entertaining	*218*
Subscription to golf club	*275*
Trade journals	*139*
Christmas party for employees	*375*
New typewriter	*850*
Donation to political party	*400*
Covenant payments to registered charity	*1,643*
	3,900

You are required to compute the Schedule D Case l adjusted profit for the year ended 31st March 1998.

Solution — Adjustment of profits

	£	£
Net profit per accounts		13,978
Add back items of expenditure disallowed		
Wages Mrs J (i)	3,500	
Bad debts (ii)	100	
Motor expenses 1/4 × 1,710	428	
Depreciation	391	
Repairs and renewals (iii)	1,750	
Legal expenses (iv)	625	
General expenses (v)	3,386	
Mortgage interest (vi)	1,100	11,280
		25,258
	£	
Less Non Case I income		
Profit on sale of fridge (capital)	386	
Garage rents (Sch. A.)	1,200	
Bank deposit interest (Case III)	187	
VAT refund (vii)	426	
PAYE refund (viii)	91	2,290
		22,968
Add value of goods (own consumption)		
Market price $1,000 + \left(\frac{20}{80}(1000)\right)$		1,250
		24,218

Notes

i) *'Wages' to Mrs J are not allowed as she is a partner in the business and taxable on her share of the profits. See Chapter 19.*

ii) *The increase in the general provision is disallowed. The defalcation by the employee is not a bad debt as such; however, it would normally be allowed as a trading expense.*

iii) *The new cash register £550, and the burglar alarm system £1,200, are capital expenditure.*

iv) *Legal expenses disallowed relate to private non-business expenditure of £75 and £550.*

v) *General expenses disallowed of £3,386 comprise:*

	£
Entertaining (not allowed)	*218*
Subscription of golf club (private)	*275*
New typewriter (capital)	*850*
Donation to political party (private)	*400*
Covenant (non business expense)	*1,643*

vi) *Mortgage interest is relieved at source at 15% and not as a business expense.*

vii) *The VAT refund is not a taxable receipt, and should be credited to the VAT account.*

viii) *The PAYE refund is not a taxable receipt.*

ix) *Goods for own consumption must be valued at market price. With a gross profit % of 20% this is equal to a mark up of*

$$\frac{20}{(100-20)}\% = \frac{20}{80} \times \frac{100}{1}\% = 25\%$$

• **Question without answer**

1. P is marketing director of K Ltd and earns a salary of £20,000 per annum. He contributes 10% of this salary to his employer's approved pension scheme. P also owns and manages a small advertising agency whose first results for the accounting year ended 31st March 1998 were as follows.

		£	£
Turnover			150,000
Less:	Advertising costs	60,000	
	Art work and materials	15,000	
	Office rent and rates	12,000	
	Bad and doubtful debts	2,500	
	Legal fees	9,500	
	Depreciation of equipment	3,700	
	Clerical salaries etc	13,200	
	HP interest	1,800	
	Repairs (all allowable)	11,400	
	Printing expenses	12,000	
	Car expenses	2,400	
	Loss on sale of old car	1,500	
	General expenses	730	145,730
	Advertising profit		4,270
Add:	Profit on sale of drawing boards	60	
	Lottery winnings	1,070	1,130
Net profit			5,400

Notes

i)   *P had received notification that a client owing £1,800 had gone into liquidation. The balance of the bad debt account written off is a general provision against further as yet unknown bad debts.*

ii) *Legal fees:*

	£
Re tax appeal on previous year's results	*2,500*
Renewal of lease on office (5 year life)	*800*
Re successfully refuting allegation of breach of contract	*6,200*
	9,500

iii) *General expenses:*

	£
Subscription to Inst. of Advertising	*100*
Donation to Oxfam	*50*
Entertaining editor of trade journal	*135*
Speeding offence fine on P	*50*
Christmas gifts of whisky	*200*
Stationery	*195*
	730

iv) *Motor expenses relate to a total mileage by P of 10,000, of which 2,000 were for private use.*

v)   *Capital allowances were agreed for the year at £7,465*

vi) *P is married and his wife has a fixed salary of £4,000 (included in clerical salaries) for part-time secretarial work in the advertising agency.*

vii) *P pays £2,400 (gross) under MIRAS per annum interest on a building society mortgage for the purchase of his house for 1997/98.*

Calculate the adjusted profits for the year to 31st March 1998 and the income tax liability for 1997/98 of P and Mrs P.

15 Income from self-employment II – basis of assessment

Introduction

1. This chapter deals with the basis of assessment of income arising from any trade, profession or vocation carried on by an individual. The special rules applicable to a partnership are discussed in Chapter 19.

Part I   new businesses after 5th April 1994 – existing 1997/98
Part II   transitional year 1996/97
Part III   existing businesses to 1995/96

Part I – Businesses started after 5th April 1994 – existing 1997/98

2. This topic is to be covered under the following headings :

         Current year basis of assessment
         Commencement provisions
         Cessation provisions

Current year basis of assessment

3. As part of the process towards the self-assessment of personal taxation the present system whereby businesses are taxed on a preceding year basis will be replaced by a current year system with effect from 1997/98. The first effects are however introduced in 1994/95 and concern all businesses starting after 5th April 1994 as noted below.

Commencement provisions

4. Where an individual starts trading after the 5th April 1994 the following rules apply for determining the basis of assessment.

a) Profits of the first year are the actual profits from the date of commencement to the 5th April.

b) Profits of the second year are normally either:

     i)   profits for the 12 months ending with the accounting date in that year or
     ii)   profits of the 12 months from the date of commencement.

Where the first accounting period ends in the third year of assessment then the second year will be assessed on an actual tax year basis.

c) For subsequent years the profits are for the 12 months ending with the accounting date.

> **Example**

T commenced trading on the 1st June 1994 with the following estimated taxable profits.

	£
1. 6. 1994 – 30. 5. 1995	6,000
1. 6. 1995 – 30. 5. 1996	10,000
1. 6. 1996 – 30. 5. 1997	12,000

Compute the taxable profits for all years of assessment.

Solution

Year of Assessment	Basis Period	Assessed Amount
1994/95	1. 6. 94 – 5. 4. 95 ($\frac{309}{365} \times 6{,}000$)	5,079
1995/96	1. 6. 94 – 30. 5. 95 (12 months to 30. 5. 95)	6,000
1996/97	1. 6. 95 – 30. 5. 96 (12 months to 30. 6. 96)	10,000
1997/98	1. 6. 96 – 30. 5. 97 (12 months to 30. 6. 97)	12,000

Notes

i) *The second year is assessed on the profit of the 12 month accounting period ending in the second year ie 12 months to 30th May 1995.*

ii) *The second year contains an 'overlap period' where profits are taxed twice. This is the period 1. 6. 1994 to 5. 4. 1995 with overlap profit of $\frac{309}{365} \times 6,000 = 5,079$.*

iii) *The amount of overlap profits is recovered on the earlier of the following:*

   a) *a change of accounting date that results in an assessment for a period of more than 12 months or*

   b) *the cessation of trading.*

iv) *Calculation should strictly be made in days and not months and fractions.*

Example

A commenced trading on the 1st May 1994 and has the following estimated results

	£
1. 5. 1994 – 31. 12. 1995	24,000
1. 1. 1996 – 31. 12. 1996	30,000

Compute the taxable profits for all years of assessment.

Solution

Year of Assessment	Basis Period	Assessed Amount
1994/95	1. 5. 94 – 5. 4. 95 ($\frac{340}{610} \times 24,000$)	13,377
1995/96	1. 1. 95 – 31. 12. 95 ($\frac{365}{610} \times 24,000$)	14,360
1996/97	1. 1. 96 – 31. 12. 96 (12 months to 31. 12. 96)	30,000

Notes

i) *The second year is assessed on the profits of the 12 months ending 31st December 1995.*

ii) *The overlap period is from 1. 1. 1995 to 5. 4. 1995, with profits of $\frac{95}{610} \times 24,000 = 3,737$.*

iii) *Assessed profits less the overlap profits to be recovered are thus equal to the actual profits. (13,377 + 14,360) – 3,737 = 24,000*

Example

T started business on the 1st January 1996 with first accounts for the 16 months to 30th April 1997 and thereafter.

	£
1.1.1996 - 30.4.1997	32,000
1.5.1997 - 30.4.1998	28,000

Compute the taxable profits for all years of assessment.

Solution

Year of Assessment	Basis Period	Assessed Amount
1995/96	1. 1.96 – 5. 4. 96 ($\frac{95}{485} \times 32,000$)	6,269
1996/97	6.4.96 – 5.4.97 ($\frac{365}{485} \times 32,000$)	24,082
1997/98	1. 5. 96 – 30.4.97 ($\frac{365}{485} \times 32,000$)	24,082
1998/99	1. 5. 97 – 30.4.98 (12 months to 30. 4. 98)	28,000

Notes

i)   There is no account ending in the second year 1996/97 therefore the actual basis applies.

ii)   The overlap period is 1.5.96 - 5.4.97 i.e. 340 days $\dfrac{340}{485} \times 32{,}000 = 22{,}433$

iii) Assessed profits less the overlap profits are thus equal to the actual profits
      $(6{,}269 + 24{,}082 + 24{,}082) - 22{,}433 = 32{,}000$

Cessation provisions

5.   These provisions apply to the cessation of businesses which commenced trading after the 5th April 1994 and existing businesses from 1997/98, the main features of which are as follows.

   i)   The final year of assessment has a basis period from the end of the previous accounting period to the date of cessation.

   ii) Any profits from the overlap period on commencement not recouped are adjusted in the final year of assessment.

   iii) The effect of the above is that over the life of a business only its actual taxable profits will be assessed.

Example

Q commenced trading on the 1st June 1994 and ceased on the 30th April 1999 with the following results.

	£
1. 6. 1994 – 31. 5. 1995	6,000
1. 6. 1995 – 31. 5. 1996	10,000
1. 6. 1996 – 31. 5. 1997	12,000
1. 6. 1997 – 31. 5. 1998	16,000
1. 6. 1998 – 30. 4. 1999	8,000

Compute the assessment for all years.

Solution

Year of Assessment	Basis Period	Assessed Amount
1994/95	1. 6. 94 – 5. 4. 95 ($\frac{309}{365} \times 6{,}000$)	5,079
1995/96	1. 6. 94 – 31. 5. 95	6,000
1996/97	1. 6. 95 – 31. 5. 96	10,000
1997/98	1. 6. 96 – 5. 4. 97	12,000
1998/99	1. 6. 97 – 31. 5. 98	16,000
1999/00	1. 6. 98 – 30. 4. 99 (8,000 – 5,079)	2,921

Notes:

i)   The overlap period is 1. 6. 1994–5. 4. 95 ie 309 days.

$$\text{Overlap profit} = \frac{309}{365} \times 6{,}000 = 5{,}079$$

ii)   The final period of profits is from 1.6. 1998 to 30. 4. 1999 assessed in 1999/2000 ie £8,000. Overlap profits of £5,079 are deducted leaving a net assessment of £2,921.

iii) Total profits over the life of the business are £52,000 which is equal to the taxable profits assessed.

iv)   When all existing businesses move to a current year basis in 1997/98 the above cessation rules will apply thereafter. The old rules will apply to any business which ceases trading before the 6th April 1997, which was trading at 5th April 1994.

Part II – Transitional year 1996/97

6.   The profits for 1996/97 are assessed on a 12 month average profits of the transitional period.

   The transitional period is the aggregate of two **separate** periods as follows.

   i)   A notional CY basis period which is the 12 months to the accounts date ending in 1996/97.

    ii) The 'relevant period' which is the period immediately beginning after the end of the basis period for 1995/96 and ending at the commencement of the period noted in (i) above.

7. For a business that has regularly made its accounts up to the 31st December the transitional period for 1996/97 will be:

    Notional period – 1.1.1996 to 31.12.1996

    Relevant period – 1.1.1995 to 31.12.1995

(**Note**: the end of the basis period for 1995/96 (year to 31.12.1994) is 31.12.1994.)

Profits assessed for 1996/97 are determined as follows:

    Appropriate % × profits of transitional basis period.

    Appropriate % = $\dfrac{365}{N} \times \dfrac{100}{1}$ where N = number of days in transitional basis period.

In the example above, the % is $\dfrac{365}{730} = \dfrac{1}{2}$ or 50% and in most cases the transitional profits will simply be 50% of the total profits for the two years ending with the accounting date in 1996/97.

Aggregation of profits and losses

8. Profits and losses within either the notional period or the relevant period must be aggregated, but an overall loss in one period must not be aggregated with the results of the other period to determine the transitional basis period profits/losses.

It should be noted that where a single accounting period of 24 months is prepared then aggregation within this period must take place.

If either period shows an overall loss then that loss is treated as nil when aggregating the two periods of the transitional period.

Where a business existing at 5.4.1994 ceases trading in 1996/97 then the old rules of cessation apply.

> **Example**

Z has been trading for many years to 30th June and has the following results.

	£
30.6.1994	12,000
30.6.1995	14,000
30.6.1996	20,000
30.6.1997	30,000

Compute the assessments for all years.

Solution

Year of Assessment	Basis Period	Assessed Amount
1995/96	1.7.93 - 30.6.94 PY	12,000
1996/97	1.7.94 - 30.6.96 TY	
	$\dfrac{14,000 + 20,000}{2}$	17,000
1997/98	1.7.96 - 30.6.97 CY	30,000

Notes

i) *The transitional year 1996/97 is equal to 50% × the profits of the 24 months to 30th June 1996.*

ii) *1997/98 is the first year of the current year basis with profits to the accounting date 30th June 1997.*

Transitional relief

9. Transitional relief is available in respect of the period from the end of the accounting period in the year 1996/97 and 5th April 1997.

Profits for this period, which in fact will be taxed as part of the accounting period ending in 1997/98, are to be computed and treated in the same way as overlap relief.

This relief is an amount intended to compensate buisinesses who on a cessation would have had a period of non taxable profits, under the old rules.

> **Example**

Z, who has been in business for many years, has the following results.

		£	
	30.6.1995	10,000	
	30.6.1996	12,000	
	30.6.1997	15,000	(after capital allowances £3,000)

Compute the assessments for all years and transitional relief.

Solution

1996/97	$\dfrac{10000 + 12000}{2}$	=	11,000	(transitional year)
1997/98	CY	=	15,000	(after capital allowances)

Transitional relief 1.07.96 – 5.4.97 = 187 days.

$$\frac{187}{365} \times 15{,}000 = £7{,}685.$$

Note: the transitional overlap relief of £7,685 is computed by reference to profits after capital allowances as these will be part of the profits taxed for 1997/98 on the CY basis.

Part III – Businesses trading at 5. 4. 1994

10. This topic is discussed under the following headings.

Main provisions	Cessation of business
Normal basis of assessment	Inland Revenue option under Section 63
Commencement of business	Averaging of profits for farmers
Taxpayer option under Section 62	

Main provisions

11. In accordance with the provisions of Sec 60–63 TA 1988, the basis of assessment for income arising under Case I or II of Schedule D is as follows.

Normal basis	Adjusted profits of the accounting period ended in the previous income tax year.
Commencement of business	Special rules apply, usually for the first three years of assessment before the normal basis comes into operation.
Cessation of business	The final period of trading and the preceding two years of assessment have special rules.

Normal basis of assessment

12. The normal basis of assessment is the adjusted profits of the business as computed from its accounts, made up to a date in the preceding income tax year.

> **Example**

T is a retailer who has regularly made his accounts up to the 31st December. The business has been trading for many years with adjusted profits as follows:

	Adjusted profits	Income tax year of assessment
	£	
12 months to 31.12.1992	10,000	1993/94
12 months to 31.12.1993	12,000	1994/95
12 months to 31.12.1994	15,000	1995/96

For this basis to apply there must be only one accounting period ending within the preceding year of assessment, and this must be for a period of 12 months. If these conditions are not met then the Revenue can determine the basis period which applies. Thus where there is a change of accounting date the normal basis is modified, *see Chapter 16.*

Commencement of business

13. The basic rules of assessment for the adjusted profits of a new business are as follows.

First year ie when business starts	Profits from the date of commencement to the following 5th April.
Second year	Profits of the first 12 months of trading.
Third year	Profits of the preceding year ie the normal basis. If no accounting period of 12 months in that year then the second years assessment is repeated.
Fourth year	Preceding year, ie the normal basis.

Example

A commenced business on 1st January 1991 and his adjusted profits for the years ended 31st December are as follows:

		£
12 months to	31.12.1991	6,000
12 months to	31.12.1992	7,000
12 months to	31.12.1993	9,000
12 months to	31.12.1994	11,000

Compute the assessment for all available years.

Solution

Year of assessment		£
1990/91	1.1.91 to 5.4.91 3/12 × 6,000	1,500
	period to end of first income tax year	
1991/92	1.1.91 to 31.12.91	6,000
	first 12 months trading	
1992/93	preceding year	
	12 months to 31.12.1991	6,000
1993/94	preceding year	7,000
1994/95	preceding year	9,000
1995/96	preceding year	11,000

Notes

i) *Although strictly speaking, calculations should be made in days to the end of the income tax year, monthly calculations are normally used for examination purposes.*

ii) *Profits are apportioned on an arithmetical basis even though there may be seasonal factors which affect the trade.*

iii) *It will be seen that the first year's profits form the basis of more than one assessment. This is illustrated in the diagram below.*

Accounting Periods

1.1.91   31.12.91 31.12.92 31.12.93 31.12.94

1990/91	├──┤	(1.1.91–5.4.91
1991/92	├────────┤	(1.1.91–31.12.91)
1992/93	├────────┤	(1.1.91–31.12.91)
1993/94	├────────┤	(1.1.92–31.12.92)
1994/95	├────────┤	(1.1.93–31.12.93)
1995/96	├────────┤	(1.1.94–31.12.94)

Example

F commenced trading on 1st March 1989 and his adjusted profits were as follows:

	£
13 months to 31.3.90	2,600
12 months to 31.3.91	2,500
12 months to 31.3.92	7,000
12 months to 31.3.93	9,000

Compute the assessments for all years.

Solution

Year of assessment		£
1988/89	1.3.89–5.4.89 1/13 × 2,600	200
1989/90	1.3.89–28.2.90 12/13 × 2,600	2,400
1990/91	Second year repeated	2,400
1991/92	1.4.90–31.3.91 preceding year	2,500
1992/93	1.4.91–31.3.92 preceding year	7,000
1993/94	1.4.92–31.3.93 preceding year	9,000

Note

In this example for 1990/91 there is no period of 12 months arising in the preceding year of assessment, only a 13 month period to 31st March 1990 so the second year of assessment is repeated.

Taxpayer's option under Section 62

14. Under this section, at the taxpayer's option, both the second and third years of assessment may be revised to an actual basis, ie from 6th April to 5th April. An election must be made within seven years of the end of the second year of assessment.

> **Example**

B started in business on the 1st July 1987 and makes accounts up to the 30th June each year. His adjusted profits were:

	£
12 months to 30.6.88	6,000
12 months to 30.6.89	4,000
12 months to 30.6.90	2,000
12 months to 30.6.91	8,000

Compute the assessment for all years.

Solution

Original assessments

1987/88	3/4 × 6,000	4,500	
1988/89	first 12 months	6,000	
1989/90	preceding year	6,000	} = 12,000
1990/91	preceding year	4,000	
1991/92	preceding year	2,000	
1992/93	preceding year	8,000	

Revised assessments

1988/89	1/4 × 6,000	1,500		
	3/4 × 4,000	3,000	4,500	
1989/90	1/4 × 4,000	1,000		= 7,000
	3/4 × 2,000	1,500	2,500	

As the revised assessments for both years, second and third, amount to £7,000, compared with the original assessments of £12,000, the taxpayer would elect under Section 62 for the actual basis.

Accounting Periods

1.7.87   30.6.88   30.6.89   30.6.90   30.6.91

1987/88	⊢———⊣ (1.7.87–5.4.88)
1988/89	⊢———⊣ (6.4.88–5.4.89)
1989/90	⊢———⊣ (6.4.89–5.4.90)
1990/91	⊢———⊣ (1.7.88–30.6.89)
1991/92	⊢———⊣ (1.7.89–30.6.90)
1992/93	⊢———⊣ (1.7.90–30.6.91)

Cessation of business

15. The basic rules of assessment in respect of a business which ceases to trade are as follows.

Final year, ie income tax year in which trade ceases	Profits from the preceding 6th April to date of cessation
Penultimate year, ie first year before final year	Normal basis, ie preceding year
Ante-penultimate year, ie second year before final year.	Normal basis, ie preceding year.

Inland Revenue option under Section 63

16. Under this section the penultimate and ante-penultimate years of assessment can be revised to an actual basis, if the Inland Revenue so decide.

> **Example**

F ceased to trade on the 30th June 1994 and his adjusted profits up to that date were as follows:

			£
12 months to 31st December	1991		3,600
12 months to 31st December	1992		3,000
12 months to 31st December	1993		4,000
6 months to 30th June	1994		1,800

Compute the assessments for all years.

Solution

Original assessments

1994/95	6.4.94–30.6.94 1/2 × 1,800		900	
1993/94	preceding year		3,000	
1992/93	preceding year		3,600	6,600

Revised assessments

1992/93	3/4 × 3,000	2,250		
	1/4 × 4,000	1,000	3,250	
1993/94	3/4 × 4,000	3,000		
	1/2 × 1,800	900	3,900	7,150

Notes

i) As the revised assessments under Section 63 amount to £7,150 compared with the original amount of £6,600, they will be made.

ii) Whichever basis of assessment is used there is always a period of profits which are not taxed on a cessation, as illustrated below.

iii) The comparisons are made for this purpose, ignoring any capital allowances claimed.

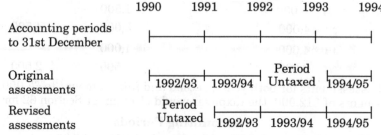

Where a business commences and ceases within a period of about four years then the actual basis is most likely to apply to all years in view of the options available under Sec 62 and 63.

Cessation in 1996/97

17. Where a business ceases trading in the year 1996/97, then the transitional rules do not apply and the existing rules noted above must be used.

Cessation in 1997/98

18. Where a business ceases trading in the year 1997/98 then initially the transitional rules will apply for 1996/97 and the new current year basis for 1997/98. However, the Inland Revenue have the right to assess 1995/96 and 1996/97 on an actual income tax year basis. It should be noted that transitional relief, outlined in paragraph 9 above, would be available.

Averaging of profits for farmers and market gardeners

19. Under Sec 96 TA 1988 farmers and market gardeners (not companies) can claim to have their adjusted profits averaged for any two years of assessment. The main provisions are:

a) Profits of the first or last year of trading cannot be included in any claim.

b) Profits are adjusted profits before capital allowances, or loss relief.

c) Once averaged the profits become fixed for all future averaging except for claims under Section 63 by the Inland Revenue.

d) Averaging is only available where the difference between the assessable profits of two successive years is 30% or more of the higher of the two years' profits.

e) There is a special rule for the year 1996/97. If it is averaged with 1995/96 the profits to be averaged will be those **before** capital allowances. If the profits for 1996/97 are to be averaged with those for 1997/98 then the profits to be averaged must be **after** capital allowances.

Example

T has the following adjusted profits:

	£
Year ended 31st December 1994	56,000
Year ended 31st December 1995	60,000
Year ended 31st December 1996	10,000

Compute the average profits for 1996/97.

Solution   **Computation of average profits**

			£
1995/96	assessment 31.12.94		56,000
1996/97	assessment $\dfrac{1.1.95 - 31.12.96}{2} = \dfrac{60,000 + 10,000}{2} =$		35,000

As the difference (56,000 − 35,000) = 21,000 is more than 30% of the higher year (30% × 56,000 = 16,800) full averaging for both years is possible.

1995/96	$\dfrac{91,000}{2} =$	45,500
1996/97	$\dfrac{91,000}{2} =$	45,500

---

f) Trading losses are to be taken as nil in making the average computation. Normal claims for loss relief are not affected by the averaging process, thus a claim under Section 380 could be made after the averaging computation.

Example

V who has been in business for many years has the following adjusted results:

		£	
12 months to 31st March	1994	25,000	
12 months to 31st March	1995	15,000	
12 months to 31st March	1996	(10,000)	loss
12 months to 31st March	1997	30,000	
12 months to 31st March	1998	*50,000	* after capital allowances

Compute the assessments with and without averaging.

Solution   **Assessments without averaging**

			£
1994/95	12 months to 31.3.94		25,000
1995/96	12 months to 31.3.95		15,000
1996/97	12 months to 31.3.96	} 40,000 ÷ 2	–
1996/97	12 months to 31.3.97		20,000
1997/98	12 months to 31.3.98		50,000
			110,000

Calculation of average profits

		Adjusted profit	Increase (decrease)	Averaged profits
1994/95	Year to 31.3.1994	25,000	(5,000)	20,000
1995/96	Year to 31.3.1995	15,000	5,000	20,000
Averaged profits $\frac{40000}{2}$		20,000		
1995/96	As averaged	20,000	–	20,000
1996/97	T.Y.	20,000	–	20,000
		40,000		
Averaged profits $\frac{40000}{2}$		20,000		
1996/97	As averaged	20,000	15,000	35,000
1997/98	Year to 31.3.1998	50,000	(15,000)	35,000
		70,000		
Averaged profits $\frac{70000}{2}$		35,000		
1997/98	As averaged	35,000		

	Averaged assessments	Assessments without averaging
1994/95	20,000	25,000
1995/96	20,000	15,000
1996/97	35,000	20,000
1997/98	35,000	50,000
	110,000	110,000

Note
The total amount of profits is the same under both methods but the averaging has smoothed out the annual figures.

20. A form of marginal averaging can be claimed where the difference between the two years' profits is between 25% and 30% of the highest year. This is effected by increasing the lower profit and reducing the higher profit by an amount equal to:

$$3 \text{ (higher profit} - \text{lower profit)} - (75\% \times \text{higher profit})$$

• Student self-testing question

P started in business on 1st October 1994 making accounts up to 30th September each year. Adjusted profits for the first three years were as follows:

12 months to 30th September 1995	8,000
12 months to 30th September 1996	4,000
12 months to 30th September 1997	2,000

Compute the assessments arising from the first three years of trading.

Solution **Original assessment**

		£
1994/95	1.10.1994 to 5.4.1995	
	$\frac{187}{365} \times 8,000$	4,098
1995/96	1.10.1994 to 30.9.1995	8,000
1996/97	1.10.1995 to 30.9.1996	4,000
1997/98	1.10.1996 to 30.9.1997	2,000

Overlap profits are: $1.10.1994 - 5.4.1995 = \frac{187}{365} \times 8,000 = 4,098$

Total profits assessed $= (18,098 - 4,098) = 14,000$.

• Questions without answers

1. X started in business on 1st July 1994. Adjusted profits for the first three years are as estimated:

Year ended 30th June 1995	12,000
Year ended 30th June 1996	14,000
Year ended 30th June 1997	16,000

   Show the assessments for all years and the overlap profits.

2. X started in business on 1st July 1994. Adjusted profits for the years to 30th September 1998 when he ceases trading are estimated:

Year ended 30th June 1995	5,000
Year ended 30th June 1996	8,000
Year ended 30th June 1997	20,000
15 months ended 30th June 1998	16,000

   Show the assessment for all years.

3. A started in business on the 1st July 1990. Adjusted profits for the first three years were:

Year ended 30th June 1991	10,000	1994	40,000
Year ended 30th June 1992	20,000	1995	50,000
Year ended 30th June 1993	30,000	1996	60,000

   Show the assessments for all available years.

4. B started in business on the 1st July 1990. Adjusted profits for the first three years were as follows:

Year ended 30th June 1991	30,000
Year ended 30th June 1992	20,000
Year ended 30th June 1993	10,000

   Show the assessments for all available years.

5. Y ceased trading on the 31st May 1996. Adjusted profits to the date of discontinuation were:

5 months ended 31st May	1996	6,000
12 months ended 31st December	1995	18,000
12 months ended 31st December	1994	24,000
12 months ended 31st December	1993	16,000

   Show the assessments for all available years.

6. F commenced trading on the 1st July 1995 with adjusted profits as follows:

6 months to 31st December	1995	12,400
12 months to 31st December	1996	12,000
12 months to 31st December	1997	15,000

   F is married and his wife has Schedule E earnings of £13,045 in respect of the year to 5th April 1998.

   F and his wife have a joint mortgage to purchase their private residence which amounts to £40,000. Interest paid under the MIRAS scheme for 1997/98 amounted to £1,500.

   F's eldest son is at university. He receives the sum of £1,000 (gross) each year from his father by way of covenant entered into in August 1992.

   i)   *Compute the assessments for the business for all available years.*

   ii) *Calculate F's income tax liability for 1997/98 and that of Mrs F.*

7. Max has been a sheep farmer for years. His adjusted trading results are as follows:

	£	
Year ended 31 December 1993	14,000	profit
Year ended 31 December 1994	44,000	profit
Year ended 31 December 1995	6,000	loss

   i)   *State the nature of the election which Max can make to reduce his liability to income tax.*

   ii) *Calculate the assessments for all the relevant years following such an election.*   **(ACCA)**

16 Income from self-employment III – change of accounting date

Introduction

1. This chapter is concerned with the effects of a change of accounting on the assessed profits of a business, and will be discussed under the following headings:

Part I   new businesses after 5.4.94 – existing 1997/98

Part II   transitional year 1996/97 and thereafter

Part III   existing businesses to 1995/96

Part I – new businesses after 5.4.94 – existing 1997/98

2. For new businesses started after 5th April 1994, and for businesses already trading at that date with effect from 1997/98, there are new rules concerning a change of accounting date.

An outline of the new rules is as follows.

a) Any change of accounting date will be ignored and assessments will be issued as if there was no change unless any of the three undermentioned circumstances apply.

     i)   The change is made in the second or third year of the business.

     ii)   The accounting period involving the change < 18 months, the Inland Revenue are notified of the change by the 31st January following the end of the year of assessment in which it is made, and the accounting date has not been changed in the previous five years.

     iii)   The accounting period involving the charge < 18 months, the Inland Revenue are notified as in (ii) above and the notice contains reasons for the change and the Inspector of Taxes is satisfied that it is being made for bona fide commercial reasons.

b) There is a right of appeal against the Inspector's decision not to accept the change as being for commercial reason.

c) Obtaining a tax advantage by such a change does not appear to be a valid commercial reason for a change.

d) Where the conditions are met the new basis period will be defined by reference to the new accounting date:

	Difference between end of preceding basis period and new accounting date	Basis period
1st year	< 12 months	12 months to new A/C date
1st year	> 12 months	Period to new A/C date
2nd year	—	12 months to new A/C date

Profits for the period of overlap will need to be computed when a change of accounting date takes place.

Example

A starts in business on 1st July 1995 and produces accounts to 5th April until 1998 when a new date of 30th June 1998 is the accounting date.

		£
Accounts	1.7.95 – 5.4.96	10,000
	6.4.96 – 5.4.97	12,000
	6.4.97 – 5.4.98	15,000
	6.4.98 – 30.6.98	2,000
	1.7.98 – 30.6.99	6,000

Compute the assessments.

Solution

		£
1995/96	1.7.95 – 5.4.96	10,000
1996/97	12 months to 5.4.97	12,000
1997/98	12 months to 5.4.98	15,000
1998/99	12 months to 30.6.98	
	1.7.97 – 5.4.98 = 279 days	

$$\frac{279}{365} \times 15,000 = \quad 11,466$$

	6.4.98 – 30.6.98 =	2,000	13,466
1999/00	1.7.97 – 30.6.99 =		6,000

Overlap Memo

There was no overlap profit arising on the commencement of the business as a fiscal year accounting date was adopted.

Overlap relief on change of accounting date:

Overlap period 1.7.1997 – 5.4.1998

$$= \frac{279}{365} \times 15,000 = \quad \underline{11,466}$$

Amount carried forward $\qquad \underline{11,466}$

Example

V started business on the 1st January 1996 with the following results.

6 months to 30.6.1996	20,000
12 months to 30.6.1997	40,000
12 months to 30.6.1998	50,000
18 months to 30.6.1999	75,000
12 months to 30.6.2000	60,000

Compare the assessments for all years and the overlap relief.

Solution

Years	Period		£
1995/96	1.1.96 – 5.4.96		
	$\frac{96}{182} \times 20,000 =$		10,549
1996/97	First 12 months trading		
	$20,000 + \frac{184}{365} \times 40,000$		
	20,000 + 20,164		40,164
1997/98	CY 30.6.1997		40,000
1998/99	CY 30.6.1998		50,000
1999/00	1.7.1998 – 31.12.1999		
	total for period	75,000	
	less overlap released	20,183	54,817
2000/01	CY 31.12.2000		60,000

Overlap Memo

Overlap profits 1.1.96 – 5.4.96 + 1.7.96 – 31.12.96 = 280 days

$\qquad = 10,549 + 20,164 = \qquad 30,713$

Overlap released 1.7.1998 – 31.12.99 = 549 days

$\qquad 549 – 365 = 184$

$$\frac{184}{280} \times 30,713 = \qquad \underline{20,183}$$

Carried forward $\qquad \underline{10,530}$

Part II – transitional year 1996/97 and thereafter

3. Where a business in existence at 5th April 1994 changes its accounting date in the transitional period, then the calculation of the profits for the notional period and the transitional period are pro-rated.

> **Example**

T has made up his accounts for many years to 30th April and decides to change to the 5th April in the year to 5th April 1997.

12 months	30.4.1994	26,000
12 months	30.4.1995	30,000
12 months	30.4.1996	32,000
11 months	5.4.1997	38,000
12 months	5.4.1998	40,000

Compute the assessments.

Solution

Year of Assessment	Basis Period	Amount
1995/96	30.4.1994 PY	26,000
1996/97	30.4.1995 – 30,000	
	+ 30.4.1996 – 32,000	
	+ 5.4.1997 – 38,000 $100,000 \times \dfrac{365}{1070}$	= 34,112
1997/98	5.4.1998 CY	40,000

Notes

i) The notional period is the 12 months to 5.4.97 = $\quad$ *365 days*

ii) The relevant period is the period 1.5.94 – 5.4.96 = $\quad$ $\underline{\textit{705} \textit{ days}}$

$\qquad\qquad\qquad\qquad\qquad\qquad\qquad\qquad\qquad\quad$ *1,070*

iii) *1996/97 is assessed on the 12 month average of the profits for the period 1.5.94 to 5.4.97.*

iv) *1997/98 is the first year on the current year basis with profits for the 12 months to 5.4.1988 assessed in 1997/98.*

Where there is no accounting date ending in 1996/97 then the relevant period will be the 12 months of the fiscal year ie 6.4.1996 to 5.4.1997.

> **Example**

B has been in business for many years with the following results.

12 months to 30.12.1995	10,000
12 months to 30.12.1996	30,000
12 months to 30.12.1997	20,000
6 months to 30.6.1998	12,000
12 months to 30.6.1999	36,000

Compute the assessments for all years and the overlap relief.

Solution

Years	Period		£
1996/97	TY $\dfrac{10,000 + 30,000}{2}$	=	20,000
1997/98	CY 31.12.97	=	20,000
1998/99	12 months to 30.6.1998		
	$12,000 + \dfrac{184}{365} \times 20,000$		
	12,000 + 10,082		22,082
1999/00	CY 30.6.1999		36,000

Overlap Memo

Transitional relief 1.1.97 – 5.4.97

$$=\frac{95}{365} \times 20,000 \qquad = \qquad 2,505$$

Overlap relief 1.7.97 – 31.12.97

$$\frac{184}{365} \times 20,000 \qquad = \qquad \underline{10,082}$$

Total c/forward $\qquad \qquad \qquad \underline{12,587}$

Part III – existing businesses to 1995/96

4. When a permanent change of accounting date occurs then the following points arise.

   a) Profits for the 12 months period ended on the new accounting date form the basis of assessment for the next income tax year, ie on the normal preceding year basis. The taxpayer has no right of appeal.

   b) Profits of the preceding income tax year may be revised by the Inland Revenue, subject to appeal by the taxpayer. This follows from the fact that

      i) If the new date is later in the income tax year than the old date then profits of some period will not come into assessment at all.

      ii) If the new date is earlier in the income tax year than the old date then the profits of some period will be assessed twice.

   c) The revision of the profits of the preceding year gives rise to a number of computational procedures which attempt to determine an intermediate profit in between the original assessment for that year, and a revised assessment based on the profits of the corresponding period to the 12 months ending with the new accounting date.

   d) Average profits for the preceding year are computed by relating the profits of the 'relevant accounting periods' to the relevant years of assessment, and deducting any original assessments.

   Relevant accounting periods are those beginning with the accounting period during which the corresponding period begins, and ending with the new accounting date.

Computational periods

In order to evaluate the effects of a change in an accounting date there are two distinct stages of computation to be made.

   Stage 1   computation of the averaged profits

   Stage 2   application of the tests of significance.

Both of these are illustrated by examples in separate sections below.

Computation of averaged profits (stage 1)

5. The following examples illustrate the principles involved in ascertaining the average profits, which is the first stage of the computation.

> **Example**

A changes his accounting date as follows:

		£
Adjusted profits	12 months to 30.9.92	10,000
Adjusted profits	12 months to 30.9.93	11,000
Adjusted profits	9 months to 30.6.94	9,000

Calculate the average profits for the preceding year.

Solution

a) Assessment 1995/96. 12 months to 30.6.94 - the new accounting date.

   Corresponding period. 12 months to 30.6.93

   Accounting period (old date) covering date when corresponding period begins, ie 1.7.92, is 12 months to 30.9.92.

b)

Relevant accounting periods	Profits £	Relevant years of assessment
12 months to 30.9.92	10,000	1993/94
12 months to 30.9.93	11,000	1994/95
9 months to 30.6.94	9,000	1995/96
33 months	30,000	36 months

Aggregate profits $= \text{Total profits} \times \dfrac{\text{relevant periods of assessment affected}}{\text{relevant periods of accounts}}$

$= £30,000 \times \dfrac{36}{33} = $ 32,727

Less final assessments:

1995/96	£9,000 + (1/4 × 11,000)	11,750	
1993/94	Previous year	10,000	21,750
1994/95	Averaged profits		10,977

Note

This solution would be subject to further tests of significance as indicated in the next section.

Example

B changes his accounting date as follows:

			£
Adjusted profits	12 months to 30.9.93		12,000
Adjusted profits	15 months to 31.12.94		16,000

Calculate the average profits for the preceding year.

Solution

a) Assessment 1995/96. 12 months to 31.12.94.
Corresponding period. 12 months to 31.12.93.
Accounting period (old date) covering date when corresponding period begins ie 1.1.93, is 12 months to 30.9.93.

b)

Relevant accounting periods	Profits £	Relevant years of assessment
12 months to 30.9.93	12,000	1994/95
15 months to 31.12.94	16,000	1995/96
27 months	28,000	24 months

Aggregate profits $= £28,000 \times \dfrac{24}{27} = $ 24,889

Less final assessment:

1995/96   12/15 × £16,000   12,800

∴   1994/95 averaged profit   12,089

Note

This solution would be subject to further tests of significance as indicated below.

Tests of significance (stage 2)

6. When the average profits have been computed it is then necessary to apply further tests of significance before deciding whether or not they are to be substituted for the preceding year as a final assessment. This is the second stage of the computation.

There are three tests to be applied as illustrated below.

Average profit for preceeding year

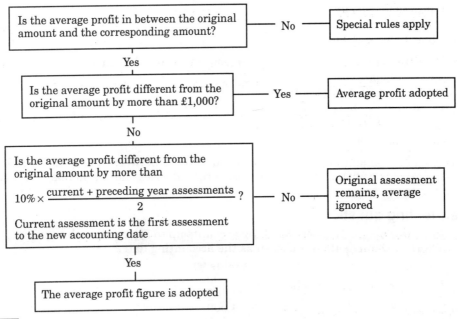

| Is the average profit in between the original amount and the corresponding amount? | — No — | Special rules apply |

Yes

| Is the average profit different from the original amount by more than £1,000? | — Yes — | Average profit adopted |

No

| Is the average profit different from the original amount by more than $10\% \times \dfrac{\text{current} + \text{preceding year assessments}}{2}$? Current assessment is the first assessment to the new accounting date | — No — | Original assessment remains, average ignored |

Yes

| The average profit figure is adopted |

Example

P changes his accounting date from 30th September to 31st December.

			£
Adjusted profits	12 months to	30.9.91	5,000
Adjusted profits	12 months to	30.9.92	12,000
Adjusted profits	3 months to	31.12.92	4,000

Calculate the average profits for the preceding year.

Solution

a) **Assessment 1993/94 12 months to 31.12.92**

	£	£
9/12 × 12,000	9,000	
3 months to 31.12.92	4,000	13,000

Corresponding period 1992/93 12 months to 31.12.91.

	£	
3/12 × 12,000	3,000	
9/12 × 5,000	3,750	6,750

b) **Average profits for 1992/93**

Relevant accounting periods	£		Relevant years of assessment	
12 months to 30.9.91	5,000		1992/93	12 months
12 months to 30.9.92	12,000		1993/94	12 months
3 months to 31.12.92	4,000			
27	21,000		24	

	£
Aggregate profits 24/27 × 21,000	18,667
Less assessment 1993/94 as above	13,000
Average profits for 1992/93	5,667

c) **Tests of significance for 1992/93**

	£
Original assessment of profits to 30.9.91	5,000
Average profits as above	5,667
Corresponding period to 31.12.91.	
3/4 × 5,000 = 3,750	
1/4 × 12,000 = 3,000	6,750

As the average profits lie in between the original assessment and the corresponding period amount, further tests are required.

Average profits for 1992/93	5,667
Less original assessment	5,000
Difference	667

As this amount is less than £1,000 it is necessary to apply the other test.

$$\frac{\text{Assessment 1993/94 + assessment 1992/93}}{2} \times 10\%$$

$$\frac{13000 + 5000}{2} \times 10\%$$

ie <u>900</u>

As this computed amount is greater than the difference between the average profit and the original assessment of £667, noted above, the original assessment remains and there is no adjustment to the preceding year.

• Student self-testing question

A starts in business on 1st May 1994 making accounts up to 5th April each year until 1998 when a new date of 30th November 1998 is chosen as the accounting date.

Relevant accounting periods	Profits (£)
1.5.94 – 5.4.95	10,000
6.4.95 – 5.4.96	12,000
6.4.96 – 5.4.97	14,000
6.4.97 – 5.4.98	16,000
6.4.98 – 30.11.98	8,000
1.12.98 – 30.11.99	20,000

Compute the assessments for all years.

Solution

				£
1994/95	1.5.94 – 5.4.95			10,000
1995/96	12 months to 5.4.96			12,000
1996/97	12 months to 5.4.97			14,000
1997/98	12 months to 5.4.98			16,000
1998/99	12 months to 30.11.1998			
	6.4.98 – 30.11.98		8,000	
	1.12.97 – 5.4.98 = 126 days			
	$\frac{126}{365} \times 16,000 =$		5,523	13,523
1999/00	1.12.98 – 30.11.99 =			20,000
Overlap relief	1.12.98 – 30.11.99			5,523
Carried forward				5,523

Total profits = 85,523 – 5,523 = £80,000

• Question without answers

1. X starts trading on 1st December 1995 with the following results:

	£
Period to 5th April 1996	7,000
Year to 5th April 1997	10,000
Year to 5th April 1998	15,000
6 months to 30th September 1998	8,000
Year to 30th September 1999	20,000

Compute the assessments for all years.

17 Capital allowances

Introduction

1. The chapter is concerned with allowances available to a taxpayer in respect of capital expenditure on fixed assets. These allowances, which are called capital allowances, consist of a mixture of annual and other allowances which are available in respect of qualifying expenditure incurred under the following headings.

Plant and machinery	Industrial and commercial buildings
Agricultural buildings and works	Patent rights
Scientific research	Know how
Mineral extraction	Dredging etc.

The chapter begins with a brief legislative summary and a definition of plant and machinery. The rules applicable to plant and machinery, and industrial and commercial buildings are then examined in detail with computational examples. An outline of the allowances available for other capital expenditures follows.

Legislative background

2. Legislation concerned with capital allowances is mainly to be found in the Capital Allowances Act 1990. However, some allowances are also enacted in the Taxes Act 1988 such as those for Patents and Know How, Sec 520–530 TA 1988.

   For income tax purposes, capital allowances have to be claimed by the taxpayer and they may be deducted from assessable income arising under:

   a) Schedule D Case I or II.

   For businesses started on or after 6th April 1994 and existing business from 1997/98 capital allowances are given as an expense in computing chargeable profits.

   b) Schedule E, where an asset is purchased for use in an employment.

   c) Schedule A, if the assets are used for the maintenance or repair of the property.

   With effect from 6th April 1995 Schedule A income for income tax purposes is computed as for Case I business income and any capital allowances available are deducted from the income as an expense.

Plant and machinery *(Part II CAA 1990)*

3. This expression is not defined in any tax statute and the definition most frequently referred to is perhaps that contained in a non revenue case, *Yarmouth* v *France* 1887 QBD. The case was brought under the Employers Liability Act 1880, and consideration given as to whether or not a horse was plant and machinery. In the course of his judgement, Lindley LJ made the following statement:

   '... in its ordinary sense it includes whatever apparatus is used by a business man for carrying on his business, not his stock in trade which he buys or makes for sale, but all goods and chattels, fixed or moveable, live or dead, which he keeps for permanent employment in his business.'

   Under Sec 66 CAA 1990, capital expenditure on alterations to an existing building, incidental to the installation of plant, may be treated as plant and machinery, where a trade is carried on. It has also long been the practice to treat as plant or machinery, items of expenditure which relate to parts usually embodied in a building structure such as: a goods or passenger lift, an overhead crane gantry, electrical wiring and motors for plant and machinery, and automatic doors. Fixtures and fittings of a permanent or durable nature such as an office desk or shop counter are also regarded as plant and machinery, but not a shop front.

   In addition to the above, there are special categories of 'building expenditure' which are to be treated as plant, and therefore qualify for the appropriate allowances. See paragraph 8 below.

Plant and machinery which are fixtures *(Sec 51–59 CAA 1990)*

4. a) These provisions endeavour to ensure that whenever expenditure is incurred on plant and machinery which becomes a fixture to a building, then capital allowances are available to someone.

b) A person incurring capital expenditure on plant or machinery, either for the purposes of a trade or for leasing otherwise than in the course of a trade, is entitled to capital allowances if:

i)   the machinery becomes a fixture, and

ii) at that time the person has an interest in the building or land of which the fixture is a part.

c) Where a person incurs expenditure and leases the fixture then the fixture is treated as belonging to that person for capital allowance purposes providing:

i)   the lessee would have been entitled to an allowance had he or she incurred the expenditure, and

ii) both parties elect for such treatment.

d) There are numerous other provisions which deal with such matters as:

– expenditure included in the consideration for the acquisition of an existing interest in land.

– expenditure incurred by an incoming lessee with an election to transfer the right to capital allowances.

– expenditure incurred by an incoming lessee where the lessor is not entitled to the capital allowances.

– fixtures ceasing to belong to the lessor or the lessee.

Plant and machinery – buildings

5.   For expenditure incurred after the 30th November 1993 plant and machinery does not include:

a)   buildings – Table 1

b)   fixed structures – Table 2

c)   interests in land.

Note The items included in column 2 of each table may still be claimed as plant and machinery subject to the existing case law criteria.

(1) **Buildings**	(2) **Assets so included, but expenditure on which is unaffected by the new rules**
A. Walls, floors, ceilings, doors, gates, shutters, windows and stairs	1. Electrical, cold water, gas and sewerage systems – a) provided mainly to meet the particular requirements of the trade, or b) provided mainly to serve particular machinery or plant used of the purposes of the trade
B. Main services, and systems, of water, electricity and gas	
C. Waste disposal systems	2. Space or water heating systems; powered systems of ventilation; air cooling or air purification; and any ceiling or floor comprised in such systems
D. Sewerage and drainage systems	3. Manufacturing or processing equipment; storage equipment, including cold rooms; display equipment; and counters, checkouts and similar equipment
E. Shafts or other structures in which lifts, hoists, escalators and moving walkways are installed	4. Cookers, washing machines, dishwashers, refrigerators and similar equipment; washbasins, sinks, baths, showers, sanitary ware and similar equipment; and furniture and furnishings
F. Fire safety systems	5. Lifts, hoists, escalators and moving stairways
	6. Sound insulation provided mainly to meet the particular requirements of the trade
	7. Computer, telecommunications and surveillance systems (including their wiring or other links)
	8. Refrigeration or cooling equipment
	9. Sprinkler equipment and other equipment for extinguishing or containing fire; fire alarm systems
	10. Burglar alarm systems
	11. Any machinery (including devices for providing motive power) not within any other item in this column

12. Strong rooms in bank or building society premises; safes
13. Partition walls, where moveable and intended to be moved in the course of the trade
14. Decorative assets provided for the enjoyment of the public in the hotel, restaurant or similar trades
15. Advertising hoardings; and signs, displays and similar assets

(1) **Structures**	(2) **Expenditure which is unaffected by the new rules**
A. Any tunnel, bridge, viaduct, aqueduct, embankment or cutting	1. Expenditure on the alteration of land for the purpose only of installing machinery or plant
	2. Expenditure on the provision of dry docks
B. Any way or hard standing, such as a pavement, road, railway or tramway, a park for vehicles or containers, or an airstrip or runway	3. Expenditure on the provision of any jetty or similar structure provided mainly to carry machinery or plant
	4. Expenditure on the provision of pipelines
	5. Expenditure on the provision of towers used to support floodlights
C. Any inland navigation, including a canal or basin or a navigable river	6. Expenditure on the provision of any reservoir incorporated into a water treatment works
D. Any dam, reservoir or barrage (including any sluices, gates, generators and other equipment associated with it)	7. Expenditure on the provision of silos used for temporary storage or on the provision of storage tanks
	8. Expenditure on the provision of slurry pits or silage clamps
	9. Expenditure on the provision of swimming pools, including diving boards, slides and any structure supporting them
E. Any dock	
F. Any dike, sea wall, weir or drainage ditch	10. Expenditure on the provision of fish tanks or fish ponds
G. Any structure not within any other item in this column.	11. Expenditure on the provision of rails, sleepers and ballast for a railway or tramway

Cases on plant and machinery

6. The following is a summary of some of the cases which have been concerned with the definition of plant and machinery:
    1. *Jarrold* v *Johngood & Sons Ltd* 1962 CA 40 TC 681. In this case movable metal partitioning used to divide office accommodation was held to be plant.
    2. *Hinton* v *Maddern & Ireland Ltd* 1959 H.L. 38 TC 391. Knives and lasts which had an average life of three years, and which were used on shoe machinery, were held to be plant.
    3. *CIR* v *Barclay Curle & Co Ltd* 1969 H.L. 45 TC 221. The company constructed a dry dock, the whole cost of which, including excavation, was held to be plant.
    4. *Cooke* v *Beach Station Caravans Ltd* 1974 CD 49 TC 524. The company constructed a swimming pool with an elaborate system of filtration, as one of the amenities at a caravan park. The cost, which included excavation, was held to be plant.
    5. *St Johns School* v *Ward* 1974 CA 49 TC 524. A special purpose prefabricated structure, for use as a laboratory and gymnasium in a school, was held not to be plant.
    6. *Schofield* v *R & H Hall Ltd* 1974 NI 49 TC 538. A grain importer built a concrete silo with gantries, conveyors and shutes, which was held to be plant.
    7. *Ben Odeco Ltd* v *Powlson* 1978 CD STC 111. Interest payments made to finance expenditure on an oil rig were held not to be plant.
    8. *Benson* v *The Yard Arm Club Ltd* 1978 CD STC 408. The purchase and conversion of an old ferry boat into a floating restaurant was held not to be plant.
    9. *Dixon* v *Fitchs Garage Ltd* 1975 CD STC 480. A metal canopy covering the service area of a petrol filling station was held to be a shelter, and not plant.
    10. *Munby* v *Furlong* 1977 CA STC 232. Books purchased by a barrister to create a library in his practice were held to be plant.

11. *Hampton* v *Fortes Autogrill Ltd* 1980 CD STC 80. A false ceiling constructed to provide cladding for electrical conduit and ventilation trunking was held not to be plant.

12. *Leeds Permanent Building Society* 1982 CD Decorative screens incorporating the society's name were held to be plant.

13. *Van Arkadie* v *Sterling Coated Materials Ltd* 1983. CD STC 95. Additional costs in pounds sterling, required to meet instalment payments on the purchase of plant and machinery, were held to be part of the cost.

14. *Thomas* v *Reynolds and another* 1987 CD STC 50. An inflatable dome which covered a tennis court was held to be the setting in which the tennis coaching business was carried on, and not plant or machinery.

15. *Wimpey International Ltd* v *Warland* 1988 CA Expenditure on items of decoration installed in the company's restaurants was held not to be plant or machinery.

16. *Hunt* v *Henry Quick Ltd: King* v *Bridisco Ltd* CHD. 1992 STC 633. The construction of mezzanine platforms in a warehouse was held to be plant and machinery.

17. *Gray* v *Seymours Garden Centre* C.H.D. 1993. The construction of a special horticultural greenhouse was held not to be plant and machinery.

Date of expenditure

7. a) To be eligible for an allowance the taxpayer must be carrying on a trade and the expenditure on plant or machinery must be incurred wholly and exclusively for the purposes of that trade.

    b) The expenditure is taken to be incurred on the date on which the obligation to pay becomes unconditional. However, if payment in whole or in part is not required until more than four months after the date on which the obligation to pay becomes unconditional, then so much of the amount as can be deferred is taken to be incurred on that date.

    c) For chargeable periods ending on or after the 30th November 1993 expenditure can only be included as plant and machinery if notified to the inspector of taxes within two years of the end of the chargeable period.

> **Example**

K orders an item of plant from X plc on the following terms:

31.12.1995 plant delivered and invoiced on same date to K.
21.1.1996   due date for payment by K, being the end of the month following date of delivery.
3.2.1996   K makes payment.

The expenditure is deemed to have been incurred on 31.12.1995.

> **Example**

L orders an item of plant from T plc costing £50,000 as follows:

31.12.1995   plant delivered and invoiced on same date.
31.1.1996   90% of invoice amount due for payment.
30.6.1996   balance of 10% due for payment.

L is deemed to have incurred the expenditure as follows:

31.12.1995   90% × £50,000 ie £45,000

30.6.1996   10% × £50,000 ie £5,000

Allowances available

8. The types of allowances which can be claimed in respect of expenditure on plant or machinery are:
   writing down allowance
   balancing allowance and related balancing charge.

Writing down allowance – rate 25%

Summary of main features

a) A writing down allowance is available in respect of expenditure incurred as follows:

businesses started after 5.4.1994 and
existing businesses from 6.4.1997 } – accounting period (AP) is the basis period

existing businesses to 1996/97 – chargeable period

b) An allowance is available whether or not the plant or machinery is in use in the basis period.

c) The writing down allowance is calculated by reference to the pool of expenditure, as shown in the specimen computation below (paragraph 11).

d) The pool is reduced by reference to the proceeds of disposal (limited to the original cost) where one of the following events occur.

   i) The plant or machinery ceases to belong to the taxpayer.

   ii) The taxpayer loses possession of the plant or machinery in circumstances where it is reasonable to assume that the loss is permanent.

   iii) The plant or machinery ceases to exist as such as a result of destruction, dismantling or otherwise.

   iv) The plant or machinery begins to be used wholly or partly for purposes which are other than those of the trade.

   v) The trade is permanently discontinued.

e) The balance remaining after deducting any proceeds of sale is written down in future years.

f) The taxpayer can claim any proportion of the allowance available.

g) If the asset has any private use then the allowance is reduced accordingly, and pooled separately.

h) A writing down allowance is not available in the year of cessation of trading.

Capital Allowances on Long Life Assets – 6%

9. For expenditure incurred on or after 26th November 1996

1) Capital allowances will be given on machinery and plant which has an expected working life when new of 25 years or more at 6 per cent a year on the reducing balance basis. This is equivalent in value to the normal accountancy treatment for an asset with a life of 25 years, which would be depreciated at 4 per cent a year on the straight line basis.

2) Capital allowances will continue to be given at 25 per cent a year on machinery or plant in a building used wholly or mainly as, or for purposes ancilliary to, a dwelling-house, retail shop, showroom, hotel or office. Motor cars will also be excluded from the new rules.

   Capital allowances will continue to be given at 25 per cent a year on sea-going ships and railway assets bought before the end of 2010, when this exclusion would fail to be reviewed by the government of the day.

3) Expenditure on long life assets which does not exceed a *de minimis* limit will also be excluded from the new rules.

   For companies, the *de minimis* limit will be £100,000 a year divided by one plus the number of associated companies.

   The *de minimis* limit of £100,000 a year will also apply to individuals and to partnerships made up of individuals provided the individual, or in the case of a partnership at least half the members, devotes substantially the whole of their time to carrying on the business.

4) The exclusion for expenditure below the *de minimis* limit will not apply to contributions to expenditure on machinery or plant, nor to expenditure on a share in machinery or plant, on machinery or plant for leasing or on machinery and plant on which allowances have been given to a previous owner at the reduced rate.

5) If a long life asset is sold for less than its tax written down value in order to accelerate allowances, it will be treated as sold for its tax written down value.

Separate pools

10. A separate pool must be kept for the following assets:
- i) assets with any private use
- ii) cars costing more than £12,000 each (£8,000 prior to 10th March 1992). Separate pool for each car
- iii) plant and machinery
- iv) short life assets
- iv) cars for employees (≤ £12,000).

Specimen computations

11. Specimen computation

	Pooled plant £
Balance of expenditure brought forward from previous year	–
Add qualifying expenditure incurred in accounting period	–
Less disposal value of plant scrapped or sold (limited to cost of acquisition)	–
Writing down allowance @ 25%	–
Balance carried forward	–

Specimen computation with FYA

	Pooled plant £
Balance of expenditure brought forward from previous year	–
Add qualifying expenditure incurred in basis period not eligible for FYA	–
Less disposal value of plant scrapped or sold (limited to cost of acquisition)	–
Writing down allowance @ 25%	–
Qualifying expenditure eligible for FYA (1.11.92 - 31.10.93)	–
Less FYA @ 40%	–
Balance expenditure carried forward	–

Businesses started after 5.4.1994 – existing businesses 1997/98

12. For new businesses commenced after the 5th April 1994 the following provisions apply.

1) Capital allowances are available in a 'chargeable period' which is the period of accounts.

2) Capital allowances are treated as a trading expense of the businesses in the chargeable period and any balancing charge is treated as a trading receipt. This means that the Schedule D Case I profit for tax purposes is after the deduction of capital allowances.

3) Where the period of account is not a 12 month period the writing down allowance is contracted or expanded on a pro-rata basis.

> **Example**

Period of account 8 months - writing down allowance $\frac{8}{12} \times 25\%$

Period of account 15 months - writing down allowance $\frac{15}{12} \times 25\%$

4) If a business has an accounting period greater than 18 months then this is split into one of 12 months and one of 6 months.

5) Any FYA's balancing allowances or charges will normally be given in the period of account in which they fall.

6) On the commencement of a new business on or after 6th April 1994, in order to deal with the taxable profits of the first and second years of assessment it will be necessary to compute the capital allowances as a first stage.

Example

P started trading on the 1st May 1994 with the following results:

Adjusted profits 1. 5. 94 – 30. 4. 1995	12,000
Adjusted profits 1. 5. 95 – 30. 4. 1996	16,000
Plant and machinery purchased 1. 5. 1994	4,000

Compute the capital allowances available and show the taxable assessments for the years 1994 / 1995 to 1996 / 97.

Solution

Capital Allowances	Plant Machinery Pool
1. 5. 1994 additions	4,000
30. 4. 95 writing down allowance 25% × 4,000 (1. 5. 94 – 30. 4. 95)	1,000
	3,000
30. 4. 96 writing down allowance 25% × 3,000 (1. 5. 95 – 30. 4. 96)	750
	2,250
30. 4. 97 writing down allowance 25% × 2250 (1. 5. 96 – 30. 4. 97)	562
	1,688

Period of Account	Adjusted Profits	Capital Allowances	Taxable Profit
1. 5. 94 – 30. 4. 95	12,000	1,000	11,000
1. 5. 95 – 30. 4. 96	16,000	750	15,250

Assessments

1994/95 (1. 5. 94 – 5. 4. 95) $\frac{339}{365} \times 11,000$	10,216
1995/96 (1. 5. 94 – 30. 4. 95)	11,000
1996/97 (1. 5. 95 – 30. 4. 96)	15,250

Notes

i) *The overlap period is from 1. 5. 94 – 5. 4. 95 ie 339 days or profits of £10,216. When the business ceases trading an adjustment in respect of this amount will be made in the final assessment.*

ii) *As all the periods of account are 12 months in length the writing down allowance is not pro-rated.*

Example

Q started trading on the 1st October 1994 with first accounts for the 15 months to 31st December 1995. Capital expenditure on plant and machinery was incurred on the 1st October 1994. Adjusted profits for the 15 months amounted to £50,000.

Capital Allowances	Plant and Machinery
Capital expenditure 1.10.1994	10,000
Period of account 1.10.94 - 31.12.95	
Writing down allowance $\frac{15}{12} \times 25\% \times 10,000$	3,125
Written down value carried forward	6,875

Assessments

Adjusted profits 1.10.94 - 31.12.95	50,000	
Capital allowances	3,125	
	46,875	

1994/95 1.10.94 - 5.4.95

$$\frac{186}{456} \times 46,875 \qquad 19,120$$

1995/96 1.1.95 - 31.12.95

$$\frac{365}{456} \times 46,875 \qquad 37,520$$

Notes

i)   The capital allowances are computed for the period of account of 15 months.

ii)   Capital allowances are deducted from the profits of the period of account before computing the assessments.

iii) Overlap profits are $\frac{95}{456} \times 46,875 = 9,765.$ (37,520 + 19,120 – 46,875)

iv)   If the first period of account had been less than 12 months' duration the capital allowances would have been pro-rated down.

Transitional year 1996/97

13.   The existing rules apply up to and including 1996/97. However, this year is the transitional year and the basis period for capital expenditure and disposals will be the aggregate of the notional CY basis period and the relevant period as defined in the previous chapter.

Example

Z makes up his accounts to 31st December each year with the following data:

	Year 31.21.95 £	Year 31.21.96 £
Adjusted profits	36,000	48,000
Plant and Machinery – additions	24,000	10,000
Plant and Machinery – dispersal	(6,000)	(5,000)
Plant pool b/f	10,000	

Compute the capital allowances and assessment for 1996/97.

Solution

		£	Plant pool £
1.1.95	(Written down value) b/f		10,000
31.12.95	Additions	24,000	
31.12.96	Additions	10,000	34,000
			44,000
31.12.95	Disposals	6,000	
31.12.96	Disposals	5,000	11,000
			33,000
	Writing down allowance (WDA) 25%		8,250
	WDV c/f		24,750

Assessment 1996/97

Adjusted profits (36,000 + 48,000) × 50%	42,000
Capital allowances	8,250
	33,750

Notes

i)   The basis period is 1.1.1995 to 31.12.1996.

ii)   The notional CY period and the relevant period is also 1.1.1995 – 31.12.1996 so the adjusted profits are divided by 50%.

iii) Any capital allowances carried forward from 1996/97 are to be treated as allowances due in the next accounting period.

Basis periods and years of assessment to 1995/96 (existing businesses)

14. Capital allowances are available in respect of what is called a 'chargeable period', which means a year of assessment, or for companies a period of account.

The allowances are granted in respect of qualifying expenditure incurred in a 'basis period', the profits of which form the basis of assessment for that chargeable period.

Thus for an established business the normal basis period is the 12 month accounting period ending in the preceding year of assessment. Relief for capital expenditure in that case is given against the profits of the same accounting period.

Example

T makes up his accounts regularly to the 31st December so that the accounts for the year ended 31.12.1994 form the basis of assessment for the income tax year 1995/96.

Capital expenditure incurred in the year to 31.12.1994, (the basis period) is available for capital allowances which are deducted from the profits assessed in 1995/96, (the chargeable period).

There are special rules for identifying capital expenditure with basis periods on the commencement and cessation of a business, noted below.

Opening years of assessment – prior to 6. 4. 1994

It is necessary to identify capital expenditure with a basis period in order that any allowance is only given once and the following rule applies.

On a commencement, where an accounting period forms the basis period for more than one year of assessment, then the capital expenditure or proceeds of sale are identified with the earliest basis period, by reference to the date of transaction.

Closing years of assessment – existing businesses

On a cessation, as noted in Chapter 16, there will always be a period of profits not assessed. If Section 63 is not invoked then capital expenditure in that period will be identified with the basis period for the penultimate year. Where Section 63 is invoked then capital expenditure in the untaxed period is identified with the basis period for the ante-penultimate year.

Example

A commenced business on the 1st January 1991. His first and subsequent accounts were made up to the 31st December each year.

Show the basis periods for all years to 1994/95.

Solution

	Accounts	Capital Allowances
	Basis Periods	
1990/91	1.1.91–5.4.91	1.1.91–5.4.91
1991/92	1.1.91–31.12.91	6.4.91–31.12.91
1992/93	1.1.91–31.12.91	–
1993/94	1.1.92–31.12.92	1.1.92–31.12.92
1994/95	1.1.92–31.12.93	1.1.93–31.12.93

Thus capital expenditure incurred on 30th March 1991 falls into three basis periods for accounts assessments, so it is allocated to the first for capital allowance purposes, ie 1990/91, the year of the expenditure.

Additions and disposals during these periods	Dealt with in these years of assessment
1.1.91–5.4.91	1990/91
6.4.91–31.12.91	1991/92
–	1992/93
1.1.92–31.12.92	1993/94
1.1.93–31.12.93	1994/95

In the above example it should be noted that there is no basis period for 1992/93 for capital allowances. However, a writing down allowance is generally allowed in practice in respect of any pool of expenditure brought forward.

If a Section 62 claim is made the basis periods would be as follows.

Basis Periods

	Accounts	Capital Allowances
1990/91	1.1.91–5.4.91	1.1.91–5.4.91
1991/92	6.4.91–5.4.92	6.4.91–5.4.92
1992/93	6.4.92–5.4.93	6.4.92–5.4.93
1993/94	1.1.92–31.12.92	–
1994/95	1.1.93–31.12.93	6.4.93–31.12.93

Additions and disposals during these periods	Dealt with in these years of assessment
1.1.91–5.4.91	1990/91
6.4.91–5.4.92	1991/92
6.4.92–5.4.93	1992/93
–	1993/94
6.4.93–31.12.93	1994/95

Example

B, who has traded for a number of years with accounts made regularly to 31st December, ceased trading on 30th June 1994.

Show the basis periods for the years 1991/92 to 1994/95.

Solution | **Basis Periods**

	Accounts	Capital Allowances
1994/95	6.4.94–30.6.94	6.4.94–30.6.94
1993/94	1.1.92–31.12.92	1.1.92–5.4.94
1992/93	1.1.91–31.12.91	1.1.91–31.12.91
1991/92	1.1.90–31.12.90	1.1.90–31.12.90

Capital expenditure in the period 1.1.92 to 5.4.94 (unassessed profits gap of 15 months) is allocated to the penultimate year, 1993/94, so that year of assessment has a capital allowance basis period from 1.1.92 to 5.4.94, that is 27 months.

Additions and disposals during these periods	Dealt with in these years of assessment
6.4.94–30.6.94	1994/95
1.1.92–5.4.94	1993/94
1.1.91–31.12.91	1992/93
1.1.90–31.12.90	1991/92

If Section 63 is invoked the basis periods would become:

Basis Periods

	Accounts	Capital Allowances
1994/95	6.4.94–30.6.94	6.4.94–30.6.94
1993/94	6.4.93–5.4.94	6.4.93–5.4.94
1992/93	6.4.92–5.4.93	1.1.91–5.4.93
1991/92	1.1.90–31.12.90	1.1.90–31.12.90

In this case capital expenditure in the period 1.1.90 to 5.4.92 (unassessed profits gap) is put into the ante-penultimate year, 1992/93, so that year of assessment has a capital allowance basis period from 1.1.91–5.4.93, ie a period of 27 months.

Additions and disposals during these periods	Dealt with in these years of assessment
6.4.94–30.6.94	1994/95
6.4.93–5.4.94	1993/94
1.1.91–5.4.93	1992/93
1.1.90–31.12.90	1991/92

15. Example

F commenced trading on 1st July 1991 and made accounts up to 30th June each year. Capital expenditure was incurred as follows:

		£
7.7.91	plant	5,000
30.6.92	private car (1/5 private use)	4,000
1.10.92	second hand van	3,500

Compute the capital allowances for all years up to and including 1994/95 with and without a Section 62 claim.

Solution

No claim made under Section 62

	Pooled plant £	Motor cars £	
1991/92 (1.7.91–5.4.92)			
Plant additions 7.7.91	5,000		
WDA @ 25% × 9/12	938		
WDV carried forward	4,062	–	
1992/93 (6.4.92–30.6.92)			
WDV brought forward	4,062	–	
Car purchased 30.6.92	–	4,000	
	4,062	4,000	
WDA @ 25%	1,016	1,000	p.u. 200
WDV c/f	3,046	3,000	
1993/94 (Nil basis period)			
WDV b/f	3,046	3,000	
WDA @ 25%	762	750	p.u. 150
WDV c/f	2,284	2,250	
1994/95 (1.7.92–30.6.93)			
WDV b/f	2,284	2,250	
Van 1.10.92	3,500	–	
	5,784	2,250	
WDA @ 25%	1,446	562	p.u. 112
WDV c/f	4,338	1,688	

Summary of capital allowances		Plant £	Cars £	Total £
1991/92	WDA	938	–	938
1992/93	WDA	1,016	800	1,816
1993/94	WDA	762	600	1,362
1994/95	WDA	1,446	450	1,896
		4,162	1,850	6,012

Notes

i) *The WDA in the first year 1991/92 is restricted to the basis period of 9 months.*

ii) *FYA is not available for the expenditure on the van as it was incurred before 1. 11. 1992.*

Solution

F. Claim made under Section 62

	Pooled plant £	Motor cars £	
1991/92 (1.7.91–5.4.92)			
Plant additions 7.7.91	5,000		
WDA @ 25% × 9/12	938		
WDA c/f	4,062	–	
1992/93 (6.4.92–5.4.93)			
WDV b/f	4,062	–	
Car purchased 30.6.92	–	4,000	
Van 1.10.92	3,500	–	
	7,562	4,000	
WDA 25%	1,891	1,000	p.u. 200
WDV c/f	5,671	3,000	
1993/94 (6.4.93–5.4.94)			
WDV b/f	5,671	3,000	
WDA 25%	1,418	750	p.u. 150
WDV c/f	4,253	2,250	

1994/95 (Nil basis period)

WDV b/f		4,253	2,250
WDA 25%		1,063	563 p.u. 113
WDV c/f		3,190	1,687

Summary of capital allowances		Plant £	Cars £	Total £
1991/92	WDA	938	–	938
1992/93	WDA	1,891	800	2,691
1993/94	WDA	1,418	600	2,018
1994/95	WDA	1,063	450	1,513
		5,310	1,850	7,160

Notes

i) The effect of an election under Section 62 is that it changes the profit assessments and accelerates the tax year in which capital allowances can be claimed.

ii) From a tax planning point of view the election for assessment under Section 62 for profit purposes should always take into consideration the effects of revised capital allowances.

iii) For 1995/96 the basis period is 6.4.94 – 30.6.94.

Expensive motor cars *(Sec 34 CAA 1990)*

16. Although motor vehicles are deemed to be plant and machinery for capital allowances purposes, there are some special rules for this type of asset.

For private cars costing more than £12,000 (£8,000 prior to 10th March 1992) the following conditions apply.

a) They must not be pooled with any other items of plant, and a separate record of each purchase must be kept.

b) The writing down allowance is restricted to £3,000 p.a. until 25% of the written down value is less than that amount. Where the accounting period is less than 12 months then a proportion of the maximum is allowed.

c) When a vehicle in this category is sold then a separate 'balancing charge or allowance' is computed.

For private cars costing £12,000 or less, a separate pool must be kept.

Example

J, a sole trader, purchased a car costing £16,000 on 1st April 1995 in his first 12 month accounting period to 31st December 1995.

Compute the capital allowances for the APs to 31st December 1997.

Solution	**Capital allowance computation**	
		£
AP 31.12.95	Cost	16,000
	Writing down allowance maximum	3,000
	Written down value c/f	13,000
AP 31.12.96	Writing down allowance maximum	3,000
	Written down value c/f	10,000
AP 31.12.97	Writing down allowance 25% × 10,000	2,500
		7,500

If a private car is hired which if purchased would cost more than £12,000, then the hiring charge allowed as a business expense is also restricted. The amount of the hire charge allowed is:

$$\text{Hire charge} \times \frac{12,000 + \tfrac{1}{2}(\text{retail price} - £12,000)}{\text{retail price}}$$

Example

C hires a car for £3,200 p.a. which if purchased would have cost £18,000.

Calculation of hire charge.

$$3,200 \times \frac{12,000 + \frac{1}{2}(18,000 - 12,000)}{18,000} \qquad \text{ie } 3,200 \times \frac{15}{18} = £2,666.67$$

The amount restricted is £3,200 – £2,667 = £533.

Note

Where the leasing agreement includes a charge for items such as repairs and maintenance, then this element of the charge should not be restricted.

Plant purchased by HP *(Sec 60 CAA 1990)*

17. With this method of purchase the interest element is allowed as an expense of trading. With regard to the capital element, any capital allowances can be claimed:

   a) Before the plant is brought in to use, for any instalment due.

   b) When the plant is brought in to use, for all instalments outstanding, as if the whole of the balance of capital expenditure had been paid on at that date.

   c) Where an HP agreement is not eventually completed after the plant has been brought into use, then an adjustment is made which claims back part of the allowance granted.

Leased plant and machinery *(Sec 61 CAA 1990)*

18. In general a lessor of plant and machinery is entitled to the full amount of capital allowances on eligible expenditure, and the rental payments of the lessee are an allowable business expense.

   Separate pooling arrangements continue to apply to leased assets within the following categories:

   a) Motor cars costing more than £12,000

   b) Assets leased outside the UK other than certain ships, aircraft and containers leased in the course of UK trade.

   The decision in *Gallagher* v *Jones : Threlfall* v *Jones* C.H.D 1993 that trade expenditure is incurred for taxation purposes when it is paid despite accepted accounting practice to the contrary was reversed in the Court of Appeal 30.6.1993.

Accounting for leased and hire purchase contracts 'SSAP 21'

19. The statement of Standard Accounting Practice for leases and hire purchase contracts (SSAP 21) does not alter the tax position of the lessee or lessor.

   Lessees are not entitled to capital allowances in respect of leased plant and machinery.

   The lessor, by incurring the expenditure and retaining ownership of the assets, will normally be entitled to the capital allowances.

   For sole traders and partnerships where SSAP 21 may not be followed, the total finance lease rental charged against the profits will be allowed for tax purposes. In this case there is no need to distinguish between capital and interest payments. Where accounts are prepared in accordance with SSAP 21, which means all companies, then for tax purposes the situation is as follows.

   a) The finance lease expense charged in the accounts is allowed for tax purposes.

   b) The normal depreciation charge on the asset in the accounts will be allowed as a deduction in computing taxable profits.

Balancing charges and allowances: general rules

20. A balancing charge arises when the disposal value (limited to the original cost) of any poolable or non-poolable asset is greater than the amount of qualifying expenditure existing in the period of the sale.

   Disposal value in the usual case is the amount of the proceeds of sale, or where the asset is lost or destroyed, any insurance or compensation moneys received. In other circumstances, eg if plant is given away, the market price is used.

Where plant or machinery is demolished and this gives rise to a balancing allowance or charge, the net cost of demolition can be added to the amount of unallowed expenditure at the time of the demolition.

A balancing allowance arises when the amount of qualifying expenditure is greater than the disposal value in the following circumstances:

a)   in the terminal period when trading permanently ceases

b)   when there is deemed to be a cessation of trade, see below.

Deemed cessation

21.   For capital allowance purposes certain assets are treated as forming a separate trade to that of any actual trade undertaken so that on a disposal the notional trade is deemed to have ceased. This applies to the following categories:

a)   expensive motor cars ie costing more than £12,000

b)   assets used only partially for the purposes of a trade, eg a private car

c)   short life assets

d)   ships

e)   each letting of machinery otherwise than in the course of trade

f)   the motor car pool for cars costing less than £12,000 (when there are no cars left).

Where capital allowances are computed on the basis of a deemed trade, this is assumed to be discontinued when a disposal has to be brought into account in respect of a single item or the last item in a pool of assets.

> **Example**

B, who has been trading for many years, has the following data relating to his year ended 31st March 1998.

		£
a)	Additions to plant	12,000
	Proceeds of sale of plant (original cost 1,500)	2,500
	Purchase of car for sales manager purchased 31/3/1998	14,000
	Sale of car used by sales staff	4,500
b)	At the 1st April 1997 the tax written down value of assets was:	

	£
Plant and machinery	2,500
Motor car pool	12,500
Motor car for B (Private use 30%)	7,400

Compute the capital allowances claimable for the AP to 31st March 1998.

Solution	**Plant pool** £	**Motor car pool** £	**Motor car (p.u.30%)** £	**Motor car costing > £12,000** £
Written down value b/f	2,500	12,500	7,400	
Additions	12,000	–	–	14,000
	14,500	12,500	7,400	14,000
Proceeds of sale	1,500	4,500	–	–
	13,000	8,000	7,400	14,000
WD allowance	3,250	2,000	1,850 (p.u. 555)	3,000
WDV c/f	9,750	6,000	5,550	11,000

Notes

i)   The proceeds of sale of the plant are limited to the original cost of £1,500.

ii)   The total allowances available to B for 1997/98 are:

	£
Plant pool	*3,250*
Motor car pool	*2,000*
Motor car (p.u. 30%)	*1,295*
Expensive motor car	*3,000*
	9,545

iii)   As the expensive car was bought after the 10th March 1992, the WD allowance is £3,000.

Plant and machinery – short life assets *(Sec 37–38 CAA 1990)*

22. The provisions of the CAA 1990 dealing with this topic may be summarised as follows.

a) The rules apply in respect of a disposal of plant and machinery but do not apply to motor cars, ships or assets leased to non-traders, or assets required to be pooled separately.

b) Where the taxpayer expects to dispose of an item of plant or machinery at less than its tax written down value, within four years of the end of the year of acquisition, then he or she can elect to have the item extracted from the general plant pool, and a separate pool created. The plant is treated as being in use for a separate notional trade.

c) The election must be made within two years of the end of the year of acquisition.

d) Any balancing adjustment arising on the disposal is calculated separately.

e) If the item of plant or machinery is not sold or scrapped by the end of four years from the end of the year of acquisition, then its tax written down value is transferred back to the general plant pool at the beginning of the fifth year.

As a general rule, it will only be advantageous to de-pool if the proceeds of sale are less than the written down value at the date of the disposal, giving a balancing allowance.

Example

T, who has traded for many years, has an accounting year end of 31st March. On the 1st May 1992 he purchases computer equipment for £10,000, electing for de-pooling.

Show the computations in the following circumstances:

a) *The plant is sold in the year to 31st March 1996 for £2,000.*

b) *The plant is sold in the year to 31st March 1996 for £5,000.*

c) *The computer equipment is not sold by the 31st March 1997.*

Solution — **Capital allowances computation**

			£
1993/94		Accounting period to 31.3.1993 cost	10,000
		Writing down allowance 25%	2,500
			7,500
1994/95		Writing down allowance 25%	1,875
			5,625
1995/96		Writing down allowance 25%	1,406
			4,219
1996/97		Writing down allowance 25%	1,055
			3,164
AP 31.3.97		Writing down allowance 25%	791
			2,373
a)	1996/97	year to 31.3.1996.	
		Proceeds of sale	2,000
		Written down value 1995/96 b/f	4,219
		Balancing allowance	2,219
b)	1996/97	year to 31.3.1996.	
		Proceeds of sale	5,000
		Written down value 1995/96 b/f	4,219
		Balancing charge	781

c) As the item of plant has not been sold within four years of the end of the year of acquisition, the written down value of £2,373 must be transferred to the general plant pool.

Alternative computation I

23. Where short life assets of a similar nature are acquired in fairly large numbers eg small tools or returnable containers, then the cost of the assets may be aggregated and treated as one sum.

> **Example**

B regularly purchases small tools for use in his trade and he has been able to satisfy the inspector of taxes that the average life of such assets in his trade is two years. He elects for short life asset treatment.

B's first accounting period is to the 30th June 1995 and purchases of tools for the three years to 31st March 1997 are as follows:

	£
Year to 30.6.95	2,000
Year to 30.6.96	1,600
Year to 30.6.97	2,800

Capital allowances computation

	Expenditure		
	1995	**1996**	**1997**
	£	**£**	**£**
Expenditure on tools	2,000	1,600	2,800
AP 30.6.95 WDA 25%	500	–	–
	1,500	–	–
AP 30.6.96 WDA 25%	375	400	
	1,125	1,200	–
AP 30.6.97 Scrap value (say)	125		
Balancing allowance	1,000		
WDA 25%		300	700
		900	2,100
AP 30.6.98 Scrap value (say)		90	
Balancing allowance		810	
WDA 25%			525
WDV c/f			1,575

Alternative computation II

24. Where assets used in a trade are stocked in large numbers and individual identification is possible but not readily practicable, then the computation can be based on the number of each class of asset retained. Assets falling under this heading could be calculators, amusement machines and scientific instruments, and videos.

> **Example**

S, whose first financial year is to 31st March 1997, uses various machines in his business which he elects to treat as short life assets. Information in respect of amusement machine type PFF is as follows:

		£
Year to 31st March 1997	purchased 50 type PFF machines	20,000
Year to 31st March 1998	sold 5 type PFF machines	1,750

Capital allowances computation

			Machine type PFF
			£
AP 31.3.97	Cost of 50 machines		20,000
	WDA 25%		5,000
			15,000
AP 31.3.98	Disposal of 5 m/c	1,750	
	5/50 × 15,000 expenditure unallowed	1,500	1,500
	Balancing charge	250	13,500
	WDA 25% × 13,500		3,375
			10,125
AP 31.3.99	WDA 25%		2,531
			7,594
AP 31.3.00	WDA 25%		1,899
			5,695
AP 31.3.01	WDA 25%		1,424
Transfer to main pool			4,271

The renewals basis

25. This is really a non-statutory method of obtaining relief on expenditure on plant and machinery, quite distinct from the capital allowance system outlined above. In fact where the renewals basis is adopted then the capital allowance system does not apply. The main points arising are:

a) The initial cost of any item of plant or machinery does not give rise to any allowances whatsoever, and no writing down allowance is available with this basis.

b) When an item is replaced then the cost of the new item, less anything received for the old one, is allowed as a deduction in computing Case I trading income. Any element of improvement or addition is excluded, and can only be claimed when it is replaced. Subsequent replacements are dealt with on a similar basis.

c) A change from the renewals basis to the normal capital allowance system can be made at any time, but the decision must apply to all items of plant in that class. In the year of the change, capital allowances can be claimed, irrespective of whether the expenditure is on a replacement or not.

The renewals basis effectively gives 100% relief in the year of expenditure on the replacement of an asset.

Industrial and commercial buildings

26. Capital allowances are available in respect of expenditure on buildings, and these may be considered under the following headings:

a) Industrial buildings and structures

b) Hotels

c) Enterprise zones.

Industrial buildings and structures *(Part I CAA 1990)*

27. Unlike plant and machinery, this does have a statutory definition which is contained in Section 18 of the CAA Act 1990 and in the main, an industrial building is a building or structure used for one or more of a number of qualifying purposes such as:

a) a trade carried on in a mill, factory or similar premise

b) a trade concerned with the manufacture or processing of goods or materials

c) a trade consisting of the warehousing and storage of goods or materials which are to be used in the manufacture of other goods

d) a qualifying trade engaged in the repair or maintenance of any goods or materials, not being part of any retail trade

e) for the purposes of a tunnel or bridge undertaking or toll road.

There are a number of appendages to the basic definition and the main points are:

a) Where the taxpayer carrying on the trade in one of the qualifying activities provides a building or structure for the welfare of workers employed in that trade, eg a canteen, and it is used for that purpose, then such a building is deemed to be an industrial building.

b) Where only a part of a building is used for a qualifying activity then only that part will rank as an industrial building.

c) A sports pavilion used by a trader for the welfare of his or her employees is treated as an industrial building whether or not the trade is in one of the qualifying activities.

d) Even where a qualifying activity is being carried on, an industrial building does not include any building or structure in use as, or part of, a dwelling house, retail shop, showroom, hotel or office. However, where 25% or less of the cost of the whole building, excluding any land cost, is attributable to the cost of such premises, then the whole building is treated as an industrial one.

e) The expression 'building or structure' is not defined, and in general, an extension or addition to a building is treated as if it were a separate building. A structure embraces such things as: walls, bridges, culverts, tunnels, roads, aircraft runways, and factory car parks. Costs of site preparation are included in the cost of a building.

f) Expenditure on the acquisition of land or rights over land is to be excluded from the cost of any industrial building or structure.

g) For details of expenditure on plant and machinery to be treated as a building or structure, see section 7.

Cases on industrial buildings

28. a) *CIR* v *Lambhill Ironworks Ltd* 1950 31 TC 93. A drawing office used by an engineering firm for workshop plans, although separate from the main workshop, was held to be an industrial building.

b) *Saxone Lilley & Skinner (Holdings) Ltd* v *CIR* 1967 HL 44 TC 22. A warehouse used for the storage of shoes, of which one third was manufactured by a group company, was held to be an industrial building.

c) *Abbott Laboratories Ltd* v *Carmody* 1963 CD 44 TC 569. An administrative unit which cost less than 10% of the whole was held to be a separate building, and not therefore an industrial one.

d) *Buckingham* v *Securitas Properties Ltd* 1980 STC 166. A building used for the purposes of wage packeting, and coin and note storage, was held not to be an industrial building, as the coins and notes were currency and not goods or materials.

e) *Copol Clothing Co Ltd* v *Hindmarch* 1982 STI 69. A warehouse used to store imported goods was held not to be an industrial building, as it was not located near to a port or airport.

Allowances available

29. The following allowances are available in respect of industrial buildings:

Initial allowance	– 20% of expenditure (1.11.92 – 31/10.1993).
Writing down allowances	– 4% of expenditure, (2% for expenditure prior to 7.11.62).
Balancing charge	– This arises where the total allowances given are greater than the 'adjusted net cost'.
Balancing allowance	– This arises where the 'adjusted net cost' is greater than the total allowances given.

An industrial building erected after the 6th November 1962 is deemed to have a maximum life of 25 years from the date when first used as an industrial building. After that period no allowance of any kind is available. For buildings erected prior to that date the maximum life is 50 years.

Writing down allowance *(Sec 3 CAA 1990)*

30. a) A writing down allowance of 4% p.a. is given providing that the building is in use as an industrial building at the end of the basis period.

b) A full writing down allowance is given unless the basis period is less than 12 months, when a proportion is available.

c) Where a writing down allowance cannot be given, ie where the building is not being used for a qualifying purpose, then a 'notional allowance' is nevertheless computed, and the life of the building is in no way affected.

Example

T, a sole trader, owns an existing factory which was constructed in 1961 at a cost of £60,000. His accounting period is the year to 31 December 1997. He incurred the following expenditure on 1 March 97:

	£
New factory (including land £50,000)	150,000
Drawing office	25,000
Retail shop being part of factory	23,000
	198,000

All buildings were in use for qualifying purposes at the 31st December 1997. The written down value of the 1961 factory was £10,000 at 1st December 1997.

Solution   **Capital allowances AP 31.12.1997**

		£
Cost of factory		100,000
Drawing office		25,000
Retail shop		23,000
		148,000
Writing down allowance	4% × 148,000	5,920
do.	2% × 60,000	1,200
Total allowances		7,120

Notes

i) *The drawing office is treated as an industrial building. The retail shop is eligible since its cost is less than 25% of the whole:*

   25% × 148,000 = £37,000

ii) *The writing down allowance is a full year's amount calculated on the cost.*

iii) *Further additions to a shop or office could negate a claim by exceeding the 25% level.*

Balancing allowances and charges *(Sec 4 CAA 1990)*

31. a) Where the building has been used for a qualifying purpose throughout the period of ownership, then a balancing adjustment arises if the proceeds of sale are greater or smaller than the 'residue of expenditure' prior to the sale.
The latter is equal to the original cost less any allowances given.

b) Where a balancing charge arises, this cannot exceed the value of the total allowances given.

c) The allowances available to a purchaser or a secondhand building are based on the residue of expenditure, plus balancing charge, minus balancing allowance, restricted where necessary to the purchase price.

> **Example**

A, who started business on 1st January 1995, purchased an industrial building new at a cost of £100,000 on 1st July 1995. The building is sold in June 2001, six years later, after allowances of £24,000 have been claimed. The sale price was (a) £20,000 (b) £120,000. A's accounting year end is to 31st December.

Compute the balancing adjustments arising on the disposal.

Solution   **Balancing adjustments AP 31.12.2001**

	£	£
a) **Balancing adjustment sale price £20,000**		
Cost	100,000	
Less allowances	24,000	
Residue of expenditure prior to sale		76,000
Proceeds of sale		20,000
Balancing allowance		56,000
b) **Balancing adjustment sale price £120,000**		
Residue of expenditure prior to sale		76,000
Proceeds of sale (limited to cost)		100,000
Balancing charge		24,000

Notes

i) *In the first case the purchaser would receive an annual allowance of*

   Residue 76,000 – BA 56,000 = $\dfrac{20,000}{19}$ ie £1,052.63.

   The remaining life of the building is 19 years.

ii) *In the second case the annual allowance would be*

   Residue 76,000 + BC = $\dfrac{100,000}{19}$ = £5,263.16 pa.

iii) *The tax life of a building is calculated to the nearest month, in this case 30th June. The age of the building on 30th June 2001 is six years and its expired life is therefore 19 years.*

Disposal after non-qualifying use *(Sec 5 CAA 1990)*

32. If a building has not been used for a qualifying purpose throughout the period, then a balancing adjustment is calculated by reference to the 'adjusted cost' of the building. The latter is equal to the original cost less any proceeds of sale, adjusted for any periods of non-qualifying use.

The comparison is made between the following:

i) the actual capital allowances given (ignoring all notional allowances) and

ii) the adjusted net cost i.e.

$$\text{(original cost} - \text{proceeds of sale)} \times \frac{\text{Periods of industrial use}}{\text{Total period of use}}$$

iii) Sale proceeds > original cost = B.C. equivalent to allowances given.

iv) Sale proceeds < original cost =

    a) B.C. where actual capital allowances > adjusted net cost.

    b) B.A. where actual capital allowances < adjusted net cost.

Example

Q, a sole trader who started in business on 1st January 1995 and whose accounting period is to 31st December, had an industrial building constructed in Dec 1995 at a cost of £100,000. It was used for the first year as an industrial building then for three years as a commercial building. After one year's further use as an industrial building it was sold on 31st December 2000 for £60,000.

Compute the balancing charge arising on the sale in Dec 2000.

Solution

		£	£
Cost of building			100,000
Writing down allowance:			
3 years notional use	4% × 100,000 × 3	12,000	
2 years qualifying use	4% × 100,000 × 2	8,000	20,000
Residue of expenditure prior to sale			80,000
Adjusted net cost to Q			
Cost of building in 1995			100,000
Less proceeds of sale			60,000
Net cost			40,000

Proportion of net cost attributable to the period of qualifying use.

2/5 × 40,000 = £16,000

Computation of balancing charge AP to 31.12.2000

		£
Net cost		40,000
Less Proportion attributable to non-business use		
3/5 × 40,000		24,000
Less Capital allowances actually given		16,000
Writing down allowances		8,000
Balancing allowance		8,000

Notes

i) *The allowances available to the purchaser would be based on the total of the residue of expenditure less the balancing allowance, restricted where necessary to the purchase price:*

Residue – Balancing allowance ie 80,000 – 8,000 = 72,000
Restricted to purchase price 60,000

ii) *Where the building is sold for more than its original cost then the balancing charge is limited to the actual allowances given, which in the above example would be £8,000.*

iii) *The age of the building on 31 Dec 2000 is five years and its unexpired life is therefore 20 years.*

Writing down allowance $\dfrac{60,000}{20}$ *ie £3,000 pa*

Hotels *(Sec 19 CAA 1990)*

33. Capital allowances are also available for expenditure incurred, in respect of what is called a 'qualifying hotel'. This is a hotel which provides accommodation in a building of a permanent nature, and which complies with the following.

a) It is open for at least four months in the season, which means April to October inclusive.

b) During the time when it is open, it has at least 10 letting rooms and the accommodation offered consists wholly or mainly of letting rooms and the normal services are provided.

The following allowances are available:

Initial allowance	20% expenditure (1. 11. 92 – 31. 10. 93)
Writing down allowance	4% of expenditure p.a. based on initial cost.
Balancing adjustments	A balancing charge or allowance can arise in similar circumstances to that for industrial buildings.

If a building ceases to be a qualifying hotel, other than by sale or destruction, for a period of two years, then a sale is deemed to take place at the end of that period, at the open market price.

Dwelling houses let on assured tenancies *(Part III CAA 1990)*

34. Capital allowances are available in respect of expenditure incurred on or after the 10th March 1982, and before the 1st April 1992, on the construction of buildings consisting of or including dwelling houses let on assured and certain other tenancies.

To qualify, a dwelling house must be let on a tenancy which is for the time being an assured tenancy within the meaning of Section 56 of the Housing Act 1980.

Rates of allowance

Writing down allowance	4% of expenditure.
Balancing adjustments	a balancing charge/allowance can arise.

Enterprise zones *(Sec 1 CAA 1990)*

35. These are areas of the country designated by the Department of the Environment, for which special provisions apply. So far as capital allowances are concerned the main features are:

a) Eligible expenditure includes the construction, extension or improvement of industrial and commercial buildings within the zone. Thus all commercial buildings, offices and hotels are included, but not dwelling houses.

b) An initial allowance of 100% is available but a reduced amount can be claimed.

c) If the building is sold within 25 years of its first use, then the normal balancing adjustments apply.

d) The allowances apply to expenditure incurred within a 10 year period beginning with the day on which the site is first designated as an enterprise zone.

Agricultural buildings and works *(Part V CAA 1990)*

36. Allowances are available on capital expenditure incurred in respect of agricultural or forestry land.

Capital expenditure includes expenditure on:

construction of farmhouses, farms or forestry buildings, cottages, fences or other works such as drainage and sewerage, water and electrical installations, broiler houses and similar buildings used for the intensive rearing of livestock.

Where expenditure is on a farmhouse then not more than a third of the expenditure can qualify as an agricultural building.

To be eligible for capital allowances the person incurring the expenditure must have the 'relevant interest' which would include an owner or tenant farmer.

The agricultural or forestry land must be in the UK.

Rates of allowance

37. Expenditure incurred

Initial allowance – 20% (expenditure 1.11.92 – 31.10.93)
Writing down allowance   4% p.a. based on cost
Balancing allowance/charge   subject to joint election

Example

D, the tenant of some agricultural land in the UK, has constructed a new farm building at a cost of £200,000, on May 1997. D's accounting period is to 30th June 1997.

Capital allowances computation AP 30.6.1997

	£
Cost of agricultural building	200,000
Writing down allowance 4% × 200,000	8,000
Written down value carried forward	192,000

In subsequent years a writing down allowance of £8,000 p.a. is available.

Balancing events

38. A balancing charge or allowance may arise in the following circumstances:

a) Where the 'relevant interest' is acquired by a new owner, and both elect for such treatment within two years of the end of the chargeable period.

b) In other cases eg where the building is destroyed or demolished or otherwise ceases to exist, if an election is made by the former owner within the two year period.

Residue of expenditure > Sale receipts = Balancing allowance
Residue of expenditure < Sale receipts = Balancing charge

Allowance to the new owner if election made: $\dfrac{\text{Residue of expenditure} + BC - BA}{\text{Remainder of twenty five years life}}$

If no election is made for a balancing adjustment the writing down allowance based on the original cost passes to the successor.

Example

E, the tenant of agricultural land in the UK, has constructed a new farm building at a cost of £200,000 on the 1st May 1996. E's first accounting period is to the 30th June 1996.

On the 1st May 1999 E sells the farm building to Z for £180,000.

Compute the capital allowances arising:
i) *if both E and Z elect for a balancing adjustment.*
ii) *if no election is made.*

Solution
a)   **Capital allowances computation**

		£
AP	year to 30.6.96 cost	200,000
	WD allowance 4% × 200,000	8,000
AP	year to 30.6.97	192,000
	WD allowance 4% × 200,000	8,000
AP	year to 30.6.98	184,000
	WD allowance	8,000
Residue of expenditure		176,000
Proceeds of sale		180,000
Balancing charge (AP year to 30.6.99)		4,000

Z would be entitled to a writing down allowance of:

$$\frac{176000 + 4000}{22 \text{ years}} = \frac{180000}{22} = 8,182 \text{ p.a.}$$

b) If no election was made the allowances available to Z would be £8,000 p.a. for a period of 22 years.

Patent rights

39. The main provisions relating to this type of capital expenditure are contained in Sec 520–522 of the TA 1988.

a) A separate pool of expenditure on the purchase of patent rights is created.

b) A writing down allowance of 25% is available for chargeable periods computed on the basis of:

$$WDV = 25\% \times (B + E - P)$$

      B   = balance of pool from previous period.

      E   = qualifying expenditure on the purchase of patent rights.

      P   = proceeds of sale limited to the cost of acquisition.

c) Where the basis period is less than 12 months' duration, (eg on a commencement or cessation) then the 25% is reduced in proportion.

d) A balancing charge arises where:

      P (restricted to cost of acquisition) > (B + E)

e) A balancing allowance arises on the permanent cessation of trade, where:

      P (restricted to cost of acquisition) < (B + E)

f) Where the proceeds of sale exceed the original cost of acquisition, then the excess is still chargeable to income tax as Schedule D Case VI income, in accordance with the provisions of Sec 380 TA 1970. The assessment can be spread over six years beginning with the year of assessment in whose basis period the sale took place.

Example

J purchased the patent rights to certain products incurring expenditure as follows:

		£
1st June 1996	patent rights of product A	10,000
25th March 1997	patent rights of product B	12,000

J sells the rights in product A to X for £15,000 in May 1998. J's first accounting period is to the 30th June 1996.

Compute the capital allowances up to the AP to 30th June 1999

Solution		£	£
AP	Year to 30.6.1996 (expenditure on product A)		10,000
	WD allowance 25% × 10,000		2,500
			7,500
AP	Year to 30.6.1997		
	Addition to pool (expenditure on product B)		12,000
			19,500
	WD allowance 25%		4,875
			14,625
AP	Year to 30.6.1998		
	Proceeds of sale product A	15,000	
	Restricted to cost	10,000	10,000
			4,625
	WD allowance 25%		1,156
			3,469
AP	Year to 30.6.1999		
	WD allowance 25%		867
	Written down value carried forward		2,602

Note

In respect of the AP to 30.6.1998 there will be a Schedule D Case VI assessment as follows:

	£
Proceeds of sale (patent product A)	*15,000*
Original cost	*10,000*
Case VI income	*5,000*

Know how

40. Know how is defined by Sec 530 TA 1988 to mean 'any industrial information and techniques likely to assist in the manufacture or processing of goods materials or in the working of a mine'. Where know how is purchased or sold as part of the sale or purchase of a business, then unless both parties to the transaction agree otherwise, the amount is treated as goodwill, and therefore subject to capital gains tax and not income tax.

The computation of capital allowances is similar to that for plant or machinery.

a) A separate pool of expenditure for know how is created.

b) A writing down allowance of 25% is available for a chargeable period computed on basis of:

$$WDA = 25\% \times (B + E - P)$$

B = balance of pool from previous period.
E = qualifying expenditure incurred in the basis period.
P = proceeds of sale, not restricted by reference to the cost of acquisition.

c) Where the basis period is less than 12 months, (eg on a commencement or cessation of trade) then the 25% is reduced in proportion.

d) A balancing charge arises where P > (B + E).

e) A balancing allowance arises where P < (B + E) on the permanent discontinuation of a trade.

Scientific research *(Part VII CAA 1990)*

41. Allowances for capital expenditure on scientific research related to a trade carried on by a taxpayer are provided by Sec 136–139 of the CAA. 1990.

Scientific research means any activities in the fields of natural or applied science for the extension of knowledge, and reference to research related to a trade includes any scientific research which may lead to an extension of that trade. Capital expenditure under this heading would include buildings and plant and machinery.

The amount of the allowance is 100% of capital expenditure.

Balancing adjustments can arise when assets representing scientific research expenditure cease to be used for such purposes and either they are sold or destroyed.

Expenditure on mineral extraction *(Part IV CAA 1990)*

42. Extensive new provisions relating to expenditure incurred on mineral extraction are contained in Sec 98–121 of the CAA 1990.

Dredging *(Part VI CAA 1990)*

43. Details of allowances available for eligible capital expenditure are contained in Sec 134–135 CAA. 1990.

For expenditure incurred on or after 1.4.86 a writing down allowance of 4% of cost allowed.

Cemeteries and crematoria

44. Particulars of the deductions allowed in respect of eligible capital expenditure are to be found in Sec 91 of the TA 1988.

• Student self-testing question

T has been trading for many years with an accounting period ending on 30th June. In respect of the years to 30th June 1996 the following data relates:

			£
1.	Pool of expenditure b/f 1st July 1992		
	Plant and machinery		3,500
	Motor car (private use 30%) VW		2,000
2.	1.8.92	New machine cost	1,500
	30.9.92	Office equipment cost	350
	1.1.93	Second-hand motor car for sales representative cost	5,000
	30.5.93	Second-hand crane cost	3,000
	30.6.93	3 new typewriters cost	1,200

			£
3.	1.7.94	BMW for T (Private use 30%)	14,000
	2.7.94	Sale of VW car used by T	2,000
4.	24.11.95	Office computer system	15,000
	12.12.95	Fork lift truck	8,500

Compute the capital allowances available to T for the years 1994/95–1996/97 and AP to 30.6.1997.

Solution

Plant and machinery pool

			£	£
1994/95	WDV b/forward			3,500
	Additions year to 30.6.1993			
	not eligible for FYA (1,500 + 350)			1,850
				5,350
	WD allowance 25%			1,338
	Additional eligible FYA (3,000 + 1,200)		4,200	4,012
	FYA @ 40%		1,680	2,520
	WDV c/forward			6,532
1995/96	WD allowance 25%			1,633
				4,899
1996/97	Additions 1.7.94 – 30.6.96 (15,000 + 8,500)			23,500
				28,399
	WD allowance 25%			7,100
	WDV c/forward			21,299
AP 30.6.97	WD allowance 25%			5,324
	WDV c/forward			15,975

		Motor car pool	Motor car (private use 30%)		Motor car costing > £12,000 (private use 30%)	
1994/95	WDV b/f	–	2,000		–	
	Additions	5,000				
		5,000	2,000		–	
	WD allowance	1,250	500	(30% 150)	–	
		3,750	1,500		–	
1995/96	WD allowance	938	375	(30% 112)	–	
		2,812	1,125			
1996/97	Additions				14,000	
	Proceeds of sale		(2,000)			
		2,812	(875)		14,000	
	Balancing charge	–	(875)	(30% 263)		
	WD allowance	703			3,000	(30% 900)
		2,109	–		11,000	
AP 30.6.97	WD allowance 25%	527			2,750	(30% 825)
	WDV c/forward	1,582			8,250	

Summary of allowances

	1994/95	1995/96	1996/97	AP 30.6.97
Plant	3,018	1,633	7,100	5,324
Motor car (private use)	350	263	(612)	–
Motor pool	1,250	938	703	527
Expensive car	–	–	2,100	1,925
	4,618	2,834	9,291	7,776

Note

The basis period for 1996/97 is 1.7.94 – 30.6.96.

• Questions without answers

1. Z, who started trading in 1995, has the following data relating to his accounting year to 31st December 1997.

		£
1.	Adjusted profits	7,000
2.	Pool of expenditure b/f 1st January 1997	
	Plant and machinery	1,500
	Motor vehicle (p.u. 20%)	2,000
3.	Additions to plant (5.10.1997)	15,000

Z is married and his wife has Schedule E income for 1997/98 of £10,000.

Compute the capital allowances Z would claim for the AP to 31.12.1997 to minimise his tax liability for that year.

2. Harry Hudson, a bicycle manufacturer, makes up annual accounts to 31st December and has been trading for several years. On 1st July 1990 Harry purchased a new building, which qualified as an industrial building, and which was brought into use immediately. The building, which was not in an enterprise zone, cost £150,000 and was used as an industrial building until 31st March 1992. Between 1st April 1992 and 30th June 1993 the factory was leased for non-industrial use as a keep-fit club because of a down turn in bicycle sales. On 1st July 1993 production of bicycles recommenced and continued until 30th June 1994 when the building was sold for £140,000 to Tommy Turpin. Tommy has been a manufacturer of refrigerators since 1980 and immediately commences production in the factory. His accounting date is 30th September.

You are required to calculate:

i) *the Industrial Buildings Allowance given to Harry Hudson for all relevant years*

ii) *the balancing adjustment on Harry Hudson on the sale of the building in 1994*

iii) *the future Industrial Buildings Allowance claimable by Tommy Turpin following his purchase of the building.* **(ACCA)**

3 Dietrich, who is 58, has been married to Marlene, who is 57 for many years. On 1 May 1994 Dietrich started a road haulage business. The profits, as adjusted for income tax but before capital allowances, are:

	£
1.5.94 to 31.12.94	25,000
1.1.95 to 31.12.95	45,000
1.1.96 to 31.12.96	50,000

Capital additions and disposals were as follows:

Additions

1.5.94	Lorry (1)	40,000
1.6.94	Car (1)	8,000
1.6.94	Car (2)	20,000
1.2.95	Lorry (2)	45,000
1.12.95	Car (3)	22,000
1.10.96	Lorry (3)	50,000

Disposals

1.12.95	Car (2)	12,500
1.10.96	Lorry (1)	20,000

Car (1) was purchased new and was for the use of Marlene. The annual mileage is 10,000 miles of which 5,000 is private.

Cars (2) and (3) are for the use of Dietrich whose annual mileage is 20,000 of which 8,000 is private.

No claim is to be made to treat any of the assets as 'short-life' assets. Marlene was employed by her husband at an annual salary of £15,000 which has already been charged in arriving at the adjusted profit figure given. PAYE of £2,600 was deducted. Although Marlene had private use of car (1) no fuel was provided for private motoring.

You are required to calculate:

(a) *the income tax assessments on Dietrich for the years 1994 – 95, 1995 – 96 and 1996 – 97,*

(b) *the 'overlap' profits.*

18 Relief for trading and capital losses

Introduction

1. This chapter is concerned with the reliefs available to a taxpayer who incurs a trading loss and 'capital losses'. A summary of the loss reliefs available for businesses trading at 5th April 1994 forms the first part of the chapter, each of which is subsequently examined in detail with examples.

Loss reliefs available for businesses started on or after the 6th April 1994 are outlined at the end of the chapter.

List of loss reliefs

2.

Section 380 TA 1988	Set against total statutory income, ie total income less charges.
Section 385 TA 1988	Carried forward and set against future trading income from the same trade.
Section 381 TA 1988	Losses incurred in the first four years of trading can be set against other total income of the three preceding years of assessment.
Section 388 TA 1988	Terminal loss relief.
Section 387 TA 1988	Carry forward of annual charges and interest.
Section 386 TA 1988	Relief for losses where a business is transferred to a limited company.
Section 574 TA 1988	Relief for capital losses.
Section 401 TA 1988	Pre-trading expenditure.
Section 72 FA 1991	Trading loss set against capital gains.

Set against 'other income' *(Sec 380 TA 1988)*

3. a) **New businesses after 5.4.94 – existing 1997/98**

  i) Capital allowances are deducted in computing adjusted taxable profits.

  ii) The current year basis of assessment applies.

  iii) Profits and losses are calculated by reference to periods of account rather than years of assessment.

  iv) Any loss which would otherwise appear in two periods of account can only appear in the first period.

  v) Relief against general income can be claimed in the year of the loss or the preceding year.

  vi) Where claims are made in respect of both years the taxpayer can choose which claim should be taken in priority. Partial claims are not permitted.

  vii) Any unused loss can be carried forward under Section 385.

b) **Existing businesses to 1995/96**

  i) The adjusted loss for an accounting period is normally available for set-off against total statutory income (ie before personal allowances) of the year of assessment in which the loss arises or the next year of assessment without any apportionment. Thus if A incurs a trading loss in his accounting period to the 31st December 1995, the whole of the loss would be available for set-off against other income of the years 1995/96 and 1996/97.

  ii) A strict statutory apportionment of the loss must be made:

  1. in the first three years of a new business or in the first four years where the taxpayer elects for the actual basis under Section 62

  2. in the year of cessation of trading

  3. in the year following one for which a claim for the strict basis was made.

  It appears however that the Inland Revenue cannot insist upon the non-statutory basis.

  iii) Loss relief must be claimed within two years of the end of the year of assessment to which the claim relates. Relief can be claimed for both years or either year.

  iv) Any unrelieved loss can be carried forward under Section 385.

c) **Transitional year 1996/97**

  i) The rules for businesses existing at 5th April 1994 continue to apply for 1996/97.

ii) As noted in Chapter 15 the assessment for 1996/97 is based on the aggregation of the profits of the notional CY period and the relevant period.

iii) If there is profit in the one period and a loss in the other then they must not be aggregated into a single overall result.

iv) Where either period shows a loss then that loss is treated as nil when aggregating the two periods of the transitional period.

v) A loss computed for the transitional year 1996/97 can be set against total income of 1996/97 and 1995/96.

vi) Where a claim is made under Section 383 to create or augment a loss then the following rules apply:

   1. If a claim is made in respect of 1995/96 then the existing preceding year basis of assessment continues to apply for 1996/97.

   2. Any allowances claimed for 1995/96 must be deducted from any allowances available for claim in 1996/97.

Example

A, who has been in business for many years, has an adjusted loss from trading for the year ended 31st December 1996 of £1,800. In respect of the transitional year of assessment 1996/97 he has other income:

	£
Schedule D Case I year to 31.12.1995 (relevant period)	10,000
Bank interest (net)	16,000
Mortgage interest paid under MIRAS (Net)	750

A is single.

Compute A's income tax liability for 1996/97 on the assumption that he claims relief for the trading loss in 1996/97.

Solution

Income tax computation 1996/97

	£
Schedule D Case I (0 + 10,000) ÷ 2	5,000
Schedule D Case III	20,000
	25,000
Section 380 loss relief 1996/97	1,800
	23,200
Personal allowance	3,765
Taxable income	19,435
Tax payable: £3,900 @ 20%	780
£15,535 @ 20%	3,107
£19,435	3,887
Less income on bank interest	5,000
Tax repayable	(1,113)

Notes

i) *1996/97 is a transitional year. A loss in the notional period (year to 31.12.1996) is not aggregated with the profit in the relevant period (year to 31.12.1995).*

ii) *In computing the Schedule D Case I income for 1996/97 the loss is treated as nil for the purposes of calculating the 'average'.*

iii) *Personal allowances are claimed after relief for a loss so that there may be unused personal reliefs.*

iv) *The whole of the loss to 31st December 1996 has been used against total income of the year of the loss, ie 1996/97.*

v) *Mortgage interest is not deducted in arriving at STI from 1994/95.*

Capital allowances

4. A claim for capital allowances can 'convert' a trading profit into a loss for loss relief purposes, under Section 383 TA 1988. However, for businesses starting after 5th April 1994 and existing ones from 1997/98 this section is redundant, as capital allowances are deducted in computing Schedule D Case I and II profits. The taxpayer does not have to claim the full allowances available in computing his or her Case I or II profits.

Example

T, who started in business in January 1995, has an adjusted trading profit for the 12 months to 31st December 1997 of £945, and capital allowances available of £4,000. T, who is married, has dividend income for 1997/98 of £5,000 (gross), and no other income. T's wife has taxable income of £32,000. T and his wife have jointly elected to transfer the whole of the MCA to T's wife.

Compute T's income tax liability for 1997/98.

Solution — **Income Tax computation 1997/98**

	£
Dividend income (gross)	5,000
Less Section 380 relief	955
	4,045
Personal allowance	4,045
	–
Schedule D Case I loss. Section 380 claim (945 – 1,900)	955

Notes

i)   There would be income tax repayable of £1,000 in respect of the taxed dividends ie 20% × £5,000.

ii)   T has claimed £1,900 of his capital allowances so that he does not waste his personal allowance. The balance of the capital allowance of £4,000 – £1,900 ie £2,100 can be carried forward to the pool for AP to 31.12.99.

iii) T's wife.

				£	£
Taxable income				32,000	
Personal allowance				4,045	27,955
Tax payable	4,100	@	20%		820
	22,000	@	23%		5,060
	1,855	@	40%		742
	27,955				6,622
Less MCA @ 15%					274
					6,348

Tax planning considerations in making a Section 380 claim

5. The following points should be taken into consideration in deciding whether or not to make a claim for loss relief under Section 380.

a) Loss of personal allowance — This cannot be carried forward, or back.

b) Transfer of married couple's allowance — This can all be transferred to the spouse, on a joint election, although only obtaining relief at the 15% rate for 1997/98.

c) Loss of personal pension plan relief *(see Chapter 20)* — Net relevant earnings are after deduction of loss relief.

d) Tax at higher rate — A claim can be made for the actual year of the loss or the preceding year.

e) Reduction in Class IV NIC — Profits for Class IV National Insurance purposes are after loss relief.

Carried forward – Section 385 TA 1988

6. To the extent that a trading loss has not been relieved it may be carried forward and set against the first available profits of the same trade.

   The loss must be set off even where this would involve a loss of personal allowances.

   The time limit for a claim under Section 385 is six years from the end of the year of assessment to which the loss relates.

> **Example**

R has taxable profits for the year to 31st December 1997 of £26,000. Trade losses brought forward under Section 385 amount to £3,955. R is married. R's wife has building society interest received for 1997/98 of £8,000 (net). R started in business on 1.7.1994.

Compute the income tax liability for 1997/98 of Mr and Mrs R.

Solution   **Income tax computation 1997/98**

				R £	Mrs R £
Earned income					
Schedule D Case I			26,000		
Section 385 losses b/f			3,955	22,045	–
Unearned income					
Building society interest (gross)				–	10,000
				22,045	10,000
Personal allowance				4,045	4,045
Taxable income				18,000	5,955
Tax Payable	4,100/5,955	@ 20%		820	1,191
	13,900/	@ 23%		3,197	–
	18,000/6,235			4,017	1,191
less income tax deducted from BSI				–	2,000
Deduct MCA @ 15% × 1,830				274	
Tax due/repayable				3,743	(809)

Losses in early years of trading – businesses commenced after 5th April 1994

7. Where a trading loss is incurred in the first year of trading then the loss may be relieved under Section 380, or carried forward under Section 385.

> **Example**

K commenced trading on the 1st January 1995 with the following results:

12 months to 31st December 1995	Loss 20,000
12 months to 31st December 1996	Profit 18,000
12 months to 31st December 1997	Profit 16,000

K makes a maximum claim under Section 380 for 1994/95 and 1995/96. *Show the computations for all available years.*

Solution   **K assessments**

1994/95	1.1.95 – 5.4.95 $\frac{94}{365} \times 20,000$		(5,150)
1995/96	1.1.95 – 31.12.95	(20,000)	
	less 1994/95	5,150	(14,850)
1996/97	C.Y. to 31.12.96		18,000
1997/98	C.Y. to 31.12.97		16,000

Notes

i) *Losses available for relief under Section 380*

1994/95	5,150	
1995/96	14,850	20,000

ii) *As the full amount of the loss has been relieved, there is none to carry forward.*

Losses in first four years of trading – Section 381 TA 1988

8. The relief which is available under this section, in addition to that under Sec 380 or 385, is as follows.

    a) Trading losses incurred in the first four years of assessment may be carried back and set against the total statutory income of the taxpayer, in the previous three years of assessment.

    b) The trading loss is to be calculated on the accounting year basis for businesses started after 5th April 1994 and existing ones from 1997/98. Previously the claim had to be made on a fiscal year basis.

    c) The loss is to be set against income of the first available year in the following order: earned income/unearned income of the claimant. For losses carried back to 1989/90 or earlier years the loss can also be set against the spouse's earned/unearned income.

    d) A claim can be made to restrict the application of relief to the claimant's income only.

    e) A claim must be made within two years of the year of assessment in which the loss is incurred.

    f) Where a claim is made for relief under Sec 380 and under Sec 381, then the loss cannot be apportioned between them. *Butt v Haxby* 1983 STC 239.

    g) The set-off is against income of an earlier year before a later year, ie on a FIFO basis.

Example

P, a single man, left his secure employment on the 31st December 1994 and commenced trading on the 1st January 1995 with the following results:

	£
12 months to 31.12.1995	(3,000)
12 months to 31.12.1996	(2,000)

Compute the losses available for set-off and show the years in which they can be utilised.

Solution

		£	£
1994/95	$1.1.95 - 5.4.95 \; \frac{95}{365} \times 3,000 =$		780
1995/96	Year ended 31.12.95	3,000	
	Less allocated to 1994/95	780	2,220
1996/97	Year ended 31.12.96		2,000

Loss relief available is as follows:

	1994/95	**1995/96**	**1996/97**
Losses available	780	2,220	2,000
Set against total income			
1991/92	780	–	–
1992/93	–	2,220	–
1993/94	–	–	2,000
1994/95	–	–	–

Notes

i) *If the losses cannot be fully used by this process then the balance can be carried forward in the usual way under Section 385.*

ii) *The loss has been shown as relieved in the earliest year available.*

Terminal loss relief – Section 388 TA 1988

9. Under this section relief is available where a cessation of trading takes place, and a loss arises in the last 12 months of trading.

    A terminal loss may be carried back and set against the trading profits (less capital allowances) of the three years of assessment prior to the year of assessment in which the trading ceases.

Example

S ceased trading on 30th June 1996 with the following results:

Adjusted profits

	£
9 months to 30.6.96	(1,500)
12 months to 30.9.95	1,200
12 months to 30.9.94	1,600
12 months to 30.9.93	2,000
12 months to 30.9.92	900

Capital allowances have been agreed as follows:

	£
1996/97	1,500
1995/96	700
1994/95	600
1993/94	800

Compute the terminal loss relief.

Solution

Calculation of terminal loss – last 12 months trading ie 1.7.95 to 30.6.96

			£	£
1996/97	1/3 × (1,500)		(500)	–
	Add capital allowances		(1,500)	(2,000)
1995/96	2/3 × (1,500)		(1,000)	
	1/4 × 1,200 profit		300	(700)
				(2,700)

Relief for terminal loss

		£	£
1995/96	Year to 30.9.94 adjusted profits	1,600	
	Less capital allowances	700	
		900	
	Less section 388 terminal loss relief	(900)	(900)
1994/95	Year to 30.9.93 adjusted profits	2,000	
	Less capital allowances	600	
		1,400	
	Less section 388 terminal loss relief	(1,400)	(1,400)
1993/94	Year to 30.9.92 adjusted profits	900	
	Less capital allowances	800	
		100	
	Less section 388 terminal loss relief	(100)	(100)
			(2,400)
Unrelieved loss			(300)
Total terminal loss			(2,700)

Note

This example assumes that Section 63 will not be invoked by the Inland Revenue.

10. Some further points on terminal losses.
    a) Capital allowances claimed including any balancing adjustments must be deducted from the assessments before terminal loss relief is applied.
    b) Normally relief under Section 380 would be claimed before any terminal loss relief, since the former is relief against total income.
    c) If there are any trade annual charges, such as patent royalties, then the terminal loss relief carried back is restricted in order to account for the income tax deducted at source.
    d) In calculating the amount of the terminal loss, capital allowances of the 12 month period not relieved elsewhere can be included. For businesses started after 6th April 1994 and existing ones from 1997/98 the terminal loss is automatically computed after deducting capital allowances.

Carry forward of annual payments and interest – Section 387 TA 1988

11. If a taxpayer makes a payment which is subject to deduction of income tax at source eg a royalty payment then the income tax must be accounted for to the Inland Revenue. Normally this is achieved by ensuring that an equivalent amount of income is actually chargeable to tax. However, if this is not possible a special Section 350 assessment is raised to recoup the income tax.

    In these circumstances, where the taxpayer incurs a trading loss and a Section 350 assessment is raised in respect of a charge made for the purpose of trade, then the Section 350 assessment can be carried forward and set against future trading income.

Transfer of a business to a limited company – Section 386 TA 1988

12. If a sole trader or partnership transfers its business to a limited company, there is a cessation of trade. Accordingly, trading losses at the date of transfer are not available for set-off against any future corporation tax profits of the new company.

    However, Section 386 provides some relief where the following conditions are met.

    a) The consideration for the business consists wholly or mainly in allotted shares of the company. In this case 80% is often taken to be equivalent to 'wholly'.

    b) The shares are beneficially held by the transferor throughout the period of any year of assessment for which a claim under Section 386 is made.

    c) The company carries on the same business throughout any year for which a claim is made.

    Relief is available in respect of trading losses (excluding capital allowances) from a former business which can be carried forward and they can be set against income received by the transferor from the company. The losses must be set against earned income first, eg directors' fees or remuneration, and then investment income, eg dividends.

    > **Example**

    D transfers his business to a limited company on the 1st August 1996 wholly for shares.

    At that date the business has trading losses of £10,000. In the year 1996/97 D receives director's remuneration of £8,000 and a net dividend of £800 from the company.

    Income tax computation 1996/97

	£
Schedule E director's remuneration	8,000
Less Section 386 loss	8,000
Schedule F dividend	1,000
Less Section 386 loss	1,000

    Notes

    i) With this example there would be trade losses to carry forward to 1997/98 of £1,000 providing the conditions noted above prevail.

    ii) In claiming the Section 386 relief for 1996/97. D has lost his personal allowances which cannot be carried forward.

    iii) A claim under Section 386 in effect involves Section 385, and is subject to most of the provisions relating to that section.

Relief for capital losses – Section 574 TA 1988

13. Under this section a loss made by an individual on the disposal of any unquoted shares can be set against his income for income tax purposes. The loss must arise from a number of shares *originally subscribed for* on the formation of the company, and not from an inheritance or subsequent acquisition.

    The claim is similar to a claim under Section 380 TA 1988, but takes precedence of relief under that section. The company must in general be a UK trading company at the date of the disposal. A qualifying loss can only be claimed in the following circumstances:

    a) on a disposal for full market value, or

    b) on a winding up, or

    c) on a claim that the shares have become of negligible value.

The loss is deducted from the taxpayer's income in the year in which the disposal takes place or in the preceding year, w.e.f. 1994/95.

Example

Z and his wife have the following data relating to 1997/98.

	£
Z Schedule E income	23,045
Mrs. Z Schedule E income	5,045
Z Building Society interest (net)	8,000
Z mortgage interest paid. MIRAS	1,500
Z allowable loss under Sec 574 TA 1988 arising from shares in A Ltd.	2,000

Compute the income tax liability for 1997/98 of Z and his wife.

Solution

Income tax computation 1997/98

	Z £	Mrs Z £
Earned income		
Schedule E Z.	23,045	-
Schedule E Mrs Z	–	5,045
	23,045	5,045
Unearned income		
Building society interest (gross)	10,000	–
	33,045	5,045
Less capital loss relief Sec 574	2,000	–
	31,045	5,045
Personal allowance	4,045	4,045
Taxable income	27,000	1,000

			Z £	Mrs Z £
Tax payable				
4,100 + 9,100 = 13,200 / 1,000	@ 20 %		2,640	200
12,900 / –	@ 23%		2,967	
900 / –	@ 40%		360	–
27,000 1,000			5,967	200
Less: income tax deducted from B.S.I.		2,000		
MCA @ 15%		274	2,274	–
			3,693	200

Notes

i)   *The relief for the capital loss is deducted from the earned income of Z in the computation. If this is insufficient it is set against his unearned income.*

ii) *As Z is paying tax at the 40% rate it would be tax efficient to transfer some of his investments to Mrs Z, to generate additional income in her own right.*

iii) *Mortgage interest has been ignored as relief is given at source at the 15% rate.*

Pre-trading expenditure – Section 401 TA 1988

14. Relief is available for expenditure incurred by a person in the seven years before he commences to carry on a trade (five years prior to 1.4.1993).

   a)   The expenditure must be allowable trading expenditure which would have been deducted in computing Case I or II trading income if incurred after the commencement of trading.

   b)   Such expenditure is treated as a trading loss of the year of assessment in which the trade commenced, to be claimed separately from any other loss relief.

   c)   The relief does not apply to pre-trading purchases of stock.

   d)   The loss may be relieved under Section 380, 385 and 381 TA 1988 for businesses started before 6th April 1995.

   e)   For businesses commencing on or after 6th April 1995 pre-trading expenditure is treated as an expense of the trade.

Example

T purchased a secondhand bookshop for £20,000 on 6th October 1996 which was closed for renovation until 6th April 1997 when trading commenced.

Trading account for the period to 5th April 1998

	£	£
Sales		95,000
Purchases	42,000	
Less Closing stock	3,500	38,500
Gross profit		56,500
Wages	23,700	
Motor expenses	3,800	
Costs of purchase of shop	5,000	
Rent and rates	2,400	
Heat and light	6,300	
Repairs and renewals	8,000	49,200
Trading profit		7,300

Notes

i) *£2,000 of the purchases were made before 6th April 1997.*

ii) *Private use of motor car has been agreed at 30%. All expenses incurred after 5th April 1997.*

iii) *Rent, rates, and heating and lighting have accrued over the period 6th October 1996 to 5th April 1997.*

iv) *Repairs includes £6,000 for repairs prior to 6th April 1997.*

Complete T's profits chargeable to income tax under Schedule D Case I for 1997/98 (ignore capital allowances).

Solution

Schedule D Case I 1997/98

	£	£	£
Trading profit per accounts			7,300
Add back:			
Cost of purchase of shop		5,000	
Motor expenses 30% × 3,800		1,140	
Pre-trading expenses	£		
Repairs	6,000		
Rent and rates 1/3 × 2,400	800		
Heat and light 1/3 × 6,300	2,100	8,900	15,040
Adjusted profit			22,340
Less Pre-trading allowable expenditure	£		
Repairs	6,000		
Rent and rates	800		
Heat and light	2,100		8,900
Case I income			13,440

Notes

i) *For businesses commencing on or after the 6th April 1995 pre-trading expenditure is treated as an expense of the business on the first day of trading.*

ii) *Capital allowances claimed would be deducted from the adjusted profits of £13,440 to arrive at the Case I profits for the period.*

Restrictions on claiming loss reliefs

15. a) A claim under Section 380 is only available to trades which are carried on with a view to profit, and on a commercial basis in year of assessment to which the claim relates (Sect 384).

b) Farmers and market gardeners cannot obtain relief under Section 380 if in the previous five years their business has incurred successive trade losses, unless it can be shown that the trade is being carried on with a view to profit, and there is a reasonable expectation of profits in the future (Section 397).

c) Loss relief under Section 385 is available in the earliest possible years only against the profits from the same trade, and not against total income or profits from any other trade.

Trading losses set against capital gains

16. Where a trading loss is incurred in the year then to the extent that it has not been fully relieved under Section 380 TA 1988, a claim for relief against any chargeable gain can be made. The amount to be claimed cannot exceed the chargeable gain for the year, before deducting the CGT exemption amount of £6,500, for 1997/98.

Example

N, who is single, has the following data relating to the year 1997/98:

	£
Schedule D Case I (CY to 31.3.98 loss)	17,000
Chargeable gains before exemption.	8,000

In the year to 31st March 1998 N has other income of £16,000.

Compute the income tax liability and CGT liability for 1997/98.

Solution

Income tax computation 1997/98

	£
Taxable income	16,000
less Section 380	16,000
	—

CGT computation 1997/98

	£
Chargeable gains	8,000
less trading losses	1,000
	7,000
less annual exemption	6,500
	500
CGT payable 200 @ 20%	100

Notes

i) *N's personal allowance of £4,045 would be wasted.*

ii) *The trading loss of £17,000 has been dealt with as follows:*

	£
Section 380 1997/98	*16,000*
Capital gain 1997/98	*1,000*

iii) *The CGT is changeable at the 20% rate in this case.*

• Student self-testing question

K who is married started trading in 1993 and has the following results:

	£
12 months to 30th June 1998	(5,000)
12 months to 30th June 1997	36,045

Mrs K has schedule E earnings for 1997/98 of £8,045 and net dividend income of £800. K pays mortgage interest (gross) of £1,000 during 1997/98 under the MIRAS scheme.

Compute the income tax liability of K and Mrs K for 1997/98 assuming he makes a claim for loss relief under Section 380.

Solution

Income tax computation 1997/98

	K £	Mrs K £
Earned income		
Schedule D Case I K (C.Y.)	36,045	–
Schedule E Mrs K	–	8,045
Unearned income		
Dividends (gross) Mrs K	–	1,000
	36,045	9,045
Less loss relief Section 380	5,000	–
	31,045	9,045
Less personal allowance	4,045	4,045
Taxable income	27,000	5,000

Tax payable	4,100 / 5,000	@ 20%	820	1,000
	22,000 /	@ 23%	5,060	–
	900 / –	@ 40%	360	–
	27,000 5,000		6,240	1,000
Less income tax deducted from dividends			–	200
Less deduction MCA @ 15%			274	–
			5,966	800

Notes

i)   *The lower rate band of £4,100 has been extended by £900, in respect of the dividend income of Mrs K which is chargeable at the 20% rate.*

ii) *The loss for the period of account 12 months to 30.6.1998 has been carried back to the preceding year under Section 380.*

• Questions without answers

1.   J, who is single, has the following data relating to 1997/98.

	£
Schedule D Case I – CY to 30.6.97	44,045
Schedule D Case I trade losses year to 30.6.1998	10,000
Dividend income (net)	800
Mortgage interest paid (net) MIRAS	800
Covenant to Oxfam (gross)	3,000

Compute J's income tax liability for 1997/98.

2.   T, who has been trading for many years, has the following results for the years ended 30th September:

	£	
30.9.95	62,000	
30.9.96	36,000	
30.9.97	(40,000)	loss
30.9.98 Estimate	20,000	

Compute the assessments for all available years.

19 Partnership taxation

Introduction

1. A partnership exists where two or more persons join together for business purposes forming an association which is not a separate legal entity.

   The main features of partnership taxation are discussed under the following main headings:

   > Part I – new businesses after 5.4.94 – existing 1997/98
   > Part II – transitional year 1996/97
   > Part III – existing businesses to 1995/96 (ie those trading at 5.4.1994)

PART I – new businesses after 5.4.94 – existing 1997/98

2. The following provisions apply to any new partnership starting after the 5th April and to partnerships deemed to start under the provisions of Section 113 TA 1988.

   a) For income tax purposes a partnership of two or more individuals is no longer treated as a separate entity distinct from the partners. The effect of this is that the partnership will no longer be assessed on the profits of the partnership. Instead each individual partner will be assessed individually.

   b) Taxable profits of the partnership are calculated in the same way as for a sole trader so that all partnership expenses and capital allowances will be given against the profits before allocation to the partners.

   c) Profits are assessed on a current year basis with the normal basis being the period of account ending in the year of assessment. The rules for computation of taxable profits in the first two and last year of the partnership are the same as for a sole trader noted in Chapter 15.

   d) Partnership profits are allocated by reference to the partnership rules applicable in the period of account and not the year of assessment.

   e) Where there is a change in the ownership of a partnership then providing that there is at least one partner carrying on the business both before and after the change then the change does not constitute a cessation for income tax purposes.

   f) The new rules apply to partnerships deemed to start after 5th April 1994 eg where an existing partnership does not make a continuation election under Section 113 TA 1988.

Adjustment and allocation of profits

3. The following points arise under this heading.

   a) Partnership profits are adjusted for income tax purposes using the same principles as for a sole trader. *See Chapter 14.* Partners' salaries and interest on capital paid to partners during the period of account are allocated to each partner individually and the balance of profit divided in profit-sharing ratios.

   b) The adjusted partnership profit is reduced by any capital allowances on partnership assets, before any allocation is made to the partners.

> **Example**

A and B formed a partnership in June 1994, sharing profits equally after charging interest of 10% p.a. on their fixed capital accounts of £8,000 and £5,000 respectively, and a salary for A of £5,000. Taxable profits for the year ended 31st December 1997 were £15,000.

Show the allocation of profits for 1997/98.

Solution   **Partnership Computation 1997/98**

Adjusted profits after capital allowances year to 31st December 1997 – £15,000

Allocation of Profit 1997/98

	Total £	A £	B £
Interest on capital: 10%	1,300	800	500
Salary – A	5,000	5,000	–
	6,300	5,800	500
Balance shared equally	8,700	4,350	4,350
	15,000	10,150	4,850

Notes

i)   *Each partner includes his share of profit, ie A. £10,150 B. £4,850 in his personal tax return, being earned income to be assessed in 1997/98.*

ii) *All amounts shown in the partnership accounts for the year to 31st December 1997, for partners' salaries, share of profits or interest on capital, will have been added back in arriving at the taxable profit of £15,000.*

| Example |

A and B enter into partnership on the 1st June 1994 with the following results:

	£	£
	Adjusted Profits	Capital Allowances
1. 6. 1994 – 31. 5. 1995	20,000	2,000
1. 6. 1995 – 31. 5. 1996	30,000	5,000

The partners have agreed to share profits equally.

Show the partners' taxable profits for the years of assessment.

Solution

	Partnership A and B		Assessments	
			A	B
1994/95	Period of account 1. 6. 94 – 5. 4. 95 $\dfrac{308}{365} \times (20,000 - 2,000)$	15,189	7,594	7,595
1995/96	Period of account 1. 6. 94 – 31. 5. 95 (20,000 – 2,000)	18,000	9,000	9,000
1996/97	Period of account 1. 6. 95 – 31. 5. 96 (30,000 – 5,000)	25,000	12,500	12,500

Notes:

i)   *The overlap period is 1. 6. 94 to 5. 4. 95 with taxable profits of £7,594 for each partner. When the partnership ceases, or a partner leaves, then the individuals' final assessment will incorporate the overlap relief*

ii) *Assessments are raised on the individuals in the partnership and not the partnership.*

Changes in partnership

4.   On a change of partners the rules are altered so that an automatic cessation or commencement will not arise, so far as the firm is concerned, on the admission, retirement or death of a partner.

No election for a continuation is required and there is an automatic continuation of the established current year basis provided at least one person is common to the partnership before and after the changes.

On a change of partners each partner is treated as having a separate share of the profits determined at the point of admission to and retirement from the firm.

| Example |

X and Y started in partnership on 1st July 1994 sharing profits equally. Their accounts are made up to 31st December each year. On 1st January 1997 Z is admitted as an equal partner, the profit ratio then becoming one third each.

Profits for the years to 31st December 1997 are as follows:

	£
1.7.1994 – 31.12.1994	20,000
12 months to 31.12.95	40,000
12 months to 31.12.96	50,000
12 months to 31.12.97	60,000

Solution

			X £	Y £	Z £
1994/95	1.7.94 – 31.12.94	20,000			
	$1.1.95 – 5.4.95 \; \frac{90}{365} \times 40,000$	9,863	29,863	14,931	14,932	–
1995/96	12 months to 31.12.95		40,000	20,000	20,000	–
1996/97	12 months to 31.12.96		50,000	25,000	25,000	–
	$1.1.97 – 5.4.97 \; \frac{95}{365} \times 60,000 \times \frac{1}{3}$		5,205	–	–	5,205
			55,205	25,000	25,000	5,205
1997/98	12 months to 31.12.97		60,000	20,000	20,000	20,000

Notes

i) When Z is admitted on 1st January 1997, there is an automatic continuation.

ii) The partners are assessed individually in respect of their shares of the profits.

iii) On Z's admission he is deemed to have started in business on 1st January 1997 and his individual overlap profit must be computed on that date. This is as follows:

1.1.97 – 5.4.97 = 95 days

$$\frac{95}{365} \times 60,000 \times \frac{1}{3} = 5,205$$

iv) When a partner retires, his or her due proportion of the overlap profits is adjusted in his or her final assessment.

v) Total profits assessed of £185,068 – Overlap reliefs (9,863 + 5,205) = actual profits.

Example

Using the data for X, Y and Z in the above example with the following results:

12 months to 31.12.98	80,000
12 months to 31.12.99	90,000
12 months to 31.12.00	100,000

Z leaves the partnership on the 30th September 2000.

Solution

			Total	X	Y	Z
1998/99	CY to 31.12.98		80,000	26,667	26,667	26,666
1999/00	CY to 31.12.99		90,000	30,000	30,000	30,000
2000/01	CY to 31.12.00	1.1.00 – 30.9.00				
		$\frac{273}{365} \times 100,000$	74,795	24,932	24,932	24,931
		Less overlap relief				(5,205)
		1.10.00 – 31.12.00				
		100,000 – 74,795	25,205	12,603	12,602	–

Notes

i) Z's assessment for the year 2000/01 comprises:

Proportion of profits from 1st January 2000 – 30th Sept 2000 =	24,931
Less overlap relief on commencement (see previous example)	5,205
	19,726

ii) There will be an automatic continuation on the retirement of Z.

Non-trading income

5. a) Non-trading partnership income has always been taxed separately on each partner according to his or her share and has never been jointly assessed. The current year basis brings no change in this respect, although there is a change in the way in which the income is

calculated. Unless the income is received net of tax, it is taxed under the current year basis rules, by reference to the same periods as the trading income, normally according to the income of the accounting year ended in the tax year.

Where a partner joins a partnership after 5 April 1994, the current year basis will apply to his or her share of non-trading income at once, despite it not applying to his or her trading income if a continuation election is made.

b) Although the transitional provisions give relief for the fact that one year's interest has been taxed twice under the previous year basis rules, by taxing only half of the 1995/96 and 1996/97 interest (and the rules of Schedule A already charge rent on an actual basis), the change to an 'accounting year basis' for non-trading income may nevertheless mean that some income might be taxed both under the old and the new rules. Overlap relief applies to eliminate the double charge.

PART II – transitional year 1996/97

5. a) The rules for the aggregation of the profits of the notional CY period and the relevant period as noted in Chapter 15 apply to partnerships.

b) For most businesses the assessment for 1996/97 will be based on 50% of the average profits for the two accounting periods ending in 1996/97, ie. 1995/96 and 1996/97.

c) Profits will be allocated amongst the partners in accordance with the profit-sharing ratios applicable in the year of assessment 1996/97.

d) The assessment for 1996/97 will be made on the partnership and not the individual partners as is the case w.e.f. 1997/98.

> **Example**

A, B and C have been in partnership for many years with the following results:

		£
Adjusted profits	31.12.1994	30,000
	31.12.1995	40,000
	31.12.1996	50,000

Profits are shared equally. Capital allowances for 1996/97 have been agreed at £6,000.

Compute the assessment for the transitional year 1996/97.

Solution

		£
1996/97 Adjusted profits 1.1.95 – 31.12.96 = $\frac{40000 + 50000}{2}$ =		45,000
Less capital allowances		6,000
		39,000
Assessment	A	13,000
	B	13,000
	C	13,000
		39,000

Note

The partnership is assessed in the sum of £39,000.

PART III – existing businesses to 1995/96

Main features

7. The main features of partnership taxation are as follows.

a) Although a partnership is not a separate legal entity like a company, a joint assessment is made in the name of the partnership in respect of its trading income.

b) Trading income is computed in accordance with the normal rules of income tax. Partnership's salaries and interest on capital charged in the accounts are added back in the computation.

c) Trading income is allocated to the partners after taking into consideration salaries and interest on capital and profit-sharing ratios pertaining to the year of assessment. The total allocation is earned income, except for a sleeping partner.

    d)   Partnership non-trading income and charges on income are not dealt with in the partnership assessment. Each partner is assessed separately in respect of his or her due proportion.

    e)   Each partner must file an individual tax return in the normal way. Personal reliefs are usually given against non-trading income first.

    f)   The normal commencement and cessation rules of assessment apply, with additional rules where there is a change of membership of a partnership.

    g)   Capital allowances are available in respect of partnership assets and these are deducted from the adjusted profits before any allocation is made. Capital allowances claimed on non-partnership assets are deducted in the individual partners personal tax computation.

Basis of assessment – existing business to 1996/97

8.   The normal basis of assessment for income arising under Schedule D Cases I and II applies, that is the preceding year. Thus the adjusted partnership trading income for the accounting year to 30th June 1994 would be assessed in the income tax year 1995/96. The allocation of profits between the respective partners is determined by reference to the profit-sharing criteria prevailing during the year of assessment and not the preceding year.

> ### Example

Adjusted trading income to 30.6.1994

Year of assessment 1995/96

Allocated according to agreement in force between 6.4.95 and 5.4.96.

The usual rules for commencement and cessation of trading apply and in particular these can be invoked where there is a change in the membership of the partnership in the circumstances noted below.

Changes in partnerships – existing businesses to 1996/97

9.   A change in a partnership arises if a partner retires or dies, or where a new partner is admitted, and special provisions apply in these situations.

Under Section 113 (2) TA 1988, an election can be made to treat the partnership as a continuing business, ie to be taxed on the preceding year basis, providing:

    a)   There is at least one partner common to both the old and the new partnership.

    b)   The election for continuation is made within two years of the date of the change.

    c)   The election is made in writing signed by all the old and the new partners.

In the absence of an election under Section 113 (2), then Section 113 (1) invokes the commencement and cessation provisions applicable to new businesses.

Commencement provisions – new partnerships

    a)   The normal cessation provisions apply, ie Section 63.

    b)   The actual basis of assessment is to be used for the year in which the change takes place and for the next three years.

    c)   The normal preceding year basis applies for the fifth and subsequent years unless the partnership elects for the fifth and sixth years to be charged on an actuals basis also.

    d)   The above changes do not apply where:
       i)   a sole trader takes on one or more partners, or
      ii)   a partnership is reduced to a sole trader.

Notes

    i)   *With effect from 1997/98 a cessation of partnership will not occur if there is at least one partner carrying on business both before and after the change.*

   ii)   *Where an existing partnership changes after 5th April 1994 without an election for continuation being made then the new rules noted in Section 15 apply.*

Summary of basis of assessment

10. (Change in partnership – no election for continuation basis)

Year of assessment	Usual basis of assessment	Basis where taxpayer elects for actual basis
First	AB	AB
Second	AB	AB
Third	AB	AB
Fourth	AB	AB
Fifth	PY	AB
Sixth	PY	AB
Subsequent years	PY	PY

Note

AB: Actual basis or current year basis, ie from 6 April in year (or date of commencement, if later) to the following 5 April.

PY: Preceding year basis, ie the profit, if any, for the 12 month accounts ending in the preceding year of assessment.

Once the assessment has been computed it is allocated between the partners as they divide profits in the year of assessment and not for the basis period.

11. | *Example* |

X and Y who have been in partnership for many years with an accounting year end to 30th June admit Z as a partner as from 1st January 1996, electing for continuation under Section 113 (2).

The following data applies:		To 31.12.95 £	From 1.1.96 £
Capital accounts:	X	10,000	10,000
	Y	7,000	7,000
	Z	–	4,000
Salaries:	X	8,000	10,000
	Y	6,000	9,000
	Z	–	7,000
Interest on capital:	X	10%	10%
	Y	10%	10%
	Z		10%
Profit-sharing ratios:		$^1/_2$	$^1/_3$
	X		
	Y	$^1/_2$	$^1/_3$
	Z	–	$^1/_3$

Adjusted profits after capital allowances for the year to 30th June 1994 were £36,000.

Compute the allocation of profits for the year 1995/96.

Solution

Allocation of profits 1995/96

	Total £	X £	Y £	Z £
9 months to 31.12.95				
$^3/_4 \times £36,000 = £27,000$				
Salaries X $^3/_4 \times £8,000$	6,000	6,000		
Y $^3/_4 \times £6,000$	4,500		4,500	
Interest on capital				
X $^3/_4 \times £1,000$	750	750		
Y $^3/_4 \times £700$	525		525	
Balance $^1/_2 : ^1/_2$	15,225	7,612	7,613	
	27,000	14,362	12,638	

	Total £	X £	Y £	Z £
3 months to 31.3.96				
$\frac{1}{4} \times £36,000 = £9,000$				
Salaries X $\frac{1}{4} \times £10,000$	2,500	2,500		
Y $\frac{1}{4} \times £9,000$	2,250		2,250	
Z $\frac{1}{4} \times £7,000$	1,750			1,750
Interest on capital				
X $\frac{1}{4} \times £1,000$	250	250		
Y $\frac{1}{4} \times £700$	175		175	
Z $\frac{1}{4} \times £400$	100			100
Balance X $\frac{1}{3}$: Y $\frac{1}{3}$: Z $\frac{1}{3}$	1,975	658	659	658
	9,000	3,408	3,084	2,508
Add 9 months to 31.12.95	27,000	14,362	12,638	–
Total assessment	36,000	17,770	15,722	2,508

Notes

i) There will be two partnership assessments for 1995/96,
    one on each partnership: X and Y

	£
X and Y	27,000
X, Y and Z	9,000
	36,000

ii) As a change occurred on the year of assessment 1995/96, agreed profits for that year must be
    allocated on the basis of profit sharing in the year 1995/96 and not the basis year to 30th June
    1994.

Partnership trading losses – existing businesses to 1996/97

12. a) Where the partnership sustains a loss, after any capital allowances, then this must be
        allocated amongst the partners in the normal way. Each partner claims and utilises his or her
        share of the loss according to personal circumstances.

b) If the partnership does not incur an adjusted loss after capital allowances, but as a result of
    the allocation, one of the partners has a 'loss', then this must be reallocated to the other
    partners.

> **Example**

X, Y and Z are in partnership sharing profits equally after salaries for 1995/96 of £8,000 for X;
£10,000 for Y; £12,000 for Z.

There was an adjusted loss for the accounting year to 30th June 1994 of £10,000, and capital
allowances available amounted to £2,000.

Show the allocation of the partnership loss for 1995/96.

Solution

Partnership computation 1995/96

	£
Adjusted loss	10,000
Add – Capital allowances	2,000
	12,000

Allocation of loss 1995/96

	Total £	X £	Y £	Z £
Salaries	30,000	8,000	10,000	12,000
Share of loss	(42,000)	(14,000)	(14,000)	(14,000)
	(12,000)	(6,000)	(4,000)	(2,000)

Notes

i) Capital allowances are added to the adjusted trading loss of £10,000 and not deducted.

ii) Each partner would be able to claim relief under Section 380 for his or her share of the
    allocated loss or carry it forward under Section 385.

> **Example**

R, S and T are in partnership sharing profits equally after salaries of £4,000 for R, £2,500 for S and £500 for T.

The adjusted profits for the year ended 31st December 1994 were £1,000, after capital allowances.

Show the allocation of profits for the year 1995/96.

Solution

Allocation of profit 1995/96

	Total £	R £	S £	T £
Salaries	7,000	4,000	2,500	500
Balance of profit	(6,000)	(2,000)	(2,000)	(2,000)
	1,000	2,000	500	(1,500)
Deficit of T allocated to R and S in ratio 2,000 : 500		(1,200)	(300)	1,500
	1,000	800	200	–

Notes

i) *As the partnership did not incur an adjusted net loss then T cannot claim any loss relief and his deficit must be reallocated to the other partners proportionately.*

ii) *Terminal loss relief is only available to a partner when he or she ceases to be engaged in the trade.*

13. If a claim for loss relief is made by a partner under Section 380 then the partnership loss is first allocated in accordance with the profit-sharing arrangements for the year of assessment in which the loss arises. This is necessary as it will be recalled that Section 380 relief is initially available against statutory total income of the year in which the loss arises. *See Chapter 17.*

Where a claim is made under Section 385, then the allocation of profits is made in accordance with the profit-sharing ratios for the accounting period in which the loss arises.

> **Example**

X, Y and Z have an adjusted loss for the year to 30.9.1993.

Section 380   This could be claimed in 1993/94, ie the year the loss is recognised, and allocated to the partners in accordance with the partnership agreement covering the period 6.4.1993 to 5.4.1994.

Section 385 relief   If a claim is made to carry the loss forward to 1994/95 then the loss is split in accordance with the partnership agreement relating to the accounting period of the loss ie 1.10.1992 to 30.9.1993.

Sleeping partners

14. A sleeping partner is one who does not actively participate in the management and business of the partnership, and in that respect is similar to a limited partner under the Limited Partnership Act 1907.

   a) Profits and losses are allocated in the normal way to each partner by reference to the profit-sharing arrangements of the period of account.

   b) The allocated share of a sleeping partner is not earned income for income tax purposes.

   c) If a loss is incurred by the partnership, a sleeping partner can make a claim for relief under Section 380 or 385.

   d) The amount of a limited partner's share of a loss of a limited partnership, that he or she may set against other income, is restricted. In effect it is limited to the amount which he or she actually has at risk in the partnership. Any balance of unrelieved loss can be carried forward and set against future profits from the partnership.

Corporate partners

15. Where a partnership exists with a company as one of the partners then the special rules outlined in Chapter 34 apply.

• Student self-testing question

X and Y started in business as partners on 1st July 1994 sharing profits equally after the provision of a salary of £5,000 to Y. Agreed taxable profits are as follows:

	£
1.7.94 – 31.12.94	12,000
12 months to 31.12.95	24,000
12 months to 31.12.96	36,000

Show the assessments for all available years.

Solution

		Total £	Y £	Z £
1994/95	1.7.94 – 31.12.94	12,000		
	$1.1.95 - 5.4.95 \frac{90}{365} \times 24,000$	6,246	18,246	
	Salary Y $\frac{90}{365} \times 5,000$	1,301		1,301
		16,945	– 8,472	8,473
		18,246	8,472	9,774
1995/96	1.1.95 – 31.12.95	24,000	24,000	
	Salary	5,000	–	5,000
		19,000	– 9,500	9,500
		24,000	9,500	14,500
1996/97	1.1.96 – 31.12.96	36,000	36,000	
		5,000	–	5,000
		31,000	– 15,500	15,500
		36,000	15,500	20,500

Notes

i) Overlap profits = £6,246 (18,246 + 24,000 + 36,000 – 6,246 = 72,000).

ii) Each partner has his own overlap profit share which in this case is £3,123 for each partner.

• Questions without answers

1. J and K started in partnership on 1st August 1994, sharing profits equally.
   L was admitted as a partner on 1st January 1997, with a one-third share of the profits.
   Results for the years to 31st December 1997 are as follows:

	£
1 August 1994 to 31st December 1994	20,000
Year to 31st December 1995	16,000
Year to 31st December 1996	24,000
Year to 31st December 1997	32,000

   Compute the assessments for all years.

2. X, Y and Z have been in partnership for many years sharing profits equally. Results for the two years ended 31st December 1996 are as follows:

	£ Profits
31.12.1995	26,000
31.12.1996	(12,000) loss

   Capital allowances for 1996/97 have been agreed at £3,000.

   Compute the profits assessable for 1996/97 and show how the loss may be dealt with.

20 Personal investment I – pensions and retirement annuities

Introduction

1. This chapter is concerned mainly with the deduction from taxable income of premiums paid to secure a personal pension by individuals in self employment. The rules applicable to personal pension plans for individuals, are also noted.

Self-employed – main provisions

2. Qualifying premiums paid to secure a personal pension plan by a self-employed person are allowed as a deduction in computing taxable income subject to certain conditions.

    a) The premiums must be made to provide for a pension payable during the life of the individual, to commence normally between the ages of 60 and 75. The pension may be payable to the individual's widow or personal representative.

    b) The relief claimed is a percentage of 'net relevant earnings' with higher percentages for those over the age of 35 at the beginning of the year of assessment, depending on the type of contract.

    c) Net relevant earnings from any trade, profession or vocation are equal to the following:

    > Taxable profits + balancing charges
    > *less*
    > Capital allowances
    > Charges on income related to business purposes
    > Loss reliefs such as those under Sections 380 and 385 TA 1988

    d) The relief for premiums paid is given in the year of assessment of the payment. However, if the taxpayer so elects before the end of the income tax year, relief may be carried back to the previous year, or to the year prior to that year in certain circumstances.

    e) Unused relief, ie where the amount of the premiums paid is less than the percentage of net relevant earnings, may be carried forward for up to six years.

    f) The relief is given as a deduction from relevant earnings in the computation.

    g) With effect from 1st July 1988 no *new* retirement annuity contracts can be taken out.

Percentage of net relevant earnings

3. The percentage of net relevant earnings available as a deduction depends upon the age of the taxpayer and whether or not he or she has a personal pension plan or retirement annuity scheme (Section 226).

    a)

    Personal pension plans 1997/98

Age at beginning of year of assessment	Maximum % of net relevant earnings
up to 35	$17\frac{1}{2}$
36–45	20
46–50	25
51–55	30
56–60	35
61–	40

    Notes

    i)   With a personal pension plan there is an upper net relevant earnings level of £84,000 for 1997/98.

    ii) The maximum tax-free lump sum taken at retirement age is set at 25% of the fund.

    b)

    Retirement annuity contracts existing at 30th June 1988

1987/88 to 1997/98	Age at beginning of year of assessment	Maximum % of net relevant earnings
	up to 50	$17\frac{1}{2}$
	51–55	20
	56–60	$22\frac{1}{2}$
	61–	$27\frac{1}{2}$

Notes

i)   With a retirement annuity contract there is no maximum amount of net relevant earnings to which the percentage is applied.

ii) The maximum tax-free lump sum taken at retirement age is currently set at 30% of the fund.

4. | Example |

Z who was born in 1968 has been in business since 1983. His adjusted profits for the year ended 31st December 1997 were £16,000.

Capital allowances have been agreed at £4,400.

During 1997/98 he made payments under an approved personal pension plan of £2,500. At 6th April 1997 there was unused relief of £250 from 1996/97. Z is married with no other income. Calculate Z's income tax liability for 1997/98, and indicate the amount of unused PP relief, if any, as at 5th April 1998.

Income tax computation 1997/98

	£	£
Schedule D Case I		16,000
Less capital allowances		4,400
		11,600
PPP 17½% × 11,600 (max)	2,030	
Premiums paid	2,500	
	470	
Unused relief b/f	250	
Unrelieved premium	220	
Total premium relief (2,030 + 250)		2,280
		9,320
Personal allowance		4,045
Taxable income		5,275
Tax payable 4,100 @ 20%		820.00
1,175 @ 23%		270.25
5,275		1,090.25
Less deduction for MCA @ 15% × 1,830		274.00
		816.25

Note:

The maximum rate for age up to 35 is 17.5% of relevant earnings with a PPP.

5. | Example |

A, who is single, aged 45, has Schedule D Case I income from his business of £27,000 for the year ended 31st December 1997, and capital allowances of £4,000.

He pays a personal pension plan premium of £4,400 and mortgage interest of £900 (net) during 1997/98. The mortgage interest is in respect of A's house and is a MIRAS Loan.

Compute A's income tax liability for 1997/98.

Solution

Relevant earnings 1997/98

	£	£	£
Schedule D case I income	27,000		
Less capital allowances	4,000	23,000	
Maximum relief 20% × 23,000		4,600	

Income tax computation 1997/98

	£	£
Schedule D Case I as above	23,000	
Personal pension plan Premiums paid		
	4,400	18,600
Personal allowance		4,045
Taxable income		14,555

Income tax payable   £

4,100	@ 20%	820.00
10,455	@ 23%	2,404.65
14,555		3,224.65

Note

Maximum relief for a person aged 45 is 20% of relevant earnings, with a personal pension plan.

Premiums related back

6. Under Section 641 TA 1988, where an individual pays a qualifying premium under personal pension plan or retirement annuity in a year of assessment he or she may elect before the end of that year that the premium (or part of it) be treated as being paid

   i) in the year of assessment preceding that year

   ii) if there was no relevant earnings for that year, in the year before that one.

   Where such election is made the premium is treated as being paid in the previous year and not in the year of the payment.

Retirement annuity relief (RAR) / personal pension plan (PPP)

7. Where the taxpayer has net relevant earnings available for relief under an existing retirement annuity contract or personal pension plan then the following should be considered:

   a) Retirement annuity premiums take precedence over personal pension contributions in allocating relief.

   b) If an individual has both types of contract then the aggregate relief is limited to the PPP relief.

   c) If the maximum payable to a PPP plus unused relief brought forward is greater than the amount paid to an RAR contract then the difference can be paid to a PPP.

> **Example**

T who is aged 40 has net relevant earnings of £100,000 for 1997/98. He pays £12,000 with an existing RAR contract and £2,000 personal pension plan.

Calculate the maximum amount of contribution for 1997/98.

Solution

	£
Maximum RAR $17\frac{1}{2}\% \times 100,000$	17,500
Maximum PPP $20\% \times 84,000$	16,800

Full relief for the payments of £14,000 (£12,000 + £2,000 PPP) can be given as they are within the PPP limit of £16,800. Additional relief in respect of £2,800 for a PPP or RAR would be available as this would bring the total to £16,800.

Early retirement ages

8. Under Section 634 TA 1988 the Inland Revenue may permit a retirement pension to commence before the annuitant's 50th birthday, if the individual's occupation is in one in which persons automatically retire before attaining the age of 50. The latest list issued by the OPB includes the following:

Boxers	35	Footballer	35	Skier	30
Cricketers	40	Golfers	40	Jockey (NH)	35
Tennis players	35	Jockeys (flat)	45	Cyclist	35

Individuals in employment

9. An outline of the new provisions under this heading is given below.

   a) From October 1987 individuals in occupational pension schemes have the right to pay 'free standing' additional contributions to a separate pension plan of their own right, up to 15% of their earnings less voluntary contributions made to the company scheme by employees (AVCS).

   b) For employees not in a company pension scheme tax relief on contributions is limited to a maximum of $17\frac{1}{2}\%$ of net relevant earnings with an increased percentage for individuals over the age of 35 at the beginning of the year of assessment. The rates for 1997/98 are:

Age	%
35 or less	17.5
36-45	20.0
46-50	25.0
51-55	30.0
56-60	35.0
61 and over	40.0

c) Net relevant earnings for an individual in employment means:
   Emoluments from any office or employment less expenses deductible under Sections 198, 201 and 332 (3) TA 1988.

d) Payments made under an approved personal pension scheme will be subject to deduction at source of an amount equal to basic rate income tax. Relief at the higher rates of tax will be given by way of adjustment in the total tax assessment for the year, usually by 'extended base rate'.

e) Where an employer makes a contribution then this must be taken into account in determining the maximum percentage deduction of $17\frac{1}{2}\%$, or higher amount for older taxpayers.

f) Any approved contributions made by the employer are not regarded as emoluments chargeable to tax under Schedule E.

g) Tax relief is limited to contributions on earnings up to a level of £82,200 (1995/96 £78,600).

h) Unused AVC relief is not available to be carried forward or backward.

Example

P was self-employed from 1992/93 to 1995/96 with the following agreed Schedule D Assessments:

	£
1992/93	14,000
1993/94	30,000
1994/95	28,000
1995/96	33,000

From 6th April 1996 P became employed with an annual salary of £35,000 from which he pays 6% to an approved company pension scheme. The company contributes 5% to the scheme.

P was born on the 6th January 1958 and has paid no previous amounts to any pension scheme.

Compute the maximum amount which P could pay to provide for a pension.

Solution

a)

	Net Relevant Earnings	%	Maximum
1992/93	14,000	$17\frac{1}{2}$	2,450
1993/94	30,000	$17\frac{1}{2}$	5,250
1994/95	28,000	20	5,600
1995/96	33,000	20	6,600
			19,900

Notes

i) *Premiums of £19,900 must be paid before 5th April 1997 and election made to carry back to 1995/96.*

ii) *Schedule D Assessment for 1995/96 is sufficient to cover the maximum premium carried back.*

b) For 1996/97 and subsequent years P could pay additional voluntary contributions computed as follows.

Maximum AVC 15% × 35,000	=	5,250
less Voluntary contributions 6% × 35,000	=	2,100
		3,150

• Question without answer

Fred has been a self-employed builder for 20 years. He was born on 31 August 1935 and is contemplating retirement in a few years' time. He consults you in early June 1996 about the payment of premiums into a personal pension scheme. He has paid annual premiums of £5,000 for each of the past seven years and assures you he has enough money to pay the maximum amount allowed.

Fred's agreed taxable profits for the past seven years are:

	£
1989-90	18,000
1990-91	20,000
1991-92	22,000
1992-93	24,000
1993-94	26,000
1994-95	28,000
1995-96	30,000

He expects his taxable profits to be at least £30,000 for the next two tax years.

Calculate the additional premiums which Fred is permitted to pay and advise him when to pay the premiums to obtain the maximum tax advantage.

(ACCA)

21 Personal investment II – miscellaneous

Introduction

1. This chapter is concerned with the income tax effects of certain forms of personal investment, dealt with under the following headings:

    Personal Equity Plans
    Enterprise Investment Scheme
    Venture Capital Trusts
    Insurance Bonds
    Purchased Life Annuities
    Capital Bonds (National Savings)
    Tax Exempt Special Savings Accounts
    Scrip Dividends
    Non-taxable income
    Income not taxed at source.

Personal equity plans

2. Under the provisions of Section 333, and Schedule 29 TA 1988, UK residents aged 18 and over may invest up to £6,000 p.a. in a general PEP and £3,000 in a company PEP, and obtain income tax relief on dividends and interest received.

    The main features of the scheme are as follows.

    a) Up to £6,000 can be invested p.a. in approved general PEP funds, and £3,000 in a company PEP.

    b) Dividends and interest accruing, which are not decreed to be part of the £9,000 annual limit, are reinvested in the PEP fund and the tax reclaimed by the fund managers on behalf of the investor.

    c) Married couples are treated as separate individuals so that each can invest the maximum amount of £9,000 p.a.

    d) Dividends arising on shares and units held in the plan are entirely free of income tax, at the 20% rate.

    e) Investment by way of subscription by an individual in a PEP plan must be in cash. However, subject to the rules of the plan, it will be possible for investors to transfer new issues and privatisation shares into their PEP plans. The value of the shares (at the offer price) will count towards the overall investment limit.

    f) PEP investments are beneficially owned by the investor but the title remains in the name of the plan manager or his or her nominee who also retains the share certificates.

    g) Income tax deducted at source from dividends is reclaimed by the plan manager and reinvested in the plan. This income is not subject to the higher rate of tax on the investor.

    h) Sales of investments under the plan are exempt from capital gains tax.

    i) When plan investments are withdrawn after the expiry of the time contained in the plan, the investor is deemed to have acquired them at market value, for CGT purposes.

    j) Details of PEPs are not required to be included in Tax Returns.

    k) Initial and annual charges may exceed the tax benefits and need to be evaluated carefully, especially for basic rate taxpayers.

Enterprise investment scheme (EIS)

3. The main features of the EIS which applies to shares issued after the 1st January 1994 are as follows.

    a) An individual can invest up to £100,000 in any tax year and obtain relief at the 20% rate against his or her taxable income.

    b) To qualify for relief the eligible shares must be held for at least five years in an unquoted trading company.

    c) 50% of the amount invested by an individual in between 6th April and 5th October in any year can be carried back to the previous income tax year subject to a maximum of £15,000.

    d) Capital gains tax on chargeable gains arising from disposals of any assets after 28th November 1994 may be deferred where such gains are invested in subscription for shares in an EIS.

Venture capital trusts

4. A new scheme for venture capital trusts is established from 6th April 1995, the main features of which are as follows.

a) The scheme is designed to stimulate individual investment in a spread of unquoted trading companies through the mechanism of quoted venture capital trusts.

b) Individuals can invest up to £100,000 p.a. attracting income tax relief at the 20% rate providing the shares are held for five years.

c) Dividends received are tax free.

d) Profits on the disposal of shares within the trust are exempt from CGT.

e) Chargeable gains arising on or after 6th April 1995 on any other asset may be rolled over into an investment in a VCT.

Life insurance bonds (non-qualifying policies)

5. a) An insurance bond is a non-qualifying life insurance policy where the investment is often made in a unit linked form. As the policy is non-qualifying there is no life assurance relief available.

b) Partial surrender of the policies is permitted on an annual basis without incurring any additional taxation payment. The maximum withdrawal that can be made each policy year is $\frac{1}{20} \times$ the original (usually single) premium.

c) If withdrawal is not made in any one year then the 5% can be carried forward and used in the next or subsequent year.

d) Where the withdrawals exceed the 5% level then the gain is subject to higher rate tax on the recipient, subject to top slicing relief. Basic rate income tax is in effect paid by the insurance company before the amount withdrawn is paid to the investor.

e) When the bond is finally cashed, the chargeable gain is equal to the policy proceeds plus all encashments less the initial investment outlay.

f) For the purposes of computing the income tax due, these chargeable event gains are deemed to fall after dividend income and before capital gains.

g) Proposals currently under discussion with the Inland Revenue may have far reaching effects on the taxation on life assurance linked investments.

Example

F, a single man, invests £16,000 in an insurance bond on 1st January 1992 and withdraws 4% in each of the next four years, cashing in the policy for £20,000 in May 1996. F's income for 1996/97 consists of £27,000 Schedule E, and Schedule D Case III £2,765.

Calculate F's income tax liability for 1996/97.

Solution

		1996/97 £
i)	**Gain on insurance bond**	
	Policy proceeds	20,000
	Add withdrawals 4% × £16,000 × 4	2,560
		22,560
	Less Original premium	16,000
	Amount assessable (chargeable event gain)	6,560
ii)	**Income tax computation 1996/97**	
	Schedule E	27,000
	Schedule D Case III	2,765
		29,765
	Less personal allowance	3,765
	Taxable income	26,000
	Tax payable 3,900 @ 20%	780
	21,600 @ 24%	5,184
	500 @ 40%	200
	26,000	6,164

Tax payable on the insurance bond   **£**

1,640 @ 40% = 656

less 1,640 @ 24% = 394

262 × 4 years =   1,048

Notes

i)   The amount of the assessable bond is top sliced by reference to the number of completed policy years at the date of the surrender ie 6,560/4 = 1,640 for 1996/97.

ii) If F's taxable income for 1996/97 together with the top sliced insurance bond had not brought him into the higher rate band of 40% there would have been no further tax to pay on surrender.

iii) For individuals whose marginal rate of tax is likely to fall in future years (eg those approaching retirement) then the bonds can be used to avoid paying tax at the higher rate.

iv) The chargeable event gain is income and must be included in the calculation of PAA restriction for income greater than £15,200.

Purchased life annuities

6.   A purchased life annuity involves the investor paying an initial capital sum for the right to receive an annual amount over either a fixed term of years or for life. Each annual receipt therefore comprises of two elements:

   i)   a repayment of part of the original capital

   ii) an income element, usually the balance.

> **Example**

Z purchased a life annuity of £3,000 p.a. in January 1998 for a capital outlay of £25,000. Assuming that the capital element of the annuity has been actuarially agreed at £2,500 p.a. with the Inland Revenue, *show the amount receivable by Z for 1997/98.*

Solution

Purchased annuity 1997/98

		£
Capital element of annuity		2,500
Balance of annuity (3000 – 2500)	500	
Less income tax @ 23%	115	385
Net amount receivable		2,885

Note

Z would be liable for any higher rate tax where this applied, on the gross amount of £500.

National savings capital bonds

7.   National Savings Capital Bonds are a government security issued by the Treasury under the National Loans Act 1968, in January 1989. They are a new form of investment, the main features of which are:

   1)   They are obtainable in multiples of £100 from a Post Office or direct from the Capital Bonds office in Glasgow.

   2)   If kept for a period of five years an investment of £100 in the latest issue would accumulate to £137.96 which is equivalent to a compound interest rate of 6.65% p.a.

   3)   At the end of the five year period the bonds are repaid in full with all the interest earned.

   4)   If the bonds are cashed within the five year period (by giving three months' notice) then a lower rate of interest is obtained.

   5)   The interest earned each year and added to the bond is taxable in that year even though there is no actual receipt of money. This recurs when the bond is either encashed or the five year period is attained.

   6)   Taxpayers will be liable to income tax at both the basic and higher rates, where appropriate.

Tax exempt special savings account (TESSA)

8.   The FA 1990 introduced this new form of savings investment which became available from 1st January 1991 to anyone over the age of 18. The main features of the scheme are as follows:

   a)   Any individual over the age of 18 will be able to open one TESSA with a bank or building society.

   b)   Up to £9,000 may be deposited over a period of 5 years. Up to £3,000 may be invested in the first year and up to £1,800 in each subsequent year provided the maximum is not exceeded.

c) During the five year period the interest will be exempt from income tax if retained in the account and need not be recorded on the Tax Returns.

d) Interest can be withdrawn up to the amount credited to the account in the five year period but this will be subject to deduction at source of income tax at the lower rate.

e) After the five year period the amount will cease to be tax exempt. However, on maturity the capital amount can be rolled over into a new TESSA, if this is done within six months of maturing.

f) Interest on the TESSA is not included in the taxpayer's income for the purpose of computing the PAA restriction where the income is greater than £15,600 for 1997/98, unless the TESSA becomes disqualified.

g) Some TESSAs allow the payment of income (net) monthly or quarterly.

Scrip dividends

9. Where a taxpayer elects to receive additional shares in a company rather than receive a cash dividend then the following rules apply.

a) The shareholder is deemed to have received gross payments of an amount equal to the cash dividend equivalent plus the lower rate income tax ie 20%. Thus if an individual receives shares worth £80.00 he or she will be treated as having received a gross dividend of £100.00 less £20.00 lower rate income tax.

b) The cash equivalent price is the value of the shares at the date of the offer subject to an adjustment to the market value on the day when dealings take place in the new shares where this is different by 15% either way.

c) Individuals liable to income tax at the lower or basic rate of income tax have no further liability to income tax.

d) Taxpayers at the higher rate will pay income tax at the difference between the higher rate and the lower rate ie 40% – 20% = 20% for 1997/98.

e) Individuals who do not pay any income tax are not entitled to reclaim any of the lower rate tax attached to the cash equivalent dividend.

Non-taxable income

10. The following types of income are exempt from taxation.

1) The first £70 of interest on deposits with the National Savings Bank held in the Ordinary Accounts. Husband and wife may each claim £70 on separate accounts. Interest on investment accounts of the NSB, and on accounts with Trustee Savings Banks are fully taxable.

2) Interest on all National Savings Certificates.

3) Interest and bonuses on Save As You Earn (SAYE) certified contractual savings schemes.

4) Premium bond prizes.

5) Interest on certain government securities held by non-residents.

6) Job release allowances if paid within one year of normal retirement age.

7) Compensation for loss of employment up to £30,000.

8) Redundancy payments.

9) War widows' pensions.

10) Interest payable on damages for personal injury or death.

11) Gambling winnings and competition prizes.

12) Scholarship awards and other educational grants.

13) Payments for services in the armed forces relating to:
   a) Wound and disability pensions
   b) Service grants, bounties and gratuities
   c) Annuities and additional pensions paid to holders of the Victoria Cross, George Cross and other gallantry awards.

14) Income reinvested in a Personal Equity Plan.

15) The widow's payment of £1,000.

16) Income retained in a TESSA.

17) Rent from the letting of part of the principal private residence up to £4,250 pa.

19) Outplacement counselling (not limited to £30,000 redundancy level).

20) National Lottery prizes.

Income not taxed at source

11. The following types of income are taxable at the 20%/40% rates, but not subject to deduction of basic rate income tax at source.

1) National Savings income bonds
2) National Savings investment account
3) National Savings ordinary account (first £70 of interest is tax free)
4) British Government securities bought through a Crown Post Office and included on the National Savings Stock Register
5) Interest on $3^{1}/_{2}$ % War Loan
6) Deposits at non-UK branches of UK or foreign banks
7) Deposits made by individuals not ordinarily resident in the UK
8) Loan interest from a private individual
9) Deposits with some off-shore building societies
10) Bank and building society accounts where the taxpayer has registered to receive the interest gross.

Student self-testing question

Z who is a single woman has the following data relating to the year ended 5th April 1997:

	£
Schedule E	26,765
Schedule D Case III (TY)	3,000
Building society interest (gross)	1,600
Investment in A Ltd.	2,500

The investment in A Ltd qualifies for relief under the EIS scheme.

Z invested £10,000 in an insurance bond on 1st January 1993. On the 1st January 1997 Z draws £5,000 having made no previous withdrawals.

Compute Z's income tax liability for 1996/97.

Solution

Income tax computation 1996/97

	£	£
Earned income		
Schedule E		26,765
Investment income		
Schedule D Case III TY	3,000	
Building society interest (gross)	1,600	4,600
		31,365
Less Personal allowance		3,765
Tax payable 6,400 @ 20%		1,280
19,100 @ 24%		4,584
2,100 @ 40%		840
27,600		6,704
Less tax on Building society interest @ 20%	320	
Less EIS: 2,500 @ 20%	500	820
		5,884

Tax payable on insurance bond

	£	
Proceeds	5,000	
Less 5% × 4(years) × 10,000	2,000	
	3,000	
Divided by (years) 3,000/4 =		750

As Z is paying tax at the higher rate for 1996/97, the liability on the bond receipt of £5,000 is:

	£
3,000 @ 40%	1,200
Less 3,000 @ 24%	720
	480

Note

Tax payable at the 20% rate is 3,900 + (4,600 – 2,100) = 6,400.

22 Estate and trust income

Introduction

1. This chapter is concerned with the income tax position of estates in the course of administration and trusts.

Estates in the course of administration (Section 659-702 TA 1988)

2. On the death of an individual as outlined in Chapter 4 income tax is calculated on the deceased's income up to the date of death with the appropriate allowances and reliefs. As regards the 'administration period' different rules apply which may be summarised as follows

   a) The administration period begins on the day following the date of the death and ends on the completion of the administration of the estate.

   b) Completion of administration is taken to occur when the residue of the estate is ascertained ie after the assets of the estate have been determined and all the debts paid.

   c) Income arising in the period of administration is taxable on the personal representative (insofar as not taxed at source) at the basic rate and not the higher rate. Personal allowances are not available to the personal representative (PR) but a claim can be made for the following.

      i) Interest on a loan to pay CTT or IHT if the loan is made to the PR before the grant of representation, and relates to tax due on 'personality'.

      ii) Loss relief in respect of any loss which the PR incurs in running a business.

   d) With effect from 6th April 1993 the liability on dividends is reduced to 20% to match the tax credit at that rate, and from 6th April 1996 this rate also applies to interest received.

   e) For payments made to beneficiaries on or after the 6th April 1995 the tax is due in the year of receipt and not spread over the period of the estate.

   Expenses of administration are not deductible in determining the 'appropriate' income tax liability of the PR, but they are in computing the income of the beneficiary.

> **Example**

Z died on 5th October 1997 leaving an estate of £500,000 all of which passed to his wife under the terms of his will. The estate consisted of properties let from 1st October with rents of £14,000 p.a. payable in advance on the normal quarter days and dividend income (net) of £8,000 for the year 1997/98 and £20,000 for the year 1998/99. The administration period is still continuing. Administration of estate's expenses amounted to £500 for 1997/98. Mrs Z received a payment of £12,820 on 4th April 1998.

Complete the income tax liability for the PR for 1997/98.

Solution   Income tax computation 1997/98

	£
Schedule A rental profits	7,000
Tax dividends (gross)	10,000
	17,000
Executorship expenses	500
Residuary income	16,500
Income tax payable : 10,000 @ 20%	2,000
7,000 @ 23%	1,610
	3,610
Less suffered at source on dividends	2,000
Tax payable by the PR	1,610

Notes

i) *In this example the residuary income belongs absolutely to the sole beneficiary Mrs Z and would form part of her taxable income for 1997/98.*

ii) The net residuary income grossed up is as follows:

	£	£
Gross income		17,000
less outgoings:		
Tax liability	3,610	
Executorship expenses	500	4,110
Net distributable income		12,890

iii) Net dividend minus expenses = 8,000 – 500 = 7,500. Gross $7,500 \times \dfrac{100}{80} = 9,375$

Dividends	*9,375*	*1,875*	*7,500*
Schedule A	*7,000*	*1,610*	*5,390*
	16,375	*3,485*	*12,890*

iv) Note that the tax borne by the PR is not the same as that attributed to Mrs Z.

Trusts

3. A trust is an arrangement whereby property is transferred to persons known as trustees, for the benefit of third parties who are known as the beneficiaries. The person transferring the property is known as the settlor or testator where the settlement is created under a will. For income tax purposes a settlement is a very broad term and includes any disposition, trust, covenant, agreement or arrangement for the transfer of assets. Settlements may be created inter vivos, by the rules of intestacy, or by will.

In this part of the chapter the income tax position of trusts and beneficiaries arising from settlements where the settlor is deceased, is outlined. The first part deals with trust income in general and the second part with accumulating and discretionary trusts.

Income of the trust

4.
a) Trustees are not individuals for income tax purposes so that there are no personal allowances or reliefs available. However, in most other respects the general principles of income tax apply also to trusts.

b) Trustees have to account to the Inland Revenue for any income tax, or other taxes, due in respect of the trust income.

c) Trustees must deduct tax from any payments made to beneficiaries.

d) For trusts in general, (ie excluding discretionary or accumulating trusts) the trust income is chargeable to income tax at basic rate 23%. The 20% rate applies to any dividend/interest income.

e) Taxable trust income is total income from all sources less charges on income paid, ie statutory total income. The only expenses allowed are those relating to specific sources of income such as property expenses under Schedule A income. General administration expenses are not allowed as an expense for income tax purposes, but they would be deducted in arriving at the net income of the trust (*Macfarlane* v *IRC* (1929) 14 TC 532).

f) Bank and building society interest is paid after deduction of income tax at the 20% rate w.e.f. 6th April 1996.

Example

The X trust has the following income and expenditure for the year 1997/98

	£
Rents receivable	3,000
Property expenses	500
Building society interest (net)	800
Trust administration expenses	550

Compute the trust income and tax liability for 1997/98. Show the net trust income available for distribution.

Solution

Income tax computation 1997/98

	£	£
Schedule A rents	3,000	
Less property expenses	500	2,500
Building society interest income (gross)		1,000
Taxable income		3,500

Income tax payable

Income tax at 23% × 2,500	575
Income tax at 20% × 1,000	200
Less income tax deducted at source on building society interest	(200)
Tax due from trustees	575

Income available for distribution

	£	£
Taxable income	3,500	
Less income tax	775	2,725
Less trust expenses		550
		2,175

Income of the beneficiary

5. The following points arise under this heading

   a) A beneficiary is entitled to personal reliefs in the same way as any other individual. Trustees are not entitled to personal reliefs.

   b) The income of a beneficiary from a trust is deemed to be the grossed up amount of the net trust income from which income tax at the appropriate rate has been deducted. Using the previous example of the X trust then the income tax of the beneficiary is as follows:

   Gross amount of BSI income less expenses payable by trustees $= 800 - 550 = 250 \times \dfrac{100}{8} = 312$

   Form R185 E for 1997/98 will show:

Savings income	312	62	250
Other	2,500	575	1,925
	2,812	637	2,175

   The beneficiary cannot reclaim the difference between the income tax borne by the trust of £775 and his or her tax credit of £637.00.

   c) Where income is paid directly to a beneficiary it is taxed in the hands of the beneficiary without the trustees paying the basic rate. This can take place with regard to rental income from land where the tenant pays rents direct to the beneficiary.

   d) Trustees are not liable for income tax at the higher rates on trust income. Beneficiaries would however be taxable in the normal way through the income tax bands.

   e) Where the trust has dividend or interest income then the tax payable is at the 20% rate and where this is passed to the beneficiary there is no further liability at the basic rate.

Accumulating and discretionary trusts

6. For trusts of the accumulating or discretionary type (ie trusts where the income is accumulated insofar as it is not applied for the maintenance, education or benefit of a beneficiary) then the following points arise.

   a) As from the 5th April 1993 a UK discretionary trust is liable to income tax at the flat rate of 34%.

   Tax credits on dividends (at the 20% rate) and other interest income (from 6th April 1996 also at 20%) can be set against the 34% liability.

   b) Income which the discretionary trustees use to meet the trust's management expenses will not be liable to income tax at the 34% but at the following rates:
      i) If paid out of dividend income and interest – 20% rate
      ii) If paid out of other income – 24% rate.

   For discretionary and other trusts, the management expenses will be treated as set off first against the savings income.

   c) Any income arising under the accrued income scheme (*see Chapter 6*) is payable at both the basic and the additional rate.

   d) Only expenses chargeable to income on the principles of trust law are deductible (*Carver* v *Duncan* 1985 STC 356).

e) Payments made by trustees for the benefit of the whole fund are to be debited against capital and not allowable eg premiums on life policies and fees paid to investment advisors. If debited to the trust income in accordance with the trust deed powers, they are not allowable for the additional rate.

f) Deposits made by discretionary trusts with a bank or building society will be subject to deduction of tax at the 20% rate at source with effect from 6th April 1996.

g) At the end of each fiscal year if the pool of tax credits including additional rate exceeds the tax certified to the beneficiaries on Form R 185E, the balance is carried forward. If the tax certified is greater than the pool an assessment under Sec 687 TA 1988 arises on the trust.

Example

The Z discretionary trust has the following income and outgoings for the year 1997/98

	£	£
Rent from property	4,500	
Property expenses	500	4,000
Dividends received		800
Mortgage interest on property gross		500
Trust administration expenses		200

Compute the tax liability of the trust for 1997/98.

Solution

Z Trust
Income tax computation 1997/98

	Saving Income	Other
Dividends (Net)	800	–
Schedule A (4,500 – 500)	–	4,000
	800	4,000
Less Trust expenses	200	–
	600	4,000

Tax liability of the trust

Schedule A 4,000 @ 34%	1,360

Savings income grossed up at $\frac{100}{80}$ @ 14%

$= 600 \times \dfrac{100}{80} \times 14\%$ — 105

Tax due by assessment	1,465
Tax deducted at source dividends	200
Total tax borne	1,665

Net revenue available for distribution

Gross income	Schedule A	4,000	
	Savings income	1,000	5,000
Less tax borne		1,665	
Trust expenses		200	1,865
			3,135

Notes

i) *If the whole of the net income has been distributed to the beneficiaries they would be deemed to be in receipt of £3,135 grossed @ 34% ie $3,135 \times \dfrac{100}{66} = 4,750$*

ii) *Mortgage interest is paid gross by the trust and set against Schedule A property profits.*

Miscellaneous points

7. a) In practice, where income is received gross by the trustees, it is sometimes paid direct to the beneficiaries who are then assessed directly rather than the trustees.

   b) Following the decision in *Baxendale* v *Murphy* 1924 9 TC 76, an amount paid to a trustee as remuneration is treated as an annual charge.

   c) Income received by a beneficiary from a trust is generally unearned income even where the trust operates a business, see *Fry* v *Sheils Trustees* 1915 6 TC 583.

   d) Distributions of income to a beneficiary by trustees must be accompanied with a certificate of deduction of income tax on form R 185E.

   e) As shown in the examples above, the gross amounts received by the beneficiaries will not be the same as the income of the trust where there are any trust administration expenses. Such expenses are not allowed as an expense of the trust for income tax purposes. However, following the decision in *Macfarlane* v *IRC* 14 TC 540, such expenses are allowed in computing the income of the beneficiary, and accordingly it is the net income available for distribution which is grossed up.

   f) Where the only beneficiaries in a trust are individuals retaining a life interest in possession, eg a life tenant, then bank deposit interest will be paid net to the trustees. However, for deposits made by discretionary trusts, and accumulation and maintenance trusts the interest will be received by them gross.

• Student self-testing question

The XYZ trust has one beneficiary who has an interest in possession as a life tenant. Trust data for the year 1997/98 was as follows:

	£
Rents received less allowable expenditure	12,000
Bank interest received	160
Dividend income (net)	800
Trust administration expenses	1,000

Compute the trust liability to income tax for 1997/98 and show the gross and net amounts due to the beneficiary.

Solution

XYZ Trust income tax computation 1997/98

		£	£
Schedule A profits			12,000
Bank interest (gross) 160 ÷ 0.8			200
Dividends (gross) 800 ÷ 0.8			1,000
Taxable income			13,200
Income tax payable	£12,000 @ 23%		2,760
	£1,200 @ 20%		240
	£13,200		3,000
Less income tax on	– dividends	200	
	– bank interest	40	240
Net payable by trustees			2,760

Income available for distribution

		£	£
Gross income			13,200
less income tax		3,000	
trust expenses		1,000	4,000
			9,200

Amount due to beneficiary

	£
Net trust income grossed up: $9,200 \times \dfrac{100}{77} =$	11,948
Less income @ 23%	2,748
	9,200

Notes

i) *The Z trust is not a discretionary or accumulating trust since the beneficiary has an interest in possession. The fixed rate of 34% is not therefore levied on the trustees.*

ii) *Interest on the bank deposit is paid net of tax at the 20% rate.*

iii) *The dividend income and bank interest are set against the trust expenses first.*

• Question without answer

The A trust is an accumulating discretionary trust, and for the year 1997/98 has the following data:

	£
Property income after expenses	7,000
Bank interest accrued	1,200
Dividend income (net)	560
Trust administration expenses	280

Compute the tax liability of the trust for 1997/98 and show the income of the beneficiaries.

23 National Insurance contributions and Social Security

Introduction

1. This chapter is concerned with National Insurance position and some aspects of the Social Security system under the following main headings:

   Classes of contribution   Statutory sick pay

   Gross pay   Statutory maternity pay

   Directors   Taxable state benefits

   Class 4 contributions   Non-taxable state benefits

   Class 1 A – Cars and Fuel

Classes of contribution

2. There are four classes of contribution payable to the Contributions Agency under the Social Security Act 1975:

   Class 1   All employed earners and their employers

   Class 1A   Employers' contributions on car/fuel benefits

   Class 2   Self-employed persons

   Class 3   Non-employed persons

   Class 4   Self-employed persons, additional contribution based on 'profits'.

   All employed persons and their employers must pay Class 1 contributions the weekly rates for which apply from 6th April 1997, are given below.

   An employed person is someone gainfully employed either under a contract of service, or as the holder of an office as defined for income tax purposes, e.g. a company director, *see Chapter 8.*

   A self-employed person is liable for Class 2 and Class 4 contributions. The Class 2 contribution is a flat rate payable each week. The Class 4 contribution is payable as percentage of 'profits' as determined for income tax purposes.

   Class 3 contributions are voluntary contributions payable weekly at a flat rate.

   Employees must be aged 16 or over before any liability to National Insurance arises.

   For persons over pensionable age (men 65; women 60) the position is as follows:

   i) Primary contributions (employees' NIC) are not due on earnings paid after 65th birthday for men (60th for women)

   ii) Secondary contributions (employers' NICS) continue as before.

   From 1991/92 employers' contributions on car and fuel benefits are payable at the full rate.

Gross pay

3. Gross pay for Class 1 National Insurance purposes includes:

   Wages/Salaries

   Bonus payments

   Fees

   Overtime pay

   Petrol allowances unless charged to a company account

   Profit-related pay

   Telephone where bill paid by employer. Can be limited to rental and business calls.

   In general most benefits in kind (eg car benefits and private health care) which are taxable under Schedule E for directors and employees earning more than £8,500 p.a. are not included in gross pay for National Insurance purposes.

National Insurance contributions

4. Class 1 Employed. From 6 April 1997

£ per week earnings Employee	Contracted in	Contracted out
Up to £61.99	Nil	Nil
Rates for earnings between		
£62 and £465		
(a) on first £62	2%	2%
plus		
(b) £62.01 to £465	10%	8.4%

Employer Select earnings band		First £62	Balance (salary related)	Balance (money purchase)
Up to £61.99	Nil	Nil	Nil	Nil
£62.00 to £109.99	3%	3%	Nil	1.5%
£110.00 to £154.99	5%	5%	2%	3.5%
£155.00 to £209.00	7%	7%	4%	5.5%
£210.00 to £465	10%	10%	7%	8.5%
Over £465	10%		£34.41 + 10%	£40.45 + 10%
			on excess over £465	

Notes

i) *The employee's contributions are known as Primary Class 1 contributions*

The employer's contributions are known as Secondary Class 1 contributions.

ii) *Separate rates apply to employers who have contracted out of the State Earnings Related Pension scheme (SERPS).*

The contracted out rates apply to employees who are members of approved occupational pension schemes where their employees have elected to be excluded from the state earnings related scheme.

Class 1A   10.0%.

Class 2   Weekly rate £6.15. No liability if earnings below £3,480 p.a.

Class 3   Weekly rate £6.05.

Class 4   See below.

NIC holidays – 1997/98

5. With effect from 6th April 1996 any employer can qualify for a full rebate of employers' National Insurance contributions for up to a year for any new employee who has been out of work for two years.

i)   Any job qualifies so long as it lasts 13 consecutive weeks.

ii) In order to obtain relief, employers must obtain a certificate authorising the NIC holiday from the Benefits Agency.

iii) The employers' rebate is paid at the not contracted-out rate even where the employer is in fact contracted out.

iv) Contributions are reclaimed from the monthly or quarterly PAYE remittance.

Directors

6. The earnings period for employees is usually the interval at which payments are made eg weekly or monthly. For directors their earnings period is annual whether they are paid weekly, monthly or at other intervals.

The following rules should be noted.

i)   The earnings period runs from 6th April to the following 5th April.

ii) Directors appointed before 6th April have an annual earnings period even if they cease to be directors in the course of the year.

iii) Where a director is appointed after 6th April then the earnings period is pro-rated using a 52 week period for the whole tax year. For example, if B is appointed in tax week 35, in 1997/98, as there are 17 tax weeks left including the week of the appointment then the earnings period is 17 weeks.

iv) NI contributions are calculated on the total earnings to date less NI contributions already paid.

v) Unlike employees, a director's NIC is calculated on a cumulative basis taking into consideration total earnings and NIC paid to date.

vi) For 1997/98 the lower earnings level is £3,224 and the upper earnings level £24,180.

Example

A is a Director of K Ltd and receives a salary of £25,000 in period 1 of 1997/98. Compute the primary and secondary NICS payable. The company has contracted out of the state earnings related pension scheme, and operates a defined salary scheme.

Solution

A National Insurance Contribution 1997/98

Primary contributions

		£
3,224	@ 2%	64.48
20,956	@ 8.4%	1,760.30
24,180		1,824.78

Secondary contributions

24,180		1,789.32 − (£34.41 × 52)
820	@ 10%	82.00
25,000		1,871.32

Notes
i) *As the earnings have already exceeded the upper earnings level there will be no further primary contribution payable for the year.*
ii) *The DSS are prepared, it seems, to accept contributions payable over a 12 month period provided that this does not lead to any overall wrong contributions, and they are not asked to approve the method!*
iii) *With effect from 1997/98 directors are treated in the same way as other employees.*
iv) *There are different rates for employers depending upon the type of pension sheme it operates.*

Class 4 contributions

7. The following are the main features of this class of contribution.

   a) Contributions are calculated and collected by the Inland Revenue together with any income tax due under Schedule D Case I or II.

   b) The Class 4 liability of a husband is calculated separately from that of his wife and is assessed independently.

   c) Where a partnership exists then each partner's liability is calculated separately and an assessment raised in the partnership name, as for income tax.

   d) The contributions are based on the profits as determined and assessed under Schedule D Case I or II, with the following deductions:
      i) Capital allowances (balancing charges are added)
      ii) Loss relief under Sections 380, 385, 388, 381, TA 1988
      iii) Annual payments not allowed in computing Case I or II income incurred wholly or exclusively for the purposes of trade.

      Personal reliefs and personal pension payments are not deductible.

   e) The rate of contribution is 6.0% of profits in between £7,010 and £24,180 for 1997/98, giving a maximum contribution of £1,030.20.

   f) Up to 1995/96, an individual can deduct 50% of the Class 4 contributions which he or she is liable to pay in respect of that year in computing his or her total income for that year. A claim for this relief must be made by the taxpayer, but in practice this is usually given in the tax assessment. This is abolished from 1996/97.

g) For the purposes of calculating Class 4 profits, losses allowed under Section 380 are set against Case I or II income of the individual. Thus any loss allowed for income tax purposes against non-trading income, can be carried forward for Class 4 purposes.

h) Where the profits of farmers are averaged in accordance with the provisions of Section 96 TA 1988, the revised amounts are used for Class 4 purposes.

i) Under self-assessment, interest on late payment of Class IV NICS will be charged at the prevailing rate of interest.

j) Where an individual is both employed and self-employed then Class 1 contributions will be paid on the employment earnings and Class 2 and Class 4 (if above the minimum level) on the self-employed earnings. As the employment earnings could in some cases also give rise to an additional Class 2 and 4 liability it is possible to apply for a deferment provided this is made before the beginning of the income tax year.

Example

X who is single has been trading for many years with an accounting year end to the 30th June. He has the following data relating to the income tax year 1997/98:

	£
Schedule D Case I CY to 30.6.1997	25,896
Agreed capital allowances	2,851
Building society interest (net)	800
Mortgage interest (MIRAS) gross	1,000

Calculate the income tax and Class 4 NHI liabilities for 1997/98.

Solution

X: Income tax computation 1997/98

	£	£
Earned income		
Schedule D case I	25,896	
Less capital allowances	2,851	23,045
Unearned income		
Building society interest (gross)		1,000
		24,045
Personal allowance		4,045
Taxable Income		20,000
Tax payable 5,100 @ 20% (4,100 + 1,000)		1,020
14,900 @ 23%		3,427
20,000		4,447
Less income tax deducted from Building society interest		200
Tax Payable		4,247
Class 4 NIC contributions payable (see note)		962.10

Note

	£
Class 4 contributions	
Schedule D Case I	25,896
Less capital allowances	2,851
	23,045
Less lower level	7,010
	16,035
6.0% × first £16,035 =	962.10

Class 1A NIC Cars and fuel

8. a) Employers are liable to pay Class 1A National Insurance contributions in respect of:
    i) a car provided for certain directors and higher paid employees (£8,500 pa including benefits and expenses) where it is available for private use
    ii) Fuel provided for private use.

b) The rate at which Class 1A NICs are calculated is the highest secondary Class 1 NIC applicable to the year in which the benefit is charged.

1994/1995	10.2%
1995/1996	10.2%
1996/1997	10.2%
1997/1998	10.0%

c) Payment of the Class 1A NICs is due on or before the 19th of June following the end of the income tax year to which they relate. If a quarterly basis for paying PAYE has been claimed the Class 1A NICs are due on or before the 19th July of the following income tax year.

Statutory sick pay

9. Since the 6th April 1983 employers have been responsible for paying statutory sick pay (SSP) to their employees. In general the amounts paid have been subsequently recouped from National Insurance contributions paid in respect of all employees.

A brief summary of the scheme, operating with effect from 6th April 1997 is as follows:

a) SSP is payable for up to 28 weeks of sickness at the undermentioned rates:

Level	Average Weekly Earnings	Weekly Rate of SSP
Standard	£62.00	£55.70

All earning at least £62.00 will be entitled to the standard rate.

b) The gross amount of sick pay paid is subject to income tax under the PAYE system and to National Insurance contributions.

c) On and from 6th April 1995 all employers can claim full reimbursement if and to the extent that their SSP payments for an income tax month exceed 13% of their gross Class 1 contribution liability for that month.

Both employers' and employees' contributions count but not the Class 1A.

d) Where the SSP recoverable is greater than the NI contributions due for the income tax month, the balance may be dealt with as follows:

i) Deducted from PAYE

ii) Carried forward to the next payment period

iii) Reclaimed from the collector of taxes by formal application.

e) Earnings for SSP purposes are the same as those used for National Insurance purposes.

f) To be eligible for SSP an employee must be incapable of work for at least four calendar days in a row, including Saturdays, Sundays and Bank holidays.

g) Any two periods of incapacity for work (PIWs) which are separated by a period of eight weeks (56 calendar days) or less are linked together for SSP purposes.

Statutory maternity pay

10. 1) A woman who has been continuously employed for at least 26 weeks continuing into the 15th week (QW) before the week when the birth is due is entitled to SMP.

2) The SMP rates are as follows

Employment ≥ 26 weeks before QW – £55.70 per week for 18 weeks.

Employment ≥ 2 years before QW

(16 hours or more per week)   90% × average pay – 6 weeks

≥ 5 years before QW   £55.70   remaining 12 weeks

(8 hours or more per week)

3) SMP is subject to National Insurance contributions and income tax in the same way as wages and salaries.

4) Small employers can recover the gross amount of SMP, plus 5.5% (wef.6.4 1996) i.e. 105.5% as compensation for the employers' NIC, other employers can recover 92%.

5) Recovery of SMP is made by reduction from monthly income tax and National Insurance payable.

6) 'Small employer' is one whose gross Class 1 NIC for the preceding year did not exceed £20,000.

State benefits taxed as Schedule E income

11. Income support payments made to the unemployed or strikers

Industrial death benefit

Incapacity benefit

Unemployment benefit[1]

Widowed mother's allowance

Non-contributory retirement pension

Retirement pension

Statutory maternity pay

Widow's pension

Note:

[1]Additions for children, housing and exceptional circumstances are excluded.

State benefits which are not taxable

12. i) *Short-term benefits*

Maternity allowance

Sickness benefit

ii) *Benefits in respect of children*

Child benefit

Child dependency additions paid with widow's pension, widowed mother's allowance, retirement pension or invalid care allowance

Guardian's allowance

One parent benefit

iii) *Industrial injury benefits*

Constant attendance allowance

Industrial injuries disablement benefit

Pneumoconiosis, byssinosis and miscellaneous disease benefits

Workmen's compensation supplement

iv) *War disablement benefits*

Constant attendance allowance

Disablement pension

Severe disablement allowance

v) *Other benefits*

Attendance allowance

Christmas bonus

Council tax benefit

Disability living allowance

Family credit

Housing benefit

Income support generally

Redundancy payment

Social Fund payments

Vaccine damage (lump sum)

War widow's or dependant's pension

Widow's payment

Minimum earnings

13.

		1996/97	1997/98
		£	£
National Insurance	Weekly	61.00	62.00
	Monthly	264.00	269.00
	Yearly	–	3224.00

• Question without answer

You are required to calculate the National Insurance contributions payable for 1997/98 by both employer and employee in the following situations.

i) Sergio is employed at an annual salary of £52,000. He is paid weekly and is not contracted out of the state pension scheme. He was provided with a 1900cc company car costing £15,000 when new, on which the business mileage was 20,000. He had use of the same vehicle for the whole of 1997/98. It was two years old. Petrol for both business and private mileage is provided by his employer.

ii) Antoinette is employed at an annual salary of £10,400. She is paid weekly and is not contracted out of the state pension scheme.

Income tax

End of section questions and answers

Income tax question No 1. P

P and his wife have the following information relating to their first self assessment tax return for 1998.

	Tax Return 1998 **(Returning income for** **year ended 5/4/98)** £
Business profits (P)	15,880
Wife's salary	17,445
Rental profits (P)	14,165
Taxed dividends (P net)	1,600
Building society interest (wife net)	480
Covenant to Oxfam by P (gross)	1,000
Covenant to son in full-time education (gross)	1,200
(executed 12/3/1991) (P)	

Additional information relating to 1997/98.

1) Mrs P maintains her widowed mother (aged 86) who is in receipt of a state retirement pension of £3,248, and also has dividend income (net) of £11,000 for 1997/98.
2) Mr P's son has part-time earnings from a weekend milk round of £1,000 and taxable unemployment benefit of £350.
3) P pays mortgage interest in respect of a qualifying loan amounting to £750 (net).
   a) *Compute the income tax liability of Mr and Mrs P for 1997/98.*
   b) *Compute the income tax liability of Mr P's mother for 1997/98.*
   c) *Compute the income tax liability of Mr P's son for 1997/98.*

Solution

a) **P. Income tax computation 1997/98**

			P		Mrs P
		£	£	£	£
Earned income					
Business profits				15,880	
Wife's salary					17,445
Unearned income					
Rental profits			14,165		–
Building society interest (gross) 480 ÷ 80			–		600
Taxed dividends (gross) 1,600 ÷ 80			2,000	16,165	
				32,045	18,045
less Charges on income:					
Covenant to Oxfam				1,000	
				31,045	18,045
Personal allowance				4,045	4,045
Taxable income				27,000	14,000
Tax payable	5,200 / 4,700	@ 20%		1,040	940
	20,900 / 9,300	@ 23%		4,807	2,139
	900 / –	@ 40%		360	–
	27,000 14,000			6,207	3,079
Add income tax on covenant to Oxfam				230	–
				6,437	3,079
Less tax on BSI 600 @ 20%					120
Less tax on dividends 2,000 @ 20%			400		
Less MCA @ 15%			274	674	
				5,763	2,959

Note

i)   *There is no tax relief for the covenant to P's son.*

b)   **P's mother. Income tax computation 1997/98**

		£	£
Schedule E pension			3,248
Taxed dividends (gross) $11,000 \times \dfrac{100}{80}$			13,750
			16,998
Personal age allowance		5,400	
less $\frac{1}{2}$ (16,998 − 15,600) =		699	4,701
Taxable income			12,297
Tax payable	12,297 @ 20%		2,459
less income tax on dividends	13,750 @ 20%		2,750
Tax repayable			(291)

Note:

The dividend income is only chargeable at the 20% .

c)   **P's son. Income tax computation 1997/98**

	£
Schedule E: part-time earnings	1000
unemployment benefit	350
	1,350
Personal allowance (restricted)	1,350
	−

Income tax question No 2. Gregg

Gregg, a married man, is a director of Gregoria Ltd. a close company of which he owns 40.0% of the issued ordinary share capital, which consists of 5,000 fully paid £1 shares. The company's trading profits for the financial year ended 31st March 1997 totalled £12,000 and its investment income comprised a dividend of £300 received in May 1996 from a United Kingdom quoted company. A dividend of 20p on its ordinary shares was paid by Gregoria Ltd. in July 1996 for the year ended 31st March 1996. A similar dividend was paid in June 1997.

The following additional matters relate to Gregg.

a)   He receives a salary of £25,000 per annum and additional remuneration dependent upon the company's financial results as under:

    For the company's year to 31.3.97   received 19.6.97   £3,329
    For the company's year to 31.3.98   received 5.7.98   £4,731

b)   His form P11D for 1997/98 showed:

	£
Entertaining expenses reimbursed	3,512
Hotel expenses reimbursed	1,209
Car – Citroen 2000 cc diesel	
List price when new	14,000
First registered 1.4.95	
Cost of repairs to Gregg's private house	596
Wages of company's cleaner for duties at Gregg's private house	314

Gregg's total mileage amounted to 12,000 and it is estimated that he used the car to the extent of one-quarter privately. All the running expenses (£1,910) were paid directly by the company.

c)   Some years ago, Gregg lent the company £4,000 on which interest at the rate of $6^{1}/4$% per annum was payable half yearly on 31st March and 30th September; all payments were made on the due dates after deduction of income tax.

d)   On 5th July 1997 Gregg granted a 21 year lease on a freehold property owned by him for many years at a premium of £10,500 with an annual rental of £1,000, payable quarterly in advance on the usual English quarter days; all outgoings were payable by the lessee.

e)   Mrs Gregg has a National Savings Bank investment account, originally opened in May 1994 and the interest credited thereon was £5,045 for the year ended 5th April 1998.

You are required to compute the total tax liability of Gregg and Mrs Gregg for the year 1997/98.

Solution

Income tax computation 1997/98

		Gregg £	Gregg £	Mrs Gregg £
Earned income	Schedule E (Note 1)		33,245	–
Unearned income	Schedule A (Note 2)	7,050		–
	Schedule D Case III			
	NSB			5,045
	Taxed interest	250		
	UK dividends (gross)			
	$400 \times \dfrac{100}{80}$	500	7,800	–
	Statutory total income		41,045	5,045
less	Personal allowance		4,045	4,045
Taxable income			37,000	1,000

Income tax payable:

4,100 @ 20%	1,000 @ 20%		820.00	200
22,000 @ 23%	–		5,060.00	–
10,900 @ 40 %	–		4,360.00	–
37,000	1,000		10,240.00	200

Less income tax on:	dividends 500 @ 20%	100.00		
	interest 250 @ 20%	50.00		
	MCA @ 15%	274.00	424.00	–
Tax borne			9,816.00	200

Note (1) **Schedule E**

	£	£
Salary		25,000
Bonus (received on 19.6.97)		3,329
Benefits in kind:		
Motor car $14,000 \times 35\% = 4,900 - \frac{1}{3}$	3,266	
Fuel diesel	740	
House repairs	596	
Cleaner's wages	314	4,916
		33,245

The bonus payments are taxed when received.

Note (2) **Schedule A profits**

	£
Lease premium	10,500
less $(21 - 1) \times 2\% \times 10,500$	4,200
	6,300
Rent accrued (3 quarters accounts basis)	750
	7,050

Note (3) **Taxed dividends**

	£
20p per share $\times$ 5,000 =	1,000
$40\% \times 1,000 =$	400
Gross dividend:	
$\dfrac{400}{1} \times \dfrac{100}{80}$	500

Note (4) NSB interest as a new source after 5.4.1994 is taxed on a current year basis.

Income tax question NO 3. Jonah

Jonah is the manager of the sales department of Whales Ltd., employed at a basic salary of £18,000 per annum plus commission on sales which amounted to £12,535 and was paid to him in the year to 5th April 1998. He contributes 9% of his basic salary to his employers' approved pension scheme.

He provides his own car for use on company business and receives an allowance of 50p per mile in respect of running expenses. They also reimburse all other expenses for which he submits approved vouchers.

In the year ended 5th April 1998 the company made a return of expense payments and benefits on form P11D as follows:

	£
Entertaining UK customers	1,500
Travelling and hotel expenses (all claimed under Section 198 TA 1988)	8320
Mileage allowance for car expenses (under FCPS)	6,000
Car: Ford Granada (2500 cc) owned by Jonah.	
First registered on 15.12.95	
Subscriptions: Clubs	820
Professional bodies (approved)	239
British United Provident Association – private health	410
Home telephone (agreed business proportion calls only)	197

Jonah's annual mileage was 14,000 and it was agreed with HM Inspector of Taxes that one-seventh of this represented private travel, for the purposes of the FCPS.

Jonah is a married man. His wife has been a freelance journalist for two years and her adjusted profits have been:

	£
Year to 31st December 1996	14,000
Year to 31st December 1997	13,445

The other income of Mr and Mrs Jonah has been:

		Year ended 5th April	
		1997	**1998**
		£	£
Jonah:	Bank Deposit interest	198	240
	(account opened in 1990)		
	National Savings Bank interest		
	(ordinary account opened in 1995)	45	50
Wife:	Interest on $3\frac{1}{2}$% War Loan purchased May 1996	300	600
Jonah:	Interest paid under the MIRAS scheme		
	on a building society mortgage in respect		
	of his only residence.	1,338	1,600

You are required to compute the income tax liability for 1997/98 of Jonah and his wife.

Solution

Income tax computation 1997/98

		Jonah		Wife	
	£		£		£
Earned income					
Schedule E (note 1)			30,745		
Schedule D Case II C.Y. 31.12.97					13,445
Unearned income					
Schedule D Case III:					
Bank deposit interest $\frac{100}{80} \times 240$			300		
National Savings Bank (50 – 70)			–		
War loan			–		600
Statutory total income			31,045		14,045
Personal allowance			4,045		4,045
Taxable income			27,000		10,000
Tax payable					
4,100 / 4,700 @ 20%			820		940
22,000 / 5,300 @ 23%			5,060		1,219
900 / – @ 40 %			360		–
27,000 10,000			6,240		2,159
Less income tax on bank deposit interest (20% × 300)	60		–		–
Less deduction MCA 1,830 @ 15%	274		334		
			5,906		2,159

Note 1: Schedule E

Salary			18,000	
Commission			12,535	
			30,535	
less Pension Cont. 9% × 18,000			1,620	28,915
Benefits in kind				
Motor car allowance			6,000	
FCPS	4,000 @ 63p	2,520		
	8,000 @ 36p	2,880	5,400	
	12,000			600
Subscriptions: Club				820
BUPA				410
				30,745

The subscriptions to approved professional bodies do not give rise to any assessable benefit.

Income tax question NO 4. Roger Thesaurus

Roger Thesaurus, a widower aged 44, has the following income and outgoings for the income tax year 1997/98.

1. Business profits as a publisher for the year to 31st December 1997 (after capital allowances). 54,845

2. Interest on a deposit account (opened 1990) with the Scotia Bank 800 (net)

3. An annual payment under a deed of covenant entered into on 1 September 1990 to a charitable organisation. 6,000 (gross)

4. An annual payment under a qualifying deed of covenant to his daughter aged 20 who is studying full-time for a degree at a UK university, entered into in October 1995. 2,000 (gross)

5. Mortgage interest payments to the Countyshires Banks plc. The payments were made outside the MIRAS arrangements. The mortgage was for £20,000 on Mr Thesaurus' only residence. 2,000 (gross)

6. Personal pension premiums. Roger had never made any pension premiums even though he had been in business as a publisher for five years and his taxable profits had always been above £20,000. 10,000

7. Interest on a National Savings Bank investment account (opened in February 1995). 200

8. Payment to his widowed mother living alone. In addition to the basic state retirement pension her only other income in 1997/98 is £50 War Loan interest. 260

You are required to calculate the income tax liability of Mr Thesaurus for 1997/98. *(ACCA)*

Solution

Roger Thesaurus. Income tax computation 1997/98

		£	£	£
a)	Schedule D Case I		54,845	
	Personal pension plan	54,845		
	Current year 20% × 54,845	10,969		
	Payments	10,000	10,000	44,845
	Bank deposit interest $800 \times \dfrac{100}{80}$			1,000
	NSB			200
				46,045
	Less Covenant to charity			6,000
	Statutory total income			40,045
	Personal allowance			4,045
				36,000

Tax payable:

	£		£
	4,100	@ 20%	820.00
	22,000	@ 23%	5,060.00
	9,900	@ 40%	3,960.00
	36,000		9,840.00
Add	income tax on covenant to charity 6,000 × 23%		1,380.00
			11,220.00
Less	income tax on bank deposit interest	200	
	APA 1,830 × 15%	274	
	mortgage interest 2,000 × 15%	300	774.00
			10,446.00

Income tax question NO 5. Muskett

F Muskett commenced trading as an antique dealer in firearms on the 1st January 1997 and his abridged trading account for the year to 31st December 1997 is as follows:

1.

		£	£
Gross trading profit			38,035
Add	Discounts received	2,700	
	Profit on sale of piano (Pte)	150	
	Lottery winnings	250	3,100
			41,135
Less	Wages shop assistant	2,500	
	Wages Mrs Muskett	3,750	
	Heating and lighting	1,205	
	Repairs and renewals	2,137	
	General expenses	275	
	Printing and stationery	311	
	Donation to Oxfam	100	
	Bad debts account	300	
	Mortgage interest (net)	1,200	
	Motor expenses	2,730	
	Depreciation	1,175	15,683
Trading profit			25,452

2. Additional information:

a) Mrs Muskett works full-time in the business and her salary for 1997/98 was £8,500.

b) Repairs and Renewals comprise:

	£
Expenditure on new warehouse necessary to make it usable	1,250
Partitioning of office (portable)	800
Storage heater	87
	2,137

3. General expenses comprise:

	£
Entertaining	121
Staff outing	75
TV Times newspaper	69
Wedding presentation to employee	10
	275

4. Bad debt account:

	£		£
Bad debts written off	150	Provisions b/f	
Loan to former employee	50	Specific	300
Provisions c/f		General	300
Specific	400	P and loss account	300
General	400	Bad debt recovered	100
	1,000		1,000

5. Mortgage interest of £1,200 relates to a loan taken out by Muskett to purchase his house. Payments under the MIRAS scheme for 1997/98 amounted to £900 (net).

6. Private use of the motor car has been agreed at 40%.

7. Capital allowances available for the accounting period have been agreed as follows:

Fixtures and fittings	736
Motor car (before private use)	600

a) *Compute the adjusted profit for the 12 months to 31st December 1997.*

b) *Compute Muskett's income tax liability for 1997/98.*

Solution

a) **F. Muskett. Adjustment of profits 31.12.97**

	£	£
Trading profit per accounts		25,452
Add back		
Repairs and renewals		
Warehouse expenditure	1,250	
Partitioning office (Plant)	800	
Storage heater	87	
General expenses:		
Entertaining	121	
Newspapers	69	
Donation – Oxfam	100	
Bad debts:		
Loan to employee	50	
Increase general reserve	100	
Mortgage interest	1,200	
Motor expenses 40% × 2,730	1,092	
Depreciation	1,175	
		6,044
		31,496
Less non-Case I income:		
Profit on sale of piano	150	
Lottery winnings	250	400
		31,096

$$1996/97 \quad \frac{94}{365} \times [31,096 - (360 + 736)] \quad = 30,000 \times \frac{94}{365} = 7,808$$

1997/98 AP to 31.12.1997 = 30,000

b) **Income tax computation 1997/98**

	F Muskett £	Mrs Muskett £
Schedule D Case I	30,000	
Schedule E (Mrs Muskett)	–	8,500
	30,000	8,500
Personal allowance	4,045	4,045
Taxable income	25,955	4,455
Tax payable: 4,100 @ 20% / 4,100 @ 20%	820	820
21,855 @ 23% / 355 @ 23%	5,027	82
25,955 4,455	5,847	902
Less deduction MCA @ 15%	274	–
	5,573	902

Income tax question NO 6. T Spark

T Spark who has carried on an engineering business for many years makes up his accounts to 30th June each year. His abridged trading and profit and loss account for the year ended 30th June 1996 is as follows:

	£	£
Gross profit from trading		44,185
Interest on $3\frac{1}{2}$% War Loan		70
		44,255

Less:

Office salaries	8,500	
Rates and insurance	1,380	
Lighting and heating	350	
Loan interest	700	
General expenses	2590	
Repairs and Renewals	400	
Audit fee	210	
Legal charges	410	
Motor car expenses	600	
Bad and doubtful debts	275	
Loss on sale of plant	90	
Depreciation	500	
T. Spark salary	3,000	19,005
Net profit		25,250

You are given the following information:

1) **Bad debts account**

	£		£
Bad debts w/off	180	Balance b/f	
Loan to former employee w/off	10	Specific	110
Balance c/f		2% other debts	240
Specific	170	Bad debts recovered	55
2% other debtors	320	Profit and loss account	275
	680		680

2) The motor car is on contract hire. Private use has been agreed at 30%.

3) Legal charges comprise:

	£
re purchase of factory premises	300
renewal of short lease	50
debt collection	60
	410

4) Repairs and renewals comprise:

	£	£
Cost of 2 new typewriters	320	
Less allowance on 1 traded in	40	280
Alteration to offices, all improvements		120
		400

Typewriters are dealt with on the renewals basis.

5) Loan interest is in respect of a business development loan used for the purchase of plant and machinery.

6) General expenses comprise:

	£
Entertaining	900
Gifts – Christmas spirits to clients	300
Company pens (£10 each)	500
Wedding gift to employee	50
Postage and stationery	125
Charitable donations	100
Staff Christmas party	450
Trade subscriptions	50
Miscellaneous	115
	2590

211

7) Capital allowances for 1996/97 have been agreed at £943.

8) The $3\frac{1}{2}$% War Loan was purchased in May 1996. Interest in the accounts represents the half years interest received on £4,000 of stock.

9) Mrs Spark has Schedule E income of £12,265 for 1996/97 and B.S.I. of £400 (net).

10) Spark's eldest son is attending university studying Biology and Modern Art. He has investment income from a discretionary trust created by his uncle which amounted to £1,056 net for 1996/97.

11) Mr Spark entered into a covenant to pay his son a gross amount of £1,500 for 1994/95 and the next 3 years.

12) Profits for the year ended 30.6.1995 have been agreed for tax purposes in the sum of £34,216.

You are required to undertake the following:

a) *Compute the adjusted profits for the year ended 30th June 1996.*

b) *Compute Spark's income tax liability for 1996/97 and that of his wife.*

c) *Compute Spark's son's income tax liability for 1996/97.*

Solution

T Spark: Adjusted profits 30.6.96

		£	£
Profit per Accounts			25,250
Add back			
Bad debts –	loan	10	
	general reserve	80	
General expenses –	entertaining	900	
	gifts	300	
	donation	100	
Repairs & Renewals –	typewriter (280 – 120)	160	
	alterations	120	
Legal charges re factory		300	
Motor car. 30% ¥ 600		180	
Loss on sale of plant		90	
Depreciation		500	
Salary – T Spark		3,000	5,740
			30,990
Less Interest $3\frac{1}{2}$% War Loan			70
			30,920

Income tax computation 1996/97

		Spark		Mrs Spark
	£		£	£
Earned income				
Schedule D case I TY (30,920 + 34,216) × 50%	32,568			
Less capital allowances	943		31,625	–
Schedule E Mrs Spark			–	12,265
Unearned income				–
B.S.I. (gross)			–	500
Case III $3\frac{1}{2}$% War Loan. CY			140	–
			31,765	12,765
Personal allowance			3,765	3,765
			28,000	9,000
Taxable income 3,900 / 3,900 @ 20%			780	780
21,600 / 5,100 @ 24%			5,184	1,224
2,500 / – @ 40%			1,000	–
28,000 9,000			6,964	2,004
Less income tax on B.S.I. 500 @ 20%			–	100
Less deduction MCA @ 15% × 1,790			268	–
			6,696	1,904

Spark's son: Income tax computation 1996/97

		£
Trust income (gross) $\dfrac{1056}{1} \times \dfrac{100}{66}$		1,600
Personal allowance (restricted)		1,600
		—
Tax deducted at source – *trust income*		
1,600 @ 34%		544.00
Repayment		544.00

Note: *Non-charitable covenants entered into after the 15th March 1988 are not liable to taxation on the recipient.*

Income tax question No 7. Lancelot

Lancelot, a dentist who is not married, provides you with the following information concerning his income.

1. Income from employment (tax years)   £
   1986–87   18,000
   1987–88   20,000
   1988–89   22,000
   1989–90   24,000
   1990–91 to 31. 12. 90   20,000

2. Income from self-employment (commenced 1. 1. 91)   £
   Year ended 31. 12. 91 – loss   (12,000)
   Year ended 31. 12. 92 – loss   (6,000)
   Year ended 31. 12. 93 – profit   9,000
   Year ended 31. 12. 94 – profit   18,000

3. Investment income (tax years)   £
   1990–91   5,000
   1991–92   4,000
   1992–93   6,000
   1993–94   8,000
   1994–95   9,000
   1995–96   10,000

You are required to show, using the figures provided, the alternative methods by which Lancelot can obtain relief for the trading losses sustained. You should assume his personal allowance for all years involved is the same as for 1992– 93.   **(ACCA)**

Solution

Computation of trading losses to be used:

1990/91	$\frac{1}{4} \times (12{,}000)$		(3,000)
1991/92	$\frac{3}{4} \times (12{,}000)$	(9,000)	
	$\frac{1}{4} \times (6{,}000)$	(1,500)	(10,500)
1992/93	$\frac{3}{4} \times (6{,}000)$	(4,500)	
	$\frac{1}{4} \times 9{,}000$	2,250	(2,250)

Section 381			Assessable before personal allowances
1990/91	Loss	(3,000)	
1987/88	Schedule E	20,000	17,000
1991/92	Loss	(10,500)	
1988/89	Schedule E	22,000	11,500
1992/93	Loss	(2,250)	
1989/90	Schedule E	24,000	21,750

213

Section 380

1990/91	Schedule E	20,000	
	Investment income	5,000	
		25,000	
1990/91	Loss	3,000	22,000
1991/92	Schedule E	—	
	Investment income	4,000	
		4,000	

Loss relief would
waste personal
allowance

| 1992/93 | Investment income | 6,000 | |
| | Loss | 2,250 | 3,750 |

Section 385

1991/92	Trade loss c/f	10,500	
1994/95	(31. 12. 93) Profit	9,000	
	loss b/f	9,000	
1995/96	(31. 12. 94) Profit	18,000	
	loss b/f (10,500– 9,000)	1,500	16,500

If no claim made under Section 380 or 381 the losses carried forward would be
as follows:

1990/91		3,000	
1991/92		10,500	
1992/93		2250	15,750
1994/95	Profits	9,000	
	Loss b/f	9,000	
		—	
		=	
1995/96	Profit	18,000	
	Loss b/f (15,750 – 9,000)	6,750	
		11,250	

Income tax question NO 8. Jones

Ben Jones has been farming for many years; his recent results (adjusted for tax) are as follows:

Year ended:	31 March 1991	Loss	£(2,000)
	31 March 1992	Profit	£10,000
	31 March 1993	Loss	£(5,000)
	31 March 1994	Profit	£20,000
	31 March 1995	Profit	£15,500

*You are required to compute the amounts assessable for 1991/92 to 1995/96 inclusive assuming
Ben elects for averaging of profits and wishes to use the losses as soon as possible. He has no other
income and the whole of his wife's income is covered by her personal allowances.*

Solution

Calculation of average profits

		Adjusted Profit £	Adjustments £	Averaged Profits £
1991/92	Year to 31.3.1991	–	5,000	5,000
1992/93	Year to 31.3.1992	10,000	(5,000)	5,000
		10,000		
	Average profits	5,000		
1992/93	As averaged	5,000	(2,500)	2,500
1993/94	Year to 31.3.1993	–	2,500	2,500
		5,000		
	Average profits	2,500		
1993/94	As averaged	2,500	8,750	11,250
1994/95	Year to 31.3.1994	20,000	(8,750)	11,250
		22,500		
	Average profits	11,250		
1994/95	As averaged	11,250	1,125 †	12,375
1995/96	Year to 31.3.1995	15,500	(1,125) †	14,375
		26,750		

† $30\% \times 15,500 = 4,650$

  $25\% \times 15,500 = 3,875$

Difference between profits 4,250 ∴ Marginal relief applies.

$3(4,250) - 0.75(15,500) = 12,750 - 11,625 = 1,125.$

Schedule D Case I assessments

		£	£
1991/92	Averaged profits	5,000	
	less Section 380 loss to 31.3.1991	2,000	3,000
1992/93	Averaged profits	2,500	
	less Section 380 loss to 31.3.1993	2,500	
1993/94	Averaged profits	11,250	
	less Section 380 loss to 31.3.1993	2,500	8,750
1994/95	Averaged profits		12,375
1995/96	Averaged profits		14,375

Notes

i)   *The loss relief for the period to 31.3.1991 could have been relieved in 1990/91 under Section 380. In the absence of data for that year relief has been given in 1991/92.*

ii) *The loss for the year to 31st March 1993 has been relieved in 1992/93 and 1993/94. Normally this would mean no assessment for the year 1993/94 on the preceding year basis. However, averaging has created this unusual situation.*

iii) *Profits are averaged before considering loss relief under Section 380.*

Part II

Corporation Tax

24 General principles

Introduction

1. In this chapter the main elements of the corporation tax system are outlined. It begins with some basic expressions and then a summary of the main features of the imputation system is provided. Forms of organisation liable and exempt from corporation tax are next examined followed by corporation tax pay and file. The remainder of the chapter deals with the corporation tax accounting periods, and the basic rates of tax. A summary of corporation tax rates and a specimen computation are provided at the end.

2. Corporation tax as a separate form of business taxation was introduced by the FA 1965. However, an entirely new set of rules for the determination of business income was not provided, and the substance of the income tax scheduler system was adroitly preserved.

   The main legislation is now contained in the TA 1988.

Basic expressions

3. **Financial year**

   A financial year runs from the 1st April to the following 31st March, and each year is known by reference to the calendar year in which the 1st April occurs. Thus the financial year 1997 covers the period from the 1st April 1997 to the 31st March 1998. Corporation tax rates are fixed by reference to financial years.

   Franked payment

   When a company pays a dividend (makes a qualifying distribution) the amount of the dividend together with the related amount of advance corporation tax, is known as a franked payment. Such payments are therefore 'gross'.

   Franked investment income

   When a UK resident company makes a qualifying distribution and the recipient is another UK resident company, then the amount of the distribution with the related tax credit is known as franked investment income, by the recipient.

   Advance corporation tax

   If a UK resident company makes a qualifying distribution, it is liable to pay to the Inland Revenue an amount related to that distribution. This is known as the ACT fraction, which for the year to 31st March 1998 is 20/80ths of the distribution and, in fact, applies to distributions made between the 6th April and the following 5th April.

   Profits

   This is the sum of the income derived in accordance with the Income Tax Schedules such as Schedule D Cases I to VI, Schedule A, investment income, and chargeable gains.

   Deductions and reliefs

   This is the total of loans, charges on income paid, group relief etc, deducted from profits.

   Profits chargeable to corporation tax

   This is profits less deductions and reliefs.

   Mainstream liability

   This is not a legal term, but is generally taken to mean the amount of corporation tax payable, after any ACT or other deductions.

   Close company

   This is a company which is owned or controlled by a small number of persons. Private family companies often fall into this category.

   Close investment holding company

   This is a close company other than one whose business consists of trading or is a member of a trading group.

   Group relief

   This is the term used to describe the set-off of a trade loss of one member of a group of companies against the profits of another member. The relief is also extended to members of a consortium.

Group income

This term is used to describe the receipt by a UK parent company, of a dividend from its UK subsidiary, without the subsidiary making any payment of ACT

Basic profits

This is the term used in the computation of the small company marginal relief and is equal to profits chargeable to corporation tax.

The imputation system

4.   The main features of this system are as follows.

a)   There are two rates of corporation tax and for the financial year 1997 they are a full rate of 33% and a 'small company' rate of 23%.

b)   The corporation tax rate is chargeable on profits whether distributed as a dividend or not.

c)   When a company pays a dividend (makes a qualifying distribution) the net amount is paid to the shareholder and at the same time the company makes a payment of advance corporation tax to the Inland Revenue.

d)   Within certain limits, the payment of advance corporation tax in an accounting period is set against the company's liability to corporation tax on its taxable profits for that period.

e)   The shareholder is regarded as having imputed to him or her a tax credit which for the income tax year 1997/98 is equal to 20% of the dividend payment.

f)   Income tax as such is not deducted from dividends. However, it is deducted from annual payments such as loan or debenture interest, royalties and deeds of covenant.

Main organisations liable to corporation tax

5.   a)   Companies resident in the UK, and this includes foreign owned companies operating in the UK through resident companies.

b)   State owned corporations such as the Bank of England.

c)   Unincorporated associations. These are not defined, but may be taken to include any form of club or society including voluntary associations.

d)   A branch or agency of a non-resident company.

e)   Building societies, provident societies, and insurance companies. Special rules apply to these organisations.

f)   Registered friendly societies. Exemption from corporation tax can be obtained in certain circumstances.

g)   Company partnerships. If a company enters into a partnership then it is charged to corporation tax in respect of its due share of the partnership profits.

Main organisations exempt from corporation tax

6.   a)   Partnerships.

b)   Local authorities.

c)   Approved pension schemes.

d)   Charities. A charity, which is defined as 'any body of persons or trust established for charitable purposes' is exempt from corporation tax in so far as the income is applied to charitable purposes only. If a charity carries on any trade then any profits arising will be exempt providing that:

i)   they are applied solely for the purposes of the charity, and

ii)   either the trade is exercised out of a primary purpose of the charity, or the work is mainly carried out by the beneficiaries of the charity.

e)   Agricultural and scientific societies.

f)   The British Museum, subject to certain restrictions.

g)   The Crown.

Corporation tax pay and file

7.   **The corporation tax return**

The main features of the new system for the payment of corporation tax and the making of returns are as follows.

a)   The new requirements apply to accounting periods ending after the 30th September 1993.

b)   Companies are responsible for the estimation and payment of corporation tax.

c) A new corporation tax return (Form CT200) must be submitted to the Inland Revenue together with accounts and computations.

Payment of corporation tax

a) Corporation tax must be paid within nine months of the end of the company's corporation tax accounting period (CTAP). This will in most cases be the same date as its accounting reference date. However, where a company ceases to trade while remaining in charge to corporation tax, then the CTAP ends on the date trading ceased.

b) Interest on unpaid corporation tax will automatically accrue in respect of any part of the liability not paid by the nine month period.

c) The company's obligation to pay arises without the issue of any assessment by the inspector of taxes. In most cases an assessment will only be raised when the return and computation are agreed by the inspector of taxes.

Self assessment

8. Self assessment for companies is not likely to apply to accounting periods ending before 1999 at the earliest.

Corporation tax return

9. a) Under the procedural arrangements the inspector of taxes issues to each company in charge to corporation tax, a notice to deliver a corporation tax return (CT203).

b) The notice to submit a return is normally issued within about three months of the end of the company's CTAP.

c) The return (form CT 200) must be completed and sent to the inspector of taxes within 12 months of the end of its accounting period, or if later within three months of the date of the request by the inspector.

d) Accounts and computation must be submitted with the return.

e) The return must be signed by the secretary, treasurer, liquidator or, in the case of a non-resident company, agent, manager etc.

f) Automatic penalties for the late submission of returns will apply as follows:

Period of delay (Months)	Penalties
1 – 3	£100
3 – 6	£200
6 – 9	£200 + 10% of tax unpaid
9 –	£200 + 20% of tax unpaid

For repeated failures to return on the due dates the fixed rate penalties are increased to £500 and £1,000.

Repayment supplement

10. Where a repayment of corporation tax or income tax of £100 or more is made more than 12 months after the material date the amount is increased by a supplement at the appropriate rate of interest for each complete tax month from the 'relevant date' to the end of the tax month in which the repayment is made.

Material date is the normal due date for payment of corporation tax ie nine months after the year end.

Relevant date is:

a) if the repayment is of corporation tax paid on or after the first anniversary of the material date – the anniversary of the material date that follows the date that tax was paid.

b) in any other case – the first anniversary of the material date.

Financial years and accounting periods

11. In accordance with Section 6 TA 1988 corporation tax is charged on the profits of companies for financial years, and these run from the 1st April to the following 31st March. Each financial year is known by reference to the calendar year in which the 1st April occurs, eg:

Financial Year	Period
1995	1st April 1995 – 31st March 1996
1996	1st April 1996 – 31st March 1997
1997	1st April 1997 – 31st March 1998

The corporation tax rates for any financial year are normally determined in the relevant FA.

Corporation tax accounting periods

12. a) A corporation tax accounting period (CTAP) is the period for which a corporation liability has to be computed and this can never exceed 12 months' duration.

b) A CTAP begins in the following circumstances:

  i) when a company comes within the scope of UK corporation tax - for example, by acquiring a source of income, starting business activities or becoming resident in the UK,

  ii) immediately after the end of a previous accounting period provided the company remains within the scope of corporation tax.

c) A CTAP ends when the earliest of the following events occurs.

  i) The company reaches its reporting 'year' end (ie its accounting date). or the end of a period for which it has not made up accounts.

  ii) It is twelve months since the corporation tax accounting period began.

  iii) The company starts or stops trading (an accounting period ends when trading starts or stops, even if other business activities continue).

  iv) The company ceases to be within the scope of corporation tax (for example, by winding up its business and selling all its income-producing assets, or in the case of non-resident companies, by ceasing to trade in the UK or to carry on mineral exploration or exploitation activities in the UK sector of the North Sea).

  v) The company goes into liquidation (once a company has gone into liquidation its corporation tax accounting periods run for consecutive periods of 12 months until the completion of the winding-up).

  vi) The company starts or stops being resident in the UK.

Accounting periods more than 12 months long

13. If a company's period of account has to be split into two or more accounting periods, the profits must be allocated between the various accounting periods. The following rules are applied:

  i) Trading income (Cases I, II or V (trades only), Schedule D) is computed for the whole period of account, before deducting capital allowances or adding balancing charges. This amount is then apportioned to the various accounting periods on a time basis. Capital allowances and balancing charges are calculated for each accounting period and the above amounts are adjusted accordingly.

  ii) For all other cases and schedules the actual income for the accounting period must be ascertained.

  iii) Chargeable gains are assessable in the accounting period in which they arise.

  iv) Charges on income are deducted from the total profits of the accounting period in which they are paid.

  v) Where the period of account exceeds twelve months, say 15 months, it will be split into two accounting periods, one of twelve months and one of three months.

> **Example**

K Ltd has regularly prepared accounts to the 31st December. With effect from the 1st January 1995 the directors decide that the year end shall be 31st March and the next set of accounts covers the period of fifteen months to the 31st March 1996.

Corporation tax accounting periods	Accounts periods
12 months to 31st December 1994	12 months to 31st December 1994
12 months to 31st December 1995	} 15 months to 31st March 1996
3 months to 31st March 1996	
12 months to 31st March 1997	12 months to 31st March 1997

Note

> There will be two return periods covering the 15 month period:
>
> 12 months to 31.12.1995 3 months to 31.3.1996.

The basic rates

14. There are two main rates of corporation tax, a full or standard rate and a 'small company rate'. The level of profits subject to corporation tax determines which rate applies, and in addition there is a form of marginal relief which links the various levels.

There are special rules for the determination of profits for the purposes of the small company rate and these are examined in detail in Chapter 31.

Profit levels

Financial Year	Full Rate		Small Company Rate		Marginal Relief
	£	%	£	%	£
1994 to 31.3.95	1,500,000	33	300,000	25	300,000 – 1,500,000
1995 to 31.3.96	1,500,000	33	300,000	25	300,000 – 1,500,000
1996 to 31.3.97	1,500,000	33	300,000	24	300,000 – 1,500,000
1997 to 31.3.98	1,500,000	33	300,000	23	300,000 – 1,500,000

Changes in the basic rate

15. Where a company's accounting period does not coincide with the corporation tax financial year, and there is a change in the rate of corporation tax, then the profits must be apportioned between the two financial years on a time basis. The profits are deemed to accrue evenly over the accounting period even though this may not reflect the actual trading experience of the company. Any apportionment must be made by reference to the number of days in the respective periods.

> **Example**

D Ltd whose accounting period ended on the 30th June 1997 had profits chargeable to corporation tax of £200,000. With a corporation tax rate of 24% for the financial year 1996 and a rate of 23% for 1997 the computation would be as follows:

Profits chargeable to corporation tax	£	£
1.7.1996 to 31.3.1997 $^{274}/_{365} \times 200,000$	150,137	
1.4.1997 to 30.6.1997 $^{91}/_{365} \times 200,000$	49,863	200,000

Corporation tax payable	
Financial year to 31.3.1996 150,137 @ 24%	36,032.88
Financial year to 31.3.1997 49,863 @ 23%	11,468.49
	47,501.37

The small company rate applies in this case, and the rates changed w.e.f. 1st April 1997.

Corporation tax – Accounting period table

16. The following table may be helpful in apportioning profit for most accounting periods which straddle financial years.

Accounting period End Date	Normal Year Days		Leap Year Days	
	FY1	FY2	FY1	FY2
30 April	335	30	336	30
31 May	304	61	305	61
30 June	274	91	275	91
31 July	243	122	244	122
31 August	212	153	213	153
30 September	182	183	183	183

..... continued

Accounting period End Date	Normal Year Days		Leap Year Days	
	FY1	FY2	FY1	FY2
31 October	151	214	152	214
30 November	121	244	122	244
31 December	90	275	91	275
31 January	59	306	60	306
28/29 February	31	334	31	335

Corporation tax rates

17.

Years to 31st March

	1994	1995	1996	1997	1998
Full Rate	33%	33%	33%	33%	33%
Small Company Rate	25%	25%	25%	24%	23%
Small Company Profit Levels £'s	250,000 to 1,250,000	300,000 to 1,500,000	300,000 to 1,500,000	300,000 to 1,500,000	300,000 to 1,500,000
Formula Fraction	$1/50$	$1/50$	$1/50$	$9/400$	$1/40$
ACT Fraction	9/31	20/80	20/80	20/80	20/80

Specimen Corporation Tax Computation (Based on FORM CT 200)

		£	£
I	**INCOME**		
	Trading profits (Schedule D Cases I and II		
	Adjusted profits		
	less Capital allowances		
	Trade losses brought forward	–	–
	Schedule D Case III		
	Income received without deduction of income tax		–
	Overseas income (Schedule D Case V		–
	Income within Schedule D Case VI		–
	Income from which income tax has been deducted		–
	Intra group income from which income tax has not been deducted by election		–
	Income from UK land and buildings		–
	Chargeable gains		–
II	**PROFITS**		
III	**DEDUCTIONS AND RELIEFS**		
	Non-trade loan relationship deficit		–
	Losses on unquoted shares	–	
	Trading losses	–	
	Management expenses	–	
	Non-trade capital allowances	–	–
	Profit before charges and group relief		–
	Charges paid		–
	Group relief		–
IV	**PROFITS CHARGEABLE TO CORPORATION TAX**		
V	**CORPORATION TAX CHARGEABLE**		
	Financial year 1996 @ 33%		–
	1997 @ 33%		–
	Total corporation tax before reliefs and set-offs in terms of tax		
VI	**RELIEFS AND SET-OFFS IN TERMS OF TAX**		
	Marginal small companies relief		–
	Double taxation relief		–
	Advance corporation tax		–
VII	**NET CORPORATION TAX CHARGEABLE**		–
	Income tax suffered by deduction		–
VIII	**CORPORATION TAX DUE**		
	(mainstream liability)		

25 The charge to corporation tax

Introduction

1. This chapter is concerned with the determination of corporation tax profits before deductions and reliefs which is, an important stage in the determination of profits chargeable to corporation tax, as indicated by the equations below.

    The chapter begins with some basic equations which identify the main components in the corporation tax computation. The main components of profits are then summarised and the chapter concludes with two comprehensive examples of the adjustment of profits for corporation tax purposes.

Basic equations

2. Any company which is resident in the UK is chargeable to corporation tax in respect of all its profits wherever they arise. In equation form profits may be defined as follows:

Profits chargeable to corporation tax	=	Profits – deductions and reliefs

Profits	=	$\begin{cases} \text{Income derived under the income tax schedules} \\ \text{Income from which income tax is deducted at source} \\ \text{Group interest} \\ \text{Chargeable gains} \end{cases}$

Deductions and reliefs	=	Trade losses etc + charges paid + group relief

    Income is to be computed and assessed under the schedules and cases as applied for income tax so that in order to understand the computation of corporation tax income, it is therefore necessary to have some knowledge of the rules and laws appropriate to each schedule. As this has already been covered in detail for income tax purposes the sections below will only indicate any significant differences which exist for corporation tax purposes. It should be noted that all income and expenditure relates to actual accounting periods for corporation tax purposes.

Schedule D Cases I and II

3. The following points should be noted under this heading.

    a) The general principles of deductible expenditure apply, but any items of expenditure which are charges on income *(see Chapter 27)* are not allowed as an expense in computing trading income. In respect of accounting periods ending after 31st March 1996, profits and losses arising from loan relationships are treated as receipts or expenses of trading and not as charges on income.

    b) Petroleum revenue tax is a deductible expense for corporation tax purposes.

    c) Incidental costs of obtaining loan finance including acceptance credits and convertible loan stock are allowed as a deduction in computing trading income. This would include such costs as fees, commissions, advertising and printing, but not stamp duty.

    d) Pre-incorporation expenses incurred up to seven years prior to the actual commencement of trading may be treated as being incurred on the first day of trading. Eligible expenditure includes all expenses which, had the company been trading would have been allowed as a trading expense such as rent, rates, wages and salaries, but not company formation expenses, stamp duties, and capital expenditure.

    e) Unpaid emoluments:
        i) A deduction for emoluments in the computation of Cases I and II of Schedule D income will not be allowed where they are paid more than nine months after the end of the period of account. Instead a deduction will be allowed in the period of account when they are paid.
        ii) Payment in this case means the same time as used to determine when emoluments are received by a person. *See Chapter 8.*

iii) Where accounts are submitted with computations within the nine month period, any unpaid remuneration at that time should not be deducted in calculating the taxable profits. If the remuneration is subsequently paid before the end of the nine month period, then an adjustment can be made to the computations, if claimed within two years of the end of the period of account.

Schedule D Case III

4. For accounting periods ending after 31st March 1996, Case III has been defined to include what was formerly Case IV. The income taxable under this heading is as follows.

   a) Profits and gains arising from non-trade loan relationships.

   b) Any annuity or other annual payment which:

   i) is payable (whether inside or outside the UK and whether annual or short) in respect of anything other than a loan relationship; or

   ii) is not a payment chargeable under Schedule A.

   Bank and building society interest normally paid gross to a company are taxed under this heading. Should a company receive an interest net, i.e. with 20% rate deducted at source, the gross amount is chargeable to corporation tax.

5. Where income is received after deduction of income tax at source, since the gross amount is chargeable to corporation tax, then the income tax deducted at source is recoverable as follows:

   a) It can be set against any income tax payable in respect of charges on income paid or a loan relationship, e.g. debenture or loan interest.

   b) If relief is not fully available under (a) then any excess may be deducted from the main corporation tax liability, or if this is exceeded, a cash repayment may be obtained.

   Taxed investment income must be accounted for under what is known as the 'quarterly return system' as outlined in Chapter 27.

Loan relationships

6. For accounting periods ending after 31st March 1996, new provisions apply to what are termed 'loan relationships', as follows.

   a) In general a loan relationship exists whenever it is a creditor or debtor for a debt which is regarded as a loan under general law. Thus the issue of a loan or debenture would fall within this definition, as well as other financial securities.

   b) The definition in (a) above encompasses practically all Government gilt-edged securities, building society PIBS (permanent interest-bearing shares), and corporate bonds and corporate debts.

   c) To give effect to the new rules there are two methods of accounting which companies are authorised to use:

   i) an accruals basis by which payments and receipts are allocated to the accounting periods in which the transaction takes place;

   ii) a market-to-market basis by which a loan relationship must be accounted for in each accounting period at a fair value.

   As a general rule, companies will be allowed to follow their accounts treatment for taxation purposes.

   d) Where companies enter into a loan relationship for the purposes of a trade, then all profits, losses and costs relating to the loan relationship will be treated as receipts or expenses of that trade and therefore included in the calculation of its Schedule D Case I trade profits or losses.

   e) Where a company enters into a loan relationship which is of a non-trade nature, ie it is not a loan relationship in the course of activities forming an integral part of the trade, the position is as follows:

   1) Any net income is assessed as Case III income.

   2) Any net loss is dealt with as below:

   i) by offset against the company's other income and gains chargeable to corporation tax for that accounting period; or

    ii) by surrender as group relief to other United Kingdom group companies. Losses can only be surrendered to the extent that these exceed the company's taxable profits for the period *before* taking account of reliefs from other periods (for example, brought forward losses); or

    iii) by carry back on a last in first out basis against the company's previous three years' net profits arising from its loan relationship to the extent that such profits arise after 31st March 1996 on a company's non-trading foreign exchange and financial instrument transactions; or

    iv) by carry forward against its future non-trading profits (including capital gains). This treatment is also extended to losses arising from non-trading foreign exchange and financial instrument transactions.

f) The new rules apply to all UK companies in charge to corporation tax, including UK branches of overseas companies.

g) A company issuing corporate debt will also be able to obtain tax relief for interest on an accruals basis provided the interest is paid within 12 months of the accounting year end.

Schedule A and Case VI property income

7.   With effect from the 6th April 1995 the income tax rules for the taxation of property income under Schedule A and Case VI are different in principle for companies to those for individuals and partnerships. The 'old' income tax rules are retained for companies and reproduced below.

Schedule A

8.   This schedule deals with rental income from leases of land or buildings situated in the UK and the main charging provisions are contained in Sec 15 TA 1988. Income is computed by reference to the 'annual profits or gains arising in respect of any rents', which means that some form of income and expenditure account is required for each type of rent.

Rental income

9.   Rent is not defined as such, but is taken to include income from lettings of house property, factories, car parks, sporting rights, and certain wayleaves. As the rental income taxable is that arising it is only assessable if actually due in the period covered by the assessment, and there are no accruals to be made except where this involves connected persons, *see Chapter 24*. Rents receivable but not actually received are taxable, but there is some relief available under Sec 41 TA 1988, where rents are not received and:

a) the non-payment is due to the default of the payer, and reasonable steps have been taken to enforce payment, or

b) the rent is waived by the landlord in order to avoid undue hardship, and there was no other consideration for the waiver.

Non-rental income

10.   The following items are not taxable income under Schedule A:

a) Income from land situated outside the UK. This is taxed under Case V.

b) Yearly interest.

c) Profits or gains arising from the use of land for one of the statutory trades referred to in Sec 55 TA 1988, which are taxable under Schedule D Case I, such as mines, quarries, canals and docks.

d) Rents under a lease which includes the use of furniture. *See furnished accommodation below*.

e) Receipts of a capital nature. *See lease premiums below*.

f) Income of hotels, cinemas, and boarding houses in practice is regarded as trading income and taxed under Schedule D Case I.

Allowable expenditure

11. Deductions are permitted for payments made in respect of the following:

a) Maintenance, repairs, insurance or management.

b) Services provided other than by way of maintenance or repair, being obligatory services for which no separate consideration is received.

c) Business rates, water rates, or other charges which the landlord is obliged to pay.

d) Any rent or ground rent.

Maintenance and repair expenditure is that needed to retain the value of the property and does not include additions, replacements or improvements. Insurance refers to the building as such, and not to the contents, but insurance premiums in respect of a leasehold redemption policy are not allowed.

Management includes all the normal expenses associated with the management of property such as costs of advertising lettings, costs of estimates for repairs, legal expenses for recovery of rent arrears etc. Where a company is landlord, then a proportion of general management expenses would be allowed. Capital allowances are available for plant and machinery used for the maintenance or repair of premises, or for management purposes.

Rents misappropriated by an agent were not allowed as an expense of management in the case of *Pyne v Stallard-Penoyre* 1964 42 TC 183.

In order to be deductible, the payment must be in respect of the premises comprising the lease, and with regard to repairs and maintenance, must relate to the period since the landlord acquired the property. Thus expenditure carried out at the beginning of a tenancy in order to make the premises habitable would not be allowed.

Classes of lease

12. The following are the three classes of lease which have significance for Schedule A purposes:

a) Landlord repairing lease at full rent.

b) A tenant repairing lease at full rent.

c) A lease at less than full rent.

Under a full rent lease the rent is sufficient, taking one year with another, to meet the landlord's expenses.

Where there is an excess of expenditure over income, then the excess may be set against other rental income in accordance with the rules noted below.

Landlord repairing lease (full rent)	1. Surplus/excess of expenditure from different leases may be set against each other, ie pooled.
	2. Any excess of expenditure not relieved may be carried forward to subsequent periods, and pooled.
Tenant repairing lease (full rent)	1. Surplus/excess of expenditure for *the current period*, may be set against any surplus arising in the same period from a landlord repairing a lease, at full rent. Any balance still outstanding can be carried forward and set off against future income from the same lease/property.
Leases at a nominal rent	1. Relief for any excess of expenditure may only be carried forward and set against income arising from the *same lease*, to the same tenant.

Void periods

13. Whenever property is neither occupied nor let to a tenant, this period is known as a void period, and expenditure incurred during this time is a permitted deduction provided that:

a) the void period follows a lease at a full rent, tenant or landlord repairing, and the property is then let at a full rent, or

b) the void period commences with the acquisition of the property and is followed by a lease at a full rent. In this case only dilapidations arising since acquisition would be permitted.

Expenditure incurred in the void period can be set against other net rental income from leases, within the restrictions noted above, or can be carried forward and set against income from the same property.

When the same property is let on a succession of different leases, then unrelieved excess expenditure may be carried forward from one lease to another provided that:

a) the successive leases are at a full rent, and

b) there is no break between the termination of one lease and the commencement of another, or if there is a break, then the property is unlet.

Lease premiums

14. One way of looking at lease premiums is to regard them as a capitalised part of future rental income which would otherwise have been received by way of annual rent. They include any sum whether payable to the immediate or a superior landlord, arising in connection with the granting of a lease, but not arising from an assignment, of an existing lease.

Under an assignment the lessee takes the position of the original lessee, with the same terms and conditions.

Where a lease is granted (but not assigned) at a premium, for a period not exceeding 50 years, then the landlord is deemed to be in receipt of a rental income equal to the premium, less an allowance of 2% of the premium for each complete year of the lease remaining, excluding the first 12 month period.

Example

B Ltd granted a lease for 24 years of its warehouse to a trader on the following terms:

A lease premium of £12,000 to be paid on 1.1.1997 and an annual rent of £1,000;

Allowable expenditure for accounting period ended 31st December 1997 was £5,800.

C. Tax AP 31.12.1997 Schedule A

	£	£
Lease premium	12,000	
Less 2% × 12,000 × (24 − 1)		
ie 1/50 × 12,000 × 23	5,520	6,480
Annual rent		1,000
		7,480
Less allowable expenses		5,800
Schedule A income		1,680

In effect the lease premium is discounted by reference to its duration, and the longer the unexpired portion, the greater the discount. Thus if a lease had 49 years to run the discount would be

$$(49 - 1) \times 2\% \text{ ie } 96\%.$$

The amount of the taxable premium may also be determined by use of the formula:

$$P - \frac{(P \times Y)}{50}$$

P = amount of premium paid; Y = Number of completed 12 months other than the first.

A premium on a lease for a period greater than 50 years would not be taxed as Schedule A income.

Lease premiums and the lessee

15. Where the lessee makes a payment of a lease premium on the granting of a lease, then a proportion of that premium may be set against the following:

a) any trading income, providing the premises are used for business purposes, Sec 87 TA 1988

b) any rental income or lease premium received from any sub lease granted by the lessee.

In effect the amount of the premium assessed as income of the lessor can be charged as an expense of trading, the taxable portion being spread over the remaining life of the lease.

Example

S Ltd is granted a lease of premises to be used for trading purposes, for a period of 20 years at an annual rent of £600 p.a. and an initial lease premium of £32,000.

	£
Lease premium	32,000
Less 2% × 32,000 × (20 − 1) ie 38% × 32,000	12,160
Lease premium charged on lessor	19,840

Relief available to S Ltd is $\dfrac{19840}{20}$ ie £992 p.a.

Schedule D Cases IV and V

16. *See Chapter 33*, International Aspects. For companies, Case IV is abolished for accounting periods ending after 31st March 1996.

Schedule D Case VI

17. There are no special features for corporation tax.

Capital gains tax

18. Companies are not liable to capital gains tax as such, but they are liable to corporation tax on any chargeable gains which must be computed in accordance with the appropriate rules, as outlined in Chapters 36 to 42.

All chargeable gains are taxed at the relevant corporation tax rate which for FY 1997 is:

Company's profits > £1,500,000	33%
Small company profits < £300,000	23%

With marginal relief for profits in between £300,000 and £1,500,000.

> **Example**
>
> K Ltd has corporation tax income of £1,500,000 for its accounting year ended 31st March 1998, and a chargeable gain of £500,000.
>
> *Compute the corporation tax payable.*
>
> *Solution*

K Ltd Corporation tax computation. AP to 31.3.1998

	£
Corporation tax income	1,500,000
Chargeable gain	500,000
Profits chargeable to corporation tax	2,000,000
Corporation tax @ 33%	660,000

Adjustment of profits

19. **Example**

S plc has the following results in respect of the year ended 31st March 1997.

Compute the Schedule D Case I adjusted profits for corporation tax purposes, before capital allowances.

	£	£
Sales		283,165
Factory cost of sales		127,333
Factory profit		155,832
Expenses: General administration	37,021	
Marketing	28,197	
Distribution	16,031	
Financial	22,000	103,249
		52,583
Non-sales revenue		14,723
Profit before tax		67,306
Corporation tax		30,000
Profit after tax		37,306
Dividends paid and proposed		23,000
Retained profits for the year		14,306

Additional information:

		£
Factory cost of sales includes:	Depreciation	17,832
	Partitioning works office	3,179
	Repairs to new premises to make usable	1,621
General expenses include:	Legal costs of tax appeal	627
	Legal costs of share issue	175
	Stamp duty	1,200
	Fines on employees, motor offences	250
Marketing expenses include:	Trade debts written off	1,211
	Loan to employee written off	250
	Increase in general bad debt provision	5,000
	Increase in specific bad debt provision	1,000
	Promotional gifts, £10 each	1,800
	Advertising on TV	6,000
Financial expenses include:	Bank interest	1,100
	Bank charges	238
	Donation to political party	250
	Subscriptions to trade associations	1,250
	Redundancy payments	11,000
Non-sales revenue comprises:	Profit on sale of assets	323
	Bad debts recovered	1,700
	Agency commission	12,700

Solution

S plc adjustment of profits. Accounting period to 31st March 1997

	£	£
Retained profits per accounts		14,306
Add back items disallowed:		
Factory cost of sales:		
Depreciation	17,832	
Partitioning	3,179	
Repairs	1,621	
General administration:		
Legal expenses	627	
Legal expenses	175	
Stamp duty	1,200	
Marketing expenses:		
Loan to employee	250	
Including general bad debt provision	5,000	
Financial expenses:		
Donation	250	
Corporation tax	30,000	
Transfer to reserves	5,000	
Dividends paid and proposed	18,000	83,134
		97,440
Less Profit on sale of assets		323
Schedule D Case I adjusted profits		97,117

Notes to answer

1. *Applications of profit are not expenses incurred in the earning of profits and accordingly the dividends and corporation tax provision have been added back. It follows that it would have been possible to commence the computation with the profits before these items, ie £67,306, and this is the normal procedure.*
2. *Depreciation £17,832 – capital allowances claimed in lieu.*
3. *Partitioning £3,879 –plant and machinery, see Jarrold v Johnson & Sons 1962 40 TC 681.*
4. *Repairs £1,621 – see Law Shipping Co Ltd, and Odeon Theatres Ltd. cases.*
5. *Legal expenses £627 – expenses of tax appeal not allowed.*
6. *Legal expenses £175 – capital expenditure not revenue.*
7. *Stamp duty £1,200 – capital expenditure not revenue.*
8. *Loan to employee £250 – non-trading debt, see Section 74(1), and Bamford v A. TA Advertising.*
9. *Increase in general provision for bad debts £5,000 – see Section 130 (i).*
10. *Donation to political party £250 – not an expense of trading.*
11. *Profit on sale of assets £323 – this is not a taxable receipt.*

• Student self-testing question

T Ltd has the following for the year ended 30th June 1997.

	£	£
Sales		160,000
Cost of sales		40,000
Gross profit		120,000
Wages and salaries	42,000	
Rent and rates	4,287	
Insurance and telephone	1,721	
Repairs and renewals	35,000	
Heating and lighting	2,897	
Professional charges	3,250	
Bank interest	1,155	
Subscriptions and donations	1,200	
Directors' emoluments (£10,000 paid in April 1998)	22,000	
Patent renewal fees	1,000	
Bad debts	1,250	
Sales commission	5,680	
Loss on sale of assets	1,000	
Miscellaneous expenses	7,251	129,691
Trading loss		(9,691)

	£	£
Other income:		
Discounts received	1,123	
Exchange surplus	12,107	
Dividends received	1,620	
Rents received less outgoings	651	15,501
Trading profit before taxation		5,810

Additional information:

Repairs and renewals:	
Repairs to newly acquired premises of which £10,000 was necessary to make usable	27,000
Furnace relining – provision for future expenditure	8,000
Professional charges:	
Audit and accounting	1,250
Architect's fees for new factory	1,750
Legal costs for renewal of short lease	250
Subscriptions and donations:	
Donation to golf club used by staff	500
Subscriptions to trade associations	150
Covenanted payment to charity	550
Directors' emoluments:	
Salaries and bonus (bonus of £10,000 paid in April 1998)	18,000
Pension scheme provisions (paid 31.8.97)	4,000
Bad debts:	
Trade debts written off	250
Increase in general provision	1,000
Miscellaneous expenses:	
Office party	410
Theatre tickets for foreign customers	725
Removal expenses of new managing director	850
Compensation to customers for damage from company's product	5,000
Interest on overdue corporation tax	266
Exchange surplus:	
Profit from currency dealings arising from trade	12,107
Rents received less outgoings:	
Net rents from letting part of factory	1,000
Deficit on property let to retired employee at a nominal rent	(349)

Compute the Schedule D Case I trading income for the AP to 30th June 1997.

Solution

T Ltd Accounting Period to 30th June 1997

	£	£
Trading profit per accounts		5,810
Add items disallowed:		
Repairs and renewals	18,000	
Professional charges	1,750	
Donation to golf club	500	
Covenant to charity	550	
Pension contribution	4,000	
Bad debt provision	1,000	
Loss on sale of asset	1,000	
Theatre tickets	725	
Interest on overdue tax	266	
Directors' remuneration - bonus	10,000	37,791
		43,601
Less: Dividends received	1,620	
Rents received	651	2,271
Schedule D Case I trading income		41,330

Notes to answer

1. *Repairs to make the premises usable are not allowable. £10,000. Round sum provisions are disallowed. £8,000.*
2. *Architect's fees for new factory are capital expenditure.*
3. *Donation to golf club, although used by staff, is not welfare or sports expenditure.*
4. *The covenant to the charity is not allowed as a trading expense, but is deducted as a charge on income in the computation.*
5. *Pension contributions are not allowed unless paid in the AP.*
6. *The increase in the bad debt provision is not allowed.*
7. *Losses on the sales of fixed assets are not trading expenses.*
8. *The theatre tickets are disallowed entertaining expenses.*
9. *Interest on overdue tax is not allowable.*
10. *Dividends received are not trading income, but 'franked investment income', which is not chargeable to corporation tax.*
11. *Rents received are taxable under Schedule A. The deficit on the nominal rented property can not be set against other Schedule A income.*
12. *As the exchange surplus has arisen through trading it is taxable as a trading receipt.*
13. *As the directors remuneration was paid more than nine months after the year end it is not allowed until CTAP 30. 6.1998.*

• Questions without answers

1. Z plc has the undermentioned results for the year ended 31st March 1998.

	£	£
Trading profits		1,900,000
3½% War loan interest (gross)	1,000	
Bank deposit interest(gross)	1,500	
Building society interest (gross)	700	3,200
		1,903,200
Less allowable expenses	50,000	
Director's remuneration	25,000	
Depreciation	8,000	83,000
Profit before tax		1,820,200

Compute the profits chargeable to corporation tax and the corporation tax payable.

2. R Ltd has schedule D Case I profits for the year ended 31st Decemnber 1997 of £91,600. The company also owns three properties which are let. All rents are receivable quarterly in advance on the usual quarter days, 25 March, 24 June, 29 September and 25 December.

   i) Property 1 is a shop which is let unfurnished on a tenant's repairing lease. The lease at an annual rental of £6,000 ended on 24 March 1997. The property was re-let from 29 September 1997 on a new lease at an annual rental of £5,000. Between Marchand September when the property was empty internal decoration work was carried out costing £3,500.

   ii) Property 2, also a shop, is let unfurnished on a landlord's repairing lease. The shop was purchased in October 1997. Immediate remedial work costing £12,000 was required to repair the foundations which had slipped in August 1997. the property was then let from 25 December 1997 at an annual rental of £20,000. The incoming tenant also had to pay a premium of £5,000 in return for the granting of a seven-year lease.

   iii) Property 3 is a house which is permanently let furnished on a landlord's repairing lease. The annual rental is £2,500.

Expenditure incurred during the year was:	£
Routine decoration and maintenance costs	2,000
Water rates	200
Council tax	400
	2,600

   A 10% wear and tear claim for furniture and fittings was to be made rather than claim the renewals basis. No election to apportion the rent between the property and the furniture will be made.

   Compute the company's charge to corporation tax for the year ended 31st December 1997.

3. P Ltd's accounts for the 12 months to 31st December 1997 showed the following:

	£		£
Wages and salaries	90,500	Gross trading profit	228,100
Rent, rates and insurance	6,000	Net rents	750
Motor expenses	2,000	Profit on sale of plant	5,500
Legal expenses	2,000		
Director's Remuneration	35,000		
Audit charges	2,500		
Miscellaneous	1,300		
Depreciations	6,000		
Premium on lease w/off	14,000		
Net profit	75,050		
	234,350		234,350

   Notes

   i) *Legal expenses comprise:*

	£
Debt collection	600
Staff service agreements	250
Issue of debentures	1,150
	2,000

   ii) *Miscellaneous expenses comprise:*

	£
Subscriptions – trade associations	150
political party	290
Interest on unpaid tax	150
Staff outing	710
	1,300

   iii) *On the 1st July 1997 P Ltd was granted the lease of additional factory premises for a period of seven years from that date, on payment of a premium of £14,000.*

   iv) *Capital allowances for the accounting period to 31.12.1997 have been agreed at £33,230.*

   v) *Gross trading profit is arrived at after deducting £50,000 paid in December 1997 under a threat of blackmail of the chief executive.*

   Calculate the mainstream liability to corporation tax for the AP to 31st December 1997.

26 Capital allowances

Introduction

1. The nature of the capital allowance system, as outlined in Chapter 17 in connection with income tax and business income, is essentially the same for corporation tax purposes. However, there are some differences, most of which will gradually disappear as the self-assessment procedures for individuals are introduced.

Main features

2. a) Capital allowances are available in respect of qualifying expenditure incurred in an accounting period, which is the basis period.

    b) Capital allowances are deducted as an expense in arriving at the Schedule D Case I trading income. A balancing charge is treated as trading income.

    c) The pool system for plant and machinery and other assets is the same for companies as for individuals, but there is no disallowance for private use of a company asset.

    d) A writing down allowance or FYA for plant and machinery can be disclaimed by a company.

    e) If capital allowances effectively create a trading loss then they are not carried forward separately but as an integral part of the Case I loss.

    f) Where the accounting period is greater than 12 months' duration then the capital allowances are computed for each separate period and not 'scaled up' as for income tax purposes.

> **Example**

K plc has the following data relating to its accounting period ended 31st March 1997.

	£
Schedule D Case I adjusted profits	1,865,550
Schedule A	173,200
Plant and machinery pool at 1.4.1996	88,000
Additions	27,000
Industrial buildings allowance	10,000

Compute the capital allowances and the corporation tax liability for AP to 31st March 1997

Solution

Capital allowances: plant and machinery

	Pool £
Written down value b/f	88,000
Additions	27,000
	115,000
Writing down allowance @ 25%	28,750
Written down value c/f	86,250

Corporation tax computation AP 31.3.1997

	£	£
Schedule D Case I adjusted profits		1,865,550
Less capital allowances:		
Plant and machinery	28,750	
Industrial buildings	10,000	38,750
Schedule D Case I		1,826,800
Schedule A		173,200
Profits chargeable to corporation tax		2,000,000
Corporation tax payable 2,000,000 @ 33%		660,000

• Questions without answers

1. Z Ltd has the following information relating to its accounting period for the 15 months to 30th April 1997. Prior to this date the company had always prepared accounts to the 31st January in each year.

		£
1.2 .1996	Pool value of plant brought forward	5,800
11.3.1996	Machinery purchased	3,000
3.7.1996	Fixtures and fittings purchased	2,000
4.8.1996	Plant and machinery sold (cost £9,000)	6,800
10.2.1997	Plant and machinery sold (cost £40,000)	35,000
15.3.1997	Office equipment purchased	30,000
12.4.1997	Micro-computers purchased	20,000

Calculate the capital allowances available to Z Ltd for the two accounting periods to 30th April 1997.

2. Palmer Pranks Limited is a manufacturing company making annual accounts up to 31 December.

On 1 July 1989 the company bought a new building, which qualified as an industrial building, and brought the building into use as an industrial building on 1 April 1990. The building was purchased for £150,000 (excluding land) and was used as an industrial building until 1 July 1991. For 2 years it was leased for non-industrial use until 30 June 1993. On 1 July 1993 Palmer Pranks Limited recommenced manufacturing in the building. On 1 October 1996 the building was sold for £225,000 (again excluding land) to Kennedy Capers Limited whose annual accounting date is 30 September and who brought the building into industrial use immediately.

The building is not located in a designated enterprise zone.

Calculate:

a)   *the industrial buildings allowances given to Palmer Pranks Limited for all years*

b)   *the balancing adjustment on the sale of the building in 1996*

c)   *the industrial buildings allowance claimable by Kennedy Capers in the chargeable accounting period ended 30 September 1997.*

27 Charges on income/quarterly returns

Introduction

1. This chapter is concerned with the charges on income such as patent royalties or covenanted payments to a charity, and their treatment for corporation tax purposes. It begins with the definition of charges on income and the conditions which must be met if they are to be allowed as deductions where payments are made to both residents and non-residents.

   The income tax aspects of charges and loan relationship interest and the manner in which such tax is collected form the remainder of the chapter.

2. In accordance with Section 338 (1) TA 1988 charges on income are allowed as a deduction in computing the profits chargeable to corporation tax for an accounting period. In equation form:

$$\begin{array}{l} \text{Profits chargeable to} \quad = \quad \text{Profits} - \text{Trading losses etc} - \text{Charges on income (paid)} \\ \qquad \text{corporation tax} \qquad\qquad\qquad\qquad\qquad\qquad\qquad - \text{Group relief} \end{array}$$

   Charges are therefore deducted from profits after trading losses etc (*see Chapter 29*) and before Group Relief (*see Chapter 32*).

Definition

3. For accounting periods ending after 31st March 1996, charges on income are defined to include:

   a) annual payments such as covenants to charities

   b) patent royalties, mining rent and royalties

   c) annuities

   d) qualifying donations to charities and company gifts (see below).

   Note that losses arising from loan relationships are not treated as charges on income but as an expense of trading.

   For accounting periods ending before 1st April 1996 charges on income included yearly interest such as loan or debenture interest.

   A sum deductible in computing trading income cannot be a charge on income. See *Wilcock v Frigate Investments Ltd*, 1982 STC 198.

Qualifying donations *Section 339 TA 1988*

4. Companies (other than close companies) can treat as a charge on income gifts to a charity up to a maximum of 3% of dividends paid on ordinary share capital, during the companies' accounting period.

   Basic rate income tax must be deducted at source from these payments which are known as qualifying donations, and accounted for under the quarterly return system.

   The above relief is in addition to any gifts made by way of a four-year covenant.

Company gifts

5. With effect from 18th March 1991 a company can make single gifts of any amount (in excess of £250) to charities within any one accounting period.

   Income tax at the basic rate must be deducted at source by the company and the gross amount is allowed as a deduction in computing the profits chargeable to corporation tax, and treated as a charge on income.

   The basic rate income tax must be accounted for under the quarterly return system.

   For non-close companies the existing relief for qualifying donations will still be available where it is more favourable.

Eligible deductions

6. To be eligible for deduction from profits the charges on income must comply with the following conditions.

   a) They must be actually paid in the accounting period and not accrued.

b) The payments must be ultimately borne by the company making the payment.

c) They must be paid out of the company's profits brought into charge to corporation tax.

d) They must be made for valuable and sufficient considerations, except for covenanted donations to charity, and qualifying donations.

e) Income tax at the basic rate must be deducted at source from each payment.

Adjustment to accounts

7. As the normal company accounts do not distinguish between charges on income and interest in arriving at profits before taxation it would be necessary to 'add back' some of the items for two reasons.

a) In the first place if they are charges on income then they are deducted from profits and not trading income.

b) Secondly, only charges actually paid in the accounting period are allowed, whereas for accounts purposes an element of accrual might have been made.

If the payments relate to an earlier accounting period, they are nevertheless allowed as a charge in the accounting period when the payments are made.

Note Interest falling within the loan relationship rules will be allowed on an accruals basis, as an expense of trade.

Collection of income tax on payments which are not distributions

8. The principles of the system for the collection of income tax, which are contained in Schedule 16 TA 1988, are as follows.

Return periods

a) A company must make returns to the collector of taxes in respect of each of its accounting periods of *payments* (not accruals) subject to the deduction of income tax at source, and of income received which has been taxed at source.

b) The returns must be made for a quarter and the dates prescribed are 31st March, 30th June, 30th September, and 31st December. These are known as standard return periods, and if a company's accounting period does not coincide with any of the quarterly dates, then an additional return is required.

Income tax is deductible from the undermentioned payments at the rates shown with effect from 6th April 1996.

	Basic rate 23%	Lower rate 20%
Yearly interest (other than to a UK bank) eg debenture/loan interest	–	✓
Interest paid by banks/building societies	–	✓
Income element of purchased life annuities	–	✓
Rents paid to non-UK residents	✓	–
Patent royalties	✓	–
Payments under deed of covenant	✓	–

> **Example**

S Ltd has an accounting year ending on the 30th November 1997. The return periods relating to that accounting period are as follows:

1996	1st December to 31st December
1997	1st January to 31st March
	1st April to 30th June
	1st July to 30th September
	1st October to 30th November

The company here has five return periods and each return must be submitted within fourteen days of the end of the return period. If there are no transactions in the period a nil return is not required.

c) The return forms must show particulars of *payments made in the period*, and income tax deducted is due on the return date without the making of any formal assessment. Particulars of any unfranked investment income, including building society interest, must also be included on the returns, and any income tax suffered at source is set against that due on any annual payments paid.

The position at the end of a return period

9. a) If the income tax payable exceeds the income tax suffered, the balance may be set against any suffered from earlier return periods, within the company's accounting period.

b) In the absence of any excess as in (a) above, then the net amount is payable on the due date.

c) Where the income tax suffered at source is greater than the income tax payable on the charges on income, then the surplus may be carried back and set against any excess of income tax paid in return periods within the company's accounting period.

Example

F Ltd has an accounting period ended 31st March 1997 and during the year the following transactions took place.

1996	April 11th	Debenture interest paid	8,000
	June 30th	Interest received on 12% Treasury stock	4,000
	August 7th	Bank interest paid	12,000
	October 11th	Debenture interest paid	8,000
1997	January 1st	Interest received on 12% Treasury stock	4,000

All transactions are shown net as entered in the company's bank account.

Show the quarterly returns for the year to 31st March 1996.

Solution

Quarter	Income tax on annual payments and interest		Income tax deducted		Net amount Paid (Received)
	Gross amount £	Income Tax £	Gross amount £	Income Tax £	£
30.6.96	10,000	2,000	5,000	1,000	1,000
30.9.96	–	–	–	–	–
31.12.96	10,000	2,000	–	–	2,000
31.3.97	–	–	5,000	1,000	(1,000)
	20,000	(4,000)	10,000	2,000	2,000

Notes

i) *In the fourth quarter, the excess of income tax suffered can be set against the payment made in quarter 1 or 3.*

ii) *Bank interest paid is not subject to deduction of income tax and is, therefore, excluded from the return system.*

iii) *Interest paid and received is taxed at the 20% rate.*

The position at the end of an accounting period

10. This may be summarised as follows.

Income tax deducted from income received net > Income tax paid on annual payments and interest.

a) (i) Excess can be set against corporation tax payable on the profits of the accounting period.

ii) If the excess is greater than the corporation tax payable then a cash repayment can be obtained.

b) Income tax deducted from income received net < Income tax paid on annual payments and interest.

i) In this case since the excess has already been paid over within the quarterly return system, no further adjustment is necessary.

Example

B Ltd has an accounting period ended 31st March 1997 and during that year, the following transactions took place, all net.

1996	June 10	Interest on unsecured loan stock paid	1,600
	July 19	Debenture interest received	2,000
	August 31	Building society interest received (Gross)	2,500
	December 10	Interest on unsecured loan stock paid	1,600
1997	January 19	Debenture interest received	2,000

The adjusted Case I trading profits for the year ended 31st March 1997 amounted to £1,795,300 Schedule A income in respect of the same period was £1,200.

Show the quarterly returns for the year to 31st March 1997 and the corporation tax computation for the same period.

The unsecured loan interest is used for trade purposes.

Solution

| | Income tax on annual payments and interest | | Income tax deducted | | Net amount | |
Quarter	Gross amount	Income Tax	Gross amount	Income Tax	Paid (Received)	Excess
	£	£	£	£	£	£
30.6.96	2,000	400	–	–	400	–
30.9.96	–	–	2,500	500	(400)	(100)
31.12.96	2,000	400	–	–	400	–
31.3.97	–	–	2,500	500	(400)	(100)
	4,000	800	5,000	1,000	–	(200)

Corporation tax computation. AP to 31.3.1997

	£
Schedule D Case I (1,795,300 – 4,000)	1,791,300
Schedule A income	1,200
Income taxed at source	5,000
Building society interest	2,500
Profit chargeable to corporation tax	1,800,000
Corporation tax @ 33%	594,000
less excess income tax as above	200
	593,800

Notes

i. *Unsecured loan interest is a deduction for Case I income purposes.*

ii. *As there was an excess of taxed income suffered, the income tax unrecovered is set against the corporation tax payable. From a cash flow point of view, the benefit will not be felt until the corporation tax becomes payable.*

Excess charges

11. It should perhaps be noted here that as charges on income are deducted from total corporation tax profits situations can arise where the charges are greater than the total profits. The excess charges give rise to a claim for loss relief and this is examined in Chapter 29, *Relief for losses*.

• Student self-testing question

K Ltd has the following data relating to its accounting period ended 31st March 1998.

	£
Schedule D Case 1	1,548,000
Building society interest (gross)	2,000
Bank interest received (net)	8,000
Qualifying donation (net)	30,800
Debenture interest accrued (net)	16,000

Compute the corporation tax payable for the AP to 31st March 1998.

Solution

Corporation tax computation AP to 31.3.1998

	£
Schedule D Case I	1,528,000
Bank interest gross	10,000
Building society interest gross	2,000
	1,540,000
Charges on income paid	
Qualifying donation gross 30,800 ÷ 0.77	40,000
Profits chargeable to corporation tax	1,500,000
Corporation tax payable	
1,500,000 @ 33%	495,000
Mainstream liability	495,000

Notes

i) Schedule D Case I   1,548,000
   Less debenture interest accrued (gross)   20,000   1,528,000

ii) *The qualifying donation is subject to deduction of basic rate income tax at source and the gross amount claimed as a charge on income. The income tax must be returned on the CT61.*

iii) *As the charges are greater than the tax income received there is no adjustment required in computing the mainstream liability.*

• Questions without answers

1. P plc has the following entries in its cash book for the year ended 31st December 1997.

Cash Book

		£				£
Jan	1 Dividend from UK company	800	Feb	1	Proposed final dividend for 1996	10,000
	31 Debenture interest	20,000	Mar	1	Debenture interest	16,000
Mar	1 Dividend from UK company	20,000	Sept	1	Debenture interest	16,000
	31 Building society interest (gross)	2,250	Oct	30	Interim dividend for 1997	30,000
Apr	30 Dividend from foreign company					
	after 45% withholding tax	825				
June	30 Bank deposit interest	12,000				
July	31 Debenture interest	25,000				
Dec	31 Bank deposit interest	5,180				

Adjusted Schedule D Case I profits for the year amounted to £1,600,000 (excluding the cash book entries) and Schedule A income £62,820.

Compute the profits charged to corporation tax for the year to 31st December 1997.

2. Stonyhurst Limited is a trading company, resident in the United Kingdom, which makes up its annual accounts to 31 March. It has no associated companies. The company's profit and loss account for the year ended 31 March 1997 was as follows:

		£	£
	Gross trading profit		372,100
1.	Add: Surplus on sale of plant etc	17,150	
	Debenture interest (gross)	3,250	
	Dividends received from UK companies (gross)	4,570	
	Building society interest received (gross)	730	
2.	Bank deposit interest	360	26,060
			398,160
	Deduct:		
	Lighting and heating	1,290	
	Repairs and renewals	1,600	
3.	Depreciation	34,650	
	Wages and salaries	24,450	
	Directors' remuneration	35,480	

4.	*Subscriptions and donations*	*1,350*	
	Postage, stationery and phone	*525*	
5.	*Loan interest payable*	*17,500*	
6.	*Professional expenses*	*6,820*	
7.	*Miscellaneous expenses*	*1,815*	*125,480*
	Net profit		*272,680*

Notes

1. The bank deposit account was opened 17 August 1996 and interest of £300 was credited to the account on 31 December 1997. £60 interest had accrued on the account at 31 March 1997.

2. Subscriptions and donations

	£
Golf club subscription for sales director	150
National Trust	50
Political party	300
Local charities	75
Works social club	750
Trade association	25
	1,350

3. Loan interest

   There was an accrued liability at 31 March 1997 for loan interest of £1,500. There was no opening accrual.

4. Professional expenses

	£
Audit and accountancy	3,000
Costs of successful tax appeal	500
Legal fees re collection of bad debts	180
Costs of defending action by a former director for wrongful dismissal	300
Legal costs on acquisition of a new seven-year lease on a warehouse	500
Architect's fees for designing a new warehouse which was not proceeded with	2,340
	6,820

5. Miscellaneous expenses

	£
Entertaining – foreign suppliers	70
– UK suppliers	340
– UK customers	180
Round-sum expense allowances to company salesmen	1,225
	1,815

6. You are also given the following information.

   a) The company paid a dividend of £18,000 to its shareholders on 13 March 1997.

   b) The written down values of capital assets at 1 April 1996 were:

	£
Plant and machinery (main pool)	72,125
1980 Pool – motor cars	10,438
Expensive car no 1 (purchased 1.1.94)	8,598
Expensive car no 2 (purchased 1.1.94)	10,520

   The following items were purchased and sold during the year ended 31 March 1997.

Purchases		£
11 August 1996	Car for salesman	6,500
23 October 1996	Moveable office partitioning	3,518
7 March 1997	Plant and machinery	42,500
28 March 1997	Plant and machinery	17,192

Sales		£
19 April 1996	Plant and machinery	31,000
29 July 1996	Expensive car No. 2	7,500
11 August 1996	Car (purchased on 13 August 1992 for £4,500)	2,150

243

Notes

i) *The private usage of the salesman's car is one-quarter.*

ii) *The company's offices do not qualify for Industrial Buildings Allowances.*

7. The industrial Buildings Allowance for the year ended 31 March 1997 is £4,106.

Compute the profits chargeable to corporation tax for the year ended 31st March 1997.   **(ACCA)**

28 Qualifying distributions ACT and FII

Introduction

1. This chapter begins with the definition of a qualifying distribution and the related advance corporation tax (ACT) implications. The meaning of franked investment income (FII) and its relationship to ACT in the computation of corporation tax payable is then examined.

   A surplus of ACT or FII: ACT and double tax relief and the collection of ACT and FII form the remainder of the chapter.

2. The treatment of dividends paid and received for corporation tax purposes is one of the main features of the imputation system. In general, where a company makes a qualifying distribution (ie pays a dividend) then an associated payment of advance corporation tax becomes payable which is subsequently deductible from any corporation tax due on the profits. Distributions, whether qualifying or non-qualifying, are not allowed as a deduction in computing corporation tax profits, and they are income in the hands of the recipient.

Qualifying distributions

3. Most of the tax laws do not in fact refer to dividends as such, but to qualifying distributions which is a general term covering a wide range of similar transactions. These include:

   a) Any dividends paid by a company including a capital dividend. Ordinary and preference dividends are thus included, together with any dividends which are described as capital dividends by the paying company, but not 'stock dividends', which are scrip shares issued in lieu of a dividend.

   b) Any other distributions out of the assets of a company whether in cash or otherwise. There are some exceptions to this rule, for example, repayments of share capital on a winding up are not qualifying distributions. However, where a company distributes in specie, assets or shares in another company, without additional consideration being received from its shareholders, then this is a qualifying distribution, as is interest in excess of a reasonable commercial return under Section 212 TA 1988.

   c) Interest on bonus securities issued in respect of shares and securities.

   d) Interest on unquoted securities convertible into shares or with rights to shares or securities. Interest on quoted convertible loan stock is not a distribution, but a charge on income.

   e) Transfers of assets or liabilities to any member, where the value of any benefit received is greater than any consideration given. This does not apply to inter-company transfers between members of a 51% group.

   f) The repayment of capital that has been originally issued by way of a bonus issue of share capital.

   g) Benefits in kind to any participator or associate of a close company except, generally, where the recipient is charged to income tax under the rules of Schedule E. The latter would be the case for most participator directors.

   h) Excessive interest payments made to associated companies may be treated as a distribution in certain circumstances.

   It should be noted that distributions which fall within the 'demerger' provisions of Section 213 TA 1988, are exempt distributions, and accordingly the advance corporation tax and income tax rules do not apply. Also exempt are payments made by an unquoted company on the purchase of its own shares, *see Chapter 34*.

Qualifying distributions and ACT

4. In accordance with Section 14 of the TA 1988, when a UK resident company makes a qualifying distribution then it is liable to pay an amount of advance corporation tax in respect of that distribution. The amount of the distribution together with the related amount of ACT is called a franked payment.

   The rate of ACT is determined annually by the Finance Act, and is in fact a fraction to be applied to the amount of any distribution made by a company. The following is a list of the ACT fractions which have applied in the last few years. Note that although the corporation tax rates are fixed for financial years the ACT fraction applies to distribution made between the 6th April and the following 5th April, ie on a fiscal year basis.

Financial years

1993	31.3.94	$\frac{22\frac{1}{2}}{77\frac{1}{2}}$ ie $\frac{9}{31}$	(6.4.93 – 5.4.94)
1994	31.3.95	$\frac{20}{80}$	(6.4.94 – 5.4.95)
1995	31.3.96	$\frac{20}{80}$	(6.4.95 – 5.4.96)
1996	31.3.97	$\frac{20}{80}$	(6.4.96 – 5.4.97)
1997	31.3.98	$\frac{20}{80}$	(6.4.97 – 5.4.98)

For 1997/98 the rate of ACT and the tax credit will be the same at 20%.

Thus when a dividend is declared the amount of the ACT and hence the franked payment can be determined.

> **Example**

Q plc pays a dividend on the 31st July 1997 of 10p per share on its ordinary share capital of 800,000 shares of 10p each.

Calculate the amount of the franked payment.

Solution

	£
Dividend payment of 10p per share	80,000
ACT $\frac{20}{80} \times 80,000$	20,000
Franked payment	100,000

A company is required to account for all ACT under what is known as the quarterly return system and this is examined later in the chapter.

ACT set-off

5. Under Section 239 TA 1988, ACT paid by a company in an accounting period can be set against its liability to corporation tax on any profits charged to corporation tax for that accounting period subject to a maximum set-off, see section 6 below:

ACT on dividends PAID in the accounting period — Set off against corporation tax on profits chargeable to corporation tax in the accounting period

*Note The distributions are those actually paid in the accounting period and **not** those proposed.*

> **Example**

T Ltd has the undermentioned profits chargeable to corporation tax for its accounting period ended 31st March 1998.

	£	£
Schedule D Case I trading income		1,796,000
Less charges on income		96,000
Profits chargeable to corporation tax		1,700,000
Dividend paid during year to 31.3.1998	240,000	
ACT $\frac{20}{80} \times 240,000$	60,000	
Franked payment		300,000

Compute the corporation tax payable.

Solution

T. Ltd AP to 31.3.98

	£
Corporation tax payable:	
Profits chargeable to corporation tax	1,700,000
Corporation tax @ 33% × 1,700,000	561,000
ACT set off 20% × 300,000 or ($\frac{1}{4}$ × 240,000)	60,000
Mainstream liability	501,000

Note

The words 'mainstream liability' have no legal connotation but are widely used to describe the corporation tax liability payable on the normal due date, ie the total liability less any ACT and other deductions.

Maximum ACT set-off

6. There is an overall limit to the amount of ACT which can be set off against the corporation tax. Under Section 238 TA 1988 this is limited to the amount of ACT that would be payable if a distribution plus ACT equal to the company's profits chargeable to corporation tax was made for the accounting period.

   Maximum ACT set off = DIVIDEND % × (profits chargeable to corporation tax)

   Dividend % = Rate of income tax on dividends (Gross) which is 20% for 1997/98.

> **Example**

A Ltd has the following data relating to the accounting period ended 31st March 1998:

	£
Schedule D Case I	350,000
Chargeable gain	1,250,000
	1,600,000
Less charges on income paid	100,000
	1,500,000

A dividend of £1,600,000 was paid on 1st January 1998.

Compute the mainstream liability.

Solution

		£
Maximum ACT set-off		
Schedule D Case I		350,000
Chargeable gains		1,250,000
		1,600,000
Less charges on income paid		100,000
Profits chargeable to corporation tax		1,500,000
Maximum ACT set-off 20% × £1,500,000		300,000
Corporation tax payable:		
£1,500,000 @ 33%		495,000
ACT on net dividend of £1,600,000	£	£
1,600,000 × $\frac{1}{4}$ =	400,000	
Maximum set-off as above	300,000	300,000
Surplus ACT	100,000	
Mainstream liability		195,000

Franked investment income

7. When a UK resident company makes a qualifying distribution, and the recipient is a person resident in the UK then he or she is usually entitled to a tax credit. This is normally equal in amount to the value of advance corporation tax payable by the company in relation to the distribution.

   If the recipient is another UK resident company then the amount of the dividend together with the tax credit is known as franked investment income, ie **FII**.

Scrip dividends are not franked investment income.

This form of income has some special rules attached to it which are given below.

a) FII is not subject to corporation tax in the hands of the recipient. However it is used to determine the 'small company' profit levels, *see Chapter 31*.

b) The calculation of any Net ACT payable is affected by any FII received, *see (e) below*.

c) An excess of FII over ACT, called a surplus of franked investment income, can be used in connection with certain loss reliefs.

d) Distributions made between members of a group of companies may be made without the ACT and related tax credit. This is known as group income.

e) For 1997/98 the value of the tax credit attached to distributions received for ACT purposes is $\frac{20}{80} = \frac{1}{4}$.

f) The tax credit for the purposes of the small company rate is also $\frac{20}{80}$ for 1997/98. *See Chapter 31*.

ACT and FII

8. Under Section 241 TA 1988, where a company is in receipt of any franked investment income, then such income is available to 'frank' distributions made by the company. Accordingly, a company is only liable to pay ACT to the extent that its franked payments exceed its franked investment income in any accounting period.

Example

B Ltd whose accounting period is to the 31st March 1998 has the following corporation tax profits:

	£
Schedule D Case I	1,450,000
Schedule D Case III	25,000
Chargeable gains	35,000
	1,510,000
Less Charges on income	10,000
	1,500,000

Dividends paid in the accounting period amounted to £600,000, and dividends received in the same period amounted to £300,000.

Compute the mainstream liability.

Solution

B Ltd AP to 31st March 1998

		£
Dividends paid		600,000
ACT 1/4 × 600,000		150,000
Franked payment		750,000
Dividends received		300,000
Tax credit 1/4 × 300,000		75,000
Franked investment income		375,000
Corporation tax payable:		
Corporation tax profits		1,500,000
Corporation tax @ 33% × 1,500,000		495,000
ACT set off:	£	
Franked payments ACT	150,000	
Franked investment income tax credit	75,000	
Set off	75,000	75,000
Mainstream liability		420,000

Note *The maximum ACT set-off is 20% × 1,500,000 = 300,000.*

Surplus FII

9. In any accounting period when there is an excess of franked investment income over franked payments, then this excess is known as 'surplus franked investment income'. In accordance with Section 241 (3) TA 1988, such a surplus may be carried forward to the next accounting period and regarded as franked investment income of that period and used for set-off against any franked payments. To the extent that the surplus is not thereby absorbed, it may be carried forward indefinitely. See also section 13(e) for use of a surplus of FII within an accounting period.

> ### Example

A Ltd has profits chargeable to corporation tax amounting to £1,800,000 for the year ended 31st March 1998. On 1st April 1997 there was a surplus of FII brought forward amounting to £50,000. A dividend of £40,000 was paid on 1st January 1998 and on 1st July 1997 dividends received amounted to £16,000.

Compute the mainstream liability.

Solution

A Ltd AP to 31st March 1998

	£	£
Franked payment 40,000 + (20/80 × 40,000 = 10,000)		50,000
Franked investment income 16,000 + ($\frac{1}{4}$ × 16,000 = 4,000)		20,000
Corporation tax payable:		
£1,800,000 × 33%		594,000
ACT set off:		
Franked payment		50,000
FII b/f	50,000	
FII during year	20,000	70,000
Surplus of FII		20,000 —
Mainstream liability		594,000

A surplus of franked investment income may also be used, in certain circumstances, by way of set off against a loss determined in accordance with Section 242 TA 1988, and this aspect is considered in Chapter 29.

Surplus ACT

10. Where the amount of ACT paid in any accounting period is greater than the maximum permitted then the surplus ACT may be dealt with as follows.

   a) It can be carried back and set against corporation tax charged on profits of accounting periods beginning within six years prior to the year in which the surplus arose. The surplus must be applied to a more recent period before an earlier period, ie on a LIFO basis.

   b) A claim for set-off against the previous six years must be made within two years of the end of the accounting period in which the surplus arose.

   c) If a company makes no claim to have a surplus of ACT carried backwards, or makes a claim which still leaves some surplus ACT unrelieved, then any surplus outstanding will be carried forward automatically.

   d) When a surplus is carried forward or backwards, then it is treated as if it were a payment of ACT in respect of a distribution, made in the period to which it is carried. It is therefore subject to the maximum set-off criteria relating to that period.

   e) It can be carried forward and set against any future corporation tax charged on total corporation tax profits. This is restricted where within any three year period:

   i) there has been both a change in the ownership of the company and a major change in the company's trade, or

   ii) after the trade has become negligible and before it revives, there is a change in ownership.

   f) It can be surrendered to a 51% subsidiary. This aspect is examined in chapter 32 dealing with groups and consortia.

Example

G Ltd has its accounting year ended on the 31st March with profits of £60,000 for 1997 and £50,000 for 1998. No dividend was paid in the year to 31.3.1997. In the year to 31.3.1998 a dividend of £56,000 was paid. The company claims to carry back any surplus ACT

Calculate the mainstream liabilities for each year.

Solution

	£	AP 31.3.98 £	AP 31.3.97 £
Corporation tax income		50,000	60,000
Corporation tax @ 23%/24%		11,500	14,400
ACT set off:			
ACT on dividend of 56,000 $\times \frac{1}{4}$	14,000		
Maximum set off 20% × 50,000	10,000	10,000	
Surplus of ACT	4,000		
Mainstream liability		1,500	14,400
Surplus ACT carried back:			
Corporation tax as above		11,500	14,400
Maximum ACT set off		10,000	–
Surplus ACT carried back		–	4,000
Mainstream liability		1,500	10,400

Notes

i)   In this example had the surplus been greater than the maximum allowed for the year to 31st March 1997 ie 20% × 60,000 ie £12,000, then the balance could be carried back five further years and used within the maximum criteria for each year.

ii) ACT on dividend of £56,000 is 20/80 × 56,000 = £14,000.

Changes in ACT rate and maximum set-off

11. Where there is a change in the rate of ACT, then if this bridges a company's accounting period, the profits chargeable to corporation tax must be apportioned on a time basis. The period up to the date of the change and the subsequent period are treated as separate accounting periods for the purpose of determining the maximum ACT set-off. This is obtained by combining the two computations.

Example

S Ltd has profits for the year ended 31st December 1994 of £400,000. The ACT fraction for the year to 31st March 1994 is $\frac{22\frac{1}{2}}{77\frac{1}{2}}$, and for the year to 31st March 1995 $\frac{20}{80}$.

Show the maximum ACT set off for the year to 31.12.1994

Solution

Calculation of maximum ACT set-off for year to 31.12.1994:   £

AP 1.1.94 to 31.3.94

$^{90}/_{365}$ × 400,000 ie 98,630 × 22½%   22,192

AP 1.4.1994 to 31.12.94

$^{275}/_{365}$ × 400,000 ie 301,370 × 20%   60,274

                                                                                          82,466

Changes in the rate of ACT do not affect the amount of any surplus ACT which can be carried back, but the maximum set-off determined for each year is based on the appropriate ACT fractions as noted in the example above.

12. a)   Where there is a change in the ACT rate the change does not apply until the 6th April of the year of the change.

     b)   Where there is a change in the rate of ACT and a dividend has been declared before April 5th, but paid after that date, or vouchers are at the printers showing the rate, ACT paid is at the new rate.

c) Where a company's accounting period straddles the 5th April then a new accounting period is deemed to commence on that date for the purposes of calculating liability for ACT. FII received after the 5th April cannot be set against franked payments made on or before that date.

The collection of ACT and FII

13. Quarterly returns of advance corporation tax and franked investment income are required in accordance with the provisions of Schedule 13 of the TA 1988. These returns have certain features in common with those required for the collection of income tax on annual payments and interest paid and received as outlined in a previous chapter.

The main provisions are as follows.

a) In respect of each accounting period, a company must make returns to the collector of taxes, of franked payments and franked investment income received. The quarterly return periods are the same as for other company payments, and will not normally exceed five in any one accounting period. A nil return is not required in any period in which there are no franked payments or franked investment income.

b) Each return must contain particulars of the amounts of any franked payments made and of any franked investment income received in the return period.

c) The amount of FII to be returned in addition to the amounts actually received in the return period should include the following:

   i) any surplus FII carried forward from the previous accounting period, and

   ii) any surplus FII carried forward from a previous return period, within the current accounting period.

d) In any return period, where there is an excess of franked payments over franked investment income, ACT is payable on the excess at the rate of ACT for the financial year in which the return period ends. Any payments of ACT must be made within 14 days of the relevant return period.

e) In any return period where there is a surplus of franked investment then it can be carried back to earlier return periods within the same accounting period and set against franked payments on which ACT has been paid. A repayment of ACT can be obtained in these circumstances.

f) If qualifying distributions are made between 1st April and the 5th April in any year *and there is a change in the rate of ACT*, then special rules apply for the set-off of ACT but a separate return period is not created.

> ### Example

T Ltd has the following dividend transactions in respect of its accounting year to the 31st March 1998. Show the amounts which would appear on the CT61.

			£
Dividends paid	1st May 1997		8,000
Dividends paid	17th February 1998		16,000
Dividend received	31st October 1997		800

Return	Amount of distribution	Franked payment	Franked investment income	Franked payments	ACT rate	Paid/ repaid	Date
1	2	3	4	3–4	5	6	7
30.6.97	8,000	10,000	–	10,000	$\frac{20}{100}$	2,000	14.7.97
30.9.97	–	–	–	–	–	–	No return
31.12.97	–	–	1,000	(1,000)	$\frac{20}{100}$	(200)	Reclaim 14.1.98
31.3.98	16,000	20,000	–	20,000	$\frac{20}{100}$	4,000	14.4.98
	24,000	30,000	1,000	29,000		5,800	

The net ACT payment for the accounting period of £5,800 can be set against profits chargeable to corporation tax in the AP to 31st March 1998, subject to the maximum criteria.

Foreign income dividends

14. Where a company elects for a dividend paid to be a foreign income dividend then the following provisions apply.

   i)   An election to treat a dividend as a FID must be made by the time the dividend concerned is paid. It cannot be revoked after payment of the FID.

   ii)   A FID is a qualifying distribution on which ACT is payable, but is not part of a franked payment.

   iii)   FIDs are treated separately from franked payments and franked investment income. Companies cannot use franked investment income received to reduce the ACT due on FIDs paid. Neither can they set FIDs received against franked payments made. But they can set FIDs received against FIDs paid.

   iv)   The recipient of a FID is not entitled to a tax credit on it, and the dividend voucher must say this.

   v)   Companies are not chargeable to corporation tax on FIDs received.

   vi)   In certain circumstances, ACT on FIDs paid can eventually be repaid if it is not needed for set-off against corporation tax.

Details of FIDs must be included in the CT61 return.

Non-qualifying distributions

15. These are defined by exception in Section 14 of the TA 1988, and comprise the following

   a)   bonus redeemable shares or securities issued in respect of shares and securities

   b)   a distribution of any share capital or securities which the company making the distribution received from another company in the form of bonus shares or securities, of a redeemable nature.

There is no ACT payable in connection with non-qualifying distributions and therefore they are not franked investment income of a recipient company. Accordingly they do not enter the quarterly return system for those types of transactions, and are not available for set-off against any ACT liability.

Example

K Ltd decided on the 1st January 1981 to capitalise some of its reserves and made a bonus issue of redeemable preference shares, comprising 100,000 10% redeemable preference shares of £1.00 each fully paid. The shares are redeemed at par on the 31st March 1995, and the company's accounting year ends on the 31st December.

In the year to 31st December 1981, there would be a non-qualifying distribution of £100,000 but no ACT liability. However, when the shares are redeemed in the year to 31st December 1995, there would be a qualifying distribution of £100,000, and ACT of $20/80 \times £100,000$ ie £25,000 would be payable in the normal way.

When a company makes a non-qualifying distribution, then it must make a return to the inspector of taxes within 14 days of the accounting period in which the distribution is made. The return must contain particulars of the transaction giving rise to the distribution, and the name and address of each person receiving any part of the distribution together with the amount received by each.

• Student self-testing question

T plc has the following data relating to the last two years.

	12 months to 31.3.1998	12 months to 31.3.1997
	£	£
Schedule D Case 1	1,550,000	50,000
Schedule A	125,000	30,000
Chargeable gains	125,000	–
Dividends paid	1,600,000	16,000
Dividend received	–	4,000

Compute the mainstream liability for 1998 and 1997 on the assumption that any surplus ACT is carried back.

Solution

Corporation Tax computation

	12 months to 31.3.1998 £			12 months to 31.3.1997 £
Schedule D Case I	1,550,000			50,000
Schedule A	125,000			30,000
Chargeable gains	125,000			
	1,800,000			80,000
Corporation tax payable:				
1,800,000 @ 33%	594,000		80,000 @ 24%	19,200
ACT set-off:				
Dividend paid	1,600,000		FP	20,000
ACT $\frac{1}{4} \times$ 1,600,000 =	400,000		FII	5,000
				15,000
Maximum set-off:				
20% × 1,800,000=	360,000	360,000	ACT 20% × 15,000	3,000
Surplus ACT	40,000		Surplus ACT from 1998	13,000 16,000
Mainstream liability		234,000	*Mainstream liability*	3,200

Notes

i) *The maximum set-off for AP to 31.3.1997 is 20% × £80,000 = £16,000.*

ii) *ACT carried back to AP 31.3.1997 is £13,000.*

iii) *Surplus ACT carried forward is £40,000 – £13,000 = £27,000.*

• Questions without answers

1. Z Ltd has the following data relating to the year ended 31st March 1998.

	£
Schedule D Case I	15,000
Schedule D Case VI	68,000
Debenture interest paid (gross)	3,000
Dividend paid	96,000

Compute the corporation tax liability for the AP to 31st March 1998.

2. Avril Showers Ltd makes up its accounts to 31 March each year. In the year to 31 March 1997 the following transactions took place:

1. 30 April 1996 — Paid loan interest of £80,000 (gross)
2. 31 May 1996 — Received interim dividend from Layne & Co Ltd (a UK company) £8,000
3. 30 June 1996 — Paid interim dividend of £160,000
4. 31 July 1996 — Received half-yearly interest on £50,000 9½% debenture stock from Lesley & Co Ltd
5. 31 October 1996 — Paid final dividend of £300,000
6. 31 October 1996 — Paid loan interest of £80,000 (gross)
7. 31 January 1997 — Received final dividend from Layne & Co Ltd (a UK company) £16,000
8. 31 January 1997 — Received half-yearly interest on £50,000 9½% debenture stock from Lesley & Co Ltd
9. 28 February 1997 — Paid deed of covenant to trade association of £1,000 (gross).

Notes

A. *There is no surplus franked investment income brought forward at 1 April 1996.*

B. *The company's adjusted trading profit for the year ended 31 March 1997 was £1,709,250.*

C. *There were chargeable gains of £135,000.*

i) *Prepare entries relating to advance corporation tax and income tax as they would appear on the forms CT61 submitted to the collector of taxes in respect of the year ended 31 March 1997.*

ii) *Prepare the corporation tax computation for the year ended 31 March 1997 showing the mainstream corporation tax payable.*

29 Relief for losses

Introduction

1. This chapter examines the various forms of loss relief available to a company which is not a member of a group of companies. As the sources of corporation tax profits can be numerous, each form of loss relief available will be considered within the framework of the schedular system. Relief available in connection with charges on income and chargeable gains is also covered.

   A company can claim to set a trading loss against other income in several ways. In summary form they may be depicted as follows:

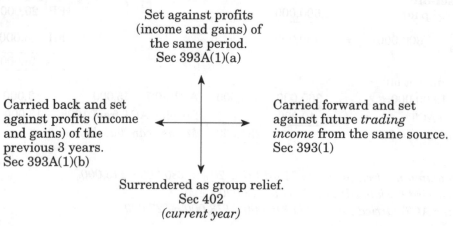

Set against profits
(income and gains) of
the same period.
Sec 393A(1)(a)

Carried back and set
against profits (income
and gains) of the
previous 3 years.
Sec 393A(1)(b)

Carried forward and set
against future *trading
income* from the same source.
Sec 393(1)

Surrendered as group relief.
Sec 402
(current year)

List of loss reliefs

2. Sec. 393A(1)(a) Set against profits chargeable to corporation tax of the same accounting period.

   Sec. 393A(1)(b) Set against profit chargeable to corporation tax of the three preceding years.

   Sec. 393(1) Carried forward and set against future trading income.

   Sec. 393(9) Excess charges carried forward and set against future trading income.

   Sec. 242/243 Treatment of surplus of FII as income and set against trading loss.

   Sec. 402 Surrender of trading losses to a 75% subsidiary (and consortium) by way of group relief, *see Chapter 32*.

   Sec. 401 Pretrading expenditure.

Schedule D Case I – trade losses

3. It is perhaps worth recalling that a Schedule D Case I trading loss is arrived at after deducting capital allowances. These may in fact turn a 'profit' into a 'loss' for tax purposes. Also, charges on income are deducted from total corporation tax profits and not Case I income.

   Trade losses Section 393A(1)(a) and (b)

   a) Under this section a company which has incurred a loss in its trade (excluding any loss brought forward) in any accounting period, may claim to set off that loss against total profits (ie including chargeable gains) of the same accounting period.

   b) Any balance of loss remaining *after this set-off* may be carried back three years prior to the accounting period in which the loss was incurred, and set off against corporation tax profits of those years.

   c) A claim for the current year must be made before claiming relief for any preceding year.

   d) A claim under this section must be made within two years of the end of the accounting period in which the loss is incurred, or within such longer period as the Inland Revenue may allow.

   e) Relief for the loss under Section 393A(1)(a) appears in the computation before charges on income and group relief are deducted.

   f) Where the accounting period of the loss is less than 12 months' duration, the loss can nevertheless be carried back 36 months.

g) Where the loss is carried back under Section 393A(1)(b) then it is set off against profits *after* deducting trade charges on income but not non-trade charges such as gifts, aid, donations and covenants. In effect this does not disturb relief obtained for trade charges in earlier years.

Example

Q Ltd has the following corporation tax profit/loss for its accounting years ended 31st March 1998 and 1997 and makes a claim for loss relief under Section 393A(1)(a) and (b).

Show the computations.

Q Ltd

	AP to 31.3.98	AP to 31.3.97
	£	£
Schedule D Case I	(30,000)	80,000
Schedule A	9,000	10,000
Chargeable gains	2,100	9,000

Solution

Claim for relief under Section 393A(1)(a) and (b)

	£	£
Schedule D Case I	–	80,000
Schedule A	9,000	10,000
Chargeable gain	2,100	9,000
Total profits	11,100	99,000
Less Section 393A(1)(a) and (b) relief	11,100	18,900
Assessment	–	80,100

Loss memorandum
The trading loss of £30,000 has been utilised as follows:

Set against other profits for the year to 31.3.1998 – 393A(1)(a)	11,100
Set against other profits for the year to 31.3.1997 – 393A(1)(b)	18,900
	30,000

Notes

i) *In making a claim under Section 393A(1)(a) for the year to 31st March 1998 it is not necessary to carry the losses back to the previous period.*

   The carryback relief is only available when the total profits of the year of the loss have been absorbed.

ii) *It is not possible to claim a partial relief for the year to 31st March 1998 and also claim relief for the period to 31st March 1997 or earlier years.*

Trade losses carried forward Section 393(1)

4. Where a company incurs a trading loss in any accounting period, then apart from any claim for relief under Sections 393A(1)(a) and (b) the loss may be dealt with as follows:

   a) It may be carried forward to succeeding accounting periods so long as the company continues to trade.

   b) A loss carried forward is only deductible from future trading income not corporation tax profits, chargeable to corporation tax.

   c) The trading profit of a succeeding period is treated as being reduced by any such loss brought forward.

   d) A claim under this section must be made within six years of the end of the accounting period in which the loss was incurred.

   e) There may be a disallowance of trading losses carried forward arising from a change of ownership. Sec 768 TA 1988 – *see Chapter 32.*

Example

D Ltd has the following results for the two years ended 30th June 1997.

	AP to 30.6.96	AP to 30.6.97
	£	£
Schedule D Case I	(12,000)	7,000
Schedule D Case III	3,000	4,000
Chargeable gain	6,000	1,000

The company makes a claim under Sections 393A(1)(a) and 393(1).

Compute the assessments.

Solution

	AP to 30.6.96 £	AP to 30.6.97 £
Schedule D Case I	–	7,000
Less Section 393(1)	–	3,000
	–	4,000
Schedule D Case III	3,000	4,000
Chargeable gain	6,000	1,000
Profits chargeable to corporation tax	9,000	9,000
Less Section 393A(1)(a)	9,000	
Assessment	–	9,000

Notes

i) *The trading loss of £12,000 incurred in the accounting period to 30th June 1996 has been utilised as indicated below.*

		£
Accounting period to 30.6.96	Section 393A(1)(a)	9,000
do. 30.6.97	Section 393(1)	3,000
		12,000

ii) *The trading loss carried forward to 30.6.97 is deducted from Case I profits and not total profits.*

Trade losses and charges on income *Section 393(9)*

5. In any accounting period where the charges on income paid exceed total corporation tax profits, and include payments made wholly and exclusively for the purposes of a trade carried on by that company, then a measure of loss relief is available under Section 393(9).

This provides that the amount of the excess charges on income or of the trade payments, whichever is the less, may be carried forward as if they were a trading loss under Section 393(1).

Payments made wholly and exclusively for the purposes of trade, include patent royalties. Covenanted payments to charities or qualifying donations would not be trade charges.

Note For accounting periods ending after 31st March 1996, interest payments such as loan/debenture interest are not charges on income but are dealt with under the loan relationship rules as expenses of trade.

Example

P Ltd has the following results for the year ended 31st March 1998.

	£	£
Schedule D Case I loss		(88,000)
Schedule D Case III		4,000
Chargeable gain		10,000
Charges on income: trade	27,000	
non-trade	5,000	32,000

The company makes a claim for loss relief under Section 393A(1)(a) and 393(1).

Compute the assessment for the AP to 31.3.1998 and show the loss relief.

Solution

P Ltd AP to 31.3.1998

	£	£
Schedule D Case III		4,000
Chargeable gain		10,000
Total profits		14,000
Less loss relief. Section 393A(1)(a)		14,000
Assessment		–

	£	£
Amount of losses carried forward:		
Trading loss for year to 31.3.98	88,000	
Less Section 393A(1)(a) relief	14,000	74,000
Charges on income the lower of:		
a) Excess charges 32,000 – 0 =	32,000	
or		
b) Trade charges only	27,000	27,000
Total trade losses carried forward		101,000

Note

Here the non-trade charges of £5,000 would not be relieved.

Example

Using the data in the previous example, if the company made no claim under Section 393A(1)(a) *recompute the losses carried forward.*

Solution

	£	£
Total profits as above		14,000
Less charges on income		32,000
Excess charges		18,000
Amount of losses carried forward:		
Trading loss for the year to 31.3.98		88,000
Charges on income the lower of:		
(a) Excess charges; or	18,000	
(b) Trade charges only	27,000	18,000
Total trade losses carried forward		106,000

Note

In this example by not claiming relief under Section 393A(1)(a), the non-trade charges are effectively relieved.

It should be noted that an excess of charges cannot be carried back like normal trade losses under Section 393A(1)(b).

Trading losses and a surplus of FII *Sections 242 and 243*

6. In an accounting period a company may incur a trading loss and, after all available loss reliefs have been claimed, still find that some proportion of the loss is unrelieved. If at the same time it has a surplus of franked investment income, then the company may elect to have the surplus treated as if it were profits chargeable to corporation tax.

For accounting periods ending after 31st March 1996, the relief extends to a non-trade deficit arising from a loan relationship.

Sections 242 and 243 of the TA 1988 enable this surplus to be used in a claim for loss relief which provides the company with a cash repayment of the tax credit attached to the surplus FII.

The main points concerning loss relief under this section are:

a) If a company has a surplus of FII for any accounting period and makes a claim, then the surplus is regarded as an equivalent amount of corporation tax profits for the purposes of making claims for loss relief under Sections 393A(1)(a), 338 (charges paid) and 75 (management expenses).

b) The surplus of FII available for relief excludes any FII brought forward.

c) In the first accounting period following that which relates to the claim, in which there is an excess of franked payments over FII, then any loss used in a Section 242 claim can be used in the normal way. Until that occasion arises any loss carried forward under Section 393(1) is restricted accordingly. The amount of the loss to be used in a normal way is the smaller of:

i) the losses claimed under Section 242, not yet released

ii) the excess of franked payments.

Example

K Ltd has the following results for the two years ending 31st March 1997, and makes a claim for loss relief under Section 242.

	AP to 31.3.1997 £	AP to 31.3.1996 £
Schedule D Case I	(15,000)	1,000
Schedule D Case III	3,000	3,000
Dividends received	18,000	

Solution   **Claim for loss relief under Section 393A(1)(a) and (b)**

	£	£
Schedule D Case I	–	1,000
Schedule D Case III	3,000	3,000
Profits chargeable to corporation tax	3,000	4,000
Less Section 393A(1)(a) and (b) relief	3,000	4,000
Assessments	–	–

Claim for relief under Section 242

		£	AP to 31.3.1997 £
Schedule D Case I loss			15,000
Less Section 393A claims:	1997	3,000	
	1996	4,000	7,000
			8,000
Less Section 242 FII $6,400 \times \dfrac{100}{80}$			8,000

Tax repaid $8,000 \times 20\%$ ie £1,600

Losses carried forward comprise:	Section 393(1)	–
	Section 242	8,000

Notes

i) The Section 242 loss cannot be treated as a trade loss carried forward under Section 393(1) until there is an excess of FP over FII.

ii) The tax repayment of £1,600 will be recouped by restricting ACT set-off at the same time as the trade loss under Section 393(1) is restored.

iii) For 1996/97 the FII is calculated for this purpose by reference to the fraction $\dfrac{20}{80}$ the same as the ACT rate.

7. ### Example

T Ltd has the following results for the two years ended 31st March 1997.

	31.3.1996 £	31.3.1997 £
Schedule D Case I	(30,000)	1,600,000
Dividend received	24,000	–
Dividend paid	–	50,000

The company makes a claim for relief under Section 242 in respect of the year to 31st March 1996. No other loss relief was available.

Show the computations.

Solution

T Ltd AP to 31.3.1996

	£
Trading loss available for relief against any FII	30,000
Surplus of FII $[24,000 + (\dfrac{20}{80} \times 24,000)]$	30,000
Loss carried forward under Section 393(1)	–
Loss carried forward under Section 242	30,000

Repayment of income tax on franked income would be:

$£24,000 \times \dfrac{20}{80}\%$ ie £6,000

AP to 31.3.1997

	£
Trading profit	1,600,000
Less loss relief under Section 242, released	30,000
	1,570,000
Corporation tax @ 33%	518,100

	£	
ACT set off:		
Dividend paid £50,000 $\times \frac{20}{80}$	12,500	
Less restriction	6,000	
Available for set off		6,500
Mainstream liability		511,600

Note

The company has had a cash flow benefit by obtaining a cash repayment of £6,000 in respect of AP to 31.3.1996 which is collected by a restriction of ACT, a year later.

Trade losses and ACT

8. Where a company makes a claim under Section 393A (1) (b) to carry back a trading loss to previous periods then this can affect the maximum ACT set-off levels and create a surplus of ACT.

> Example

Z Ltd has the following data:

	APs (12 months)			
	31.3.97	**31.3.96**	**31.3.95**	**31.3.94**
Schedule D Case I	(250,000)	80,000	30,000	200,000
Corporation tax	–	20,000	7,500	50,000
Dividend paid				150,000
ACT paid ($\frac{9}{31} \times 150,000$)				43,548

Z Ltd claims loss relief under Section 393A(1)(a) and (b).

Solution

		31.3.97	**31.3.96**	**31.3.95**	**31.3.94**
Schedule D Case I		–	80,000	30,000	200,000
Less Section 393A(1)(a) and (b)		–	(80,000)	(30,000)	(140,000)
		–	–	–	60,000
CT payable @ 25%					15,000
ACT set off					
Dividend Paid	= 150,000				
ACT $\frac{9}{31} \times 150,000$	= 43,548				
Max 22.5% × 60,000	13,500				13,500
Surplus ACT	30,048				
Mainstream liability			Nil	Nil	Nil	1,500
Tax repaid		–	20,000	7,500	4,952

Notes

i)   *The carry back of the trade loss has created a surplus of ACT for the AP to 31.3.1994 of £30,048.*

ii) *The surplus ACT could not be carried back beyond 31st March 1994, as a claim must be made within 2 years of 31.3.1994.*

iii) *The trade loss of £250,000 has been fully carried back.*

iv) *Tax repaid for 31st March 1994 = 50,000 – 43,548 = 6,452 – 1,500 = 4,952, plus a repayment supplement.*

Transfer of losses Section 343

9. When a company ceases trading and another company takes over the same trade, then unrelieved losses can be carried forward to the successor company providing that certain conditions are met, which are:

   a) On or at any time within two years after the succession and within one year prior thereto, at least 75% of the interest in the trade is held by the same persons. This means that three quarters of the ordinary share capital in both companies must be held by the same persons throughout the three year period. Throughout the same period the same trade must be carried on by a company in charge to corporation tax.

   b) It follows from this provision that the transfer of a trade from an individual to a company precludes the transfer of trading losses between the entities. However, in that case under Section 386 some relief for an individual is available whereby part of a business loss may be set against income which he or she receives from the company. *See Chapter 17.*

   Where there is a transfer of trade then the following applies.

   a) The trade is not treated as if it had been discontinued and a new one started.

   b) Loss relief under Section 393(A) (1)(b) is not available to the company ceasing to trade. If the second company ceases to trade within four years of the succession, then loss relief can be carried back, where appropriate, to the first company.

   c) Relief under Section 393(1) for the carry forward of losses is available subject to any claim by the company ceasing to trade, under Section 393(A) (1)(a) ie set off against corporation tax profits chargeable to corporation tax.

   Where a trade or part thereof is transferred between two companies so that Section 343 applies, then relief to successor for losses brought forward is restricted where the amount of the 'relevant liability' immediately before the transfer exceeds the open market value of the 'relevant assets' at that time.

   d) No balancing adjustments are raised on the transfer.

   e) Unused capital allowances can also be carried forward under Section 77 CAA 1990.

   f) Losses can not be carried forward where at any time before the change in ownership the scale of activity becomes small or negligible and the change takes place before any considerable revival has occurred.

   g) Schedule D Case VI losses or capital gains tax losses cannot be transferred.

   The main provisions relating to the transfer of trades are contained in Sections 343 and 344 of the TA 1988.

Pre-trading expenditure – Section 401 TA 1988

10. Relief is available for expenditure incurred after the 31st March 1993 by a company in the seven years before it commences to carry on a trade (five years prior to 1.4.1993).

    a) The expenditure must be allowable trading expenditure which would have been deducted in computing Case I or II trading income if incurred after commencement of trading.

    b) Such expenditure is treated as a trading expenditure on the first day on which the trade commences.

    c) The relief does not apply to pre-trading purchases of stock.

    d) With effect from the 1st April 1993 charges on income paid by a company are also eligible for treatment as pre-trading expenditure. They will be deemed to be paid as a charge on the first day that trading commences.

Chargeable gains

11. The amount of any chargeable gain arising in an accounting period is reduced by any allowable capital losses of the same period and by those brought forward from a previous period.

> **Example**

R Ltd has the following data relating to its AP to 31st March 1998.

	£
Capital losses brought forward 1.4.97	3,000
AP to 31.3.1998 – Schedule D Case 1	41,000
– Chargeable gains	22,000

Compute the corporation tax payable.

Solution

R Ltd AP to 31st March 1998

	£	£
Schedule D Case 1		41,000
Chargeable gains	22,000	
Less losses b/f	3,000	19,000
Profits chargeable to Corporation tax		60,000
Corporation tax payable: $60,000 \times 23\%$		13,800

Non-trading losses and deficits

12. Schedule D Case III

Since there are no permitted expenses allowed against income from this source there can be no loss or deficit for tax purposes.

Schedule D Cases IV and V

Losses would not normally arise under these cases but when a trade falls to be taxed under this part of the schedule, then the loss relief under Section 393A(1)(a) and (b) is not available. A Case V loss may only be carried forward and set against income from the same source.

Note that for accounting periods ending after 31st March 1996 Case IV is merged with Case III for corporation tax purposes.

Schedule D Case VI

When a loss is incurred under this case, then it may be set against other Case VI income of the same or future accounting periods. Such a loss may not be carried back, or set against any non-Case VI income.

Schedule A

As explained in an earlier chapter, excess expenditure under this schedule can only be dealt with in accordance with the special rules of Schedule A.

• Student self-testing question

Z Ltd has the following results for the four years to 31st March 1998.

	1995 £	1996 £	1997 £	1998 £
Schedule D Case I	100,000	40,000	(200,000)	60,000
Chargeable gains	10,000	20,000	5,000	8,000
Loan interest paid	7,000	7,000	–	–

Show the assessments for all the years assuming that loss reliefs are claimed as soon as possible.

Solution

	1995 £	1996 £	1997 £	1998 £
Schedule D Case I	100,000	40,000		60,000
Less Section 393 (1)	–	–	–	39,000
	100,000	40,000	–	21,000
Chargeable gains	10,000	20,000	5,000	8,000
Corporation tax profits	110,000	60,000	5,000	29,000
Less Trade charges	7,000	7,000	–	–
	103,000	53,000	5,000	29,000
Less Section 393A(1)(b)	103,000	53,000		
Assessments	Nil	Nil	Nil	29,000
Trade charges c/f				

Loss memorandum

	£	£
Trade loss for year to 30.6.97		200,000
Section 393A(1)(a) 30.6.97	5,000	
Section 393A(1)(b) 30.6.96	53,000	
Section 393A(1)(b) 30.6.95	103,000	
Section 393(1) 30.6.98	39,000	200,000

Notes

i) *Loss relief for the current period is set against income and gains before charges.*

ii) *For the three year carry back the relief is set against income and gains after trade charges and before non-trade charges.*

iii) *A claim for 1997 must be made before seeking relief for earlier years.*

Questions without answers

1. O plc has the following results for the periods to 31st March 1997.

	1994 12 months to 31.12.94 £	1995 3 months to 31.3.95 £	1996 12 months to 31.3.96 £	1997 12 months to 31.3.97 £
Schedule D Case I	35,000	(17,000)	4,500	8,000
Schedule A	1,000	2,000	3,000	2,000
Chargeable gain			5,000	(8,000)
Debenture interest paid	1,000	1,000	1,000	

Compute the assessment for each year assuming all available loss reliefs are claimed.

2. T Ltd has the following results to 30th June 1997.

	30.6.97 £	30.6.96 £	30.6.95 £	30.6.94 £	30.6.93 £
Schedule D Case I	51,000	(180,000)	35,000	7,500	5,000
Chargeable gains	75,000	7,500	7,500	–	–

Compute the assessments for all years, assuming all loss reliefs are claimed under Section 393A(1) (a) and (b), and 393 (1).

30 Close companies

Introduction

1. This chapter is concerned with the special rules of taxation introduced by the FA 1989 which apply to close companies which are close investment companies (CICs). The rules apply in respect of accounting periods beginning after 31st March 1989.

   The topic is dealt with under the following headings:
   - Meaning of close company
   - Meaning of close investment holding company
   - Property investment companies
   - The charge to corporation tax
   - Loans to participators.

What is a close company Section 414 TA 1988?

2. A close company is defined as a company resident in the UK:

   a) Under the control of five or fewer participators, or

   b) Under the control of any number of participators who are also directors of the company, or

   c) Where five or fewer participators, or any number of participators who are directors together possess or are entitled to acquire:

      i) such rights as would on a notional winding up entitle them to receive more than 50% of the assets of the company available for distribution to the participators, or

      ii) such rights as would entitle them as in (i) disregarding any rights which any one has as a loan creditor.

   Within this statement there are clearly a number of terms which require further explanation in order to gain an understanding of the three basic definitions, and these are given below.

Control Section 416 TA 1988

3. Under this section a person has control of a company if he or she is able to exercise, or is entitled to acquire, control, whether direct or indirect, over the company's affairs.

   Control is also established if a person is entitled to acquire:

   a) the greater part of the share capital or issued share capital, or voting power of the company.

   b) such part of the issued share capital as would entitle him or her to receive the greater part of the income of the company if it were distributed amongst the participators, ignoring the rights of loan creditors.

   c) such rights as would on a winding up of the company, or in any other circumstance, entitle him or her to the greater part of the assets of the company, available for distribution among the participators.

   For the purposes of determining whether or not a person has control of a company, then the rights and powers of the following classes of person are to be taken into consideration: any nominee; any company of which the person or his or her associates have control; any associate; any nominee for an associate.

Participator Section 417 TA 1988

4. This is a person having a share or interest in the capital, or income of a company and includes:

   a) any person who possesses, or is entitled to acquire, now or in the future, share capital or voting rights in the company

   b) any loan creditor of the company such as a debenture holder, but excluding any bank indebtedness lent to the company in the ordinary course of business

   c) any person who possesses, or is entitled to acquire a right to receive, or participate, in distributions of the company, or any amounts payable by the company by way of premium on redemption of any loan

   d) any person who is entitled to secure that any income or assets of the company will be applied directly or indirectly for his or her benefit.

Associate Section 417 TA 1988

5. In relation to a participator an associate is defined to mean:

   a) Any direct relative ie parents and remote forebears, children and remoter issue, brothers and sisters, and spouse.

   Relatives *excluded* for this purpose include: son or daughter in law, issue of brothers or sisters, relatives of spouse, brothers or sisters in law and uncles and aunts.

   b) Any partner.

   c) The trustees of any settlement made or entered into by the participator or any of his or her direct relatives whether living or dead.

   d) The trustees or personal representatives interested with the participator in any shares or obligations of the company which are subject to any trust or part of any estate of a deceased person. In *Willingdale* v *Islington Green Investment Co* 1972 CA 48 TC 547, one of the three executors and trustees of a deceased shareholder in a close company was also a participator, and his co-trustees were held to be associates.

   Where the participator is a company, an associate is any other company interested in the shares or debentures of that company.

Director Section 417 TA 1988

6. This includes any person occupying the position of director by whatever name called; any person in accordance with whose directions or instructions the directors are accustomed to act; and any person who:

   a) is a manager of the company or otherwise concerned in the management of the company's trade or business, and

   b) is remunerated out of the funds of that trade or business, and

   c) is either on his own or with associates, the beneficial owner of, or able through the medium of other companies, to control 20% or more of the ordinary share capital of the company.

Ordinary share capital is defined as meaning all issued share capital by whatever name called, other than capital having a right to a dividend at a fixed rate, with no other right to share in the profits of the company. It follows that participating preference shares would be classified as 'ordinary share capital' for this purpose only. Section 832 TA 1988.

Example

L Ltd has an authorised an issued share capital of 100,000 ordinary shares of £1.00 each fully paid. The shareholders, none of whom are associated, are as follows:

	Number of Shares
A Director	15,000
B	10,000
C	5,000
D Director	20,000
E	20,000
F	20,000
G Director	10,000
	100,000

Since fewer than five participators, namely D, E, and F hold more than 50% of the share capital and therefore have control, the company is a close company.

Example

S Ltd has the following authorised and issued share capital and shareholdings:

   10,000 ordinary shares of £1.00 each fully paid.
   5,000 10% participating preference shares of £1.00 fully paid.

		Ordinary Shares	10% Participating Preference Shares
A	Director	1,000	
B	Director	500	
C		500	
D		500	
E		100	
F	Works manager	1,000	2,000
G		800	1,000
H		1,000	1,000
I		800	1,000
J		200	
K	A's brother	500	
L	A's sister in law	1,000	
M	B's wife	1,000	
N	B's partner	1,100	
		10,000	5,000

The directors of the company are A and B.

F is also deemed to be a director by reason of his total shareholding which is: $\dfrac{3,000}{15,000}$ ie 20%

The directors and their associates hold the following voting shares:

A		1,000
K	A's brother	500
B		500
M	B's wife	1,000
N	B's partner	1,100
F		1,000
Total		5,100

Since the control of the company is in the hands of the participator directors it is a close company.

The notional winding up test

7. In such a notional winding up the assets provided as being available for distribution to a participator are the aggregate of:

   a) any assets he or she would receive in the extent of the winding up of the company, and

   b) any other assets he or she would receive if another company participator were itself wound up, and that company's assets distributed pro rata.

> **Example**

Z Ltd has the following shareholders:

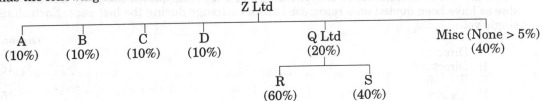

R owns 60% × 20% ie 12% of Z Ltd.

S owns 40% × 20% ie 8% of Z Ltd.

Z Ltd is under the control of 5 participators. A, B, C, D and R with a total of 52% and is therefore a close company.

Quoted companies which are not close companies

8. Even though a company may satisfy the criteria for control contained in the basic definition, it may nevertheless not be a close company if certain conditions prevail. These are as follows.

   a) If shares in the company carrying not less than 35% of the voting power have been allocated, or acquired unconditionally, and are beneficially held by the public. Shares entitled to a fixed rate of dividend are ignored.

b) Any such shares have within the last twelve months, been the subject of dealings on a recognised Stock Exchange, and quoted in the Official List.

Shares are deemed to be held by the public if they are beneficially held by a UK resident, or non-resident open company (ie a non-close company) or if held on trust for an approved superannuation scheme.

Shares held by a principal member, who is normally one of the five largest shareholders (see below), are also deemed to be held by the public providing that such a member is:

a) an open company, or

b) an approved superannuation scheme not for the benefit of the company's directors or employees.

Shares are not held by the public if they are held by the following persons.

a) Directors, their associates or any company controlled by such persons.

b) Any associated company. This is a company which has been under the same control as the company being reviewed, within the previous twelve months.

c) Any fund the capital or income of which is applied for the benefit of employees, directors, or their dependants. Thus a self-administered company pension scheme owning shares in its contributor company would not be deemed to be held by the public whoever the trustees.

Quoted companies which are close companies

9. Any company whether quoted or not, which does not fall within the basic definitions of control, would clearly not be a close company. Further, as noted in the previous section, a company may be director controlled and nevertheless still not be a close company, if the 35% criteria applies. However, there is a very important exception to this rule which involves the shareholding of the 'principal members' and can in fact override the 35% concept.

This rule states that where the total percentage of the voting power of the 'principal members' in a company exceeds 85%, then despite the 35% rule the company is deemed to be a close company.

Principal member

10. A principal member is defined in Section 415 TA 1988 as a person who possesses more than 5% of the voting power in a company. If there are more than five such principal members, then he is one of the five who possess the greater percentage of the voting power. If there are no such five persons because two or more have equal percentages of the voting power, then the principal member is one of the six or more who possess the greatest percentage of voting power.

A principal member's holding consists of his or her own holding and any attributed voting power of nominees, controlled companies or associates.

Example

S Ltd has the undermentioned shareholdings. It is a public quoted company and its ordinary shares have been quoted on a recognised stock exchange during the last year. Each share carries a single vote.

		Ordinary Shares
A	Director	15,000
B	Director	16,000
C	B's wife	9,000
D	A's son	15,000
E		1,000
F Ltd	Pension fund not for benefit of S Ltd employees	4,000
G		2,000
H Ltd	an open company	10,000
I		1,000
J		2,000
K		5,000
L	a large number of shareholders each with less than 100 shares	20,000
		100,000

The company is controlled by its directors and their associates, and by fewer than five participators so that prima facie it is a close company.

In order to establish whether or not the 85% rule applies it is necessary to compute the amount of the public interest as follows:

	Ordinary Shares
E	1,000
F Ltd	4,000
G	2,000
H Ltd	10,000
I	1,000
J	2,000
K	5,000
L	20,000
	45,000

As this is more than the 35% criteria the company is not a close company unless the principal members control more than 85% of the votes.

Principal members' shares	Ordinary Shares
A	15,000
A's son	15,000
B	16,000
B's wife	9,000
H Ltd	10,000
K	5,000
F Ltd	4,000
Total	74,000

As this interest is only 74%, the overriding 85% rule does not apply and the company is not a close company. Notice that the shareholdings of H Ltd and F Ltd are included as both public interest and principal members' interest.

Non-close companies

11. The following companies are not close companies:

a) Any company not resident in the UK

b) A registered industrial and provident society, or building society.

c) Any company controlled by or on behalf of the Crown

d) Any company which is controlled by a non-close company, and which cannot be treated as a close company except by taking as one of the five or fewer participators that non-close company

e) Any company which can only be treated as a close company by reason of the fact that it is under the control of persons who are entitled to the greater part of the assets of the company in a winding up, and which would not be a close company if the participators did not include loan creditors who are not themselves close companies.

> **Example**

D Ltd has the following shareholders: there are no associates or other shares.

	Ordinary Shares
A Ltd a non-close company	19,000
B Director	3,500
C	2,500
D Director	2,000
E Director	2,000
F	2,000
G	2,000
H	2,000
Total	35,000

As the company is not director controlled, and can only be under the control of five or fewer participators by the inclusion of A Ltd an open company, then the company is not a close company.

Close investment holding company

12. A close investment holding company is a *close company* as defined earlier in this chapter, which is *not*:

    a) a trading company, or

    b) a member of a trading group.

    Trading company

    This is a company that exists wholly or mainly for the purposes of trading which must be carried out on a commercial basis. In order to satisfy this test a company will not necessarily have to trade in an accounting period.

    Member of a trading group

    The following categories fall within this definition:

    i) a non-trading parent company of a trading group or single trading subsidiary company

    ii) a non-trading parent company which makes loans to subsidiary trading companies

    iii) a parent company which holds property used by trading subsidiaries, or provides other services or trades itself.

Property investment companies

13. The following are not to be treated as close investment holding companies:

    a) a company that carries on property investment on a commercial basis

    b) a company which *both* trades and invests in property

    c) a trading member of a trading group where the subsidiaries are property investment companies

    d) companies which deal in land shares or securities, where this constitutes a trade.

    Where a company invests in land or property that company will be a close investment holding company where the tenant is any of the following:

    i) an individual who controls the company

    ii) an individual who, acting with any other person controls the company

    iii) the brother, sister, grandparent or grandchild of the individual in (i) and (ii);

    iv) the spouse of the individual in (i), (ii) and (iii)

    v) a company which is controlled by or is under the control of the landlord company

    vi) a company that is controlled by the same person (or group of persons) as the landlord company.

The charge to corporation tax

14. For accounting periods commencing after the 31st March 1989 a close investment holding company will be charged to corporation tax at the full rate of 33% (FY to 31.3.1997) whatever the level of its taxable profits.

    The small company rate of 23% (FY to 31.3.1998) and the marginal relief bands do not apply to CIC's.

Example

    T Ltd, a close company, has the following data relating to its accounting year ended 31st March 1998:

	£
Schedule A income	207,000
Bank interest	3,000
FII	4,000

    The company's Schedule A income is derived from investment properties managed on a commercial basis, with none of the tenants being connected.

    Compute the corporation tax payable.

Solution

i) Close investment holding company test

As the company is a property investment company then it does not fall within the definition of a CIC and the normal rates of computation apply.

ii) Corporation tax payable AP to 31.3.1998

	£
Schedule A	207,000
Schedule D Case III	3,000
Profits chargeable to CT	210,000
Corporation tax payable 210,000 @ 23%	48,300

Note There is a surplus of FII of £4,000.

Example

K Ltd has the following data relating to its financial year to 31st March 1998:

	£
Bank interest	70,000
Dividends received (net)	30,000
Chargeable gain	18,000
Charges paid	8,000

The chargeable gain arose from the sale of the company's former offices, and is after indexation and all allowable costs. K Ltd has never traded.

Compute the corporation tax payable.

Solution

i) Close investment holding company test

As the company does not trade and is not a property investment company it is prima facie a CIC.

ii) Corporation tax payable AP to 31.3.1998

	£
Bank interest	70,000
Chargeable gain	18,000
	88,000
Less: Charges paid	8,000
Profits chargeable to CT	80,000
Corporation tax payable 80,000 @ 33%	26,400

Notes

i) *The full rate of corporation tax applies.*

ii) *There is a surplus of FII of £40,000*

Loans to participators (quasi distributions)

15. Under Section 419 TA 1988, where a close company, otherwise than in the ordinary course of its business which includes the lending of money, makes an advance or loan to an individual who is a participator, then with some important exceptions, the company is charged to an amount of income tax on the loan.

References to an individual also include:

i) a company receiving the loan or advance in a fiduciary or representative capacity

ii) a company not resident in the UK.

The tax to be paid is calculated in the same way as ACT, but cannot be deducted from any corporation tax liabilities or in any way treated as ACT. If the loan is repaid then the company is entitled to a repayment of the tax.

Circumstances in which a close company is regarded as making a loan to a person include those where that person incurs a debt due to the close company or where a debt due from a person to a third party is assigned to a close company. This does not apply to a debt incurred from the supply of goods or services in the ordinary course of trade unless the credit given exceeds six months, or is longer than that normally given to customers.

Accounting periods ending on or after 31st March 1996

16. a) Tax due in respect of a loan to a participator is payable by the company nine months after the end of the accounting period.

   b) A repayment of tax levied under Section 419(3) becomes due for repayment nine months after the end of the accounting period in which the repayment of the loan is made.

   c) Where a loan is repaid in full before the date falls due, i.e. nine months after the year end, then no tax will be payable.

Exemptions

17. It is important to note that none of the above provisions apply where:

   a) the company's business includes that of lending money.

   b) the loan or advance is made to a full-time director or employee of the company and

      i) he or she does not have a material interest in the company, ie more than 5% of the ordinary share capital, and

      ii) the loan or advance made together with any previous loans, including any made to a spouse, does not exceed £15,000.

   Any loan or advance greater than the £15,000 exemption is assessable to tax on the company, but only on the excess.

Loans to participators which incur the charge to taxation based on the ACT rates are not distributions for corporation tax purposes.

> **Example**

M Ltd, a close trading company with no banking interests, lends the sum of £1,600 to a participator in August 1996. £800 was repaid in October 1997, and the balance was written off as irrecoverable at the same time. The participator is neither an employee or director of the company. The company's accounting period is to the 31st December each year.

Solution

M Ltd AP to 31st December 1996

August 1996	Loan to participator	1,600
	Notional ACT assessment 20/80 × 1,600	400

AP to 31st December 1997

October 1997	Loan repaid to company	800
	ACT repayment 20/80 × 800	200

Notes

i) *The notional ACT paid in respect of the loan not repaid by the participator of £200 is irrecoverable.*

ii) *Repayment of notional ACT is at the same rate as that paid in August 1996 ie 20/80ths of the notional distribution.*

iii) *The participator is deemed to be in receipt of dividend income of £1,000 gross for 1997/98 in respect of the loan written off which will be subject to the higher rates of income tax.*

iv) *If the participator was a director or higher paid employee then the beneficial loan provisions noted in* Chapter 8 *are likely to be involved where all the employees' loans total more than £5,000 during the accounting period.*

31 Corporation tax rates and the small company

Introduction

1. This chapter is concerned with the taxation of 'small companies'. It begins with a summary of the basic rates and the meaning of profits for small company purposes. The marginal relief provisions are then examined with reference to associated companies and accounting periods of less than twelve months' duration. The chapter ends with an example of the effects of a change in the rate of marginal relief.

   A small company is defined in Section 13 TA 1988 as any company whose 'profits' for any accounting period do not exceed the lower maximum amount. Where the profits are greater than the lower maximum amount but less than an upper maximum amount, then the marginal relief provisions apply. A claim for the lower rate or marginal relief must be made under Section 13, and this must be evidenced by adequate reference in the computations. The number of associated companies (*see section 7 below*) must be specifically mentioned, and is required on Form CT 200.

Basic rates

2.

Financial Years	Rate	Relevant Maximum Amounts	
		Lower Level	Upper Level
	%	£	£
1993 to 31.3.1994	25	250,000	1,250,000
1994 to 31.3.1995	25	300,000	1,500,000
1995 to 31.3.1996	25	300,000	1,500,000
1996 to 31.3.1997	24	300,000	1,500,000
1997 to 31.1.1998	23	300,000	1,500,000

Definition of small company profits

3. The definition of profits for small company rate purposes is the sum of:

   a) profits chargeable to corporation tax ie total profits less charges on income, and group relief, *plus*

   b) franked investment income.

   Group income is excluded from the definition.

   > **Example**

   AP Ltd has the following income and charges relating to the year ended 31st March 1998.

	£
Schedule D Case I	127,000
Chargeable gain	3,500
Charges on income paid	1,500
Dividends received	14,400
Group income	3,000

   Calculate the corporation tax payable for the AP to 31st March 1998.

   Solution

   Corporation tax computation AP to 31.3.98

	£
Schedule D Case I	127,000
Chargeable gain	3,500
	130,500
Less charges on income	1,500
Profit chargeable to corporation tax	129,000
Add franked investment income 14,400 + $(\frac{20}{80} \times 14,400)$ ie 3,600	18,000
Small company profits	147,000
Corporation tax payable:	
£129,000 @ 23%,	29,670

   Note *The small company profit threshold for the year to 31.3.1998 is £300,000.*

Marginal relief

4. Where the small company profits exceed the lower maximum amount, but fall below the upper maximum amount, then the position is as follows:

a) Corporation tax profits are chargeable at the full rate of 33%.

b) $[(M - P) \times \dfrac{B}{P} \times \text{a fraction}]$ is deducted from (a)

M	=	Upper maximum amount ie £1,500,000. F.Y. to 31. 3. 98.
P	=	Profits chargeable to corporation tax + FII.
B	=	Basic profits ie profits chargeable to corporation tax.
P	=	B + FII.

c) The fraction is determined with respect to financial years, and the recent years to 31.3.1998 are as follows:

Financial Years	Marginal Relief Fraction	Financial Years	Marginal Relief Fraction
1992 to 31.3.1993	1/50	1995 to 31.3.1996	1/50
1993 to 31.3.1994	1/50	1996 to 31.3.1997	9/400
1994 to 31.3.1995	1/50	1997 to 31.3.1998	1/40

d) Thus in respect of accounting periods for the financial year to the 31st March 1998 the formula is:

$$(1,500,000 - P) \times \frac{B}{P} \times \frac{1}{40}$$

Example

Z Ltd has the undermentioned data relating to its accounting year ended 31.3.1998.

	£
Schedule D Case I	453,100
Chargeable gains	2,250
Charges on income	5,350
Dividend received	1,600
Dividend paid	24,000

Compute the mainstream liability.

Solution   Calculation of small company profits

	£
Schedule D Case I	453,100
Chargeable gain	2,250
	455,350
Less charges on income	5,350
	450,000 ie B
Add franked investment income	2,000
	452,000 ie P

Computation of marginal relief:

$$(1,500,000 - 452,000) \times \frac{450,000}{452,000} \times \frac{1}{40}$$

	26,084

Z Ltd Corporation tax computation AP 31.3.1998

	£
Schedule D Case I	453,100
Chargeable gains	2,250
	455,350
Less charges on income	5,350
	450,000
Corporation tax @ 33% × 450,000	148,500
Less Marginal relief	26,084
	122,416

Less ACT set off: Dividend paid 24,000 × $\frac{1}{4}$ =	6,000	
Dividend received 1,600 × $\frac{1}{4}$ =	400	5,600
Mainstream liability		116,816

Notes

i)   *From this example it will be noted that the marginal relief is in fact a calculated amount which is deducted from the profits charged at the full rate of 33%.*

ii)   *As P > £300,000, marginal relief should be claimed.*

Marginal rate of corporation tax

5.   The marginal rate of corporation tax refers to the rate of corporation tax borne on profits in between £300,000 and £1,500,000, and for the financial year to the 31st March 1998 this is 35.50%.

Example

B Ltd has profits chargeable to corporation tax of £400,000 for the year ended 31st March 1998. Calculate the corporation tax payable and show the marginal rate of tax.

Solution

	£
Profits chargeable to corporation tax	400,000
Corporation tax @ 33%	132,000
Less marginal relief	

$$(1,500,000 - 400,000) \times \frac{1}{40}$$

	27,500
	104,500

Mainstream liability

This can be shown to be equivalent to:

300,000 @ 23%	69,000
100,000 @ 35.50% (marginal rate)	35,500
400,000	104,500

The marginal rate of 35.50% compares with a marginal rate of income tax for 1997/98 of 40%.

Associated companies

6.   A company is treated as an associate of another at a given time, if at that time, or at any time within one year previously, either one of the two has control over the other, or both are under the same control. Control has the same meaning as that used in connection with close companies, *see* Chapter 30.

If a company has one or more associated companies in the accounting period, then the upper and lower relevant maximum and minimum amounts are divided equally between the company and the number of associates. Thus a company with two associates would have to allocate the relevant amounts threefold:

FY to 31.3.1998	Lower Level £	Upper Level £
The company	100,000	500,000
First associate	100,000	500,000
Second associate	100,000	500,000
	300,000	1,500,000

In determining the number of associated companies the following points should be noted.

a)   An associated company which was not a trading company or has not carried on a trade at any time in the accounting period is to be disregarded.

b)   A company which is only an associate for part of an accounting period is to be counted.

c)   Two or more companies are to be counted even if they were associated for different parts of the accounting period.

d)   Overseas subsidiaries are included in determining the number of associates.

Accounting periods of less than 12 months

7. As already indicated, for corporation tax purposes a company's accounting period cannot exceed 12 months in duration. If the accounting period is less than 12 months in length then the relevant maximum amounts are reduced accordingly.

   Thus with an accounting period of three months' duration ending in the financial year to 31.3.1996 the lower profit level would be £300,000/4 ie £75,000, and the upper profit level would be 1,500,000/4 ie £375,000. If the situation arises where a company has an accounting period of less than 12 months' length, and is an associated company, then the respective profit levels are first divided by the number of companies and then reduced in proportion to the length of the accounting period.

Changes in the marginal rates

8. Where there is a change in the marginal rate levels or fractions and a company's accounting period straddles the tax year, then in order to apply the appropriate reliefs, total profits are apportioned on a time basis and the relevant maximum levels reduced pro rata.

> **Example**

S Ltd has the following results for the year ended 31st December 1997.

	£
Schedule D Case I	220,000
Chargeable gains (£50,000 – 31.3.97. £230,000 – 30.6.97)	280,000

Compute the corporation tax payable.

Solution

	Period 31.3.97 £	Period 31.12.97 £
Apportionment of profit		
Schedule D Case I	55,000	165,000
Chargeable gains	70,000	210,000
	125,000	375,000

Marginal relief computation

	£
Period to 31.3.97 $(375,000 - 125,000) \times \dfrac{9}{400}$	5,625
Period to 31.12.97 $(1,125,000 - 375,000) \times \dfrac{1}{40}$	18,750
	24,375

Corporation tax payable:	£	£
125,000 @ 33%	41,250	
375,000 @ 33%	123,750	165,000
Less marginal relief		24,375
Mainstream liability		140,625

Notes

i)

FY to 31.3.97	$\dfrac{1,500,000}{4}$	= 375,000
FY to 31.3.98	$\dfrac{1,500,000}{4} \times 3$	= 1,125,000

ii) *Cross check:*

$$\frac{300000}{4} = 75,000$$

$$\frac{300,000}{4} \times 3 = \underline{225,000}$$

75,000 @ 24%	18,000
225,000 @ 23%	51,750
(125,000 – 75,000) @ 35.25%	17,625
(375,000 – 225,000) @ 35.50	53,250
	140,625

iii) Total profits chargeable to C. T. are apportioned on a time basis including the chargeable gains.

• Student self-testing question

K plc has the undermentioned data relating to its accounting period ended 31st March 1998.

	£
Schedule D Case I	327,000
Schedule A	13,000
Chargeable gains	45,000
Charges on income paid	10,000
Dividend received	16,000
Dividend paid	24,000

Calculate the mainstream liability for the AP to 31st March 1998.

Solution   Corporation Tax computation AP to 31.3.1998

	£
Schedule D Case I	327,000
Schedule A	13,000
Chargeable gains	45,000
	385,000
Less charges on income paid	10,000
Profits chargeable to corporation tax	375,000 = B

Corporation tax payable

	£
375,000 @ 33%	123,750
Less marginal relief	26,226
	97,524

ACT set off:	£	
Dividend paid $24,000 \times \frac{1}{4}$	6,000	
Dividends received $16,000 \times \frac{1}{4}$	4,000	2,000
Mainstream liability		95,524

Note

Marginal relief computation.

$$B = 375,000$$
$$P = B + FII = 375,000 + 20,000 = 395,000$$
$$(1,500,000 - 395,000) \frac{375,000}{395,000} \times \frac{1}{40}$$
$$= 1105,000 \times \frac{375}{395} \times \frac{1}{40} = 26,226.$$

• Questions without answers

1. D Ltd has the following data relating to its accounting year ended 31st March 1998.

	£
Schedule D Case I	440,000
Schedule D Case VI	10,000
Schedule A	20,000
Chargeable gain	20,000
Group income	8,000
Debenture interest paid (gross)	10,000
Dividend received	4,000
Dividend paid	24,000

Compute the corporation tax mainstream liability for the AP to 31st March 1998.

2. The following information has been extracted from the records of Nerston Ltd, a UK resident company, for its trading year to 31st March 1998.

	£
Trading profits	180,000
Schedule A	200,000
Debenture interest paid	32,000
Chargeable gain	24,000
Dividends paid in the year, final dividend for the year to 31st March 1997.	300,000

Debenture interest was paid on 7th July 1997 and dividends were paid 1st December 1997.

Compute mainstream corporation tax payable for the accounting period to 31st March 1998.

32 Groups and consortia

Introduction

1. This chapter considers the main aspects of corporation tax where a company is a member of a group or consortium. It begins with a summary of the topics to be examined, each of which is considered in detail subsequently.

Topics to be considered

2. a) **Group relief** (75% subsidiaries and consortia) — The set-off trading losses against profits within a group is known as group relief.

   b) **Surrender of ACT** (51% subsidiaries) — ACT may be surrendered from a parent to its subsidiaries, but not the reverse.

   c) **Group income** (51% subsidiaries and consortia) — The payment of inter-company dividends without the payment of any ACT is known as group income.

   d) **Inter-company charges** (51% subsidiaries and consortia) — The payment of inter-company charges on income without accounting for income tax thereon.

   e) **Inter-company transfer** (75% subsidiaries) — The transfer of assets between group companies without any chargeable gain or loss arising.

   f) **Company reconstructions** — Without change of ownership.

   g) **Change in ownership** — Disallowance of trading losses.

Group relief (groups and consortia) *Section 402*

3. This is the term used to describe the amount of trading losses, excess charges on income, or surplus management expenses which one company in a group of companies may surrender and another company in the same group may claim to be set against its corporation tax profits. The main provisions which deal with this form of relief are found in the TA 1988 Sections 402–413.

Meaning of group

4. Two companies are deemed to be members of a group of companies if the following four conditions all prevail.

   a) Both are resident in the UK.

   b) One is the 75% subsidiary of the other, or both are 75% subsidiaries of a third company. A 75% subsidiary is defined under Section 838 TA 1988 in terms of the direct or indirect ownership of not less than 75% of the ordinary share capital, ordinary shares meaning all shares other than fixed rate preference shares.

   c) The parent company is beneficially entitled to not less than 75% of the profits available for distribution to equity holders of the subsidiary company. An equity holder is any person who holds ordinary shares or is a loan creditor in respect of a loan which is not a commercial loan. Loan creditor has the same meaning as that used in connection with close companies except that the proviso in favour of bank normal borrowings is not excluded and therefore is within the definition for the purposes of these conditions. A normal commercial loan is one which carries a reasonable rate of interest, with no rights to conversion.

   d) The parent company would be entitled beneficially to not less than 75% of any assets of the subsidiary company available to its equity shareholders on a winding up.

> **Example**
>
> B Ltd owns 75% of the ordinary share capital of W Ltd who in turn owns 75% of the ordinary share capital of Z Ltd All companies are UK residents.
>
> Since B Ltd would only be entitled to 56.25% of the profits available for distribution by Z Ltd the three companies do not constitute a group for the purposes of group relief. B Ltd and W Ltd however would constitute a group, as would W Ltd and Z Ltd.

Example

T Ltd is the USA parent of two 100% subsidiaries, A Ltd and B Ltd, both being UK resident companies.

As A Ltd and B Ltd are owned by a non-resident parent company, group relief would not be available between any of them. In this case if a UK parent was interposed to own A Ltd and B Ltd then group relief would be available.

Meaning of consortia

5. A company is owned by a consortium if 75% or more of its ordinary share capital is beneficially owned by UK resident companies, none of which:
   a) beneficially owns less than 5% of the ordinary share capital,
   b) would be entitled to less than 5% of any profits available for distribution to equity holders,
   c) would be entitled to less than 5% of any assets available to equity holders on the wind up.

6. Group relief is also available to a consortium of companies in the following circumstances:
   a) Where the company surrendering the loss is a trading or holding company owned by a consortium (not being a 75% subsidiary of any company) and the claimant company is a member of the consortium. A loss may also be surrendered from a member of the consortium to trading or holding company.
   b) Where a trading company is the 90% subsidiary of a holding company, which itself is owned by a consortium.

Example

A loss in X, Y or Z could be transferred to the consortium members in proportion to their interests. In addition a loss by any of the consortium members could be claimed by X, Y or Z, and in this case the amount would be restricted to the profits of each claimant proportionately. However, *see Section 12 below*.

What may be surrendered

7. The following may be given by a surrendering company as group relief:
   a) trading losses computed as for set off in accordance with Section 393A(1)(a) ie excluding any losses brought forward, but after claims for capital allowances.
   b) any excess of capital allowances normally given against income of a special class, such as agricultural buildings allowances.
   c) any excess of charges on income, whether trading or non-trading, over profits including chargeable gains.
   d) any excess of management expenses of an investment company, other than a close investment holding company.
   e) a net loss arising from a loan relationship.

   In each of the above cases no amounts arising from earlier or succeeding accounting periods can be surrendered.

   The surrendering company does not have to make any claim for loss relief, eg under Section 393A(1)(a), before surrendering any loss to claimants, although this is frequently done in practice.

The claimant

8. In the corresponding accounting period of the claimant company, the surrendered loss may be set against the claimant's total profits including chargeable gains determined as follows:
   a) After taking into consideration any relief for losses from trading (or charges) brought forward from previous years under Section 393(1). These would be deducted in arriving at the normal Schedule D Case I trading income.

b) After taking into consideration any loss relief under Section 393A(1)(a) for the current accounting period, whether claimed or not.

c) Before any loss relief under Section 393A(1)(b) in respect of a loss brought back from a subsequent accounting period.

d) After deducting charges on income, whether trade or non-trade.

Relief is to be set against the current profits of the claimant, and it cannot be either carried forward or backward to other accounting periods.

General points

9. a) Group relief is limited to the smaller of the surrendering company's losses relief, or the claimant company's profits available for group relief. Where the surrendering company's losses are greater than the claimant's available profits then the excess cannot be carried forward or backward as group relief. This does not prevent any other form of loss relief being obtained by the surrendering company, eg carry forward under Section 393(1).

   b) More than one company in the group may make a claim relating to the same surrendering company.

   c) If any payment takes place between the claimant and the surrendering company, and such a payment is not necessary to support a claim, then this transaction is:
      i) ignored for all corporation tax purposes as regards both payer and recipient
      ii) not treated as a distribution or as a charge on income.

Example

H Ltd has a wholly owned subsidiary company M Ltd and the results of both companies for their current accounting period of the same 12 months are given below:

	H Ltd £	M Ltd £
Schedule D Case I	(75,000)	70,000
Less loss b/f under Section 393(1)	–	30,000
	(75,000)	40,000
Schedule D Case III	15,000	–
Chargeable gain	10,000	5,000
Charges on income	–	25,000

H Ltd decides to make a claim for loss relief under Section 393A(1)(a) and to surrender as much as possible of the balance of its loss to M Ltd.

Show the effects of the claims on H Ltd and M Ltd.

Solution

H Ltd

	£
Schedule D Case III	15,000
Chargeable gain	10,000
	25,000
Less Section 393A(1)(a) relief	25,000
Assessment	–
Utilisation of losses.	
Available trade loss	75,000
Less Section 393A(1)(a)	25,000
Available for group relief	50,000
Less surrendered to M Ltd under Section 402	20,000
Carried forward under Section 393(1)	30,000

M Ltd

	£
Schedule D Case I	40,000
Chargeable gain	5,000
	45,000
Less charges on income	25,000
Available for group relief	20,000
Group relief claimed under Section 402	20,000
Assessment	–

Smaller amount taken for group relief

Notes

i) In this example the group relief is limited to the claimant's profits of £20,000, as these are the lower amount.

ii) Group relief is deducted after charges on income by the claimant.

Corresponding accounting periods

10. Where the accounting periods of the surrendering company and the claimant company do not coincide, but they have been members of the same group throughout their respective accounting periods, then the group relief is in effect restricted to the proportion of the loss/profit of the common period. This may, in fact, cover two accounting periods of either company.

> **Example**

X Ltd has a 75% subsidiary, Y Ltd, and the results of both companies for the last two accounting periods are as follows:

X Ltd

AP to 31.3.1996 Schedule D Case I	10,000
AP to 31.3.1997 Schedule D Case I	(16,000)

Y Ltd

AP to 31.12.1996 Taxable profits	6,000
AP to 31.12.1997 Taxable profits	24,000

Compute the group relief available.

Solution

In this example the period of the loss by X Ltd covers two accounting periods of Y Ltd and it will be necessary to determine the lower of the profit or loss in each corresponding period.

Group Relief Available

	£	£
Common period 1.4.1996 to 31.12.1996		
X Ltd ¾ × (16,000)	(12,000)	
Y Ltd ¾ × 6,000	4,500	
Restricted to the lower amount		4,500
Common period 1.1.1997 to 31.3.1997		
X Ltd ¼ × (16,000)	(4,000)	
Y Ltd ¼ × 24,000	6,000	
Restricted to the lower amount		4,000
Total		8,500

Companies joining or leaving a group

11. Group relief is generally only available if the claimant and surrendering companies are members of the same group (or fulfil the conditions relating to a consortium) throughout the accounting periods of both companies. However, when a company either joins or leaves a group or consortium, then some relief is available and a new accounting period is deemed to end or commence on the occurrence of that event.

Normally the profits/losses are apportioned on a time basis. However, if it appears that such an apportionment would produce an unreasonable result, then a more reasonable basis must be used.

> **Example**

D Ltd, a trading company, acquires a 100% interest in W Ltd on the 30th June 1996. Both companies have the same year end and the results for the year to 31st December 1996 are as follows:

	D Ltd £	W Ltd £
Schedule D Case I	17,000	(40,000)
Schedule D Case III	3,000	–
Chargeable gain	15,000	–
Chargeable loss	–	(10,000)
Charges on income	5,000	–

Compute the amount of group relief available.

Solution

On the acquisition of W Ltd who then with D Ltd forms a group, there is deemed to be a commencement of an accounting period for group relief purposes.

	£
Loss to be surrendered by W Ltd	
Loss for 12 months to 31.12.1996	40,000
Proportion for deemed accounting period from	
1.7.1996 to 31.12.1996 $^6/_{12} \times 40,000$	20,000
Loss to be claimed by D Ltd	
Schedule D Case I	17,000
Schedule D Case III	3,000
Chargeable gain	15,000
	35,000
Less charges on income	5,000
	30,000
Proportion from 1.7.1996 $^6/_{12} \times 30,000 =$	15,000

Since this is smaller than the amount of the loss of the surrendering company, this is the maximum available for group relief.

The computations for the year to 31st December 1996 are:

	£
D Ltd	
Taxable profits as above	30,000
Less group relief	15,000
Assessment	15,000
W Ltd	
Schedule D Case I loss	40,000
Less surrendered	15,000
Unused loss	25,000

Notes

i) *The balance of the loss of W Ltd is not available for future group relief, but it can be used by W Ltd under Section 393A(1)(b) or 393(1).*

ii) *The capital loss of W Ltd may not be set against the chargeable gain of any other company.*

Similar provisions apply when a company leaves a group, and the profits and losses up to the date of the demerger must be apportioned to determine the amount of any group relief available.

Consortium relief

12. Where there is a consortium of companies as defined in section 6 above, then the following types of relief may be available:

   a) surrender to consortium members

   b) surrender by the consortium members

   c) a mixture of group/consortium relief

   d) relief through a link company.

Surrender to a consortium member

13. K Ltd is owned by four companies A Ltd (20%), B Ltd (30%), C Ltd (10%) and D Ltd (40%).

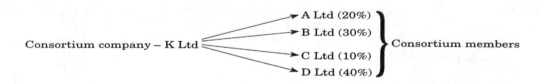

If K Ltd incurs a trading loss it may be surrendered to the consortium members A, B, C, D in proportion to their shareholding in K Ltd. Thus if K Ltd makes a loss of £20,000, the amount that can be surrendered to the consortium members is:

		£
A Ltd	20% × 20,000	4,000
B Ltd	30% × 20,000	6,000
C Ltd	10% × 20,000	2,000
D Ltd	40% × 20,000	8,000
		20,000

The amount of the loss that can be surrendered by K Ltd is reduced to the extent that it has profits of the same accounting period available to relieve the loss under Section 393A(1)(a). It should be noted that K Ltd does not have to make the claim under Section 393A(1)(a) but the consortium relief is restricted as though this had taken place whereas with group relief this restriction does not apply.

Surrender by the consortium members

14. Where a consortium member makes a loss then this can be surrendered to the consortium company. However, in this case the amount that can be surrendered is limited to the percentage of the *profits* of the consortium company.

> **Example**

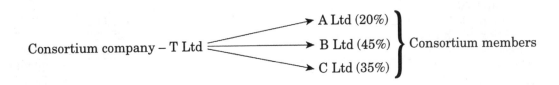

If C Ltd makes a loss then the amount that can be surrendered to T Ltd is restricted to 35% of the profit of T Ltd.

For example, if C Ltd makes a loss of £25,000 and T Ltd has profits of £50,000 then the amount of the loss that can be surrendered is limited to 35% × £50,000 ie £17,500.

In this case it is not necessary for C Ltd to consider any other profits available for set-off under Section 393A(1)(a).

A mixture of group/consortium relief

15. Under Sections 405 and 406 TA 1988 the position is as follows.

a) Where a consortium owned company is also a member of a group of companies then that company is known as a 'group/consortium company'.

b) If a group/consortium company incurs a loss then the amount that can be surrendered pro rata to the consortium members must first be reduced by:

   i) any potential claim under Section 393(A)(1)(a) (set-off against other profits of the same period)

   ii) any potential group relief claims that could be made under Section 402.

   The potential loss claims do not have to be made, but their availability restricts the loss to be surrendered by the group/consortium company.

c) Where the group/consortium company has taxable profits and wishes to claim loss relief from any of its consortium members then the available profits must first be reduced by any potential group loss claims within the group/consortium company's own group.

Example

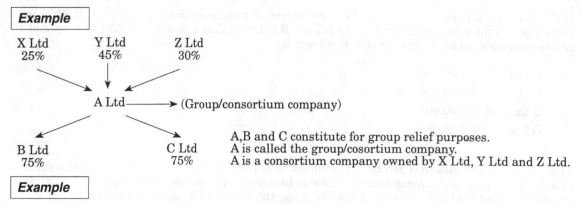

X Ltd 25% Y Ltd 45% Z Ltd 30%

A Ltd ──────► (Group/consortium company)

B Ltd 75% C Ltd 75%

A,B and C constitute for group relief purposes.
A is called the group/cosortium company.
A is a consortium company owned by X Ltd, Y Ltd and Z Ltd.

Example

The following results relate to the year ended 31.12.1996.

			£
A Ltd	Trading loss		80,000
	Chargeable gain		12,000
B Ltd	Trading profits		25,000
C Ltd	Trading loss		10,000
	Chargeable gains		3,000

Compute the amounts that could be surrendered to X.

Solution

		£	£
a)	A Ltd trading loss		80,000
	Less potential reliefs:		
	Section 393A(1)(a) A Ltd	12,000	
	Section 402 B Ltd	25,000	
	Section 402 C Ltd	3,000	40,000
			40,000
	25% × 40,000 =		10,000
b)	A Ltd trading loss		80,000
	Less potential reliefs:		
	Section 393A(1)(a) A Ltd	12,000	
	Section 402 B Ltd	18,000	30,000
			50,000
	25% × 50,000 =		12,500

Notes

i) In (a) the inter-group relief by B & C and the possible claim under Section 393A(1)(a) by C has not been exercised.

ii) In (b) the amount of potential group relief is after taking:
        C Ltd Section 393A(1)(a)   £10,000 – £3,000 = £7,000 loss
        B Ltd group relief with C Ltd   £25,000 – £7,000 =£18,000 profit.

Relief through a link company

16. A link company is defined as a company which is a member both of a consortium and of a group.

Example

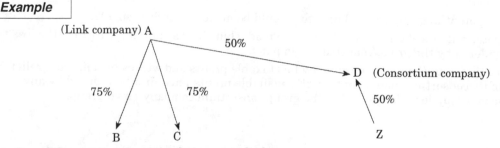

(Link company) A

75%   75%   50%

B   C   D (Consortium company)

50%

Z

A, B and C constitute a group for group relief purposes.
A and Z jointly own the consortium company D.
A is a member of a group and a consortium.

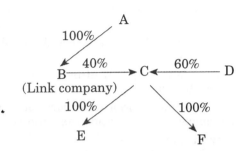

A and B constitute a group. C, E and F constitute a group. C is owned by a consortium of two members B and D. C is also a group consortium company.

In respect of the year ending 31st December 1996 the companies have the following results:

	£
A Ltd	100,000
B Ltd	(30,000) loss
C Ltd	(20,000) loss
D Ltd	Nil
E Ltd	12,000
F Ltd	(4,000) loss

Calculate the possible claims for group relief and consortium relief.

Solution

AP to 31st December 1996

E Ltd	Profits before relief		12,000
	Less Group relief surrendered by F	4,000	
	do. C	8,000	12,000
	Assessment		–
A Ltd	Profits before relief		100,000
	Less Group relief surrendered by B	30,000	
	Consortium relief C:		
	40% × (20,000 – 8,000)	4,800	34,800
	Profits chargeable to corporation tax		65,200

Notes

The consortium relief available to A Ltd from C Ltd is the lower of:
A Ltd profits after group relief ie   100,000 – 30,000   = 70,000
B Ltd share of C Ltd loss ie   40% (20,000 – 8,000)   =   4,800

The surrender of surplus ACT (groups only) Section 240 TA 1988

17. Where a UK resident company has paid a dividend (but not any other qualifying distribution) and has paid ACT in respect of that dividend, then it may surrender either the whole or any part of the ACT to its 51% subsidiary. For this purpose a UK resident company is a subsidiary of another, its parent, in the following circumstances:

a) If more than 50% of its ordinary share capital, ie all share capital excluding fixed rate preference shares, is owned directly or indirectly by the parent company, and

b) The parent company is beneficially entitled to more than 50% of any profits available for distribution to equity holders of the subsidiary company, and

c) The parent company would be beneficially entitled to more than 50% of any assets of the subsidiary company, available for distribution to its equity holders, on a winding up.

18. The ACT which is available for surrender:

a) is only that of the current accounting period

b) excludes any ACT brought forward or back from other accounting periods

c) need not be surplus ACT

d) is available in only one direction as from parent to subsidiary, and not the reverse

e) is not available for a member of a consortium.

A claim for surrender of ACT, in accordance with Section 240 TA 1988, must be made within six years of the relevant accounting period and the consent of the subsidiaries concerned is required.

Surrendered ACT and the 51% subsidiary

19. So far as the 51% subsidiary is concerned, the amount of the ACT surrendered by its parent is treated as follows.

a) It is treated as if it were a payment of ACT by the subsidiary and therefore, available for set-off against its own corporation tax liability.

b) To the extent that the surrendered ACT cannot be fully utilised in the accounting period then any surplus may be carried forward in the usual way.

c) In determining what surplus ACT, if any, there is in a subsidiary company's accounting period, then the set-off against that company's corporation tax liability is as follows:

   i) first, against ACT surrendered by the parent

   ii) second, against any ACT arising on any distributions made by the subsidiary itself.

d) No surplus ACT arising from that surrendered by the parent may be carried back by the subsidiary.

e) Any payment made for surrendered ACT by the subsidiary is to be ignored for tax purposes.

f) No surrender is available for any part of an accounting period in which the company was not a subsidiary.

g) Where a change in ownership occurs on or after the 16th March 1993 ACT in the period after the change cannot be carried back to earlier periods.

Example

F Ltd owns 51% of the ordinary share capital of B Ltd and in respect of the year ended 31st March 1998, they have the following details:

	F Ltd £	B Ltd £
Schedule D Case I	900,000	800,000
Dividends paid (net)	800,000	–

F Ltd decides to surrender any surplus ACT for the year to its subsidiary.

Show the computations.

Solution

F Ltd

	£	£
Corporation tax @ 33% × £900,000		297,000
Less ACT set off:		
Dividend payment $\frac{1}{4}$ × £800,000	200,000	
Maximum set off 20% × £900,000	180,000	180,000
Surrendered to B Ltd	20,000	
Mainstream liability		117,000

B Ltd

	£
Corporation tax @ 33% × £800,000	264,000
Less ACT surrendered from F Ltd	20,000
Mainstream liability	244,000

Note

As there are two companies in the group, the marginal relief rate does not apply:

$$\frac{1,500,000}{2} = £750,000$$

Example

P Ltd owns 100% of Q Ltd and in respect of the year ended 31st March 1998 they have the following details:

	P Ltd £	Q Ltd £
Schedule D Case I	60,000	25,000
Dividends paid (net)	8,000	
Surplus ACT b/f	25,000	

P Ltd decides to surrender as much ACT as possible to Q Ltd.

Solution

P Ltd AP to 31.3.1998

	£	£
Profits chargeable to CT		60,000
Corporation tax @ 23%		13,800
ACT set off		
Dividend paid	8,000	
ACT @ $\frac{1}{4} \times 8,000$	2,000	
Surrendered to Q Ltd	2,000	
Surplus ACT b/f	25,000	
Maximum set off 20% × 60,000	12,000	12,000
Surplus c/f	13,000	
Corporation tax payable		1,800

Q Ltd AP to 31.3.1998

	£
Profits chargeable to CT	25,000
Corporation tax @ 23%	5,750
ACT set off surrendered from P Ltd	2,000
Corporation tax payable	3,750

Notes

i) *The surplus ACT of £25,000 brought forward by P Ltd cannot be surrendered to Q Ltd.*

ii) *If Q Ltd pays a dividend then the ACT surrendered by P Ltd is utilised first.*

20. It is a fundamental condition of the claim for relief under Section 240, that the subsidiary is a 51% subsidiary throughout the period during which the surrendering company made the ACT payment. Further, no surrendered ACT can be set against the subsidiary company's corporation tax liability for any accounting period, or part, in which that company was not a 51% subsidiary of the parent. If a 51% subsidiary relationship is terminated then any surrendered ACT being carried forward by the subsidiary at that date cannot be used, unless the parent/subsidiary relationship is reconstructed at a later date.

Group income (groups and consortia) Section 247 TA 1988

21. This term is used to describe the receipt by a UK parent company of a dividend from its UK subsidiary without that company making any payment of advance corporation tax. It also applies to dividends received in similar circumstances by fellow subsidiaries, and members of a consortium, providing that all the companies concerned are UK residents. As with the surrender of ACT this section only applies to dividends and not other qualifying distributions.

Who may elect

22. Companies may elect to pay inter-company dividends without the consequent payment of ACT providing the company paying the dividend is:

a) A 51% subsidiary of another company receiving the dividend, or

b) A 51% subsidiary of a company which itself owns 51% of both the paying and receiving company. This covers the payment of dividends to fellow subsidiaries, or,

c) A trading or holding company (which is not a 75% subsidiary of any other company) owned by a consortium of which the recipient is a member.

The 51% subsidiary is defined in terms of the ownership of ordinary share capital excluding fixed rate preference shares, any share capital owned through a non resident company, and shares held for trading purposes. The parent must also be beneficially entitled to more than 50% of any profits available for distribution to the equity holders of the subsidiary company and to more than 50% of the assets on a winding up.

Group income treatment is also available to a consortium on similar terms to those which apply to group relief.

An election for the treatment of inter-company dividends as group income must be made jointly by both companies concerned to the inspector of taxes. While the election is in operation, the companies may nevertheless notify the inspector that they do not wish the election to apply to particular transactions.

Effect of an election

23. When an election is in operation the effects are as follows.

a) Dividends received are not franked investment income of the recipient.

b) Group income is not chargeable to corporation tax in the hands of the recipient.

c) Dividends are not franked payments, and they do not enter into the quarterly return system for ACT and there is no set-off against any corporation tax liability.

d) Group income is ignored in determining whether or not the small company rate of corporation tax applies, and also in applying the tapering relief formula.

It is usually advantageous for inter-company dividends to be paid as group income since there is a cash flow benefit if ACT does not have to be paid on the quarterly return system.

Example

F Ltd has a 100% subsidiary, S Ltd, and their results for the year ended 31st March 1998 without any election for group income treatment, are as follows:

	F Ltd £	S Ltd £
Corporation tax income	1,600,000	1,500,000
Dividends paid	200,000	400,000
Investment income from S Ltd (net)	400,000	–
Corporation tax @ 33% × 1,600,000/1,500,000	528,000	495,000
Less ACT set off:		
400,000 @ $\frac{1}{4}$	–	100,000
Mainstream liability	528,000	395,000

F Ltd has a surplus of FII.

Show the effects of an election for group income treatment.

Solution

Election for group income treatment. The results for the year would be as follows:

	F Ltd £	S Ltd £
Corporation tax income	1,600,000	1,500,000
Dividends paid	200,000	–
Group income	400,000	–
Group payment		400,000
Corporation tax @ 33% × 1,600,000/1,500,000	528,000	495,000
Less ACT set off:		
200,000 @ $\frac{1}{4}$	50,000	–
Mainstream liability	478,000	495,000

Notes

i) *In this example there is a saving of ACT payable with an election of £50,000 although the total payments of ACT and mainstream liability are the same (£1,023,000) for the group thus providing a cash flow advantage.*

Example

R Ltd has a wholly owned subsidiary, S Ltd, and in respect of the year to 31st March 1998 they have the following results:

	R Ltd £	S Ltd £
Profits chargeable to CT	40,000	30,000
Dividend paid (net)	40,000	–
Dividend paid to outside preference shareholders (not R Ltd)		24,000
Dividend paid to R Ltd (under group election)		10,000

R wishes to surrender any surplus ACT arising for the year to 31st March 1998 to S Ltd.

Solution

R Ltd AP to 31st March 1998

	£	£
Profits chargeable to CT		40,000
CT payable 40,000 @ 23 %		9,200
ACT set off:		
Dividend paid	40,000	
ACT $\frac{1}{4} \times 40,000$	10,000	
Maximum set off 20% × 40,000	8,000	8,000
Surrendered to S Ltd	2,000	
	10,000	
CT payable		1,200

S Ltd AP to 31st March, 1998

	£	£
Profits chargeable to CT		30,000
CT payable 30,000 @ 23%		6,900
ACT set off:		
Dividend paid	24,000	
ACT @ $\frac{1}{4} \times 24,000$	6,000	
ACT surrendered by R Ltd	2,000	
Own ACT used	4,000	6,000
CT payable		900

Notes

i) *S Ltd has surplus ACT of £6,000– £4,000 = £2,000 which may be carried forward or backward by S Ltd. Maximum set off is 20% ×30,000 = 6,000.*

ii) *S Ltd uses the ACT surrendered before its own ACT.*

iii) *Group income does not affect the ACT computations.*

Inter-company charges on income (groups and consortia) *Section 247 TA 1988*

24. Where the conditions outlined in the previous section exist so that companies may elect for group income treatment, then they may also elect to make any inter-company charges on income payments, without the deduction of income tax. The main provisions which deal with this treatment, are:

a) Companies eligible for group income treatment are also eligible for this election.

b) Once an election is made it must be applied to all transactions and there is no option as there is for dividend payments.

c) So far as the recipient is concerned the receipt of charges on income under an election means that they are still chargeable to corporation tax, but there is no income tax credit to set against the corporation tax liability.

d) The payment of charges on income under an election does not enter the quarterly return system.

e) While inter-company dividend payments are normally only between parent and subsidiary, charges can be in any direction.

f) In respect of payments made the recipient company income chargeable under Schedule D Case III is treated as being received on the date of the payment.

g) Interest payable within multinational groups to UK resident companies is to be taxable on the accruals basis rather than on receipt.

Inter-company charges are frequently dealt with by means of this election, as the income tax does not have to be paid and there is normally a cash flow advantage.

For accounting periods ending after 31st March 1996 under the loan relationship rules inter-group interest payments will still be subject to the deduction of income tax at the 20% rate in the absence of an election.

Transfer of assets between group companies (groups only)

25. There is no method of group relief applicable to chargeable gains and losses which arise within different members of a group of companies. Accordingly, when a company disposes of a chargeable asset outside the group, then any capital gain arising will be chargeable to corporation tax. However, if the disposal is by a member of a group of companies to another group company then the provisions of Section 171 TCGA 1992 enable the transaction to be construed as if the disposal does not give rise to any chargeable gain or loss. This is achieved by deeming the consideration for the disposal of the asset to be such an amount that neither a gain nor a loss accrues to the company disposing of the asset. When the asset is ultimately disposed of outside the group, then a normal liability to corporation tax on any gain would arise.

Companies eligible

26. a) A group comprises of a principal company and all of its 75% subsidiaries.

b) A 75% subsidiary means a company whose ordinary share capital is owned by another company either directly or indirectly to the extent of at least 75%. Again ordinary share capital comprises all shares other than fixed preference shares.

c) Where the principal company is itself a 75% subsidiary of another company, then both its parent and its subsidiaries, together with the principal company, constitute a group.

d) All members of the group must be UK residents.

e) A company will not be a member of a group unless the principal member of the group has itself directly or indirectly a more than 50% interest in its profits and assets.

Members of a consortium are not eligible for treatment as a group for the purposes of this section, nor are close investment holding companies, unless the transfer is between close investment holding companies.

Assets available for group treatment

27. The disposal of any form of property contained in Section 21 TCG ACT 1992 could give rise to the no gain or loss treatment, but there are some exceptions which are as follows.

a) Where the disposal is of redeemable preference shares in a company, on the occurrence of the disposal.

b) Where the disposal is of a debt due from a member of a group, effected by satisfying the debt or part of it.

c) Where the disposal arises from a capital distribution on the liquidation of a company.

d) Where the company is a dual resident member of a group of companies and any gain made by that company would be exempt.

If the transfer is of an asset which the recipient company appropriates to its trading stock, then that company is deemed to have received a capital asset and immediately transferred that asset to its trading stock. There would thus be no capital gain or loss arising on the inter-company transfer, as it would fall within the provisions noted above.

Where the asset transferred to a group company was trading stock of the transfer or company, then the latter is treated as having appropriated the asset as a capital asset immediately prior to the disposal. The value placed on the asset for trading purposes under Section 161 TCG ACT 1992 would be the transfer value giving rise to a 'no gain or loss' situation.

Miscellaneous points

28. a) When an asset is disposed of by a group company to a company outside the group, then any capital allowances granted to any member of the group relating to the asset are taken into consideration in computing any gain or loss.

b) If a company to which an asset has been transferred ceases to be a member of a group within six years of the date of the transfer the position is as follows.

i) At the date of the acquisition of the asset by the company leaving the group or if later the beginning of the accounting period when the company left the group, it is deemed to have sold and reacquired the asset at its market value.

ii) There will therefore, be a chargeable gain or loss on the difference between the market value and the original cost to the group of the asset.

This provision does not apply if a company ceases to be a member of a group by being wound up.

c) The provisions of Section 152 TCG Act 1992 (rollover relief) is extended to groups and enables all trades carried on by the group to be treated as one.

d) Capital losses brought into a group as a result of joining that group are restricted in respect of any losses set against gains on or after the 16th March 1993. This applies to losses generated by a company which joined the group after the 31st March 1987.

Company reconstruction without change of ownership Section 393–394 TA 1988

29. When a company ceases trading and another company takes over the same trade, then unrelieved losses can be carried forward to the successor company providing that certain conditions are met, which are:

a) On or at any time within two years after the succession and within one year prior thereto, at least 75% of the interest in the trade is held by the same persons. This means that three quarters of the ordinary share capital in both companies must be held by the same persons throughout the three year period. Throughout the same period the same trade must be carried on by a company in charge to corporation tax.

b) Throughout the same period the same trade must be carried on by a company in charge to corporation tax.

30. Where there is a transfer of trade then the following applies.

a) The trade is not treated as if it had been discontinued and a new one started.

b) Loss relief under Section 393A(1)(b) is not available to the company ceasing to trade. If the second company ceases to trade within four years of the succession, then terminal loss relief can be carried back, where appropriate, to the first company.

c) Relief under Section 393(1) for the carry forward of losses is available subject to any claim by the company ceasing to trade, under Section 393A(1)(a) ie set off against corporation tax profits.

Where a trade or part thereof is transferred between two companies after so that Section 343 applies, then relief to successor for losses brought forward is restricted where the amount of the 'relevant liability' immediately before the transfer exceeds the open market value of the 'relevant assets' at that time.

d) No balancing adjustments are raised on the transfer.

e) Unused capital allowances can also be carried forward.

f) Losses can not be carried forward where at any time before the change in ownership, the scale of activity becomes small or negligible and the change takes place before any considerable revival has occurred.

g) Schedule D Case VI losses or capital gains tax losses cannot be transferred.

The main provisions relating to the transfer of trades are contained in Section 343 and 344 of the TA 1988.

Change in ownership – disallowance of trading losses Section 768 TA 1988

31. No relief for trading losses carried forward under Section 393(1) is available where:

a) within any period of three years there is both a change in the ownership of the company *and* (either earlier, later or simultaneously) a major change in the nature or conduct of a trade carried on by the company, *or*

b) there is a change in the ownership of the company at *any time* not just within a three year period – after the scale of the activities in a trade have become small or negligible and before any revival of the trade.

These provisions prevent the set-off of a loss incurred by a company in an accounting period beginning before the change of ownership against trading income of an accounting period ending after the change of ownership.

There is a change in the ownership of a company when:

a) a single person acquires more than 50% of the ordinary share capital of the company

b) two or more persons each acquire more than 5% or more of the ordinary share capital and together they own more than 50% of the ordinary share capital.

A major change in the nature of the trade is defined as

a) a major change in the type of property dealt in, or services or facilities in the trade, *or*

b) a major change in customers, outlets or markets of trade.

On a change in ownership, if the company fails to pay its corporation tax liability for an A.P. then it may in certain circumstances be assessed on the person who had control of the company before the change.

• Student self-testing question

The results of A Ltd and its wholly owned subsidiary B Ltd for the three years ended 31st March 1998 are as follows:

		31.3.1996 £	31.3.1997 £	31.3.1998 £
A Ltd	Schedule D Case I	1,200	(7,500)	4,800
	Schedule A	500	500	500
B Ltd	Schedule D Case I	2,500	3,500	5,000

A Ltd makes a claim for loss relief under Section 393A(1)(a) and (b) and then claims group relief under Section 402.

Show the computations.

Solution   **Corporation tax computations**

	31.3.1996 £	31.3.1997 £	31.3.1998 £
A Ltd			
Schedule D Case I	1,200	–	4,800
Less Section 393(1)	–	–	1,800
	1,200	–	3,000
Schedule A	500	500	500
	1,700	500	3,500
Less Section 393A(1)(a) and (b)	1,700	500	–
Assessments	–	–	3,500
B Ltd			
Schedule D Case I	2,500	3,500	5,000
Less group relief Section 402	–	3,500	–
Assessments	2,500	–	5,000

Loss memorandum		£	£
Loss year to 31st March 1997			7,500
Section 393A(1)(a)	31.3.1997	500	
Section 393A(1)(b)	31.3.1996	1,700	
Section 393(1)	31.3.1998	1,800	
Section 402	31.3.1997	3,500	7,500

(group relief surrendered to B Ltd)

Note: The maximum amount has been surrendered to B Ltd.

• Question without answer

1. Z Ltd, a UK trading company, acquired a 75% interest in Q Ltd on the 30th September 1990. Both companies have the same year end and their results for the A.P. 31.3.1998 are as follows:

	Z Ltd £	Q Ltd £
Schedule D Case I	75,000	(30,000)
Schedule A	15,000	–
Chargeable gain	10,000	–
Debenture interest paid (gross)	5,000	5,000

Compute the amount of group relief available for the AP to 31st March 1998, and show the corporation tax computations.

33 International aspects

Introduction

1. This chapter deals with some of the more common features of corporation tax arising from overseas operations under the following headings:

> Company residence
> Schedule D Case IV
> Schedule D Case V
> Computation of underlying taxes
> ACT and double tax relief
> Foreign tax credit and loss relief
> Foreign income dividends
> Controlled foreign companies.

Company residence

2. a) A company is deemed to be resident in the UK for taxation purposes in the following circumstances:

   i) Where the company is incorporated in the UK, wherever its central management and control is situated.

   ii) Where the company is not incorporated in the UK but its central management and control is situated in the UK. This could apply, for example, to the branch of a foreign registered company whose central management and control is located in the UK.

   b) The tests for determining the residence of a company will still therefore be relevant for non-UK incorporated companies and these may be summarised as follows:

   i) A company is resident where the central management and control actually abides. That is a pure question of fact per *L Loreburn in De Beers Consolidated Mines v Howe* 5 TC 198.

   ii) The place of control management and control is ascertained by reference to such factors as:
      1) the place of residence of the director and senior management
      2) the place where board and management meetings are held
      3) the determination of which individuals actually manage and control the company ie provide effective management
      4) whether there is parent/subsidiary relationship or branch organisational structure.

   c) Dividends from a UK incorporated company whose management and control is exercised overseas will be franked investment income if received by another UK company. Any qualifying distribution paid by that company will be subject to ACT in the usual way.

   d) It is possible for a company belonging to a group to be resident of two countries for taxation purposes ie dual resident.

Schedule D Case IV – APs ending before 31st March 1996

3. Income arising from securities outside the UK is chargeable to corporation tax under Case IV, excluding any income which is taxed at source under Schedule C. Security income means income from a mortgage or debenture, but not from stocks or shares.

   a) The amount assessed to corporation tax is the gross income arising before any deduction for any foreign tax paid.

   b) A UK resident company is entitled to claim a credit for any foreign tax charged directly on security interest paid to it, such as a withholding tax. This credit may be set against the tax liability arising on the Case IV income.

   c) The amount of the credit cannot exceed the corporation tax liability on the gross income. This entitlement is known as 'unilateral relief', and is available where no Double Taxation Agreement is in existence, or exceptionally, where such an agreement does not permit a credit.

   d) For accounting periods ending after 31st March 1996 the interest receivable under Case IV is brought within the loan debt relationship arrangements, and any profit taxed as Case III income.

> **Example**

K Ltd has the following data relating to the 12 months AP to the 31st March 1998.

	£
Schedule D Case I	1,280,000
Schedule D Case IV :	
(foreign interest after 15% withholding tax)	85,000
Chargeable gains	250,000

Calculate the MCT for the AP to 31st March 1998.

Solution

K Ltd Corporation tax computation AP 31.3.1998

	£
Schedule D Case I	1,280,000
Schedule D Case IV (gross) $\frac{85,000}{85} \times \frac{100}{1}$	100,000
Chargeable gains	250,000
Profits chargeable to CT	1,630,000

	£
Corporation tax payable	
1,630,000 @ 33%	537,900
Less Double tax relief	15,000
Mainstream liability	522,900

Note

The double tax relief is the lower of the following:

Foreign income	*100,000*
UK tax @ 33 %	*33,000*
Foreign tax	*15,000*

Schedule D Case V

4. Income arising from possessions outside of the UK, not being income consisting of any emoluments of any office or employment, are chargeable to corporation tax under this case. Income from possessions embraces all income from trades, professions and vocations, income from stocks and shares, and foreign bank interest.

   With Case V income the form of unilateral relief available under Section 790 TA 1988 is extended to 'underlying taxes' in special circumstances. Underlying taxes means taxes on profits out of which dividends have been declared attracting the withholding tax. The special circumstances are:

   a) The UK company must control not less than 10% of the voting power of the overseas company paying the dividend.

   b) The 10% holding can be established through the medium of sub-subsidiaries, providing that the direct and indirect linkage gives the minimum percentage.

   c) Unilateral relief can be extended to cover provincial, state and municipal taxes.

Computation of underlying taxes

5. Underlying tax is the tax attributable to the relevant profits out of which the dividend has been paid, and following the rules outlined in the case of *Bowater Paper Corporation Ltd* v *Murgatroyd* 1969 the rate is calculated as follows:

$$\frac{\text{Actual tax paid}}{\text{Actual tax paid + Relevant profits}} \times 100 = \text{Rate \%}$$

   Relevant profits = Profits after tax per accounts.

   The actual amount of the underlying tax may be computed from the following formula:

$$\frac{\text{Overseas tax paid}}{\text{Relevant profits}} \times \text{Dividend (including withholding tax)}.$$

Example

T Ltd received a dividend of £9,000 (after withholding tax of 10%) from its wholly owned subsidiary V Ltd. The profit and loss account of V Ltd for the AP to 31st March 1998 translated into sterling is as follows:

	£	£
Operating profit before taxation		30,000
Deduct:		
Taxation provision	12,000	
Deferred taxation	3,000	15,000
Profit after taxation		15,000
Proposed dividend (gross)		10,000
Retained Profits		5,000

The actual tax paid on the profits of V Ltd was £10,000.

T Ltd had case I income for the AP to 31st March 1998 of £30,000.

Compute the MCT.

Solution

i) **Calculation of Case V income**

$$\text{Underlying tax rate} = \frac{10,000}{10,000 + 15,000} \times 100 = 40\%$$

	£	
Cash received	9,000	
Add withholding tax	1,000	
	10,000	= 60%
Add underlying tax	6,667	= 40%
Case V income	16,667	= 100%

ii) **T Ltd Corporation tax computation AP 31.3.1998**

	£
Schedule D Case I	30,000
Schedule D Case V (gross)	16,667
Profits chargeable to CT	46,667
CT payable: 46,667 @ 23%	10,733
DT relief	
Foreign income 16,667 @ 23%	3,833
MCT	6,900

Notes

i) *The excess foreign tax suffered, and unrelieved is:*

	£
Case V income	16,667
Less dividend received (net)	9,000
Total foreign tax	7,667
Less DTR	3,833
Unrelieved foreign tax	3,834

ii) *The amount of the underlying tax is also computed as follows:*

$$\frac{\text{Overseas tax paid}}{\text{Relevant profits}} \times \text{Dividend} = \frac{10,000}{15,000} \times 10,000 = £6,667$$

Example

T plc, a UK company, has corporation tax profits of £1,472,000 for the year ended 31st March 1998. During the same period T plc received a dividend from its foreign subsidiary Z Ltd of £17,850 after a deduction of 15% withholding tax, and underlying tax of 25% on its profits.

Calculate the gross amount of the foreign dividend and the CT computation for the AP to 31.3.1998.

Solution

		£	£
Foreign income grossed up			
Net dividend received		17,850	
Withholding tax: $15\% \times \dfrac{17,850}{100-15} \times \dfrac{100}{1}$		3,150	21,000
Underlying tax: $25\% \times \dfrac{21,000}{100-25} \times \dfrac{100}{1}$			7,000
			28,000

Corporation tax computation AP 31.3.1998

	£
Schedule D Case I	1,472,000
Schedule D Case V foreign income gross	28,000
	1,500,000
Corporation tax @ 33%	495,000

		£	£
Less double tax relief:	withholding tax	3,150	
	underlying tax	7,000	
		10,150	
Restricted to lower UK tax:			
28,000 @ 33%		9,240	9,240
Unrelieved foreign tax		910	
Mainstream liability			485,760

Patent royalties received

6. Where they arise in respect of a UK registered patent then the royalties are deemed to arise within the UK and are not eligible for DTR.

   Statutory concession number B8 enables payments made to a person resident abroad, for use of a UK registered patent to be treated as arising outside the UK for DTR purposes – except to the extent that it represents consideration for material services rendered in the UK. When the royalties arise in respect of a foreign registered patent they are deemed to arise from a foreign possession and are assessable under Schedule D Case V.

ACT and Double Tax Relief

7. As noted above corporation tax is payable on UK and foreign trading profits under Schedule D Case I and foreign interest and possessions under Schedule D, Case V.

   The foreign trading profits and other income are 'grossed up' by reference to the foreign taxes which may include both underlying and withholding taxes.

   Relief for the foreign tax, insofar as it does not exceed the UK rates, is allowed with the following provisions:

   a) Charges on income management expenses and trade losses (Section 393A(1) set off) may be allocated against any income or chargeable gains. Section 797 TA 1988.

   b) The foreign tax credit is deductible first from the corporation tax attributable to that income and then the ACT set-off is made.

   c) The maximum ACT set-off criteria of Section 239 TA 1988 applies to each source of income in the normal way, including chargeable gains. However the maximum ACT set off against foreign income is the *lower of*:

      i) the net UK tax on the foreign income after any DT Relief, or

      ii) the UK ACT rate tax multiplied by the gross foreign income, ie using the normal criteria.

> **Example**

P Ltd, a UK resident company, has the following data relating to its AP to 31st March 1998:

	£	
Schedule D Case I	1,000,000	
Schedule A	500,000	
Schedule D Case V (gross)	300,000	F. Tax £105,000
Dividend paid	3,000,000	

Calculate the MCT for the AP to 31.3.1998.

Solution

P Ltd Corporation tax computation AP 31.3.1998

	£
Schedule D Case I	1,000,000
Schedule A	500,000
Schedule D Case V	300,000
Profits chargeable to corporation tax	1,800,000
Corporation tax payable:	
1,800,000 @ 33%	594,000
less DT Relief (see below)	99,000
	495,000

ACT set off		
Dividends Paid	3,000,000	
ACT $\frac{20}{80} \times 3,000,000$	750,000	
Maximum set off	300,000	300,000
Surplus ACT	450,000	
Mainstream corporation tax		195,000

Calculation of DT relief and maximum act set off

	Schedule DI £	Schedule A £	Schedule DV £	Total £
CT income	1,000,000	500,000	300,000	1,800,000
Corporation tax	330,000	165,000	99,000	594,000
DT Relief			99,000	99,000
	330,000	165,000	–	495,000
ACT set off				
Maximum UK income 20%	200,000	100,000	–	300,000

Notes

i) *Maximum ACT set off in respect of the foreign income is the lower of:*

Case V Net UK tax $\quad = \quad 0$

$20\% \times 300,000 \quad = \quad 60,000 \quad = 0$

ii) *Case V unrelieved foreign tax is £105,000 – £99,000 = £6,000.*

Foreign tax credit and loss relief

8. Where a UK company has foreign income then in order to preserve the maximum amount of DT relief the consideration of loss relief claims should be considered carefully.

Example

W Ltd and its wholly owned UK subsidiary X Ltd have the following results for the year ended 31st March 1998.

	W Ltd £	X Ltd £
Schedule D Case I	(30,000)	20,000
Schedule D Case V	16,000	
(gross before withholding tax of 15%)		
Chargeable gains	2,000	1,000

Calculate the MCT in the following situations:

a) *W Ltd claims loss relief under Section 393A(1)(a) and surrenders the maximum loss to X Ltd.*

b) *W Ltd makes no claim under Section 393A(1)(a), and surrenders as much loss as possible to X Ltd.*

Solution

(a) **Corporation Tax computations AP 31.3.1998**

	W Ltd £	X Ltd £
Schedule D Case I	–	20,000
Schedule D Case V	16,000	–
Chargeable gains	2,000	1,000
	18,000	21,000
Less Section 393A(1)(a)	(18,000)	
Section 402		(12,000)
Profits chargeable to CT	–	9,000
CT Payable @ 23%	–	2,070
Unrelieved foreign tax £2,400		
MCT	–	2,070
(b) Schedule D Case I	–	20,000
Schedule D Case V	16,000	–
Chargeable gain	2,000	1,000
	18,000	21,000
Less Section 402	–	(21,000)
Profits chargeable to CT	18,000	–
CT payable @ 23%	4,140	–
Less DTR	2,400	–
MCT	1,740	–

Notes

i) *By not claiming loss relief under Section 393A(1)(a) the DT relief of £2,400 has been obtained.*

ii) *W Ltd loss relief carried forward under Section 393(1) is 30,000 – 21,000 = £9,000.*

Foreign income dividends

9. The main features of the FID scheme which applies to dividends paid on or after the 1st June 1994 are as follows.

a) The scheme is optional and may be applied to any of the dividends paid by a company within its accounting period.

b) Foreign source profits out of which a FID may be paid are those of the current or immediately preceding accounting periods.

c) FIDs are treated separately from franked payments and franked investment income. Companies cannot use F11 received to reduce the ACT due on FIDs paid. Neither can they set FIDs received against franked payments made. FIDs received can be set against FIDs paid.

d) Companies are not chargeable to corporation tax on FIDs received.

e) Shareholders are treated as receiving a FID grossed up at the lower (20%) rate of income tax. Lower and basic rate taxpayers have no further tax liability but there is no repayable tax credit.

f) An international headquarter's company may pay a FID without paying ACT. An IHC is in general a company wholly owned throughout the accounting period by a non-UK resident company.

Controlled foreign companies

10. Under Section 747 TA 1988 certain UK resident companies with interests in a controlled foreign company (CFC) may be charged to corporation tax on an apportionment of the profits of the CFC. Some of the main features of the legislation are noted below.

Controlled foreign company

The charge due to corporation tax, which only occurs on the direction of the Board of Inland Revenue, is applicable where the company is a controlled foreign company (CFC). The latter is defined to mean:

a) an overseas resident company which is under the control of persons resident in the UK, and,

b)   the overseas resident company is subject to a lower level of taxation in its country of residence than it would be in the UK. Lower in this case means that the tax paid in the country of residence < 75% of the tax payable had the company been resident in the UK.

Tests of exclusion

11.   No direction will be made to apportion the profits of the CFC if that company satisfies any one of the following tests of exclusion.

   a)   ***Pursues an acceptable distribution policy***

   In general this means that a trading CFC must have paid to UK residents by way of dividends at least 90% of its available profits for accounting periods beginning on or after 28th November 1995. Prior to that date the percentage was 50%. For all other companies 90% of taxable profits less capital gains and foreign tax must be distributed.

   b)   ***Is engaged in exempt activities***

   Under this heading a CFC is engaged in exempt activities if it has, throughout the accounting period, a business establishment in its territory of residence and its business affairs are effectively managed there. The latter is evidenced, amongst other things, if it has a sufficient number of employees in the territory to deal with its volume of business locally. Certain non-trading activities have to meet other criteria to benefit under this heading.

   c)   ***Fulfils the public quotation condition***

   This is met where the CFC has at least 35% of its shares which have voting power, quoted on a recognised stock exchange in the country of residence. As for close companies in the UK, this requirement is not met where 85% of the company's voting power is in the hands of its principal members.

   d)   ***Satisfies the motive test***

   Under this heading there are two conditions to be met if the CFC is to satisfy the motive test.

   i)   The existence of the CFC was not made mainly for the purposes of achieving a diversion of profits from the UK, and

   ii)   Any reduction of UK tax resulting from transactions is either minimal or is not the main reason for undertaking those transactions.

   e)   ***Has chargeable profits <£20,000***

   Where the chargeable profits of the CFC are less than £20,000 for a 12 month accounting period then it automatically falls within the exclusion category.

   Chargeable profits, including capital gains, if the company was resident in the UK, would be chargeable to corporation tax.

Assessable profits

12.   a)   Where a direction to apportion chargeable profits is made then corporation tax at the 'appropriate rate' is assessed on the following:

   | The apportioned amount of chargeable profits | – Any creditable tax attributable to the apportioned profits such as DT relief. |

   The appropriate rate of corporation tax is the average rate applicable to the company's UK profits for the accounting period in which the accounting period of the CFC ends.

   b)   Deductions at the appropriate rate can be made where the UK company has reliefs which have not been fully utilised against its UK taxable profits. The reliefs are:
   i)   relief for trading losses (sec. 393a(1)(2))
   ii)   relief for excess charges (sec. 393(9))
   iii)   group relief (sec. 402)
   iv)   relief for management expenses (Sec. 75(1)).

   c)   No assessment will be made unless the amount apportioned to a UK company and its associates of the CFC's chargeable profits amount to at least 10% of those chargeable profits.

   ACT set-off is available against the apportioned amount subject to the normal maximum criteria for ACT set-off.

13. Inland Revenue press releases have provided a list of what are known as 'excluded countries'. Where a company carries on a trade in one of these countries it is deemed to fall outside the charging provisions noted above.

• Student self-testing question

A Ltd, a UK company, owns one third of the voting shares in B, a foreign company. The profit and loss account of B for the AP 31.3.98 in sterling was:

	£	£
Profit before tax		1,000,000
Tax on profits	300,000	
Deferred tax	100,000	400,000
		600,000
Dividend (net)	240,000	
Withholding tax	60,000	300,000
Retained profit		300,000

Actual tax liability was agreed at £270,000. A Ltd has Schedule D Case I income for the AP 31.3.98 of £1,355,000. *Compute the DTR and MCT.*

Solution

A Ltd Corporation tax computation AP 31.3.98

	£
Schedule D Case I	1,355,000
Schedule D Case V	145,000
Profits chargeable to CT	1,500,000
CT payable @ 33%	495,000
Less DT relief	47,850
Mainstream CT liability	447,150

Notes

i) *Calculation of underlying tax*

$$\frac{270,000}{270,000 + 600,000} = 31.034\%$$

	£
Net dividend received $\dfrac{240,000}{3} =$	80,000
Add withholding tax @ 25%	20,000
	100,000

Add underlying tax		
$\dfrac{100,000}{100 - 31.034} \times 100 =$	145,000	
less	100,000	45,000
Case V income		145,000

The amount of the underlying tax is also computed as:

$$\frac{270,000}{600,000} \times 100,000 \ ie \ 45,000.$$

ii) *Unrelieved foreign tax amounts to the following:*

	£
Case V income	145,000
Foreign taxes	65,000
UK tax 145,000 ×33%	47,850
Unrelieved tax	17,150

• Question without answer

1. T Ltd, a UK company, owns 20% of A, a foreign resident company. T Ltd has the following results for the year ended 31st March 1998:

	£
Schedule D Case 1	2,000,000
Chargeable gains	66,000
Schedule D Case V (gross)	280,000
Debenture interest paid (gross)	140,000
Dividend paid (net)	500,000

The foreign income is subject to overseas taxation of 45%.

Compute the MCT for the AP to 31st March 1998.

34 Miscellaneous

Introduction

1. This chapter is concerned with the corporation tax aspects of the following:

    Investment companies; companies in liquidation and companies in partnership; purchase by an unquoted company of its own shares.

Investment companies (other than close investment holding companies)

2. An investment company is defined in Section 130 TA 1988 as 'any company whose business consists wholly or mainly in the making of investments, and the principal part of whose income is derived therefrom'. This definition it should be noted is not the same as that contained in Section 266 of the Companies Act 1985. Further provisions are contained in Section 75.

3. Savings banks, other than Trustee Savings Banks, are treated as investment companies, as are investment trusts. Authorised unit trusts are also taxed as if they were investment companies by Section 468 TA 1988.

4. An investment company is not a trading company taxable under Schedule D Case I so that any expenses incurred must be either deductible from a particular source of income eg Schedule A, or fall within the category of 'management expenses' to be allowable. In this context a company which trades in investments will normally be assessed under Schedule D Case I also. Where a trading company invests its surplus cash this does not thereby mean that it becomes taxable as an investment company. While in general the principles of corporation tax apply to investment companies, there are some special features noted below.

    a) The total profits of a UK resident investment company for any accounting period are computed as for corporation tax purposes, from which may be deducted 'management expenses' for that period.

    b) 'Management expenses' include commissions and expenses of managing the company, eg salaries, directors' fees, rent rates, printing and stationery.

        Exchange losses on investments and expenses such as brokerage fees on the change of investments are not allowable expenses. Professional charges for investment advice would be allowable.

    c) Expenses which relate to the management and maintenance of property are not management expenses of the investment company.

    d) Management expenses are deducted from total profits chargeable to corporation tax. Excess management expenses can be dealt with as follows:

        i)   carried forward and treated as management expenses of the next succeeding accounting period

        ii) surrendered as group relief to a fellow subsidiary

        iii) relieved against a surplus of franked investment income.

    e) Expenses deductible in computing Schedule A income are expressly excluded from management expenses. Sums deductible in computing profits under any other section of the Taxes Acts are also expressly excluded from management expenses.

    f) For accounting periods ending after 31st March 1996, loan and bank interest are dealt with according to the loan relationship rules and not as charges on income. Where the loan relationship is not for trade purposes, the net loss can be set against other income.

    g) Special rules apply to close investment companies. *(See Chapter 30.)*

    h) Relief for management expenses and charges carried forward is withdrawn where ownership of an investment company changes after the 28th November 1994 and

        i)   there is a major change in the nature or conduct of the business during a three year period or

        ii) its business revives having been negligible before the change or

        iii) there is a significant increase in the company's capital in the year before or three years after the change or

        iv) an asset is acquired from a company in the purchasing group after the change of ownership and disposed of within three years of the change.

Example

B Ltd is a UK investment company with the following income and expenditure relating to its accounting period ended 31st March 1998.

	£
Rents due	1,025,000
Bank deposit interest	50,000
Chargeable gain	480,000
Franked investment income	80,000
Maintenance and repair of properties	10,000
Management expenses	30,000
Debenture interest paid (gross)	9,000
Property expenses	6,000

Compute the corporation tax liability for the AP to 31.3.1998.

Solution

	£	£
Rental income		
Schedule A rent		1,025,000
Less property expenses	6,000	
maintenance and repair	10,000	16,000
		1,009,000

	£
Computation for AP to 31st March 1998	
Property income	1,009,000
Schedule D Case III (50,000 – 9,000)	41,000
Chargeable gain	480,000
	1,530,000
Less management expenses	30,000
Assessable profits	1,500,000
Corporation tax payable 33% × 1,500,000	495,000

Notes

i)   *In this example there would be a surplus of franked investment income of £80,000.*

ii) *The debenture interest of £9,000 has been set against the bank interest of £50,000 under the loan relationship rules, and the net income assessed as Case III income, as B Ltd is assumed to be a non-trading company.*

Companies in liquidation

5.   **General points**

When a company goes into liquidation then from a taxation point of view there are a number of consequences which arise, and these are outlined below.

a)   An accounting period ends on the commencement of a winding up, and thereafter every 12 months until the winding up is completed. Section 12 TA 1988.

b)   Where assets are vested in a liquidator under Section 538 of the Companies Act 1985, no disposal by the company takes place.

c)   Distributions made in respect of shares in the course of a winding up are not liable for any ACT but they are disposals from the shareholders' point of view, for CGT purposes.

d)   Profits, if any, arising in the course of a winding up are chargeable to corporation tax, as are any chargeable gains arising from the disposal of assets.

e)   Liquidation terminates the 'group structure' for corporation tax purposes so that group relief and group income are no longer permitted. However, for CGT purposes the group relationship is not affected.

f)   Loss relief under Section 393A(1)(a) and (b) could be available up to the date of the commencement of the winding up.

Example

R Ltd has been trading unsuccessfully for a number of years and its results for the four accounting periods to the 31st December 1998, are:

	31.12.95 £	31.12.96 £	31.12.97 £	31.12.98 £
Schedule D Case I	(3,000)	(5,000)	(17,000)	(25,000)

A liquidator was appointed on the 1st January 1999, and further trading losses were incurred up to the 31st March 1999 amounting to £5,000. On that date the company ceased trading, and the business assets were sold giving rise to a chargeable gain of £25,000 after indexation.

Show the corporation tax computation for the AP to 31.3.99.

Solution

Corporation tax computation for the three months to 31st March 1999

	£
Chargeable gain	25,000
Less Section 393A(1)(a) relief loss for the period	5,000
Assessable profits	20,000
Corporation tax payable 23% × 20,000 =	4,600

Notes

i) *Here the trade losses brought forward are not available for set-off against the chargeable gain.*

ii) *If chargeable gains arise during a liquidation, outside any trading period, they can only be set against capital losses.*

iii) *Under Section 15A.CAA.1990, where a trader sells an industrial building after the cessation of the trade in which it has been used, any balancing charge arising may be set against losses brought forward under Section 393(1) or 393(9).*

Companies in partnership

6. Where a partnership exists with one or more of the partners being a company, then special rules apply to the determination of the profits chargeable to corporation tax. In the main these are to be found in Section 114 TA 1988, and include the following.

a) Profits of the partnership are ascertained as if the partnership was a company, ie by reference to accounting periods falling within financial years, and not on the preceding year basis. With the introduction of a current year basis for partnerships these periods will eventually be the same.

b) The profits are computed using normal corporation tax principles, except for certain items which are initially ignored, such as distributions to the partners, capital allowances, charges on income, and losses of other accounting periods. The profits after these adjustments are divided amongst the partners in accordance with the partnership agreement.

c) Capital allowances are calculated for each accounting period on corporation tax principles, and allocated to the partners, as are any charges on income.

d) Any non-trading income of the partnership would also be shared amongst the partners.

Example

W and X are in partnership with A Ltd and the partnership results and data for the transitional year ended 31st March 1998 are as follows:

	£
Schedule D Case I before capital allowances	27,000
Capital allowances	3,000
Schedule D Case III	5,000

Interest on partnership capital accounts is: W £2,000, X £1,000 and A Ltd £5,000. Partnership profits are to be shared equally after the provision of interest on capital.

Show the allocation of profits.

Solution

Allocation of profits. Accounting period to 31.3.1998

	W £	X £	A Ltd £	Total £
Interest on capital	2,000	1,000	5,000	8,000
Share of balance	8,000	8,000	8,000	24,000
Total profits	10,000	9,000	13,000	32,000
Less capital allowances	1,000	1,000	1,000	3,000
	9,000	8,000	12,000	29,000
Total profits to be shared				
Schedule D Case I		27,000		
Less capital allowances		3,000		24,000
Schedule D Case III				5,000
				29,000

Notes

i) *The total profits to be shared of £29,000 are not divided equally by one third, since the interest on capital accounts varies.*

ii) *A Ltd is chargeable to corporation tax on profits of £12,000 for the accounting period to 31st March 1998. If this is not the same accounting period as for the company's non-partnership business, then an apportionment must be made.*

iii) *Capital allowances are deducted from profits for 1997/98 onwards.*

Partnership loss relief and ACT set-off

7. Subject to the special provisions noted below, a company's share of a partnership loss is available for relief against other non-partnership income, including group relief, in the usual manner. Further any ACT arising on qualifying distributions of the company may be set against any corporation tax liability due on the share of the partnership profits. However, both loss relief and ACT set-off are not generally available where arrangements are in existence whereby:

   a) any member of the partnership (or a person connected with that member) receives any payment or other benefit related to the company partners' share of the profit or loss, or

   b) the company, or any connected person, receives any payment or other benefit (other than a payment for group relief) in respect of its share of the partnership loss.

   These rules, which are contained in Section 116 TA 1988, are generally designed to prevent artificial transactions involving the exploitation of the group relief and loss relief provisions, particularly where a first year allowance is available.

Purchase by an unquoted company of its own shares

8. a) Under Section 219 TA 1988 certain companies are permitted to purchase, redeem or repay their own shares, subject to certain conditions. Where these are met then the transaction is not treated as a distribution, so that no ACT is payable by the company and no income tax liability arises on the recipient. The transaction does amount to a disposal by the shareholder for capital gains tax purposes.

   b) The following are the main conditions which apply

      i) The company must be an unquoted company. Shares dealt with on the unlisted securities market qualify as unquoted shares. A company which is a 51% subsidiary of a quoted company is a quoted company.

      ii) The company must be a trading company or a member of a trading group.

      iii) The redemption repayment or purchase must be made either

         1) wholly or mainly with the purpose of benefiting a trade carried on by the company or by its 75% subsidiary, or

         2) the whole or substantially the whole of the payment (apart from any sum paid by way of CGT) is applied by the person to whom it is made in discharging a liability of his or hers for inheritance tax charged on death, and is so applied within two years of the death.

iv) The transaction must not form part of a scheme or arrangement, the main purpose of which is:

    1)   to enable the owner of the shares to participate in the profits of the company without receiving a dividend, or

    2)   the avoidance of tax.

c) With regard to the vendor the following points should be noted.

    i)   The shares must have been owned for at least five years at the time of purchase by the company – three years where the shares were acquired under a will or intestacy.

    ii)   Where shares are acquired from the vendor's spouse then the latter's period of ownership is counted towards the five year period.

    iii)   The vendor's interest in the company must either be completely eliminated or substantially reduced as a result of the purchase by the company. A reduction is not substantial if it is less than 25%. For these purposes the holdings of associates are taken into consideration.

d) Advance clearance of proposals for the purchase by a company of its own shares can be obtained by applying in writing to the Inland Revenue. Subject to any request for additional information the Inland Revenue must notify the company of their decision within 30 days of the date of the application or provision of further information.

e) The vendor of the shares is subject to the normal rules of CGT with regard to his or her disposal to the company.

• Student self-testing question

O Ltd, an investment and property company, has the following results for its year ended 31st March 1998.

	£
Bank deposit interest	17,500
Dividends received	8,000
Rents receivable	68,000
Property maintenance and repair	7,500
Debenture interest paid (net)	4,000
Chargeable gain	20,000
Management expenses	17,000
Dividends paid (net)	16,000
Management expenses b/f	3,000

Compute the corporation tax liability for the AP to 31.3.1998.

Solution

Corporation Tax computation AP to 31.3.1998

		£	£
Schedule A Rent		68,000	
Less property expenses		7,500	60,500
Schedule D Case III (17,500 – 5,000)			12,500
Chargeable gains			20,000
			93,000
Less Management expenses	b/f	3,000	
	paid in year	17,000	20,000
Profits chargeable to corporation tax			73,000

Corporation tax payable		
73,000 @ 23%		16,790
Less ACT set-off:		
Dividends paid $16,000 \times \frac{20}{80}$	4,000	
Dividends received $8,000 \times \frac{20}{80}$	2,000	2,000
Mainstream liability		14,790

Notes

i) *Debenture interest is paid less tax at the 20% rate.*

ii) *Case III income is bank interest received of £17,500 less debenture interest paid of £5,000 (gross), i.e. £12,500.*

• Question without answer

F Ltd, an investment company, has the following data relating to its financial year to 31st March 1998.

	£
Rents received	74,000
Bank deposit interest	7,000
Dividends received	2,400
Property expenses	22,000
Audit fee (25% property)	1,000
Directors' remuneration (25% property)	25,000
General office expenses (25% property)	15,000
Dividends paid	8,000

Excess management expenses brought forward from previous year amounted to £5,000.

Compute the profits chargeable to corporation tax for the AP to 31st March 1998.

Corporation tax
End of section questions and answers

Corporation tax rates

	Years to 31st March				
	1994	**1995**	**1996**	**1997**	**1998**
Full rate	33%	33%	33%	33%	33%
Small companies rate	25%	25%	25%	24%	23%
Small company profit levels:					
Lower relevant amount	250,000	300,000	300,000	300,000	300,000
Higher relevant amount	1,250,000	1,500,000	1,500,000	1,500,000	1,500,000
Formula fraction	1/50	1/50	1/50	9/400	1/40
ACT fraction	9/31	20/80	20/80	20/80	20/80

Corporation tax question No 1. Advance Ltd

Advance Limited, a trading company, makes up its accounts annually to 31st January. The company had the following results for the year ended 31st January 1998.

		£	£
Sales			1,565,204
Less: Purchases		1,044,134	
Add: Stock at 1.2.97		264,216	
		1,308,350	
Less: Stock at 31.1.98		390,208	
			918,142
			647,062
Less: Salaries, NHI, pension contributions		244,778	
Rent, rates, light, heating		104,324	
Delivery expenses		43,211	
Sundry expenses (note 1)		14,409	
Professional charges (note 2)		12,602	
Repairs and maintenance (note 3)		8,040	
Interest payable (note 4)		7,491	
Depreciation plant and machinery		3,620	
			438,475
Trading profits			208,587
Investment income (note 5)			42,000
Profit before taxation			250,587
Taxation			120,000
			130,587
Dividend (note 6)			70,000
			60,587
Add: Retained earnings brought forward			201,266
Retained earnings carried forward			261,853

1. Sundry expenses

	£
Stationery, postage, telephone	4,866
Office teas, coffees etc	1,982
Entertaining – UK customers	1,856
– Staff	2,514
Office cleaning	864
Removal expenses	1,256
Hire of vehicles	1,031
Donation (non-trade)	40
	14,409

2. Professional charges
    Audit and accountancy
    Legal charges re new lease
    Legal charges – re unfair dismissal claim
    Debt collecting

	£
Audit and accountancy	7,420
Legal charges re new lease	2,650
Legal charges – re unfair dismissal claim	1,500
Debt collecting	1,032
	12,602

3. Repairs and maintenance

	£
Building alterations to new premises	3,200
Decoration of new premises	1,250
Annual maintenance contract	1,900
Sundry repairs	1,690
	8,040

4. Interest payable (to UK Bank)

	£
Accrued at 1.2.1997	(2,444)
Paid during year	6,524
	4,080
Accrued at 31.1.1998	3,411
	7,491

5. Investment income

	£
Franked investment income	30,000
Debenture interest (received) gross – trading purposes	12,000
	42,000

6. Dividend
    This was paid on 2nd January 1998.   £70,000

7. The pool written down value at 1st February 1997 was £32,080. During the year items of plant and machinery were sold for £16,400 and the company acquired a secondhand polishing machine for £26,000 and new items of plant costing £3,400, on the 1st January 1998.

8. Advance Limited moved premises during the year acquiring a 99 year lease on 1st May 1997 of a showroom for a consideration of £180,000.

    You are required to compute the profits subject to corporation tax for the year ended 31st January 1998 on the assumption that all available reliefs are claimed.   **(INST. TAX)**

Solution

Advance Ltd AP to 31st January 1998

Schedule D Case I

		£
Adjustment of profits		
Profits before taxation		250,587
Add back:		
Entertaining	1,856	
Donation	40	
Legal charges re new lease	2,650	
Alterations to new premises	3,200	
Decoration of new premises	1,250	
Depreciation	3,620	12,616
		263,203
Less non-Case I income investment income		30,000
		233,203

	Plant and Machinery Pool
	£
Capital allowances	
Balance b/f	32,080
Less proceeds of sale	16,400
	15,680
Additions	29,400
	45,080
WA allowance @ 25%	(11,270)
WDV c/f	33,810

Corporation tax computation. AP to 31st January 1998

	£	£
Schedule D Case I. adjusted profits	233,203	
Less : capital allowances	11,270	221,933
Profits chargeable to corporation tax		221,933

Notes

i)   The amount invested in the new showroom was:

	£
99 year lease	180,000
legal charges	2,650
	182,650
non-revenue expenditure:	
alterations	3,200
decoration	1,250
	187,100

ii)   There would be no capital allowances available in respect of the new showroom nor any relief for the lease premium being greater than 50 years' duration.

iii) Small company profit rate of 23% would apply in this case.

iv) Debenture interest is deducted as an expense in computing the Case I profit.

Corporation tax question NO 2. Threadbare Ltd

Threadbare Ltd is a manufacturer of quality clothing which makes its accounts up to the 31st March each year.

Its trading and profit and loss account for the year ended 31st March 1998, its centenary year, is as follows:

	£	£
Sales		787,315
Cost of sales		731,118
Gross profit		56,197
Add Miscellaneous income		5,142
		61,339
Less Expenses:		
Salaries	4,705	
Rent rates and insurance	1,650	
Lighting and heating	1,291	
Motor expenses	7,402	
Repairs and renewals	10,011	
General expenses	8,117	
Depreciation	5,483	
Debenture interest paid (gross)	7,500	
		46,159
Profit before taxation		15,180

You are given the following information:

1. Miscellaneous income comprises:

	£
Profit on sale of plant and machinery	1,642
Dividend from UK company (net) received 15.6.97	800
Building society interest received (gross)	1,800
Bank interest received (gross)	900
	5,142

2. Repairs and renewals comprise:

	£
Repairs to new premises, necessary to make them usable	2,502
Portable office partitioning	2,509
New microcomputers	5,000
	10,011

3. General expenses comprise:

	£
Bad debts written off	1,123
Increase in general bad debt provision	1,000
Legal costs of renewal of lease for 20 years	557
Entertaining	1,532
Promotional gifts of bottles of wine	2,055
Covenanted payment to charity (gross)	100
Theatre outing for staff	1,750
	8,117

4. Capital allowances in respect of all qualifying expenditure have been agreed at £1,919.

5. During the year to 31st March 1998 the company paid two dividends:

		£
1.6.1997	Proposed final 1997 (net)	8,000
28.10.1997	Interim dividend (net) 1998	4,000

a) *Compute the profits chargeable to corporation tax.*

b) *Calculate the mainstream liability.*

c) *Show the due dates for any ACT payable.*

Solution

Threadbare Ltd AP to 31st March 1998

Schedule D Case I adjustment of profits	£	£
Profit before taxation		15,180
Add back:		
Repairs to make premises usable	2,502	
Office partitioning	2,509	
New microcomputers	5,000	
Increase in general bad debt provision	1,000	
Entertaining	1,532	
Promotional gifts	2,055	
Covenant to charity	100	
Depreciation	5,483	20,181
		35,361
Less non-Case I income		5,142
		30,219

Corporation tax computation AP to 31st March 1998

	£	£	£
Schedule D Case I adjusted profits		30,219	
Less: capital allowances		1,919	28,300
Building society interest gross		1,800	
Bank interest		900	2,700
			31,000
Charges on income paid			
covenant (gross)			100
Profits chargeable to corporation tax			30,900

Corporation tax payable:

30,900 @ 23 %			7,107

ACT set off

	£		£
Dividends paid $(12,000 \times \frac{1}{4})$	3,000		
Dividends received $800 \times \frac{1}{4}$	200		2,800
Mainstream liability			4,307

Due dates for payment

		£	£
ACT	14th July 1997	1,800	
	14th January 1998	1,000	2,800
Mainstream liability 1st January 1999.			4,307

Note

Debenture interest is allowed as an expense of trading for APs ending after 31.3.1996.

Corporation tax question No 3. XYZ Ltd

XYZ Limited, a non-close company with no associated companies, has been trading since 1980, making up its accounts to 31st March.

In arriving at a profit from all sources of £509,000 for the year ended 31st March 1998, the following items were included:

Income:	£	
Rent received	10,000	
Premium on a lease granted to a tenant	8,000	(note 1)
Interest on deposit account	700	
Debenture interest (received net in June 1997)		
Gross amount	1,000	
Dividend from UK company (received net 4,000 in August 1997)		
Gross amount	5,000	
Profit on sale of freehold property	126,850	(note 3)
Items charged in the accounts:		
Depreciation	5,900	(note 5)
Legal charges:		
Negotiation of a new lease taken by the company	700	(note 2)
Blackmail payment made in 1.12.97.	600	
Sale of premises	850	
General expenses	2,400	(note 4)

Notes

1. The premium received was in respect of the granting of a lease for 21 years. (Ignore CGT in respect of this transaction.)

2. The new lease took effect from 1st April, 1997 for a term of 21 years.

3. The chargeable gain arising on the sale of the property has been agreed at £29,200.

4. General expenses included:

	£
Deed of covenant to charity (gross)	200
Staff Christmas party	400
Thefts by staff	1,000
Sundries (all allowable)	800
	2,400

5. Capital allowances have been agreed at £61,200.

6. Dividends paid:

    a) For year ended 31.3.97 £60,000 paid 20.7.97.

    b) Interim for year ended 31.3.98 £20,000 paid 1st January 1998.

Compute the corporation tax payable.

Solution

XYZ Ltd Corporation tax computation. AP to 31st March 1998

	£	£
Schedule D Case I income		
Profit from all sources		509,000
Add back:		
Depreciation	5,900	
Legal charges: New lease	700	
Blackmail payment	600	
Sale of premises	850	
General expenses: Covenant	200	8,250
		517,250
Less non-Case I income		
Rent received	10,000	
Premium on lease	8,000	
Interest on deposit a/c non-trading	700	
Dividends	5,000	
Profit on sale of factory	126,850	150,550
		366,700
Less capital allowances		61,200
		305,500

	£
Schedule A	
Lease premium	8,000
Less $(21 - 1) \times 2\% \times 8,000$	3,200
	4,800
Rents received	10,000
	14,800

Corporation tax computation. AP to 31.3.1998

	£
Schedule D Case I	305,500
Schedule A	14,800
Schedule D Case III	700
	321,000
Chargeable gains	29,200
	350,200
Less charges on income paid:	
Deed of covenant	200
Profit chargeable to corporation tax	350,000
Corporation tax payable:	
£350,000 @ 33%	115,500

Less marginal relief:

$$(1,500,000 - 355,000) \times \frac{350000}{(350,000 + 5,000)} \times \frac{1}{40}$$

$$= 1,145,000 \times \frac{350000}{355000} \times \frac{1}{40}$$

	28,222
	87,278

Less ACT set off:

Dividends paid 80,000 $\times \frac{1}{4}$	20,000	
Dividends received 4,000 $\times \frac{1}{4}$	1,000	
	19,000	19,000
		68,278

Less excess income tax suffered: (1,000 @ 20%) = £200 – (200 @ 23%) = 46

	154
	68,124

Corporation tax question NO 4. Ultimate Upholsterers Ltd

Ultimate Upholsterers Ltd is a United Kingdom resident trading company which manufactures leather upholstered chairs. It has been trading for many years and has no associated companies.

The company's results for the year ended 30 September 1997 are summarised as follows:

	£
Trading profits (before capital allowances)	375,864
Dividend from UK company (29 May 1997)	22,400 (net)
Loan interest received (30 June 1997)	12,000 (gross)
Debenture interest paid (31 July 1997)	24,000 (gross)
Writing-down allowances on plant and machinery	49,000

The company operates from two factories, both of which meet the definition of 'industrial building' in the Capital Allowances Act. Neither building is situated in an enterprise zone.

Factory 1 was first occupied by Ultimate Upholsterers Ltd on 1 October 1980 under the terms of a 25 year lease which had been acquired for £50,000, premium.

Factory 2 was purchased on 1 January 1997 for £300,000. The factory cost £150,000 on 1 January 1988 and had been used continuously as an industrial building by the previous owner until it was sold. An extension to Factory 2 was completed on 1 July 1997 at a cost of £125,000 to provide extra production facilities following increased demand and brought into use on 8 August 1997.

Notes

i) *The company paid a dividend of £80,000 on 17 February 1997.*

ii. *The company had no surplus of franked investment income, advance corporation tax or losses to carry forward on 1 October 1996.*

Calculate the mainstream corporation tax payable for the year ended 30 September 1997. **(ACCA)**

Solution

Ultimate Upholsterers Ltd. Corporation tax computation AP to 30.9.97

Schedule D Case I	£	£	£
Trading profit			363,864
Less capital allowances			
Plant	49,000		
Ind Blgs	13,824	62,824	
Lease premium		1,040	63,864
Profits chargeable to CT			300,000
CT payable:			
FY96 150,000 @ 33%	49,500		
FY97 150,000 @ 33%	49,500		99,000

Marginal relief:

FY to 31.3.97 $(750,000 - 150,000) \times \dfrac{9}{400}$ (13,500)

FY to 31.3.98 $\dfrac{1}{40} \times [750,000 - (150,000 + 28,000)] \times \dfrac{150,000}{178,000}$

$= 572,000 \times \dfrac{1}{40} \times \dfrac{150,000}{178,000}$ (12,050)

                                                                                                73,500

ACT set off

Dividend paid $80,000 \times \dfrac{1}{4}$ 20,000

Dividend received $22,400 \times \dfrac{1}{4}$ 5,600

                                                                                                14,400

Mainstream liability   59,100

Notes

i)   *Capital allowances – Industrial buildings*
         Cost 1.1.1989   *150,000*
         Cost 1.1.1997   *300,000*

     Allowances to purchaser limited to cost $\dfrac{150,000}{(25-8)} =$ *8,824*

     Factory extension $125,000 \times 4\%$ *5,000*
                                                                                            13,824

ii) *Lease premium*
         1.10.1980 payment   *50,000*
         Less (25 – 1) × 2%   *24,000*
                                                                      26,000

     Annual amount $\dfrac{26,000}{25}$ *1,040*

iii) *Schedule D Case I – adjusted profits*   *375,864*
              Add loan interest received   *12,000*
                                                                      387,864
              Less debenture interest paid   *24,000*
     Case I   *363,864*

Corporation tax question No 5. Unassailable Undertakings Ltd

Unassailable Undertakings Limited is a United Kingdom resident trading company which has been trading for many years. It has no associated companies. Accounts have always been prepared to 30th June but in 1997 the accounting date was changed to 30th September. The company's summarised results are as follows:

	12 months to 30.6.96 £		15 months to 30.9.97 £	
Schedule D Case I				
Adjusted profit/(loss)	450,000		(175,000)	
Capital (loss)/gain	(20,000)	(31.3.96)	2,000	(31.7.97)
Bank interest received	2,000	(31.12.95)	1,500	(31.12.96)
Building society interest received	3,000	(31.5.96)	6,000	(31.7.97)
Dividends from UK company (net)	6,000	(31.1.96)		

Notes

i)   *Trading losses of £75,000 were brought forward at 30th June 1995.*

ii) *Capital losses of £5,000 were brought forward at 30th June 1995.*

iii) *Dates shown in brackets are the dates on which the transactions occurred.*

iv) *Interest received is from non-trade sources.*

Calculate the amount of any profits chargeable to corporation tax for all relevant accounting periods and to show the amounts of any losses carried forward at 30th September 1997 assuming relief for losses is claimed as early as possible.   ***(ACCA)***

Solution

Unassailable Undertaking Ltd Corporation tax computations

	£	30.6.96 (12 months) £	30.6.97 (12 months) £	30.9.97 (3 months) £
Schedule D Case I		450,000		
Less losses b/f 393(1)		75,000		
		375,000		
Bank interest		2,000	1,500	–
BSI (gross)		4,000	–	8,000
Less relief 393A(1)(a)(b)		381,000	1,500	8,000
CAP 30.6.97		138,500	1,500	–
CAP 30.9.97		–	–	8,000
Profits chargeable to CT		242,500		

i) Loss memorandum		£	£
loss for 15 months to 30.9.97		175,000	
available for relief Sec 393A(1)(b)	$^{12}/_{15} \times 175,000$ =		140,000
CAP to 30.6.97		1,500	
CAP to 30.6.96		138,500	140,000
loss relief CAP 30.9.97 393A(1)(a)			8,000
loss c/f 393(1) (35,000 – 8,000)			27,000
			175,000

ii) Capital losses		£	£
b/f 30.6.95		5,000	
b/f 30.6.96		20,000	25,000
set off 30.9.97			2,000
c/f			23,000

Corporation tax question No 6. Andrell Ltd

Andrell Ltd was incorporated on 1st April 1990 and has always prepared accounts to the 31st March each year. The company have now decided to change their accounting date to the 30th June and the accounts for the 15 months to the 30th June 1997 are as follows:

		£	£
Gross trading profits			177,310
Add:	Bank deposit interest received (note 1)	3,450	
	Rents receivable (note 2)	1,000	
	Profit on sale of plant (note 3)	6,000	10,450
			187,760
Deduct:	Wages and salaries	43,000	
	Light and heat	23,000	
	Legal and professional charges (note 4)	1,860	
	Depreciation	3,000	
	Bad debts (note 5)	4,600	
	Debenture interest (gross) (note 6)	11,250	
	Rent and rates	10,000	96,710
			91,050

Andrell Ltd is a non-close company with no associates and the following information is given in relation to the above accounts.

1. The bank short-term interest was received on the following dates:

		£
30th June 1996		1,200
31st December 1996		1,850
30th June 1997		400

2. On the 1st June 1997 the company negotiated to rent out part of its storage facilities, the annual rent of £1,000 being payable in advance on the 10th June. Due to an industrial dispute however, the first payment was not received by Andrell Ltd until the 10th July 1997.

3. An extract from the asset disposal account relating to the sale of plant showed:

	£
Cost (purchased 1st March 1996)	12,000
Less accumulated depreciation	2,500
	9,500
Sale proceeds (sold 12th February 1997)	15,500
Profit on sale	6,000

The chargeable gain has been agreed at £2,300

4. The legal and professional charges were made up of:

	£
Accountancy charge re annual audit	1,500
Accountancy charge for negotiating successful tax appeal	150
Legal charge for negotiating successful appeal against rates	210
	1,860

5. Bad debts comprise:

	£
Increase in specific reserve	1,800
Increase in general reserve	2,000
Bad debts written off	1,200
	5,000
Less Bad debts recovered	400
	4,600

6. The debenture interest paid related to an issue of debentures, the interest on which is payable half yearly on the 30th June and 31st December and includes an accrual of £2,500 as at the 30th June 1997.

The company had a pool balance brought forward for plant and machinery of £276,000 and the only capital additions during the period of account were:

	£
1st December 1996 purchased new plant	3,000
1st May 1997 purchased 16 saloon motor cars for use by the company salesmen, each car costing £12,000	192,000

Compute the mainstream corporation tax payable and show the due dates for payment. Assume that all allowances and reliefs are claimed as soon as possible. **(ACCA)**

Solution

Andrell Ltd AP 15 months to 30.6.1997

Adjustment of profits	£	£
Net profit per accounts		91,050
Add back: Legal and professional fees	150	
Depreciation	3,000	
Bad debts	2,000	
		5,150
		96,200
less non-case I income		
Bank deposit interest	3,450	
Rents receivable	1,000	
Profit on sale of plant	6,000	10,450
		85,750

Corporation tax computation AP

	12 months to 31.3.1997 £	3 months to 30.6.1997 £
Adjusted profits $\frac{12}{15}$ ¥ 85,750	68,600	
$\frac{3}{15}$ ¥ 85,750		17,150
less capital allowances	66,750	24,516
Schedule D Case I	1,850	(7,366)
Schedule D Case III	3,050	400
Schedule A	–	1,000
	4,900	1,400
Chargeable gain	2,300	
	7,200	1,400
less Section 393A(1)(a)(b) (Total 7,366)	(5,966)	(1,400)
	1,234	–
Corporation tax @ 24%	296	

Mainstream liability

Due dates for payment

Mainstream liability	–	
	1st January 1998	1st April 1998
	AP to 31.3.97 £	AP to 30.6.97 £

Capital allowances

Pool balance b/f	276,000		200,250
Proceeds of sale (restricted to cost)	12,000		–
	264,000		200,250
Additions (1.12.96)	3,000		
	267,000		
WD allowance 25%	66,750	25% × ¼	12,516
Balance c/f	200,250		187,734

Motor car pool

Cost	192,000
WD allowance 25% × $\frac{1}{4}$	12,000
	180,000

Summary of allowances

		AP to 31.3.97 £	AP to £30.6.97 £
Plant and machinery	W.d. allowance	66,750	12,516
Motor cars	W.d. allowance	–	12,000
		66,750	24,516

Notes

i) *The loss of £5,966 is carried back to the accounting period to 31.3.1997 under Section 393A(1)(b).*

ii) *As the motor vehicles do not cost more than £12,000 each they are pooled collectively.*

Corporation tax question NO 7. XYZ Ltd

XYZ Limited has a 100% subsidiary, PQR Limited, and each company prepares its accounts annually for the year ended 31st March.

The following are summarised results of each company for the year ended 31st March 1998:

	XYZ Limited £	PQR Limited £
Adjusted trading profit/(loss) before capital allowances	279,600	(110,000)
Deposit interest received	4,000	2,000
Chargeable gains/(losses)	7,900	(4,000)
Capital allowances	2,400	1,800

XYZ Limited has a capital loss brought forward of £2,700.

You may assume that neither company paid any dividend and that there are no balances of Advance Corporation Tax or Franked Investment Income to consider.

a) *Show how the losses of PQR Limited may be most effectively utilised, assuming that it is not expected to make a profit for several years.*

b) *Calculate the mainstream corporation tax payable by XYZ Limited;*

c) *State with reasons the advice that should have been given in respect of the capital transactions of PQR Limited.*

(ICMA)

Solution

a) **Corporation tax computation**

	£	XYZ Ltd £	PQR Ltd £
Schedule D adjusted profit	279,600		–
Less capital allowances	2,400	277,200	
Schedule D Case III		4,000	2,000
		281,200	2,000
Chargeable gain:			
Chargeable gain	7,900		
Less losses b/f	2,700	5,200	–
		286,400	2,000
Less Section 393A(1)(a)	–	–	2,000
		286,400	–
Less Group relief Section 402		109,800	
Profits chargeable to corporation tax		176,600	–

b) **Corporation tax payable:**

	£
£176,600 @ 33 % =	58,278

Marginal relief:

$$(750,000 - 176,600)\ \frac{176,600}{176,600} \times \frac{1}{40}$$

	£
$= 573,400 \times \dfrac{1}{40}$	14,335
Mainstream liability	43,943

Loss memorandum:

	£
Trading loss	110,000
Add capital allowances	1,800
	111,800
Less section 393A(1)(a)	2,000
Group relief	109,800

Notes

1) If PQR Ltd did not claim relief under Section 393A(1)(a) there would be £2,000 more available for group relief giving an overall group tax saving of £2,000 × (35.5% – 23%) ie £250. The 35.5% rate is the marginal rate where there is no FII.

2) Small company rate for two companies in $\dfrac{1,500,000}{2} = 750,000$ and $\dfrac{300,000}{2} = 150,000$

3) The capital loss incurred by PQR Ltd cannot be surrendered to XYZ Ltd by way of group relief. It can be carried forward and set against future gains incurred by PQR Ltd. In view of the group relationship it would have been more advantageous to channel all the transactions giving rise to a capital gain or loss through one company which remains within the group. Initially this would require a transfer of assets in accordance with Section 172 TCG Act 1992. If PQR Ltd had transferred the asset giving rise to the capital loss of £4,000 to XYZ Ltd then the position would have been:

	£
Net gain per computation	5,200
Less transferred from PQR Ltd	4,000
	1,200

Corporation tax question No 8. Hardcastle (Investments) Ltd

Hardcastle (Investments) Limited is an investment company and a wholly owned subsidiary of Dennis (Holdings) Limited. The group comprises the Holding Company, two UK trading companies and the investment company. The income of Hardcastle (Investments) Limited is derived from the management of investments, and the letting of residential and commercial property both within the Dennis Group and also to unconnected persons.

During year ended 31st December 1995, Hardcastle (Investments) Ltd had the following results:

	£
Franked investment income	67,405
Taxed interest (gross)	193,240
Untaxed interest	54,560
Rents from managed properties	445,240
Chargeable gains	85,714
Management expenses	156,390
Managed property expenses	40,315

You are given the following information.

1. There were excess management expenses at 31st December 1994 of £135,410.
2. The management property expenses include a general provision for repairs of £12,500. The remaining expenditure relates to rates, repairs and maintenance and surveyors fees for letting and rating purposes.
3. On 5th July 1995 Hardcastle (Investments) Limited acquired an industrial building for £145,000 (including £12,500 site cost). This property was immediately let to Andrews (Forging) Limited for five years. Under the terms of the lease Hardcastle (Investments) Limited was required to install a central heating system which it did at a cost of £14,750. The cost of the central heating was paid for by 31st December 1995.
4. All interest was received in the year and is shown gross.

Compute the corporation tax for the year ended 31st December 1995. **(INST. TAX)**

Solution

Hardcastle (Investments) Ltd
Corporation tax computation AP to 31st December 1995

	£	£
Schedule A property income	417,425	
Less capital allowances	8,987	408,438
Taxed interest		193,240
Schedule D Case III		54,560
Chargeable gains		85,714
		741,952
Less management expenses	156,390	
Management expenses b/f	135,410	291,800
Profits chargeable to corporation tax		450,152
$\frac{1}{4} \times 450,152 = 112,538$ @33%		37,137
$\frac{3}{4} \times 450,152 = \underline{337,614}$ @33%		111,413
$450,152$		148,550
Less income tax on taxed interest		
$\frac{1}{4} \times 193,240 = 48,310$ @25%	12,078	
$\frac{3}{4} \times 193,240 = \underline{144,930}$ @25%	36,232	48,310
$193,240$		
Mainstream liability		100,240

Notes

i)   Property income is computed as follows:

	£	£
Rents from managed properties		*445,240*
Less managed property expenses	*40,315*	
Less round sum provision	*12,500*	*27,815*
		417,425

ii) **Capital allowances**
     Industrial building

	£	£
Cost less site cost	132,500	
WD allowance 4% × 132,500 = 5,300	5,300	5,300
WD value c/f	127,200	

Plant and machinery

	£	£
Central heating cost	14,750	
WD allowance 25%	3,687	3,687
Total allowances	11,063	8,987

iii) *Corporation tax rates (four companies).*

$$FY \text{ to } 31.3.1995 \quad \frac{1,500,000}{4} \times \frac{1}{4} = 93,750$$

$$FY \text{ to } 31.3.1996 \quad \frac{1,500,000}{4} \times \frac{3}{4} = 281,250$$

As the profits without FII of £450,152 exceed the above limits there is no marginal relief and profits are taxable at the full rates.

There is a surplus of FII of £67,405.

Corporation tax question NO 9. Fell Ltd

Fell Ltd, a UK resident company, commenced trading in 1965 and makes up accounts to 31 December each year.

The accounts for the year ended 31 December 1996 show a net profit of £649,885. A detailed examination of the accounts reveals that the following items of income and expenditure have been included in arriving at that figure.

	£
Income	
Bank interest received December 1996	683
Building society interest received November 1996 (net)	420
Dividends from UK companies received November 1996 (including tax credits)	1,125
Expenditure	
Depreciation	22,000
Deed of covenant to charity (gross)	1,000
Staff Christmas Party (20 staff @ £32.50 each)	650
Provision for bad debts @ 5% of debtors	2,500
Debenture interest payable (gross)	3,250

Capital allowances are due in the sum of £10,500.

Fell Ltd has two UK resident trading subsidiaries, in which it has the following shareholdings:

Moor Ltd   100%
Hill Ltd   70%   (the balance of 30% being held by Jones Ltd, an unconnected UK company)

The results of the subsidiary companies for the year ended 31 December 1996 were as follows:

	Schedule D Case I (loss) £	Charges £	Schedule A £
Moor Ltd	(25,000)	(5,000)	–
Hill Ltd	(50,000)	–	3,000

All charges are trade charges.

Compute the tax payable by each company for the year ended 31 December 1996, assuming that all reliefs are claimed as soon as possible and show the losses to be carried forward, if any.

(INST TAX)

Solution

Fell Ltd Corporation tax computation AP 31.12.96

			£	£
Schedule D Case I	Adjusted profits		673,157	
	Capital allowances		10,500	662,657
Schedule D Case III				683
BSI $\dfrac{420}{.8}$				525
				663,865
Less charges paid:	Covenant			1,000
				662,865
Less	Group relief	Moor Ltd	30,000	
	Consortium relief	Hill Ltd	32,900	62,900
Profits chargeable to CT				599,965
Corporation tax payable	599,965 @ 33%			197,988

Notes

i) Net profit per accounts 649,885

Add back:	Depreciation	22,000	
	Deed of covenant	1,000	
	Bad debt provision	2,500	25,500
			675,385
Less:	Bank interest	683	
	BSI	420	
	Dividends	1,125	2,228	673,157

ii) **Group relief. Moor Ltd**

Schedule D Case I loss	25,000	
Charges on income	5,000	30,000

Both trade and none trade charges may be group relieved.

iii) **Consortium relief. Hill Ltd**

Schedule D Case I loss	50,000
Schedule A	3,000
Less Section 393A(1)(a)	3,000
	–
Loss available for consortium relief	47,000
70% × 47,000 =	32,900
Loss c/f	14,100

iv) *With three companies in the group the upper levels of profits are:*

FY to 31.3.1996	$\dfrac{1,500,000}{3} \times \dfrac{1}{4} =$	125,000
Profits chargeable to CT	$\dfrac{599,965}{4} =$	149,991
FY to 31.3.1997	$\dfrac{1,500,000}{3} \times \dfrac{3}{4} =$	375,000
Profits chargeable to CT	$\dfrac{599,965}{4} \times 3 =$	449,973

Therefore, the full rates of corporation tax apply.

Corporation tax question NO 10. Mettle Ltd

A student in the tax department of your firm has handed you the following computations for review. Unfortunately, the computations contain various errors.

Mettle Ltd Accounting period to 30 September 1997

	Deduct £	Add £
Profit per accounts		73,100
Depreciation		12,430
Profit on sale of fixed assets	300	
Entertaining – UK customers		375
– staff annual party		610
Luncheon vouchers supplied to staff (excess over 15p per day)		1,147
Charitable deed of covenant (6th annual payment – £921 gross)		700
Bank interest receivable (including £400 accrued at 30.9.97)	3,145	
Rents receivable (on new letting; £7,000 received less in advance £1,500)	5,500	
Capital allowances	11,400	
	20,345	88,362
		20,345
		68,017
Trading profit for year		
Losses brought forward – under 393(1) TA 1988	94,172	
– under 393(9) TA 1988 re deed of covenant	1,000	(95,172)
		(27,155)
Schedule D Case III – interest receivable	3,145	
Schedule A	5,500	8,645
		(18,510)
Add: Payments under deed of covenant		700
Losses carried forward		(19,210)

Capital allowances	Pool £	Total allowances £
WDV 1.10.96	18,000	
Additions – motor car (Nov 1996)	12,200	
– new photocopier (August 1997)	7,800	
	38,000	
Sale of motor car purchased in November 1993 (cost of £6,000 being the only motor car purchased in past seven years)	(2,000)	
	36,000	
	(9,000)	9,000
Writing-down allowance		
WDV 30.9.97	27,000	
Add: writing-down allowance on industrial building which is let		2,400
		11,400

Prepare a revised corporation tax computation, correcting the errors which you have detected. Give a brief explanation of the reasons for making the adjustments. Mettle Ltd has no associated companies.

(INST. TAX)

Solution

Mettle Ltd Corporation Tax Computation. AP 30.9.1997

	£	£	£	£
Schedule D Case I		68,312		
Less Section 393(1) losses b/f		68,312		–
Schedule D Case III				3,145
Schedule A				3,100
				6,245
Less charge on income paid				921
Profits chargeable to corporation tax				5,324
Corporation tax payable: 2,662 @ 24%			638.88	
2,662 @ 23%			612.26	1,251.14

Notes

i)   Schedule D Case I adjusted profits

	£	£	£
Profit per accounts		73,100	
Add back:			
Depreciation	12,430		
Entertaining	375		
Deed of covenant	700	13,505	
		86,605	
Less non-Case I income:			
Profit on sale of assets	300		
Bank interest	3145		
Rents	5,500	8,945	
		77,660	
Capital allowances (per note ii)		9,348	68,312

ii)   Capital allowances

	Plant & Machinery Pool £	Motor Car Pool £	Motor Car > 12,000 £	Total Allowances £
WDV b/f	18,000			
Less Motor car pool	2,531	2,531	–	
	15,469			
Additions				
Photocopier	7,800			
Motor car		–	12,200	
	23,269	2,531	12,200	
Proceeds of sale	–	2,000		
	23,269	531	12,200	
WD allowance 25%	5,817	BA 531	3,000	9,348
WD value c/forward	17,452	–	9,200	9,348

iii)   Written down value of motor car as at 30 September 1996

	£
Cost November 1993	6,000
WD allowance 30.9.94	1,500
	4,500
WD allowance 30.9.95	1,125
	3,375
WD allowance 30.9.96	844
WD value 30.9.96	2,531

iv)   Schedule A

	£
Rent profit accrued	5,500
Less industrial buildings allowance	2,400
	3,100

v)   Section 393(1) loss relief

	£
Trade losses b/f	94,172
Less utilised AP to 30.9.1997	68,710
Carried forward	25,462

vi)   *The charitable deed of covenant loss brought forward under Section 393(9) is not a trade charge and therefore not available for loss relief.*

vii)   *The motor car pool does gives rise to a balancing allowance, as a separate trade. The disposal of the last item in the pool is assumed to be a cessation of a trade.*

Part III

Taxation of
Chargeable Gains

35 General principles

Introduction

1. A comprehensive form of capital gains tax was introduced by the Capital Gains Tax Act 1965, and applied to all 'chargeable gains' arising after the 5th April 1965. The law was consolidated in the Capital Gains Tax Act 1979 which has now been replaced by the Taxation of Chargeable Gains Act 1992 (TCGA 1992). This Act consolidated the law as at the 5th April 1992.

Rebasing

2. The base date was changed from the 6th April 1965 to the 31st March 1982 and for disposals after the 5th April 1988 only gains or losses accruing from 31st March 1982 need be brought into charge to tax.

   For assets held on 31st March 1982 re-basing means that the asset is assumed to be sold and immediately re-acquired on 31st March 1982 at that date.

   In general, if the gain under the re-basing method is greater than it would be under the 'old rules' then the latter may be used. The taxpayer can make a once and for all election that all gains and losses acquired before 31st March 1982 are to be computed by reference to the 31st March 1982 re-basing method.

Persons chargeable

3. The following classes of persons are chargeable to capital gains tax:

   > Individuals and personal representatives
   > Companies, who pay corporation tax at the company rate
   > Trusts and trustees.

   To be chargeable a person must be resident or ordinarily resident, in the UK, or carrying on a business there. In general the terms residence, ordinary residence and domicile have the same meaning as for income tax as noted in Chapter 5.

   A UK domiciled person, not resident and not ordinarily resident, is not liable to CGT on assets situated in the UK or abroad.

   A non-UK domiciled person, resident or ordinarily resident or both, is liable to CGT on all UK assets but only in respect of remittances for assets situated abroad.

   Husbands and wives are assessed and charged to capital gains tax independently from 5th April 1990.

   A partnership is not a taxable person for capital gains tax. Any chargeable gain of the partnership must be apportioned to each partner in the normal profit-sharing ratios.

Rates of tax 1997/98

4. Person	Exemption	Rate of tax
Individuals	£6,500	Chargeable gains after exemption treated as top slice of income and taxed at income tax rates (23%–40%). Husband and wife are taxed separately.
Companies	Nil	Chargeable gains taxed at company rate ie small company rate, marginal rate or full rate.
Personal representatives	£6,500	Exemption applies to year of death and next two years. Chargeable gains taxed at basic rate of income tax (23%).
Trusts (Mentally disabled)	£6,500	Accumulation and discretionary trusts – taxed at 34%.
Trusts (General)	£3,250	Other trusts – taxed at 23%.

Chargeable assets

5. In accordance with Sections 21 and 22 of the TCGA 1992 all forms of property are assets for the purposes of capital gains tax, whether situated in the UK or not, including:

   a) options, debts, and incorporeal property in general

   b) currency other than sterling

   c) any form of property created by the person disposing of it, or coming to be owned without being acquired

   d) capital sums derived from assets.

Property

6. This includes anything capable of being owned such as freehold and leasehold land, shares and securities, and other tangible assets and intangible assets such as goodwill.

Options section

7. An option is a right of choice and where a person grants an option to another person then this is a disposal of a chargeable asset. If an option is exercised, any consideration received is added to any made with the initial grant, to form a single transaction.

   Where an option is abandoned then this is not a disposal by the grantee so that he or she cannot establish a capital loss, except where the option is to subscribe for shares in a company or to acquire a business asset. The abandonment of a traded option in gilt edged securities, bonds, or loan stocks can also produce an allowable CGT loss.

Debts section

8. An ordinary debt is not a chargeable asset in the hands of the original creditor, his or her personal representative or legatee. However, a person acquiring a debt say by an assignment, obtains a chargeable asset.

   A debt on security is a chargeable asset and this includes any holding of loan stock of a government, local authority or company.

   A loan to a trader, or payment by way of guarantee, where it is not a debt on a security, if irrecoverable, can be used to establish a capital loss.

Incorporeal property

9. This is other intangible property such as a tithe or easement, or a right to exploit a copyright.

Currency section

10. Any currency other than sterling is a chargeable asset, but foreign currency acquired by an individual for personal use is exempted.

Created property

11. This would include such assets as goodwill, copyright, patents and trade marks or know how. Goodwill, trade marks and copyright are chargeable assets.

    Patents are not chargeable assets since any excess over cost is taxed as Schedule D Case VI income.

    Know how is treated as a chargeable asset where its disposal includes any part of a trade, with some exceptions. *See Chapter 16.*

Capital sums

12. These are defined to include:

    a) Any capital sums received by way of compensation for any kind of damage or injury, to assets or for the loss, destruction or dissipation of assets or for any depreciation of an asset

    b) Capital sums received under a policy of insurance of the risks of any kind of damage or injury to, or the loss or depreciation of assets.

    c) Capital sums received in return for forfeiture or surrender of rights, or for refraining from exercising rights.

d) Capital sums received as consideration for use or exploitation of assets.

A disposal of a chargeable asset occurs when a person derives any capital sum from assets. If any part of the amount received is used to restore or replace the original asset then special reliefs apply. *See Chapter 39.*

Non-chargeable assets and exemptions

13. The following assets are either exempt assets or chargeable assets, on whose disposal there may not be a chargeable gain or loss.

a) Private motor vehicles.

This includes private cars and vintage cars purchased for investment.

b) Savings certificates.

All non-marketable securities are included under this heading such as National Savings Certificates, and Defence Bonds.

c) Gambling winnings.

This covers winnings from pools, lotteries, premium bonds and bingo prizes.

d) Decorations for valour.

These are exempt assets if disposed of by the individual to whom they were awarded, or their legatee. If purchased they become chargeable assets.

e) Currency.

Foreign currency acquired for personal use is exempt.

f) Compensation.

Any compensation or damages obtained for any wrong or injury suffered by a person, or in connection with his or her profession or vocation.

g) Life assurance and deferred annuities.

No chargeable gain arises on the disposal of any rights under a life assurance policy or deferred annuity, providing the disposal is made by the original owner. The acquisition of such rights from an original owner is a chargeable asset.

h) British government securities and qualifying corporate bonds.

i) Private residence. *See Chapter 37.*

j) Chattels. *See Chapter 37.*

k) Gifts to a recognised charity.

l) Certain disposals conditionally exempt from IHT eg works of art.

m) Tangible moveable property with a useful life of less than 50 years, not used for trade purposes.

Exempt persons

14. The undermentioned persons are exempted from capital gains tax:

a) Pension funds approved by the Inland Revenue.

b) Registered charities providing the gains are used for charitable purposes.

c) Registered friendly societies.

d) Local authorities.

e) Scientific research associations.

Administration

15. The self assessment rules apply first to capital gains for the year 1996/97. Particulars of chargeable assets acquired do not have to be entered on the personal income tax return. Details of any gains where these exceed £6,500 or proceeds where they exceed £13,000 in any year are required.

In general appeals can be made to either the General or Special Commissioners except:

a) appeals in respect of the valuation of any land, which will be heard by a Lands Tribunal.

b) appeals in respect of the valuation of unquoted shares which will be heard by the Special Commissioners.

c) Where an election to appeal to the Special Commissioners is disregarded by the General Commissioners.

Payment of tax

16. Capital gains tax is due when the final balancing payment is made under the income tax rules for self assessment, as described in Chapter 2. The due date is as follows:

1995/96	–	31st December 1996
1996/97	–	31st January 1998
1997/98	–	31st January 1999

It is possible to pay capital gains tax by instalments where the consideration is payable over a period exceeding 18 months, and payment of capital gains tax in one sum would cause undue hardship. Payment of tax by ten equal instalments is also available in respect of tax due on gifts not eligible for holdover relief (*see Chapter 41*).

Outline computation

17. In general a chargeable gain or loss is computed as follows:

	£	1997/98 £
Gross consideration or market value		
Allowable deductions:		
† Initial cost of asset plus incidental expenses	–	
Enhancement expenses (not repairs)	–	
Incidental costs of disposal	–	–
Unindexed gain		–
Indexation allowance (based on cost + enhancement)		–
Chargeable gain		–
Less Annual exemption (£6,500 for 1997/98)		–
Taxable gain		–

† Assets acquired before 31st March 1982 can be revalued at 31st March 1982 and that value substituted for the initial cost plus incidental expenses, under the re-basing principle.

The indexation allowance is calculated by reference to changes in the Retail Prices Index which was re-based to 100 in January 1987.

Where an asset was held on the 31st March 1982 then indexation allowance is automatically based on the higher of the original cost or market value at 31st March 1982.

For disposals on or after the 30th November 1993 indexation cannot be used to create or increase a capital loss, with transitional relief of £10,000 for disposals between 30th November 1993 and 5th April 1995.

Retail price index

18.	**1982**	**1983**	**1984**	**1985**	**1986**	**1987**	**1988**	**1989**	**1990**	**1991**	**1992**	**1993**	**1994**	**1995**	**1996**	**1997**
Jan	–	82.61	86.84	91.20	96.25	100.0	103.3	111.0	119.5	130.2	135.6	137.9	141.3	146.0	150.2	154.4
Feb	–	82.97	87.20	91.94	96.60	100.4	103.7	111.8	120.2	130.9	136.3	138.8	142.1	146.9	150.9	155.0
Mar	79.44	83.12	87.48	92.80	96.73	100.6	104.1	112.3	121.4	131.4	136.7	139.3	142.5	147.5	151.5	
Apr	81.04	84.28	88.64	94.78	97.67	101.8	105.8	114.3	125.1	133.1	138.8	140.6	144.2	149.0	152.6	
May	81.62	84.64	88.97	95.21	97.85	101.9	106.2	115.0	126.2	133.5	139.3	141.1	144.7	149.6	152.9	
June	81.85	84.84	89.20	95.41	97.79	101.9	106.6	115.4	126.7	134.1	139.3	141.0	144.7	149.8	153.0	
July	81.88	85.30	89.10	95.23	97.52	101.8	106.7	115.5	126.8	133.8	138.8	140.7	144.0	149.1	152.4	
Aug	81.90	85.68	89.94	95.49	97.82	102.1	107.9	115.8	128.1	134.1	138.9	141.3	144.7	149.9	153.1	
Sep	81.85	86.06	90.11	95.44	98.30	102.4	108.4	116.6	129.3	134.6	139.4	141.9	145.0	150.6	153.8	
Oct	82.26	86.36	90.67	95.59	98.45	102.9	109.5	117.5	130.3	135.1	139.9	141.8	145.2	149.8	153.8	
Nov	82.66	86.67	90.95	95.92	99.29	103.4	110.0	118.5	130.0	135.6	139.7	141.6	145.3	149.8	153.9	
Dec	82.51	86.89	90.87	96.05	99.62	103.3	110.3	118.8	129.9	135.7	139.2	141.9	146.0	150.7	154.4	

36 The basic rules of computation

Introduction

1. This chapter is concerned with the basic rules of computation used in the taxation of chargeable gains. It begins with an examination of the meaning of consideration and market price, and the allowable deductions. The principles of the indexation allowance are then covered followed by the treatment of assets held on 31st March 1982, and part disposals.

Consideration and market price

2. As a general principle a chargeable gain is computed by deducting from the total consideration obtained the initial cost of acquisition, any allowable expenditure, and what is known as the 'indexation allowance'. Consideration is taken to be the gross sales price without any deduction for expenses of sale. However, in the undermentioned cases the disposal is deemed to be at market price:

   a) where the disposal is by way of a gift

   b) where the transaction is not at arms length, eg between connected persons such as husband and wife or group companies

   c) where an asset cannot be readily valued, or is acquired in connection with a loss of employment

   d) on a transfer into a settlement by a settlor.

3. Where the market value for a disposal is used, then the person who acquires the asset is also treated as acquiring at the market value.

   Market value means the price which assets might reasonably be expected to fetch in a sale on the open market. There are a number of special rules which relate to particular assets, and these are noted below.

Deferred consideration

4. The general rules of computation are not affected where the consideration is payable by instalments as the whole of the consideration is brought into account with no discount for the future receipt of monies. Where all or part of the consideration is deferred because it cannot be quantified at the date of the original disposal, the value of the right to receive that additional amount is included with any ascertainable consideration at the date of the original disposal. The value of this right (known as a 'chose in action') is deducted from the deferred consideration when that is received at a later date. See *Marren v Ingles* 1980 STC 500. *Marson v Marriage* 1980 STC 177.

Allowable deductions Section 38–39

5. The following may be deducted from the consideration:

   a) The cost of acquisition, including incidental expenditure. (*See below for assets held on 31.3.1982.*)

   b) Any enhancement expenditure, but not repairs or maintenance.

   c) Expenditure incurred in establishing or protecting the right to any asset.

   d) Incidental costs of disposal (*see below*).

   e) The indexation allowance (*see below*).

6. Incidental costs include: fees, commission, or professional charges such as legal accountancy or valuation advice: costs of transfer and conveyance including stamp duty: advertising to find a buyer or seller. The following items of expenditure are specifically disallowed:

   a) Costs of repair and maintenance.

   b) Costs of insurance against any damage injury or loss of an asset.

   c) Any expenditure allowed as a deduction in computing trading income.

   d) Any expenditure which is recouped from the Crown or public or local authority.

Indexation allowance

7. In addition to the allowed deductions noted above, an indexation allowance applies to disposals made on or after the 6th April 1982, or 1st April 1982 for companies. The main general provisions relating to disposals are as follows.

    a) The indexation allowance is calculated by reference to the change in the Retail Price Index between the date of the disposal and:

        i) the date of acquisition, or

        ii) the 31st March 1982 if that is later than the date of acquisition.

    b) The indexation applies to the initial cost of acquisition and any enhancement expenditure but not to the incidental costs of disposal.

    c) Where an asset was held on the 31st March 1982 indexation will automatically be based on the market value at that date or the actual allowable expenditure whichever is the greater.

    d) On a part disposal the indexation allowance is calculated by reference to the apportioned cost, before determining the actual gain. The allowable cost carried forward is not indexed at that stage.

    e) For disposals made on or after 30th November 1993 indexation cannot be used to create or increase a capital loss, subject to transitional relief of £10,000 for disposals between 30th November 1993 and 5th April 1995.

Calculation of indexation allowance

8. The calculation of the indexation allowance commonly called the 'indexation factor' is made according to the following formula rounded to three decimal places:

$$\frac{\text{RPI in month of disposal} - \text{RPI in month of acquisition (or if later 31st March 1982)}}{\text{RPI in month of acquisition (or if later 31st March 1982)}}$$

> **Example**

N purchased an additional property, not being his main residence, for £10,000 in January 1983. Legal charges and other allowable costs of acquisition amount to £500. In January 1984 an extension to the property was built for £3,000, and major repairs undertaken amounting to £1,000. The whole property was sold for £50,000 in September 1997 with incidental costs of disposal of £1,500. RPI January 1983 82.61, January 1984 86.84, September 1997 say 155.0.

Compute the chargeable gain for 1997/98.

Solution

Calculation of indexation allowance

	£	£	£
Cost of acquisition January 1983	10,000		
Acquisition expenses January 1983	500	10,500	
Enhancement expenditure January 1984		3,000	13,500
Indexation allowance:			
Cost 1983	10,500		
$\dfrac{155.0 - 82.61}{82.61}$			
$= 0.876 \times 10,500 =$		9,198	
Cost 1984	3,000		
$\dfrac{155.0 - 86.84}{86.84}$			
$= 0.785 \times 3,000 =$		2,355	11,553

CGT computation 1997/98

	£	£
Proceeds of sale		50,000
Less: Cost of acquisition	10,000	
Expenses of acquisition	500	
Enhancement expenditure	3,000	
Expenses of disposal	1,500	15,000
Unindexed gain		35,000
Indexation allowance as above		11,553
Chargeable gain		23,447

Example

A purchased a painting for £75,000 in March 1982 which he sold for £170,000 on 25th March 1998. Retail prices index March 1982 was 79.44: March 1998 say 155.0.

Compute the chargeable gain for 1997/98.

Solution

Calculation of indexation allowance

	£	£
Market value at 31.3.1982 $\times \dfrac{155.0 - 79.44}{79.44}$ ie $75,000 \times 0.951$	71,325	

CGT computation 1997/98

	£
Proceeds of sale	170,000
Cost 31.3.1982	75,000
Unindexed gain	95,000
Less indexation allowance as above	71,325
Chargeable gain	23,675

Calculation of market value

9. Quoted shares or securities

Market value is determined by reference to prices quoted in the Stock Exchange Daily Official List, in one of two ways:

a) One quarter of the difference between the lowest and the highest average quotations for the day is added to the lowest average.

b) The half way point between the highest and the lowest prices at which bargains were recorded, other than those made at a special price. If there are no bargains on the day, then method a) will be used.

Example

The following data was extracted from the Official List in relation to four shares:

Share	Quotations	Bargains made
A	28p – 36p	29p 30p 31p
B	109p – 120p	–
C	53p – 59p	54p 56p 57p (special price)
D	247p – 265p	249p 253p 255p

Market values	Lowest price plus $\frac{1}{4}$	Mean of bargains	Lowest value
A	28 + 2 = 30	30	30
B	109 + $2^{3}/4$ = $111^{3}/4$	–	$111^{3}/4$
C	53 + $1^{1}/2$ = $54^{1}/2$	55	$54^{1}/2$
D	247 + $4^{1}/2$ = $251^{1}/2$	252	$251^{1}/2$

Unit trusts

Market value means the lowest price (or buying price) as published on the relevant day, or nearest day if not published on that day. Where regular monthly savings in unit trusts (and investment trusts) are made then for indexation purposes they may be treated as a single annual investment in the seventh month of the trust's year.

Unquoted shares

There are no precise rules for the valuation of unquoted shares, which must be determined on the basis of professional advice, and agreed with the share valuation division of the Capital Taxes Office.

New issues - calls

10. Where a new issue of shares or securities takes place, as in privatisation issues, then the date for indexation of any instalment payments depends on the nature of the issue.

a) If the shares are issued as fully paid with the price payable in instalments then indexation is taken from the date of the initial payment and not the dates of the stage payments.

b) Where the shares are issued as partly paid with calls due on specified dates then indexation is determined as follows:

calls paid within 12 months of issue - date of original issue

calls paid after 12 months - treated as separate item of expenditure for indexation purposes.

Assets held on 31st March 1982

11. For assets held on 31st March 1982, the following rules apply.

a) The asset is assumed to be sold on 31st March 1982 and immediately re-acquired at its market value at that date. This is the general re-basing rule and applies to all taxpayers.

b) The general basing rule is *not applied* to a disposal in the undermentioned cases:

i) Where a gain would accrue on the disposal if the general re-basing rule applied, and either a smaller gain/loss would accrue if the old pre-FA 1988 rules applied.

ii) Where a loss would accrue if the general re-basing rule applied, and either a smaller loss or gain would accrue if the old pre-FA 1988 rules applied.

iii) Where quoted securities were held on 6th April 1965 and neither a gain nor a loss would accrue if the general re-basing rule did not apply.

c) Where the effect of the general re-basing rule is to substitute a gain for a loss, or a loss for a gain, then on a disposal there is a no gain/no loss situation.

d) Taxpayers can make a once and for all election that all gains and losses acquired before 31st March 1982 are to be computed by reference to the March 1982 value, and the old rules would not then be considered.

e) Taxpayers could make an election, whether or not they make a disposal, at any time up to and including 5th April 1990. In addition if an election is not already in force it will be possible to make one within two years of the end of the accounting period or year of assessment in which the first disposal on or after 6th April 1988 of an asset held at 31st March 1982 takes place. It appears that the disposal of the principal private residence activates this two year period.

f) Where an election is made and a loss arises under the re-basing rules this is not overruled where there is a gain under the old pre-FA 1988 rules.

In the case of groups of companies the election will have to be made by the principal company in the group on behalf of all other members.

g) The pre-1988 FA rules have now been incorporated into Section 35 TCGA 1992.

h) For disposals made after 30th November 1993 the indexation allowance restriction for losses applies to 'no gain/no loss' situations.

Summary of rules

General re-basing at 31.3.82	Old rules (Pre-FA 1988)	Chargeable gain/loss
Gain	Smaller gain than general re-basing	Smaller gain (old rules)
Gain	Larger gain than general re-basing	Smaller gain (re-basing)
Gain/Loss	Loss/gain	No loss/no gain
Loss	Smaller loss than general re-basing	Smaller loss (old rules)
Loss	Larger loss than general re-basing	Smaller loss (re-basing)

Example

X purchased a painting in 1979 for £10,000 which he sells for £85,000 in August 1997 after incurring expenses of disposal amounting to £5,000. The market value at 31st March 1982 was £36,000. Assume indexation of 95% and no general election for re-basing.

Calculate the chargeable gain for 1997/98.

Solution

Chargeable gains tax computation 1996/97

	£	Re-basing 31.3.82 £	£	Pre-FA 88 Rules £
Proceeds of sale		90,000		90,000
Less cost of acquisition		–	10,000	
MV at 31.3.82	36,000		–	
Cost of disposal	5,000	41,000	5,000	15,000
Unindexed gain		49,000		75,000
Indexation allowance				
95% × 36,000		34,200		34,200
Chargeable Gain		14,800		40,800

Note

The smaller gain of £14,800 obtained from re-basing will be taken as the chargeable gain. Where the March 1982 value is greater than the original cost the FA 88 computation will not normally be required.

Example

B bought 1,000 shares in Minor Ltd, a private company, in 1975 for £12,000 which he sold in August 1997 for £50,000. The market value at 31st March 1982 has been agreed at £10,000.

Assume indexation of 95% and no general election for re-basing.

B. Chargeable gains tax computation 1997/98

	Re-basing 31.3.82	Pre-FA 88 Rules
B. Proceeds of sale	50,000	50,000
Less cost of acquisition		12,000
MV at 31.3.82	10,000	
Unindexed gain	40,000	38,000
95% × 12,000	11,400	11,400
Chargeable gain	28,600	26,600

Note
The smaller gain of £26,600 obtained by using the old rules will be taken as the chargeable gain.

Disposal on or after 30.11.93 – Indexation

12. For disposals made on or after 30th November 1993 the following rules apply.

   a) Subject to the transitional relief noted below the indexation allowance cannot be used to turn a gain into a loss or to increase a loss. It now applies to reduce or extinguish capital gains.

   b) For disposals in between 30th November 1993 and 5th April 1995 transitional relief of £10,000 is available.

   c) Indexation losses on disposals in 1993/94 must first be used to reduce the net chargeable gains for that year to the level of the taxpayer's annual exemption of £5,800.

   d) Any unused indexation loss for 1993/94 can be carried forward to 1994/95 and used with indexation losses for that year to reduce the net chargeable gains for that year to £5,800.

   e) Any unused indexation loss existing at 5th April 1995 will be unusable.

   f) The indexation loss is the indexation allowance on disposals made in between 30th November 1993 and 5th April 1995 which is reduced as a result of the general restriction on indexation.

   g) The transactional relief is available to individuals and trustees but not companies.

Example

P had the following data relating to 1993/94 and 1994/95.

	1993/94	1994/95
Chargeable gains (after 30.11.93)	13,000	10,000
Indexation losses	12,000	6,000

Compute the taxable gain for each year.

Solution	1993/94	1994/95
Chargeable gain	13,000	10,000
Indexation loss	7,200	2,800
	5,800	7,200
Annual exemption	5,800	5,800
Taxable gain	Nil	1,400

Notes

i)   The transitional loss relief of £10,000 is used as follows:

1993/94	7,200
1994/95	2,800
	10,000

ii)   The excess indexation allowance for 1994/95 of £6,000 is not usable.

Example

B owns freehold property which has a market value of £20,000 on 3rd March 1982. The property was sold on 1st May 1997 for:

   a) £30,000   b) £19,000

Assume indexation of 95%. Compute the chargeable gain/loss for 1997/98.

Solution

B. Chargeable gains tax computation 1997/98

a)	Proceeds of sale	30,000
	March 1982 value	20,000
	Unindexed gain	10,000
	I.A. 95% × 20,000 = 19,000	
	Restricted to unindexed gain	10,000
	Net gain	Nil
b)	Proceeds of sale	19,000
	March 1982 value	20,000
	Unindexed loss	(1,000)
	I.A. restricted to nil	–
	Net loss	(1,000)

Disposals still treated as no gain/no loss

13.   The following transactions are still to be treated as no gain/no loss disposals:
   i)   Acquisitions of quoted securities before 6th April 1965 where the substitution of the market value at 6th April 1965 converts a gain into a loss or vice versa.
   ii)   Disposals between spouses.
   iii)   Transfers within a group of companies.
   iv)   Deemed disposals on the death of a life tenant.
   v)   Company reconstruction and amalgamations.
   vi)   Gifts etc involving heritage property.

Previous no gain/no loss disposals

14. Where a person disposes of a chargeable asset after 5th April 1988 which he or she did not own at 31st March 1982, nevertheless, the general re-basing provisions apply provided the following conditions are met.

   i) The disposal itself is not a no gain/no loss disposal (eg transfer between spouses).

   ii) The acquisition by the taxpayer and any prior transfers after the 31st March 1982 were all on a no gain/no loss basis.

> **Example**

T purchased a piece of porcelain in 1980 for £2,000 which he gave to his wife in July 1984 when it was worth £3,500. T's wife sells the porcelain for £12,000 on the 10th August 1997. The market value at 31.3.1982 has been agreed at £4,800. Assume indexation of 95%.

Solution

CGT computation 1997/98

	£	Mrs T £
Proceeds of sale		12,000
MV at 31.3.82	4,800	
IA 95% × 4,800	4,560	
		9,360
Chargeable gain		2,640

Note The value on the date of the interspouse transfer at July 1984 is ignored.

Part disposals Section 42

15. Where the part disposal of an asset takes place then the attributable cost of acquisition is determined by the following general formula:

$$\text{Attributable Cost} = \text{Cost of Acquisition} \times \frac{A}{A + B}$$

A is the consideration for the disposal, excluding any expenses of sale.
B is the market value of the undisposed portion.

For assets held on the 31st March 1982, the general formula is:

$$\text{Attributable Cost} = \text{Market Value at 31.3.1982} \times \frac{A}{A + B}$$

No apportionment is required where expenditure is wholly attributable to the part disposal, or to the part retained.

> **Example**

F purchased a chargeable asset in June 1970 for £5,000. On 7th November 1997 he sold a part for £8,000 and at that time the remainder had a value of £12,000. Compute the chargeable gain. Assume indexation of 95%. MV at 31.3.82 of whole asset was £14,000.

Computation 1997/98 Re-basing 31.3.1982.

	£	£
Proceeds of sale		8,000
Market value 31.3.82: $14,000 \times \frac{8,000}{8,000 + 12,000}$		5,600
Unindexed gain		2,400
Indexation allowance: 95% × 5,600 = 5,320 Restricted to		2,400
Chargeable gain		Nil

Note

In this case the indexation allowance is restricted as the disposal was after 30th November 1993.

Computation 1997/98 Pre-FA 88 Rules

	£	£
Proceeds of sale		8,000
Attributable cost: $5,000 \times \dfrac{8,000}{8,000 + 12,000}$		2,000
Unindexed gain		6,000
Indexation allowance: $95\% \times 5,600$		5,320
Chargeable gain		680

Notes

i) *If a general election for re-basing is made the zero gain for 1997/98 remains.*

ii) *With no general election for re-basing as the gain is smaller under re-basing (zero) for 1997/98 there will be no chargeable gain.*

Assets held on the 6th April 1965

16. As capital gains tax initially only applied to disposals made after 5th April 1965 special rules of computation were introduced to deal with chargeable assets acquired before that date.

   In effect there are two alternative methods of computation which can be applied to all assets other than:

   i) land with development value

   ii) quoted securities.

   Methods of computation

   a) The time apportionment method.

   b) The market value at 6th April 1965 method.

   a) *Time apportionment method*
   Under this method the total gain, calculated in the normal way after the indexation allowance, is apportioned as follows:

$$\text{Total Gain} \times \frac{\text{Period from 6th April 1965 to date of disposal}}{\text{Total period of ownership}}$$

   The earliest date of acquisition is deemed to be 6th April 1945 where the acquisition took place prior to that date.

   If there is enhancement expenditure in addition to the original cost the computational procedure is as follows:

   First   – Compute the total gain in the normal way after indexation.

   Second – Apportion the gain by reference to the separate amounts of expenditure, excluding the indexation allowance.

   Third   – For each apportioned gain, (as determined at the second stage) apply the time apportionment method.

   b) *Value at 6th April 1965*

   Under this method the value of the asset at 6th April 1965 plus the indexation allowance, which may be based on the March 1982 value, is deducted from the disposal value to compute the chargeable gain.

   The 6th April 1965 basis must be used where there is land with development value.

   With regard to losses, then the following principles apply:

   i) If there is a loss by reference to 6th April 1965 basis, and a gain with the time apportionment method, then the result is treated as a no gain/no loss transaction.

   ii) If both the methods produce a loss then the loss is limited to the actual loss suffered ie before time apportionment.

   It should be noted that in general negotiations with the Inland Revenue about a valuation at 6th April 1965 cannot take place before an election is made.

17. These rules still apply to disposals after 5th April 1988 unless an election has been made to treat all such disposals at their March 1982 values. The re-basing rules only apply if it reduces a gain or a loss. Thus the taxpayer in possession of assets held at the 5th April 1965 has the following computations to make:

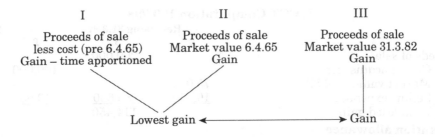

I	II	III
Proceeds of sale less cost (pre 6.4.65) Gain – time apportioned	Proceeds of sale Market value 6.4.65 Gain	Proceeds of sale Market value 31.3.82 Gain

Lowest gain ← → Gain

Notes

i) *The lowest overall gain can be taken.*

ii) *The normal indexation rules apply to the three situations, subject to (iv) below.*

iii) *Following the decision of Smith v Schofield HL1993 the indexation allowance is to be applied before the time apportionment rules are applied.*

iv) *For disposals on or after 30th November 1993 indexation cannot increase or create a loss, subject to the transitional relief for indexation losses.*

Example

Y purchased a painting in March 1945 for £10,000 which he sold for £200,000 on the 6th October 1997. Assume indexation of 95%. The painting had an estimated value of £64,000 at the 31st March 1982 and £30,000 at the 6th April 1965. *Compute the chargeable gain.*

Solution

CGT computation 1997/98 (Pre-FA 1988 rules)

i)	Proceeds of sale		200,000
	Cost of acquisition	10,000	
	Indexation allowance – 95% × 64,000	60,800	70,800
	Total gain		129,200
	Time apportionment:		
	$\dfrac{6.4.65 - 6.10.97}{6.4.45 - 6.10.97} = \dfrac{32.5}{52.5} \times 129,200$		79,981
ii)	Proceeds of sale		200,000
	MV at 6.4.65	30,000	
	Indexation allowance (as above)	60,800	90,800
	Total gain		109,200

Note *Under the old rules the time apportionment method would be taken.*

CGT computation 1997/978 (Re-basing)

Proceeds of sale		200,000
MV @ 31.3.82	64,000	
Indexation allowance @ 95%	60,800	124,800
Total gain		75,200

Summary of computations:

Time apportionment	79,981
MV at 6.4.65	109,200
Re-basing	75,200

In this example the re-basing method produces a lower gain and the chargeable gain therefore becomes £75,200.

• Student self-testing question

Z purchased a painting for £100,000 in August 1974 which he sold for £200,000 on the 3rd March 1998. Selling expenses amounted to £10,550. The painting was valued for insurance purposes at £75,000 on the 31st March 1982.

Compute the chargeable gain. Assume that the RPI March 1998 is 155.0.

Z. CGT Computation 1997/98

	Re-basing 31.3.82			Pre-FA 1988 Rules
	£	£	£	£
Proceeds of sale		200,000		200,000
Less Cost of acquisition	–		100,000	
Market value 31.3.82	75,000		–	
Selling expenses	10,550	85,550	10,550	11,0550
Unindexed gain		114,450		89,450
Indexation allowance				
Based on higher cost				
$\dfrac{155.0 - 79\ 44}{79.44} \times 100,000 = 0.951 \times 100,000$		95,100		89,450
Chargeable gain		19,350		Nil

Notes

i. *In this example the pre-FA 1988 rules give a zero chargeable gain which becomes the gain for 1997/98.*

ii. *The indexation allowance of £95,100 is restricted to £89,450 in this example under the Pre-FA 1988 rules.*

• Question without answer

A purchased a piece of land in June 1978 for £15,000, incurring legal costs of acquisition of £200. On 6th May 1997 he sold part of the land for £35,000, the remainder having a value at that time of £40,000. Selling expenses amounted £1,100. Assume indexation of 95%. The land had a market value of £30,000 at 31st March 1982.

Compute the chargeable gain for 1997/98 before annual exemption.

37 Land and chattels

Introduction

1. This chapter deals with the CGT rules applicable to land and chattels under the following headings:

   Freehold/leasehold land and buildings   Granting a lease from a freehold interest
   Part disposals of land   Private residence
   Small part disposals of land   Chattels
   Disposals of short leases

Freehold/long leasehold land and buildings

2. There are no special rules for the computation of capital gains arising on the disposal assets under this heading.

   A long lease is a lease with more than 50 years to run.

   Land includes houses, hereditaments and buildings.

   Where the property is also the main residence of the owner then exemption is normally available. *See below.*

Part disposals of land

3. Where there is a part disposal of freehold or long leasehold land then unless the disposal is 'small', *(see below)* the normal part disposal formula applies.

$$\text{Attributable cost} = \text{Cost of acquisition} \times \frac{A}{A+B}$$

$$\text{Attributable cost} = \text{Market value at 31.3.1982} \times \frac{A}{A+B} \quad \text{(Assets held on 31.3.82)}$$

Example

G purchased a plot of land of 10 acres for £10,000 in May 1976, and an adjacent further 2 acres for £5,000 in June 1980. In December 1997 a sale of 5 acres was made for £60,000, from the original 10 acres, the remaining 5 acres being worth £75,000 at that time. Take indexation at 95%. *Compute the chargeable gain.* The market value of the 10 acres of land at 31st March 1982 was £22,000.

Solution

CGT computation 1997/98

	£
Proceeds of sale	60,000
Market value 31.3.82: $22,000 \times \dfrac{60,000}{60,000 + 75,000}$	9,778
Unindexed gain	50,222
Indexation 95% × 9,778	9,289
Chargeable gain	40,933

In this case, since the disposal was out of the first identifiable plot, there is no need to combine the acquisition costs of the two plots.

If the sale had been 5 acres out of the total of 12 acres (valued at £25,000 at 31.3.82) with the remaining 7 acres being valued at £85,000 at the date of disposal then the computation would be:

	£
Proceeds of sale	60,000
Market value 31.3.82: $25,000 \times \dfrac{60,000}{60,000 + 85,000} =$	10,345
Unindexed gain	49,655
Indexation 95% × 10,345	9,828
Chargeable gain	39,827

Small part disposals of land Section 242

4. There are some special rules which relate to land where:
   a) the value of the part disposal does not exceed £20,000.
   b) the part disposal is small relative to the market value of the entire property, before the disposal. Small in this context means 20% of the value immediately prior to the disposal.

   Given these conditions, then the taxpayer can claim to have any consideration received for the part disposal deducted from the allowable expenditure of the whole property. In this case there would be no chargeable gain on the part disposal.

   The £20,000 exemption does not apply to a compulsory purchase by a public authority.

   The taxpayer's total consideration for disposals of land in an income tax year must not exceed £20,000, for him or her to be eligible to claim relief under this section.

> ### Example
>
> Z owns land which he acquired in April 1982 for £20,000 comprising some 10 acres. The costs of the acquisition amounted to £500. In August 1997 Z sells 1.5 acres for £6,500 incurring disposal costs of £750. At the date of sale the remainder of the land had a market value of £135,500.
>
> *Compute the chargeable gain arising in 1997/98. If Z makes a claim under Section 242 show the computations. Assume indexation of 95%.*

Solution

CGT computation 1997/98

	£	£
August 1997 Proceeds of sale		6,500
Deduct – allowable cost $\frac{6,500}{6,500 + 135,500} \times 20,500$	938	
Cost of disposal	750	1,688
Unindexed gain		4,812
Indexation 95% × 938		891
Chargeable gain		3,921
Claim under Section 242 TCGA 1992		
Cost of acquisition		20,500
Less proceeds of sale August 1997 (6,500 – 500)		6,000
Revised allowed cost		14,500

Notes

i) *In this example, rather than claim relief under Section 242 it might be more advantageous to accept the chargeable gain since it falls within the exemption level of £6,500 for 1997/98 which might otherwise go unused.*

ii) *The election under Section 242 TCGA 1992 can be made where the proceeds of sale are less than 20% of the value of the entire property before the disposal.*

$$\frac{Disposal\ value}{Total\ value\ before\ sale} = \frac{6500}{142000} = 4.6\%$$

Disposal of a short lease

5. On the sale of a short lease (ie one with less than 50 years to run) the cost of acquisition must be written off in accordance with the special table contained in Schedule 8 TCGA 1992, as reproduced below. This table effectively writes off the lease at an increasing rate p.a., and excludes from the attributable expenditure the following amount:

$$\text{Total cost} \times \frac{P(1) - P(3)}{P(1)}$$

   P(1) is the % from the table, applicable to the length of the lease at the time of its acquisition.
   P(3) is the % from the table, applicable to the length of the lease at the time of its disposal.

   The fraction of any additional enhancement expenditure which is not allowed is given by:

$$\text{Additional cost} \times \frac{P(2) - P(3)}{P(2)}$$

   P(2) is the percentage derived from the table for the duration of the lease at the time when the item of expenditure is first reflected in the nature of the lease. P(3) is as defined above.

   If the duration of the lease is not an exact number of years the percentage from the table is that for the whole number of years plus 1/12 the difference between that percentage and the next higher number of years for each odd month, counting an odd 14 days or more as one month.

If a lease was acquired before 6th April 1965 and an election to use the MV (market value) at 6th April 1965 is made, then that date is treated as the date of acquisition for depreciation purposes ie P(1) = 6.4.1965. Similarly, where the March 1982 value is used for indexation and/or re-basing then 31st March 1982 is taken to be the date of acquisition, ie P(1) = 31.3.1982.

Example

On 1st January 1990 C acquired a thirty year lease on a factory for £30,000. On the 10th February 1998 the lease of the factory is sold for £45,000. Assume indexation of 50%. *Compute the chargeable gain.*

Solution

Computation 1997/98

	£	£
Proceeds of sale 10.2.98		45,000
Less: Cost of acquisition 1.1.1990	30,000	
Proportion not allowed:		
$\dfrac{87.330 - 76.252}{87.330} \times 30,000$	3,805	26,195
Unindexed gain		18,805
Indexation 50% × 26,195		13,097
Chargeable gain		5,708

Notes

i) *1.1.1990 – 1.1.2020 = 30 years; 1.1.1990 – 10.2.1998 = 8 years, 1 month, 9 days*

ii) *At 10th February 1998 the unexpired life of the lease is*

21 years, 10 months and 19 days	=	*21 years 11 months*
Percentage for 21 whole years	=	*74.635*
Addition for 11 months is: $^{11}/_{12} \times (76.399 - 74.635)$	=	*1.617*
		76.252

iii) *The percentage for a 30 year lease is 87.330.*

iv) *The percentage for 22 years is 76.399: 21 years 74.635.*

v) *Instead of deducting the proportion not allowed the calculation of the allowed cost can be computed directly by the following:*

$$\text{Cost} \times \frac{\text{\% relating to number of years left at date of assignment}}{\text{\% relating to number of years when lease first acquired}}$$

ie $30,000 \times \dfrac{76.252}{87.330} = £26,195$

Example

On 31st March 1979 Q acquired a 40 year lease of a shop at a premium of £5,000. Q sold the shop lease for £40,000 on the 31st March 1998. Market value at 31st March 1982 is estimated at £15,000. Assume indexation of 95%.

Solution

Q. CGT computation 1997/98

		Re-basing 31.3.82 £	Pre-FA 88 Rules £
Proceeds of sale		40,000	40,000
Cost 31.3.78	5000		
Allowable amount			
$\dfrac{74.635}{95.457} \times 5000$			3,909
MV @ 31.3.82	15,000		
Allowable amount			
$\dfrac{74.635}{93.497} \times 15,000$		11,974	———
Unindexed gain		28,026	36,091
Indexation allowance 95% × 11,974		11,375	11,375
Chargeable gain		16,651	24,716

Notes

i)   31.3.1998 – 31.3.2019   =   *21 years - Number of years remaining on disposal*

     31.3.1982 – 31.3.2019   =   *37 years - Number of years since 31.3.1982*

     95.457   =   *40 years*

     74,635   =   *21 years*

     93.497   =   *37 years = Number of years from 31.3.1982*

ii)   *Indexation is based on the market value at 31.3.1982 less the wastage percentage to the date of disposal.*

iii)   *The chargeable gain under the re-basing method will be taken as it gives a smaller gain.*

Short lease depreciation table

6.   **TCGA 1992, Schedule 8**

Table

50 (or more)	100	25	81.100
49	99.657	24	79.622
48	99.289	23	78.055
47	98.902	22	76.399
46	98.490	21	74.635
45	98.059	20	72.770
44	97.595	19	70.791
43	97.107	18	68.697
42	96.593	17	66.470
41	96.041	16	64.116
40	95.457	15	61.617
39	94.842	14	58.971
38	94.189	13	56.167
37	93.497	12	53.191
36	92.761	11	50.038
35	91.981	10	46.695
34	91.156	9	43.154
33	90.280	8	39.399
32	89.354	7	35.414
31	88.371	6	31.195
30	87.330	5	26.722
29	86.226	4	21.983
28	85.053	3	16.959
27	83.816	2	11.629
26	82.496	1	5.983
		0	0

Grant of a lease from a freehold interest

7.   Where a lease of land is granted from a freehold interest, and this requires payment of a premium, then the transaction amounts to a part disposal of the freehold interest. Accordingly, the part disposal formula applies. If the premium is brought into account as a receipt of a Schedule A business then in order to avoid double taxation, the consideration is reduced by that amount.

Example

F purchased freehold property on 1st July 1983 for £10,000 and on 1st September 1997 granted a 21 year lease to P for a premium of £8,000. The market value of the freehold subject to the lease at 1st September 1997 was £15,000. Assume indexation of 90%. *Compute the chargeable gain.*

Solution

F. Computations 1997/98

	£
Schedule A assessed premium:	
Premium received	8,000
Less: $8,000 \times 2\% \times (21-1)$	3,200
Chargeable to income tax	4,800
Chargeable gain:	
Disposal value	8,000
Less: Assessed under Schedule A	4,800
	3,200

Less: Proportion of cost:

$$10,000 \times \frac{8000 - 4800}{8000 + 15000}$$

ie $10,000 \times \dfrac{3200}{23000} =$ 1,391

Indexation allowance $90\% \times 1,391 =$	1,252	2,643
Chargeable gain		557

Notes

i) *The proportion of cost calculation has a numerator of £3,200 ie the part of the lease premium not charged to income tax but the denominator uses the gross premium ie £8,000.*

ii) *Where there is a grant of a sublease from an existing short lease, then the part disposal formula does not apply.*

Summary of CGT treatment of leases

8.   i)

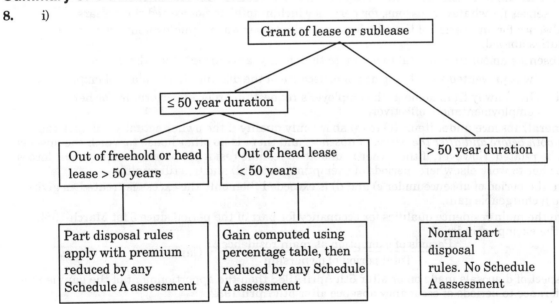

ii)

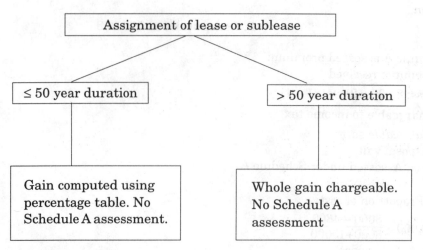

Private residence Section 222–226

9. Any gain accruing to an individual on the disposal of his or her only or main residence can be exempt from capital gains tax. The exemption also extend to one other residence provided for a dependent relative, if the property is rent free and without other consideration up to 5 April 1988.

Residence includes a dwelling house (or part) together with land up to half a hectare in area, or more if justified, and a mobile home. See *Makins v Elson* 1981 STI 326.

Full exemption is available where there has been a continuous period of ownership, and the following are to be taken into consideration in determining the total periods of exemption.

a) Actual periods of occupation.

b) Any period of absence during the last three years of ownership providing that at some time the residence has been occupied as the principal private residence of the taxpayer. This period of absence applies even where the occupancy was only before 31st March 1982.

c) Absences for whatever reasons, for periods which in total do not exceed three years.

d) Absence for any period of time during which the owner was in employment, carrying out duties abroad.

e) Absences amounting in total to not more than four years during which the owner:

   i) was prevented from living at home because of the distance to the place of employment.

   ii) lived away from home at the employer's request, in order to perform his or her employment more effectively.

In general, absence under items (c) to (e) above only qualify if the owner actually occupies the home *both before and after the period of absence*, and there is no other house to which the absence could be related. However, if the owner is unable to resume residence because employment forces him or her to work elsewhere, periods of exemption under (d) and (e) still qualify.

Where the period of absence under c) and d) is exceeded then only the excess is treated as giving rise to a chargeable gain.

Where the main residence qualifies for occupancy for part of the period since 31st March 1982, then the exempt gain is:

$$\frac{\text{Periods of exemption as main residence}}{\text{Total period of ownership}} \times \text{Gain}$$

In respect of disposals made on or after 6th April 1988 then the apportionment of the gain is made by reference to periods of occupancy/absence after 5th April 1982.

Example

A purchased a house for £6,000 on 6th April 1978 which he used as his main residence until 5th April 1982 when the property was unoccupied for 10 years while he visited relatives in Canada. He resumed occupancy on the 6th April 1992 until the house was sold for £79,000 on the 31st March 1998. Assume indexation of 95%. The value of the house at March 1982 has been agreed at £15,000.

Compute the chargeable gain.

Solution

A. CGT computation 1997/98

	£	Re-basing 31.3.82 £	£	Pre-FA 88 Rules £
Proceeds of sale		79,000		79,000
Cost of acquisition			6,000	
Market value 31.3.82	15,000			
Indexation allowance – 95% × 15,000	14,250	29,250	14,250	20,250
Total gain		49,750		58,750
Exempt gain $^9/_{16}$ × 49,750		27,984		
$^9/_{16}$ × 20,250				11,391
Chargeable gain		21,766		47,359

Notes

i) *Period of ownership:*

	Years
6.4.78 – 31.3.98	20
31.3.82 – 31.3.98	16
Occupancy since 31.3.82:	
6.4.92 – 31.3.98	6
Last three years of ownership: 6.4.95 – 31.3.98	3
Absence abroad preceded and followed by occupancy	3
Total periods of exemption (6 + 3)	9

ii) As the re-basing method gives a smaller gain the old rules will not apply.

iii) Where the house was owned before the 31st March 1982, the period of ownership is taken from the 31st March 1982 under the re-basing method, and the pre-FA 1988 rules.

iv) The last three years includes in this case, the final period of occupancy and is not therefore counted twice.

10. The following additional points should be noted.

   a) If part of any house is used *exclusively* for business purposes, then that part of any gain attributable to the business portion is not eligible for any exemptions.

   b) If a house, or part of it, is let for residential purposes then the part of the gain attributable to that letting is exempt up to the smaller of:

      i) the gain otherwise exempt

      ii) £40,000

      iii) the gain attributable to the letting period.

Example

A purchased a house on 1st July 1982 for £25,000 in which he lived until the 31st March 1983. The property was then let for five years, followed by occupancy by A until he sold the house for £325,000 on the 31st March 1998. Assume indexation of 90%.

Compute the chargeable gain.

Solution

Computation 1997/98

	£	£
Proceeds of sale		325,000
Cost of acquisition	25,000	
Indexation 90% × £25,000	22,500	47,500
Total gain before exemption		277,500
Less: Exemption:		
Proportion of total gain $\frac{165}{189}$ × 277,500		242,262
		35,238
Less Let property exemption: Lower of:		
maximum amount	40,000	
gain otherwise exempt	242,262	limited to 35,238
letting gain	35,238	
		Nil

Note

		Years	Months	Total months
Period of ownership	1.7.82 – 31.3.98	15	9	189
Period of absence	1.4.83 – 31.3.88	5	–	60
Periods of occupancy	1.7.82 – 31.3.83	–	9	9
	1.4.88 – 31.3.98	10	–	120

			Months
Last three years			36
Period of absence preceded and followed by occupancy			36
Occupancy additional to last three years 1.7.82 – 31.3.83	9		
1.4.88 – 31.3.95	84		93
			165

c) A husband and wife can only have one residence for the purposes of any exemptions. If they are permanently separated or divorced, then each qualifies individually for the residence exemption.

d) Exemption is extended to the trustees of a settlement where a person is entitled to occupy the house under the terms of the settlement.

e) The exemption also applies to an individual who lives in job-related accommodation and who intends in due course to occupy a house owned by that individual, as his or her main residence. It also applies to self-employed people living in job-related accommodation.

Chattels Section 262

11. The chattels discussed here are personal chattels or tangible movable property which for capital gains tax purposes are put into three categories.

  a) Chattels which are specifically exempt from capital gains tax, eg private cars, or decorations for valour.

  b) Chattels which are wasting assets.

  c) Chattels, not being wasting assets, disposed of for £6,000 or less.

Chattels which are wasting assets

12. A wasting asset is one with an estimated useful life of less than 50 years at the time of the disposal. A chattel which is a wasting asset is exempt from capital gains tax unless:

  a) the asset has been used since first owned, for the purposes of a trade, profession or vocation, and capital allowances were available in respect of the expenditure, whether claimed or not, or

  b) it consists of commodities dealt with on a terminal market.

Where capital allowances have been claimed, then no chargeable gain will arise unless the disposal value is greater than the original cost. If the proceeds are less than £6,000 then the exemption noted below can be claimed.

Chattels disposed of for £6,000 or less – marginal relief

13. Any gain arising on the disposal of a chattel, not being a wasting asset, is not a chargeable gain where the gross disposal value is £6,000 or less.

Marginal relief applies where the disposal value is greater than £6,000 and the cost less than £6,000. The marginal relief limits the gain to:

$$\frac{5}{3} \times (\text{gross proceeds} - £6,000)$$

Thus the maximum assessable gain is the lower of:

i) $\frac{5}{3} \times$ (gross proceeds – £6,000) or

ii) The actual gain ie gross proceeds less (costs + indexation).

> **Example**

H buys a piece of pottery for £800 in June 1982 which he sells in October 1997 for (a) £4,800, (b) £6,800. Assume indexation of 90%.

Compute the chargeable gains.

Solution

H. CGT computation 1997/98

a)   As the proceeds of sale are less than £6,000 no chargeable gain arises.

b)

	£	£
Proceeds of sale		6,800
Less: cost of acquisition	800	
Add: indexation 90% × 800	720	1,520
Chargeable gain		5,280
Limited to $\frac{5}{3}$ (6,800 − 6,000)		1,333
Net chargeable gain		1,333

Restriction of loss

14.   If the chattel which cost more than £6,000 is sold for less than £6,000 then the allowable loss is calculated by reference to £6,000 and not the actual disposal value. If both the disposal price and the cost price are less than £6,000 then the loss is not allowed at all.

Where two or more chattels form part of a set, then any disposal of part of the set is to be aggregated with any disposal of the other parts, and treated as a single transaction.

Capital allowances

15.   Where there is a disposal of an asset in respect of which capital allowances were available (whether claimed or not) then any loss on disposal is restricted by reference to the available capital allowances.

For plant and machinery the capital allowances are taken to be the difference between the disposal value and the cost of the capital expenditure incurred.

> **Example**

A purchased plant for use in his business in May 1988 for £50,000 which was sold for £15,000 in July 1997. Assume indexation of 50%.

Solution

Chargeable gains tax computation 1997/98

	£
Proceeds of sale	15,000
Cost of acquisition	50,000
Gross loss	(35,000)
Less restriction by net capital allowances	35,000
	−
Indexation allowance 50% × 50,000	−
Allowable loss	Nil

Notes

i)   *As the disposal took place after the 30th November 1993, indexation cannot be used to create or increase a loss.*

ii)   *Where the disposal takes place after 5th April 1988 and the asset was owned on 31st March 1982 then the general re-basing provisions apply.*

iii)   *Where the proceeds of sale are less than the original cost, which would be the normal situation for plant and machinery, the loss is equal to the indexation allowance for disposals prior to 30th November 1993.*

• Student self-testing question

T purchased a house on 1st May 1970 for £15,000 in which he lived until 30th April 1980. The property was then let until sold on 31st March 1998 for £185,000. Assume indexation of 90%. The market value of the house at 31st March 1982 was £36,000. *Compute the chargeable gain.*

Solution

T. CGT computation 1997/98

	£	Re-basing 31.3.82 £	£	Pre-FA88 Rules £
Proceeds of sale		185,000		185,000
Cost of acquisition			15,000	
MV @ 31.3.82	36,000			
Indexation allowance – 90% × 36,000	32,400	68,400	32,400	47,400
Total gain		116,600		137,600
Less: Exemption:				
$^{36}/_{192} × 116,600$		21,862		
$^{36}/_{192} × 137,600$				25,800
Gain attributable to letting		94,738		111,800
Less: Exemption:				
lower of exempt gain	21,862		25,800	
Maximum	40,000	21,862	40,000	25,800
Chargeable gain		72,876		86,000

Notes

		Year	*Months*
i)	*Period of ownership since 31.3.82*		
	1.4.82 – 31.3.98	*16*	*192*
	Occupancy since 31.3.82	*0*	*0*
	Last three years	*3*	*36*

ii) *The smaller gain under the re-basing rules would be taken.*

iii) *As the property was not occupied before and after the letting the three year period of absence cannot be claimed.*

• Questions without answers

1. K purchased a painting for £500 on the 1st June 1975. The painting was sold for £7,500, after sales commission of 10% in May 1997 at auction. The market value at 31st March 1982 was £4,000.

   Compute the chargeable gain for 1997/98. Assume indexation of 95%.

2. A purchased his private residence for £20,000 on the 1st August 1978. The property was immediately let at a rent of £2,000 p.a. until the 1st January 1987 when A occupied the house. The house was sold for £300,000 on the 30th April 1997, with costs of disposal amounting to £1,500. At 31st March 1982 the property had an estimated value of £40,000.

   Compute A's CGT liability for 1997/98 before annual exemption. Assume indexation of 95%

3. James purchased a house in Oxford, 'Millhouse', on 1st July 1981 and took up immediate residence. The house cost £50,000. On 1st January 1983 he went to work and live in the United States where he stayed until 30th June 1985. On 1st July 1985 James returned to the UK to work for his United States employers in Scotland where it was necessary for him to occupy rented accommodation. On 1st July 1986 his mother became seriously ill and James resigned from his job to go and live with her. His mother died on 30th September 1987 leaving her house to James. James decided to continue to live in his mother's house and finally sold 'Millhouse' on 30th June 1997 for £300,000. The value of the house on 31st March 1982 was £75,000.

   Calculate, before annual exemption, the capital gains assessable on James for 1997/98. No election has been, or will be, made under 35 TCGA 1992, to have all pre-31st March 1982 acquisitions re-based to 31st March. Assume indexation of 95%.

   (ACCA)

38 Stocks and securities

Introduction

1. This chapter is concerned with the CGT rules applicable to stocks and securities and begins with the general method of computation and indexation for shares or securities of the same class and then examines bonus and rights issues and takeover bids. The rules for quoted securities held on 6th April 1965, and qualifying corporate bonds are also outlined.

General method of computing – shares or securities of the same class

2. The following are the main provisions which apply to disposals of shares or securities of the same class, where they are held by one person in the same capacity.

   a) Separate pools must be established as follows.
      i) Shares or securities acquired on or after the 6th April 1982 (1st April for companies). This is called the New Holding.
      ii) Shares or securities acquired prior to 6th April 1982 (1st April for companies) held at 6th April 1985. This is called the 1982 Holding.

   b) The re-basing rules apply to shares and securities held at the 31st March 1982 and the market value at that date forms the basis of valuation of the 1982 Holding. As with other assets, the old rules can be used where this gives a smaller gain/loss and the taxpayer has not elected for only the re-basing method to be adopted.

   c) Securities within the accrued income provisions, deep discount securities, qualifying corporate bonds and certain securities in offshore funds are excluded from the new pooling arrangements.

   d) For disposals on or after 30th November 1993, indexation cannot increase or create a loss, subject to the transitional relief for indexation losses for 1993/94 and 1994/95.

New holdings – rules for shares of the same class

3. a) The pool consists of:
      i) the cost of acquisition of shares acquired on or after 6th April 1982, plus
      ii) the indexation allowance.

   b) Additions to the pool either by acquisition or by rights issue will need to take into account an addition in respect of the indexation allowance. This is determined by the formula

   $$\frac{RE - RL}{RL}$$

   RE = RPI for month in which pool is increased.

   RL = RPI in month when pool created, or when last operative event occurred.

   (Rounding to the third decimal place is not a legal requirement for quoted securities.)

   c) When part of the share holding is disposed of, the cost of acquisition relating to the disposal is the proportionate part of the cost of all the shares in the holding. A weighted average cost is computed.

   > **Example**

   Q has the following transactions in the 25p ordinary shares of Z plc.

				£
6th April 1982	purchased	3,500	shares at cost	2,500
31st March 1984	purchased	1,000	shares at cost	500
31st January 1998	purchased	2,000	shares at cost	3,500

   Calculate the indexed pool value of the 'new holding' at 31st January 1998.

   RPI April 1982 81.04: March 1984 87.48: January 1998 say 155.0

Solution

Q. Ordinary shares in Z plc

	Retail Price Index	Number of Shares £	Qualifying Expenditure £	Indexed Pool £
6.4.82	81.04			
Purchased		3,500	2,500	2,500
31.3.84	87.48			
Indexation allowance				
$\dfrac{87.48 - 81.04}{81.04} = 0.079$				198
$0.079 \times 2,500$				
		3,500	2,500	2,698
31.3.84 Purchase		1,000	500	500
		4,500	3,000	3,198
31.1.98	155.0			
Indexation allowance				
$\dfrac{155.0 - 87.48}{87.48} = 0.772 \times 3,198$				2,469
		4,500	3,000	5,667
31.1.98 Purchase		2,000	3,500	3,500
Pool values at 31.1.1998		6,500	6,500	9,167

Notes

i) *The indexation allowance is calculated immediately before there is a change in the pool by acquisition or disposal, subject to the rule noted for disposals on or after the 30th November 1993.*

ii) *It is possible to omit the intermediate stages and compute the pool values as illustrated below:*

	RPI	Number of Shares	Qualifying expenditure	Indexed Pool
6.4.1982	81.04	3,500	2,500	2,500
Indexation allowance				
$\dfrac{155.0 - 81.04}{81.04} = 0.913 \times 2,500$				2,283
31.3.84 Purchase	87.48	1,000	500	500
Indexation allowance				
$\dfrac{155.0 - 87.48}{87.48} = 0.772 \times 500$				384
31.1.98 Purchase	155.0	2,000	3,500	3,500
		6,500	6,500	9,167

1982 Holdings

4. a) The pool consists of shares or securities acquired prior to 6th April 1982 which are deemed to have been sold and reacquired at their market value on 31st March 1982.

b) Indexation is based automatically on the cost or market value at 31st March 1982, *whichever is the greater*.

c) A part disposal from the pool is computed by using the weighted average cost principle.

d) Acquisitions of additional shares cannot be added to this pool and they must be treated as a 'new holding'. But *see Rights issues below*.

e) Taxpayers can make a once and for all election that all gains and losses acquired before 31st March 1982 are to be computed by reference to the March 1982 value, and the old rules would not then be considered.

f) Taxpayers were able to make such an election, whether or not they made a disposal, at any time up to and including 5th April 1990. In addition, if an election is not already in force it will be possible to make one within two years of the end of the accounting period or year of assessment in which the first disposal on or after 6th April 1988 of an asset held at 31st March 1982 takes place.

Identifying disposals with acquisitions

5. **a)** **General rules**

First	with shares acquired on the same day
Second	with shares acquired in the previous nine days
Third	with shares in the new holdings pool (ie acquired on or after 6th April 1982)
Fourth	with shares in the 1982 pool (ie acquired before 6th April 1982)
Fifth	with shares acquired before 6th April 1965 on a LIFO basis.

b) **Shares or securities bought and sold within a 10 day period**

The main rules of identification under this heading are as follows.

i) The number of securities acquired = number sold. The securities are not regarded as forming part of a new or existing holding, and there is no indexation allowance.

ii) The number of securities acquired > number sold. The excess constitutes a new holding and acquisitions within the 10 day period are identified on a FIFO basis.

iii) The number of securities acquired < number sold. The excess is identified in accordance with general rules for identification noted above, ie on a LIFO basis.

c) **Bed and breakfast transactions**

When shares or securities are sold and subsequently re-purchased they do not fall within the 10 day rule for identifying disposals with acquisitions. The disposal is deducted from the pool and the re-purchase added to the pool in the normal way. Where the market price is greater than the pool average indexed cost, a disposal and 'immediate' re-purchase can utilise the annual exemption of £6,500 and raise the average cost of the pool for future disposals.

Example

Q has the following transactions in the 25p ordinary shares of K plc.

				£
1.6.1975	purchased	1,000	shares at cost	525
1.9.1980	purchased	500	shares at cost	575
2.1.1983	purchased	2,500	shares at cost	3,500
10.10.1997	sold	3,000	shares, proceeds	36,000

RPI March 1982 79.44, January 1983 82.61, October 1997 say 155.0. Market value of shares at 31st March 1982 110p per share. A general election for re-basing has not been made by Q.

Calculate the chargeable gain for 1997/98 before annual exemption.

Solution

Q. CGT computation 1997/98

						£	£
10.10.1997	Proceeds of sale of 3,000 shares						36,000

New holdings	Retail Price Index	Nominal Value £	Qualifying Expenditure £	Indexed Pool £	
2.1.1983 Purchase	82.61	2,500	3,500	3,500	
10.10.1997 Indexation allowance 155.0					

$$\left(\frac{155.0 - 82.61}{82.61}\right) \times 3,500$$

$$= 0.876 \times 3,500$$

				3,066	
		2,500	3,500	6,566	
Disposal		2,500	3,500	6,566	6,566
Pool carried forward		–	–	–	

1982 Holding				Re-basing MV 31.3.82	
1.6.1975 Purchase		1,000	525	1,100	
1.9.1980 Purchase		500	575	550	
		1,500	1,100	1,650	

10.10.1997 disposal 500 shares

Proportion of MV $\dfrac{500}{1,500} \times 1,650 =$ 550

Indexation allowance:

$$\frac{155.0 - 79.44}{79.44} \times 550 = 0.951 \times 550 \qquad\qquad \underline{523} \qquad \underline{1,073}$$

Total allowable expenditure $\qquad\qquad\qquad\qquad\qquad\qquad \underline{7,639}$

Notes

i)   The 1982 unindexed pool of expenditure carried forward consists of 1,000 shares at weighted average cost (based on market value at 31.3.82) of 1,650 – 550 = £1,100.

ii) Disposals are matched with the new holding before the 1982 holding.

iii) The proceeds of sale are apportioned between the 1982 holding and the new holding by reference to the number of shares sold from each pool.

Capital gains tax computation 1997/98

			£	£
New Holding	Proceeds of sale	$\frac{2,500}{3,000}$ x 36,000	30,000	
	less pool cost		6,566	23,434
1982 Holding	Proceeds of sale	$\frac{500}{3,000}$ x 36,000	6,000	
	less pool cost		1,073	4,927
Chargeable gain				28,361

iii) Re-basing has been chosen for the 1982 holdings as the shares had a greater market value than cost at that date.

Example

V had the following transactions in the quoted shares of Z plc.

23.11.1980	Bought	6,000	shares costing	£14,000
7.1.1983	Bought	800	shares costing	£5,600
30.10.1997	Sold	1,000	shares for	£6,000

The market value of the shares at the 31st March 1982 was £2.75. No general basing election has been made.

Compute the chargeable gain. Assume RPI October 1997 was 155.0.

Solution

V CGT computation 1997/98

New Holding	RPI	Nominal Value	Qualifying Expenditure	Indexed Pool
			£	£
7.1.1983	82.61	800	5,600	5,600
30.10.1997	155.0			
I.A. $\frac{155.0 - 82.61}{82.61}$				
0.876 × 5,600				4,906
		800	5,600	10,506
Disposal		800	5,600	10,506
		–	–	–

30.10.97 Proceeds of sale 800 shares $\frac{800}{1000} \times$ £6,000 = $\qquad$ 4,800

Cost without indexation $\qquad\qquad\qquad\qquad\qquad\qquad$ 5,600

Allowable loss $\qquad\qquad\qquad\qquad\qquad\qquad\qquad$ (800)

Note *As the disposal is after 30.11.93 indexation cannot be used to increase the loss.*

1982 holding	Nominal Value	Qualifying expenditure	Re-basing 31.3.1982
		£	£
23.11.1980	6,000	14,000	16,500
30.10.1997 Disposal	$\frac{200}{6000} \times 16,500$		550

IA $\frac{155.0 - 79.44}{79.44} \times 550$

0.951×550

			523
			1,073
			1,200
30.10.97 Proceeds of sale 200 shares $\frac{200}{1000} \times 6,000$			
Indexed cost as above			1,073
Chargeable gain			127

V CGT tax computation 1997/98

30.10.97 Proceeds of sale 100 shares			6,000
Less allowable expenditure			
New holding		5,600	
1982 holding + IA		1,073	6,673
Allowable loss			673

Note *This is equal to (800 – 127) = 673 as above.*

Bonus issues of similar shares

6. When a company makes a bonus or scrip issue of shares of the same class, then the average cost (or market value at 31.3.1982) of all the shares held is not affected, but their number is increased, and hence the average cost per share is reduced. The indexation allowance principle is not affected by a bonus issue, so that the normal rules for identification noted above apply. The number of shares in each pool is increased by the bonus issue.

Example

T Ltd makes a bonus issue of 1 for 5 in respect of its ordinary shares on 1st August 1984. A had acquired 500 ordinary shares in T Ltd on 1st May 1972 at a cost of £1,000. In June 1997 A sells 250 of the shares for £6,500. Assume indexation of 95%. The market value of the shares before the bonus issue at 31.3.1982 was £2.50 per share. *Compute the chargeable gain.*

Solution
Cost of shares, 1982 holding

		Cost £	Market value at 31.3.82 £
1.5.1972 cost of	500 ordinary shares	1,000	1,250
1.8.1984 cost of	100 bonus shares	–	–
	600	1,000	1,250

The deemed date of acquisition of the bonus shares is the date of the original purchases.

CGT computation 1997/98

Proceeds of sale June 1997		6,500
MV of 250 shares sold as at 31.3.1982:		
$\frac{250}{600} \times 1,250$	521	
Indexation allowance: 95% × 521	495	1,016
Chargeable gain		5,484

353

Notes

i)   *The value of the 250 shares sold, as at 31.3.1982, is 250 × £2.083 = £521 (£1,250 ÷ £600 = £2.083)*

ii) *The unindexed value of the 350 shares carried forward is £1,250 − 521 ie £729.*

iii) *If the pre-FA 1988 rules applied the computation would be:*

	£	£
Proceeds of sale		*6,500*
Cost of 250 shares sold $\frac{250}{600} \times 1,000$	*416*	
Indexation allowance (as above)	*495*	*911*
Chargeable gain		*5,589*

As there is a smaller gain under the re-basing method than under the old rules the chargeable gain is £5,484.

Example

AB Ltd makes a scrip issue of 1 for 10 on the 30th June 1987. Z had acquired 10,000 ordinary shares in AB Ltd in April 1980 at a cost of £14,000. Z sells 2,000 shares in May 1997 for £6,000. The market value of the shares in issue at 31st March 1982 was £1.50 per share, i.e. before the bonus issue. *Compute the chargeable gain under the re-basing provisions. Assume indexation of 95%.*

Solution

CGT computation 1997/98

		£
Proceeds of sale – 2,000 shares		6,000
MV at 31.3.1982:		
10,000 @ £1.50 =	15,000	
$\frac{2000}{11000} \times 15,000$ (ie 2,000 × £1.364)	2,727	
IA 95% × 2,727	2,591	5,318
Chargeable gain		682

Notes

i) **1982 Holding:**

	Number	*Cost*	*MV 31.3.82*
April 1980 cost	*10,000*	*14,000*	*15,000*
June 1987 bonus	*1,000*	*Nil*	*Nil*
	11,000	*14,000*	*15,000*

Market value of shares plus the bonus issue is $\frac{£15000}{11000}$ *= £1.364 per share ie the price as adjusted for the bonus issue. 2,000 shares @ £1.364 = £2,727.*

ii) *The unindexed MV carried forward is £15,000 − £2,727 = £12,273.*

Bonus issues of shares or debentures of a different class

7.   A bonus issue of shares of a different class, or debentures, gives rise to two distinct classes of holdings, and the original cost of the shares must be apportioned. The method of apportionment is as follows:

a)   Quoted investments.   Apportionment by reference to the market value of the new holding on the first day a price is quoted on the stock exchange.

b)   Unquoted investments.   The part disposal formula is applied as and when a disposal occurs.

Example

T plc, a quoted company, made a bonus issue on the 31st August 1997 of 1 new ordinary shares for every 5 held, and £1.00 of 8% debenture stock for every 2 shares held. First day dealing prices on 1st September were 160p for the ordinary, and par for the debentures. A acquired the shares from his father's estate on 1st July 1983: 1,000 ordinary shares in T plc value £1,500.

Compute the apportioned cost.

Solution   £

Calculation of apportioned cost

After bonus issue of 1 for 5. 1,200 shares held at a cost of   1,500

	Market Value 1.9.1997 £	*Apportioned Cost* £	
1,200 ordinary shares @ 160p	1,920	1,190	see below
£500 8% debenture @ £100	500	310	
	2,420	1,500	

Ordinary shares: $\dfrac{1,920}{2,420} \times 1,500$ ie   1,190

Debentures: $\dfrac{500}{2,420} \times 1,500$ ie   310

Note

On a disposal indexation will apply to each holding, in this example from 1st July 1983, subject to the limitation rules noted earlier.

Rights issues of the same class

8. Where a company makes a rights issue of the same class of shares as existing ones, and they are taken up, then for CGT purposes the following rules apply.

   a) The consideration paid for the shares by way of the rights issue is deemed to take place at the time when the cost of the rights becomes due.

   b) Where the rights issue relates to a 'new holding' then the pool cost is increased accordingly.

   c) If the rights issue relates to a 1982 holding then the cost of the rights must be treated as an addition to that holding.

   d) The indexation allowance is computed from the date the rights become due and payable whether they relate to a new holding or a 1982 holding.

> *Example*

T plc makes a rights issue on the 7th February 1984 of 1 new ordinary share for every 2 held, at a price of 125p per share. J acquired 1,000 ordinary shares in T plc for £1,300 on the 1st October 1982. He sells 750 shares for £10,000 on the 25th October 1997. *Compute the chargeable gain.* RPI October 1982 82.26, February 1984 87.20, October 1997, say 155.0

Solution

CGT computation 1997/98

Pool value at 25.10.1997	Retail Price Index	Nominal Value £	Qualifying Expenditure £	Indexed Pool £
1.10.1982 Acquisition	82.26	1,000	1,300	1,300
25.10.1997 Indexation allowance:	150.0			
$\dfrac{155.0 - 82.26}{82.26} \times 1,300 = 0.884 \times 1,300$				1,149
7.2. 1984 Rights issue	87.20	500	625	625
25.10.1997 Indexation allowance:	150.0			
$\dfrac{155.0 - 87.20}{87.20} = 0.778 \times 625$				486
Pool value before disposal		1,500	1,925	3,560
25.10.1997 Disposal 750 shares		750		
$\dfrac{750}{1,500} \times 1,925$			963	
$\dfrac{750}{1,500} \times 3,560$				1,780
Value of pool c/f		750	962	1,780

CGT computation 1997/98

	£
Proceeds of sale	10,000
Less indexed cost	1,780
Chargeable gain before exemption	8,220

Notes

i) The rights issue of 1 for every 2 is 500 new shares at a cost of 125p per share ie £625.00.

ii) Indexation applies from the date of the rights issue for the new shares, ie 7th February 1984.

Rights issues of a different class

9. Where the shareholder is offered shares of a different class, or securities, by way of a rights issue, then the same rules apply as for a bonus issue of shares of a different class, noted above. The different treatment for quoted and unquoted shares also applies to this type of rights issue. For indexation purposes the additional consideration becomes a separate asset as for rights issues in general.

Takeover bids

10. Where a company makes a bid for the shares of another company the following situations could arise.

a) The consideration is satisfied entirely by cash. In this case a shareholder who accepts the offer has made a chargeable disposal.

b) The consideration is a share for share exchange. In this case an accepting shareholder is deemed to have acquired the new shares at the *date and cost of the original holding*, or the 1982 value.

c) The consideration is either a partial cash settlement, or it consists of two or more shares or securities by way of exchange. In both cases it will be necessary to use the market value of the separate components of the bid, in order to apportion the original cost.

> **Example**

A owns 1,000 ordinary shares in P Ltd which he acquired for £1,500 on 27th June 1983. On the 30th May 1997 Z plc makes a bid for P Ltd on the following terms:

For every 200 shares: £30.00 in cash, 100 ordinary shares in Z plc, and £50.00 of 7% unsecured loan stock. MV when first quoted: ordinary 375p, 7% loan stock at par.

Assume indexation of 90%. *Compute the apportioned cost and CGT computation for 1997/98.*

Solution

	Market Value £	Apportioned Cost £
Cash 5 × 30	150	99
7% loan stock 5 × 50	250	165
500 ordinary share 500 × 375p	1,875	1,236
	2,275	1,500

CGT computation 1997/98

Disposal cash receipt		150
Less apportioned cost	99	
Indexation 90% × 99 = 89. Restricted	51	150
Chargeable loss		Nil

Notes

i) The cost apportionments are as follows:

Cash $\frac{150}{2,275} \times 1,500 = 99$

7% loan stock $\frac{250}{2,275} \times 1,500 = 165$

Ordinary shares $\frac{1,875}{2,275} \times 1,500 = 1,236$

ii) Indexation is limited as the disposal took place after the 30th November 1993.

iii) See 11 below for treatment of 'small' disposals. In this case $\frac{150}{2,275} = 6.5\%$.

Example

Using the data in the previous example A sells all his 500 ordinary shares in Z plc for £10,000 on the 1st December 1997. *Compute the chargeable gains.* Assume indexation of 2%.

Solution

CGT computation 1997/98

	£	£
Proceeds of sale 500 shares in Z plc		10,000
Less cost of acquisition (as above)	1,236	
Indexation allowance: 2%	25	1,261
Chargeable gain before exemption		8,739

Small capital distributions Section 122

11. Where a person receives cash by way of a capital distribution, eg on a takeover bid, in the course of a liquidation, or by the sale of any rights, then there is a part disposal for capital gains tax purposes. However, if the cash received is small relative to the value of the shares, then it may be deducted from the cost of acquisition. Small here is taken to be not exceeding 5% of the value of the shares, before the sale of rights and in other cases after the distribution is made.

Example

T acquired 5,000 ordinary shares in A Ltd at a cost of £1,500 on 8.2.1978. On the 12th June 1997 the company made a rights issue of 1 for 10 at a price of 25p. T sold his rights for 60p each on the 1st August 1997 when the market value of the 5,000 ordinary shares was £7,000. *Compute the allowed cost carried forward, and any CGT liability for 1997/98* MV at 31.3.82 was 75p per share.

Solution

T. CGT computation 1997/98

	£
Proceeds of sale of rights. 500 × 60p	300

As this is less than 5% of the market value of the shares of £7,000, the cost of acquisition can be reduced for any future disposal:

1982 holding

	£
5,000 × 75p of 5,000 ordinary shares	3,750
Less sale of rights	300
Allowed value carried forward (unindexed)	3,450

Note

i) *As there is no part disposal there is no CGT liability for 1997/98.*

ii) *5% of MV of £7,000 = £350.*

Example

A holds 100,000 ordinary shares in Beta plc which he bought in 1987 for £5,000. In May 1997 there was a rights offer of 1 for 10 which A did not take up. The rights were sold for £2,000, nil paid when the ex rights price of the shares was £12,000.

Compute the chargeable gain for 1997/98.

Assume indexation of 50%.

Solution

A CGT Computation 1997/98

		£
Proceeds of sale of rights		2,000
Allowable cost		
$5,000 \times \dfrac{2000}{2000 + 12000}$	714	
I.A. 50% × 714	357	1,071
Chargeable gain		929

Note: *5% × ex rights price £12,000 = £600 which is less than the proceeds of sale from the rights.*

Quoted securities held on 6th April 1965 – no election for pooling

12. If no general election for re-basing is made then the undermentioned rules apply:

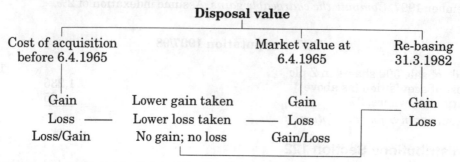

Notes

i) The comparison is made before indexation.

ii) If the re-basing shows a loss and the old rules show a profit then the result is a no gain / no loss.

iii) If the re-basing shows a gain and the old rules show a gain then the smaller gain is taken. The smaller loss is taken where both show a loss.

iv) If the old rules show a no gain no loss situation then re-basing does not apply.

Example

B had the following transactions in the quoted shares of K plc.

				£
5.3.1964	purchased	1,000 ordinary shares	cost	1,500
3.2.1980	purchased	1,000 ordinary shares	cost	2,500
31.3.1998	sold	2,000 ordinary shares	proceeds	20,000

The market values were 6.4.1965 £2.00 per share, 31.3.1982 £3.50 per share.

Assume RPI at 31.3.1998 at 155.0. No election has been made for general re-basing or under Schedule 2 TCGA 1992.

Solution

CGT Computation 1997/98 – shares held 6.4.1965

	Cost of Acquisition £	MV 6.4.1965 £
31.3.98 Proceeds of sale 1,000 × £10.0	10,000	10,000
Allowable cost		
MV 6.4.1965	–	2,000
Cost	1,500	–
Unindexed gain	8,500	8,000

IA $\dfrac{155.0 - 79.44}{79.44} = 0.951$

$0.951 \times (1,000 \times 3.50)$

	3,329
	4,671

Note the lower gain comparison is made before indexation and in this case is the MV as at 6.4.1965.

March 1982 Re-basing	£	£
31.3.1998 Proceeds of sale 1,000 shares		10,000
Cost of acquisition:		
1,000 shares MV 31.3.1982	3,500	
IA 3,500 × 0.951	3,329	6,829
Gain		3,171

Note

As there is a smaller gain with re-basing this will be taken for 1997/98 @ £3,171.

CGT computation 1997/98– shares held 31.3.82

			Re-basing £		Pre-FA 88 rules £
Proceeds of sale			10,000		10,000
Cost	1,000 @ 2.50			2,500	
MV	1,000 @ 3.50	3,500			
IA	3,500 × 0.951	3,329	6,829	3,329	5,829
Loss/gain			3,171		4,171

Note

As there is a smaller gain under re-basing this will be taken for 1997/98 @ £3,171.

Quoted securities held on 6th April 1965 – *election for pooling*

13. Under Schedule 2 TCGA 1992 a taxpayer can elect to have the original purchase price of the shares or securities ignored. Instead the market value at 6th April 1965 is substituted and pooled with all subsequent purchases, up to 5th April 1982. At that date, as noted earlier, the pool is frozen.

   a) A separate election must be made for this treatment for each class of holding in a company eg ordinary shares, preference shares, loan capital.

   b) The election is irrevocable and applies to all disposals. Originally the election had to be made within two years of the end of the year of assessment in which the first disposal takes place after 19th March 1968. Under Section 109 TGCA 1992, a person can now elect to pool quoted securities held at 6th April 1965 when they would be treated either as an accretion to an existing 1982 holding or constitute a new 1982 holding. The time limit for making an election is two years after the end of the year in which the first disposal of securities occurs after 5th April 1985 (31st March for companies).

   c) Separate elections are required from husband and wife.

   d) The election applies to companies as well as other persons.

   e) The pool is effectively frozen at 6th April 1982 and treated as a separate asset. Subsequent purchases must be treated according to the rules outlined earlier for new holdings.

Example

A had the following transactions in the quoted shares X plc.

7.6.1961	purchased	600 ordinary shares	cost	900
23.3.1964	purchased	400 ordinary shares	cost	850
30.6.1975	purchased	1,000 ordinary shares	cost	2,500
21.4.1997	sold	500 ordinary shares	proceeds	6,000

The market values were 31.3.1982 £3.50 per share, 6.4.1965 £1.85 per share. An election under Schedule 2 TCGA 1992 has been made but no general election for re-basing.

Compute the chargeable gain for 1997/98. Assume indexing of 95%.

Solution

CGT Computation 1997/98

				1982 Holding £
6.4.1965	1,000	shares at MV of £1.85		1,850
30.6.1975	1,000	shares at cost		2,500
	2,000			4,350
				6,000
Proceeds of sale (500 shares)				
MV at 31.3.1982 500 × £3.50			1,750	
IA 95% × 1,750			1,663	3413
Chargeable gain				2,587

Notes

i) *As the market value at 31st March 1982 of £3.50 is greater than the 'cost' of £2.175 re-basing will give a smaller gain. (4,350 ÷ 2,000 = 2.175)*

ii) *The shares acquired before 6th April 1965 form part of the 1982 Holding by reason of the election for pooling under Schedule 2 TCGA 1992.*

Qualifying corporate bonds

14. The disposal of a qualifying corporate bond is exempt from capital gains tax.

A qualifying corporate bond is a marketable security denominated in sterling such as a debenture on unsecured loan stock which:

i) is issued by a company (or other body). For disposals prior to 14th March 1989 it was necessary that they were listed on the Stock Exchange or dealt in on the Unlisted Securities Market.

ii) is a normal commercial loan. In general this is a loan without any conversion rights, which bears a commercial rate of interest.

Inter-company loans between members of the group (ie parent companies and 75% subsidiaries) cannot be qualifying bonds.

Where qualifying corporate bonds are received by way of capital reorganisation (eg on a takeover bid) in exchange for shares then the CGT position is as follows.

i) The gain on the shares exchanged is frozen at the date of the reorganisation with indexation up to that date.

ii) When the qualifying corporate bonds are sold or redeemed the deferred CGT on the shares becomes payable.

Unquoted shares and securities

15. An election under Schedule 2, noted above, is not available in respect of unquoted shares or securities held at 6th April 1965. For those assets the computation of any chargeable gain or allowable loss is made by reference to:

a) the time apportionment method, or

b) the market value as at 6th April 1965, or

c) the market value as at 31st March 1982.

• Student self-testing question

T has the following transactions in the 10p ordinary shares of W plc.

					£
11.10.1977	purchased	500	shares cost		600
10.11.1980	purchased	1,000	shares cost		800
20.5.1983	purchased	500	shares cost		750
25.10.1983	purchased	500	shares cost		1,000
30.3.1998	sold	1,700	shares proceeds		10,000

The market value at 31st March 1982 was 165p per share. RPI March 1998 say 155.0.

Compute the CGT liability for 1997/98.

Solution

T. CGT computation 1997/98

Calculation of cost of 1,700 shares sold 30.3.1998

New holding	Retail Price Index £	Nominal Value £	Qualifying Expenditure £	Indexed Pool £	Total Cost £
20.5.1983 Purchase	84.64	500	750	750	
30.3.1998 Indexation allowance: 155.0					
$\dfrac{155.0 - 84.64}{84.64} = 0.831 \times 750$				623	
		500	750	1,373	
25 10.1983 Purchase	86.36	500	1,000	1,000	
30.3.1998 Indexation allowance: 155.0					
$\dfrac{155.0 - 86.36}{86.36} = 0.795 \times 1,000$				795	
		1,000	1,750	3,168	
30.3.1998 Sale		1,000	1,750	3,168	3,168
Pool carried forward		–	–	–	

1982 Pool	Nominal Value £	Cost £	Market Value 31.3.82 £
11.10.1978 Purchase	500	600	825
10.11.1980 Purchase	1,000	800	1,650
	1,500	1,400	2,475
30.3.1998 Sale	700		

$MV \times \dfrac{700}{1,500} \times 2,475$ 1,155

30.3.98   Indexation allowance:

$\dfrac{155.0 - 79.44}{79.44} = 0.951 \times 1,155$ 1,098   2,253

                                                              5,421

CGT Computation 1997/98

New Holding   Proceeds of sale $\dfrac{1,000}{1,700} \times 10,000$ 5,882

                 Pool cost   3,168   2,714

1982 Holding   Proceeds of sale $\dfrac{700}{1,700} \times 10,000$ 4,118

                 Pool cost   2,253   1,865

Chargeable gain   4,579

Note

In respect of the 1982 Holding it would not be beneficial to use the old rules of computation rather than re-basing as this would give a higher gain, the market value at 31.3.1982 being greater than the original cost.

• Questions without answers

1. F acquired 10,000 ordinary shares in T plc on 12th May 1980 for £1,500. On 15th December 1983, T plc made a rights issue of 1 for 5 at a price of 130p. F took up the rights and then sold half of his total holding on 10th May 1997 for £12,000.

   The market value of the shares at 31st March 1982 was £1,300. *Compute the CGT liability of F for 1997/98. Assume RPI May 1997 was 152.0.*

2. T has the following transaction in the 10p ordinary shares of B plc, a quoted company.

					£
4.5.80	purchased	5,000	@	80p	4,000
4.12.81	purchased	300	@	75p	225
16.5.82	purchased	1,000	@	104p	1,040
30.4.83	purchased	3,000	@	125p	3,750
5.9.85	purchased	2,000	@	150p	3,000
31.3.98	sold	9,000	@	180p	16,200

   The market value as at 31st March 1982 was £1.00.

   Assume the RPI to be 155.0 at March 1998. *Compute CGT liability for 1997/98.*

3. Adrienne sold 2,000 ordinary shares in the Paramount Printing Company plc, a quoted company, on 4th August 1997 for £18,000. She had bought ordinary shares in the company on the following dates:

	No of shares	Cost £
12th May 1959	1,500	4,000
1st May 1987	1,500	5,000

   The value of each of these shares on 31st March 1982 was £4 and on 6th April 1965 £7.

   No election has been made under Schedule 5, para. 4, Capital Gains Tax Act prior to 6th April 1965 to be treated as acquired on 6th April 1965 at their market value on that day. Neither has any election been made under s.96(5), Finance Act 1988 to have all pre-March 1982 acquisitions re-based to March 1982. Assume RPI August 1997 was 153.0.

   Calculate, before annual exemption, the capital gain assessable on Adrienne for 1997/98.

39 Taxable persons

Introduction

1. This chapter is concerned with the persons who are responsible for chargeable gains tax liabilities. It states the CGT position of individuals, husband and wife and personal representatives, with examples showing the effects of the unification of the income tax rates and capital gains. The CGT aspect of other persons is outlined.

Individuals

2. An individual is liable to capital gains tax if he or she is resident, or ordinarily resident in the UK in an income tax year, wherever he or she may be domiciled. If domiciled outside the UK, then any capital gains tax arising from the disposal of foreign assets is only chargeable to the extent that the sums are remitted to the UK. For this purpose the terms residence, ordinary residence and domicile, have the same meaning as for income tax. *See Chapter 8.*

Rates   1997/98   –   First £6,500 (£6,300 – 1996/97) of net gains in the income tax year is exempt. The balance is taxed at the taxpayers marginal rate of income ie 20% – 25% – 40%.

The following points should be noted.

a) Net gains are added to an individual's taxable income ie after all charges on income and personal allowances.

b) Where a taxpayer has no taxable income any unused allowances and reliefs cannot be deducted from the chargeable gains.

c) Depending upon the level of an individual's taxable income chargeable gains above the exemption of £6,500 will be chargeable at rates equivalent to the lower rate, the basic rate, the higher rate or partly at one and partly at another.

d) Husband and wife are treated separately.

e) For the purpose of determining the rate of income tax to apply to capital gains (after exemption) the order in which income and capital gains are taken is as follows:

   i)   non-dividend income

   ii) dividend income

   iii) life assurance policy gains/termination payments

   iv) capital gains.

> **Example**

T, who is single, has Schedule E income for 1997/98 of £18,000 and pays a covenant to Oxfam of £1,540 (net). Chargeable gains for 1997/98 have been agreed at £7,500.

Compute the CGT liability.

Solution

CGT computation 1997/98

	£
Schedule E	18,000
Covenant (gross) 1540 ÷ 0.77	2,000
	16,000
Personal allowance	4,045
Taxable income	11,955
Chargeable gain	7,500
Less Annual exemption	6,500
Taxable Gain	1,000
CG tax payable 1,000 @ 23% =	230

Note

The £4,100 level @ 20% has been used and (11,955 – 4,100) £7,855 of the basic rate band of £22,000. CGT is therefore payable @ the 23% rate.

Example

M who is single has Schedule D Case I income for 1997/98 of £20,045 and bank deposit interest of £800 (net). Chargeable gains for 1997/98 have been agreed at £18,000.

Compute the CGT liability.

Solution

M. CGT computation 1997/98

	£
Schedule D Case I	20,045
Bank interest (gross) $800 \times \dfrac{100}{80}$	1,000
	21,045
Less Personal allowance	4,045
Taxable income	17,000
Chargeable gain	18,000
Less Annual exemption	6,500
Taxable gain	11,500
CGT payable	
(26,100 – 17,000) = 9,100 @ 23%	2,093
2,400 @ 40%	960
11,500	3,053

Note

As the net gain after the exemption has increased the taxable income for CGT purposes above the lower level and basic rate band of £26,100, the balance is chargeable at the higher rate of 40%.

Losses

3. Losses of the current year must be set against any gains of the same year.

    Losses cannot be carried back except on death.

    Losses brought forward are only utilised to the extent that they are used to reduce any net gains to the £6,500 level.

    Realised losses brought forward from 1991/92 and earlier years are available for set-off against gains computed under the re-basing method.

    The restriction of the indexation allowance to increase or create a loss for disposals after 30th November 1993 does not affect losses brought forward before that date.

    As from 1996/97, relief is given first for losses arising in or after 1996/97. Only after these have been used up is relief given for pre-1996/9 losses.

Example

B makes a chargeable gain of £12,000 in 1997/98 and a capital loss excluding indexation in the same period of £2,500. B's taxable income for 1997/98 is £1,700 after all allowances.

Compute the CGT liability for 1997/98.

Solution

B. CGT computation 1997/98

	£	£
Chargeable gain	12,000	
Less Capital loss	2,500	9,500
Less exempt amount		6,500
Taxable gain		3,000
CGT payable 4,100 – 1,700 = 2,400 @ 20%		480
600 @ 23%		138
3,000		618

Notes

i) *In this case part of the gain has been taxed at the lower rate of 20% and the balance at the 23% rate.*

ii) *Indexation cannot be used to increase the capital loss of £2,500.*

Husband and wife

4. The following points should be noted.
   a) Husband and wife are treated as separate individuals, each with an exemption allowance of £6,500 for 1997/98.
   b) Assessments to CGT are made individually on husband and wife.
   c) The transfer of chargeable assets between husband and wife in any year of assessment does not give rise to any CGT charge where they are living together in the year of assessment.
   d) The position with regard to losses is as follows.
      i) Losses of one spouse cannot be set against the gains of the other.
      ii) Losses brought forward at 6th April 1990 can only be used by the spouse to whom they belong.
   e) Where assets are jointly owned then in the absence of a declaration of beneficial interest, the 50–50 rule applies and each is treated as owning 50% of the assets.
   f) Husband and wife are 'connected persons', so the market value rule applies.
   g) Where a married couple live together they can have only one residence which can qualify as their principal private residence.
   h) Where a spouse disposes of an asset which she acquired from her husband before 30th November 1993, the base cost to the spouse includes any indexation up to the date of the inter-spouse transfer.

Example

Mr and Mrs J have the following data relating to the year ended 5th April 1998:

	Mr J £	Mrs J £
Capital gains	13,500	9,000
Capital losses	–	1,500
Taxable income	20,000	16,500

Compute the CGT liabilities for 1997/98.

Solution

CGT computation 1997/98

	Mr J £	Mrs J £
Capital gains	13,500	9,000
Less losses	–	1,500
	13,500	7,500
Less exempt amount	6,500	6,500
Chargeable gain	7,000	1,000
CGT payable: 26,100 – 20,000 = 6,100 @ 23% / 1,000 @ 23%	1,403	230
900 @ 40% / –	360	–
7,000	1,763	230

Notes

i) *Assessments will be raised on Mr and Mrs J individually.*
ii) *It is not possible to transfer any of the loss of £1,500 to Mr J, to save him paying tax at the 40% rate.*

Trading losses set against chargeable gains

5. Where a trading loss is incurred in the year then to the extent that it has not been fully relieved under Section 380 TA 1988 a claim for relief against any chargeable gain can be made. The amount to be claimed cannot exceed the chargeable gain for the year, before deducting the exemption amount of £6,500.

Example

N, who is single, has the following data relating to the year 1997/98:

	£
Schedule D Case I 1997/98 (year to 31.3.1998)	15,000
Chargeable gains (before exemption)	8,500

In the year to 31st March 1999 N has a trading loss of £16,000, and no other income.

Compute the income tax liability and CGT liability for 1997/98.

Solution

N Income tax computation 1997/98

	£
Schedule D Case I	15,000
Less Section 380 Loss relief	15,000
Assessment	–

CGT computation 1997/98

	£
Chargeable gain	8,500
Less trading loss	1,000
	7,500
Less annual exemption	6,500
	1,000
CGT payable £1000 @ 20% =	200

Notes

i) N's personal allowance of £4,045 would be wasted.

ii) The trading loss of £16,000 has been dealt with as follows:

	£
Section 380 1997/98	15,000
Capital gain 1997/98	1,000

The trading loss for the year ended 31st March 1999 can be used in either 1998/99 or 1997/98.

iii) The first £4,100 tax band has not been used so CGT is payable at that rate.

Personal representatives

6. The executor or administrator of a deceased person's estate is deemed to have acquired all the chargeable assets at the market value at the date of death, but there is no disposal. Legatees are also deemed to have acquired assets passing to them, at their market value at the date of death, so that any transfer to a legatee is not a chargeable disposal.

Rates   The first £6,500 of net gains is exempt in the year of assessment in which the death occurs and the subsequent two years of assessment.

Balance within the time scale noted above, at 23%. There after all at 23% with no exemption.

Losses   Losses of the personal representative cannot be set against previous gains of the deceased.

Losses of the deceased in the year of his or her death can be carried back against the previous three years of assessment.

Within the time scale of the year of death and the next two years, losses need only be utilised to the extent that they reduce the net gains to the exempt amount of £6,500.

Qualifying corporate bonds are exempt in the hands of the personal representative, and a legatee, irrespective of the time they or the deceased have held them.

Example

K is appointed executor to the estate of TP deceased, who died on the 1st January 1996. In order to provide cash funds to pay estate debts he disposed of the following assets:

31.3.1996	Sold shares in X Ltd. for £9,000.	Value at death £7,000.
28.10.1996	Sold shares in T Ltd. for £15,000.	Value at death £10,000.
28.10.1996	Sold shares in Q Ltd. for £10,000.	Value at death £6,000.

Compute the CGT liabilities arising. RPI Jan 1996 150.0, Mar 1996 151.0, Oct 1996 155.0.

Solution

Computation 1995/96

	£	£	£
31.3.96 Disposal of shares in X Ltd.			9,000
Less Market value at 1.1.1996	7,000		
indexation $\frac{151.0 - 150.0}{150.0} = 0.007 \times 7,000$	49		7,049
			1,951
Less exempt amount			1,951
Chargeable gain			–

Computation 1996/97

	£	£	£
28.10.1996 Disposal of shares in T Ltd.		15,000	
Less Market value at 1.1.1996	10,000		
indexation $\frac{155.0 - 150.0}{150.0} = 0.033 \times 10,000$	330	10,330	4,670
28.10.1996 Disposal of shares in Q Ltd.		10,000	
Less Market value at 1.1.1996	6,000		
indexation $0.033 \times 6,000$	198	6,198	3,802
			8,472
Less exemption			6,300
Chargeable gain			2,172
CGT payable 2,172 @ 24%			521

Trustees

7. In general there are two classes of UK trustees:

    a) Nominee or bare trustees who look after property on behalf of some other person who has absolute title to the property, or who would have such a title but for some disability or is an infant.

        In these cases the acts of a trustee are deemed to be those of the person on whose behalf the trustee acts, and accordingly the rates, exemptions and rules applicable to an individual apply.

    b) Other trustees are considered to be a single continuing body of persons quite distinct from the persons beneficially interested in the trust property. The taxable position of this class of trustee is as follows.

        #### Exemptions – 1997/98

Trusts for mentally disabled and those receiving attendance allowance	First £6,500 of net gains in any year exempt
Other trusts	First £3,250 of net gains in any year exempt. Amount split between all trusts with same settlor.

        #### Rates – 1997/98

Accumulation and discretionary trusts	Basic rate of income tax + additional rate. ie 24% + 10% = 34%.
Other trusts	Basic rate of income tax ie 23%.

    The 20% band rate does not apply to trusts.

    Losses from trusts may be carried forward and set against future gains, and they are only used to the extent that they reduce any net gains to the appropriate exemption level, as for individuals.

    Other occasions on which a capital gains tax liability may arise in connection with settled property are referred to in Chapter 40.

Foreign trusts

8. A trust is regarded as being resident abroad if a majority of the trustees are resident abroad, and the general administration of the trust is carried on overseas. In general, a foreign trust is exempt from capital gains tax wherever the disposal of chargeable assets takes place. However, where the trust was created by a settlor who is or (at the time of the creation of the trust) was domiciled and

resident, or ordinarily resident in the UK, then the beneficiaries can be assessed to capital gains tax, if they receive capital payments from the trust.

Companies

9. Companies are not liable to capital gains tax as such, but they are liable to corporation tax on the disposal of any chargeable assets. This aspect of the subject is covered in Chapter 25.

Partners

10. A partner is assessed as an individual in respect of his or her share of any chargeable gains accruing from the disposal of partnership assets. Accordingly any personal chargeable gains can be set against his or her share of any partnership capital losses, and vice versa.

• Student self-testing question

R bought a painting for £2,500 in June 1973 which he sold for £45,000 on the 8th May 1997. Incidental costs of acquisition amounted to £200, costs of disposal £2,200.

R's wife has capital losses of £3,500 for 1997/98. The painting had a market value of £15,000 on 31st March 1982. R's taxable income for 1997/98 is £28,000, ie after all allowances and reliefs.

Compute the 1997/98 CGT liability. Assume indexation of 95%.

Solution

CGT computation 1997/98

	£	£
Proceeds of sale 8.5.1997		45,000
Less MV 31.3.82	15,000	
Cost of disposal	2,200	17,200
Unindexed gain		27,800
Indexation allowance:		
95% × 15,000		14,250
		13,550
Less Exempt amount		6,500
CGT assessment		7,050
CGT payable @ 40% × 7,050		2,820

Note The losses of Mrs R can only be used against her own future gains.

• Questions without answers

1. F has chargeable gains of £7,500 for the year 1997/98, and capital losses of £500. His wife sells a piece of land for £10,000 on 10th May 1997 being part of a larger plot purchased in 1975 for £3,000. The remaining part had a value of £30,000 on 10th May 1997. F's taxable income for 1997/98 is £21,300 and his wife's £1,000.

    The market value of the land at 31st March 1982 was £2,500. Assume indexation of 95%.

    Compute the CGT liability for 1997/98 of Mr and Mrs F.

2. A purchased a painting in 1970 for £2,000 which he sells for £50,000 in January 1998. The painting was valued at £20,000 in 1982.

    A's wife owned the lease of a flat which she acquired for £15,000 on the 1st January 1982. The lease then had 40 years to run. On the 1st January 1998 she sells the flat for £35,000, incurring disposal costs of £200.

    The market value as at 31st March 1982 was £16,000.

    Assume the RPI at January 1997 to be 155.0.

    A's taxable income for 1997/98 is £20,000 and his wife's is £12,000.

    Compute the CGT liability of A and his wife for 1997/98.

40 Chargeable occasions

Introduction

1. A chargeable gain or loss arises on the occasion of a disposal of a chargeable asset. For this purpose a disposal takes place in the following circumstances, each of which is examined in this chapter:

    a) on a sale by contract

    b) on the compulsory acquisition of assets

    c) where capital sums are derived from assets destroyed or damaged, eg from insurance claims

    d) where assets have negligible value

    e) on the part disposal of an asset

    f) by value shifting

    g) on a death

    h) where a gift is made

    i) in connection with settled property.

Disposal by contract

2. Where an asset is disposed of by way of a contract then the date of the disposal is the time the contract is made and not, if different, the time when the asset is conveyed or transferred. For shares and securities the date of the contract note is the disposal date, and for land and buildings and house property the date of the contract to sell is the relevant date, and not the date of completion.

Compulsory acquisition

3. Where there is a compulsory acquisition of an interest in land, then the date of the disposal is the date when the amount of compensation is formally agreed.

Capital sums derived from assets Section 22

4. Compensation or insurance monies received in respect of an asset, amounts to a disposal by the owner. Thus if A has property which is damaged or destroyed by fire, then any insurance money received constitutes a disposal for CGT purposes. However, this is varied to some extent where the capital sum is used for the following purposes:

    a) to restore a non-wasting asset or

    b) to replace a non-wasting asset lost or destroyed.

Restoration of a non-wasting asset Section 23

5. If a capital sum is received in respect of a non-wasting asset, which is not lost or destroyed, the taxpayer can claim to have the sum deducted from the cost of acquisition, rather than treated as a part disposal. Such a claim can only be made if:

    a) the capital sum is used wholly for restoration, or the amount not restored is small relative to the capital sum or

    b) the capital sum is small relative to the value of the asset.

    Small is normally taken to be 5% or less.

> **Example**

T purchased a picture for £10,000 in June 1970, which was damaged by fire in May 1997. Insurance proceeds of £1,000 were received in December 1997, the whole amount being spent on restoring the picture. T claims to have the sum of £1,000 not treated as a disposal. The value of the painting after the fire was estimated at £8,000. Market value at 31.3.1982 was £35,000.

Show the computation of the allowable expenditure carried forward.

Solution

Computation 1997/98

	£
Market value 31.3.82	35,000
Less insurance sum	1,000
	34,000
Add expenditure on restoration	1,000
Allowable expenditure c/f	35,000

Note

From a capital gains tax point of view, T is in exactly the same position as he was before the picture was damaged.

Example

S purchased a piece of antique furniture for £10,000 in May 1977. The item was damaged by water in January 1997 for which £1,500 was received by way of insurance in July 1997. The amount spent on restoration was (a) £1,500 (b) £1,430. The market value at 31.3.1982 was £12,000. *Compute the allowable costs in each case.*

Solution

a) As the whole sum was spent on restoration there is no disposal if S so claims, and no overall adjustment to the cost of the antique.

b) In this case the whole sum was not spent, but the unused amount of £70 is less than 5% of the capital sum, ie £75. The £70 not spent on restoration need not be treated as a disposal, but may be deducted from the allowed cost.

Computation 1997/98

	£	£
MV of antique 31.3.1982		12,000
Less insurance claim:		
Spent on restoration	1,430	
Not spent	70	1,500
		10,500
Add expenditure on restoration		1,430
Allowable expenditure		11,930

Note

This is equivalent to the MV at 31.3.1982 less the amount not spent ie £12,000 – £70 = £11,930.

Example

V has a collection of rare books purchased in February 1991 for £70,000 which were damaged by fire in May 1996 when they were estimated to be worth £100,000. The value of the collection as damaged by the fire was £70,000. In July 1996 V received £30,000 insurance compensation and the collection was restored.

Compute the CGT effects of a) restoring and b) not restoring the book collection.

RPI Feb. 1991 130.9, July 1997, say, 155.0.

Solution

a) **Restoring**

CGT computation 1997/98

	£
Original cost of collection	70,000
Less insurance claim	30,000
	40,000
Add expenditure on restoration	30,000
Allowed expenditure c/f	70,000

As the whole sum has been spent on restoration there is no disposal if V so claims and no adjustment to the cost of acquisition.

b) **Not restoring**

CGT computation 1997/98

	£
Insurance proceeds	30,000
Apportioned cost (as above) $\dfrac{30,000}{30,000 + 70,000} \times 70,000$	21,000
Unindexed gain	9,000
Indexation allowance	
$\dfrac{155.0 - 130.9}{130.9} = 0.184 \times 21,000$	3,864
Chargeable gain	5,136

Replacement of non-wasting assets Section 23

6.   Where an asset is lost or destroyed and a capital sum is received by way of compensation, or under a policy of insurance, then if it is spent on a replacement asset within 12 months of the receipt of the sum (or such longer period as the Inspector of Taxes may allow), and the owner so claims, then:

a)   the consideration for the disposal of the lost or damaged asset is taken to be such that neither a gain or loss arises after indexation.

b)   the cost of the replacement asset is reduced by the excess of the capital sum over the total of the consideration used in (a) above, plus any residual or scrap value of the old asset.

> **Example**

Q purchased a picture for £3,000 in 1968 which was destroyed by fire in July 1997. Insurance of £20,000 was received in December 1997 and Q decided to purchase another picture using the full amount of the insurance money. The scrap value of the picture was £100.

Show the computations, with and without a claim under Section 23. Assume indexation of 95% and a market value of £8,000 at 31st March 1982.

Solution   CGT Computation 1997/98

		£	£
a)	**If no claim is made**		
	Capital sum received December 1997	20,000	
	Add residual value	100	20,100
	Less MV at 31.3.82	8,000	
	Indexation 95% × 8,000	7,600	15,600
	Chargeable gain		4,500
b)	**If a claim is made**		
	Deemed proceeds of sale December 1997		15,600
	MV at 31.3.1982 + indexation		15,600
	No gain or loss		–
	Replacement picture at cost		20,000
	Less capital sum	20,000	
	Less deemed proceeds	15,600	
		4,400	
	Add scrap value	100	4,500
	Allowable cost carried forward		15,500

Note

Rather than waste £4,500 of the exempt amount of £6,500 for 1997/98 Q should consider making a claim.

Where the whole sum is not spent on a replacement asset, then some relief is available providing that the amount not spent is less than the amount of the gain.

Assets whose value becomes negligible Section 24

7.   The occasion of the entire loss, destruction, or extinction of an asset (wasting or non-wasting) amounts to a disposal of that asset, whether or not any capital sum is received. Where the value of an asset has become negligible, and the inspector is satisfied that such is the case, then the owner

may make a claim to the effect that the asset has been sold and immediately required for a consideration equal to the negligible value. Thus if P owns a building which is destroyed by fire, and it was not insured, then he may claim to have made a disposal and reacquisition at the scrap value. An allowable loss for capital gains tax purposes would arise, assuming that the building was not an industrial building eligible for capital allowances.

The replacement of business assets Sections 152–158

8.   Where a 'business asset' is disposed of, including the occasion of the receipt of a capital sum, then special provisions apply if the assets are either wholly or partially replaced. This aspect which relates to assets used for the purposes of a trade is covered in Chapter 42.

Value shifting Sections 29–30

9.   Under these sections a disposal is deemed to occur where for example the value of a controlling interest in a company is 'watered down' in such a way that the value is passed into other shares or rights, without the occurrence of a disposal.

Hire purchase Section 27

10.   Where a person enters into a hire purchase or other transactions, whereby he or she enjoys the use of an asset for a period of time, at the end of which he or she may become the owner of the asset, then the acquisition and disposal is deemed to take place at the beginning of the period of use. If the transaction is ended before the property is transferred then 'suitable adjustments' are to be made in agreement with the Inspector of Taxes. See *Lyon* v *Pettigrew* March 1985 STI 107.

Part disposals Section 42

11.   In general any reference to a disposal also includes a part disposal, and where this occurs it is necessary to make some apportionment of the cost of acquisition. This is explained in Chapter 35.

Death Section 62

12.   On the death of a person there is no disposal of any chargeable assets for capital gains tax purposes. The personal representative is deemed to have acquired any assets at their market value at the date of death, and any legatee also acquires the assets at the same market value, the date of acquisition being the date of death.

   If a personal representative disposes of any assets other than to a legatee, eg in order to raise funds to pay any inheritance tax, then a chargeable occasion arises. However, in the year of death and in the two following years of assessment, the personal representative is entitled to the same annual exemption as an individual.

   Losses incurred by a personal representative cannot be set against any previous gains of the deceased. However, if the deceased had incurred any losses in the year of his or her death, then if they cannot be relieved in that year, then they can be carried back and set against gains in the previous three years.

Gifts

13.   A gift of a chargeable asset does amount to a disposal, and this aspect together with the special reliefs available is examined in Chapter 41.

Settled property

14.   Property held on trust for the benefit of others is known as settled property, and the creation, administration, and operation of such a trust gives rise to a number of capital gains tax occasions.

   a)   On the creation of a trust there is a disposal of property by the settlor and it is a chargeable occasion for him or her as an individual. The market value of the disposal is used here.

   b)   If the trustees dispose of assets, for example to pay any taxation, then this is a chargeable occasion. The exemptions and rates of tax applicable to trusts are noted in Chapter 39.

   c)   On the death of a life tenant the following is the position.
      i)   Where a person becomes absolutely entitled to any part of the property, as against the trustees eg a remainderman, there is a deemed disposal and reacquisition by the trustees

at market value at the date of death of the life tenant, who then hold the property as nominees for the beneficiary. No chargeable gain or loss arises on the deemed disposal.

ii) Where on the death of a life tenant the property continues to be held for the benefit of any continuing life tenants, there is a deemed disposal and reacquisition at market value but no chargeable gain or loss arises.

iii) Where the property in the settlement reverts to the settlor the settlor is deemed to have acquired the assets at a no gain or loss price, from the trustees.

The death of a person in receipt of an annuity and the termination of the annuity is regarded as the death of a life tenant.

d) In general, the interest of beneficiaries under trusts are not chargeable assets unless they were acquired by way of purchase. In the latter case a chargeable occasion arises when the beneficiary becomes absolutely entitled to the assets of the trust.

• Student self-testing question

J has a collection of rare prints which cost £3,000 in May 1983. They were damaged by water in November 1996 and J received £17,000 by way of insurance compensation in May 1997. He spent £15,000 on restoration. The value of the prints in a damaged state was £6,000. Assume indexation of 90%.

Compute any CGT liability arising and the amount of allowable expenditure carried forward.

Solution

CGT computation 1997/98

	£	£
Capital sum received May 1997		17,000
Less spent on restoration		15,000
Part disposal		2,000
Proportion of cost: $3,000 \times \dfrac{2,000}{2,000 + 6,000} =$	750	
Add indexation of 90% × 750	675	1,425
Chargeable gain		575
Allowable expenditure carried forward		
Cost of acquisition		3,000
Less part disposal cost		575
		2,425

Note

The indexation allowance can be applied to the allowable expenditure carried forward of £2,425, on a subsequent disposal subject to the restriction concerning losses.

• Question without answer

Z had a painting which was badly damaged by fire in January 1997. The picture was originally purchased for £1,000 in July 1972. In May 1997 Z received insurance compensation of £20,000 which he decides to spend on a new painting. The scrap value of the damaged painting was £50.

Show the CGT position on the basis that

a) *Z makes a claim under Section 23 TCGA 1992*

b) *Z makes no such claim.*

Assume indexation of 95% and a market value of the painting at 31st March 1982 of £10,000.

41 Gifts – holdover relief

Introduction

1. This chapter is concerned with capital gains tax arising from gifts of chargeable assets. It begins with a list of exempt gifts and then examines the general holdover relief available for gifts made after 13th March 1989. The effect of retirement relief on a gift and the gift of business assets to a company form the remainder of the chapter.

2. A gift or a bargain not made at arm's length of a chargeable asset amounts to a disposal for capital gains tax purposes and is deemed to be made for a consideration equal to its market value. Thus in the case of *Turner* v *Follett* 1973, 48 TC 614, a gift of shares to the taxpayer's children was held to be a disposal at their market value.

   The indexation allowance applies to gifts, subject to the normal rules.

Exemptions

3. The following gifts do not give rise to any chargeable gain or loss.

   a) A gift to a charity or other approved institution such as the National Gallery, or the British Museum. Such a transfer is deemed to take place on a no gain or loss basis.

   b) Gifts of works of art, manuscripts, historic buildings, scenic land etc, if the conditions required for inheritance tax exemption are satisfied.

   c) A gift of a chattel with a market value of less than £6,000. *See Chapter 37.*

   d) A gift of an exempt asset such as a private motor car, or the principal private residence of the taxpayer, unless otherwise taxable.

   e) Gifts between husband and wife.

   f) Transfers between members of a group of companies. *See Chapter 42.*

Gifts of business assets made after 13th March 1989 – Section 165

4. The following are the main provisions relating to disposals made on or after 14th March 1989.

   a) Holdover relief is available to an individual who makes a transfer at less than market price to a person of:

      i) business assets used for the purposes of a trade, profession or vocation carried on by:
         1. the transferor, or
         2. his or her personal company
         3. a member of a trading group of which the holding company is his or her personal company.

      ii) Shares or securities of a trading company, or of the holding company of a trading company where:
         1. the shares are neither quoted nor dealt in on the AIM/USM or,
         2. the trading company or the holding company is the transferor's personal company.

      iii) agricultural property qualifying for the 100% IHT relief.

   b) A personal company is one in which the individual is entitled to exercise 5% or more of the voting rights.

   c) The relief must be claimed jointly by the transferee and the transferor, within six years of the date of transfer.

   d) The relief is only available in respect of chargeable business assets such as goodwill, factory premises or plant. Investments, stocks, debtors, cash etc are 'excepted' or non-business assets.

   e) Holdover relief is not available:

      i) if the donee is non-resident or is exempt from CGT by reason of a Double Tax Treaty.

      ii) if the recipient is a company controlled by non-residents who are connected with the donor.

   f) Special provisions apply to the capital gains tax liability where there has been a deferral of tax on a transaction between 31st March 1982 and 6th April 1988. This applies to held over gains from gifts and to rollover relief for the replacement of business assets. 50% of the held over gain is excluded from the computation.

g) If the transferor is entitled to any retirement relief then this is given before computing the held over gain, so that no relief is available where the gain is wholly relieved by retirement relief.

Example

B purchased the goodwill and freehold property of a retail business for £12,000 in 1970, which he gave to his son in May 1997 when it was worth £185,000.

The market value of the business at 31st March 1982 was £90,000. Assume indexation of 95%.

Compute the chargeable gain that can be held over.

Solution

Computation 1997/98

	£	£
Disposal at market price		185,000
Less MV at 31.3.82	90,000	
Indexation allowance 95% × 90,000	85,500	175,500
Chargeable gain held over		9,500

Acquisition by B's son

	£
Market value of assets transferred	185,000
Less held over gain	9,500
Deemed cost	175,500

Example

W purchased his business premises in October 1973 for £10,000, which he gave to his son in May 1983 when it was worth £50,000. The election for hold over relief was given. In May 1997 W's son sold the premises for £200,000.

The March 1982 value was £40,000.

Compute the chargeable gain before exemption for 1997/98.

RPI May 1997 say 155.0

Solution

CGT 1983/84

	£	£
Value of premises		50,000
Cost of acquisition	10,000	
IA $\dfrac{84.64 - 79.44}{79.44}$		
$0.065 \times 40,000$	2,600	12,600
		37,400
Held over gain		37,400
Chargeable gain		NIL

CGT 1997/98

	£	£
Proceeds of sale		200,000
Base cost $50,000 - \dfrac{37,400}{2} =$	31,300	
IA $\dfrac{155.0 - 84.64}{84.64}$		
$0.831 \times 31,300$	26,010	57,310
Chargeable gain		142,690

Notes

i) *Indexation allowance for 1983/84 is based on 1982 M value of £40,000.*

ii) *50% of the held over gain is deductible as the deferral took place in between 31st March 1982 and 5th April 1988.*

Gift of shares in personal company

5. If the transfer by an individual is of shares in his or her personal company then the held over gain is restricted to the amount of:

$$\text{Chargeable gain} \times \frac{\text{Chargeable business assets of the company}}{\text{Chargeable assets of the company}}$$

> **Example**

T acquired all the shares of X Ltd, a trading company, for £9,000 in 1984, and transferred them by way of a gift to Z in May 1997 when they were worth £140,000. At the date of the gift the company's assets were valued as follows:

	£
Freehold land and buildings	30,000
Goodwill	30,000
Plant and machinery - all items > £6,000	25,000
Investment in quoted company	60,000
Stocks, debtors and cash	18,750

Assume indexation of 85%.

Solution

Computation 1997/98

	£	£
Proceeds of sale of shares		140,000
Less cost of acquisition	9,000	
Indexation 85% × 9,000	7,650	16,650
Chargeable gain		123,350
Held over gain: $\frac{85,000}{85,000 + 60,000} \times 123,350$		72,309
Assessable gain		51,041

Notes

i) *The deemed cost to Z is £140,000 – 72,309 ie £67,691*

ii) *Plant and machinery is assumed to have made no gain on disposal. Plant and machinery items valued at less than £6,000 per item are exempt and not chargeable business assets.*

iii) *Stock, debtors and cash are exempt from capital gains tax.*

iv) *A business asset is an asset used for the purpose of trade.*

v) *The investment is not a chargeable business asset.*

vi) *Chargeable assets are any assets on the disposal of which any gain would be a chargeable gain, and excludes, therefore, motor cars and items of moveable plant purchased and sold for £6,000 or less.*

Chargeable assets
(open market value at date of disposal)

	Business £	Non-Business £
Freehold land	30,000	
Goodwill	30,000	
Investment		60,000
Plant and Machinery	25,000	
	85,000	60,000

Gifts of non-business assets, works of art etc. Section 258

6. Holdover relief is also available to gifts, where both the transferor and the transferee are individuals or a trusts for:

i) gifts which are immediately chargeable transfers for IHT purposes ie gifts to discretionary trusts.

ii) gifts which are either exempt or conditionally exempt for IHT purposes eg gifts to political parties or gifts of heritage property, but not PETs.

Gift relief and retirement relief

7. Where a gift is made and retirement relief is made available in respect of any part of the chargeable gain arising on the disposal then the following rules apply.

    a) Retirement relief must be deducted from the indexed gain *before* considering any holdover relief.

    b) Holdover relief is only available in respect of the balance of any gain arising.

Example

Z gave his controlling shares in his family company to his son on 1st July 1997 when Z was 56. Z had been in business for the previous nine years. The chargeable gain after indexation has been agreed at £400,000.

Compute the amount of gain eligible for holdover relief.

Solution

Z. CGT computation 1997/98

		£
Chargeable gain		400,000
Less retirement relief:		
90% × 250,000 =	225,000	
50%(400,000 − 225,000) =	87,500	312,500
Amount of gain eligible for holdover relief		87,500

Note *The computation of retirement relief is covered in the next chapter.*

Payment of tax by instalments

8. a) Chargeable gains tax on gifts not eligible for full holdover relief may be paid by ten equal annual instalments where an election is made in writing. This only applies to the following assets:

    i) Land or any interest in land.

    ii) Shares or securities in a company which immediately before the disposal gave control to the person making the disposal.

    iii) Shares or securities of a company (not falling in (ii)) and not quoted on a recognised stock exchange nor dealt in on the USM AIM.

    b) Where the gift is to a connected person, tax and accrued interest become payable where the donee subsequently disposes of the gift for a valuable consideration.

    c) The first instalment is due on the normal due date. Instalments are not interest free unless the gifted property is agricultural land qualifying for IHT agricultural property relief.

• Student self-testing question

K purchased shares in 1973 which he gave to M in March 1984 when the market value was £25,000. Both K and M elected to hold over £5,000 of the computed gain. M sold the shares in May 1997 for £80,000. Assume an increase in RPI of 90%. *Show the CGT computations.*

Solution

Computation 1997/98

	£	£
Proceeds of sale (May 1997)		80,000
Market value (March 1984)	25,000	
Less 50% of gain held over – 50% × 5,000	2,500	22,500
Unindexed gain		57,500
IA 90% × 22,500		20,250
Chargeable gain		37,250

Note

As the gain takes place after 6th April 1988 and the asset was acquired before 31st March 1982 and was also subject to holdover relief in between 31st March 1982 and 5th April 1988, 50% of any held over gain is excluded from the computation.

• Question without answer

F purchased a controlling interest in N Ltd, a trading company, for £20,000 in 1971 which he gave to his son on his retirement in May 1997 when he was 70 years of age. The market value of the interest at the date of the gift was £500,000. A joint claim under Section 165 TCGA 1992 was made.

The estimated market value of the controlling interest at 31st March 1982 was £100,000. There were no non-business, chargeable assets. Ignore retirement relief.

Taking the indexation allowance at 95% compute the chargeable gain.

42 Business assets and businesses

Introduction

1. The disposal of a business or of any business, assets requires special consideration for chargeable gains tax purposes as there are valuable reliefs available to the owners. In this chapter the following topics will be examined:

    a) Replacement of business assets. Sections 152 to 158.

    b) Reinvestment relief for individuals.

    c) Transfer of a business on retirement. Schedule 6.

    d) Transfer of a business to a company. Section 162.

    e) Transfer of assets between group companies.

    f) Trading stock.

    g) Loans to traders.

    The holdover relief in respect of a gift of business assets is outlined in the chapter on gifts, *see Chapter 41*.

Replacement of business assets Sections 152–158

2. Relief under these provisions enables a taxpayer to 'roll over' any gain arising on the disposal of a 'business asset', by deducting it from the cost of a replacement. The main rules are:

    a) A business asset is one used for the purposes of a trade and falling within the undermentioned classes:

    > land and buildings occupied by the taxpayer; fixed plant and machinery; satellites, space stations, space craft; ships, aircraft and hovercraft; goodwill; milk and potato quotas; E.C. agricultural quotas.

    b) The assets disposed of must be used throughout the period of ownership, and the latter includes assets held by a 'personal company'.

    c) The new asset must be acquired within 12 months of the disposal, or within three years after, although the Inspector of Taxes has power to extend these limits.

    d) Where a trader re-invests in business assets to be used in a new trade then relief is available providing the interval between the two trades is not greater than three years.

    e) Partial relief is available where the whole of the proceeds of sale are not used in the replacement. In these circumstances the gain attracting an immediate charge to tax is the lower of:

    i) the chargeable gain, and

    ii) the uninvested proceeds.

    By concession the Inland Revenue regard proceeds net of disposal costs for this purpose.

    f) There are special provisions where the replacement asset is a depreciating asset. *See below.*

    g) The relief is also available to non-profit making organisations such as trade and professional associations.

    h) Where a person carrying on a trade uses the proceeds from the disposal of an 'old asset' on capital expenditure to enhance the value of other assets, such expenditure is treated for the purposes of these provisions as incurred in acquiring other assets provided:

    i) the other assets are used only for the purposes of the trade, or

    ii) on completion of the work on which the expenditure was incurred the assets are immediately taken into use and used only for the purposes of the trade.

    i) Where a 'new asset' is not, on acquisition, immediately taken into use for the purposes of a trade, it will nevertheless qualify for relief provided:

    i) the owner proposes to incur capital expenditure for the purpose of enhancing its value;

    ii) any work arising from such capital expenditure begins as soon as possible after acquisition, and is completed within a reasonable time;

    iii) on completion of the work the asset is taken into use for the purpose of the trade and for no other purpose; and

    iv)   the asset is not let or used for any non-trading purpose in the period between acquisition and the time it is taken into use for the purposes of the trade.

j)   Special provisions are contained in the FA 1988 to halve the rolled over tax liability where there has been a deferral of tax on a replacement of business assets between 31st March 1982 and 6th April 1988.

k)   As a general rule rollover relief should not be claimed by an individual where the gain would be covered by the annual exemption of £6,500.

Example

P purchased the goodwill of a retail business in 1970 for £5,000 and sold it on 1st December 1997 for £40,000. On 31st December 1997 P purchased the goodwill of a new business for £50,000. Assume an increase in the RPI of 95%. The market value of the business at 31st March 1982 was £15,000. *Compute the chargeable gain.*

Solution

Computation 1997/98

	£	£
Proceeds of sale		40,000
Less market value 31.3.82	15,000	
Indexation allowance 95% × 15,000	14,250	29,250
Chargeable gain		10,750
Cost of new business		50,000
Less rolled over gain on old business		10,750
Deemed cost		39,250

Example

K purchased a freehold factory for his business use in 1971 for £22,000. This was sold for £250,000 in March 1998, and a new factory acquired for £230,000. Assume an increase in RPI of 95%.

The market value of the factory at 31st March 1982 was £75,000. *Compute the chargeable gain.*

Solution

Computation 1997/98

	£	£
Proceeds of sale		250,000
Less market value at 31.3.82	75,000	
Indexation allowance 95% × 75,000	71,250	146,250
		103,750
Less rollover relief:		
Unrelieved gain	103,750	
Less amount of consideration not invested	20,000	83,750
Chargeable gain		20,000

Notes

i)   *The base cost for subsequent disposals would be £230,000 – £83,750 ie £146,250.*

ii)   *The rolled over gain is restricted by any part of the consideration not reinvested, ie (250,000 – 230,000) = 20,000.*

iii)   *Indexation on a future disposal is also based on the net cost of £146,250.*

Assets held on 6th April 1965

3.   Where the original asset was held on 6th April 1965 and the time apportionment basis is used in comparison with re-basing, then there is a proportion of the total gain which is not taxed ie the period prior to 6th April 1965. If part of the proceeds of sale have not been reinvested then for rollover relief purposes the amount not invested is also apportioned. An immediate liability to CGT arises by reference to the following:

$$\text{Proceeds of sale not reinvested} \times \frac{\text{Chargeable gain}}{\text{Total gain}}$$

The balance of the chargeable gain could still be rolled over.

Replacement with a depreciating asset

4. Where the asset is replaced with a depreciating asset then the gain is not deducted from the cost of the asset, ie the replacement asset, but is frozen until the earliest of the following occurs:

   a) the depreciating asset is itself sold, or

   b) the depreciating asset ceases to be used by the person in his or her trade, or

   c) the expiry of 10 years from the date of the replacement.

   A depreciating asset is one with an estimated life of 50 years or less, or one which will have such a life expectancy within 10 years from the date of acquisition, ie a total of 60 years at the date of acquisition.

   Where a gain on a disposal is held over against a depreciating asset then provided that a non-depreciating asset is bought before the held over gain on the depreciating asset crystallises, it is possible to transfer the held over gain to a non-depreciating replacement.

   | **Example** |

   J sold his freehold shop property used for trade purposes for £120,000 on 1st August 1997. The property was bought for £50,000 on 1st May 1982. In December 1997 J acquired a 50 year lease on alternative premises for £130,000 which he occupied immediately for trade purposes until he ceased trading altogether on 31st March 1999. Assume indexation of 95%.

   Compute the chargeable gain for 1997/98 and 1998/99 in respect of the freehold shop.

   ### Solution

   #### J. CGT computation 1997/98

		£	£
1.8.1997	Proceeds of sale of property		120,000
1.5.1982	Cost of acquisition	50,000	
	IA 95% × 50,000	47,500	97,500
Chargeable gain			22,500
Less amount held over			22,500
Assessable gain			Nil

   #### J. CGT computation 1998/99

	£
Held over gain	22,500

   ### Notes

   i) *There would be no indexation of the held over gain from 1st August 1997 to 31st March 1999.*

   ii) *As the business ceased to trade the held over gain has crystallised.*

Reinvestment relief for individuals

5. For disposals on or after 30th November 1993 individuals can claim relief for chargeable gains arising from the disposal of *any asset* subject to the following condition.

   i) A new qualifying investment is acquired within the period beginning 12 months before the disposal and ending three years after the disposal.

   ii) A qualifying investment is any holding of eligible shares (ie ordinary shares with no present or future rights to dividends) in an unquoted company which carries on certain types of business, mainly trading.

   iii) Relief is granted by reducing the consideration for the disposal of the asset by the smallest of the:
   a) chargeable again otherwise arising
   b) consideration for the qualifying investment
   c) amount specified in the claim.

   Thus the amount reinvested need not be the same as the proceeding sale to obtain the relief.

   iv) The deferred gain will become taxable:
   a) if the new shares cease to be eligible shares
   b) if the individual ceases to be both resident and ordinarily resident in the UK
   c) if the company ceases to become a qualifying company.

Transfer of a business on retirement Schedule 6 TCGA 1992

6. On retirement from a business an individual may be eligible for retirement relief in respect of any capital gains tax arising from the material disposal of business assets. The main provisions in respect of disposals are as follows:

a) **Amount of relief (Disposals on or after 30th November 1993)**

For disposals on or after 30th November 1993 the amount of retirement relief available is the aggregate of the following:

i) Full relief   –   First £250,000 of gain $\times$ AP

ii) 50% relief   – $\frac{1}{2} \times$ [Gain – (£250,000 $\times$ AP)], with upper limit (£1,000,000 – 250,000) $\times$ AP

AP = Appropriate % = % of ten year qualifying period

Maximum relief = £250,000 + $\frac{1}{2} \times$ (£1,000,000 – 250,000) = £625,000.   AP = $\frac{10}{10}$

Minimum relief p.a. = $\dfrac{250000}{10} + \dfrac{\frac{1}{2}(1,000,000-250000)}{10}$ = 25,000 + $\frac{1}{2} \times$ 75,000 = £62,500.

b) Relief is available where a material disposal of business assets is made by an individual, who at the time of the disposal:

i) has attained the age of 50 for disposals after 27.11.1995 (55 prior to that date)

ii) has retired on grounds of ill health before the age of 50.

c) A disposal of a business includes:

i) part disposal of a business

ii) a disposal of assets used for the purpose of the business

iii) a disposal of shares or securities in a trading company.

d) For disposals on or after 16th March 1993 relief will be available for any full-time working officer or employee who owns at least 5% of the voting shares. This is defined as an individual's personal company.

For disposals before 16th March 1993 relief is available in respect of a family company defined as one in which the voting rights are:

i) not less than 25% of the total exercised by an individual or

ii) not less than 50% of the total exercised by an individual and his or her family with the individual holding at least 5%.

Under these provisions the relief did not apply to employees.

e) Relief is only granted where a part of the business is disposed of rather than some of its assets. *See Mc Gregor* v *Adcock 1977 WLR. 864. Atkinson* v *Dancer, Manmon* v *Johnston CD. 1988.*

f) A disposal is a material disposal if throughout a period of at least 12 months ending with the date of the disposal the business is owned by the individual making the disposal, or by his or her personal company.

g) Relief is only available in respect of the disposal of interests in chargeable business assets such as goodwill, factory premises or plant and machinery which have been used for the purposes of the trade, profession or vocation. Assets such as shares and securities held by the business as investments, stocks, debtors and cash balances are not chargeable business assets.

h) The amount of relief is reduced proportionately where, at the date of the disposal, the period of continuous ownership of the business is less than 10 years' duration.

i) Relief is available in respect of the transfer by gift or sale of a sole trader's business, an interest in a partnership, or shares in a personal company.

j) The relief is also available in the following cases:

i) disposals involving receipts of compensation or insurance proceeds.

ii) disposals of shares in a personal holding company of a trading group.

iii) disposals by trustees of a settlement of assets used for the purpose of a business if the business was carried on by a beneficiary who retires and has an interest in possession (other than for a fixed term) in the settlement.

k) The relief is mandatory and is given without a formal claim.

Successive businesses

7. a) Where an individual has owned more than one business prior to retirement and the period of ownership of the last business has been less than 10 years then the periods of ownership of the two businesses may be added together to produce 'an extended qualifying period'.

    b) An earlier business period can be added to an original qualifying period provided that the earlier business period:

        i) ended not more than two years before the start of the original qualifying period, and

        ii) falls in whole or in part within a 10 year period prior to the date of disposal qualifying for retirement relief.

    c) A taxpayer is entitled to only one amount of retirement relief (maximum for disposals on or after 30th November 1993 of £625,000) in his or her lifetime.

    If an earlier disposal does not fully use up the maximum entitlement then the balance can normally be obtained in respect of a later disposal.

Example

A sold his business on 30th June 1997 when he was 50 years of age, to Q Ltd for £850,000. The business had been purchased by A for £300,000 on 1st July 1990. All the assets of the business are chargeable business assets. Assume indexation rate of 70%.

Compute the chargeable gain for 1997/98.

Solution

Computation 1997/98

	£	£
Proceeds of sale		850,000
Less cost 1.7.90	300,000	
Indexation allowance 70% × 300,000	210,000	510,000
Chargeable gain		340,000
Retirement relief:		
Duration of ownership 7 years = $\dfrac{7}{10}$		
250,000 × 70%	175,000	
Amount available for 50% relief		
340,000 − 175,000 = 165,000		
50% × 165,000	82,500	257,500
Chargeable gain		82,500

Notes

i)   *The full relief band of £250,000 is restricted to 70% × £250,000 as the qualifying period is seven of the ten years 1.7.90 – 30.6.97.*

ii) *The upper limit of the 50% relief band is (1,000,000 – 250,000) × 70% = 525,000 As the gain is less than that amount (ie £340,800) there is no restriction.*

iii) *The 50% relief band becomes 340,800 – 175,000 ie £165,000.*

Example

T, who is a full-time working director in Z Ltd, sells his 100% holding of ordinary shares for £678,000 on 6th May 1997, having acquired them for £9,000 on 6th April 1969. The value of the assets of Z Ltd on 6th May 1997 is given below. Assume indexation rate of 95%.

The shares had a market value of £110,000 at 31st March 1982.

	6th May 1997 £
Freehold property	400,000
Goodwill	215,000
Quoted investments in O Ltd	25,000
Stocks, debtors and cash less creditors	38,000
	678,000

T was 59 at the date of the disposal, and had been a full-time working director since 6th April 1969.

Compute the chargeable gain.

Solution

T. CGT Computation 1997/98

	£	£
Proceeds of sale of shares		678,000
Less market value at 31.3.82	110,000	
Indexation allowance 95%	104,500	214,500
Gross gain		463,500
Gain eligible for relief:		
$\dfrac{615000}{640000} \times 463,500$	445,395	
Retirement relief:		
Full amount	250,000	
$50\% \times (445,395 - 250,000)$	97,698	347,698
Chargeable gain		115,802

Notes

i) The retirement relief is restricted by the proportions of the gain:

$$\frac{\text{Chargeable business assets}}{\text{Total chargeable assets}}$$

ie $\dfrac{400,000 + 215,000}{400,000 + 215,000 + 25,000} = \dfrac{615,000}{640,000} \times 463,500 = £445,395.$

ii) An asset is not a chargeable business asset if on a disposal of it any gain which might accrue would not be a chargeable gain. Stocks, debtors, cash and investments do not enter the calculations.

iii) The maximum retirement relief band is £445,395 as this is less than £1,000,000.

iv) Where all the assets are chargeable business assets, there is no restriction of retirement relief.

Transfer of a business to a company Section 162

8. The transfer of a business to a company is a disposal of the assets of the business and can therefore give rise to a chargeable gain or loss.

A form of rollover relief is available where an individual transfers the whole of his or her business to a company in exchange for shares, wholly or partly. In effect the held over gain is deducted from the costs of the shares acquired. The gain to which this section relates is that arising on the transfer of chargeable business assets, and the amount deferred is equal to:

The net gain $\times \dfrac{\text{Value of shares received}}{\text{Total value of consideration ie shares and cash}}$

All assets of the business must be transferred although cash balances and other non-business assets may be retained as a general rule.

Example

A transfers his business to T Ltd on 6th April 1997 in exchange for 100,000 ordinary shares of £1 each fully paid, having a value of par, and £25,000 in cash. Chargeable gains on the transfer of business assets to T Ltd amounted to £75,000, after indexation.

Compute the chargeable gain.

Solution

Calculation of rolled over gain 1997/98

	£
$75,000 \times \dfrac{100,000}{100,000 + 25,000} =$	60,000

Computation 1997/98

	£
Chargeable gain	75,000
Less amount rolled over	60,000
Assessed gain	15,000

	£
Deemed cost of shares carried forward	
Value of shares	100,000
Less rolled over gain	60,000
Net cost	40,000

Transfer of assets between group companies (groups only)

9. There is no method of group relief applicable to chargeable gains and losses which arise within different members of a group of companies. Accordingly, when a company disposes of a chargeable asset outside the group, then any capital gain arising will be chargeable to corporation tax. However, if the disposal is by a member of a group of companies to another group company then the provisions of Section 171 TCGA 1992 enable the transaction to be construed as if the disposal does not give rise to any chargeable gain or loss. This is achieved by deeming the consideration for the disposal of the asset to be such an amount that neither a gain nor a loss accrues to the company disposing of the asset. When the asset is ultimately disposed of outside the group, then a normal liability to corporation tax on any gain would arise.

Companies eligible

10. a) A group comprises a principal company and all of its 75% subsidiaries.

    b) A 75% subsidiary means a company whose ordinary share capital is owned by another company either directly or indirectly to the extent of at least 75%. Again ordinary share capital comprises all shares other than fixed preference shares.

    c) Where the principal company is itself a 75% subsidiary of another company, then both its parent and its subsidiaries, together with the principal company, constitute a group.

    d) All members of the group must be UK residents.

    e) With effect from the 14th March 1989 a company will not be a member of a group unless the principal member of the group has itself directly or indirectly more than 50% interest in its profits and assets.

    Members of a consortium are not eligible for treatment as a group for the purposes of this section, nor are close investment holding companies, unless the transfer is between close investment holding companies.

Assets available for group treatment

11. The disposal of any form of property could give rise to the no gain or loss treatment, but there are some exceptions which are as follows:

    a) where the disposal is of redeemable preference shares in a company, on the occurrence of the disposal

    b) where the disposal is of a debt due from a member of a group, effected, by satisfying the debt or part of it

    c) where the disposal arises from a capital distribution on the liquidation of a company.

    If the transfer is of an asset which the recipient company appropriates to its trading stock, then that company is deemed to have received a capital asset and immediately transferred that asset to its trading stock. There would thus be no capital gain or loss arising on the inter-company transfer, as it would fall within the provisions noted above.

    Where the asset transferred to a group company was trading stock of the transfer or company, then the latter is treated as having appropriated the asset as a capital asset immediately prior to the disposal. The value placed on the asset for trading purposes under Section 161 TCGA 1992 would be the transfer value giving rise to a 'no gain or loss' situation.

Miscellaneous points

12. a) When an asset is disposed of by a group company to a company outside the group, then any capital allowances granted to any member of the group relating to the asset are taken into consideration in computing any gain or loss.

    b) If a company to which an asset has been transferred, ceases to be a member of a group within six years of the date of the transfer the position is as follows.

       i)   At the date of the acquisition of the asset by the company leaving the group, it is deemed to have sold and reacquired the asset at its market value.

       ii) There will therefore be a chargeable gain or loss on the difference between the market value and the original cost to the group of the asset.

       This provision does not apply if a company ceases to be a member of a group by being wound up.

c) The provisions of Section 175 TCGA 1992 (rollover relief) are extended to groups and enable all trades carried on by the group to be treated as one.

d) Where a company is a dual resident member of a group of companies detailed provisions exist which are designed to prevent:

   i) the transfer of assets at a no gain/no loss value where the dual resident company would be exempt from CGT

   ii) the granting of rollover relief for the replacement of business assets where the replacement assets are required by a dual resident company.

e) Capital losses brought into a group as a result of a company joining the group after 31st March 1987 will be 'ring fenced' for disposals made on or after 16th March 1993. In effect such capital losses will only be available for unrestricted set-off against gains on:

   i) assets held by the company at the date that it joined the group or

   ii) assets acquired by that company from outside the new group and used in a trade carried on by that company before joining the group.

Trading stock

13. Trading stock is not a business asset for capital gains tax purposes as it is normally taken into consideration in computing taxable trading income.

   Where an asset is appropriated to stock in trade then there is a deemed disposal at the date of the appropriation if a gain or loss would have arisen from a sale of the asset at its market value. An election can be made to have the gain (or loss) deducted (or added) from the value of the asset so that the ultimate profit is taxed as trading income.

   If an asset is appropriated from trading stock for any purpose then it is deemed to be acquired for CGT purposes at the value taken into account in computing the Schedule D income.

   ### Example

   K purchased an asset in 1988 for £20,000 which he held as an investment until 31st July 1996 when it was transferred to trading stocks. Market value at 31st July was £45,000. It was sold as trading stock in December 1996 for £60,000.

   Show the effects of the above both with and without an election. Assume indexation at 70%.

   ### Solution

   Without election. CGT computation 1996/97

	£	£
July 1996 Market Value		45,000
Less cost of acquisition	20,000	
Indexation allowance 70%	14,000	34,000
Chargeable gain		11,000
Schedule D Case I:		
Sale of trading stock		60,000
Less cost		45,000
Case I income		15,000

   With election. CGT computation 1996/97

	£	£
Schedule D Case I:		
Sale of trading stock		60,000
Market value on appropriation	45,000	
Less gain (as above)	11,000	34,000
Case I income		26,000

   ### Notes

   i) *The asset must be of a kind sold in the ordinary course of trade.*

   ii) *The appropriation must be made with a view to resale at a profit.*

   iii) *An election is only available by a person taxable under Schedule D Case I.*

Loans to traders

14. Under Section 253 TCGA 1992 loans made to traders may be claimed as a CGT loss in the following circumstances:

i) where a loss is incurred on a qualifying loan.

ii) where the taxpayer has to meet a guarantee made on a qualifying loan, or

iii) where a loss is incurred on a qualifying corporate bond.

The borrower must be resident in the UK and the money advanced must be used wholly for the purposes of the trade or profession carried on, or for letting qualifying holiday accommodation.

The loss arises at the time the claim is made, and not the date of the loan transaction so that indexation does not arise.

• Student self-testing question

B, a full-time working director of Z Ltd, sells his controlling interest of 100% of the ordinary share capital for £800,600 on 10th May 1997 in Z Ltd. Net assets consisted of the following as at 10th May 1997.

	£
Goodwill	360,000
Plant and machinery (all items > £6,000)	150,000
Freehold factory premises (cost £50,000)	140,000
Investments (long term)	90,000
Net current assets	60,600
	800,600

B purchased the shares in Z Ltd for £50 000 in May 1972. B is 57 years of age. The market value of the shares at 31st March 1982 was £130,000. *Compute the chargeable gain arising on the sale of his shares.* Assume indexation of 95%.

Solution

CGT computation 1997/98

	£	£
Proceeds of sale of shares		800,600
Less Market value at 31.3.82	130,000	
Indexation allowance 95% × 130,000	123,500	253,500
Total gain		547,100
Gain eligible for retirement relief :		
$\frac{650000}{740000} \times 547,100$	480,560	
Retirement relief: exempt band	250,000	
50%(480,560 − 250,000)	115,280	365,280
Chargeable gain		181,820

Notes

i) Total chargeable business assets comprise:

	£
Plant and machinery	*150,000*
Goodwill	*360,000*
Freehold factory	*140,000*
	650,000

Total chargeable assets comprise:

	£
Plant and machinery	*150,000*
Good will	*360,000*
Freehold factory	*140,000*
Investments	*90,000*
	740,000

ii) *The retirement relief is limited in this example as not all of the company's assets were chargeable business assets. Net current assets and investments are not chargeable business assets.*

iii) *Plant and machinery is not covered by the 'Chattels exemption' in this example.*

• Questions without answers

1. Z sold his business on 10th May 1997 when he was 50 ½ years of age. The proceeds of sale amounted to £1,500,000 for the chargeable business assets. Z had purchased the business for £200,000 on 9th May 1980. Assume indexation of 95%. The market value of the business at 31st March 1982 was £250,000.

    Z's wife has agreed capital losses for 1997/98 of £7,500.

    Compute the chargeable gain.

2. T purchased a grocery business on 1st June 1977 which he is considering selling in December 1997 for an estimated price of £400,000. The sale price is allocated between the business assets on the following basis.

	Consideration £	Cost 1.6.1977 £
Freehold premises	275,000	15,000
Flat above premises occupied by T since acquisition	40,000	5,000
Goodwill	50,000	1,500
Trading stock	20,000	6,000
Shop fixtures	15,000	3,000
	400,000	30,500

    The value of the business at 31st March 1982 was estimated to be £150,000 comprising the following:

	£
Freehold premises	60,000
Flat above premises	30,000
Goodwill	40,000
Trading stock	15,000
Shop fixtures	5,000

    T was born on 1st May 1955 and pays an annual retirement annuity premium of £2,500. His taxable income for 1997/98 is £25,000.

    Calculate the CGT liability which would arise should T sell the business and retire. Assume the RPI at December 1997 to be 155.0.

Taxation of chargeable gains
End of section questions and answers

Chargeable gains tax question No 1. T

An examination of the books and records of T, a retired Army officer aged 58, and his wife for the year ended 5th April 1998 showed the following.

i) December 16th. Sale of 4,000 ordinary £1.00 shares in Beta Ltd at a price of 835p per share. T's records showed that his total holding prior to the sale consisted of the following:

			£
1.6.1969	purchased 300 ordinary shares, cost		300
30.9.1975	purchased 1,500 ordinary shares, cost		1,750
1.10.1980	rights issue of 1,800 shares at cost		2,000
30.10.1984	purchased 1,400 ordinary shares cost		1,800

The market value of the ordinary shares at 31st March 1982 was 150p.

ii) December 30th. Sold painting for £9,500 which he had purchased in 1970 for £2,100. The painting had an estimated value of £4,800 at 31st March 1982.

iii) December 30th. Sale of entire holding of ordinary shares in Kornet Ltd an ice cream business, for £42,000. Mrs T had purchased the shares in Kornet Ltd, an unquoted company, for £8,000 on 6th April 1970. Their market value at 31st March 1982 was £18,000.

T is married and his taxable income (after all allowances and reliefs) for 1997/98 amounted to £26,100. His wife's taxable income for 1997/98 was £14,000.

Calculate the CGT liabilities for 1997/98 arising. Assume RPI December 1997 155.0.

Solution

T. Capital gains tax computation 1997/98

i) **Sale of 4,000 shares in Beta Ltd**

New holding		Retail Price Index £	Nominal Value £	Qualifying Expenditure £	Indexed Pool £	Total Cost £
30.10.1984	purchase	90.67	1,400	1,800	1,800	
16.12.1997		155.0				

Indexation allowance:

$\left(\dfrac{155.0 - 90.67}{90.67}\right) = 0.709 \times 1,800$

					1,276	
			1,400	1,800	3,076	
16.12.1997	sale		1,400	1,800	3,076	3,076
Pool carried forward			–	–	–	

1982 Pool

		Nominal value £	Cost £	Re-Basing market value 31.3.82 £
1. 6.1969	purchase	300	300	450
30.9.1975	– do –	1,500	1,750	2,250
1.10.1980	– do –	1,800	2,000	2,700
		3,600	4,050	5,400
16.12.1997	sale	2,600		

Proportionate cost: $\dfrac{2,600}{3,600} \times 5,400$

			3,900	

Indexation allowance:

Market value 31.3.1982: $2,600 \times 150p = £3,900$

$\left(\dfrac{155.0 - 79.44}{79.44}\right) = 0.951 \times 3,900$

		3,709	7,609

388

Chargeable gain

New Holding	Proceeds of sale $\frac{1,400}{4,000} \times 33,400$		11,690	
	Less pool cost		3,076	8,614
1982 Holding	Proceeds of sale $\frac{2,600}{4,000} \times 33,400$		21,710	
	Less pool cost		7,609	14,101
				22,715

Note Proceeds of sale are 4,000 × £8.35 = £33,400.

ii) **30.12.1997 Sale of painting**

	£	£
Proceeds of sale		9,500
Market value at 31.3.82	4,800	
Indexation		
$\left(\dfrac{155.0 - 79.44}{79.44}\right) = 0.951 \times 4,800$	4,565	9,365
		135

Marginal relief

$$740 - \left(\frac{5}{3} \times 9,500 - 6,000\right)$$

$$740 - 5,833 = -5,093$$

Chargeable gain	—
	135

iii) **Mrs T Sale of shares in Kornet Ltd**

		Cost £	Market value 31.3.82 £
30.12.1997	Proceeds of sale	42,000	42,000
6.4. 1970	Cost	8,000	
31.3.1982	Market value		18,000
		34,000	24,000

Indexation allowance			
Market value 31.3.1982	18,000		
$= 0.951 \times 18,000$		17,118	17,118
Capital gain		16,882	6,882

Chargeable gain taken as the smaller gain of £6,882.

T. Capital gains tax computations 1997/98

	T £	Mrs T £
Shares in Beta Ltd	22,715	–
Painting	135	–
Shares in Kornet Ltd	–	6,882
	22,850	6,882
Less exemption	6,500	6,500
Chargeable gain	16,350	382
CGT payable 26,100 − 14,000 = 12,100 ∴ 382 @ 23%	–	88
16,350 @ 40%	6,540	–
	6,540	88

Chargeable gains tax question No 2. Fred Baker

Fred Baker had the following transactions during the year ended 5th April 1998.

i) On 15th April 1997 he sold for £165,000 leasehold premises in which his fishing tackle business had been carried on for a number of years. The leasehold premises were acquired by him for £30,000 on 15th March 1976 when the lease had 40 years to run. Improvements to the premises were carried out on 15th April 1981 at a cost of £15,000. The percentages relating to leases in Schedule 8 CGTA 1992. 1979 includes 40 years 95.457; 34 years 91.156; 19 years 70.791.

The business was transferred to freehold premises which had been acquired previously on 31st March 1994 at a cost of £80,000. Due to continued expansion of the business a new branch was opened on 1st January 1999 in freehold premises acquired for £150,000 on that date.

At 31st March 1982 the leasehold premises had an estimated value of £52,000. Assume RPI April 1997 155.0.

ii) Fred gave his daughter a painting on 20th October 1997 which he had purchased for £250 in May 1944. The following valuations have been made in connection with the painting:

6th April 1965	12,250
31st March 1982	25,000
20th October 1997	50,000

Assume RPI October 1997 155.0.

Compute any capital gains tax liability arising from the above transactions in 1997/98. Fred's taxable income for 1997/98 was £28,000.

Solution

i)

Fred Baker CGT computation 1997/98

		£	£
15.4.1997	Proceeds of sale leasehold premises		165,000
	Less cost of lease less reduction		
15.3.1976	MV @ 31.3.1982	52,000	
	Less $52,000 \times \dfrac{91.156 - 70.791}{91.156}$	11,617	40,383
			124,617

Indexation allowance

$$\left(\frac{155.0 - 79.44}{79.44}\right) \times 40,383$$

		£
$= 0.951 \times 40,383$		38,404
		86,213

***Less* rollover relief:**

	£	£
Unrelieved gain	86,213	
Less proceeds not invested		
(165,000 – 150,000)	15,000	71,213
Chargeable gain		15,000

Notes

i) *The investment in the freehold premises of £80,000 was made more than 12 months before the date of the disposal and is not therefore eligible for rollover relief unless the Revenue at their discretion extend the time limit.*

ii) *The investment in the new branch premises of £150,000 made on 1st January 1999 is eligible for rollover relief.*

ii)

	Cost £	Market value 6.4.1965 £
20.10.1997		
Deemed proceeds of sale of painting	50,000	50,000
Less cost	250	
Market value 6.4.1965		12,250
Unindexed gain	49,750	37,750
Indexation allowance		
Market value at 31.3.1982 25,000		
$\left(\dfrac{155.0 - 79.44}{79.44}\right) \times 25,000 = 0.951 \times 25,000$	23,775	23,775
	25,975	13,975
Re-basing		
Proceeds of sale		50,000
MV @ 31.3.1982	25,000	
IA (as above)	23,775	48,775
Capital gain		1,225

Note

The comparison of cost and MV at 6.4.1965 is made before indexation. In this case the lower MV is taken and compared with the re-basing gain.

CGT computation 1997/98

	£
Leasehold properties (as above)	15,000
Gift of painting	1,225
	16,225
Less exempt amount	6,500
Chargeable gain	9,725
Capital gains tax 9,725 @ 40%	3,890

Chargeable gains tax question No 3. David Plaine

David Plaine resigned as a full-time working director of Plaine Sailing Ltd, an unquoted personal company, on 1st July 1997, his 50th birthday, to become non-executive chairman and president of the company. He had joined the company on 1st July 1976, acquiring 30% of the ordinary shares at a cost of £95,000.

On 1st July 1997 he sold his entire interest for £800,000.

The following is a summary of the balance sheet of Plaine Sailing Ltd as at 30th June 1997 at market values:

	£
Freehold land and buildings	800,000
Goodwill	105,000
Plant and machinery (all items > £6,000)	300,000
Quoted investments	395,000
Stocks and working progress	300,183
Trade debtors	210,146
Cash in hand	32,000
Trade creditors	100,184
Bank overdraft	164,239

Plaine's 30% interest has been valued at £180,000 at 31st March 1982.

Compute the chargeable gain for 1997/98 after any claim for relief Plaine could make. Assume RPI for July 1997 of 155.0.

Plant and machinery was sold at a loss.

Solution

David Plaine. CGT computation 1997/98

		£	£
1st July 1997	Proceeds of sale of shares		800,000
	Less market value at 31.3.82	180,000	
	Indexation allowance		
	0.951 × 180,000	171,180	351,180
	Capital gain		448,820
	Gain eligible for retirement relief:		
	$\frac{1,205,000}{1,600,000} \times 448,820 =$		338,018
	Relief 1st	250,000	
	$\frac{338018 - 250000}{2} =$	44,009	294,009
			154,811
	less exemption		6,500
	Chargeable gain		148,311

Notes

i) *Chargeable business assets comprise:*

	£
Freehold land and buildings	800,000
Goodwill	105,000
Plant machinery (not covered by chattels exemption)	300,000
	1,205,000

ii) Total chargeable assets comprise:
   Chargeable business assets (as above)   1,205,000
   Quoted investments   395,000
                                                                           _____
                                                                           1,600,000

Chargeable gains tax question No 4. Robert Jones

Robert Jones held 140,000 shares in MNO plc. He sold 125,000 shares on 5 October 1997 for £2.20 per share. He had acquired the shares as follows:

Date	Number acquired	Price per share
21 June 1980	30,000	£1.30
9 December 1983	70,000	£1.35

In June 1988 there was a rights issue of 2 ordinary shares for every 5 held at £1.10 per share. Robert took up his full rights issue. The shares were quoted at £1.25 on March 1982.

No election has been made under S. 35(5) TCGA 1992.

Assume RPI October 1997 is 155.0

Calculate the amount of chargeable gain on the disposal.   (ATT)

Solution

New holding

	RPI	No of shares	Indexed pool
9/12/83 Bought	86.9	70,000	94,500
5/10.97 IA	155.0		
$\frac{155.0 - 86.9}{86.9}$			
0.783×94500			73,994
		70,000	168,494
6/88 RI 2 for 5	106.6	28,000	30,800
I A $\frac{155.0 - 106.6}{106.6}$			
$0.454 \times 30,800$			13,983
		98,000	213,277
Sale		98,000	213,277
Carried forward		Nil	Nil

1982 Pool

	No of shares	Cost	MV 31.3.82
21/6/80 Cost	30,000	39,000	37,500
6/88 RI	12,000	13,200	13,200
	42,000	52,200	50,700
5/10/97 Sale	27,000	33,557	32,593
C/forward	15,000	18,643	18,107

Chargeable gains computation

New holding.	Proceeds of sale 98,000 @ 2.20	215,600	
	Index pool cost	213,277	
			2,323
1982 Holding proceeds of sale 27,000 @ 2.20		59,400	
less cost (> MV at 31.3.82)		33,557	
	Unindexed gain	25,843	
I Allce			
$33,557 \times \frac{39000}{52200} \times 0.951 =$		23,843	
$33,557 \times \frac{13200}{52200} \times 0.454 =$		3,853	
		27,696	
Restricted		25,843	25,843
Total gain			2,323

Chargeable gains tax question No 5. Michael Oliver

Michael Oliver, who is resident and ordinarily resident in the UK, had the following transactions in the year ended 5 April 1998.

a) On 30th June 1997 he sold a house for £132,000. The house had been purchased on 1st August 1979 for £23,000 and Michael lived there until 31st March 1982. No other residence was owned during this period. On 1st April 1982 Michael purchased a flat which he had elected to be his main residence from that date. The house was not rented out at any time and had an estimated market value of £27,000 at 31st March 1982.

b) On 30th June 1997 he sold by auction a grandfather clock which had been left to him by his grandfather. The probate value on his grandfather's death on 1st July 1967 was £300. The clock was sold for £8,500, and the auction expenses were £720. The market value of the clock at 31st March 1982 was estimated at £4,000.

Losses for capital gains tax purposes for 1996/97 brought forward were £43,741.

Calculate the capital gains tax payable for 1997/98. Assume indexation to June 1996 of 95%. His taxable income for 1997/98 was £20,000.

(ACCA)

Solution

Michael Oliver Capital gains tax computation 1997/98

a)

	£	Re-basing £	Old Rules £	£
Proceeds of sale – house 30.6.97		132,000		132,000
Cost of acquisition	–		23,000	
Market value 31.3.82	27,000		–	
Indexation allowance				
$0.95 \times 27,000$	25,650	52,650	25,650	48,650
Capital gain		79,350		83,350
Exemption				
$\dfrac{36}{183} \times 79,350$		15,609		
$\dfrac{36}{183} \times 83,350$				16,397
Chargeable gain		63,741		66,953

The smaller gain of £63,741 under rebasing would be taken.

Periods of ownership since 31.3.82	31.3.82 – 30.6.97 = <u>183</u> months
Period of exemption	1.7.94 – 30.6.97 = <u>36</u> months

Note

Although occupation was before 31st March 1982, the last 36 months exemption period can be claimed.

b)

	£	£
Proceeds of sale – clock 30.6.1997		8,500
Market value 31.3.82	4,000	
Expenses of disposal	720	
Indexation allowance 95% × £4,000 (restricted)	3,780	8,500
		Nil
	–	–
Chargeable gain		Nil

Capital gains tax computation 1997/98

		£
Chargeable gains: house		63,741
Less losses b/f		43,741
		20,000
Less annual exemption		6,500
Total chargeable gain		13,500
CG tax payable		
Taxable income		20,000
6,100 (26,100 – 20,000)	@ 23%	1,403
7,400	@ 40%	2,960
13,500		4,363
CG tax payable 31/1/1999		4,363

Part IV

Inheritance Tax

43 General principles

Introduction

1. In this chapter the basic features of the inheritance tax are outlined, most of which are developed in detail in later chapters.

    A summary of the rules for the distribution of an estate on an intestacy is also provided together with the administrative arrangements for the assessment and collection of the tax.

    The main consolidating legislation is to be found in the Inheritance Tax Act 1984 (IHTA 1984).

Basic rates

2. There is one table of scale rates of IHT which apply to transfers of value. The rates applicable to transfers made on or after 6th April 1996 together with 'grossing up' tables are reproduced at the end of this chapter.

    Where tax is chargeable in respect of any gift inter vivos, eg a gift by an individual to a discretionary trust, then the rate of tax used is 50% of the death scale rates.

Transfers of value

3. A transfer of value occurs where an individual's estate is reduced in value as a result of a gift or disposition and the amount of that decrease in value is the value transferred.

    In the case of transfers on a death the value transferred is the value of the estate immediately prior to the death.

Chargeable transfers

4. A chargeable transfer is a transfer which is not an exempt transfer or a potentially exempt transfer (PET).

Potentially exempt transfers (PETs)

5. A potentially exempt transfer is a transfer of value made by an individual:

    i)   to another individual, or

    ii) to an accumulation or maintenance trust, or

    iii) to a trust for the disabled, or

    iv) a transfer involving an interest in possession.

    Although a PET is a transfer of value no inheritance tax is due at the time the transfer. is made. IHT falls due for payment only if the transferor dies within seven years of the date of the transfer.

    A PET made more than seven years before death is an exempt transfer.

    Tax payable on a PET, which may be subject to taper relief, is the responsibility of the recipient first, and secondly the personal representative (to a lesser extent) of the donor.

    A PET is assumed to be an exempt transfer during the seven years following the transfer or, if earlier, until immediately before the transferor's death.

Other chargeable transfers

6. Other chargeable transfers made by an individual are not PETs and these would include:

    i)   transfers by an individual to a discretionary trust

    ii) transfers by an individual to a company.

    IHT is chargeable on these transfers at the time the transfer is made, at 50% of the death scale rates.

Taper relief

7. Any inheritance tax payable in respect of chargeable transfer made within seven years of the death of the donor is reduced by reference to the following table

Years between date of transfer and date of death	% of normal tax charged	% of normal tax deducted
0 – 3	100	–
3 – 4	80	20
4 – 5	60	40
5 – 6	40	60
6 – 7	20	80

Gifts with reservation

8. Where an individual makes a transfer of value, and still retains some interest in the property, then in general on his or her death the property is treated as part of the estate. He or she is deemed to be beneficially entitled to the property and it is taxed together with the rest of the possessions.

Examples of gifts with a reservation are:

i) a gift of a house where the donor remains in residence.

ii) a gift to a discretionary trust where the donor retains an interest as a beneficiary.

9. Property is subject to a reservation if:

i) possession and enjoyment of the property is not bona fide assumed by the donee at or before the beginning of the 'relevant period', or

ii) at any time in the 'relevant period' the property is not enjoyed to the entire exclusion, or virtually so, of the donor and of any benefits to him or her by contract or otherwise.

The relevant period is the period ending on the date of the donor's death and beginning seven years before then, or, if later, the date of the gift.

General scope of the tax

10. If the individual making the transfer of value is domiciled in the UK, tax applies to his or her property wherever it is situated.

Where the transferor is domiciled outside the UK then in general only property situated in the UK is chargeable. For IHT purposes there are special rules by which an individual is deemed to be domiciled in the UK where:

a) he or she was domiciled in the UK on or after 10th December 1974 and within three years prior to the date of the transfer, or

b) he or she was resident in the UK on or after the 10th December 1974 and in at least 17 of the 20 years ending in the year of the transfer.

Excluded property

11. The following items of property are not liable to IHT on a lifetime transfer and do not form part of an individual's estate on death:

a) property situated outside the UK where the owner is also domiciled outside the UK.

b) reversionary interests in a settlement except those acquired for money or money's worth or those where either the settlor or his or her spouse is beneficially entitled to the reversion.

Thus if property is settled on X for life with remainder to Y, then Y has a reversionary interest in the property which is ignored for IHT purposes.

X's interest is deemed to be an absolute interest in the property and is not excluded property.

c) property of individuals killed on active service.

Location of assets

12. To qualify as excluded property owned by a non-UK domicile, the individual assets must be situated outside the UK. The location of assets is determined in accordance with the general principles of law as follows:

Land	— Land including leasehold property is situated where the land is physically located.
Tangible moveable property	— Assets such as furniture and paintings are situated where they are located.
	Coins and bank notes are situated where they are at the time of the transfer.
Shares/securities	— These are situated where the register is kept.
Bearer shares	— These are situated where the certificate of title is kept.
Debts	— These are located where the debtor resides.
Business assets	— Assets of a business are located where the place of business is situated.
	An interest in a partnership is located where the head office is found.
Goodwill	— This is located where the business is carried on.
Trademark	— This is situated where it is registered.

General exemptions and reliefs

13. The following are the main exemptions and reliefs available in respect of lifetime and death transfers.

	PET/other lifetime transfers	Death
a) Transfers between husband and wife (no limit).	✓	✓
b) Transfers each year up to £3,000.	✓	
c) Small gifts to any one person not exceeding £250.	✓	
d) Transfers by way of normal expenditure out of taxed income.	✓	
e) Gifts in consideration of marriage	✓	
£5,000 max: donor is parent to one of the parties to the marriage		
£2,500 max: donor is grandparent/great grandparent		
£1,000 max: donor is in any other relationship.		
f) Gifts to charities	✓	✓
£ no limit: whenever made.		
g) Gifts to political parties	✓	✓
£ no limit: whenever made.		
h) Gifts for national purposes or for public benefit.	✓	✓
i) Gifts made during lifetime for family maintenance including the education of children.	✓	

Business and agricultural property reliefs

14. These important reliefs are available in respect of both transfers inter vivos (PETs and other transfers) and on death. They are given effect to by a reduction in the value transferred.

a) Relief for business property.

   Percentage reductions available are as follows:

	%
i) Transfers of a business or partnership interest	100
ii) Transfers of business assets	50
iii) Transfers of shares in unquoted companies including USM, AIM	100
(Prior to 6.4.1996: holdings over 25%	100
holdings under 25%)	50
iv) Transfers of a controlling interest in a quoted company	50

b) Relief for agricultural property
Percentage reductions available are as follows: %

i) Where the transferor has the right to vacant possession or could obtain it
within 12 months after a transfer ... 100

ii) Where the transferor does not have the right to vacant possession or cannot
obtain it within 12 months of the transfer, eg tenanted property from 1.9.95 ... 100
prior to 1.9.95 ... 50

Growing timber

15. Where land in the UK, not subject to agricultural or business relief, includes growing timber then the value of the timber may be excluded from a person's estate at death. IHT becomes payable on the later sale or lifetime transfer of the timber on the value at the date of the disposal.

Quick succession relief

16. This is available in respect of property transferred on the death of a person which has borne inheritance tax within the preceding five years. The relief is given by way of a percentage reduction or the original tax paid as follows:

	% Reduction
Death within 1 year	100
Death within 2 years	80
Death within 3 years	60
Death within 4 years	40
Death within 5 years	20

Sale within 1 or 4 years of death

17. Where shares are sold within one year of death, or land sold within four years of death and the proceeds of sale are less than their market vale at the date of death, then a reduction of IHT payable may be claimed.

Liabilities and expenses

18. In general, liabilities are taken into account in computing the value of an estate for IHT purposes insofar as they have been incurred for a consideration in money's worth or imposed by law. Liabilities forming a charge on any property, such as a mortgage on a house, are deducted from the value of that property.

Post-death events

19. The beneficiaries under a will or intestacy can vary the terms of the disposition where it is not in the interests of all concerned. Under Section 142 IHTA 1984 the 'Deed of Variation' must satisfy the following conditions.

a) The instrument in writing must be made by the persons or any of the persons who benefit or would benefit under the dispositions of the property comprised in the deceased's estate immediately before his or her death.

b) The instrument must be made within two years after the death.

c) The instrument must clearly indicate the dispositions that are the subject of it, and vary their destination as laid down by the deceased's will, or under the law relating to intestate estates, or otherwise.

d) A notice of election to vary the will must be given within six months of the date of the instrument, unless the Board sees fit to accept a late election.

e) The notice of election must refer to the appropriate statutory provisions.

Any liability to IHT on death will be calculated on the basis of the revised estate distribution resulting from the Deed of Variation.

Intestacy

20. Where a person dies without making a will then there are rules of intestacy which prescribe the manner in which an estate must be distributed. A summary of some of the main provisions to be found in the Administration of Estates Act 1925, are given below.

Spouse survives alone

21. (No issue, parents, brothers or sisters of the whole blood)

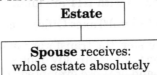

> **Estate**
>
> **Spouse** receives:
> whole estate absolutely

Note

Remember relatives, such as grandparents, uncles and aunts have no interest in the estate.

Spouse survives with issue

22.

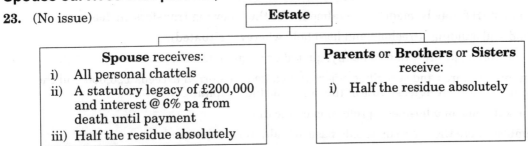

> **Estate**
>
> **Spouse** receives:
> i) All personal chattels
> ii) A statutory legacy of £125,000 and interest @ 6% pa from death until payment
> iii) A life interest in half the residue
>
> **Issue** receive:
> i) Half the residue absolutely
> ii) A reversionary interest in the life interest of the spouse

Note

Personal chattels includes furniture fixtures and fittings, household effects, paintings, private motor cars, jewellery etc. (Prior to 1st December 1993 the legacy was £75,000).

Spouse survives with parents, brothers and sisters of whole blood

23. (No issue)

> **Estate**
>
> **Spouse** receives:
> i) All personal chattels
> ii) A statutory legacy of £200,000 and interest @ 6% pa from death until payment
> iii) Half the residue absolutely
>
> **Parents** or **Brothers** or **Sisters** receive:
> i) Half the residue absolutely

Note

The half share of the residue passes to the parents absolutely or, if there are none, to the brothers and sisters of the whole blood. Issue of brothers or sisters take shares in place of their parents where the latter are deceased. (Prior to 1st December 1993 the legacy was £125,000.)

No surviving spouse

24.

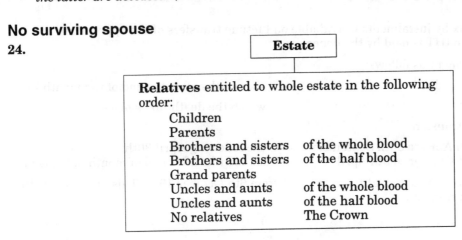

> **Estate**
>
> **Relatives** entitled to whole estate in the following order:
>
> Children
> Parents
> Brothers and sisters   of the whole blood
> Brothers and sisters   of the half blood
> Grand parents
> Uncles and aunts   of the whole blood
> Uncles and aunts   of the half blood
> No relatives   The Crown

Administration and payment

25. a) The Inland Revenue Offices which deal with IHT are known as the Capital Taxes Offices.

b) Reporting lifetime transfers to the Capital Taxes Office is carried out as follows.

    i) In the case of a chargeable transfer, the transferor must report unless some other person such as the donee liable for the tax has already done so. There is no requirement to report transfers within the nil rate band or those exempted. The account must be delivered within 12 months or, if later three months from the date on which he or she first becomes liable for the tax.

    ii) In the case of a PET it is the transferee's duty to report the transfer within 12 months after the end of the month in which death occurs.

c) Appeals against an assessment are to the Special Commissioners or to the appropriate Land Tribunal.

d) For transfers on death, probate or letters of administration are not given until the appropriate account (provisional, if necessary) has been rendered and any IHT due paid. However, under the Administration of Estates (small payments) Act 1965 certain assets with a total value of £5,000 may be handed over to the persons beneficially entitled to them without a grant of probate or letters of administration. This unusually applies to assets held by statutory authorities, trustee savings banks and similar organisations.

e) Where the estate is 'excepted', then there is no duty to make a return on death. This applies where:

    i) the gross value of the property < £180,000.

    ii) there is no settled property.

    iii) not more than 10% (or if higher £30,000) is situated outside the UK.

    iv) the deceased died domiciled in the UK.

f) Payments of IHT may be made by instalments for the following transfers on death:

    i) land and buildings (freehold and leasehold wherever situated)

    ii) a controlling interest in a company, quoted or unquoted.

    iii) unquoted shares and securities where the value transferred exceeds £20,000 and the shares represent at least 10% of the nominal share capital.

    iv) the net value of a business, profession or vocation

    v) timber where the proceeds of sale basis of valuation is not used.

g) Instalments are payable by 10 equal yearly amounts. Interest on IHT due on land other than land used for business or agricultural purposes is calculated on the whole amount outstanding and added to each instalment.

IHT due on other property payable by instalments only incurs interest when an instalment is in arrears.

The payment of tax by instalments is available on lifetime transfers of the appropriate property where the IHT is paid by the donee.

h) IHT is due for payment as follows:

    i) On a transfer on death   – six months after the end of the month in which the death takes place.

    ii) On a lifetime transfer

        made from 6th April to 30th September   – the following April 30th
        made from 1st October to 5th April   – six months after end of month of transfer.

i) Interest accrues on overdue tax at the rate of 5% from 6th October 1994. This applies to both lifetime and death transfers.

Inheritance tax rates

Death rates

	Chargeable transfers (gross)		IHT %	Tax on band	Cumulative tax	IHT on transfer (net)
	£		%	£	£	
on or after 6.4.97	0	– 215,000	nil	nil	nil	nil
	215,001	–	40	-	-	2/3
6.4.96 – 5.4.97	0	– 200,000	nil	nil	nil	nil
	200,001	–	40	-	-	2/3
6.4.95 – 5.4.96	0	– 154,000	nil	nil	nil	nil
	154,001	–	40	-	-	2/3

Lifetime transfers

	Chargeable transfers (gross)		IHT %	Tax on band	Cumulative tax	IHT on transfer (net)
on or after 6.4.97	0	– 215,000	nil	nil	nil	nil
	215,001	–	20	-	-	1/4
6.4.96 – 5.4.97	0	– 200,000	nil	nil	nil	nil
	200,001	–	20	-	-	1/4
6.4.95 – 5.4.96	0	– 154,000	nil	nil	nil	nil
	154,001	–	20	-	-	1/4

44 Basic rules of computation

Introduction

1. In this chapter the basic rules of IHT computations ignoring exemptions are examined under the following headings:

        Grossing up procedures
        Taper relief and gifts inter vivos
        Chargeable lifetime transfers
        Chargeable lifetime transfers – death within seven years
        Potentially exempt transfers within seven years of death
        Death with no chargeable transfers within seven years of death
        Transfers of value made within seven years of death and earlier transfers .

Grossing up procedures

2. Where a life time transfer is made and any IHT is paid by the donor, eg on a transfer to a discretionary trust, then it is necessary to 'gross up the net transfer' as IHT is payable on the gross amount.

> **Example**

A makes a net lifetime gift of £250,000 on 15th May 1997. *Compute the amount of the gross transfer.*

Solution

		£
15.5.1997 Net gift		250,000
IHT is $\frac{20}{80} \times (250,000 - 215,000) = \frac{35,000}{4}$		8,750
Gross transfer		258,750
Check Gross transfer		258,750
IHT $(258,750 - 215,000) \times 20\%$		8,750
Net transfer		250,000

Taper relief and gifts inter vivos

3. The inheritance tax payable in respect of transfers of value made within seven years of the death of an individual is reduced by reference to the following table.

Years between date of transfer and date of death	% of normal tax charged	% deduction of tax charged
0 – 3	100	–
3 – 4	80	20
4 – 5	60	40
5 – 6	40	60
6 – 7	20	80

4. For potentially exempt transfers no tax is payable unless death occurs within seven years of the date of the transfer. When this arises IHT calculated at the death rates subject to any taper relief is payable by the donee.

Other chargeable transfers (non-PETs) are taxed at 50% of the death rate at the time of making the transfer. If death occurs more than seven years after the date of the transfer then the position is as follows.

i)   The chargeable transfer is ignored in computing the IHT payable on the value of the estate.

ii)   There is no additional tax payable by the donee.

iii) IHT already paid when the transfer was made is not recoverable.

Taper relief does not affect the amount of inheritance tax payable on an estate by the executors.

The computational principles of taper relief are illustrated in the examples given below.

Chargeable lifetime transfers (non-PETs)

5. These transfers are chargeable at half the death rate at the time of the transfer, and where necessary must be grossed up.

Example

X makes a transfer of £400,000 to a discretionary trust on 1st December 1997 agreeing to pay any IHT. All exemptions had been used and X had made no previous transfers. *Compute any IHT payable.*

Solution

	£
1.12.97 Gift to discretionary trust.	400,000
IHT on net gift of £400,000	
$(400,000 - 215,000) \times \frac{1}{4}$	46,250
Gross transfer	446,250
IHT payable by X at lifetime scale rate	46,250
Check (446,250 − 215,000) at 20% =	46,250

Chargeable lifetime transfers (non-PETs) – death within seven years

6. When the transferor dies within seven years of making a chargeable transfer then the gift is retaxed at the death rates, together with any taper relief. Any IHT payable when the gift was first made is then deducted in arriving at any additional tax due by the donee.

The value of the transfer is taken at the date of the gift but any additional tax arising on the death of the donor can be calculated by reference to the *lower* of:

i) the market value at date of donor's death, or

ii) the proceeds of an earlier sale.

Example

X dies leaving an estate valued at £100,000 on 11th June 2000. On 1st June 1997 he made a gift of £310,000 gross to a discretionary trust, inheritance tax of £20,000, being paid by the trustees.

Calculate the IHT due in respect of X's estate and any additional tax payable on the chargeable lifetime transfer. Assume rates in 2000 the same as 1997.

Solution

		£
11.6.2000 Value X's estate		100,000
Chargeable transfers within previous 7 years		310,000
		410,000
IHT payable FA 1997 death scale rate		
215,000 – Nil		–
195,000 @ 40%		78,000
410,000		78,000
Less notional tax on transfers of £310,000 within last 7 years.		
215,000 per table		–
95,000 @ 40%	38,000	38,000
310,000		
Payable by executors		40,000
Additional tax payable on gift:		
1.6.97 Gross transfer		310,000
11.6.00 IHT (as above)		38,000
Less taper relief:		
(3–4 years) 20% reduction. 20% × 38,000		7,600
		30,400
Less paid by trustees on gift by X		20,000
Additional tax due by trustees		10,400

Notes

i)   If the additional tax payable is a 'negative amount', none is payable.

ii) There can be no refund of the IHT payable on the original gift.

iii) Tax on the estate is borne at the highest slice, ie after taking into consideration gifts within seven years of death.

iv) Where the cumulative lifetime transfers exceed the exempt band then the estate will simply be the value of the estate × the death rate. In this example £100,000 @ 40% = £40,000.

v)   The IHT paid by the trustees on the gift by X is (310,000 – 215,000) × 20% = 19,000.

Potential exempt transfer within seven years of death

7.   There is no inheritance tax payable when the transfer is made. At the date of death where this is within seven years of the transfer, the PET is taxable at the death rate subject to any tapering relief. In addition the PET is added to the value of the estate to determine the rates of tax payable.

     As with all lifetime transfers brought into charge, the estate is treated as the highest slice and the cumulative transfers in the previous seven years, as the lowest slice.

8.   For the purposes of calculating the tax payable by the donee, then the market value at the date of death or the proceeds of an earlier sale may be used if lower than the value of the PET at the date of the transfer.

Example

A dies on 10th October 2001 leaving a net estate valued at £125,000. On 1st of December 1997 A made a gift to his son of £250,000 after having used all his exemptions. A had made no previous transfers of value.

Calculate the IHT payable.

Solution

		£
10.10.2001 Value of A's estate		125,000
Add Cumulative transfers in previous 7 years		250,000
		375,000

		£
IHT thereon (375,000 – 215,000) × 40% (FA 1997 Death Rates)		64,000
Less notional tax on transfers within previous 7 years	£250,000	

	£		
215,000 per table	–		
35,000 @ 40%	14,000		
250,000	14,000		14,000
IHT payable on estate			50,000
Tax payable by A's son			
1.12.1997 Value of gift			250,000
IHT thereon as above			14,000
Less taper relief: (3–4 years) 20% × 14,000			2,800
IHT payable			11,200

Example

Using the data in the previous example compute the IHT payable if the value of the gift to A's son was only worth £150,000 at the date of A's death.

Solution

		£
10.10.2001	Value of A's estate	125,000
	Add Cumulative transfers in previous 7 years	250,000
		375,000
IHT payable on estate		50,000 (as above)

IHT payable by A's son	£
1.12.97 Value of gift	250,000
Less fall in value	100,000
10.10.2001 Value	150,000
IHT on £150,000	
$(150,000 - 215,000) \times 40\%$	Nil
Less taper relief $20\% \times 0$	Nil
IHT payable	Nil

Notes

i)   The value of the **original gift** is included in calculations for the IHT payable on the estate.

ii) The reduced value of £150,000 is used to determine the amount of additional tax borne by the donee, which in this case is nil.

Death with no chargeable transfers or PETs within previous seven years

9. On the death of a person who has not made any chargeable transfers within the previous seven years, the death scale rates are applied to the value of the estate, subject to any permitted exemptions and reliefs.

> **Example**

T died on 14 June 1997, leaving a chargeable estate of £255,000. He had made no lifetime transfers. *Compute the IHT payable.*

Solution

T deceased IHT computation 14.6.1997

	£
Total value of estate:	255,000
Tax payable: (FA 1997 rates)	
215,000	–
40,000 @ 40%	16,000
255,000	16,000

Notes

Estate rate of IT $= \dfrac{16,000}{255,000} \times 100 = 6.27\%$

This is required where there is any IHT payable by instalments eg UK land, or by different persons.

Transfers of value made within seven years of death, and earlier

10. Transfers of value made more than seven years before the date of death are not accumulated to arrive at the IHT rate at the date of death. However, where a transfer of value is made within the seven years before the date of death, then in determining any additional IHT payable on death by the recipient, any transfers made in the seven years before the date of that transfer must be considered.

> **Example**

K makes a gross chargeable transfer to P of £150,000 on 1st February 1992. On 1st November 1995 K gives his son £75,000. K dies on 30th August 2000, leaving an estate of £300,000. *Calculate the IHT payable on the estate of K and on the PET of £75,000.*

Solution

	£
30.8.2000 **Value of K's estate**	300,000
Add transfers of value made within previous 7 years	
1.11.95 Gift to son	75,000
	375,000
IHT payable: (FA 1997 Rates)	
215,000	–
160,000 @ 40%	64,000
375,000	64,000

		£	£
Less notional tax on transfers within previous 7 years		£75,000	
£75,000 per table		Nil	–
Payable by Executors			64,000

Tax payable by A's son

		Gross	**IHT (FA 1997 Death rates)**
1.2.92	Gross transfer to P	150,000	–
1.11.95	Gift to son	75,000	4,000
		225,000	4,000

IHT	215,000		–
	10,000 @ 40%	4,000	
	225,000	4,000	

Deduct transfers made more than 7 years prior to date of death	150,000	–
	75,000	4,000

less taper relief	
4–5 years 40% × 4,000	1,600
IHT payable	2,400

Notes

i)   *The IHT payable at the death rate is calculated by reference to the value of **all** chargeable transfers in the seven years before the date of the gift.*

ii) *The tax due on the PET of £2,400 is not the amount deducted in computing the IHT payable on the estate by the executors, which in this example is nil.*

iii) *The taper relief for a transfer made in between four and five years is 40%.*

• Student self-testing question

Z dies on 22nd October 2000 leaving a net estate of £150,000. During his lifetime he had made the following transfers of value, after using all available exemptions.

1st December 1994	Gift to his daughter of £130,000.
20th June 1997	Gift to an accumulation and maintenance trust of £140,000.

Compute the IHT payable on the death of Z.

Solution

	£	£
22.10.2000 Z's estate		150,000
Add transfers of value made in previous 7 years		
1.12.94 Gift to daughter	130,000	
20.6.97 Gift to trust	140,000	270,000
		420,000

IHT payable (FA 1997 Rates):

215,000 per table		–
205,000 @ 40%	82,000	
420,000	82,000	82,000

Less notional tax on lifetime transfers of £270,000	
(270,000 – 215,000) × 40% =	22,000
IHT payable by executors	60,000

IHT payable by donees:		
1.12.94 gift to daughter	130,000	
(130,000 – 215,000) × 40%		Nil

	£
20.6.97 **Gift to Accumulation and maintenance trust**	140,000
Add Gifts in previous 7 years	
Gift to Z's daughter (1.12.94)	130,000
	270,000

IHT payable:

$(270{,}000 - 215{,}000) \times 40\%$	22,000
Less notional IHT on gift to Z's daughter of £130,000	–
	22,000
Less taper relief: (3–4 years) $20\% \times 22{,}000$	4,400
Tax payable by trustees	17,600

Cumulative transfers	**Gross** £	**Tax** £	
1.12.1994 Gift to daughter	130,000		
IHT payable @ FA 1997 death rates	–	–	
	130,000	–	
20.6.97 Gift to accumulation trust	140,000	22,000	subject to taper relief
	270,000	22,000	
Less transfers made more than 7 years prior to 22.10.2000	Nil	Nil	
	270,000	22,000	

Notes

i) *Both of the transfers during Z's lifetime are PETs.*

ii) *The tax due in respect of each gift is* computed separately beginning first with the one furthest from the date of death, within the seven years period.

iii) IHT payable on the second gift is calculated after deducting any notional tax on the previous gift to Z's daughter which in this cas*e is nil*.

iv) Taper relief 20.6.97–22.10.00 is three–four years.

• Questions without answers

1. S died on the 1st June 1997 leaving a net estate after allowable liabilities of £250,000. On 3rd July 1991 S had made a gross gift to his son of £400,000. S had made no other gifts inter vivos.

   Calculate the IHT payable on the estate and any additional tax due in respect of the gift to his son.

2. J makes a transfer of £50,000 to a discretionary trust set up for the benefit of his grandchildren, on 1st January 1997. On 5th August 1997 he gives his son in law £275,000 to assist him in establishing a fish farm. J dies on 17th September 2001 leaving a net estate of £225,000.

   Calculate any IHT liabilities arising on J's death.

45 General exemptions and reliefs

Introduction

1. There are a number of general exemptions and reliefs available, some of which only relate to lifetime transfers and others which relate to both lifetime transfers and those arising on death. This chapter begins with a summary of exemptions and reliefs, all of which are later discussed in detail.

Summary of exemptions and reliefs

2.

	PET/Other	Death
Small gifts not exceeding £250	✓	–
Gifts up to £3,000 p.a.	✓	–
Transfers out of normal expenditure	✓	–
Gifts and bequests between husband and wife	✓	✓
Gifts in consideration of marriage	✓	–
Gifts and bequests to charities	✓	✓
Gifts and bequests to political parties	✓	✓
Gifts and bequests for national purposes	✓	✓
Gifts for family maintenance	✓	–
Transfer to an employee's trust	✓	–

Small gifts lifetime only

3. Small gifts not exceeding £250 in any one income tax year to any one person are exempt if the total of gifts made to that person does not exceed £250. If the gift exceeds £250, there is no small gift exemption and the first part of a larger gift is not exempt. Thus if A makes a gift to Z of £200 then the small exemption applies. If the gift to A was £600 the £250 exemption is not applicable and A has made a potentially exempt transfer of £600.

Gifts up to £3,000 p.a. lifetime only

4. This annual exemption applies to the first £3,000 of transfer (PET or others) in any one income tax year so that, in effect, it can be deducted from a larger transfer.

If the annual exemption is not used in a particular income tax year it can be carried forward, wholly or partially, for one year but no longer.

It is generally held that where both potentially exempt transfers and chargeable transfers are made in the same income tax year, then when allocating the annual exemption the PETs are ignored in the first instance.

The Capital Taxes Office appears to take a contrary view, and considers that the exemption should be allocated to the first transaction in the income tax year, PET or chargeable transfer. As the latter view also seems to be expected in examinations, then this has been utilised in the examples in this book.

Where a chargeable life time transfer is to be 'grossed up' the annual exemption is applied before the gross gift is computed. Any subsequent reallocation is made to the original gross gift.

> **Example**

During 1996/97 T used his small gift exemption, and made a gift to P of £10,000. He had made no previous transfers. On 1st May 1997 T makes a gift of £303,000 (gross) to a discretionary trust the trustees to pay any IHT on the transfer.

Show the IHT computation for 1997/98.

Solution

IHT Clock

			£	£	Gross £	IHT (Life time rate) £	Net £
1996/97	Gift to P is a PET			10,000			
	Less annual exemption	1996/97	3,000				
		1995/96	3,000	6,000			
	Left out of account			4,000	–	–	–

			Gross	IHT	Net
1997/98	Gift to discretionary trust	303,000			
	Less annual exemption 1997/98	3,000	300,000	17,000	283,000
	Cumulative total		300,000	17,000	283,000

Notes

i)   *The gift to P is a PET and is initially left out of the cumulative totals.*

ii) *The annual exemption is applied to the PET.*

iii) *IHT on the gross transfer of £300,000 is (300,000 – 215,000) × 20% = £17,000.*

iv) *The cumulative total is required for the seven year period or death if earlier.*

Example

T makes a gift to his son of £306,000 on 31st May 1997. T dies on 7th June 2001 leaving a net estate of £150,000. T made no other lifetime transfers.

Calculate any inheritance tax payable in respect of the gift.

Solution

IHT Clock

				Gross	IHT	Net
1997/98.	Gift to T is a PET		306,000			
	Less AE 1997/98	3,000				
	1996/97	3,000	6,000			
	Left out of account		300,000	–	–	–

IHT Clock rewritten

	Gross £	Gross £	IHT (Death scales) £
31.5.1997 Gift to son		306,000	
Less exemption 1997/98	3,000		
1996/97	3,000	6,000	
		300,000	34,000

IHT payable (FA 1997 Rates):

215,000	Nil	
85,000 @ 40%	34,000	
300,000	34,000	34,000
Less taper relief: (4–5 years) 40% × 34,000		13,600
IHT payable by T's son		20,400

Example

K who has made no previous transfers of value makes the following gifts:

1st May 1996 — Gift of £200 to his nephew
30th December 1996 — Gift of £50,000 to his daughter
30th September 1997 — Gift of £283,000 gross to a discretionary trust – trustees to pay any IHT

K dies on 29th January 2001 leaving a net estate of £100,000.

Compute any IHT due in respect of the gifts and the estate.

Solution

K. IHT Clock

			Gross	IHT (Lifetime scale)	Net
1996/97					
1.5.1996	Gift to nephew		200		
	Small exemption		200		
30.12.1996	Gift to daughter PET		50,000		
	Less AE 1996/97	3,000			
	1995/96	3,000	6,000		
	Left out of account		44,000	–	–	–

1997/98

30.9.1997	Gift to discretionary trust	283,000			
	Less AE 1997/98	3,000			
		280,000	280,000	13,000	267,000
			280,000	13,000	267,000

IHT $(280,000 - 215,000) \times 20\% =$ ⎯ 13,000

IHT Clock rewritten

		£	£	Gross £	IHT (Death scale) £
1996/97					
30.12.1996	Gift to daughter		50,000		
	AE 1996/97	3,000			
	AE 1995/96	3,000	6,000	44,000	–
1997/98					
30.9.1997	Gift to trust		283,000		
	AE 1997/98		3,000	280,000	43,600
				324,000	43,600

$324,000 - 215,000$ @ 40% = 43,600

29.1.2001	*IHT payable on estate of*	100,000	
	Free estate	100,000	
	Add chargeable transfers		
	within previous 7 years	324,000	
		424,000	

IHT Payable (FA 1997 rates)

IHT on 424,000 = $(424,000 - 215,000) \times 40\%$	83,600	
Less IHT on gifts as above	43,600	
IHT payable on estate	40,000	

IHT Payable on gifts

30.12.1996	Gift to daughter	44,000	Below exemption level of £215,000
30.9.1997	Gift to discretionary trust	280,000	
	IHT (as above)	43,600	
	Less taper relief		
	(3–4 years) 20% × 43,600	8,720	
		34,880	
	Less paid (1997/98)	13,000	
	Payable by trustees	21,880	

Notes

i) *The IHT on gift to the discretionary trust of £13,000 is payable on 30.4.1998.*

ii) *The IHT of £21,880 (and the £40,000) arising on the death is payable on 31.7.2001.*

iii) *As the lifetime transfers were greater than the exempt band of £215,000 the estate of £100,000 will be taxed at the 40% rate ie £40,000.*

Transfers out of normal expenditure *Lifetime only*

5. Transfers of value under this heading are exempt, providing that they are:

a) part of the normal expenditure of the transferor, and

b) made out of taxed income leaving sufficient income to maintain the transferor's usual standard of living.

Transfers between husband and wife *Life and death*

6. Lifetime transfers and those arising on death between husband and wife are exempt from IHT. However, if the wife is not domiciled in the UK then the first £55,000 of transfers to her are exempt.

Gifts in consideration of marriage *Lifetime only*

7. Gifts made in consideration of marriage are exempted at different amounts, depending upon the relationship of the donor to the marriage partners.

   £5,000 maximum: Donor is parent to one of the parties to the marriage.

   £2,500 maximum: Donor is grandparent or great grandparent to one of the parties to the marriage.

   £1,000 maximum: Donor is in any other relationship to one of the parties to the marriage.

   The limits apply to all gifts made by a person in respect of a single marriage and they do not have to be grossed up.

   Thus a husband and wife can each give £5,000 to their son and daughter on the occasion of their respective marriages. They could also give £1,000 to their respective son-in-law, and daughter-in-law.

   Where a gift is made in consideration of a marriage which is to take place, then the exemption is conditional on that event occurring. The exemption is deducted before any annual exemption.

Gifts and bequests to charities *Life and death*

8. Transfers of value to charities, whether lifetime or on a death, are exempt without any limit.

Gifts and bequests to political parties *Life and death*

9. Gifts to political parties made after 14th March 1988 are exempt without any limitation.

   To be eligible a political party must have:

   a) at least two members of the House of Commons or

   b) one member of the House of Commons and have polled not less than 150,000 votes in respect of all its candidates at the last general election.

   The following political parties are currently recognised by the Inland Revenue:

Conservative	Scottish National
Labour	Plaid Cymru
Ulster Unionist	Liberal Democratic

National Heritage property

10. The following forms of relief are available in respect of national heritage property transferred either on death or inter vivos.

    a) Conditional exemption from IHT in respect of certain designated national heritage property providing specified undertakings are given.

    b) Exemption from IHT where the property is transferred to certain specified bodies such as:

       The National Gallery; The British Museum; any UK college or university; any local authority. The full list is contained in Schedule 3 IHTA 1984.

    c) Acceptance of national heritage property in payment of IHT.

    d) Exemption from IHT on the transfer of value for the creation of a fund for the maintenance of historic buildings.

11. For the purposes of the conditional exempt transfer the following types of property are within the term national heritage property, providing they are so designated by the Board of Inland Revenue.

    a) Any pictures, prints, books, manuscripts, works of art, scientific collections or other things not yielding income which appear to the Board to be of national, scientific, historic or artistic interest.

    b) Any land which in the opinion of the Board is of outstanding scenic or historic or scientific interest.

    c) Any building for the preservation of which steps should in the opinion of the Board be taken by reason of its outstanding historic or architectural interest.

    d) Any area of land which in the opinion of the Board is essential for the protection of the character and amenities of such a building as is mentioned in (c) above.

    e) Any object which in the opinion of the Board is historically associated with such a building as is mentioned in (c) above.

The following undertakings must be given in connection with a conditional exemption

12. a) In respect of property in 11(a) above it must be kept permanently in the UK and cannot leave temporarily except with the approval of the Board. In addition, steps must be taken for the preservation of the property and for securing reasonable access to the public.

b) For property falling within the other categories reasonable steps must be taken for the maintenance and preservation of the land, buildings and associated objects, and for securing reasonable access to the public.

13. As noted above the conditional exemption applies to both death and lifetime transfers. However, where a lifetime transfer is made the property must have been owned for six years by the transferor or his wife, or be inherited property which qualified for conditional exemption on the earlier death.

Gifts for family maintenance *Lifetime only*

14. In general any gift by one party in a marriage to another is not a transfer of value providing that:

a) it is a provision of maintenance for the spouse or a dependant relative, or

b) it is for the maintenance, education or training of children.

The transfers of value to a spouse would normally be exempt anyway and this section covers provision of maintenance to an ex-spouse and to a spouse domiciled outside the UK.

Transfers to employee's trust *Life time only*

15. Transfers to an employee's trust by an individual are exempt, provided a number of conditions are met.

a) The trust capital must not be applied for the benefit of the settlor or any person connected with him or her.

b) The property transferred must be shares in a company.

c) The trustees must hold more than 50% of the company's ordinary share capital and have a controlling interest.

Allocation of exemptions and IHT

16. The following points arise under this heading.

a) A testator may state in his or her will that certain gifts passing on death are to be made 'free of IHT' while other gifts are to bear their own IHT. In the former case, any tax arising in respect of the gift will be a testamentary expense payable out of the residue.

b) In the absence of the contrary intention in a will IHT attributable to freehold property (realty) and other free estate in the UK, is a general, testamentary and administration expense. Section 211, IHTA 1984.

c) A specific gift is any other than residue and, if it is not an exempt gift (eg to a spouse), the IT will normally be paid from the residue. In these circumstances, the gift must be grossed up at the death scale rate to compute the amount borne by the residue.

d) There are special rules for attributing the value of net gifts where agricultural or business property relief apply.

> **Example**

Z died on 1st June 1997 leaving a net estate of £400,000. In his will he left £35,000 free of tax to his son and the residue to his wife. During the previous seven years Z had made chargeable transfers amounting to £215,000. *Show the IHT computations.*

Solution

		Gross £	Tax £	Net £
1.6.97	Cumulative transfers	215,000	–	215,000
	Gift to son	58,333	22,333	35,000
		273,333	22,333	250,000

£250,000 grossed up at death rate of 40% from the band level of 215,000 is:

[Nil + (250,000 − 215,000) × $^{40}/_{60}$]   ie £23,333 + 250,000 = 273,333.

Check: £273,333 @ death rate   = (273,333 − 215,000) @ 40%
                                = 58,333 @ 40% = £22,333

	£	
	£	
Value of estate	400,000	
Less gross value of gift	58,333	IHT payable of £23,333
		'out of residue'
Residue to spouse	341,667	

In the previous example, if the legacy to Z's son had to bear its own IHT, as directed in the will, then the calculation would be as follows:

1.6.97	Cumulative lifetimes transfers	215,000
	Specific gift	35,000
		250,000

IHT at death rates:

	£	£
	215,000	–
	35,000 @ 40%	14,000
	250,000	14,000

	£	
Value of estate	400,000	
Less gift to son	35,000	IHT payable of £14,000 by Z's son
Residue to spouse	365,000	

• Student self-testing question

L dies on 3rd of May 2002 leaving a net estate of £100,000. During his lifetime L had made the following gifts.

30th April 1994	Gift to a discretionary trust of £60,000 gross after all exemptions.
7th May 1996	Gift to his son of £106,000.
27th December 1997	Gift to an accumulation and maintenance trust of £78,000.

Calculate the inheritance tax payable on the death of L in respect of the gifts.

Solution

Lifetime transfers IHT Clock				Gross £	Tax £	Net £
1994/95	30.4.1994 Gift to discretionary trust		60,000			
	AE 1994/95	3,000				
	1993/94	3,000	6,000	54,000	–	54,000
1996/97	7.5.1996 Gift to son PET		106,000	–	–	–
	AE 1996/97	3,000				
	1995/96	3,000	6,000			
	Left out of account		100,000	–		–
1997/98	27.12.1997 Gift to accumulation and maintenance trust PET		78,000			
	AE 1997/98		3,000			
	Left out of account		75,000	–	–	–
				54,000	–	54,000

IHT Clock rewritten

		Gross £	Tax £
30.4.1994	Gift to discretionary trust	54,000	–
7.5.1996	Gift to son PET	100,000	
27.12.1997	Gift to accumulation and maintenance trust	75,000	5,600
		229,000	5,600

IHT (229,000 − 215,000) × 40% = 5,600
Less transfers made more than 7 years before
date of death, ie before 3.5.1995

54,000	–
175,000	5,600

IHT payable on estate of L 3.5.2002

			£
Value of net estate			100,000
Add transfers within previous 7 years			175,000
			275,000
IHT payable	215,000 @ Nil		–
	60,000 @ 40%		24,000
	275,000		24,000

Less IHT on life time gifts of £175,000 = Nil

IHT payable by estate		24,000

Notes

i) *Gifts within the last seven years of each gift are taken into consideration in determining the amount of IHT payable by the donees.*

ii) *As the gifts are below the threshold of £215,000, there is no further tax to pay.*

• Questions without answers

1. A gives his daughter £4,500 on 1st May 1997 in consideration of her marriage planned to take place in August 1997. On 30th November 1997 he makes a gift of £175,000 gross to a discretionary trust. A dies on 23rd July 2002 leaving a net estate of £260,000

    Compute the IHT arising on the death of A.

2. T died on the 3rd July 1997 leaving a net estate of £450,000. He made the following bequests:

    a) £50,000 to his son free of tax.

    b) £175,000 to his daughter free of tax.

    c) Residue to his wife.

    T had made no previous lifetime transfers of value.

    Compute the IHT liability arising on T's death and indicate how it will be borne.

46 Principles of valuation

Introduction

1. In general, property is valued for IHT purposes at the open market price at the date of the transfer. However, there are a number of variations to this rule and also some relief is given by way of a reduction in valuation. This chapter begins with a list of topic headings each of which is then examined in detail. Relief for business property, agricultural property and growing timber is covered in later chapters.

List of topics

2. Basic rules
   Related property
   Quoted shares and securities
   Quoted shares and securities sold within 12 months of death
   Land and house property
   Land and buildings sold within four years of death
   Quick succession relief
   Life assurance policies
   Liabilities
   Funeral expenses

Basic rules

3. The basic rule of valuation is contained in Section 160, IHTA 1984. This states that property is to be valued at the price it might reasonably be expected to fetch if sold in the open market. Market value is a question of fact to be ascertained at the date of the transfer. Market price is not to be assumed to be reduced on the grounds that the whole property is to be placed on the market at one and the same time. Thus a higher value might be placed on a very large block of shares transferred on a death than if the shares were actually sold in a single bargain where the price could be lower. As a general rule the price realised for the sale of property after a transfer gives some indication of the value to be placed on the transfer.

Related property

4. Where an individual makes a transfer then related property consists of other connected property:

   a) owned by the transferors' spouse

   b) transferred as an exempt transfer to a charity, political party or national public body by either spouse within the preceding five years.

   If there is related property on a transfer, all the related property is then valued as a proportionate part of the whole.

   > **Example**

   X owns 25% of the ordinary share capital of Q Ltd and his wife owns 50%. X's interest is valued at £5,000 and his wife's at £7,000, both being minority holdings. Their combined majority holdings of 75% are valued at £30,000.

   X transfers his shares to his son on 1st August 1997. *Calculate the value of the potentially exempt transfer.*

   Solution

	£
Shares in Q Ltd X 25% value	5,000
Mrs X 50% value	7,000
X and Mrs X 75% value	30,000

   X's related value $\dfrac{5,000}{5,000 + 7,000} \times 30,000 = 12,500$:

   The value of the PET by X to his son for IHT purposes is therefore £12,500.

> **Example**

A owned a pair of vases with a market value of £6,000 and his wife owned a similar pair with the same market price. As a collection all four vases would be worth £20,000. A's wife transfers her vases to her grandson on 1st July 1997.

Calculate the value of the transfer.

Solution

	£
Related value of vases A	6,000
Mrs A	6,000
Combined value A and Mrs A	20,000
Mrs A's related value $\frac{6,000}{6,000 + 6,000} \times 20,000 =$	10,000

The value of the transfer for IHT purposes is therefore £10,000.

Quoted shares and securities

5.   In the absence of specific IHT rules, the CGT principles are followed which means that the market price is the lower of:

a)   one quarter up from the lower to the higher limit of the quotation, or

b)   halfway between the lowest and the highest bargains recorded for the day, ignoring any special prices.

> **Example**

T died on 14th April 1997 and his estate included 1,000 ordinary shares in O plc. According to the Stock Exchange Daily Official list, on 14th April the quotation was 206p/212p. Normal bargains were transacted at 214p and 204p.

Calculate the value of the shares for IHT purposes.

Solution

O plc $\frac{1}{4}$ up from lower to the higher quotation

ie $\frac{212p - 206p}{4} = 1\frac{1}{2}$ ie $206 + 1\frac{1}{2} = 207\frac{1}{2}$p

$\frac{1}{2}$ way from lowest to highest price

$\frac{214p - 204p}{2} = 204 + 5p = 209p$

∴ Value of 1,000 shares = $1,000 \times 207\frac{1}{2}$p = £2,075.00

If shares are quoted ex dividend the cash dividend due on the shares must be added to the ex dividend price in determining the estate value.

Dealings in shares suspended

6.   Where dealings in quoted shares are suspended within a year of the death of an individual then the value at the date of the first anniversary may be substituted for that at the date of death.

This applies to deaths occurring up to 12 months before 16th March 1993, and subsequently.

Quoted shares and securities sold within 12 months of death

7.   a)   Where quoted shares or securities are sold by the personal representative within 12 months of a death, the selling price realised may be substituted for the estate value, if it is lower.

b)   If a claim is made to substitute the selling price the principle must be applied to all investments sold, not just those which have been sold at a lower value.

c)   The difference in value is calculated by comparing the estate value and the proceeds of sale exclusive of any expenses of sale. The net loss arising is deducted from the value of the property at death and the IHT recomputed.

d)   The above provisions also apply where shares or securities become valueless within the first 12 month period.

Example

X died on 1st June 1997 leaving net estate of £400,000 which included quoted shares with an estate value of £250,000. These were sold on 15th December 1997 for £210,000 excluding expenses. X had made no previous transfers of value during his lifetime.

Calculate the IHT payable on X's death and any adjustment due as a result of the sale of the quoted shares.

Solution

	£	£
1st June 1997. Value of X's estate		400,000
IHT payable:		
215,000 Nil	–	
185,000 @ 40%	74,000	
400,000	74,000	74,000
Net value of estate		326,000
15th December 1997. Value of estate 1.6.97		400,000
Less relief for loss on sale of shares:		
Value of shares at 1.6.97	250,000	
Value of shares at 15.12.97	210,000	40,000
		360,000
IHT payable:		
215,000 Nil	–	
145,000 @ 40%	58,000	
360,000	58,000	58,000
		302,000

Note

The adjustment of the IHT payable on the estate is therefore 74,000 – 58,000 = 16,000 which is equivalent to the reduction in value of 40,000 @ 40%.

Where quoted shares or securities are sold within the 12 month period and the proceeds reinvested within two months of the sale (within the 12 month period) in other quoted shares or securities then the loss on sale is *reduced* by the following amount:

$$\text{(Proceeds of sale} - \text{Probate value)} \times \frac{\text{gross amount reinvested}}{\text{gross sale proceeds}}$$

Thus, where the whole of the proceeds of sale are reinvested within the 12 month period then the loss is reduced to nil.

Example

Y died on 2nd May 1997 leaving an estate of £360,000, of which £50,000 consisted of quoted shares. On 12th December 1997 the executor sold the shares for £44,000, after expenses of £1,000. After paying off liabilities of £30,000 the balance was reinvested in quoted shares on 23rd January 1998.

Show the computations for the revised value of the estate.

Solution

	£
Value of Y's estate at 2.5.97	360,000
23rd January 1998. Calculation of relief	
Probate value of shares	50,000
Less gross proceeds	45,000
loss on sale	5,000
Reduced by: $5,000 \times \dfrac{14,000}{45,000}$	1,556
Net loss	3,444
Value of estate at 2.5.97	360,000
Less reduction in value of shares	3,444
Revised value of estate	256,556

Notes

i)   The gross value of the sale proceeds is £45,000.

ii) The amount reinvested is £44,000 – 30,000 = £14,000.

Land and house property

8. a) The principal basis of land valuation is the market value of similar properties or by means of a multiple of the anticipated rental values. All property values have to be agreed with the District Valuation Office.

   b) Jointly held property is valued as a proportionate share of the whole.

   c) Property situated overseas is valued at death on normal principles less an allowance of up to 5% of the valuation to compensate for additional expenses of realisation.

Land or buildings sold within four years of death

9. Where land or buildings are sold by the personal representative within four years of a death and there is a fall in the value, the gross proceeds of sale may be substituted for the probate value and the value of the estate for IHT purposes recomputed. The following conditions apply.

   a) The loss must be greater than £1,000 or 5% of the value on death whichever is the lower.

   b) All sales of land within the four year period must be aggregated and only a net loss taken into account.

   c) Where reinvestment in land takes place between the date of death and within four months of the last sale, within the four year period, then the loss is *reduced by*:

$$\text{(Probate value} - \text{Proceeds of Sale)} \times \frac{\text{Gross amount reinvested}}{\text{Gross sale proceeds}}$$

   d) The four year rule (previously 3 years) introduced by the FA 1993 applies to disposals after 16th March 1993.

Quick succession relief

10. a) Where a person dies within five years of the transfer to him or her of property (whether by way of a life time transfer or on a death) and IHT becomes payable for the second time, relief is available under this heading.

   b) The relief is given in the form of a IHT credit calculated by reference to the first transfer as follows:

$$\frac{\text{Net amount}}{\text{gross amount}} \times \text{IHT charged x\% reduction}$$

   Net amount   = actual value of original transfer to the deceased within the five year period.

   Gross amount = gross value of transfer, whoever paid the IHT within the five year period.

   % reduction = scale reduction depending upon the time intervals:

Period between transfers	%
Up to 1 year	100
1 to 2 years	80
2 to 3 years	60
3 to 4 years	40
4 to 5 years	20

Example

T died on 1st May 1997 leaving a net estate of £250,000. He had made no lifetime transfers. On 1st June 1992, T had received a painting from Z worth £20,000 on which Z paid IHT of £4,000 using his lifetime scale. The painting was valued at £25,000 on 1st May 1997.

Compute the amount of quick succession relief and the IHT payable on T's death.

Solution

Computation of quick succession relief: £

$$\frac{20,000}{24,000} \times 4,000 \times 20\% =$$ 667

The 20% reduction figure is used as the death occurred in between four and five years of the original transfer.

		£
IHT payable on T's estate on 1.5.1997		
Net value of estate		250,000

IHT payable:

£		£
215,000 Nil		Nil
35,000 @ 40%		14,000
250,000		14,000
Less quick succession relief		667
IHT chargeable on death		13,333

Note

The relief is a calculated amount which is then deducted in the IHT computation.

If the amount of quick succession relief exceeds the amount of the IHT attributable to the transfer on the deceased's estate, then the shortfall can be carried forward by a beneficiary. It could be set against any liability for IHT arising on his or her death if it occurs within five years of the original transfer which gave rise to the first calculation of quick succession relief.

Double tax relief

11. Double tax relief is available in respect of overseas tax borne on either death or lifetime transfers.

   a) The relief applies only to foreign taxes similar to the UK IHT and not local taxes.

   b) The amount of the tax credit is the lower of:

      i) IHT on the foreign property; or

      ii) overseas tax on the foreign property.

   c) Relief is deducted from the IHT payable on the estate and after the determination of the estate rate %. DTR therefore only reduces the IHT on the foreign property and not the tax borne on other property in the estate.

Example

R died on 1st of November 1997 leaving the following estate:

		£
Foreign property. Apartment in Paris	FFs	2,000,000
UK Free estate	£s	150,000

Death duty paid in France amounted to £20,000 and realisation costs £8,222.

At the date of death the French franc exchange rate was quoted $8 - 9 = £1$ sterling.

Calculate the IHT payable.

Solution

R's estate 1st November 1997

	£	£
UK Free estate		150,000
Apartment in Paris		
French francs $\dfrac{2,000,000}{9} =$	222,222	
Less costs of realisation	8,222	214,000
		364,000
IHT payable		59,600
$(364,000 - 215,000) \times 40\%$		
DT Relief		
Foreign property	214,000	
Foreign tax	20,000	20,000
UK IHT		39,600

Notes

i) The estate rate is $\dfrac{59,600}{364,000} = 16.37\%$

ii) IHT on the foreign property is $214,000 \times 16.37\% = £35,032$ therefore the lower foreign tax of £20,000 is deducted.

iii) Conversion into £1 sterling is made at the rate to give the lowest UK value ie FFs 9 = £1 sterling.

iv) Realisation expenses not exceeding 5% of the value of the foreign property are deductible for the purposes of calculating IHT. $5\% \times 222,222 = £11,111$.

v) The net UK tax borne by the foreign property is $£35,032 - £20,000 = £15,032$.

Life assurance policies

12. a) Life assurance policies payable on the death of an individual form part of his or her estate and are valued at their maturity value.

b) Life assurance policies which mature on the death of another individual also form part of the deceased's estate and are valued at the open market value.

c) If an individual transfers a policy on his or her own life upon which he or she has paid some premium, then the value is the greater of:

   i) the premium or other consideration paid for the policy, or

   ii) the surrender value at the date of the transfer.

d) A whole life assurance policy written in trust for the beneficiaries of an estate does not form part of the deceased's estate. The proceeds are paid direct to beneficiaries who could, for example, use the money to pay any IHT due on the estate. The annual premiums may be able to be covered by the normal expenditure exemption.

Liabilities

13. The following points should be noted under this heading.

a) Liabilities forming a charge on any property (realty) are to be deducted from the value of that property rather than from the estate in general. This would apply, for example, to a mortgage on a home.

b) Only debts unpaid by law or incurred for a consideration are debts of the estate.

c) Debts payable at a date after death are valued as a discounted sum.

d) Rent, rates and taxes due to the date of death are deductible from the estate.

e) Liabilities due to persons outside the UK (and not charged on UK property) must be deducted from the value of non-UK property as far as possible.

f) Additional costs, incurred by an executor in administering or realising foreign property, are deductible from the value of that property, subject to a maximum of 5% of the gross value of that property.

g) Debts incurred by an executor are not deductible from the value of the estate for IHT purposes.

h) Incidental costs of transferring assets are not included in the computation of any value transferred except where they are borne by the transferee. In this case, since they reduce the value of the amount transferred, they are deductible.

Funeral expenses

14. a) Reasonable funeral expenses are allowed as a deduction from the value of the estate for IHT purposes.

b) Where death takes place abroad then special expenditure incurred in transporting the body back to the UK would be deductible.

c) The cost of mourning or of a tombstone is not part of funeral expenses. However, by concession, reasonable expenditure for the mourning of the deceased's family and servants is allowed.

• Student self-testing question

J died on 7th June 1997 leaving the following estate:

	£
Freehold property	185,000
Household furniture and effects	10,000
10,000 ordinary shares in T plc (a quoted company)	35,000
Life assurance policy on J's life	50,000

J owned the freehold property until March 1990 when he gave it to his son by way of a gift. J continued to live in the property with his son, rent free until the date of his death. The value of the property in March 1990 was £95,000.

There was a mortgage on the freehold property amounting to £35,000. Funeral expenses amounted to £1,500. J had made no lifetime transfers of value. The executor sold the shares in T plc for £30,000 after expenses of £1,000, in December 1997 in order to pay estate debts.

Compute the IHT liability arising on J's death.

Solution

J's estate 7th June 1997

	£	£	£
Freehold property (gift with reservation)		185,000	
Less mortgage		35,000	150,000
Household furniture and effects			10,000
10,000 ordinary shares in T plc:			
at valuation		35,000	
Less loss on sale		4,000	31,000
Life assurance policy			50,000
			241,000
Less funeral expenses			1,500
			239,500

IHT payable:

		£	£
215,000 @ Nil		Nil	
24,500 @ 40%		9,800	
239,500		9800	9,800

Notes

i)   *The sale of the quoted shares within 12 months of the date of J's death has shown a loss which may be deducted from the estate value.*

ii) *The loss on the ordinary shares is £35,000 – £31,000 = £4,000 ie before expenses. There is no restriction through reinvestment of the proceeds, since this did not take place.*

iii) *The gift with reservation forms part of J's estate as he retained an interest in it.*

• Question without answer

G died on 21st June 1997 leaving a net estate of £480,000, having made no previous lifetime transfers. On 5th May 1995 G received property worth £200,000 on which IHT of £80,000 was paid. The property was valued at £250,000 on G's death and included in the net estate of £480,000.

Compute the IHT payable on G's death.

47 Business property relief

Introduction

1. Relief is available for transfers of value inter vivos or on a death of an individual, of relevant business property.

The relief is given by way of a percentage reduction from the valuation of the property.

This chapter begins with a summary of the relief available, followed by a definition of relevant business property and the associated rules. Worked examples then show the computations to be made.

Summary of relief – transfers after 6th April 1996

2.

a) Property consisting of a business or interest in a business such as a partnership or sole trader. A business includes total assets including goodwill, less liabilities.   100%

b) Shares or securities in unquoted companies including USM/AIM after 6th April 1996.   100%

c) Shares or securities of a quoted company which gave the transferor control of the company immediately before the transfer.   50%

d) Business assets such as land and buildings, plant and machinery owned by the transferor as a sole trader, partner, or as a controlling director, and used in that business.   50%

e) Business assets such as land and buildings, plant and machinery used by the transferor in a business which was settled property in which he or she had an interest in possession.   50%

Relevant business property

3. In addition to the details shown in the summary above, the following points should be noted.

a) To qualify for relief, the property must have been owned by the transferor for at least two years immediately prior to the transfer. Where property replaces other property and the two years criteria cannot be met then relief is still available, provided aggregate ownership is greater than two years out of the previous five.

b) Assets not used wholly or mainly for the purposes of the business within the two year period noted in (a) above are excepted assets e.g. investments or surplus cash and relief is not available for those items.

c) Relief is not available for a transfer of business property which is used wholly or mainly for the following purposes:

   i) Dealing in stocks, shares or securities. (Stock jobbers and discount houses are, however, eligible for relief.)

   ii) Dealing in land or buildings.

   iii) Making or holding investments.

d) The expression business includes a profession or vocation but does not include a business carried on otherwise than for gain.

e) Shares in a holding company qualify if the subsidiaries themselves qualify for relief.

f) The original property (or if sold, its replacement) must be owned by the transferee throughout the period beginning with the chargeable transfer and ending on the transferor's death to retain the full benefit of the relief.

g) Where the original property is disposed of before the transferor's death and the proceeds are used to purchase replacement property full relief is available if:

   i) the whole of the proceeds are used to purchase a replacement

   ii) both sale and purchase take place within three years of each other.

h) If only part of the original property (or its replacement) is in the transferee's possession on the death of the transferor, then only that part will be eligible for relief.

i) Relief reduces the value of the transfer before any available exemptions are given.

j) Where any of the relief is clawed back the additional tax payable by the transferee is calculated on the transfer before BPR. However, the net transfer ie after BPR included in the transferor's cumulative total remains unchanged.

Holdings in unquoted companies and the USM / AIM

4. Business property relief is increased from 50% to 100% for transfers made from 6th April 1996 on all unquoted shares held for at least two years.

PET and business property relief

5. If the property eligible for business property relief is transferred by a PET then tax will only become payable on the death of the transferor within seven years of the date of the transfer. For other chargeable transfers, tax is due at the date of the transfer and at the date of death if within the seven year period.

> **Example**

A who had made no previous transfers gave his controlling interest in Z Ltd, a private company, to his son on April 12th 1997. The interest was valued at £440,000. A's controlling interest was acquired for £50,000 in 1984. A died on the 10th August 2001 leaving an estate of £380,000. A's son has retained the controlling interest in Z Ltd.

Compute the IHT arising on A's death.

Solution

	£	£
10.8.2001. Value of A's estate		380,000
Add transfers made within previous 7 years		
12.4.97 gift to son	440,000	
Less business property relief 100% × 440,000	440,000	–
		380,000
IHT payable thereof FA 1997 rates:	£	£
	–	
215,000 @ Nil		
165,000 @ 40%	66,000	66,000
380,000	66,000	66,000
Less notional IHT on gift to son of	440,000	Nil
		66,000
IHT payable by executors		Nil

IHT payable on PET

Notes

i) *IHT is not payable in respect of the transfer on 12th April 1997 as the transfer of value is a PET.*

ii) *As the business property relief of 100% applied there would be no IHT payable by A's son on the death of his father.*

iii) *BP relief is given at the rate appropriate to the property at the time the gift was made.*

• Student self-testing question

B dies on 7th April 2000 leaving the following estate:

	£
20% interest in Q Ltd, an unquoted private company	125,000
Freehold land used by Q Ltd	35,000
Shares in Z plc, a quoted company (< 1% holding)	15,000
Other property (net)	312,500

Three years before his death B had transferred a 15% interest in the shares in Q Ltd to his son. B has made no other transfers but has used all his annual exemptions. B's son has retained his interest in Q Ltd which at the date of the gift was valued at £40,000, and on B's death was worth £280,000.

Calculate the IHT arising on B's death.

Solution

	£	£
7.4.2000 value of B's estate:		
20% interest in Q Ltd	125,000	
Less business property relief100% × 125,000	125,000	–
Freehold land used by Q Ltd		35,000
Shares in Z plc		15,000
Other property		312,500
		362,500
Add transfer within previous 7 years		
Gift of shares in Q Ltd	40,000	
Business property relief 50% × 40,000	20,000	20,000
		382,500
IHT thereon FA 1997 Rates:		
215,000 per table	Nil	
167,500 @ 40%	67,000	
382,500	67,000	67,000
Less notional IT on gift within last 7 years	20,000	–
IT payable executors		67,000

Notes

i)   There is no inheritance tax payable in respect of the gift as it was below the threshold level of £215,000.

ii) The BP rate of 100% applies to the shares in Q Ltd.

iii) No relief is available for the freehold land used by Q Ltd as B did not have a controlling interest.

iv) The PET is valued at the date of the transfer and not the date of B's death for estate purposes. Where the death value is lower than the transfer value, that value is used to compute any IHT on the transfer at death.

• Question without answer

S died on 17th June 1997 leaving the following estate:

	£
Leasehold house property	239,000
Household furniture and effects	10,000
10,000 ordinary shares in T plc, a quoted public company (<1% holding)	25,000
Life assurance policies on his own life	35,000
A controlling interest in F Ltd, an unquoted private manufacturing company which he had owned for 10 years	266,000

S had made no lifetime transfers.

Compute the IHT arising on the death of S.

48 Agricultural property and woodlands relief

Introduction

1. Relief is available for transfers of value inter vivos or on a death, of 'agricultural property'. The relief is given by way of a percentage deduction from the valuation of the property.

    In this chapter a summary of the agricultural relief available is first given, followed by a definition of agricultural property. Examples of how to work out the relief in computations are given. The rest of the chapter deals with relief available in respect of growing timber.

Summary of relief

2. Transferor has right to vacant possession, or right to obtain vacant possession within the next 12 months, eg owner occupied farmlands and farm tenancies.   100%

    Transferor does not have right to vacant possession either immediately or within next 12 months eg tenanted farmland, owned by the transferor – from 1.9.95.   100%

    Prior to that date relief was at 50%.

Agricultural property

3. The following points should be noted under this heading.

    a) Agricultural property includes agricultural land and pastures; woodlands ancillary to the occupation of agricultural property; buildings used for the intensive rearing of fish or livestock or milk quotas. Farm building houses and cottages are excluded, see *Starke* v *IR CHD* 1994.

    b) Animals, plant and machinery, feeding stocks and seeds are not agricultural property.

    c) Relief is only available in respect of the 'agricultural value' of the property and not in respect of any potential development value.

    d) The relief is available in respect of inter vivos and death transfers.

Conditions for relief

4. a) The property must be either:

        i) occupied by the transferor for the purposes of agriculture throughout the last two years or,

        ii) owned by the transferor throughout the previous seven years prior to the date of the transfer and occupied by him or her or someone else for the purposes of agriculture, throughout the seven years.

    b) Where property is replaced then condition (a) (i) is satisfied by occupation of both properties for two of the previous five years. Condition (a) (ii) is satisfied if the property is owned and occupied for seven of the previous ten years.

    c) If the transferor has a controlling interest in a company which owns agricultural property and he or she meets the occupancy conditions above, then the relief is available.

    d) The original property (or if sold, its replacement) must be owned by the transferee throughout the period beginning with the chargeable transfer and ending on the transferors death. For transfers of value made on or after the 30th November 1993 the replacement period is three years or such longer period as the Inland Revenue allow.

    e) If only part of the original property (or its replacement) is in the transferee's possession on the death of the transferor, then only that part will be eligible for relief.

    > **Example**

    P owns and farms agricultural property which he transfers to his son on 1st May 1997. P has farmed the property for 10 years. The agricultural value at 1st May 1997 was £440,000. P had made no previous transfers and had used up all his exemptions. P dies on 4th October 1998 leaving a net estate of £350,000.

    Compute the IHT arising on the death of P.

Solution

		£	£
4.10.98	Value of P's estate		350,000
	Add chargeable transfers within last 7 years		
1.5.97	Gift to son	440,000	
	Less agriculture relief 100% × 440,000	440,000	–
			350,000

IHT thereon FA 1997 Rates:

			£	£
215,000	per table		Nil	
135,000	@ 40%		54,000	
350,000			54,000	54,000

Less notional IHT on gifts on transfers within last 7 years

Gift to son (440,000 – 440,000 (BPR))	Nil
IHT paid by executors	54,000

Note

There is no IHT payable in respect of the gift of P's son as it is owner occupied farmland and therefore eligible for the 100% AP relief.

Where the agricultural property has a greater value than its 'agricultural value' then it is usually possible to obtain business property relief on the non-agriculture value.

Woodlands

5. The relief available under this heading amounts to a postponement of the payment of tax. The following points should be noted.

   a) The relief is only available in respect of a transfer on death.

   b) If the relief is claimed then the value of the growing timber (but not the land) is excluded from the deceased's estate. When the timber is subsequently sold or gifted with or without the land, then IHT becomes payable.

   c) The relief is available in the following circumstances.

      i) Where an election is made within two years of the death by the person who would otherwise have to pay the tax on the timber. The time period may be extended at Inland Revenue discretion.

      ii) Where the deceased was the beneficial owner of the woodlands including the land, for at least the five years immediately prior to death, unless he or she received it by way of gift or inheritance.

   d) The net proceeds of sale are added to the value of the deceased's estate and the tax calculated at the marginal rate. If there is a change in the IHT rates the calculations are made with the *latest rates, where these are lower than at the date of death*.

   e) Net proceeds of sale are after any expenses of disposal and expenses of replanting within three years of disposal.

Example

K dies on 23rd June 1988 leaving growing timber worth £40,000 to his son P. His other estate amounted to £100,000 and land of £20,000. There were no previous transfers of value. The executors elect for woodlands relief.

On 1st July 1997 P sells the whole of the timber for £300,000.

Compute the IHT payable in respect of the timber.

Solution

		£	£	£
23.6.88	K's estate excluding timber			
	Land			20,000
	Other estate			100,000
	Chargeable estate			120,000

IHT payable at 1988 rates:

		£
90,000		Nil
30,000	@ 30%	9,000
120,000		9,000

		£	£	£
1.7.97	IHT arising on sale of timber			
	Proceeds of sale			300,000
	K's chargeable estate at 23.6.88			120,000
	Revised estate value			420,000

IHT payable at 1997 rates:

215,000 per table		–	
205,000 @ 40%		82,000	
420,000		82,000	

1.7.97	IHT on estate of 420,000		82,000
23.6.88	IHT on estate of 120,000		–
	IHT payable on sale of timber		82,000

Notes

i) *IHT on £120,000 at rates prevailing at 1.7.1997 is Nil.*

ii) *Where the rates of IHT change, tax is charged at the death rate at the time of the sale.*

iii) *Where the woodlands are managed commercially then business property relief is usually available in respect of both land, and the proceeds of sale of the timber.*

iv) *The IHT is payable by the person entitled to the proceeds of sale in this case P.*

• Student self-testing question

Z owned agricultural property which was farmed by a tenant. On 1st June 1997 Z died leaving the agricultural value of the property at £100,000 subject to a mortgage of £25,000. The agricultural property was subject to a 20 year lease which did not terminate until 1999. Z left other net estate with a value of £262,500. On 21st April 1993 Z had made a gift of £260,000 to his daughter after using all his annual exemptions.

Calculate the IHT arising on Z's death.

Solution

Z's estate 1.6.1997

	£	£
Agricultural value of property	100,000	
Less mortgage	25,000	
	75,000	
Less agricultural relief		
100% × 75,000	75,000	–
Value of other property		262,500
Add gift within last 7 years: 21.4.1993 Gift to daughter		260,000
		522,500

		£	£
IHT arising thereon: FA 1997 rates			
215,000 per table		–	
307,500 @ 40 %		123,000	
522,500		123,000	123,000
Less IHT on gifts within last 7 years: Gift to daughter 21.4.1993		260,000	
IHT (260,000 – 215,000) × 40%			18,000
Tax payable by executors			105,000

Notes

i) *The 100% agricultural property relief applies to a transfer on or after 1st September 1995.*

ii) *IHT on gift to daughter of £260,000 = 260,000 – 215,000 at 40% = 18,000*

Less taper relief 4–5 years 40% × 18,000	7,200
IHT payable by daughter	10,800

• Question without answer

V died on 6th April 1989 leaving a net estate of £250,000 which included growing timber valued at £30,000. V had made no previous lifetime transfers. Under his will the timber was left to his brother.

The executors elect for woodlands relief under Section 125 IHTA 1984. On 12th July 1997 V's brother sells the whole of the timber for £300,000.

Compute the IHT payable in respect of the timber.

49 Settlements

Introduction

1. A trust is an organisational structure with a separate legal identity which owns property and is administered by trustees on behalf of beneficiaries. For IHT purposes the term settlement embraces a number of different types of trust. There is also an important distinction made between settlements with an interest in possession and those without; the latter are often called discretionary settlements.

   This chapter begins with a summary of some important expressions. It then deals with the main features of settlements with an interest in possession and those without. A detailed survey of this topic is not provided.

Some basic expressions

2. a) Settlement (Section 43 IHTA 1984)
   This is defined as any disposition of property as a result of which the property is for the time being:

   i) held in trust for persons in succession eg property left for life to A, with remainder to B, or

   ii) held in trust for a person subject to a contingency eg property held in trust for A until he or she attains the age of 35, or

   iii) held in trust with powers to accumulate income or make payments of the income of the trust at the discretion of the trustees.

   b) Interest in possession.

   An interest in possession in settled property exists where the person holding the interest has the immediate entitlement to income, eg an ordinary life annuitant or life tenant.

   c) Relevant property (Section 58 IHTA 1984)

   This is settled property in which there is no qualifying interest in possession (eg a discretionary settlement) other than the following.

   i) Property held for charitable purposes only.

   ii) Property held in an approved maintenance fund for historic buildings.

   iii) Property held in accumulation and maintenance settlements.

   iv) Property held in superannuation schemes.

   v) Property held in trust for employees.

   vi) Property held in trust for disabled persons.

   vii) Excluded property.

Creation of settlements

3. a) Transfers by an individual to the following trusts are PETs:

   i) accumulation and maintenance trusts

   ii) trusts for disabled persons

   iii) trusts where there is a beneficial interest.

   IHT is not payable in respect of these transfers unless the settler dies within seven years of the transfers.

   b) Transfers other than PETs are chargeable to IHT at the date of the transfer.

   c) Transfers into a settlement by a settlor are subject to the normal rules of computation. If the settlor agrees to pay the IHT on a transfer to a trust then the grossing up procedures must be applied.

   d) There is no chargeable transfer where the settlor retains beneficial interest in possession since in this case for IHT purposes he or she is treated as the owner of the trust property. The estate has therefore not been diminished as a result of the transfer.

Example

T settled the sum of £250,000 on a discretionary trust on 6th June 1997, after using his annual exemptions. In the previous year on 10th May, T has given his son £30,000 after exemption.

Compute any IHT arising on the creation of the discretionary trust.

Solution

		Gross £	Tax £	Net £
6.6.1997	Accumulated transfers within last 7 years	30,000	–	30,000
	Transfer to trust	266,250	16,250	250,000
		296,250	16,250	280,000

IHT on net transfer of £280,000
$\frac{1}{4}(280,000 - 215,000) =$ 16,250

Check gross transfer of £296,250

215,000 per table	–	
81,250 @ 20%	16,250	16,250
296,250		

Thus T will pay inheritance tax of £16,250 on the transfer to the discretionary trust of £250,000. Additional tax may be payable by the trust if T dies within seven years of the date of transfer.

Settlements with an interest in possession

4. a) For IHT purposes, a person having an interest in possession is treated as the owner of the trust property which provides him or her with income. Thus the life tenant of a trust is deemed to be the owner of the trust assets which provide him or her with income for life (eg an annuity).

   b) A chargeable event arises where the interest in possession is terminated, in the following circumstances:

   i) Where the person entitled to the interest in possession dies.

   ii) Where the interest is disposed of by way of a gift, sale or surrender.

   iii) Where the interest is terminated at a particular date or on the occasion of a particular event.

   c) The amount of IHT payable on the termination of an interest in possession depends upon the lifetime cumulative total of transfers and, where necessary, the death scale rates, of the person entitled to the interest.

Example

J died on 1st July 1997 leaving the following estate:

	£
Life interest in Alpha trust remainder to J's brother	90,000
Other net estate	210,000

He has made no lifetime transfers.

Compute the IHT payable on J's death.

Solution

		£	£
1.7.97	Value of J's estate:		
	Life interest	90,000	
	Other estate	210,000	300,000
	IHT on death scale. $(300,000 - 215,000) \times 40\%$		34,000

Estate rate is $\frac{34,000}{300,000} = 11.33\%$

IHT is apportioned as follows:

		£
Trustees of the Alpha trust	90,000 @ 11.33%	10,197
Executors of J's estate	210,000 @ 11.33%	23,803
	300,000	34,000

Notes

i) *The death of J constitutes a termination of his interest in possession in the Alpha trust and the value of the property in that trust forms part of his estate.*

ii) *IHT due in respect of the life interest is payable by the trustees of the Alpha trust.*

5. The following additional points should be noted.

a) Where the life tenant become absolutely entitled to the trust property there is no IHT liability, since the life tenant deemed to own the property before the transfer to him or her (in the capacity of life tenant) and then becomes the actual owner.

Thus if property is held in trust for M until he reaches the age of 25 and then it passes to him absolutely there will be no IHT charge when he becomes 25.

b) On the termination of an interest in possession the following exemptions and reliefs could be available:

i) the annual exemption of £3,000 for a lifetime transfer

ii) business property relief where the interest is business property.

iii) transfer to a spouse exemption

iv) quick succession relief.

Settlements with no interest in possession *Discretionary trusts*

6. As noted above, Section 58 IHTA 1984 defines relevant property as settled property where there is no interest in possession and these settlements are often referred to as discretionary trusts. Special IHT rates apply to relevant property and the definition particularly excludes certain categories of discretionary trust which would otherwise be taxable in the same way, eg accumulation and maintenance settlements.

IHT charge on 10 year anniversary

7. A liability to IHT arises on the 10th anniversary of the creation of a discretionary trust and in general is computed as follows.

a) The amount on which tax is charged is the value of the relevant property held by the trust on the 10th anniversary.

b) IHT is charged at 30% of the effective rate.

c) The effective rate is equal to:

$$\frac{\text{IHT on life time scale at marginal rate}}{\text{hypothetical transfer}} \times \frac{100}{1}\%$$

i) The IHT is calculated on the cumulative total of lifetime transfers of the settlor made within seven years of the creation of the trust plus the value of the assumed transfer noted in (ii) below.

ii) The hypothetical transfer is the sum of the following:
1. value of property at 10 year anniversary
2. value of trust property at date of creation of trust which has not subsequently become relevant property
3. value of property in any other trusts created by settlor at same date.

Example

N settled property worth £60,000 in a discretionary trust on 1st May 1997 which had a value of £216,000 on 1st May 2007. No other trusts were created by N. On 1st May 1997 N had made chargeable transfers of £84,000 within the previous seven years.

Compute the IHT payable on the 10 year anniversary.

Solution

Calculation of effective rate (FA 1997 rates)

		£
1.5.2007	Value of trust property	216,000
	Cumulative total of transfers to 1.5.97	84,000
		300,000

IHT using lifetime scale rates

	Gross £	Tax £
Prior transfers	84,000	–
Value of trust property	216,000	17,000
	300,000	17,000

$(300,000 - 215,000) \times 20\% = 17,000$

Effective rate $= \dfrac{17,000}{216,000} = 0.0787\%$

Rate of IHT $30\% \times 0.0787\% = 0.0236\%$

IHT payable £216,000 $\times$ 0.0236% = **£5,097.60**

Example

On 31st May 1997 Y settled property of £30,000 on each of two trusts, A and B. The trust A was a discretionary trust and the B was subject to a life interest. On 31st May 2007 each trust is assumed to have a value of £60,000. In the seven years prior to 31st May 1997 Y had accumulated transfers of £185,000 gross.

Compute the IHT liability arising on the first 10 year anniversary of the trust.

Solution

Computation of effective rate

	£
Assumed transfer:	
Value of relevant property 31.5.2007	60,000
Value of property in related settlement	
on creation 31.5.97	30,000
Chargeable transfer in previous 7 years	185,000
	275,000

IHT using lower scale rates FA 1997

IHT on transfer of 275,000:

215,000 per table	–
60,000 @ 20%	12,000
275,000	12,000

Effective rate $= \dfrac{12,000}{90,000} = 0.1333$

Rate of IHT $30\% \times 0.1333 = 0.0399\%$

IHT payable by trustees £60,000 $\times$ 0.0399% = £2,394

Property ceasing to be held on discretionary trusts *Before 10 year anniversary*

8. a) Where property leaves a discretionary trust, for example where the trustees distribute part of the capital, then a charge to IHT arises.

   b) The donor grossing up principle applies where the trustees agree to pay any IT arising under this heading.

   c) The effective rate is multiplied by an appropriate fraction. The latter is equal to:

   $$\frac{\text{no. of quarters since commencement of settlement}}{40 \text{ quarters}}$$

Thus if a charge arises seven years after the commencement of a settlement then the fraction is $\dfrac{28}{40}$.

Example

R settled £200,000 on a discretionary trust on 29th April 1997 at which date he had made cumulative chargeable transfers of £75,000 within the last seven years. On 1st May 2001 the trustee's appointed the sum of £85,000 to an accumulation and maintenance settlement.

Compute the proportionate charge.

Solution

	£
Assumed transfer:	
Value of property at creation of settlement 29.4.97	200,000
Cumulative transfers to 29.4.97	75,000
	275,000
IHT at lower scale rates: $(275,000 - 215,000) \times 20\%$	12,000

Effective rate $\dfrac{12,000}{200,000}$	$= 6.0\%$
No. of completed quarters to 1st May 2001	$= 16$
Proportionate charge $= \dfrac{16}{40} \times 6.0\% \times 30\%$	$= 0.7\%$
IHT payable £85,000 $\times 0.7\%$	$= £595$

Note

If the IHT is paid out of relevant property, and not by the donees, then the chargeable transfer must be grossed up in accordance with the normal rules.

Miscellaneous points

9. a) Where property is added to a discretionary settlement there are a number of adjustments to be made to the computations outlined in the previous sections.

   b) There are slightly different rules applicable to discretionary trusts made before 27th March 1974.

Accumulation and maintenance settlements

10. These are normally settlements without an interest in possession and would be treated in the same way as 'relevant property' of a discretionary trust but for special excluding provisions.

These provisions contained in Section 71 IHTA 1984 apply where:

a) one or more persons will become entitled to an interest in possession or to the settled property absolutely on or before attaining a specified age not exceeding 25 years of age.

b) income is accumulated for the maintenance, education or benefit of a beneficiary and there is no interest in possession.

c) either not more than 25 years have elapsed since the trust was created or all the persons who are or have been beneficiaries have a common grandparent.

11. The main consequence of these types of trusts are the following.

a) IHT is not payable on the creation of the trust as the transfer is a PET.

b) No tax is payable on the 10 year anniversary.

c) No tax is payable when capital is advanced to a beneficiary.

d) There is no charge to tax when a beneficiary becomes entitled to the property absolutely or obtains an interest in possession.

• Student self-testing question

M died on 13th August 1997 leaving the following estate:

Life assurance policy on his own life	27,000
Cash and bank balances	12,500
Freehold property	234,000
Partnership interest in M.N. & Co Solicitors	70,000
Life interest in Zebra Trust	17,500

Funeral expenses amount to £2,000

Compute the IHT arising on the death of M who had no lifetime transfers, and show the amount borne by the trustees of the Zebra trust.

Solution

M's estate 13th August 1997

	£	£
Freehold property		234,000
Life interest in Zebra trust		17,500
Life assurance policy		27,000
Cash and bank balances		12,500
Partnership interest	70,000	
Less business property relief		
100% × 70,000	70,000	
		291,000
Less funeral expenses		2,000
		289,000

IHT payable on £289,000: FA 1997 rates

215,000 per table	–	
74,000 @ 40%	29,600	
289,000	29,600	29,600

Effective rate $\dfrac{29,600}{289,000}$ = 10.24%

IHT apportioned as follows:

Trustees of Zebra trust 10.24% ×	17,500	1,792
Executors of M's estate 10.24% ×	271,500	27,808
	289,000	29,600

• Question without answer

R settled property worth £80,000 in a discretionary trust on 21st June 1997 which had a value of £200,000 on 21st June 2007. On 21st June 1997 R had made chargeable transfers within the previous seven years of £150,000.

Compute the IHT payable by the trust on the first 10 year anniversary of the creation of the trust.

Inheritance tax
End of section questions and answers

Inheritance tax question No 1

On 12th August 1997 P made a gift of £255,000 gross to a discretionary trust after using all his exemptions. P dies on 14th June 2001 leaving a net estate of £120,000 having made no other lifetime transfers.

Calculate the IHT arising from the above transactions.

Solution

			£
1997/98 Gift to discretionary trust (gross)			255,000
IHT payable thereon at lower scale rates			

£		£	
215,000 per table		–	
40,000 @ 20%		8,000	
255,000		8,000	

		£
IHT payable by P on gift		8,000
14.6.2001 P's estate value		120,000
Add transfers within previous 7 years		
12.8.97 Gift to discretionary trust		255,000
		375,000

IHT thereon FA 1997 rates

215,000 per table		–	
160,000 @ 40%		64,000	
375,000		64,000	64,000

Less notional IHT on gifts within last 7 years of £255,000

215,000 per table		–	
40,000 @ 40%		16,000	
255,000		16,000	16,000

IHT payable by executors		48,000
IHT payable on gift of	255,000	
as computed at death scale rates		16,000
Less taper relief		
(3–4 years) 20% × 16,000		3,200
		12,800
Less tax already paid 1997/98		8,000
Additional IHT payable by trustees		4,800

Inheritance tax question No 2

T, who has made no previous transfers of value, makes the following gifts during the year 1997/98.

April 10th	Gift of £1,000 to T's sister-in-law on the occasion of her wedding in June 1997.
July 1st	Gift of £15,000 to his son to assist with wedding preparations. The wedding took place in December 1996.
August 12th	Gift of £250 to his gardener.
November 5th	Gift of £295,000 to discretionary trust (trustees to pay the tax).

T dies on 9th April 1999 leaving a net estate of £250,000.

Calculate any IHT arising in respect of the gifts and T's estate.

Solution

IHT Clock

			£	Gross £	Tax £	Net £
1997/98						
10.4.97	Gift to T's sister-in-law		1,000			
	Less Marriage exemption		1,000	–		
1.7.97	Gift to son		15,000			
	Less Marriage exemption		5,000			
	PET		10,000	–		
	Less AE 1997/98	3,000				
	1996/97	3,000	6,000			
	Left out of account		4,000	–	–	–
12.8.97	Gift to gardener		250			
	Small gift exemption		250			
5.11.97	Gift to discretionary trust [IHT: (295,000 – 215,000) x 20% = 16,000]		295,000	295,000	16,000	279,000
				295,000	16,000	279,000

IHT Clock rewritten

		Gross	IHT (Death rate)
1.7.97	Gift to son	4,000	–
5.11.97	Gift to discretionary trust	295,000	33,600
		299,000	33,600

IHT (299,000 – 215,000) × 40% = 33,600

T's estate 9th April 1999

	£
Free estate	250,000
Transfers within previous 7 years	299,000
	549,000

IHT payable (FA 1997 rates):

(549,000 – 215,000) × 40%	133,600
Less IHT on life time transfers (as above)	33,600
Payable by executors	100,000

IHT payable on gift to discretionary trust

5.11.97	Value of gift	299,000
	IHT as above	33,600
	Less taper relief (less than 3 years)	Nil
		33,600
	Less paid – 31. 5. 1998	16,000
	Payable by trustees 31. 10. 1999	17,600

Inheritance tax question No 3

Reg Plowman, who has been employed for many years as a salesman with a food manufacturer, died on 18th October 1997. His estate as valued for inheritance tax comprised:

	£
Leasehold residence	245,000
Quoted investments	See below
Household effects	5,700
Cash at bank	1,409
Life policy (including bonuses)	16,321

Quoted investments consisted of the following:

£2,000 nominal, of $2\frac{1}{2}$ % Consols. quoted 24 – 25

5,000 ordinary shares in T plc quoted ex-dividend at 150 – 162p

Recorded bargains being made at 151, 157, 159, 160. A dividend of 2p per share is payable on 1st December 1997 (the shareholding is less than 1% of the total).

In addition, he owned agricultural property with no development potential valued at £43,750 on 18th October 1997 on which date the rent due from the tenant amounted to £1,250. He acquired the agricultural property in December 1995 and it has been occupied by the tenant for agricultural purposes since that date. His liabilities were:

	£
Personal debts	875
Income tax 1997/98	323

Funeral expenses amounted to £967. His liability to capital gains tax for 1996/97 is estimated to be £500. He had made no gifts during his lifetime.

Under the terms of his will, he left pecuniary legacies to friends totalling £3,500, a gift of £10,000 to a charity, a pecuniary legacy of £30,000 to his wife, the agricultural property to his brother and the residue of his estate to his children for life and thereafter to his grandchildren equally.

You are required to compute the inheritance tax payable on the estate of Reg Plowman.

Solution

18th October 1997. Estate of Reg Plowman

	£	£
Leasehold premises		245,000
Household effects		5,700
Life policy		16,321
Agricultural property		43,750
Accrued rent		1,250
Cash at bank		1,409
Quoted investments:		
$2\frac{1}{2}$% Consols £2,000 × £24¼ per £100		485
5,000 shares in T plc at lower of:		
¼ up. $162 - 150 = \frac{12}{4}$ ie 153		
½ way. $160 - 151 = \frac{9}{2}$ ie 155½		
5,000 @ 153		7,650
Accrued dividend 5,000 × 2p (net)		100
		321,665
Less Personal debts	875	
Income tax 1997/98	323	
CGT 1996/97	500	
Funeral expenses	967	2,665
Chargeable estate		319,000
Less Exemption		
Legacy to charity	10,000	
Legacy to wife	30,000	40,000
		279,000

IHT payable

215,000	–		
64,000 @ 40 %	25,600		
279,000	25,600		25,600

Notes

i) *There is no agricultural relief available as the property has not been owned for two years.*

ii) *The net dividend is added to the ex-dividend price of the T plc shares for IHT purposes.*

Inheritance tax question No 4

A owns and farms Blackacres which consists of 800 acres of arable farm land.

On his 60th birthday, 15th April 1997, he retires and gives his son the farm land valued at £900,000.

A's son continues to farm the land, which his father bought in 1950 for £100 per acre. On 31st December 1998 A's son sells 80 acres to a property developer for £180,000.

A dies on 9th October 1999 leaving a net estate of £175,000.

A had made no other lifetime transfers, and had regularly used all of his exemptions.

Calculate the IHT payable on A's death.

Solution

	£	£
9.10.1999 Value of A's estate		175,000
Add transfers with previous 7 years		
15.4.1997 Gift to son	900,000	
Less Agricultural relief restricted		
$100\% \times \dfrac{720}{800} \times 900,000$	810,000	90,000
		265,000
IHT arising thereon: 215,000	–	
50,000 @ 40%	20,000	
265,000	20,000	20,000
Less notional IHT payable on gift		
Value as above	90,000	
Below exemption level of 215,000	Nil	
IHT payable on residue		20,000

Notes

i)   *As part of the land has been disposed of the agricultural property relief is restricted to the proportion of the original gift held at the date of death ie 720 acres not 800 acres*

ii) *The transfer of value on A's retirement is a PET.*

iii) *The agricultural relief of 100% applies.*

Inheritance tax question No 5

a)   Leonardo, who was born in and whose home country is Italy, has lived in the UK since 1980, but plans to return to Italy following his retirement.

In June 1991 he gifted capital to his granddaughter amounting to £71,000 after deducting available exemptions. As this figure was within the exempt band, no IHT was payable.

On 31 January 1997 he made a chargeable transfer of £200,000 before deducting exemptions, paying the inheritance tax due himself on the due date.

His estate, at current values, comprises:

a)   10,000 £1 shares is Exodus plc quoted on the Stock Exchange at 134p–140p with recorded bargains of 134, 135 and 136.

b)   10,000 no par value bearer shares in Canadian Timber Ltd. The company register is in Ontario, Canada, and the shares are quoted on the Ontario Stock Exchange at the sterling equivalent of 90–92.

c)   A half share in a painting in the UK which Leonardo and his brother, Vincento, had bought in 1975, each providing one half of the purchase money. Its value is £48,000 but a half share is worth £22,000.

d)   A house in Pisa, Italy, valued at 40,000,000 lire. (2,000 lire = £1)

e)   Three insurance policies with a UK insurance company on his life:
   i)   Taken out in 1975; the proceeds of £50,000 will be left to his wife, who will receive nothing else;
   ii) Taken out in 1977 on which he had paid the premiums and under which £15,000 will become payable to his executor;
   iii) Taken out in 1984 in the name of his granddaughter under which £6,000 becomes payable on his death. Leonardo had paid each annual premium of £220 himself.

f)   Debts owing to him of:
   i)   £1,500 by Michael living in the UK, and
   ii) 2,000,000 lire by Manolo living in Italy.

g)   Cash held in bank accounts:
   i)   In the UK £4,500.
   ii) In Italy 6,000,000 lire.

h)   His gold watch valued at £800 and gold ring valued at £200 both held in the UK.

j)   His private dwelling-house in London valued at £70,000 plus furniture valued at £2,500.

k)   His UK trading business which he has run as a sole trader since 1980, valued at £160,000.

All share certificates and house deeds are held by Leonardo's solicitor at his office in Italy.

Compute the inheritance tax payable by Leonardo following the January 1997 transfer, stating the date it falls due, and the inheritance tax which would be payable if Leonardo were to die unexpectedly within the week following the transfer. Explain the basis for any exemptions or exclusions which apply to Leonardo's estate.

In the case of tax payable on death you should also identify the amounts which can be paid in instalments, the period over which instalments are payable, and the extent to which relief from interest is given on tax so payable.

Solution

Leonardo's estate as at February 1997

a)	10,000 £1 shares in Exodus plc @ 135			13,500
	$^1/_4$ up on 134 = 135 $^1/_2$			
	Mid point = 135			
b)	10,000 bearer shares in Canada Timber Ltd. Documents of title outside UK excluded			–
c)	$^1/_2$ share in painting			22,000
d)	House in Italy excluded			–
e)	Insurance policies – widow exempt			–
	– self			15,000
	– daughter excluded			–
f)	Debts due – Michael			1,500
	– Manolo excluded			–
g)	Cash – UK banks			4,500
	– Italian banks excluded			–
h)	Gold watch and ring			1,000
i)	House furniture in UK			2,500
j)	Private house in UK			70,000
k)	UK Business		160,000	
	Less BPR 100%		160,000	–
	Net estate			130,000

Lifetime transfers			Gross	Tax	Net
1.6.91 Gift to granddaughter			71,000	–	71,000
31.1.97 Transfer		200,000			
AE 1996/97	3,000				
1995/96	3,000	6,000	194,000	16,250	177,750
			265,000	16,250	248,750

IHT (265,000 – 200,000) × $^1/_4$ = 16,250

IHT payable on estate

Net estate	130,000
Add Transfers within last 7 years	265,000
	395,000
IHT (395,000 – 200,000) × 40%	78,000
Less IHT on transfers 65,000 @ 40%	26,000
Payable on estate	52,000

Payable by instalments:

House $\dfrac{70,000}{130,000} \times 52,000 = £28,000$. Interest runs from 31.8.97

Inheritance tax question No 6

You have been asked to provide tax advice at today's date (which you should assume to be 1st February 1997) to the personal representatives of Richard. Richard was aged 65 and died on 2nd November 1996, leaving the following assets:

	Probate Value £	Current Value £
1,000 shares in Bluechip plc (a quoted company with a share capital of 2,000,000 shares)	22,000	17,000
2,500 shares in Giltedge plc (a quoted company with a share capital of 3,000,000 shares)	15,000	20,000
6,000 shares in Nobody Ltd (a private investment company with a share capital of 100,000 shares)	39,000	30,000
Private residence	190,000	230,000
Holiday home	55,000	40,000
	321,000	337,000

Potential selling costs are estimated at 2% of selling price in respect of each asset.

Richard made the following transfers prior to his death:

i) Annual gifts of £3,000 made out of capital to his nephew, Oscar, on 6th April of each year.

ii) A gift of £90,000 cash to a discretionary trust on 3rd September 1988. All taxes on the gift were borne by the trustees.

iii) A gift of £210,000 cash to his son Boris on his marriage on 1st September 1993.

iv) A gift of 10 acres of farmland to his son, Christian, on 1st July 1994. The land was valued at £150,000 and was subject to a mortgage of £55,000. Richard had occupied the land and farmed it since January 1980. Christian sold the land to an unconnected party on 11th October 1996 for £120,000. He used the proceeds to pay off the mortgage and also to buy himself a yacht.

In his will Richard left all his assets to his sons Boris and Christian. He appointed his brother Nigel as his executor. He was confident that his sons would look after his widow, Maria, who is aged 73 and owns no assets in her own right. Maria is in very poor health and is not expected to live much longer.

a) Calculate the IHT arising as a result of Richard's death.

b) Explain whether the IHT arising could be reduced by disposing of all or any of Richard's assets before winding up his estate. Indicate any possible disadvantage in such a course of action.

c) Explain whether it would be advisable from an IHT viewpoint to alter the terms of Richard's will. Outline the conditions which must be satisfied for such an alteration to be valid for IHT purposes.

ACCA

Solution

	£	£
1. **Estate of Richard (deceased) on 2.11.1996**		
Probate value of estate		321,000
Add Transfer within previous 7 years		
Gift 1.9.1993	210,000	
Less marriage exemption	5,000	205,000
Gift 1.7.1994	150,000	
Less mortgage	55,000	95,000
		621,000
IHT (621,000 – 200,000) @ 40%		168,400
Less IHT on gifts (300,000 – 200,000) @ 40%		40,000
		128,400
2. **IHT on gifts**		
1.9.1993 net gift		205,000
Add gift in previous 7 years 3.9.1988		90,000
		295,000
IHT (295,000 – 200,000) @ 40%		38,000
Less taper relief 20% (3 – 4 years)		7,600
		30,400
1.7.1994 Sale price - lower than PET value		120,000
Less mortgage		55,000
		65,000
IHT @ 40%		26,000

441

2. Possible IHT savings

a) Sale of Bluechip plc before 1.11.1997 (22,000 – 17,000) @ 40% = £2,000 (ie within one year of death).

b) Sale of holiday home before 1.11.2000 (55,000 – 40,000) @ 40% = £6,000 (ie within four years of death).

c) Deed of Variation so that, say, £200,000 passes to spouse Maria. £200,000 @ 40% = £80,000. This would not affect the exempt band of £200,000.

Part V

Value Added Tax

50 General principles

Introduction

1. Value added tax is a tax on the supply of goods and services made by a registered taxable person within the UK.

    This chapter begins with a summary of the headings under which the tax will be examined.

Summary of topic headings

2. Legislative background

    VAT rates

    Classification of goods and services

    Zero rated goods and services

    Exempted goods and services

    Land and buildings

    Taxable persons

    Business splitting

    Mandatory registration

    Date of registration

    Voluntary registration

    Voluntary de-registration

    Group registration

    Companies organised into divisions

    Accounts and records

    Accounting for VAT

    Administration

    Offences and penalties

    Default surcharge

    Errors on VAT returns

Legislative background

3. Value added tax was first introduced in the UK with effect from 1st April 1973, superseding purchase tax and selective employment tax. The main provisions of the VAT legislation are now contained in the Value Added Tax Act 1994. In addition to that Act there are a large number of Statutory Instruments which have introduced changes and provided information about the detailed machinery of the Act.

VAT rates

4. VAT has to be paid on the supply of goods and services within the UK by a taxable person unless they are exempt supplies. There are two positive rates of tax:

	After 31.3.91	Before 31.3.91
Standard rate supplies	17.5%	15%
Zero rated supplies	0%	0%

    The tax element of an SR VAT-inclusive price is $7/47$ (previously $3/23$).

    From 1st April 1994 VAT on supplies of fuel and power for domestic use is 8%.

Classification of goods and services

5. For VAT purposes goods and services are classified into three broad groups:

    Standard rate supplies — These are goods and services not zero rated or exempt, chargeable at the standard rate of 17.5%.

    Zero rated supplies — These are goods and services which are subject to a positive rate of tax of nil% eg publications and most food.

    Exempt supplies — These are goods and services which are not subject to VAT, such as postal services and insurance.

    Details of the zero rated and exempted supplies are contained below.

    A taxable supply is a supply of goods or services made in the UK, other than exempt supplies.

Zero rated goods and services

6. Particulars of the goods and services which are zero rated are contained in Schedule 8 to the VAT Act 1994 and there are seventeen broad groups classified as follows.

    Group 1   Food. Most food for human consumption is zero rated unless supplied as a meal when it is taxable. However, hot food for consumption off the premises is taxable. In addition, some food products such as ice cream, sweets and chocolate, fruit juice and minerals are taxable. Pet foods are taxable but not general animal feeding stuffs.

Group 2   Sewerage services and water. The supply of water is zero rated but not distilled and mineral water. The supply of water and sewerage services to industry is standard rated.

Group 3   Books etc. The supply of books and magazines, newspapers, music, maps and charts is zero rated. Diaries and stationery are taxable.

Group 4   Talking books for the blind and handicapped, and wireless sets for the blind. Zero rated items include magnetic tapes, tape recorders and accessories, if supplied to approved agencies such as the Royal National Institute for the Blind and similar charities.

The supply of information other than photographs to newspapers or to the public by news agencies is zero rated.

Group 5   Construction of buildings. The position under this heading may be summarised as follows.

Zero rated

i)   Construction of new domestic buildings.

ii)   Approved alterations to domestic listed buildings.

Standard rated

i)   Construction of new non-domestic buildings (previously zero rated).

ii)   Repair, maintenance or alteration of existing buildings.

iii)   Civil engineering services or new work.

iv)   Civil engineering services or repair, maintenance or alteration of existing buildings.

v)   Demolition of domestic and non domestic buildings.

vi)   The construction of a building for own use in business.

Group 6   Protected buildings.

Group 7   International services. The supply of certain services such as professional advice or entertainment outside the UK with exceptions for EEC residents, is zero rated.

Group 8   Transport. Zero rating applies to a wide range of activities such as the supply of passenger transport both inland and international, international freight transport, and the supply, repair and maintenance of certain ships and aircraft. Standard rating applies to taxis and hire cars, car parking and luggage storage.

Group 9   Caravans and house-boats. Caravans are zero rated if they exceed 7 metres in length or 2.3 metres in width, the size permitted for use on public roads. The smaller towable caravans are taxable as is the supply of caravan accommodation. House-boats if suitable for permanent habitation are also zero rated.

Group 10   Gold. The supply of gold coins which are legal tender is taxable at the standard rate. The supply of gold held in the UK, by a central bank to another central bank or a member of the London Gold Market, and reciprocal transactions are zero rated.

Group 11   Bank notes. The issue of bank notes payable to bearer is zero rated.

Group 12   Drugs, medicines, aids for the handicapped etc. The following supplies are zero rated: goods dispensed by a registered pharmacist on prescription, medical and surgical appliances, electrical and mechanical appliances for a handicapped person. Other drugs and medicines dispensed without prescription are taxable.

Group 13   Imports, exports etc. The supply of imported goods before the 'delivery of an entry' within the meaning of Section 37 Customs and Excise Management Act 1979, is zero rated. The transfer of goods or services from the UK, by a person carrying on a business both inside and outside the UK, to the overseas business is also zero rated. This would cover, for example, the transfer of parts to be assembled from a UK company to its overseas branch.

Group 14   Tax-free shops.

Group 15   Charities etc. Zero rating applies to the supply by a charity established primarily for the relief of distress or the benefit or protection of animals, of goods donated for sale, any exports, medical or scientific equipment used solely in medical research, and appliances for the handicapped. The supply of goods and services purchased for resale are taxable in the ordinary way as there is no general exemption for charities.

Group 16   Clothing and footwear. Children's clothing and footwear are zero rated. Protective boots and helmets are standard rated when supplied to a person for use by his or her employees. Supplies of protective boots and helmets to any other person for industrial use remain zero rated. Also zero rated are motor cycle helmets.

Exempted goods and services

7.   Particulars of the goods and services which are exempt supplies are contained in the 9th Schedule to the VAT Act 1994 and there are 12 groups classified as follows.

Group 1   Land. See separate heading below.

Group 2   Insurance. All forms of insurance are exempted and this includes insurance broking and agency services.

Group 3   Postal services. The conveyance of postal packets other than telegrams, by the post office is exempted. Services rendered by persons other than the post office are taxable.

Group 4   Betting gaming and lotteries. Examples of exempt services under this group are bookmakers, charges for bingo and profits from casino games. Admission charges to any premises where betting or the playing of games of chance takes place are however taxable as are takings from gaming or entertainment machines.

Group 5   Finance. In general, banking services such as those relating to the receipt and transfer of money are exempt. Specific services offered such as executorship and trustee work, portfolio management etc are taxable as are the commissions from stockbroking, and management fees of unit trusts.

Group 6   Education. Educational services provided by schools, colleges, universities and youth clubs are exempted as are the supply of goods and services to those establishments. Services provided by organisations with a view to profit such as correspondence courses are taxable.

Group 7   Health and welfare. The supply of goods and services by registered persons such as doctors, dentists, opticians, occupational therapists etc. is exempted. Goods supplied under a prescription by a pharmacist are zero rated.

Group 8   Burial and cremation. The services of undertakers in connection with a funeral or cremation are exempt, and within limits this includes charges for the supply of a coffin, shroud etc. but not flowers.

Group 9   Trade unions and professional bodies. Exemption is covered for membership, services and related goods supplied by a trade union and most non-profit making professional, learned or representational bodies.

Group 10   Sports competitions. The grant of a right to enter a competition in sport or physical recreation, where the consideration for the grant consists in money which is to be used wholly for the provision of prizes, is exempt.

Group 11   Works of art etc. The disposal of works of art in circumstances where there is no liability to capital transfer tax or capital gains tax is exempt.

Group 12   Fund raising activities by charities.

Land and buildings

8.   *Exempt*

i)   The sale of used domestic and non-domestic buildings

ii)   Leases of used domestic and non-domestic buildings

iii)   Leases of new domestic buildings

iv)   The sale of building land for domestic building

Zero rated

i)   Sales of new domestic buildings provided that the seller is the person constructing the building

ii)   Leases of new domestic buildings where the lease is capable of exceeding 21 years.

Standard rated

i)   Sales of new non-domestic buildings

ii)   Sales of building land for non-domestic building

iii)   The grant of any interest, right or licence consisting of a right to take game or fish

iv)   The provision in an hotel, inn, boarding house or similar establishment of sleeping accommodation or of accommodation in rooms which are provided in conjunction with sleeping accommodation or for the purpose of a supply of catering

v)   The provision of holiday accommodation in a house, flat, caravan, house-boat or tent

vi)   The provision of seasonal pitches for caravans, and the grant of facilities at caravan parks to persons for whom such pitches are provided

vii)   The provision of pitches for tents or of camping facilities

viii)   The grant of facilities for parking a vehicle

ix)   The grant of any right to fell and remove standing timber

x)   The grant of facilities for housing, or storage of, an aircraft or for mooring or storage of, a ship, boat or other vessel

xi)   The grant of any right to occupy a box, seat or other accommodation at a sports ground, theatre, concert hall or other place of entertainment

xii)   The grant of facilities for playing any sport or participating in any physical recreation.

Taxable persons

9.   A taxable person is any person registered for VAT purposes. Person includes an individual, partnership, company, club, society or trust.

Business splitting

10.   Customs and Excise have indicated that the following factors will be taken into consideration in deciding whether or not an independent business exists for VAT registration purposes.

i)   Appropriate premises and equipment for the business should be provided by the person carrying on the business.

ii)   Day-to-day records identifying the business should be kept and where appropriate separate annual accounts.

iii)   Purchase and sales invoices should be in the name of the person carrying on the trade who should be legally responsible for all trading activities.

iv)   A separate bank account should be opened for the business.

v)   All payroll payments should be paid by the person carrying on the business.

vi)   The business should be treated as an independent business for income tax purposes.

vii)   The person carrying on the business should be legally responsible for all trading activities.

At present, Customs cannot require separate businesses to register as a single trader for VAT purposes unless it can show that the main reason (or one of the main reasons) for keeping those businesses separate was to avoid a liability to be registered.

This limitation will be removed, with effect from Royal Assent to the Finance Act 1997, and 'connected businesses which have avoided liability for VAT by artificially separating will be liable to be treated as one, whatever the purported reason for the separation'. For example, a series of limited companies running a pub, launderette or other retail outlet for only one month a year in order to keep the turnover of each company below the registration threshold will be treated as one business.

Mandatory registration – with effect from 27.11.1996

11.   Registration is mandatory in the following circumstances.

a)   At the end of any month if the value of the taxable supplies in the past 12 months has exceeded £48,000 unless the turnover in the next 12 months will not exceed £46,000.

b)   At any time if there are reasonable grounds for believing that the value of taxable supplies in the next 30 days will exceed £48,000.

Taxable supplies include standard and zero rated supplies but not exempt supplies or the sale of capital assets. (For the period from 29.11.95 the registration level was £47,000.)

12. Event	Notification to Customs and Excise
Turnover in past 12 months exceeds £48,000 (£47,000)	Within 30 days of the end of the relevant month (*see below*). Registration is effective from the end of the month following the relevant month or such earlier date as may be mutually agreed.
Turnover in next 30 days exceeds £48,000	Before the end of the 30 day period. Registration is effective from the beginning of the 30 day period.

Note *Relevant month is the month at the end of which liability to registration arises.*

Voluntary registration

13. Where a person who is not liable to be registered satisfies the Customs and Excise that he or she:

i) makes taxable supplies; or

ii) is carrying on a business and intends to make such supplies in the course or furtherance of that business;

then, if the person so requests, he or she will be registered, with effect from the day on which the request is made or such earlier date as may be mutually agreed.

Voluntary de-registration

14. From 27th November 1996 a registered person may apply for de-registration if his or her taxable turnover excluding VAT is not expected to exceed £46,000 (£45,000 previously) in the next year.

Group registration

15. Under Section 43 VATA 1994 two or more UK resident companies are eligible to be treated as members of a group if either:

i) one controls each of the others or,

ii) one person (being either a company, an individual or partnership) controls all of them.

Control exists where a person controls the composition of the board of directors of a company or holds more than 50% of the company's voting rights.

Applications for the VAT group registration must satisfy the definition contained in the Companies Act 1985.

A company is a subsidiary if another company:

i) holds a majority of the voting rights in it, or

ii) is a member of it and has the right to appoint or remove a majority of its board of directors, or

iii) is a member of it and under an agreement with other shareholders or members controls alone a majority of the voting rights in it, or

iv) is a subsidiary of a company which is itself a subsidiary of that other company.

In general, the effects of a group registration are as follows.

i) The VAT affairs are vested in one group company known as the representative member and only one VAT return is required.

ii) Inter-group supplies are not subject to VAT.

iii) All members of the group are jointly and severally liable for the VAT due from the representative member.

Companies organised into divisions

16. A UK resident company carrying on business in several divisions may be registered in the name of its divisions as follows.

i) All divisions of the company must be registered separately. It is not possible to exclude certain divisions eg where they fall below the registration limits.

ii) Separate returns are made by each division.

iii) The separate divisions are not separately taxed persons and the company remains liable for the whole VAT.

iv) Inter-divisional transfers are not subject to VAT.

v) Each division should be an independent unit with its own accounting and administration, carrying on business activities in separate locations.

vi) Input tax attributable to exempt supplies (exempt input tax) by the corporate body as a whole must be less than the limits referred to in Chapter 50 (Section 20).

Divisional registration is subject to the approval of Customs and Excise.

Accounts and records

17. There are a number of detailed regulations concerning the 'book-keeping' arrangements required for VAT purposes, and some of these are noted briefly below.
    a) Any standard or zero rated supply of goods or services must be supported by a 'tax invoice', which is described in the next chapter.
    b) At regular intervals, usually quarterly, a return must be completed showing the amounts of output and input tax for the period and the net amount payable or receivable from the Customs and Excise. The period covered by a return is known as a tax period and each return must be submitted not later than one month after the end of that tax period. A separate VAT account must be sent for each quarter. A specimen return is produced at the end of Chapter 51.
    c) Adequate records and accounts of all transactions involving VAT must be maintained to support both the amount of output tax chargeable, and the claim, for deductible input tax. These will be checked from time to time by Customs and Excise officers.
    d) Books and records must be kept for a period of six years. Business records include the following:
       Orders and delivery notes
       Relevant business correspondence
       Purchase and sales books
       Cash books and other account books
       Purchase invoices and copy sales invoices
       Records of daily takings eg till rolls
       Annual accounts – balance sheet and profit and loss accounts
       Import and export documents
       Bank statements and paying-in-slips
       Any credit/debit notes issued or received.
    e) There are some special schemes for retailers for VAT purposes and these are outlined in Chapter 52.

Accounting for VAT

18. The following is an extract from the Statement of Standard Accounting Practice No. 5 concerning the treatment of VAT for persons exempt or partially exempt.
    a) **General**
       VAT is a tax on the supply of goods and services which is eventually borne by the final consumer but collected at each stage of the production and distribution chain. As a general principle, therefore, the treatment of VAT in the accounts of a trader should reflect his or her role as a collector of the tax and VAT should not be included in income or in expenditure whether of a capital or of a revenue nature. There will however be circumstances, as noted below, in which a trader will bear VAT and in such circumstances the accounting treatment should reflect that fact.
    b) **Persons not accountable for VAT**
       Persons not accountable for VAT will suffer VAT on inputs. For them VAT will increase the cost of all goods and services to which it applies and should be included in such costs. In particular, the VAT on fixed assets should be added to the cost of the fixed assets concerned and capital allowances claimed accordingly.
    c) **Accountable persons who also carry on exempted activities**
       In the case of persons who also carry on exempted activities there will be a residue of VAT, which will fall directly on the trader and which will normally be arrived at by division of his or her activities as between taxable outputs (including zero rated) and those which are exempt. In such cases, the principle that such VAT will increase the costs to which it applies and should be included in such costs will be equally applicable. Hence the appropriate portion of the VAT allocable to fixed assets should, if irrecoverable, be added to the cost of the fixed assets concerned and the proportion allocable to other items should, if practicable and material, be included in such other items. In some cases, for example where financial and VAT accounting periods do not coincide, an estimate may be necessary.

d) **Non-deductible inputs**

All traders will bear tax in-so-far as it relates to non-deductible inputs (for example, motor-cars, other than for resale, and certain business entertaining expenses). Such tax should therefore be included as part of the cost of those items.

e) **Amounts due to or from the revenue authorities**

The net amount due to or from the revenue authorities in respect of VAT should be included as part of debtors or creditors and will not normally require separate disclosure.

Administration

19. The department of Customs and Excise is the government department responsible for the administration and collection of VAT. In the event of a dispute between a taxable person and the VAT office it is possible to appeal to a VAT tribunal, providing that it is concerned with one of a number of prescribed matters. The main areas which can be dealt with are as follows.

a) Registration or cancellation of registration.

b) Assessment of tax.

c) Amount of tax chargeable.

d) Amount of input tax deductible.

e) Bad debt claims.

f) Group registration matters.

g) Matters concerned with the value of supplies.

On questions of law an appeal can be made to the High Court from the tribunal.

Late registration

20. a) Failure to notify the Custom and Excise at the proper time that a business should be registered for VAT purposes may incur a penalty, subject to a minimum of £50.00 based on the following rates.

Number of months late for registration	% of VAT due w.e.f. 1.1.95
0 – 9	5%
10 – 18	10%
19 –	15%

The amount of VAT due is the sum due from the date the registration should have been made.

The penalty is not due if the trader can satisfy the Custom and Excise that there was a reasonable excuse for the failure.

The following does not amount to reasonable excuses:

i) insufficiency of funds to pay the tax

ii) reliance on a third party to pay the tax

iii) ignorance of the law relating to registration.

b) Custom and Excise have indicated that the following *guidelines* show circumstances where there might be a reasonable excuse for *late registration.*

i) **Compassionate circumstances** where an individual is totally responsible for running a small business and he or she, or a member of the immediate family, was seriously ill or recovering from such illness at the time notification was required.

ii) **Transfer of a business as a going concern** where such a business is taken over with little or no break in the trading activities and returns have been submitted and tax paid on time under the registration number of the previous owner.

iii) **Doubt about liabilities of supplies** where there is written evidence of an enquiry to Custom and Excise about the liability of supplies and liability has remained in doubt. *See G Davies, LON/ 84/174 (2126).*

iv) **Uncertainty about employment status** where there are genuine doubts as to whether a person is employed or self-employed or where correspondence with the Inland Revenue can be produced about these doubts.

v) **Effective date of registration earlier than required** where a person has requested registration from an earlier date than was legally required in the mistaken belief that he or she had to do so to recover input tax on stocks and assets for the business. This excuse could only apply if there was no reason to believe that taxable turnover would exceed the registration threshold from the required date.

The default surcharge – Section 59 VATA 1994

21. The following points should be noted under this heading.

a) A person will be in default if by the last day on which a return is required, the Customs and Excise have not received that return, or the tax.

b) Taxpayers can be in default for two return periods (ie quarters or months) in any 12 month period without incurring a monetary penalty.

c) Where the taxpayer is in default for the first time then a surcharge liability notice will be issued. The surcharge liability notice once issued remains in force for a period of 12 months during which time there must be no default.

d) While the notice is in force a default charge will arise in any quarter in which a default occurs, at the following rates, if greater than £30.00, w e f 30. 9. 1993

	% of Vat
1st default	2%
2nd default	5%
3rd and subsequent defaults	15%

e) A person is not liable to a surcharge if he or she satisfies the Commissioners that in the case of a default which is 'material to the surcharge' :

i) the return, or as the case may be the tax shown on it, was despatched at such time and in such manner that it was reasonable to expect that it would be received within the appropriate time limit, or

ii) there is a reasonable excuse for the return or tax not having been despatched.

The following are not reasonable excuses (FA 1985 Sec. 33(2)):

i) Insufficiency of funds to pay any tax

ii) Where reliance is placed on any other person to perform any task, the fact of that reliance or any other dilatoriousness or inaccuracy on the part of the person relied upon.

Errors on VAT returns

22. a) With effect from 11th March 1992 the procedures for the *voluntary disclosure of errors* are as noted below:

Errors amounting to £2,000 or less	Separate disclosure not required.
	No interest charged on underpayments whether notified or not.
Errors amounting to more than £2,000	Customs and Excise must be notified in writing by letter or using VAT Form 652.
	Interest is chargeable from date when VAT was outstanding.
Default interest	This will be charged on net payments to the Customs and Excise at the prescribed rate of interest.
	The interest charge is not an expense of trade for income tax purposes.

b) A Serious Misdeclaration Penalty can arise if the Customs and Excise find as a result of their enquiries that VAT has been misdeclared.

A penalty of 15% from 11th March 1992 of the VAT due can be imposed but this will only apply where:

Amount misdeclared for a VAT accounting period $\geq$ which is the lesser of:

(i) 30% of the true amount of tax payable, or

(ii) the greater of £1.0 million and 5% of the true amount of tax for the period

c) A Serious Misdeclaration Penalty will not normally be imposed:

i) during the period from the end of an accounting period to the due date for furnishing the VAT return for the following accounting period

ii) when a VAT return is misdeclared but this has been corrected by a compensating misdeclaration in respect of the same transaction for the following accounting period, with no overall loss of VAT.

51 The VAT system

Introduction

1. This chapter contains the main features of the VAT system covered under the following main topic headings:

The VAT return
Zero rated and exempt supplies
Taxable supply of goods and services
Taxable persons
The supply of goods and services
Place of supply
Tax point
Tax invoice
Value of goods and services
Input tax – deductions
Input tax – no deduction
Private motoring

Imports – removal from warehouse
Exports
Goods for personal use
Partial exemption
Bad debts
Transfer of business
Sale of business assets
Business assets – capital allowances
VAT on capital goods – partly exempt businesses
Self supplies
Cash/annual accounting
Rents
Changes in tax rates

The VAT return

2. A taxable person is required to charge VAT on taxable supplies to customers, called output tax, but he or she is also able to claim credit for the tax paid on business purchases and expenses, and assets known as the input tax.

At the end of an accounting period, usually a month or three months, a business has to submit a return of Value Added Tax to the Customs and Excise. This must show the total taxable supplies made and the VAT charged, together with the total purchases and expenses and any VAT paid. If the tax charged exceeds the amount paid then the balance is payable to the Customs and Excise. Where the output tax is less than the input tax then a repayment can normally be obtained.

Example

	£	£
Total taxable turnover for the period	100,000	
Output tax @ 17.5%		17,500
Total taxable inputs for the period	80,000	
Input tax @ 17.5%		14,000
Balance payable to Customs and Excise		3,500

Zero rated and exempt supplies

3. Goods or services which fall within the zero rated or exempt supplies categories are not subject to VAT at the standard rate. However, there are some important differences between the two supplies.

a) Zero rated goods or services are taxable at a nil rate of output tax. It follows that any input tax incurred in providing those outputs can be reclaimed since there is no output tax to give a normal means of set-off.

b) Supplies of exempt goods and services are really outside the VAT system and therefore any input tax incurred cannot be reclaimed, and there is no available set-off. However, such input tax would in effect be an allowable expense for business taxation purposes in most circumstances.

c) A business which makes only exempt supplies cannot normally register for VAT.

d) Details of the implications of being partially exempt are noted below.

Taxable supply of goods and services

4. Tax is chargeable on any supply of goods and services which are made in the UK or imported where the supply counts as being taxable. The supply must be made by a taxable person in the course of a trade, profession or vocation.

Taxable persons

5. A taxable person is any person who has registered for VAT, and this is required if the total value of his or her taxable supplies for any one year are greater than £45,000. All business activities must be aggregated in order to determine whether or not a person should register. Registration can be for an individual, partnership or limited company. The total of taxable business supplies is called taxable turnover.

The supply of goods and services

6. The supply of goods can include any of the following:

a) sale by ordinary commercial transaction

b) sale by auction or through agents

c) sale under a credit sale agreement or by hire purchase.

d) goods supplied for further processing

e) goods supplied for personal use.

The supply of services covers any which are provided for money or money's worth, and includes the hire, lease or rental of any goods. Services which are ancillary to the supply of goods such as postage and packing and delivery are normally treated as services and not as part of the goods sold, if they are shown separately on the sales invoice.

Place of supply

7. In general only goods and services supplied in the UK are chargeable to VAT so that the determination of the place of supply is important. If the goods to be supplied are physically located in the UK then they are liable to VAT even where they may be subsequently exported. However, if the goods are located overseas and remain there, then the supply is outside the UK and hence not subject to VAT. This could arise, for example, where a shipping company arranges for a consignment of goods to be sold and transferred from one country to another.

With regard to the supply of a service then this is treated as occurring where the supplier 'belongs', which is usually the place of business. If this is the UK then any service provided from that place could be liable to VAT, and using the example noted above, the provision of the shipping facility would be a taxable supply.

For VAT purposes the UK includes the Isle of Man but not the Channel Isles.

Time of supply – tax point

8. The tax point determines the period in which a supply falls, and is therefore taxable. For goods the basic taxpoint is generally the date when the goods are removed or made available, and for services the basic tax point is the date of the performance. However, there are two key exceptions.

a) If an invoice is issued within 14 days after the time when the goods are removed or made available, then the date of the invoice normally becomes the actual tax point. This practice is widely followed and enables the VAT return to be completed from copy invoices.

b) If payments are made in advance of the date when the goods are removed or made available, then it is the date of the invoice or payment which determines the actual tax point.

The same rules apply for deciding the period in which the inputs arise, and in general relief for input tax is available before the invoice is paid. Although in principle tax on imports is due at the date of importation, a business is allowed to pay tax with the next return providing the imports are included in the VAT return for the period in which the importation occurs.

Under the standard method of accounting for VAT by retailers the actual tax point is the date on which the retailer receives payment for goods sold.

A system of cash accounting available. *See below.*

Tax invoice

9. A tax invoice is a sales invoice issued by a registered person in respect of any goods or services supplied by him or her to another taxable person. The invoice must contain:

a) supplier's name, address and VAT registration number

b) customer's name and address

c) type of supply ie whether a sale, sale by HP, hire or rental

d) description of goods or services supplied together with the amount payable excluding VAT

e) total amount payable without VAT

f) particulars of any cash discounts offered

g) total amount of tax chargeable.

A less detailed invoice may be used where individual supplies by a retailer amount to less than £100 including VAT with effect from 9th April 1991 (previously £50).

Credit notes

10. During 1996 regulations were issued requiring all businesses to issue credit or debit notes whenever a price adjustment alters the amount of VAT due on an invoice.

Value of goods and services

11. The general rule is that the value on which VAT is chargeable is the amount of money (excluding VAT) which a customer has to pay for the goods or services supplied. The following should be noted.

   a) Cash discounts must be deducted from the invoiced amount to determine the VAT value.

   b) If the supply is not made for money then the open market value less any VAT should be taken.

   c) The cost of the goods to the supplier may be used to determine the value of a taxable supply. This would apply to goods appropriated from trading stock for personal use, and to the trader's own built plant and machinery.

Mixed supplies

12. A mixed supply occurs where a single inclusive price is charged for a number of separate supplies of goods and services. Where all the supplies are taxable at the same rate then the normal rules of computation apply. However, where different rates apply then an apportionment must be made which is 'fair and justifiable'.

> **Example**

B makes a mixed supply of goods at a VAT-inclusive price of £160.00. The product costs show zero rated goods costing £30.00 and standard rated goods costing £50 (exclusive of VAT)

Solution

Computation of VAT

Proportion of total cost at SR $\dfrac{50 + \text{VAT}}{(50 + \text{VAT}) + 30} = \dfrac{58.75}{58.75 + 30} = \dfrac{58.75}{88.75}$

VAT inclusive price of standard rated goods $\dfrac{58.75}{88.75} \times £160 = £105.90$

VAT included $= 106 \times \dfrac{7}{47} = 16$

Value of zero rated supply $= 160 - 106 = 54$.

Analysis of total price as apportioned

	£
Value of standard rated supply (106 – 16)	90
VAT on standard rated supply 17.5% × 90	16
Zero rated supply	54
Mixed supply	160

Other methods of apportionment eg based on market values can be used. Apportionment must not be made where the supply is a composite supply. *See below*.

Examples of mixed supply are:

Annual subscription to the AA *(C & E v AA QB 1974 STC 192)*

Fees for correspondence courses (*Rapid Results College Ltd 1973 VAT TR 197*)

(Books are zero rated. Tuition is standard rated).

Composite supply

13. This occurs where goods and services supplied together make up a single indivisible supply, and apportionment must not be made.

    Composite supplies include:

Services of a launderette (supplies of water, heat, use of machinery)	*Mander Laundries Ltd 1973 VAT TR 136*
A course in dress design (material & guidance notes)	*Betty Foster (Fashion Sewing) 1976 VAT TR 229*

Input tax – *Deduction*

14. Input tax is the VAT charged on business purchases and expenses including imported goods, goods removed from a warehouse, and capital expenditure.

    To be deductible, the input tax must be in respect of goods and services for the purposes of the business and not of a class where the tax is specifically non-deductible.

    Input tax can be reclaimed providing that it is attributable to:

    i)   standard or zero rated supplies

    ii) supplies made in the course of business which are outside the scope of UK VAT but would have been subject to standard or zero rate if made in the UK

    iii) supplies or warehoused goods.

    Input tax incurred in relation to exempt supplies may be wholly recoverable where it falls within the de minimis rules. (*See partial exemption section below.*)

    Input tax incurred in respect of any other activity not covered by (i) to (iii) above is not reclaimable.

    Input tax on business overheads or research and development expenditure can be claimed as input tax provided that it is attributable to the three activities noted above. If the expenditure is partially attributable to exempt supplies or to activities outside the three categories then only part of the input tax attributable to the three activities is reclaimable.

Input tax – *No deduction*

15. Input tax charged in respect of the following is non-deductible.

    a) The purchase of private motor cars except where they are bought for re-sale. VAT on the purchase of commercial vehicles is allowable, as is the tax on leasing payments for private cars which are used for business purposes.

        With effect from 1st August 1995 leasing companies (and other buyers where the car is used *wholly* for business purposes) can reclaim the VAT on their purchases of motor cars.

    b) Motor accessories. When a motor is purchased, VAT on the accessories is not reclaimable even if invoiced separately. VAT on accessories purchased and fitted later is deductible provided that the car remains in business ownership.

    c) Business entertainment expenses. Input tax on this kind of expenditure is only allowable where it is incurred for staff entertainment for the purposes of the business eg provision of meals and seasonal entertainment.

Private motoring

16. Input tax on all road fuel purchased for business or private use is reclaimable providing that it is attributable to the specified supplies. For example, where exempt supplies are made, part of the input tax may not be recoverable.

    With effect from accounting periods beginning after the 6th April 1987 a fuel scale charge was introduced for fuel for private use in a similar manner to that used for Schedule E purposes. Output tax is charged on the deemed taxable supply, by reference to the following scales.

    VAT fuel rates 1997/98

    The following rates apply to VAT accounting periods beginning on or after the 6th April 1996, ie the first Return Period after that date.

Engine size(cc)		3 month period				1 month period		
	Scale charge diesel	VAT due per car	Scale charge petrol	VAT due per car	Scale charge diesel	VAT due per car	Scale charge petrol	VAT due per car
	£	£	£	£	£	£	£	£
1400 or less	185	27.55	200	29.78	61	9.08	66	9.82
More than 1400 but not more than 2000	185	27.55	252	37.53	61	9.08	84	12.51
More than 2000	235	35.0	372	55.40	78	11.61	124	18.46

The above rates are the same as those use for income tax purposes and benefits in kind.

Imports – removals from the warehouse

17. Imports of goods

VAT is charged on most goods imported into the UK whether or not the importer is registered for VAT. The tax is in addition to any customs duty or other charges which might be incurred and is calculated on a value which includes all such charges.

Payment of VAT on imported goods is due at the time of importation or removal from a warehouse unless deferment arrangements have been made.

A registered trader approved by Custom and Excise may defer payment of tax on goods imported in the course of business during a calendar month until the 15th of the following month (or the next working day after the 15th if that day is a holiday). The VAT is normally collected by a direct debit mandate which forms part of the procedure an application for department must comply with.

VAT on imported goods can be claimed as input tax subject to the normal rules. The claim for the VAT as input tax must be made in the return for the accounting period during which the importation or removal from warehouse occurs.

Warehoused goods

As a general rule when goods are warehoused for customs and excise purposes then payment of any VAT is suspended. VAT becomes payable when the goods are removed from the warehouse for use in the UK.

Imports of services

Where services such as banking, insurance, and business consultancy are received from outside the UK then the taxable person may have to account for the output tax on those transactions as if he or she had made the supply personally. In this case there would be a set-off of input tax of an equivalent amount.

Exports

18. The export of goods and services to an overseas customer are mainly zero rated under group 15. Where goods are sent to a final exporter in the UK then in general they will not be zero rated, but this does not include delivery to a port or central clearance depot for shipment.

EC Trade

19. With effect from 1st January 1993 charges in the regulations affecting EC trade were introduced. The concepts of imports and exports were changed for intra-community trade. Imports became 'acquisitions', and exports because 'transactions for acquisition'. Numerous other changes are being made since the abolition of the fiscal frontiers.

Goods for personal use

20. Where goods which belong to a business are put to private use outside the business then a taxable supply is made and output tax is chargeable. Thus if trading stock is withdrawn from the business for private use or an employee uses a business asset for private purposes, a taxable supply occurs.

VAT is chargeable on the cost (for income tax purposes it is the market value) of the supply or service to the business and the tax point is the time when the goods or services are made available for non-business use.

There are special rules for the private use of motor cars (*see above*).

Partial exemption

21. New rules for the determination of partial exempt supplies came into effect from 1st April 1992, which are outlined below.

i) Where a business makes exempt supplies of financial or land related services, and these are not incurred in the course of carrying on a business in the financial sector, then all exempt input tax can be recovered provided it has been incurred in relation to any of the following supplies:

- the granting of any lease or tenancy of land, or any licence to occupy land (provided that the exempt input tax related to all such supplies made by the business is less than £1,000 per tax year, and that the business does not incur any exempt input tax other than that related to those supplies listed in this paragraph)
- any deposit of money
- any services of arranging insurance
- any services of arranging mortgages
- any services of arranging hire-purchase, credit sale or conditional sale transactions
- the assignment of any debt in respect of a supply of goods or services by the assignor.

If the exempt input tax is incurred in relation to supplies other than those listed above, then the tax must be taken into consideration in determining the 'de minimis limit'.

ii) A business can be treated as fully taxable providing its exempt input tax is not more than £625 per month on average, with effect from 30.11.1994.

In addition businesses must also satisfy the additional condition that exempt input tax is no more than 50% of the VAT on all purchases.

iii) Exempt input tax must be considered where financial businesses are carried on, such as a bank, building society, money lender, credit card company etc.

iv) The standard method of calculation to be used where the business cannot be treated as fully taxable is as follows.

a) Identify the non-attributable input tax.

b) Calculate percentage rounded up to the next whole number of such input tax which is equal to:

$$\frac{\text{value of supplies (excl. VAT)}}{\text{value of taxable supplies (excl. VAT)} + \text{value of exempt supplies}}$$

Example

A Ltd had the following transactions in the quarter to 30th June 1997:

	£
Standard-rated supplies (excluding VAT)	150,000
Zero-rated supplies	50,000
Exempt supplies	100,000

Input tax has been paid as follows:

	£
Standard-rated supplies	12,000
Zero-rated supplies	–
Exempt supplies	17,000
General overheads	4,000

The general overhead input tax cannot be directly attributed to any of the listed supplies.

Compute the VAT payable for the quarter to 30th June 1997.

Solution

A Ltd VAT Return: Quarter to 30th June 1997

			£
Output tax 150,000 @ 17.5%			26,250
Input tax:	Standard-rated	12,000	
	Zero-rated	–	
	Overheads	2,680	
			14,680
VAT due			11,570

Notes

i) *VAT attributable to overheads:*

$$\frac{150,000(SR) + 50,000(ZR)}{150,000(SR) + 50,000(ZR) + 100,000(EX)} \times 4,000 = 67\% \times 4,000 = 2,680$$

ii) *As the de minimis levels for exempt input tax have been exceeded, the business is partially exempt.*

iii) *An annual computation is required to adjust any quarterly fluctuations.*

Bad debts

22. Relief is available for bad debts incurred by a taxable person, and a claim for a refund of the appropriate output tax can be made where:

a) the goods or services were supplied for a monetary consideration, and VAT on the supply was paid.

b) the customer has become insolvent. This means an official determination of inability to pay debts such as bankruptcy, or the winding up of a company.

c) a trader can obtain a certificate from the 'administrator' or 'administrative receiver' of a company stating that in his or her opinion if the company went into liquidation its assets would be insufficient to pay secured and preference debts.

d) any debt which is more than six months old which has been written off in the trader's accounts can be claimed as a bad debt for VAT purposes. The six-month period is from the date the payment was due (previously the time of supply).

Bad debts – *Claim*

23. The amount of the claim will usually be readily ascertainable by reference to the actual debt outstanding. However, where there are payments on account (not allocated by the debtor to any particular supply) then these are allocated to the earliest supplies in the account after adjusting for any mutual supplies ie contra items.

Example

R Ltd is registered for VAT. One of its customers, X Ltd, went into liquidation on 31st July 1997.

The sales ledger account for the last two months to 31st July 1997 was as follows:

R Ltd Sales ledger account with X Ltd

		£			£
1.5.97	Balance b/f	12,000	30.6.97	Cheque May a/c paid	12,000
25.5.97	1. Goods (including VAT)	36,000	23.7.97	Cheque payment on a/c	10,000
15.6.97	2. Goods (zero rated)	9,000	31.7.97	Balance c/f	50,000
20.7.97	3. Goods (including VAT)	15,000			
		72,000			72,000
31.7.97	Balance b/d	50,000			

Compute the bad debt relief available to R Ltd.

Solution

Amount due from X Ltd at 31st July 1997, £50,000

		Gross £	VAT £
Invoice	No. 3	15,000	2,234.04
	No. 2	9,000	–
	No. 1 (part)	26,000	3,872.34
		50,000	6,106.38

Notes

i) *VAT on Invoice No.1 36,000 $\times \,^{7}/_{47}$ = 5,361.70*

Proportion $\frac{26,000}{36,000} \times 5,361.70 = 3,872.34$

ii) *VAT recoverable is £6,106.38.*

Transfer of a business as a going concern

24. a) The sale of the assets of a business as a going concern is not a supply of goods on services and not therefore chargeable to VAT provided that:

   i) the assets are to be used by the purchaser in carrying on the same kind of business whether as part of an existing business or not.

   ii) in a case where the seller is a taxable person, the purchaser if not already registered must register immediately.

b) A sale of part of a business is also not subject to VAT provided that the part sold is capable of separate operation.

c) The purchaser cannot claim any input tax in respect of the purchase of the business even where this has been incorrectly charged to him or her.

d) The provisions do not apply where the business is a different one after the transfer to that carried on by the seller.

e) The transfer of a sole trader's business to a limited company or into partnership with one or more other persons falls within the transfer provisions and is therefore not chargeable to VAT.

f) Where the business is transferred as a going concern then it is possible for the VAT Registration number of the vendor to be transferred to the purchaser subject to certain conditions, and the approval of the Custom and Excise.

g) Where a business carried on by a taxable person is transferred to another person who is not registered at the time of the transfer then the taxable supplies limit of £47,000 for registration is calculated by reference to the 12 months beginning with the month of the transfer. The previous owner's turnover is not taken into consideration.

Sale of business assets

25. The sale of assets used by a person in the course of business, eg plant and machinery, is subject to VAT as a taxable supply. This also applies where a person ceases to trade and the business assets are sold.

VAT is not chargeable on the disposal of a motor car unless it is sold for more than the price paid when purchased. Where the latter occurs VAT is chargeable to the disposer on the difference between the purchase and sale price.

Business assets – *Capital allowances*

26. In general there is no difference between the treatment of capital goods and other inputs for VAT purposes and in most cases the input tax can be set against the output tax in the normal way. However, where a trader's supplies are exempt, or partially exempt or the taxable turnover is below the threshold limits, he or she will not be able to recover all or part of the input tax on the capital goods. In such cases the VAT not reclaimable can be added to the cost of the asset for capital allowance purposes.

For motor cars the VAT is not recoverable input tax and is therefore added to the cost of the asset for capital allowance purposes.

VAT on capital goods – *Partly exempt businesses*

27. With effect from 1st April 1990 new regulations came into force whereby input tax recovered by a trader on certain assets when first acquired can be repaid where there is a change in the use to which they are applied eg from taxable to exempt use.

The assets to which these rules apply are:

a) computers and computer equipment worth over £50,000, if their use changes within five years of acquisition.

b) land and buildings worth over £250,000, if their use is changed within ten years of acquisition.

Self supplies

28. The following are the main circumstances when self supply of goods or services gives rise to a taxable supply.

   i) Self supply of stationery by an exempt or partially exempt supplier where the self supply exceeds £48,000 p.a.

   ii) Self supply of motor cars by vehicle manufacturers or car dealers. Where this takes place there is a self supply at cost to the trader (excluding any input tax recovered).

Cash accounting

29. A scheme of cash accounting is optional for all businesses with a turnover of less than £350,000 w.e.f 1.4.93. p.a. The main features are as follows.

   a) VAT on inputs and outputs can be accounted for by reference to cash paid and received rather than on the basis of invoice dates as under other systems.

   b) Applications for the scheme, once approved, remain in force for two years.

   c) The problem of VAT on bad debts does not arise in the first place.

Annual accounting

30. This scheme is available to all businesses which regularly pay VAT tax, have been registered for at least one year and whose turnover is < £300,000 p.a. with effect from 9th April 1991 (previously £250,000) excluding VAT. The main features of the proposed scheme are as follows.

   a) Businesses choosing the scheme will make only one VAT return a year instead of the usual four.

   b) There will be nine equal payments on account by direct debit and a tenth balancing payment with the annual return.

Rents

31. With effect from 1st August 1989 landlords can elect to charge VAT on rents from non-domestic buildings. The election must be made on a building by building basis, and once made will apply to all future transactions in the property, ie lettings or sales by the landlord. Businesses which are fully taxable will not be greatly affected by this change but those which are exempt or partially exempt may be effected, such as Group 2 Insurance and Group 5 Finance.

Changes in the tax rates

32. When a change in the standard rate of VAT occurs or a new rate is introduced, the following rules apply.

   a) Output tax is calculated under the normal rules i.e. by reference to the tax point unless the special change of rate provisions are applied

   b) Under these provisions where the rate goes up, the tax at the old rate can be charged on goods removed or services performed before the date of change even though a tax invoice would normally have been issued after the date of change.

   c) Where a supply of services takes place which crosses the threshold date of change in rate then the supply can be apportioned by reference to normal costing or pricing procedures. Tax at the old rate would be charged on the services performed before the date of the change.

   d) Input tax following a change in rate is obtained from the supplier's invoice and only the amount charged can be reclaimed. For less detailed tax invoices which do not show the VAT separately, the amount of input tax can be computed at the rate appropriate at the tax point.

Annual Returns and Payments

33. With effect from 1st December 1995 traders whose turnover is below the registration threshold but who have registered voluntarily will be required to adopt the Annual Returns and Payments system (ARP). This involves a single annual return and one lump sum payment of VAT.

ARP will be extended by way of option to other traders whose turnover is less than £100,000 from 1st December 1996.

Pre-registration expenditure

34. Input tax on pre-registration business expenditure can be included in the first VAT return. In the case of input tax on goods (as distinct from services) the goods must either be retained or converted into other goods still retained. For services the expenditure must have been incurred six months prior to registration.

Business gifts

35. In general traders are not required to account for VAT as a taxable supply on the value of small business gifts such as diaries and calendars. With effect from 29th November 1995 the limit on such goods is increased from £10.00 per item to £15.00.

Value Added Tax Return

For the period

to

HM Customs and Excise

Your VAT Office telephone number is 0181–748 8010

For Official Use

Registration Number	Period

You could be liable to a financial penalty if your completed return and all the VAT payable are not received by the due date.

Due date:

For Official Use

ATTENTION

If you are using Retail Scheme B1, D or J, please remember to carry out your annual adjustment at the appropriate time.

Before you fill in this form please read the notes on the back and the VAT leaflet *"Filling in your VAT return"*. Fill in all boxes clearly in ink, and write 'none' where necessary. Don't put a dash or leave any box blank. If there are no pence write **"00"** in the pence column. **Do not** enter more than one amount in any box.

For official use			£	p
	VAT due in this period on **sales** and other outputs	**1**		
	VAT due in this period on **acquisitions** from other **EC Member States**	**2**		
	Total VAT due **(the sum of boxes 1 and 2)**	**3**		
	VAT reclaimed in this period on **purchases** and other inputs (including acquisitions from the EC)	**4**		
	Net VAT to be paid to Customs or reclaimed by you **(Difference between boxes 3 and 4)**	**5**		
	Total value of **sales** and all other outputs excluding any VAT. **Include your box 8 figure**	**6**		00
	Total value of **purchases** and all other inputs excluding any VAT. **Include your box 9 figure**	**7**		00
	Total value of all **supplies** of goods and related services, excluding any VAT, to other **EC Member States**	**8**		00
	Total value of all **acquisitions** of goods and related services, excluding any VAT, from other **EC Member States**	**9**		00

Retail schemes. If you have used any of the schemes in the period covered by this return, enter the relevant letter(s) in this box.

If you are enclosing a payment please tick this box.

DECLARATION: You, or someone on your behalf, must sign below.

I, ...declare that the

(Full name of signatory in BLOCK LETTERS)

information given above is true and complete.

Signature ....Date ....19............

A false declaration can result in prosecution.

S

CD 2859/N3(08/93)   0052416   F 3790 (February 1994)

VAT 100

52 Special schemes for retailers

Introduction

1. In order to facilitate the calculation of retailer's output tax in many different sets of circumstances, there are 12 alternative schemes available. Some of the schemes are only suitable for the smaller business, and others have special conditions attached so that in reality the choice for any one retailer is not one of 12 main methods. An outline of the schemes, labelled alphabetically, is given in this chapter.

In most retail establishments a tax invoice is not given in respect of cash sales, and the gross takings figure is used as a basis for determining the appropriate output tax. For VAT purposes there are two basic methods in use.

a) The standard method of calculating gross takings is based on payments received from customers, and that includes credit customers as well.

b) An optional method which is also based on payments received, but credit sales are included when the customer is actually invoiced and not when the account is paid.

Under the standard method of accounting for VAT by retailers the actual tax point is the date on which a retailer receives payment for goods sold. For this purpose payment includes external credit card transactions. However, where an 'in store' credit card is used, the tax point is when the payment is actually received by the retailer.

Changes in retail schemes

2. On 27th November 1996, Retail Scheme B was closed to traders with a retail turnover exceeding £1 million. Large traders already using Retail Scheme B are required to migrate to another scheme by 1st April 1997.

The fixed mark-up schemes (B2 and C) will be withdrawn on 31st March 1998. Other schemes will be simplified and rationalised between July 1997 and March 1998.

The standard method of calculating gross takings (SMGT) was withdrawn on March 1st 1997. SMGT currently allows traders selling goods on self-financed credit to account for tax as instalments are received from customers. VAT due on outstanding balances as at 28th February 1997 is payable by instalments over the ten months March to December 1997.

Cash accounting

3. The system of cash accounting for businesses with a taxable turnover of not more than £350,000 p.a. is not likely to be advantageous for most retailers who already account for VAT on the basis of cash receipts. They would lose the advantage of reclaiming VAT on purchases as soon as they are invoiced and could only claim set-off at the end of the accounting period in which the payment was made.

Scheme A

4. This scheme is available for any size of retailer whose supplies of goods and services are all at the standard rate.

A full record of daily takings must be kept and the output tax is: gross takings × 7/47.

Scheme B

5. This scheme is also available for any size of retailer whose supplies of goods and services are subject to two rates of tax, zero rating counting as a positive rate of tax. With this scheme sales at the zero rate must not be greater than 50% of the total sales.

The output tax is calculated as follows.

a) The gross takings, that is standard and zero rated supplies, must be recorded in the normal way.

b) The value of goods purchased for resale at the zero rate of VAT is priced at selling prices, including VAT, and after adjustment for bad debts and losses.

c) Takings at the standard rate are the difference between (a) and (b) above.

d) Output tax is the estimated standard rated takings as determined above, multiplied by 7/47.

> **Example**

	Quarter ending 31.3.1997
	£
Gross takings (standard and zero)	172,500
Less valuation of zero rated goods received for resale at selling price	55,000
Estimated takings at standard rate	117,500
Output tax is 117,500 × 7/47	17,500

Scheme B1

6. Under this scheme the main differences from Scheme B are as follows.
   a) There is no 50% rule.
   b) There are no turnover restrictions.
   c) An annual stock adjustment is required.

Scheme B2

7. Under this scheme taxable turnover (ie total value of standard and zero rated supplies plus VAT) must be £750,000 p.a. or less from 1.10.91 (previously £500,000). The turnover level has a 25% tolerance level ie to £937,500.

Scheme C

8. This scheme is only available to retailers with a taxable turnover of £125,000 or less p.a. where there is more than one rate of tax. The scheme is not available for retailers with any hirings, leases, or rentals. With this scheme sales are calculated by reference to average fixed mark-ups. The turnover has a 25% tolerance level, ie to £156,250.

   The output tax is computed as follows.

   a) The cost of sales for each rate of goods supplied is multiplied by an approved mark-up percentage, which may be different from the actual business mark-up percentage.
   b) Output tax is 7/47 × the standard rate sales.

> **Example**

	Quarter ending 31.3.1997	
	Standard rate	Zero rate
	£	£
Cost of goods purchased incl. VAT	20,000	16,000
Add approved mark-up 20%	4,000	–
Assumed sales	24,000	16,000

Output tax is £24,000 × 7/47 ie £3,574.

Scheme D

9. This scheme applies to retailers with a taxable turnover of £1,000,000 p.a. or less with more than one rate of taxable supply. This scheme is not available for retailers with any hirings, leases, or rentals. There is a tolerance level of 25%, i.e. turnover of £1,250,000. The output tax is calculated as follows.

   a) The gross takings, zero and standard, are recorded in the normal way.
   b) The cost of goods received including VAT at each positive rate is recorded, and the proportion at each rate is applied to the total takings.

> **Example**

	Quarter ending 31.3.1997
	£
Gross takings, standard and zero rated	480,000
Cost of goods with VAT standard rate	250,000
Cost of goods with VAT zero rate	90,000
Total cost	340,000
Output tax is $\frac{250,000}{340,000} \times 480,000 \times 7/47 =$	52,566

Note
With this scheme an annual adjustment to the computation must be carried out.

Scheme D1

10. Under this scheme the main differences from Scheme D are as follows.

a) The value of purchases from unregistered supplies and suppliers who offer prompt payment discounts *which are not taken up* should not exceed 25% of the total purchases of goods for resale.

b) Supplies of self-made goods or supplies of catering must be dealt with outside the scheme.

Scheme E

11. This scheme is available for any size of business with more than one rate of taxable supply, but cannot be used for services including goods on hire, lease or rental.

The output tax is computed as follows.

a) In the first tax period, the total of the opening stock and the goods purchased for resale at each positive rate must be valued at the appropriate selling price including VAT.

b) Tax at the standard rate is determined by applying the fraction 7/47 to the standard rate sales.

c) In the second and subsequent tax periods the opening stock figure is omitted.

> **Example**

	Quarter ending 31.3.1997	
	Std. rate	Zero rate
	£	£
Opening stocks at SP and VAT	17,000	6,000
Purchases at SP and VAT	43,000	8,000
	60,000	14,000

Output tax is $60,000 \times 7/47$ ie £8,936.

Scheme E1

12. Under this scheme the main differences from Scheme E are the following.

a) Detailed stock records are required.

b) This is a complicated scheme which involves a certain amount of detailed paperwork to support the calculations.

Scheme F

13. This scheme is available for any size of business with more than one rate of taxable supply, where the distinction between the types of supply can be identified at the point of sale.

As the total sales at each positive rate are required, the output tax is the standard rate sales multiplied by the fraction 7/47.

Scheme H

14. This scheme may be used by any size of retailer where there is more than one positive rate of tax, but is not available for services or goods on hire, lease or rental.

Output tax is calculated as follows.

a) A full record of daily gross takings must be kept.

b) For each positive rate, the opening stock and purchases for resale must be valued at their VAT inclusive selling prices.

c) Output tax is equal to the following:

$$\frac{\text{SP with VAT of SR goods}}{\text{SP with VAT of all goods}} \times \text{Gross takings} \times 7/47$$

d) For the first three quarters the opening stock must be included in the computation.

Example

	Third quarter to 31.3.1997	
	Std. rate	Zero rate
	£	£
Opening stock 1.7.96 at SP and VAT	30,000	10,000
Purchases from 1.7.96 at SP and VAT	120,000	40,000
	150,000	50,000

Gross takings for the quarter to 31.3.1997 £50,000.

Output tax is $\dfrac{150,000}{200,000} \times 50,000 \times 7/47$

ie $37,500 \times 7/47 = £5,585$.

Scheme J

15. This scheme is more applicable to large retailers where there is more than one positive rate of tax, but is not available for use with supplies of services, goods on hire, lease or rental.

Output tax is calculated in a similar manner to that for Scheme H, as follows.

a)   A full record of daily takings is required.

b)   For each positive rate, the opening stock and purchases must be valued at their VAT-inclusive selling prices.

c)   Output tax is equal to:

$$\frac{\text{SP with VAT of SR goods}}{\text{SP with VAT of all goods}} \times \text{Gross takings} \times 7/47$$

At the end of the VAT year the closing stock for each positive rate must be evaluated at their VAT-inclusive selling prices. The output tax is then recomputed by reference to a derived sales value.

	Std rate goods at SP with VAT £
Opening stock	–
Add purchases for resale	–
	–
Less closing stock	–
Sales at standard rate	–

d)   If the annual output tax on the computed sales is different from the total amounts determined by the quarterly returns, an adjustment is made.

Miscellaneous

16. a)   It should perhaps be noted that it is possible for a retailer to have more than one scheme in operation at a time, and a combination of schemes could be used, for example, where there are separate departments of a large store.

b)   In general only Schemes A and F, and in certain circumstances B, can be used for retailers who supply services including hirings, leases and rentals.

c)   Goods applied for personal use are to be included in gross takings at cost price plus VAT.

d)   Schemes C and D cannot be used by retailers in respect of goods which they manufacture or grow themselves, since they are based on an evaluation of the goods purchased for resale, at their VAT-inclusive selling prices.

e)   Adaptations to Scheme J and others are available.

53 VAT worked examples

Introduction

1. This chapter provides some worked examples of VAT under the following headings:

> Registration
> VAT return – non-retailing
> Bad debt recovery
> Partial exemption
> Retail scheme D

Registration

2. **Example**

A has been the owner of a retail store for a number of years. He has not previously registered for VAT as his turnover has consistently been below the minimum criteria. However he now feels that he should register and seeks your advice. Turnover since January 1995 has been as indicated below:

	1995 £	1996 £	1997 £
January	1,125	2,775	8,000
February	950	1,450	12,000
March	1,000	2,400	15,000
April	950	2,550	
May	1,450	3,700	
June	1,150	4,200	
July	1,400	3,900	
August	1,425	4,500	
September	1,500	4,000	
October	1,550	2,000	
November	1,675	1,500	
December	2,500	1,500	

Solution

Moving annual total sales

	£
12 months to 30.9.96 =	35,200
12 months to 31.10.96 =	35,650
12 months to 30.11.96 =	35,475
12 months to 31.12.96 =	34,475
12 months to 31.1.97 =	39,700
12 months to 28.2.97 =	50,250
12 months to 31.3.97 =	62,850

As the annual total to 28th February 1997 has exceeded £48,000 A must notify the Customs and Excise by 31st March 1997. Registration will be effected from 31st March 1997.

3. **Example**

D commenced trading on 1st January 1997 with the following taxable turnover.

	£
Quarter to 31st March 1997	8,000
Quarter to 30th June 1997	9,000

As a result of an unexpected UK order, obtained on 1st May 1997, budgeted sales evenly spread for the remainder of the financial year to 31st December 1997 are as follows:

	£	
Quarter to 30th September 1997	100,000	(budget)
Quarter to 31st December 1997	120,000	(budget)

D wants to know when he should register for VAT.

Solution

When the order was obtained in May 1997 it was clear that the annual turnover would exceed £48,000 the level for registration from 27th November 1997.

With the sales evenly spread the cumulative sales for the month of July would be:

		£
Quarter to 31.3.97		8,000
Quarter to 30.6.97		9,000
July 1997 $\dfrac{100000}{3}$		33,333
		50,333

Registration would be required either:
a) by 30th August 1997, or
b) at an earlier mutually agreed date.

VAT return – *non-retailing*

4. **Example**

Z runs his own manufacturing business and submits VAT returns for the quarters ended 31 March, 30 June, 30 September and 31 December. The following relates to transactions for the quarters to 30 June 1996. The actual tax point dates have been agreed with the local VAT office.

Sales invoices

No.	Date	Tax point	Value excluding VAT £
133	15.4.96	15.5.96	4,500
134	17.5.96	21.5.96	5,500
135	1.6.96	1.6.96	4,000
136	30.6.96	17.7.96	1,500
			15,500

Purchases and expenses invoices

No.	Date	Tax point	Value excluding VAT £
1	1.4.96	1.4.96	1,200
2	1.5.96	6.5.96	1,250
3	13.6.96	30.6.96	2,500
4	11.7.96	24.6.96	2,700
			7,650

Compute the net VAT payable for the quarter to 30th June 1996.

Solution

VAT quarter to 30.6.96

			£		£
Output tax:	Sales invoices 133		4,500		
	134		5,500		
	135		4,000		
			14,000	£14,000 @ 17.5%	2,450.00
Input tax:	Invoices	1	1,200		
		2	1,250		
		3	2,500		
		4	2,700		
			7,650	£7,650 @ 17.5%	1,338.75
VAT payable					1,111.25

Note

The time of supply for VAT purposes is the actual tax point and not the date of the invoice although these will invariably be the same.

Bad debt recovery

5. T, a trader registered for VAT, has made the following supplies to P Ltd.

Date	Rate	Value of goods	VAT	Gross value
25.1.96	Zero	3,000	–	3,000
3.2.96	SR	1,200	210	1,410
5.3.96	Exempt	450	–	450
22.3.96	SR	1,600	280	1,880
2.4.96	SR	2,500	438	2,938
10.4.96	SR	2,000	350	2,350
		10,750	1,278	12,028

T has received the following payments on account:

	£
15.3.96	1,646
11 .5.96	1,000
20.5.96	1,000

P Ltd was the subject of a creditors' voluntary winding up order on the 30th May 1996. *Calculate the amount of bad debt relief for VAT.*

Solution

Amount of debt outstanding 12,028 – 3,646 = 8,382

This would be represented by the following:

	Gross value	VAT
10.4.96	2,350	350
2.4.96	2,938	438
22.3.96	1,880	280
5.3.96	450	–
3.2.96	764	114
	8,382	1,182

Proportion of invoice dated 3.2.96

$$\frac{764}{1,410} \times 210 = 114$$

VAT recoverable £1,182

Partial exemption

6. S Ltd has the following data relating to the quarter ended 30th June 1997

	£
Sales standard rated (excluding VAT)	95,000
Zero rated	15,000
Exempt	28,000
Input tax	
Attributable to taxable supplies	9,500
Attributable to exempt supplies	1,100
Attributable to overheads	2,500
	13,100

Apportionment of overhead expenditure	%
Standard rate supplies	50
Zero rate supplies	35
Exempt supplies	15
	100%

Calculate the VAT payable for the quarter ending 30th June 1997.

Solution

VAT payable quarter to 30 June 1997

	£	£	£
Output tax £95,000 @ 17.5%			16,625
Input tax			
Attributable to taxable supplies		9,500	
Attributable to overheads 85% × 2,500		2,125	
Attributable to exempt supplies	1,100		
Add % of overheads 15% × 2,500	375		
		1,475	13,100
VAT Payable			3,525

Note

As the input tax attributable to the exempt supplies of £1,475 (1,475 ÷ 3 = 492) is less than £625 on average per month and the exempt input tax of £1,475 is less than 50% of the total input tax of £13,100, the total input tax is recoverable.

VAT retail scheme D

7. | *Example* |

P is registered for VAT as a retailer and uses Scheme D. His data for the four quarters to 31st March 1997 are as follows:

	Gross takings	Cost of goods Standard rate (inc. VAT)	Total cost of goods (inc. VAT)
	£	£	£
Quarter to 30.6.96	19,500	9,500	14,200
Quarter to 30.9.96	25,500	12,300	19,150
Quarter to 31.12.96	14,700	4,200	9,100
Quarter to 31.3.97	20,500	8,500	15,100
	80,200	34,500	57,550

Compute the output tax for each quarter together with the annual adjustment.

Solution

Quarter to 30.6.96

Output tax $= \dfrac{9,500}{14,200} \times 19,500 =$ £13,046.00

Output tax $= 13,046 \times \dfrac{7}{47} =$ £1,942.98

Quarter to 30.9.96

Output tax $= \dfrac{12,300}{19,150} \times 25,500 =$ £16,378.00

Output tax $= 16,378 \times \dfrac{7}{47} =$ £2,439.27

Quarter to 31.12.96

Output tax $= \dfrac{4,200}{9,100} \times 14,700 =$ £6,785.00

Output tax $= 6,785 \times \dfrac{7}{47} =$ £1,010.53

Quarter to 31.3.97

Standard output $= \dfrac{8,500}{15,100} \times 20,500 =$ £11,540.00

Output tax $= 11,540 \times \dfrac{7}{47} =$ £1,718.68

Annual adjustment

Standard output $= \dfrac{34,500}{57,550} \times 80,200 =$ £48,078.00

Output tax $= 48,078 \times \dfrac{7}{47} =$ £7,160.58

Less: recorded Quarter 1	1,942.98	
Quarter 2	2,439.27	
Quarter 3	1,010.53	
Quarter 4	1,718.68	7,111.46
Under declaration		49.12

• Questions without answers

1. P operates a café in a busy holiday resort which is open from March to October each year on a full-time basis and the remainder of the year on special occasions. Turnover since the business started on 1st January 1996 is as follows:

	1996 £	1997 £
January	100	300
February	–	150
March	500	1,100
April	3,200	4,400
May	2,900	3,800
June	4,500	5,500

	1996 £	1997 £
July	2,500	10,200
August	2,700	9,500
September	4,900	14,200
October	200	15,000
November	–	16,000
December	400	

Advise P as to when, if at all, he should register for VAT.

2. T is a small manufacturer registered for VAT. The following information relates to transactions for the quarter to 30th June 1997.

Sales invoices		Value excluding VAT £
No. 1	Standard rate goods	75,000
No. 2	Standard rate goods	42,000
No. 3	Zero rate goods	19,000
No. 4	Exempt goods	56,000

Purchase invoices		Value excluding VAT £
No. 1	Raw materials	39,500
No. 2	Raw materials	65,300 (15% attributable to exempt supplies)
No. 3	Printing and stationery	1,250
No. 4	Canteen food	3,500
No. 5	Repairs to factory roof	9,500
No. 6	Gas and Electricity	12,000
No. 7	Rates	1,500
No. 8	Transport and delivery costs	7,500

Overhead expenditure is to be apportioned on the following basis:

SR goods (70%) zero rated goods (10%)
exempt goods (20%)

Calculate the VAT payable for the quarter to 30th June 1997.

3. Andrew Poser is a self-employed management consultant.

On 1st December 1994 he registered for Value Added Tax as an intending trader.

He has made the following additions to fixed assets

		Gross cost £	VAT £	Net cost £
22 December 1994	Office equipment and furniture	5,450	711	4,739
28 February 1995	Vauxhall motor car	8,250	1,076	7,174
15 June 1995	Photocopier and equipment	2,180	324	1,856
31 December 1995	Metro motor car for full-time employee	4,500	670	3,830
1 June 1996	Office fixtures	288	43	245
31 July 1996	Word processor	2,185	325	1,860
1 August 1996	BMW motor car	13,500	2,010	11,490

The Vauxhall was sold on 1st August 1996 for £4,790. The photocopier and office equipment were of poor quality and were scrapped in August 1996 for no consideration. Mr Poser's full-time employee used the Metro motor car for business 60% of the time. The remainder represented private use. The Vauxhall and BMW were used exclusively by Andrew. The Inspector of Taxes has accepted that 40% of the use of these vehicles was for private purposes.

No claims are to be made to treat any of the fixed assets as short life assets for capital allowances purposes.

Andrew moved into his offices and started to trade on 1st January 1995.

Calculate the capital allowances due for all years of assessment.

Part VI

Elements of Tax Planning

54 Elements of tax planning

Introduction

1. This chapter is concerned with some basic principles of tax planning which can be applied to most situations where a taxpayer has a choice of alternative courses of action.

What is tax planning?

2. Given a set of circumstances or a situation where a decision is to be made which involves the incidence of taxation, then tax planning is concerned with achieving the best result with respect to that decision from the taxation perspective. The 'best result' is usually taken to mean achieving the least amount of tax payable consistent with any cash flow advantages which are also often important.

There is no set body of knowledge called tax planning as it usually requires the application of threads of tax law and practice from across the whole spectrum of taxation and law. An exercise in tax planning therefore involves the following.

a) Identification of the specific problem to be considered.

b) Identification of the relevant parts of the tax statutes which have relevance to the problem.

c) Application of the tax rules identified to the problem.

d) Evaluation of the various options available in order to minimise the incidence of taxation.

e) Identification and examination of any other factors of a legal, commercial or financial nature which should be taken into consideration.

Objectives of tax planning

3. Tax planning objectives for individuals may be summarised as follows.

a) To reduce taxable income and/or chargeable gains falling to be assessed.

b) To lower rate of tax which is applicable to taxable income or chargeable gains.

c) To defer the date on which tax becomes payable, thereby gaining a cash flow/interest advantage.

For companies in general, similar objectives can be applied. However, for family companies with shareholder directors/employees, tax planning for the individual must inevitably be considered together with that for the family company. This arises because in many cases most of the income of the family director/employee shareholder is in fact derived from family company sources, in the form of remuneration, benefits in kind and dividends.

Tax planning caveats

4. The following points should be borne in mind when undertaking any tax planning exercise.

a) Tax planning, sometimes called tax avoidance, should not be confused with tax evasion. The latter, which is unlawful and may lead to criminal prosecution, is associated with fraudulent or dishonest plans to avoid taxation.

b) Commercial factors should not be ignored just for the sake of a business tax planning exercise. For example, there is no point in investing in additional capital expenditure to obtain capital allowances if the capital project itself shows negative returns on investment.

c) Future financial security should not be put at risk. The making of substantial gifts inter vivos to mitigate IHT on the death of the donor should be balanced against the possible shortfall in annual income which might ensue.

d) Possible changes in the law in the future may render current tax planning exercises less advantageous.

e) Tax plans should be flexible to accommodate, if possible, changes in circumstances. There is no permanent long-term relationship between capital and income which will meet all the requirements of all taxpayers.

Example 1

Z, who has been trading for many years, has the following data relating to his accounting years ended 31st December 1996.

	31.12.95 £	31.12.96 £
Adjusted profits	3,500	6,000
Additions to plant	–	16,000

Plant pool brought forward 1st January 1995 was £1,500.

Motor car (private use 30%) brought forward 1st January 1995 was £3,000.

Z is married with no other income for 1996/97. His wife has Schedule E income for 1996/97 of £10,000.

Compute Z and his wife's income tax liability for 1996/97.

Solution

Income tax computation 1996/97

		Z £		Mrs Z £
Schedule D Case I $\frac{3,500 + 6,000}{2}$		4,750	Schedule E	10,000
Capital allowances		985		
		3,765		10,000
Personal allowance		3,765		3,765
Taxable income		–		6,235
Tax payable	3,900 @ 20%	–		780
	2,335 @ 24%	–		560
	6,235	–		1,340
Less MCA 1,790 @ 15%		–		268
		Nil		1,072

Notes

i) *Capital allowances*

	Plant £	Motor car (PU 30%) £
WDV b/f	1,500	3,000
Additions	16,000	
	17,500	3,000
WD allowance (restricted)	985	–
	16,515	3,000

By claiming a reduced amount of capital allowances Z has not wasted his personal allowance which cannot be carried forward.

ii) *The maximum claim for capital allowances is:*
Plant 25% × 17,500

		4,375
Motor 25% × 3,000 =	750 less p.u. 225 =	525
		£4,900

iii) *By not claiming the full amount the value of pool carried forward is enhanced for subsequent years.*

iv) *The MCA can be transferred to Mrs Z by election.*

v) *1996/97 is a transitional year and the profits are averaged before computing capital allowances.*

vi) *By claiming capital allowances Z has reduced his relevant earnings eligible for PPP.*

Example 2

P is the 100% owner of Alpha Ltd, an unquoted trading company with a year end of 30th April 1996.

Schedule D Case I profits of Alpha Ltd are £280,000 for the year ended 30th April 1996 after directors remuneration to P of £80,000. There were no dividend payments.

P would like to have available cash of about £60,000 by June 1996 and requests advice as to the best method of obtaining this sum from the company. Advise P.

Solution

The following factors should be taken into consideration:

		£
i) Additional remuneration net		60,000
Gross up at 40% rate		40,000
		100,000
Employer's NIC 10.2%		10,200
		110,200

Less corporation tax @ 24%/25%

$$\frac{110,200}{12} \times 11 \times 25\% = \qquad 25,254$$

$$\frac{110,200}{12} \times 1 \times 24\% = \qquad 2,204 \qquad\qquad 27,458$$

	82,742
Net cost to company	
ii) Dividend paid by company to give net of £60,000 is	80,000 (net)
Gross dividend to P 80,000 × 100 ÷ 80 =	100,000
Higher rate @ 40%	40,000
Net amount received	60,000

iii) Based on the above, the net cost to the company (which is owned 100% by P) is £2,742 more for the additional remuneration rather than a dividend.

iv) If the dividend is paid before 30th April 1996 the ACT of £20,000 will be available for set-off against the company's corporation tax liability for the accounting period ended 30th April 1996. ACT will be due for payment on or before 14th May 1996.

v) If the dividend is paid after 6th April 1996, it will fall into the income tax year 1996/97, and the higher rate will not be due until 31st January 1998. If paid before 6th April 1996, the higher rate tax will be due on 1st December 1997.

Conclusion

P should be advised to adopt the policy of providing the additional £60,000 required by the means of a dividend rather than additional remuneration.

Tax planning summary

5. Individuals

I Income tax	Employees	Self-employed	Directors
1. Claim expenses of employment	✓	–	✓
2. Claim capital allowances for privately owned asset/FPCS	✓	✓	✓
3. Company pension scheme: consider AVC	✓	✓	✓
4. No company pension scheme: consider PP Plan	✓	✓	✓
5. Inter-spouse transfer of assets to use PA's and MCA. PA + MCA	✓	✓	✓
6. Car fuel benefit/payment business mileage	✓	–	✓
7. Phase capital expenditure to save Class IV NIC income tax	–	✓	–
8. Employ staff with earnings below NI thresholds	–	✓	–
9. Consider PEP/TESSA – tax-free	✓	✓	✓
10. Consider Enterprise Investment scheme – tax saving at 20%	✓	✓	✓

	Employees	Self-employed	Directors
II Capital gains tax			
1. Bed and breakfast – utilise A exemption	✓	✓	✓
2. Inter-spouse transfer of assets to minimise CGT	✓	✓	✓
3. Phase disposals between tax years to use A exemption	✓	✓	✓
4. With takeover consider cash/shares to minimise CGT	✓	✓	✓
III Inheritance tax			
1. Maximise use of general exemptions – £250	✓	✓	✓
£3,000	✓	✓	✓
Normal expenditure – for marriage	✓	✓	✓
inter-spouse	✓	✓	✓
charitable bequests	✓	✓	✓
2. Consider gifts intervivos – personal assets	✓	✓	✓
business assets	–	✓	–
3. Deeds of Variation to change distribution of estate	✓	✓	✓
IV VAT			
1. Consider voluntary registration to claim input tax	–	✓	–
2. Phase capital expenditure to benefit cash flow from input tax	–	✓	–
3. Consider payment for private fuel rather than scale charge	–	✓	–
4. Consider turnover levels as it approaches registration point	–	✓	–

6. Companies

1. Timing of dividend payments – cash flow benefits.
2. Extended account period, e.g. 18 months to 6 and 12.
3. Phasing capital expenditure to maximise small company relief.
4. Consider group election for dividends and interest – cash flow benefits.
5. Consider payment of additional remuneration/dividend – NI saving for latter.

Questions without answers

1. Sonya Rich is the managing director of Wealthy Ltd, an unquoted trading company. She owns all of the shares in the company. Sonya has asked for your advice regarding tax planning measures that both she and Wealthy Ltd should take during the next six months. You should assume that today's date is 1 January 1996.

Sonya is a 47-year-old widow, her husband having died several years ago. She has one daughter, Kate, aged 23. You have the following information.

1. Wealthy Ltd is forecast to have Schedule D1 trading profits of £285,000 for the year ended 30 April 1996. This is after taking into account Sonya's directors' remuneration of £95,000 p.a. Wealthy Ltd has not paid any dividends during the year ended 30 April 1996.

   At some time during the next six months, Sonya would like to draw an additional amount from Wealthy Ltd, either by way of directors' remuneration or as a dividend, sufficient to leave her with additional post-tax income of £60,000.

2. During the next six months, Wealthy Ltd will need to purchase new computer equipment costing £80,000 and a new freehold office building costing £95,000. In the case of the office building, Sonya might acquire this herself and rent it to Wealthy Ltd at a market rent of £7,500 p.a. should this be beneficial.

3. Sonya's investments include the following.

   i) £11,800 in a TESSA account with her local building society. This account was opened on 5 January 1991.

   ii) Ordinary shares in quoted companies worth £162,400. Included in this figure are a number of shareholdings which are currently standing at a substantial capital gain.

   iii) £14,500 in two personal equity plans that were opened on 15 March 1993 and 2 April 1994.

   iv) £10,000 in National Savings Certificates which were acquired on 1 February 1991.

   Sonya does not wish to increase her overall exposure to equity investments. She has not disposed of any assets during 1995–96.

4. Kate is to get married on 30 April 1996, and Sonya would like to make a gift worth £20,000 to her on or before the date of the wedding. Sonya has already made substantial lifetime transfers of value to Kate, the last of which was four years ago. Kate is the sole beneficiary under the terms of Sonya's will.

Advise both Sonya and Wealthy Ltd of tax planning measures that they should take during the period 1 January 1996 to 30 June 1996.

*Your answer should be confined to the information given in the question, and you should pay particular attention to the **timing** of any tax planning measures that you have recommended. Where possible, a calculation of the tax saving that will result from each aspect of your advice should be included.*

ACCA

2. Highrise Ltd is an unquoted trading company. Highrise Ltd has always had an accounting date of 30 June, with its most recent accounts being prepared to 30 June 1994. However, the company now plans to change its accounting date to 31 December. Highrise Ltd has forecast that its results for the 18 month period to 31 December 1995 will be as follows:

   1. Tax adjusted Schedule D1 trading profits, before capital allowances, per six monthly period will be:

	£
Six months to 31.12.94	141,000
Six months to 30.6.95	126,000
Six months to 31.12.95	165,000

   2. The tax written-down value of plant and machinery at 1 July 1994 is £20,000. On 31 May 1995 Highrise Ltd will purchase plant costing £120,000.

   3. Highrise Ltd owns two freehold office buildings which have always been rented out unfurnished. These are both to be sold. The first building at Ampton will be sold on 31 December 1994 resulting in a chargeable gain of £42,000, whilst the second building at Bodford will be sold on 31 May 1995 resulting in an allowable capital loss of £25,000.

   4. The building at Ampton is currently let at £48,000 p.a., rent being due quarterly in advance on 1 January, 1 April etc. The building at Bodford was let until 31 March 1994, but has been empty since then. It will be decorated at a cost of £9,000 during May 1995 prior to its disposal. Both lettings are at a full rent and Highrise Ltd is responsible for all repairs.

   5. A dividend of £50,000 (net) will be paid on 10 October 1994.

   6. Highrise Ltd has a 20% shareholding in Shortie Ltd, an unquoted trading company. A dividend of £10,000 (net) will be received from Shortie Ltd on 15 June 1995.

Advise Highrise Ltd of whether it would be beneficial to:

i) prepare one set of accounts for the 18 month period to 31 December 1995, or

ii) prepare separate accounts for the six month period to 31 December 1994 and for the year ended 31 December 1995.

Your answer should include a calculation of Highrise Ltd's total mainstream corporation tax liability for the 18 month period to 31 December 1995 under each alternative.

Part VII

Case Law

55 Case law

This chapter provides a summary of the cases referred to in the text, under the following headings:

Income tax and Corporation tax

- Schedule E
- Schedules A and B
- Schedule D Case III
- Schedule D Case Vl
- Schedule D Cases I and II: The concept of trading; Exchange profit and losses; Insurance claims; Compensation and voluntary payments; Allowable expenditure; Losses and defalcations; Stock and work in progress; Capital expenditure – Plant and machinery, industrial buildings; Losses; Trust income.

Capital gains tax

Inheritance tax

Income tax and Corporation tax

Schedule E

1. ***Edwards* v *Clinch*. HL 1981. STI**

   The taxpayer was appointed to act as an inspector at a public enquiry. The Inland Revenue claimed that he held a public office within Section 181(1) TA 1970.

   Held. Taxpayer did not hold an office since the post had no existence independent of him, and there was neither continuity nor permanence.

2. ***Fall* v *Hitchen*. 1972. 49. TC 433.**

   The taxpayer was a ballet dancer with Sadlers' Wells with a contract in the standard form approved by the British Actors' Equity Association.

   Held. Contract was of service rather than for service hence the artiste was taxable under Schedule E and not Schedule D Case II.

3. ***Reed* v *Seymour*. 1927. HL 11. TC 625.**

   A country cricket club designated a match as a benefit match for one of its professionals and handed the net proceeds (gate money less expenses) to him. The benefit did not arise from any contractional obligation.

   Held. The proceeds were in the nature of a personal gift and therefore not assessable income.

4. ***Moorhouse* v *Doorland*. 1954. CA 36. TC 1.**

   The taxpayer was a professional cricketer in the Lancashire League, the rules of which provided for collections from spectators for meritorious performances by professional players.

   Held. The collections were profits arising from the players' employment and therefore taxable.

5. ***Ball* v *Johnson*. 1971. 47. TC 155.**

   A bank expected its male clerks to take the Institute of Bankers examinations and cash awards were made to those who passed.

   Held. The awards were not remuneration for services rendered but a gift and therefore not assessable as income.

6. ***Moore* v *Griffiths*. 1972. 48. TC 475.**

   The taxpayer was a member of the English squad in the successful 1966 WORLD CUP competition. He was assessed on (1) £1000 he received out of a bonus of £22,000 paid by the FA to the squad on winning the competition and (2) £750 paid by a manufacturer as a prize for the best player.

   Held. The amounts were not rewards for services rendered and not therefore assessable income.

7. ***Calvert* v *Wainwright*. 1947. 27. TC 475.**

   The taxpayer was a taxi driver employed by a taxi hire company. During the course of his employment he received tips from customers.

   Held. The tips were remuneration for services rendered and assessable income.

8. ***Cooper* v *Blakiston*. HL 1908. 5. TC 347.**

   'Easter offerings' were given to a vicar by his parishioners and others in response to an appeal made by the Bishop and supported by the churchwardens.

   Held. The offerings were assessable income.

9. ***Tenant* v *Smith*. 1892. HL 3 TC 158.**

   A bank required its agent to live on the bank premises in appropriate residential accommodation. The agent's total income from other sources amounted to £375, and the 'value' of the occupation of the bank premises was placed at £50. Where a taxpayer's income was below £400 he was entitled to an abatement.

Held. He was not assessable in respect of the occupancy of the premises and therefore entitled to the abatement. Lord Halsbury stated that the thing sought to be taxed 'was not income unless it can be turned into money'. Occupancy of the bank premises could not be converted into money and the agent was forbidden to sublet.

10. *Wilkins v Rogerson*. 1961. 39. TC 344.

A company decided to give certain employees a suit, overcoat or raincoat as a Christmas box.

Held. The suit given to the taxpayer was a perquisite or profit of the employment and the measure of the emolument was the value of the suit to the employee ie its secondhand value.

11. *Rickets v Colquhoun*. 1926. 10. TC 118.

A barrister residing and practising in London was Recorder of Portsmouth. He claimed a deduction for his travelling expenses between London and Portsmouth and hotel expenses.

Held. The travelling expenses were attributable to the Recorder's own choice of residence and were not necessary to the Office nor incurred in the performance of his duties as Recorder.

12. *Garforth v Newsmith Stanton Ltd*. 1978. 52. TC 552.

The Company placed sums of money at the disposal of one of its directors by crediting a bonus to his current account.

Held. The payment was made at the time the bonus was credited to the current account and not when drawings against that bonus were made.

13. *R v IRC ex parte Chisholm*. 1981. STC. 253.

The taxpayer was directed to pay tax which should have been deducted by X Ltd from his emoluments as a director. He claimed that there was no evidence on which it could be claimed that he had received the emoluments knowing that X Ltd had wilfully failed to deduct tax under Regulation 26(4) Income Tax (Employments) Regulations 1973.

Held. There was ample evidence on which the Commissioners could have based their decision. Construing regulation 24(4). 'Knowing' meant 'knowing' not 'ought to know.' 'Wilfully' means intentionally or deliberately .

14. *Reed v Clarke*. 1985. STC. 323.

The taxpayer was a British subject domiciled in England who before and after 1978/79 was resident in the UK. He planned to spend 1978/79 working outside the UK. He was advised that he could avoid UK income tax on the sale of certain copyrights if he was physically absent from the UK throughout 1978/79. The taxpayer left England shortly before April 5th 1978 and returned after 6th April 1979.

Held. The taxpayer was not resident in the UK for the year 1978/79 and Section 49 TA 1970 did not bring the taxpayer into charge to tax.

15. *IRC v Lysaght*. 1928. 13. TC 511.

Until 1919 the taxpayer lived in England. He then retired, retaining an advisory post with his former company, sold his residence and from 1920 resided in Ireland with his family. He claimed relief for 1922/23 and 1923/24 in each year of which he visited the UK for about 100 days for business purposes.

Held. He was resident and ordinarily resident in the UK for the years of the claim.

16. *IRC v Addison*. CD 1984. STC. 540.

The taxpayer was a British subject resident in Zimbabwe with no foreign income in his own right, but whose wife had foreign earnings of her own. He claimed that he was entitled to unrestricted personal allowances.

Held. His total income within the meaning of Section 27(2) TA 1970 (ie total world income) did not include his wife's foreign earnings.

17. *Brown v CIR* 1965. 42. TC 583.

The taxpayer, considering it wrong to combine his wife's income with his own for surtax purposes deliberately omitted certain dividends of his wife from his income tax returns. In 1962 assessments to surtax on the amounts omitted for years back to 1950/51 were raised.

Held. Taxpayer's contention that the law requiring his wife's income to be included in his total income was invalid. In deliberately omitting the dividends he had been guilty of wilful default.

18. *Clixby v Pountney*. CD. 1967. 55. TC 515.

The taxpayer had been assessed on the basis of accounts and returns submitted on his behalf by an accountant. Following the latter's death there was a back duty investigation and assessments were made on the taxpayer under the extended time limits for fraud or wilful default.

Held. The legislation extended to cases where fraud or wilful default was committed by an agent and it could not be proved that the taxpayer was privy to it.

19. *R v CIR ex parte Cook R v CIR ex parte Keys*. QB May 1987.

The company had two directors who were its only shareholders. In 1982 it went into liquidation and the Inland Revenue issued directions under Regulation 26(4) for the recovery of income tax which should have been deducted for directors' remuneration under the PAYE system. The directors claimed that the operation of PAYE had been delegated to accountants who had failed to deduct the tax in error. They applied for a judicial review of the Court, seeking an order of certiorari to quash the directions.

Held. That the decision of the Inland Revenue to make the directions was entirely reasonable and could not be faulted and the directors were properly held liable for the tax not deducted.

20. *Shilton v Wilmhurst*. 1991 HL STC.

A well-known footballer received the sum of £75,000 from his old club Nottingham Forest FC as part of the transfer arrangements for joining Southampton FC. The General Commissioners found that the payment was an inducement to play for Southampton and therefore an emolument of office taxable under Section 19 (1) TA 1988.

Held. The payment did not flow from services rendered to the Southampton club and the charge as an emolument did arise under Section 19 (1) TA 1988. This decision reversed the ruling of the Court of Appeal.

21. *Elderkin* v *Hindmarsh*. *1988 STI*

The taxpayer was an inspector who was required to live away from home for long periods. A weekly living allowance of a fixed sum was provided which did not exceed the expenditure he was to incur. The General Commissioners found that his living expenses were incurred wholly exclusively and necessarily in the performance of his duties.

Held. The expenditure was incurred in order to put the taxpayer into the position of being able to do the work he was employed to do, and not incurred in the performance of his duties. He did not live in nearby accommodation in the course of performing those duties.

22. *Parikh* v *Sleeman*. *1990 CA STC 233*

The taxpayer who was a general medical practitioner also held a post as clinical officer to three separate hospitals. He claimed travelling expenses in the performance of his clinical appointments against the Schedule E assessments.

Held. Taxpayer's duties did not commence until he arrived at the hospitals so that the travelling expenses were not incurred in the performance of his duties. This confirmed the decision of the lower court and of the Special Commissioner.

23. *Pepper* v *Hart*. *1992 HL STC 898*

The taxpayer was an assistant master at Malvern College where his son was being educated. The fees charged were reduced by 80% and the Inland Revenue sought to tax the difference under Section 154 TA 1988, as a benefit in kind.

Held. The cost of providing a benefit should be based on the marginal cost of providing that benefit and not on an appropriate proportion of the total costs to the employer ie average cost.

24. *O'Leary* v *McKinlay*. *1990 HC STC*

O'Leary, a professional footballer with Arsenal, is domiciled in the Republic of Ireland. In 1979 the club loaned £266,000 to the trustees of a Jersey settlement for O'Leary's benefit. The sum was put on deposit and the interest paid to the player. As he was domiciled outside the UK it was thought that only remittances to the UK would be taxable.

Held. The source of the income was O'Leary's contract of employment and in view of the special conditions attached to the loan the interest was taxable as Schedule E income.

25. *Delaney* v *Staples*. *HL 1992*.

A payment in lieu of notice was first paid over, but the cheque was stopped and the employee had to take action to recover the sum. The employee argued that as the payment arose in connection with her employment it could be subject to a ruling by an industrial tribunal.

Held. Such payments are connected with the termination of employment and do not arise as a result of obligations under a continuing employment.

26. *Fitzpatrick* v *IRC*. *HL 1994*.

Four journalists who worked for national newspapers claimed the cost of purchasing newspapers and periodicals as a deduction under Section 198 TA 1988.

Held. The newspapers and periodicals were not purchased to put the taxpayers in a position to carry out their employment.

27. *Hall* v *Lorimer*. *CA 1994 STC.33*

Payments were made to a television mixer who over a period of four years had 574 engagements mostly for one day duration, claimed that he should not be taxed under Schedule E.

Held. The contracts were for services to be rendered and as such taxable under Schedule D.

Schedules A and B

1. *Pyne* v *Stallard-Pendyre*. *1964. 42. TC 183*.

Rents collected by an agent who was managing an estate for the taxpayer were misappropriated by him.

Held. The loss of rent was not admissible as maintenance expenditure.

2. *Collins* v *Fraser*. *1969. 46. TC 143*.

A timber merchant operated by converting round timber at this sawmill first into planks, some of which was sold in that form and some as wooden boxes.

Held. Up to and including the planking stage the taxpayer was doing no more than market his timber. Thus the Schedule B charge on the woodland covered the profit on the timber up to that stage.

Schedule D Case III

1. *Parkside Leasing Ltd* v *Smith*. *1984. STI. 740*.

The company received a cheque for compensation and interest on the 9th April 1979 in respect of the compulsory acquisition of its premises. The cheque was presented to the bank on April 11th and the company started a new trade on April 10th. The Inland Revenue claimed that the interest was taxable as income on the date of receipt ie the 9th April.

Held. Receipt of a cheque did not place the money at the payee's disposal. Only when the proceeds (cash or crediting the company's bank account) had been received was there receipt of interest for taxation purposes.

2. ***IRC v Crawley and Others***. *1987. STI. 4*

Payments made to a charity under deed of covenant had fallen into arrears and those due for 1974 to 1976 were not made until later years. In February 1984, the Charity claimed repayment of income tax deducted from payments due in the year to 5th April 1977, and paid in 1979/80, 1980/81 and 1982/83.

The Inland Revenue refused the claim on the basis that the income related to the year when the payments were due, and the claim was therefore outside the six year limit.

Held. The payments were the taxpayer's income for the year in which the payment became due, and therefore the repayment claim was out of time.

3. ***Shaw v Tonkin***. *1987 CH.D*

Mrs Shaw incurred expenses in her capacity as chairperson of the Association of Teachers' Widows and claimed to set the expense against her Case III Trustee Savings Bank account interest.

Held. There were no grounds at all for allowing a deduction.

4. ***Minsham Properties Ltd v Price***. *1990 STI 896*

Two questions were raised in this case:

i) Whether interest paid was short or yearly interest.

ii) Whether the interest actually paid was within the meaning of Section 248 TA 1970.

The Special Commissioner dismissed the company's Appeals and the latter appealed to the High Court.

Held. i) There were no grounds at all for allowing a deduction.

ii) Although a book entry could constitute payment it was not always the case that an entry crediting an amount to a payee would constitute a payment. In the present case the interest was added to the principal thereby increasing the loan account and this was held not to constitute a payment within the meaning of Section 248.

Schedule D case VI

1. ***Leeming v Jones***. *1930. 15. TC 333.*

Two individuals jointly purchased undeveloped land in 1935 and 1937 which they gave to their respective wives who then sold it at a profit to development companies controlled by their husbands.

Held. There was evidence for the finding that there was no trading and not enough to compel the Commissioners to find that the profits were income.

2. ***Hobbs v Hussey***. *1942. 24. TC 152.*

The taxpayer sold serial rights in his life story to a newspaper for £1500, payable in instalments.

Held. The £1,500 less expenses was assessable as Case VI income.

Schedule D cases I and II

The concept of trading

1. ***Martin v Lowry***. *HL. 1927. 11. TC 297.*

A merchant in agricultural machinery with no previous experience of the cotton trade purchased 44 million yards of linen, being Government surplus stock. Negotiation for a direct sale proved to be abortive and as a consequence he set up an organisation in order to dispose of the stock in lots. A number of purchasers acquired the linen which was sold within a year.

Held. Merchant was carrying on a trade. The contention that the profits were not 'annual profits or gains' was rejected.

2. ***IRC v Reinhold***. *SCIS. 1953. 34. TC 289.*

The taxpayer purchased and sold four houses in between 1945 and 1947, and he conceded that the intention was to resell the houses. On an appeal to the General Commissioners they allowed the appeal against an assessment made by the Inspector of Taxes.

Held. The fact that the properties were purchased with a view to resale did not of itself establish trade.

3. ***Wisdom v Chamberlain***. *CA. 1969. 45. TC 92.*

A well-known actor purchased a quantity of silver ingots in 1961/62 as a hedge against anticipated devaluation, and sold them within little more than a year at a profit.

Held. On the facts of the case, the nature of the transactions was an adventure in the nature of trade.

4. ***Taylor v Goode***. *CA. 1974. 49. TC 277.*

The taxpayer made a bid at an auction for a large country house which he had admired when younger. Unexpectedly he acquired the property for £5100 in 1959 and tried unsuccessfully to persuade his wife to live there. Subsequently he applied for and obtained planning permission for 90 houses; he then sold the property to a developer for £54,500 in 1963.

Held. That on the facts found or conceded there was not evidence of an adventure in the nature of trade. The Crown accepted the taxpayer's contention that the property was not acquired with a view to resale, but claimed unsuccessfully that the property had subsequently been appropriated to trading.

5. ***Ransom v Higgs***. *HL. 1974. STC. 539.*

The taxpayer sold land at a considerable undervalue to a partnership, one of the partners being his wife. She subsequently transferred her interest in the partnership to trustees of a discretionary trust, which had been created for the benefit of the taxpayer's family. The trustees subsequently sold the land to a company unconnected with the taxpayer, for £170,000 and the taxpayer was assessed to tax on this sum.

Held. That the taxpayer did not himself engage in trading. The fact that he procured others to enter into a scheme, some aspects of which involved trading by them, did not mean that the taxpayer himself had been trading.

6. *Tempest Estates Ltd* v *Warmsley*. *CD. 1976. STC. 10.*

In 1946 a company acquired from trustees some undeveloped land near Bolton, the main reason for the transaction being the saving of estate duty. Until 1958 only nominal sales of land took place but from that date a considerable proportion was sold including one sale to a subsidiary company which was a developer.

Held. That the fact that the acquisition was part of a scheme to save estate duty was not inconsistent with the conclusion that the land was acquired for trading.

7. *Gordon and Blair* v *CIR* *SCIS. 1962. 40. TC 358.*

The company ceased the brewing of beer and began selling beer supplied to its specification by another brewer.

Held. A new trade of beer selling had commenced and accordingly unrelieved trade losses from brewing could not be set against profits of the new trade.

8. *Rutledge* v *CIR*. *SCIS. 1929. 14. TC 490.*

In an isolated transaction the taxpayer purchased and sold a large quantity of toilet rolls.

Held. The transaction was an adventure in the nature of trade.

9. *Cannon Industries Ltd* v *Edwards*. *1965. CD 42. TC 625.*

The company that previously manufactured gas cookers commenced the assembly of electric food mixers for retail sale.

Held. The new activity amounted to an extension of its existing trade and not the creation of a new one.

10. *Marson* v *Morton*. *1986. The Times. 7.8.86.*

In June 1977 the taxpayers purchased land for £65,000, for which they borrowed £30,000 at 17% interest. In September 1977 the land was sold for £100,000 and the Inspector of Taxes issued an assessment under Schedule D Case I in respect of dealing in land. Mr Morton, a potato merchant, and his brother had never invested in land before and the General Commissioners found in favour of the taxpayers.

Held. A single transaction could be an adventure in the nature of trade but the responsibility for making that decision rested ultimately with the General Commissioners. In such cases the Court had no right to interfere with their findings.

11. *Kirkham* v *Williams*. *STC February 1989*

The taxpayer, a general dealer and demolition plant hire contractor, bought a 10 acre site, a small part of which was used to provide office and storage space. The remainder of the land was used for a limited farming activity. A house was built on the land and

sold realising a profit of £90,000 and another property acquired. Assessments were raised under Schedule D Case I and alternatively under Case VI (Section 778 TA 1988).

Held. The whole profit was attributable to a single adventure in the nature of trade, and taxable as Case I trading income.

Exchange profits and losses

1. *Imperial Tobacco Co of Gt Britain and Ireland* v *Kelly*. *CA 1943. 25. TC 292.*

The company accumulated dollars for the eventual purchase of American tobacco leaf as part of its normal trading practice. However, due to war-time restrictions the arrangement ceased and the company was obliged to sell its surplus dollars to the Treasury which resulted in an exchange surplus.

Held. There was a taxable profit as the dollars had been purchased with an intention to exchange them for trading materials.

2. *Davies* v *The Shell Co of China Ltd*. *CA. 1951. 32. TC 133.*

Some overseas agents of the company were required to deposit sums of money which were to be repaid on the termination of the agency. When the event occurred a substantial exchange surplus arose.

Held. This was held to be a capital profit and not one from trading. The deposits were considered to be part of the fixed capital of the company.

3. *Pattison* v *Marine Midland Bank Ltd*. *1984. STC. 10.*

The company issued $15 million of unsecured loan stock to banks within the same group to be redeemed at par in 1981, but with a right to repurchase earlier. The proceeds, which were never converted into sterling, were used to make loans in dollars and other currencies. Exchange gains and losses were brought into account even though there was no actual conversion into sterling. The company repurchased its loan stock in 1976 at an exchange loss and was assessed to corporation tax on the basis that the exchange loss was a capital loss, and the exchange profits on matching were revenue gains.

Held. Company did not make a capital loss when it repaid the loan stock nor did it make any income or profit from lending the $15 million to customers. There was no exchange profit because the company did not make any relevant currency transactions.

4. *Beauchamp* v *FW Woolworth plc*. *1990 HL.*

The company raised a loan of £50m Swiss francs in 1971 and a further loan of £50m Swiss francs in 1972. On repayment of the loans exchange losses of £11.4m arose due to the depreciation of sterling during the loan period, which the company claimed were deductible for corporation tax purposes.

Held. Reversing the decision of the Court of Appeal, that the exchange losses were not deductible for corporation tax purposes.

Insurance claims

1. ***Green* v *Gliksten J & Son Ltd.** HL. 1929. 14. TC 364.*

   For commercial reasons, timber trading stock destroyed by a fire was not entirely replaced with the proceeds of the insurance claim.

   Held. The whole sum receivable was a trading receipt.

2. ***Gray & Co Ltd* v *Murphy**. KB. 1940. 23. TC 225.*

   As a result of a fatal accident to one of its employees the company received a sum of money under its accident insurance policy.

   Held. The insurance recovery was a trading receipt and accordingly taxable as such.

3. ***Keir & Cawden Ltd* v *CIR**. SCIS. 1958. 38. TC 23*

   The company insured the life of a partner in a firm of consulting engineers, engaged by the company to advise on the construction of a dam. On the partner's sudden death the company received the sum of £50,000.

   Held. The sum received was a revenue receipt arising from trade.

Compensation and voluntary payments

1. ***Murray* v *Goodhews**. CA. 1978. STC. 191.*

   A brewing company terminated a number of tied tenancy agreements and made an ex-gratia payment to the former tenants calculated by reference to the rateable value of the premises.

   Held. The payments were held to be voluntary and unsolicited and not to arise from trading.

2. ***CIR* v *Falkirk Ice Rink Ltd**. SCIS. 1975. STC. 434.*

   The company received a donation of £1,500 from a club anxious to ensure that special facilities it used for curling would not be withdrawn.

   Held. The donation was a trading receipt.

3. ***Simpson* v *John Reynolds & Co (Insurance) Ltd**. CA. 1975. 49. TC 693.*

   As a result of a takeover, the company lost an important client who, in order to recognise long and valuable service, decided to pay the company the sum of £5,000, in five annual instalments of £1,000 each.

   Held. That the payments were gifts and not a reward for services rendered, and therefore not taxable.

4. ***Creed* v *H & M Levinson Ltd**. CD 1981. STI. 133.*

   The company manufactured hats and supplied a considerable quantity of them to a large chain store. In 1961 the store ceased the sale of hats and offered to assist the company in changing its business to light clothing manufacture. This arrangement did not prove to be satisfactory and in an action for damages in 1965 the company was awarded the sum of £22,500 for 'loss of goodwill' which was assessed to corporation tax as a trading receipt. The company appealed claiming that the receipt was either a capital receipt or an ex-gratia payment.

   Held. The receipt was held to be a trading receipt and accordingly charged to corporation tax.

5. ***Poulter* v *Gayjon Processes Ltd**. STI 1985*

   The taxpayer manufactured shoes and received a government subsidy (temporary employment subsidy and supplement) which was claimed as a non-taxable receipt.

   Held. On the facts, the subsidy was paid to the company in order to allow it to employ work people who would otherwise have been made redundant. It was therefore a revenue receipt.

Allowable expenditure

1. ***Strick* v *Regent Oil Co Ltd**. 1965. 43. TC 1.*

   A petrol company entered into a number of agreements with garages which took the form of a lease by the garage proprietor to the company of his premises for a premium, and a nominal rent and sub lease of the premises to the garage proprietor at a nominal rent.

   Held. The premiums were capital payments and not deductible.

2. ***IRC* v *Carronco**. HL 1968. 45. TC 65.*

   Expenditure was incurred by the company (incorporated by Royal Charter in 1773) in modifying its charter to obtain a better administrative structure and modernise its borrowing powers.

   Held. This was held to be revenue expenditure as no new asset was created.

3. ***Mitchell* v *Noble (BW) Ltd**. CA 1927.11 TC 373.*

   An instalment of £19,200, on account of compensation amounting to £50,000, was paid to a permanent director of the company in consideration for his retirement.

   Held. This was held to be revenue expenditure and not a capital payment.

4. ***Associated Portland Cement Manufacturers Ltd* v *Kerr**. CA 1946. 27. TC 103.*

   Lump sum payments were made to retiring directors in consideration of covenants that they would not carry on a similar business.

   Held. This was held to be capital expenditure. The expenditure was made with a view to bringing into existence an advantage for the enduring benefit of the trade, ie buying off potential competition.

5. ***The Law Shipping Co* v *IRC**. SCIS 1924. 12. TC 621.*

   The company purchased a ship in 1919 for £97,000 which at the time of purchase was ready for sale and had freight booked. Exemption from the periodical maritime survey was postponed until after the voyage when £51,558 was spent on repairs. Of this sum £12,000 was agreed as being applicable to the period of ownership by the company.

   Held. The balance was capital expenditure and not a deductible expense. 'If the ship had not been in need of repair when purchased a correspondingly higher price would have been paid', Lord Cullen.

6. *Pitt* v *Castlehill Warehousing Co Ltd.* CD 1974.
    49. TC 638.

    The company owned warehouses, the access road to
    which ran through a residential area. In order to
    placate the residents a new access road was built,
    the cost of which was claimed as an allowable
    expense.

    Held. That it was capital as the company had
    acquired an asset.

7. *Harrods (Buenos Aires) Ltd* v *Taylor Gooby.* CA
    1964 41. TC 450.

    The company owned a commercial establishment in
    the Argentine and in accordance with that country's
    laws was obliged to pay a tax annually of one per
    cent of its share capital, in order to be entitled to
    carry on business there.

    Held. That the expenses were incurred to enable
    the company to carry on its trade and
    therefore deductible.

8. *Strong & Co Romsey Ltd* v *Woodifield.* HL 1906.
    5. TC 215.

    A brewery company paid damages and costs of
    £1,490 to a guest at one of its houses on account of
    injuries caused by the falling of a chimney.

    Held. That the expenditure was not incurred for
    the purpose of earning profits and was not
    allowable.

9. *Smiths Potato Estates* v *Bolland.* HL 1948. 30.
    TC 267.

    The company claimed as a deduction from profits
    the legal and accountancy expenses of an appeal
    against an assessment to income tax.

    Held. That the expenditure was incurred to
    determine the amount of tax payable on the
    profits, not in order to earn profits.

10. *Morgan* v *Tate & Lyle Ltd.* HL 1955. 35. TC 367.

    Expenses incurred by the company in a campaign to
    prevent the nationalisation of their industry were
    claimed to be allowable as a deduction against
    profits.

    Held. That the expenditure was made to enable
    the company to carry on its trade. The
    Crown view that a trade could survive a
    change of ownership was not accepted.

11. *Copeman* v *Flood (William) & Sons Ltd.* 1941.
    KB. 24. TC 53.

    A private company engaged in pig trading had as its
    directors the controlling director's daughter aged 17
    and son aged 23. Each were paid £2,300 by way of
    remuneration. It was contended by the Crown that
    having regard to the age and duties of the children
    the remuneration should be considered by the
    General Commissioners.

    Held. That although the sums were paid as
    remuneration it did not follow that they
    were expended wholly and exclusively for
    the purpose of the company's trade. The case
    was remitted to the Commissioners to
    determine whether or not some proportion of
    the remuneration was so expended.

12. *Odeon Associated Theatres Ltd* v *Jones.* 1972.
    CA 48. TC 257

    In 1945 the Company purchased the Regal Cinema,
    Marble Arch for £240,000. Repair and maintenance
    work had not been carried out to any great extent
    during the previous five years, but this had not
    affected the purchase price nor the use of the cinema
    by the public. In between 1945-54 sums of money
    spent on repairs were allowed as deductions but
    £7,969 spent on deferred repairs was disallowed
    following the Law Shipping authority.

    Held. That the expenditure was allowable. The
    nature of the repairs did not mean that it
    had to be done to make the asset
    commercially viable. Accountancy evidence
    was given that in accordance with
    established principles of sound commercial
    accounting the disputed items of
    expenditure were a charge to revenue.

13. *ECC Quarries Ltd* v *Watkins.* CD 1975. STC. 578.

    The company claimed unsuccessfully for planning
    permission to extract sand and gravel from certain
    sites. Abortive expenditure amounting to £24,000
    was charged by the company as revenue expenditure
    and disallowed by the Inspector of Taxes on the
    grounds that it was capital expenditure.

    Held. That the expenditure was capital. The
    expenditure was a once and for all sum, and
    would have secured enduring advantage to
    the company. Although expert evidence was
    given to the effect that the treatment of the
    expense was in accordance with sound
    accountancy practice this was not decisive of
    the question.

14. *Tucker* v *Granada Motorway Services Ltd.*
    1977. CD. STC. 342–362.

    The company secured a change in its lease of a
    motorway service station, and in consideration
    agreed to pay the landlord the sum of £122,220. This
    was equivalent to six times the amount of additional
    rent due for 1973, which would no longer be payable
    under the amended lease. The company claimed that
    the payment was of a revenue nature, and the
    Special Commissioners agreed.

    Held. That the lump sum which was paid to secure
    an improvement in a fixed capital asset,
    such as a lease, was capital expenditure
    even though the improvement had been
    necessary to enable the taxpayer to continue
    his trade and had resulted in a reduction of
    his revenue expenses.

15. *Heather* v *PE Consulting Group Ltd.* 1972. CA
    48. TC 393.

    The company agreed to pay 10% of its annual profits
    to a trust created to give its staff the opportunity of
    acquiring shares in the company, and to remove the
    possibility of the company being taken over. In the
    Chancery Court the expert opinion of accountants on
    the treatment of this item as a revenue expense was
    held to be conclusive.

Held. That the expenditure was for the purposes of trade and not capital. Again the position was made clear that it is the Courts who must decide what is capital and revenue expenditure as these are matters of law.

16. ***Garforth v Tankard Carpets Ltd.*** *1980. CD STC. 251.*

The company granted a mortgage over some of its premises in order to secure loans made to a connected company. When the mortgage was foreclosed the company paid over £41,920 which it claimed as a business expense.

Held. That the expenditure was not incurred wholly and exclusively for the purpose of the company's trade. Further, since the company had acquired an asset, namely the right to proceed for recovery of the satisfied debt from the connected company, the expenditure was capital and not revenue.

17. ***CS Robinson v Scottbader Co Ltd.*** *1980. CD STC. 241.*

An employee of the company was seconded to its French subsidiary in order to provide technical and marketing expertise. The parent company claimed the salary expenses and social costs of the employee whilst in France as a business expense.

Held. That the expenditure was to further the parent company's (and not the subsidiary's) business in France and Europe and was therefore allowable as an expense of trading.

18. ***Dollar v Lyon***. *1981. STC. 333.*

D and his wife had difficulty in obtaining farm labour and paid each of their four children (aged between 7 and 12) £2 per week and £250 in National Savings Certificates for working on the farm.

Held. Payments to children were not an expense of trade.

19. ***Walker v Joint Credit Card Co Ltd.*** *1982. STI. 76.*

A payment of £75,000 was made by a credit card company (ACCESS), to a competing company (EUROCARD) in consideration of EUROCARD ceasing to carry on business. Access claimed the expense as a deduction in computing its profits.

Held. Payment was not an expense of trading. It was made to obtain a permanent result and advantage rather than a short term one.

20. ***Whitehead v Tubbs (Elastic) Ltd.*** *1983. STI. 496.*

The company made a payment of £20,000 to ICFC Ltd in order to obtain release from the onerous terms of a capital loan agreement.

Held. The payment was capital expenditure.

21. ***Watkiss v Ashford, Sparkes and Hayward.*** *1985. STC.*

The taxpayer was a large firm of solicitors with several branch offices. Weekly lunchtime meetings were held to discuss partnership business, at which a modest lunch was provided. In addition an annual conference was held at an hotel at which expenditure on the provision of accommodation and meals was incurred.

Held. 1) Expenditure on partnership lunches were not deductible.

    2) Annual conference costs were deductible expenses.

22. ***Jeffs v Ringtons Ltd.*** *1985. STC. 809.*

The company made payments to a trust fund to acquire shares for the benefit of its employees.

Held. The expenditure was of a revenue nature and not capital.

23. ***Mackinlay v Arthur Young McCelland Moores & Co.*** *HL 1989. STC 898*

The taxpayer reimbursed two of its partners the sum of £8,568 being removal expenses incurred as a result of being asked to move to another part of the UK. This was established practice for both employees and partners. The Inland Revenue refused to accept the payments as business expenses as they served a dual business and private purpose.

Held. Reversing the decision of the Appeal Court, that the expenditure could not be treated as wholly and exclusively for the business of the firm as a separate entity.

24. ***Rolfe v Wimpey Waste Management Ltd.*** *CA 1989 STC 454*

The company incurred substantial expenditure in acquiring rights to use land for tipping waste material. The life of each site varied from between seven and ten years and the company claimed an annual proportion as an expense in computing its corporation tax liability.

Held. Upholding the decision of the High Court, that the expenditure was capital and not therefore allowable as an expense of trading.

25. ***Donald Fisher (Ealing) Ltd v Spencer.*** *STI February 1989 CA*

The taxpayer's rent review was settled in excess of the market value and the company received £14,000 by way of compensation from their agent. The company claimed that the receipt was not trading income and not chargeable to CGT.

Held. Upholding the decision of the High Court, that the amount had been paid to compensate the company for a diminution in profits and accordingly was taxable as a revenue receipt. In this case there was a variation in the rent payable. In the *Tucker v Granada Motorway Services Ltd (STC 1979)* case, by contrast, there had been a change in the terms of the lease.

26. ***Lawson v Johnson Matthey plc.*** *1992 HL*

As part of a financial rescue operation Johnson Matthey plc injected £50m into a subsidiary company Johnson Matthey Bankers Ltd immediately prior to the sale of that company to the Bank of England. JM plc claimed the sum as a trading expense incurred solely to preserve its trade which would have collapsed had JMB Ltd gone into liquidation.

Held. The payment was an allowable trading expense of JM plc. The money had been paid to preserve the trade. The decision of the lower court was reversed.

27. **Gallagher v Jones: Threlfall v Jones** *CA 1994*

The two taxpayers were hirers of narrow boats under leasing agreements and claimed to charge the actual amounts paid in the first two years, rather than spreading them as per SSAP 21, in order to evade losses to be carried back to years when the rate of tax was higher.

Held. The trade expenditure is allowed for taxation purposes when it is incurred in accordance with SSAP 21 in this case.

28. **Vodafone Cellular Ltd v Shaw** *CH.D. ST1 219 1995*

The company paid £30m to cancel an agreement to pay 10% of the group's pre-tax profit in return for know-how which was no longer needed.

Held. Payment was revenue expenditure but as it benefited the whole group, it was not wholly and exclusively for the companys' trade.

29. **Stone & Temple Ltd v Walters** *CH.D. ST1 1656 1994*

The company entered into a joint venture to acquire and develop a restaurant in Canada. The restaurant was sold and loans made to the purchaser to keep the restaurant open and protect the lease value.

Held. The advances were not deductible for corporation tax purposes.

Losses and defalcations

1. **English Crown Spelter Co Ltd v Baker.** *1908. KB. 5. TC 327.*

An advance to a subsidiary company to finance the acquisition and development of mines, proved to be irrecoverable on the failure of the subsidiary.

Held. The advance was not a trading expense.

2. **Henderson v Meade-King Robinson & Co Ltd.** *1938. K.B. 22. TC 97.*

An advance to a firm managing certain whaling companies proved to be irrecoverable on the loss of the selling agency to those companies.

Held. This was held to be a loss of capital and not an allowable expense.

3. **Milnes v J Beam Group Ltd.** *1975. CD STC. 487.*

A payment was made by a company of £20,048 under its guarantee of a loan to an associated company.

Held. This was held to be capital and not wholly and exclusively for the purpose of trade.

4. **Owen & Gadsdon v Brock.** *1951. HC. 32. TC 206.*

A loss was incurred by a firm of solicitors due to the purchase and sale of a house used temporarily by an employee.

Held. This was held to be of a capital nature and not allowable.

5. **Roebank Printing Co Ltd v CIR.** *1928. SCIS 13. TC 864.*

Excess drawings on account of commission by a managing director proved to be irrecoverable.

Held. The loss was not a trading expense.

6. **Curtis v Oldfield J & G Ltd.** *1925. 9. TC 319.*

Following the death of the managing director of a family company debts due from the deceased for private transactions amounting to £14,584 were discovered.

Held. Debt was not allowable in computing company's profits.

Stock and work in progress

1. **IRC v Cock Russell & Co Ltd.** *1949. KB. 29. TC 287.*

A firm of wine merchants sought to value some of its stock at cost and some of the items at market value.

Held. That the company had used a correct method of valuation and, therefore, the whole of the stock need not be valued on the same basis. CROOME-JOHNSON, J. quoting from Lord Porter in ABSALOM v TALBOT. 1944. A.C. 204, said '*profits are to be ascertained on ordinary commercial principles subject to such provisions of the Income Tax Acts as require a departure from those principles*'.

2. **BSC Footwear Ltd v Ridgway. HL 1971.** *47. TC 495.*

The company retailed shoes, and for its final accounts purposes claimed to be entitled to value some of its closing stock by reference to its replacement value, this being less than its original cost. This method which had been applied by the taxpayer for the period of 30 years consisted of ascertaining a notional purchase price which would yield a normal or requisite gross profit percentage at the expected selling price. Expert accountancy opinion in the form of the Principal Advisory Accountant to the Inland Revenue, and a partner in the firm's auditors, was given, but in fact conflicted.

Held.
1) That in the absence of statutory authority, the long established practice of valuing stock at the lower of cost or market value was the correct principle to follow.

2) The firm's method of stock valuation was incorrect. Market value meant the selling price of the stock less marketing expenses and not a 'mathematical' price, wholly unreal.

3. **Duple Motor Bodies Ltd v Ostime.** *1961. HL 39. TC 537.*

The company had valued its work in progress on the same basis for a number of years, and this consisted of the inclusion of labour and materials only with no allowance for any overhead or indirect costs. This method is frequently referred to as the direct cost method. The Inland Revenue challenged the method and claimed that a due proportion of overhead expenditure should be included in the valuation of work in progress.

Held. The Inland Revenue were not justified in requiring the company to change its method of valuation by the inclusion of overhead expenditure.

4. ***Sharkey v Wernher***. *1955. 36. TC 275.*

The taxpayer's wife carried on a stud farm within Case I and also horse racing and training which are not within Case I. Five horses were transferred from the stud farm to the racing stables.

Held. The market value of the horses should be credited to the stud farm profits.

Capital expenditure

Plant and Machinery

1. ***Derby (Earl of) v Aylmer***. *1915. KB 6. TC 665.*

A claim for an allowance in respect of the diminished value of some stallions, year by year, was refused.

Held. That a stallion did not diminish in value by reason of wear and tear. The court was not asked to decide whether or not a horse was plant or machinery in this case.

2. ***Daphne v Shaw***. *1926. KB 11. TC 256.*

The books which formed a law library for a solicitor were claimed as plant and machinery.

Held. They were not plant or machinery, not being apparatus or implements used in carrying out an operation of the vocation .

3. ***Jarrold v Johngood & Sons Ltd.*** *1962. CA 40. TC 681.*

In this case some movable metal partitioning used to divide office accommodation was claimed as plant.

Held. The Crown's contention, that such partitioning was the setting within which operations were carried out and not the apparatus used in it, was not accepted. Partitioning was plant.

4. ***Hinton v Maddern & Ireland Ltd***. *TD. 1959. HL 38. TC 391.*

A shoe manufacturer claimed an investment allowance on its knives and lasts used on its machinery. These items had an average life of three years.

Held. That they were plant.

5. ***CIR v Barclay Curle & Co Ltd***. *1969. HL 45. TC 221.*

The company constructed a dry dock for its business of shipbuilders and repairers, the cost being excavation, £186,928; concrete work etc. £500,380; £243,288 ancillary plant and machinery.

Held. That the whole cost was plant or machinery, the dock being regarded not as a passive receptacle for ships, but a device by which a ship was transferred from the river for the purpose of repair.

6. ***Cooke v Beachstation Caravans Ltd.*** *1974. C. D. 49. TC 514.*

The company constructed a swimming pool with an elaborate system of filtration, as one of the amenities at a caravan park. The cost included £3,353 for excavating, concreting and lining the pools and the surrounding terrace, which the company claimed as plant.

Held. That the whole expenditure was on plant and machinery.

7. ***St John's School v Ward***. *1974. CA 49. TC 524.*

A special purpose prefabricated structure for use as a laboratory and gymnasium in a school was claimed as plant.

Held. Not to be plant. The structure was to be considered a building in which the trade was carried on rather than the apparatus of the trade.

8. ***Schofield v R & H Hall Ltd***. *1974. Northern Ireland. 49. TC 538.*

A grain importer built a concrete silo with gantries, conveyors and chutes.

Held. To be plant. The silos were not simply storage containers but holders from which grain could be conveniently loaded into conveyances.

9. ***Ben-Odeco Ltd v Powlson***. *1978. HL STC. 111.*

The company made payments of nearly £500,000 for interest and commitment fees to obtain essential finance to construct an oil rig and claimed a first year allowance in respect of the expenditure.

Held. That the expenditure was not on the provision of machinery or plant but on the provision of finance, by the use of which machinery or plant was acquired.

10. ***Benson v Theyard Club Ltd.*** *11978. CD STC.*

The company purchased and converted an old ferry boat into a floating restaurant and claimed the expenditure as machinery or plant.

Held. That the boat was merely a place or setting where the business of running a restaurant was carried on, rather than the apparatus by which the business was carried on.

11. ***Dixon v Fitch's Garage Ltd.*** *1975. CD STC. 480.*

A metal canopy covering the service area of a petrol filling station was constructed.

Held. To be a shelter, and not plant or machinery.

12. ***Munby v Furlong***. *1977. CA STC. 232.*

A barrister created a library for the purpose of his practice and claimed capital allowances as plant and machinery.

Held. Reversing the lower court decision and overruling *Daphne v Shaw* , that 'plant' has acquired a special meaning and covered whatever apparatus or chattels a business man used for carrying on his business.

13. ***Leeds Permanent Building Society v Proctor.*** *1982. STI. 372.*

The company had designed and manufactured decorative screens incorporating the Society's name, for display in particular premises.

Held. The screens were plant, being part of the apparatus by means of which the Society carried on its business.

14. ***Vanarkadie v Sterling Coated Materials Ltd.*** *1983. CD STC. 95.*

The company incurred additional costs in sterling in meeting instalment payments on the purchase of plant and machinery.

Held. The additional costs were part of the cost of plant.

15. ***Thomas v Reynolds and Another.*** *1987. CD. STI. 50*

The taxpayers carried on the business of tennis coaching and in 1982 incurred expenditure on an inflatable polythene dome to enable winter coaching to take place.

Held. The airdome was no more than the setting in which the tennis coaching business was carried on and the expenditure was not therefore on plant. The General Commissioners did find that the dome had a function to fulfil in the taxpayers' business and this view was not disturbed by the court.

16. ***Wimpey International Ltd v Warlan D.*** *CA 1988 STI.*

The company owned and operated a chain of fast food restaurants and money was spent on improving and modernising the premises. The disputed items consisted of the following main categories of expenditure:
 i) Flooring (tiling, carpeting, linoleum, raised areas)
 ii) Wall surfacing (tiling brickwork, panels, mirrors)
 iii) False ceilings
 iv) Lighting and associated wiring
 v) Shop fronts and fascia board.

Held. Confirming the decision of the Lower Court, the Court of Appeal found as follows:
 i) Only carpeting was plant.
 ii) Wall panels, mirrors and decorative brickwork were plant. Wall tiling was not plant.
 iii) A particular false ceiling made of metal strips was plant. All other false ceilings were not plant.
 iv) Lighting and associated wiring were plant.
 v) None of the shop fronts were plant. The fascia boards were plant.

17. ***Carr v Sayer.*** *1992 STI. 458.*

The taxpayer claimed capital allowances as plant and machinery on the provision of quarantine dog kennels.

Held. The kennels were not plant and machinery eligible for capital allowances.

18. ***Hunt v Henry Quick Ltd: King v Bridisco Ltd*** *CH.D 1992 STC 633*

In each case the company carried on the business of wholesale merchants operating from a large single storey warehouse. Mezzanine platforms were installed to increase storage capacity

Held. The mezzanine platform floors were plant and machinery. Ancillary lighting which provided general illumination was held not to be plant and machinery.

19. ***Gray v Seymours Garden Centre*** *CHD. 1993*

The taxpayer had constructed a special horticultural greenhouse to keep plants for sale at a garden centre and claimed the expenditure as plant and machinery.

Held. The building was part of the premises in which the taxpayer carried on his business and was not therefore plant and machinery.

Industrial buildings

1. ***CIR v Lambhill Ironworks Ltd.*** *1950. SCS. 31. TC 93.*

A drawing office was used by a firm of structural engineers, which was separate from the main workshop, and consisted of the upper storey of a two storey building.

Held. To be an industrial building and not an office or ancillary to an office. The drawing office was predominantly used for workshop plans.

2. ***Dale v Johnson Bros.*** *1951. KB (NI) 32. TC 487.*

A warehouse was used by selling agents for commodities of various manufacturers.

Held. Not to be an industrial building.

3. ***Saxone Lilley & Skinner (Holdings) Ltd v CIR.*** *1967. HL 44. TC 22.*

In this case the company, which was a member of a group which manufactured and retailed shoes, constructed a warehouse for the central storage of shoes of which approximately one third were manufactured by a group company, the balance being supplied by third parties.

Held. To be an industrial building or structure.

4. ***Kilmarnock Equitable Co-operative Society Ltd v CIR.*** *1966. SC/S 43. TC 675.*

The Society had erected a separate building to screen and pack coal which was sold in paper bags, as one part of its business.

Held. To be an industrial building.

5. ***Abbott Laboratories Ltd v Carmody.*** *1968. CD 44. TC 569*

The company, engaged in the pharmaceutical industry, carried on its business from blocks of buildings on a 53 acre site. These blocks included an administrative unit, which cost less than 10% of the whole and was connected to a manufacturing unit by a covered passage.

Held. That on the facts the administrative block was a separate building and not an industrial building.

6. ***Buckingham v Securitas Properties Ltd.*** *1980. STC. 166.*

A building was used for the purposes of wage packeting and coin and note storage.

Held. The building was not an industrial building as the coins and notes were currency and not goods or materials.

7. **Copol Clothing Co Ltd v Hindmarch.** *1982. STI. 69.*

The company owned a warehouse in Manchester which it used to store imported clothing and claimed the building as an industrial building used for the storage of goods.

Held. The building was not an industrial building as it was not located near to a port or airport.

Losses

1. **CIR v Scott-Adamson.** *1932. 17. TC 629*

A taxpayer commenced trading on 1st June 1929 and made up his accounts to 31st March. For the 10 months to 31st March 1930 he made an agreed loss of £61 and for the year to 31st March 1931 a profit of £142. For the first twelve months his actual loss was £61 - (1/6 x 142) 24 = £37.

Held. The loss available for carry forward to 1931/32 was £37 and not £98 claimed by the taxpayer.

2. **Butt v Haxby.** *1983. STC. 239.*

H commenced trading in 1978 while continuing to be in employment. His Schedule E income for 1978/79 was over £4,600 while the capital allowances and losses of the trade amounted to £4,100. He elected to use £3,500 of the losses under Section 168 TA 1970, and the balance under Section 30 FA 1978.

Held. While relief can be claimed under both sections, in either order, the loss cannot be apportioned between them .

Trust income

1. **Macfarlane v IRC.** *1929.14. TC 532.*

The taxpayer's share of income from a trust created by a will, was calculated after deducting the management expenses of the trust.

Held. General management expenses are not allowed as an expense of the trust for income tax purposes but should be deducted in arriving at the net trust income.

2. **Baxendale v Murphy.** *1924. 9. TC 76.*

Under a deed of settlement each trustee was entitled to £100 p.a. as remuneration for his services. The trustees made the payments less tax, out of the trust income.

Held. The payments were annual payments within Case III.

3. **Fry v Shiel's Trustees.** *1914. 6. TC 583.*

Testamentary trustees were assessed on the profits of a business carried on by them for the benefit of minors.

Held. The profits were not earned income of the beneficiaries.

Capital gains tax

1. **Lyon v Pettigren.** *1985. STI. 107.*

The taxpayer owned eleven taxis and agreed to sell six of them plus licences for £6,000 each to be paid by 150 instalments of £40 each per week. He appealed against CGT assessment for 1979/80 arguing that the contract only took effect when all the money had been paid.

Held. The contracts were not conditional and tax was therefore due for the year 1979/80, the year in which the contract for the disposal was made.

2. **Turner v Follett.** *1973. 48. TC 614.*

The taxpayer gave his children shares and was assessed on the basis of a disposal of the shares at their market value at the time.

Held. The gift was a disposal for CGT purposes.

3. **Marron v Ingles** *1980 STC 500*

Shares were sold for a fixed price per share plus an amount to be determined later by reference to the company's profits.

Held. There were two disposals, the first when the shares were sold for a fixed price and the second when the capital sum was determined at a later date.

4. **Marson v Marriage** *1980 STC 177*

In March 1965 the taxpayer sold 47 acres of land for £47,040 plus an additional £7,500 per acre subsequently developed, this latter amount not being qualifiable in March 1965. The taxpayer received £348,250 in 1976 and was assessed to CGT on £250,000.

Held. There were two separate disposals, one in 1965 and the other in 1976 when the capital sum was received in respect of the chose in action. The second disposal was properly chargeable to capital gains tax. The other disposal occurred before capital gains tax was introduced.

5. **Atkinson v Dancer/Mannion v Johnston.** *CD 1988*

Two farmers both aged over 60 years sold some of their land when ill health made it difficult for them to manage their respective farms. Both were assessed to CGT and given no retirement relief.

Held. They were not entitled to retirement relief as the disposals amounted to a disposal of business assets and not a disposal of the business. There had not been a material change in the farmers' businesses.

6. **Lewis v Ladyrook.** *1990 STC 23*

In 1968 the taxpayer purchased a property which comprised the main house, 10.5 acres of land, some agricultural land and two cottages. One of the cottages was sold in 1979 after occupation by the taxpayer's gardener, and the Inland Revenue claimed that the cottage did not form part of the dwelling house.

Held. The cottage formed part of the taxpayer's principal private residence whilst occupied by the gardener.

The following similar cases were referred to in the judgment:

Batey v Wakefield 1981 STC 512;
Markey v Sanders 1987 STC 256

7. ***Smith v Schofield***. *H,L. 1993*

The taxpayer bought a Chinese cabinet and a French mirror for £250. In 1987 she sold them for £15,800.

Held. That indexation should be applied first before applying the time apportionment rules for the periods before and after 6th April 1965.

8. ***Campbell Connelly & Co Ltd v Barnet.*** *1992.*

The company sold its premises and moved into the same building as its parent company. Later on, new premises were acquired but they could not be occupied for a period of nine months.

Held. A claim for roll over relief under Section 152 TCGA 1992 was not eligible as the premises were not capable of being brought into immediate use.

9. ***Capcount Trading v Evans.*** *CH D 1992*

The company acquired and disposed of Canadian Dollars at a loss, by converting the net loss into sterling for CGT purposes.

Held. Where an asset was acquired and disposed of incurring other than sterling then the cost of acquisition and proceeds of disposal should both be converted at the rate of exchange prevailing at the respective dates.

10. ***Jarmin v Rawlings.*** *CH D STI 1373 1994*

A dairy farmer with 34 cattle sold his milking parlour and yard at auction in October 1988. The grazing land was retained and by January 1984 14 cows had been sold, the remainder were transferred and dairy farming ceased.

Held. The October sale was a part disposal of the business for retirement relief purposes.

Inheritance tax

1. ***Starke v I.R.*** *C.H.D 1994*

Executors of a deceased farmer claimed agricultural property relief in respect of a farmhouse and fenced enclosures close to the farm.

Held. That farmhouses and surrounding land are not agricultural property for the IHT purposes and the full value of such property is therefore liable to IHT.

Index

	Chapter	Paragraph
Accrued income scheme	10.	6
Administration Chapter	2.	1–11
Advance Corporation Tax	28.	1–14
Age allowance	3.	12–
Agricultural buildings	17.	36–39
Annual payments and charges	5.	1–13
Appeals	2.	5–6
Benefits in kind	8.	5–13
British subject resident abroad	9.	8–12
Building society interest		
paid	5.	9–11
received	6.	1–2
Business assets	42.	1–
Business expansion scheme	21.	3–
Capital allowances	17.	1–51
Chargeable gains tax		35– 42.
administration	2.	1–11
	35.	15–
allowable deductions	36.	4–5
assets held on 31.3.82	36.	9–
	38.	1–
bonus issues	38.	6–7
business assets	42.	1–
capital sums	35.	9–
	37.	4–
chattels	37.	11–14
chargeable assets	35.	5–
	37.	2–
chargeable occasions	40.	1–
computation	36.	1–12
consideration	36.	3–
death	40.	12–
exempt assets	35.	13–
exemptions	35.	13–
gifts	41.	1–
gifts of business assets	41.	6–
general principles	35.	1–
government securities	38.	App.
husband and wife	39.	3–
indexation allowance	36.	7, 8, 11
individuals	39.	2–
land	37.	
leases	37.	5–8
market price	36.	2–
	36.	7–
parallel pooling	38.	12–13
part disposals	36.	11–
persons chargeable	35.	2–
	39.	1–
personal reps	39.	5–
private residence	37.	9–10
qualifying corporate bonds	38.	15
quoted securities held on 6.4.65	36.	14–15
	38.	12
rates of tax	35.	3–
re-basing	36.	9–
relief for gifts – holdover relief	41.	1–
replacement of assets	42.	6–
restoration of assets	41.	5–6
retail prices index	35.	18–
retirement relief	42.	4–
rights issues	38.	8–9
settled property	40.	14–
small disposals	37.	4–
stocks and securities	38.	11–14
takeover bids	38.	10–
time apportionment	36.	App.
transfer of business	42.	5–
trustees	39.	6–7
unquoted shares and securities	38.	16–
Case law Chapter	54.	
Charitable gifts and donations	4.	13
Charges on income	5.	1–13
Close investment holding co's.	30.	
Corporation tax	24–34.	
accounting periods	24.	9–
advance corporation tax	28.	1–14
bank interest	25.	5–
	27.	2–
building society interest	25.	8–
capital allowances	26.	1–2
capital gains tax	25.	12–
charges on income	27.	1–13
charge to corporation tax	25.	1–
close companies	30.	1–
close inv. holding companies	30.	12–14
companies in liquidation	34.	5–7
companies in partnership	34.	8–9
consortia	32.	5–6
		12–16
controlled foreign companies	33.	10–15
distributions	28.	3–
double tax relief	33.	10–
financial year	24.	9–
franked investment income	28.	7–
groups and consortia	32.	1–
group income	32.	17–20
group relief	32.	3–12
imputation system	24.	4–
income tax	27.	9–
international aspects	33.	
investment companies	34.	1–4
loan relationships	25–26.	
loss relief	29.	
management expenses	33.	4–
payment of tax	23.	7–
pay and file	24	7–
rates of tax	24.	10–12
small company rates	31.	2–4
specimen computation	24.	12–
surplus of ACT	28.	10–
	32.	13–
surplus of FII	28.	9–
	29.	13–
terminal loss relief	29.	11–
unfranked investment income	25.	6–

	Chapter	Paragraph		Chapter	Paragraph
Death	4.	8–9	dwelling house allowance	17.	34–
	40.	12–	emoluments of office	8.	3–4
Deduction at source	1.	7	enterprise zones	17.	36–
	6.	1–	estate income	22.	12–
Directors	28.	3–	extended basic rate	5.	13
Distributions	28.	3–	farmers profits averaging	15.	9–10
Dividends	6.	8–	first year allowance	17.	11
Domicile	9.	4–	furnished accommodation	11.	8
			higher paid employees	8.	6–
Double tax relief	12.	4–5	hotels	17.	33–
	25.	10–	husband and wife	3. & 4.	
	28.	12–	independent taxation	3. & 4.	
	47.	11	industrial buildings	17.	24–33
			interest on overdue tax	2.	8–9
Earned income	1.	3	interest paid	5.	10–13
Emoluments	7.	3–4	interest on bank deposits	6.	8–12
Employment	8.	3–	know how	17.	45–46
Enterprise zones	17.	36–	leased plant	17.	14–15
Enterprise Investment Scheme	21.		leases	11.	7–9
Estate income	22.		liability insurance relief	8.	23
			life annuities	21.	6–
Foreign income	12.	1–5	life assurance relief	21.	4–5
	25.	10–	loss relief	18.	1–16
	28.	12–	medical insurance	4.	6
Furnished lettings	11.	12–	MIRAS	5.	10–12
			motor vehicles	17.	11–12
Gifts	41.	1–	non-taxable income	1.	17–
Golden handshakes	8.	17–	non-resident landlords	11.	12
Group relief	32.	3–12	overseas employment	9.	
			partnership taxation	19.	
Higher paid employees	8.	6–	patents and royalties	17.	41–44
Husband and wife	3. & 4.		pay as you earn system	10.	
	32.	3–	payroll deduction for charities	8.	19
			personal allowances and reliefs	3. & 4.	
Income tax	1–23.		plant and machinery	17.	3–21
accrued income charge	7.	3–14	personal equity plans	21.	2–
accumulating trusts	22.	4–	post-cessation expenditure	14.	21
additional rate	1.	9	profit related pay	8.	26
	22.		qualifying loans	5.	10–11
administration	2.	1–7	rates of tax	1.	End of
agricultural buildings allce.	17.	37–40			chapter
allowable business expenditure	14.	8–19	renewals basis	17.	22–
annual payments	5.	1–13	residence and domicile	9.	3–4
assessments	1.	6–	retirement annuities	20.	1–7
	2.	1–4	retirement from office	8.	17–
asset values	14.	20–	schedule A	11.	1–11
benefits in kind	8.	5–13		25.	3-12
British subjects overseas	9.	8–12	schedule D Cases I and II	14.	1–20
building society interest	6.	9–11		15.	1–11
business expansion schemes	21.	4–	schedule D Case III	7.	1–16
capital allowances	17.	1–51	schedule D Cases IV and V	12.	1–5
change of accounting date	16.	1–7	schedule D Case VI	13.	1–9
charges on income	5.	1–13	schedule E	8.	1–21
charitable gifts and donations	4.	13		9.	1–13
classification of income	1.	4	schedule F	6.	7–
deduction at source	1.	7	scientific research	17.	47–
	6.	1–	separation and divorce	4.	10
deduction of trading expenses	14.	8–19	small workshops	17.	35–
de-pooling	17.	19–21	specimen computation	1.	2
dividend income	6.	8–	stocks and work in progress	14.	21–
double taxation relief	12.	4–5	taxable income	1.	5–
due dates for payment	2.	7–	trading	14.	4–5

	Chapter	Paragraph
trading income	14.	6–
trading overseas	15.	11–
transfer of business to company	18.	13–
trust income	22.	
waste disposal	14.	21
Indexation allowance	36.	6–
Industrial buildings	17.	25–34
Inheritance tax	43–49.	
accumulations and maintenance		
settlements	49.	10–
administration	43.	24–
agricultural property	48.	1–5
agricultural property relief	43.	14–
	48.	1–5
annual exemption	43.	14–
	45.	4–
business property	43.	14–
	47.	1–3
business property relief	43.	14–
	47.	1–3
chargeable transfer	43.	5–7
death scale rates	43.	End of chapter
deeds of variation	43.	20–
double tax relief	46.	11–
discretionary trusts	49.	6–9
excluded property exemptions	43.	1–
family maintenance	45.	14–
funeral expenses	46.	13–
general exemption and reliefs	43.	13–
	45.	1–16
gifts to charities	43.	13–
	45.	8–
gifts to political parties	43.	13–
	45.	9–
gifts for national heritage	43.	13–
	47.	10–13
gifts with reservation	43.	9–
grossing up procedures	44.	2–
interest in possession	49.	4–
intestacy	43.	19–
land and house property	46.	8–9
liabilities	43.	18–
	46.	13–
life assurance policies	46.	12–
life time scale rates	43.	End of chapter
life time transfers	43.	3–
location of assets	43.	13–
national heritage property	43.	10–13
normal expenditure	43.	5–
payment	43.	20–
potentially exempt transfers	43.	6–
	44.	4–7
quick succession relief	43.	16–
	46.	10–
quoted shares and securities	46.	5–6
related property	46.	4–
relevant property	49.	2–
settlements	49.	1–11

	Chapter	Paragraph
scale rates	43.	3–
	43.	End of chapter
small gifts	43.	14–
	45.	3–
taper relief	44.	3–
transfers of value death	43.	4–
transfers of value life time	43.	4–
valuation principles	46.	1–13
woodlands	43.	15–
	48.	5–
woodlands relief	43.	15–
	48.	5–
Interest paid	5.	10–13
	27.	3–
Investment company	34.	1–4
Know how	17.	45–46
Leased plant	17.	14–15
Leases	11.	7–9
Legal expenses	14.	18–
Life assurance relief	21.	13–
Liquidation of company	34.	5–7
Loan relationships	25–27.	
Losses:		
trading	18.	1–14
	29.	1–17
capital	18.	15–
Machinery and plant	17.	3–21
Management expenses	34.	1–4
Medical insurance	4.	6
Mortgage interest	5.	9–11
Motor vehicles	17.	11–12
National insurance	23.	1–4
Office	8.	3–
Ordinary resident	9.	3–
Overseas employment Chapter	9.	1–13
Patent rights	17.	41–44
Pay as you earn	10.	
Personal equity plans	21.	2–
Personal investment	20–21.	
Personal reliefs	2.	
Purchased annuities	21.	6–
Purchase of own shares	34.	10
Qualifying distributions	28.	3–
Rent	11.	3–
Repairs and renewals	14.	11–
Retirement annuities	15.	1–7
Royalties	7.	3–4
Schedule A	11.	1–11
Schedule D case I and II	14.	1–20
	15.	1–11
Schedule D case III	7.	1–16
Schedule D case IV and V	12.	1–5

	Chapter	**Paragraph**
Schedule D case VI	13.	1–9
Schedule E	8.	1–21
	9.	1–13
Schedule F	6.	7–
Shares and securities	38.	1–16
Statutory sick pay	23.	8–
Statutory maternity pay	23	9–
Statutory total income	1.	9–
Social Security	23.	9–
Stock and work in progress	14.	20–
Tax planning	54	
Terminal losses	18.	10–
Terminal payments	8.	17–
Total income	1.	8–
Trading	14.	4–5
Trading expenditure	14.	8–19
Trading income	14.	6–
Trusts	22.	47–

	Chapter	**Paragraph**
Value added tax	50–52.	
accounting for VAT	50.	16–17
administration	50.	18–
bad debts	51.	19–20
company cars	51.	13–
computation	51.	11–
exempt goods and services	51.	7–
imports and exports	51.	24–
input tax	51.	11–16
offences and penalties	50.	19–20
partial exemptions	51.	17–18
place of supply	51.	15–
rates of tax	50.	4–
registration	50.	10–15
special schemes for retailers A, B, C, D, E, F, G, H, J	52.	1–12
specimen VAT return	50.	End of chapter
standard rate	50.	4–
taxable supply	50.	4–10
tax invoice	50.	9–
tax point	50.	8–
zero rated goods and services	49.	22–
Venture Capital Trust	24.	
Waste disposal	14.	21
Widows	4.	6–